For Colin an[...]

With much [...]

for their frien[...]

and my love

Jones   2013

G000048696

Freddy Temple: a portrait

Dedication:

For Michael Frederick Temple,
a dearly loved little boy
who was such a light to many in his short life

Freddy Temple

A PORTRAIT

by Christopher Dobb

Foreword by the Most Revd
and Rt Hon Dr Rowan Williams,
Archbishop of Canterbury

Rooftop Publishing UK

2006

First published in Great Britain in 2006
by Rooftop Publishing UK:
Kingsbury Hall, Calne, Wiltshire. SN11 8DG.

Copyright © Christopher Dobb 2006

The right of Christopher Dobb to be identified as the author of this work has been as-serted by him in accordance with the Copyright, Designs and Patents Act 1998.

All rights reserved. No part of this publication may be reproduced, stored in a retrieval system, or transmitted, in any form or by any means without the prior written permis-sion of the publisher, nor be otherwise circulated in any form of binding or cover other than that in which it is published and without a similar condition being imposed on the subsequent purchaser.

A catalogue record for this book is available from the British Library.

ISBN 0-9553285-0-0

Typographic design by Steve Hammett
www.sustainabledesign.co.uk

Printed on Cyclus 100% recycled fibre paper
by Biddles Ltd
Kings Lynn
Norfolk PE 30 4LS

Grateful acknowledgement is made to the editors of the following newspapers:
the Church Times, the Jerusalem Post, the London Evening Standard, the Portsmouth News, the Swindon Advertiser, the Sunday Times and the South China Morning Post.
Also to the Rt Revd Christopher Chessun, Bishop of Woolwich, Stephen Fry, the es-tate of the late Sir Edward Heath, Roger McGough, Pink Floyd and Lyn Smith of the Im-perial War Museum. The copyright holder/s of the former Associated Rediffusion television company could not be ascertained.

Foreword

by the Most Revd and Rt Hon Dr Rowan Williams, Archbishop of Canterbury

In my study - and often in my hand - is Freddy Temple's pastoral staff, a gift from his widow which I greatly treasure. As I read these pages, I thought often about the pastoral heart of which this simple wooden staff was an outward sign; and I thought rather soberly and repentantly what I have to live up to. Because to read this book is to learn so much about being a pastor - to learn not by lengthy theorising or by nagging exhortation but just by the example of unfailing generosity and sensitivity and joy.

And having said that, I realise this is to say that reading this book is about learning to be a Christian. Generosity and sensitivity and joy are at the centre of all discipleship worth the name. So this is not a book for specialists, not a book for clerical historians, but a book of inspiration for any and every believer. It brings alive so vividly a man who had at his disposal an amazing family heritage of distinction and learning and who put it at the service of all who asked for it, whether in the humblest of parishes or in the rarefied air of Lambeth and Westminster.

Chris Dobb has written a book that is thoroughly worthy of a loving and loveable man, a book full of entertainment and wisdom in equal measure. It is wonderful to have this tribute not only to a great man but also - if you might put it like this - to a certain spirit or ethos in the Church not always in great supply these days: something of the 'unbearable lightness' of faith, perhaps. Read it with delight.

+ Rowan Cantuar:

Contents

Author's acknowledgements

It was an enormous privilege to have been entrusted to write this Portrait of Freddy Temple. What follows is obviously a very personal view of Freddy's life; it will be equally obvious that it is written from a standpoint of great affection. My brief was to 'write something not too stodgy and something that can be read with profit and enjoyment by the widest range of people'. I hope I have fulfilled these criteria: the book was never intended to be a work of great scholarship, but rather one to give glimpses of the sort of person Freddy was.

The archive material was a little intimidating; the very task of sorting and filing Freddy's papers took a great deal of time. Freddy once complained that his family were like squirrels, in that they hoarded even the most inconsequential pieces of paper. This smacks of the pot calling the kettle black! Then, whenever I thought I had more than enough to get on with the task of writing, more material would come my way, often from the most unlikely of sources - and sometimes putting a slightly different slant on things.

When I originally appealed for information and reflections about Freddy, I was totally unprepared for the four hundred or so letters, faxes, e-mails and telephone calls I received. To all those who responded I was, and am, very grateful. Many contributions complemented each other: I could have laughed till I cried whenever mention was made of Freddy's idiosyncratic laugh! So I must first thank all those who took the trouble to contact me and say that, even if they are not acknowledged personally in the text, every contribution was valuable and added to, or underlined, the perception so many had of Freddy.

Sir Edward Heath was to have written an appreciation of Freddy for inclusion in this book; sadly, he did not complete it before he died. I was grateful to him for the interest he showed in the book, for his generous hospitality and for the time he so willingly gave me to talk about life with Freddy at Balliol and his views on William Temple (not to mention a host of other people who shall remain nameless!).

My thanks, too, to Wendy and Kenneth Jennings for their encouragement - especially to Wendy for reading some of the early manuscript and giving me wise suggestions as to how to proceed.

I am indebted, too, to Bishop Stephen Verney for allowing me a totally free hand to edit the correspondence with Freddy about pacifism, printed as appendix ii - and similarly to Stephen Temple for giving me permission to edit the letters his father sent to him over the years (appendix iii). The correspondence in both these cases was voluminous and needed a great deal of paring. Mina Temple, too, gave me some fascinating insights into the life of her father.

As soon as he learnt that I was writing Freddy's 'Life', Professor Leslie Houlden rang to offer whatever assistance and advice he could - for which I was immeasurably grateful. Over the time I have been writing the book he has offered invaluable help and guidance. At times he has had to be very long-suffering with me! Nothing was too much trouble for him. Perhaps, above all, he gave me the supreme gift of confidence to proceed. My thanks to him for all that he has done - and also for offering to write his Evaluatory Introduction. I think he realised that my great affection for Freddy blinkered me somewhat to some things that ought perhaps to be said.

Patience, too, was the hallmark of Steve and Susie Hammett. I am indebted to them for putting up with my missing deadlines - and also for their professionalism. It has been good to work so closely with them over the production of this book.

I am specially grateful, too, to Dr. Rowan Williams, the Archbishop of Canterbury, not only for contributing a Foreword, but also for the very encouraging things he said about the book in private correspondence.

Without Joan Temple's active help and encouragement, this book would not have been written. We have met (and will continue to do so) at least once a week since Freddy died, and have just talked - about Freddy, about life, about love, about death, about everything. I am so grateful for the many happy (and some sad) hours that we have spent together. But more than that, I am indebted to Joan for what I can only call her courage in giving me complete, unrestricted access to all of Freddy's extant letters, diaries and personal papers - and well as her own personal diaries. Joan gave me carte-blanche to use the material in any way I wanted, and held nothing back. Much of the material that I found she had not read before, and did not even know existed.

Finally, I must say thank you to David Woodhouse, closest friend and partner for over thirty five years of ministry in the Church. While this book was in preparation, David put up with my rather erratic working hours with (on the whole!) good humour and understanding.

Christopher Dobb

Introduction

by the Revd Dr Leslie Houlden
Professor Emeritus of Theology, King's College, London

Christopher Dobb has generously allowed me to write what we are calling an evaluative introduction to his fascinating account of Freddy Temple's life — which, after the first few chapters, is also a life of his wife Joan, his partner and co-worker. I bring detachment to the task, for I never knew Freddy — though, after reading the book, I can almost believe that I did. It is striking to me that, though I was born only ten years or so after Freddy, I feel that I belong to an almost unrecognizably different world, both socially and ecclesiastically.

First, socially. Freddy was the grandson and nephew of Temple Archbishops of Canterbury. He was therefore from the very heart of the Anglican aristocracy, both clerically and in his place in the world in general. His family background makes itself felt on almost every page of what follows. It was a legacy almost wholly benign and admirable in its effects. How could being William Temple's nephew be otherwise? All the same, it had interesting consequences in relation to both church and society.

By my time, things had already begun to change, though not radically. I myself was from a lower middle class Cheshire family that was churchgoing but not in the least clerical. I went to grammar school, and then (it was magic!) to Oxford — in fact to Queen's, where William Temple had been a Fellow at the beginning of the century. However, when I got to Cuddesdon in 1953 to train for ordination, I found myself (as I recall) the only student not from an independent school — and only one of us (a different one!) was not Oxbridge. Many of my contemporaries there went on to be priests recognizably of the Freddy Temple mould: devout, eager, committed to pastoral work and the bettering of society, often working in urban slums, at least to begin with, some of them moving eventually into senior posts both in the Church and in social work (all the same managing to send their own children to public schools, though often after much heart-searching).

By the 1970s, when I returned to Cuddesdon as Principal (and first met the author of this book), the place had changed in this respect out of all recognition. If there were products of independent schools, it scarcely showed. A few were Oxbridge graduates and others became so while at Cuddesdon; but the social 'feel' was entirely different and much more typical of society as a whole.

Now, only a few years after Freddy's death, you would look hard to find clergy of his social class, my contemporaries having all retired or died. I can think of only one present bishop who is at all comparable in that way (let wild horses stay in their stable!). You would also search long to find many Oxbridge or other graduate ordinands going straight on from university to train for the priesthood. The scene is dominated by men and women of decidedly mature years and lots of experience of life.

What difference does this make (difference, that is, that bears on Freddy Temple's life and style)? I identify two factors and I sketch boldly (though, to contradict myself, hesitantly). If one comes to the priesthood from the making of (and sometimes the achieving of success in) another career, it is hard not to bring a sense of career-making to one's new path of life; not least because of financial need and of habits acquired. Often of course this is scarcely observable, and one can rightly admire; but we do hear more of clerical ambition, like it or not, and one can sense it in the behaviour of the up-and-coming, who, when they do 'come up', find themselves sometimes in social and cultural environments and areas of experience that are quite beyond their ken; and then they must 'pronounce' and they must conduct themselves as best they can where they never thought they would be. They are not of course alone in experiencing this situation: it is a mark of a more mobile society where old snobbery recedes (though surely new snobbery advances!). If the Etonian learns to speak Cockney, the Cockney may find it desirable to learn to speak Etonian!

Freddy's 'lot' seem devoid of all such impulses. It is of course partly true that they could quietly expect promotions to come their way (though any hint of resentment if it did not was out): on the whole, they had no need to worry and to scheme. So they were freed — to serve, often dashingly and sacrificially, as the life that follows illustrates again and again. And one has the feeling that, for all the often only half-conscious assumption of 'classiness', they were genuinely not much concerned with 'office'. They were indeed, in this sense, the cream of their class and of their kind, living by expectations and ideals long bred in their race in various ways. Such men were entering the Anglican priesthood in noticeable numbers down to the early Sixties.

This wonderful generosity of spirit, often (as in the Temple case) shared fully and practically by their wives and sometimes passed on in one shape or another to their offspring, did have a downside. It is a recognizable class-characteristic that survives, though often now modified for the worse. To call it 'gush' is to trivialize, but it is also to mark it recognizably. It hit me between the eyes when I came to read the sermons printed as the first appendix in this volume, but it had been there, especially in letters, throughout. The sermons particularly, palpably delivered without notes (why is this so often seen as a mark of sincerity?), typify what I sum up as 'gush'. How many such utterances — mostly from senior clergy — have I experienced down the years, but not, I think, for quite a long time. It is a style once much favoured by speakers and audiences alike: rambling, emotional, unlearned but with a dash of supposedly learned information, kind-of candid but not revealing much, devout, but not closely based in either scripture or doctrine, or indeed in discernible thought. It has had parallels in other spheres of English life: headmasters, headmistresses, politicians, openers of occasions of all kinds used to speak similarly — and all produced a certain frisson which could count as inspiration, making one's life better. I confess that it always (or nearly always) made me squirm (as some attempts at it still do — I write in the midst of an election campaign), and I am glad that it has largely gone: as, I think, the audience for it has also gone. Perhaps they just stay away, in despair. There is no doubt, however, of its popularity in its day. Freddy was widely admired as a great preacher and no doubt did much good.

Younger readers than myself will probably share my surprise at the great assurance in the Church's future felt by Freddy Temple and his friends as recently as the 1970s. They felt they were on the edge of a golden age. Buoyancy is the word. This surprised me, and I do not either recall or understand it. Perhaps it was not present in my environment, perhaps I am overborne by later developments. But, unless these men were whistling in the dark to encourage one another, they misread the signals terribly. Their feeling comes, in part, from a certain brand of spirituality, commoner among Evangelicals, which, in its assurance of God's power and blessing, is filled with optimism, as if success were a covenanted gift from Heaven, never denied to the truly faithful. And it can certainly be said that tepid religion, not unknown among Anglicans, brings its own negative reward. But Freddy's generation and companions set much store by sheer, constant enthusiasm — perhaps not always on the surface or felt in the emotions, but desirable and justified. There is no doubt of the devotion which enabled them to bring to both individuals and public audiences much encouragement and spiritual help — far more than is often brought by more sober or academic voices.

But surely they had not taken the measure of either modern secularism or reasoned unbelief. How many English people of their circle in those days took refuge in being 'agnostic' when they often meant 'not feeling very keen'; and now they would be candidly atheist. The theological equipment of these good men was often superficial or outdated — and audiences were coming to recognize that in the later decades of the twentieth century. It is a paradox, however, that precisely in the years of the widespread decline in religious practice in all the churches, the study of theology and religion in British universities and colleges has greatly increased, matched by growing numbers of A level RE students. It is untrue to say that only charismatic styles of religion can achieve anything: numbers of people, who are not keen on 'gush' want to understand and are not content with what strikes them as superficial enthusiasm. And of course good pastoral work and intelligent preaching still produce notable results, even in secularized England, quite apart from the less sober Evangelical successes.

Could Freddy Temple's generation have done better, more to help? They might have been less incurably optimistic! They could have been more sober and willing to take the force of good contrary arguments, which they seem to have parried with rather glib and outworn, unconvincing little arguments that failed to impress even those who loved and admired them. And perhaps sometimes they argued with an authority that was still not only religious but somewhat social, even hereditary. But they had their own kind of brilliance and even of sanctity, giving themselves without reserve. It is good that the story of one of their brightest and best has been laid out for us to read with such care and imagination.

Leslie Houlden

1 Meet the Ancestors

After the announcement in 1973 that Her Majesty the Queen had approved the appointment of Freddy Temple as Bishop of Malmesbury, one of the many hundreds of letters which were sent to him was from Janet Lacey, C.B.E., the Director of Christian Aid. She began her letter:

I saw in The Times *that you are to be the Bishop of Malmesbury and I am delighted. I do not think that it matters a bit that your name is Temple, but it matters a lot that it is going to be you.*

Many of the other letters that Freddy received alluded to his ancestry; the Temple family has traced its forebears back through many centuries. On being asked once whether it was true that one of his ancestors was Lady Godiva, Freddy replied in the affirmative and continued, 'but I think I'll draw a veil over that, just as it would have been more seemly if the good lady had done so over herself.'

From Lady Godiva onwards, Freddy's ancestry can be traced through the family trees of those who built and lived in many of the great houses of England, including Althorp, Arundel, Blenheim, Burghley House, Castle Howard, Hatfield, Longleat and Woburn. In his biography of William Temple, Iremonger quotes Frederick Temple, grandfather of Freddy, saying, after his marriage to Beatrice Lascelles, 'When I first entered the Lords [as a Bishop] I treated them all with respect; after I got married I treated them as cousins; and was generally right.'

From the ecclesiastical point of view, Freddy's more immediate ancestry was what the Director of Christian Aid had in mind. The lives of his uncle, William, and of William's father, Frederick, both of whom were Archbishops of Canterbury, have been well documented in biographical and historical writings, and need not be rehearsed in great detail here. Instead, there are some Temple family anecdotal stories which deserve a light airing. Whenever he was asked to talk about his ancestry, Freddy himself directed his enquirers to the history books and biographies and then would need little encouragement to start recounting some personal and lighter stories which had rarely surfaced elsewhere.

His maternal great-grandfather, Richard Chenevix-Trench (1807-86), was successively Professor of Theology at King's College, London, Dean of Westminster and Archbishop of Dublin. His two books on the Gospels, *Notes on the Parables of our Lord* and *Notes on the Miracles of our Lord*, were both recognised as scholarly and stimulating and created a fresh interest in the Gospels. Almost unbelievably, his mother chose to read these two books to the young Freddy as bedtime reading at the age of six or seven, and the boy thought them 'wonderful'. Many years after their publication, Freddy often referred to them and recommended them to ordinands, curates and parish priests as 'good material for sermons - with the added bonus of keeping the congregations within the diocese at least within a hundred or so years of being theologically up-to-date.'

Trench's many theological writings were eclipsed by his works in philology and poetry. In philology he popularised the scientific study of words; he was also responsible for spearheading the creation of the *New English Dictionary*. While at Westminster, Trench used to hold literary breakfasts at the Deanery; Browning, Tennyson and Clough were often amongst those present.

Like some other scholars and thinkers, Trench was absent-minded. There was an occasion when he, well after his preferment to the Archbishopric of Dublin, returned to the Deanery at Westminster Abbey as guest of honour at a dinner party. In these familiar surroundings he forgot the passage of the years and took advantage of a pause in the conversation around him to say to his wife, 'I am sorry to say, my dear, that we must call the new cook one of our failures.'

It was Trench's practice, as Archbishop, to ask ordinands to stay at the Palace for the weekend. This was naturally something of an ordeal for the young men, especially as it included taking a service in his private chapel and preaching a sermon. Brigadier Richard Chenevix-Trench, in a short family memoir of his father, tells how one weekend an ordinand went to Mrs. Trench, Freddy's great-grandmother, in great distress, since he had left his manuscript behind and was lost without it. She begged him not to distress himself; he had only to go to the Archbishops's study, where he would find a sheaf of sermons; she told him to take his choice. 'You need have no fear of his recognising it; His Grace always sleeps throughout the sermon.'

This time, however, the Archbishop did wake during the sermon, stirred, listened for a time and then turned to his wife and said in a loud voice, 'Damn it, Mary; the fellow has got hold of my Samaritan Woman.'

Freddy used to recount these two stories often, accompanying them with great snorts of glee, even if he had told them three times already that particular day.

When Trench died he was buried in Westminster Abbey; his tomb is just beside that of the Unknown Warrior.

One of the Trenches' daughters, Edith, married Reginald Copleston in 1882. Copleston had been ordained priest in 1875 and immediately rose in meteoric fashion in the hierarchy of the Church. In the very same year, two days after his thirtieth birthday, the canonical age for being consecrated as a bishop, he was consecrated Bishop of Colombo. He earned himself the sobriquet 'the Boy Bishop'. Four days after the consecration he sailed for Colombo, making use of the rather tedious voyage to Ceylon to learn Tamil (perhaps the most difficult of the principal Indian tongues); he addressed the clergy in it on his arrival, greatly to the delight and amazement of his new diocese, though he did, apparently, make one grammatical error!

Freddy once said he remembered his grandmother, charmingly Irish, on being told a true, funny story, saying what a delightful story it was and adding, 'I think I will borrow that for myself and embroider it a little.' Similarly, Freddy delighted in telling the story of the enthronement of Copleston; if he did embellish it a little, there is obviously far more than a grain of truth in it, for the *Overland Ceylon Observer* reported:

> At the end of the procession walked Reginald Stephen Copleston, DD, Lord Bishop of the Diocese, with clasped hands, bowed head, pale face and most solemn cast of countenance. But the Bishop was thrown into the shadow by what followed. Close upon His Lordship's heels came his Chaplain, who held high aloft a most gallant crook, worked with cunning artifice and apparently set with precious stones of large size. The manner in which this was borne and the general demeanour of the priest showed that religious processioning was no novice's work to him. Bravely aloft was it borne, but alas! he had not calculated upon the punkah [the ceiling fan] which was swinging to and fro in the upper air of the building, and for a moment crook and calico (or whatever the material of the punkah may be) came into contact. The crook was at once lowered, but elevated again the moment the watchful eye of its bearer saw the large punkah was passed. Some of those at worship declared that they detected the makings of a smile straining to be unleashed from His Lordship's face, and his eyes certainly appeared to those closest to be alert with merriment.

It should not be forgotten that Victorian colonial bishops were not renowned for their sense of humour. Copleston was well aware that his sense of humour could land him in trouble. In his obituary, *The Times* reported, 'He was no less watchful of his keen sense of humour, knowing that in the East this quality is apt to be misunderstood.'

Edith Copleston was, to put it mildly, a little vague - but delightfully so. Freddy delighted in recounting stories of her as the Bishop's wife; there were times when, in the words of Freddy, 'my dear Grandmother was totally living in another world.' Freddy continued: 'On one occasion, grandmother was responsible for the arrangements for a rather select and posh garden party in the grounds of Bishop's House. A magnificent military band was organised to play on the Bishop's lawn throughout the proceedings. They, according to family tradition, played with great panache and competence. Unfortunately, however, they played only to themselves and to my grandfather and grandmother. The latter, poor dear, had omitted to send out the invitations to the garden party; they were later found in a bureau in the library.'

Copleston remained at Colombo for twenty-seven years, before being appointed Bishop of Calcutta and Metropolitan of India in 1902. (He was succeeded as Bishop of Colombo by his younger brother, Ernest Arthur Copleston, Freddy's great-uncle.)

The Metropolitan of India with his wife, Edith, and family. Freddy's mother has her hand on her own mother's knee.

Freddy could only remember his grandfather as somebody who seemed 'extremely old and white-haired and for whom I had to be very quiet.' He was always being told by his family that he looked like his grandfather, and portraits and photographs of Copleston certainly confirm this. As a child, Freddy once said, rather querulously, 'I don't want to look like him; I want to look like me.' His great-uncle Ernest was much in favour with the young Freddy; he remembered being taken to Lords one day to watch cricket, and on the same evening being taken to the play *The Three Musketeers*; the duel scene made an indelible impression on his young mind.

Bishop and Mrs. Copleston, though they had wished to remain in India, retired to London, on the advice of the Bishop's doctors. During his many years abroad, he had kept closely in contact with the Oxford men of his time, including Mandell Creighton, Henry Scott Holland (who had been best man at his wedding) and Edward Talbot; correspondence shows how such men were always unburdening themselves by post to their 'dear Cop' - sometimes using what *The Times* obituarist of Bishop Copleston called 'delightful freedom' in describing one another and others. Although one cannot be sure exactly what was meant by this phrase, one can make an informed guess. Many would say, on reading his correspondence, that Freddy inherited this trait from his grandfather. Be that as it may, some of the correspondence is very funny; witty and perspicacious, but stopping short of being hurtful. Mandell Creighton had died in 1901, but it was a delight now for Copleston to spend some time with his other friends. Copleston died in 1925 and his wife, Edith, in 1942. Meanwhile, Freddy's mother, Frances Mary

Copleston, had been born in Colombo in June, 1883.

Freddy's paternal grandfather was Frederick Temple, born in 1821, the thirteenth child of Octavius and Dorcas Temple. Octavius Temple died at the age of 40 whilst serving as Governor of Sierra Leone, leaving Freddy's great-grandmother a widow at a young age. They owned a farm in Devon and Dorcas brought Frederick up very strictly and did her best to start him with a good education, something which she herself had not been fortunate enough to acquire. She did not know any mathematics herself, but she did have an answer book; Frederick had the questions and he could not go to bed until he had the answers right. She simply struck the answer through if it was wrong, but could not help him in getting it right. Frederick knew all the proofs of the theory of Pythagoras by the age of eight; once, when a visitor came and refused to believe this, the young boy was woken from sleep, brought downstairs and made to recite. This may help to explain why, a few years later, he acquired a First in Maths and Greats in the same year at Oxford.

His mother once asked him when he was still a very small boy to go and buy some nails from the nearest town, which was some four or five miles away; she gave him half a crown. Frederick did not know how many nails to buy, and so used up the whole half-crown. His mother became worried when he had not returned after a long period of time. She then looked out to see a small boy humping an enormous sack, full of nails, a step at a time on his way home. It was one of the few times she was known to run out in tears and kiss him. On another occasion Frederick was sawing wood in the farmyard when he cut off a bit of his finger. He went inside, received little sympathy from his mother, and was told, 'Silly boy, go and find the end.' Fortunately a pig was eating it; there might well have been a problem with tetanus had she just tried to stick it back on.

While at Oxford, Frederick had to be very economical and could often not afford a fire or a light in his rooms, so sat studying in a greatcoat and mittens on the stairs. He would write to his mother one way on the paper and then turn it round the other way with a letter to his eldest sister, Netta. The Temple family still have such letters, and also some which are pre-penny postage, from his time at Blundells School. The family have a wonderful eight-page letter describing his first journey up to Oxford, by coach and horse. Another letter to his mother tells of an immensely studious day starting early in the morning and just having a little time for a walk in the afternoon. Frederick says that he 'does hope that she will feel he is not idling.'

When Frederick became a young Headmaster of Rugby he realised, as he looked out one evening from his study window in the Headmaster's House, that every energetic boy would want to climb trees, so he decided that he had better see for himself whether they were safe. Accordingly, when the whole school was safely locked up in the evening, the Headmaster would go out and climb each tree in turn to see that it was all right. In outward appearance, Frederick gave the impression of being a very gruff and rather stern man, and was always proud to repeat a sentence from a letter one of the boys sent home to his mother, after he had beaten the boy: 'Temple is a beast, but a just beast.' There are many picturesque descriptions of the character of Frederick Temple: 'Granite on fire' and 'A tiger in a state of grace' are two of the most famous. The Rugby story of 'a beast, but a just beast' is misleading because it was said of a headmaster, and the schoolboy use of the word 'beast' has more bark than bite. Rather longer, but incomparably vivid, is Scott Holland's account of 'the enormous moral energy of the man, which, breaking out through every obstacle, in a voice that was hardly a voice so much as a sound, would shake the soul of his hearers with a violence and a passion which were unlike anything else in the whole wide world. The whole heart of religion was in him. His soul was given to his Master with all the complete surrender of a child.'

There was a tremendous uproar when the volume *Essays and Reviews* was published in 1860. Frederick Temple made a contribution in which there was a small paragraph suggesting that the Gospel would not be in danger if it were discovered that certain parts of the Old Testament were not word for word literally true and Genesis was not actually true scientifically. When he was appointed by Gladstone to the see of Exeter enormous petitions went to the Archbishops of Canterbury and York and to Gladstone, protesting against the appointment. When finally the opponents realised they were not going to succeed, they took Netta, Frederick Temple's older sister, into a law court and made her swear that her brother had been born in wedlock. The fuss over the appointment of David Jenkins as Bishop of Durham in 1984 was perhaps as nothing compared to the fuss created at Freddy's grandfather's appointment to Exeter over a hundred years earlier.

Temple could be quite acerbic. Sandford, in his *Memoirs of Archbishop Temple*, tells of the occasion when Temple, as Bishop of Exeter, was approached by somebody who asked, 'My aunt was suddenly prevented from going on a voyage in a ship that went down; would you call that Providential interference?' 'Can't tell; didn't know your aunt', replied the Bishop brusquely.

When he was Bishop of London, a vicar came to see him on being appointed to a new parish and said, 'My Lord, my wife and I do not care for the vicarage; it is not a suitable house for us to live in. We have found another house just outside the parish, but only two miles from the Church as the crow flies. Have we your permission to live in it?' 'You have not', replied the Bishop, 'you are not a crow.'

On the other hand, Frederick Temple wrote absolutely lyrical letters to his wife. The letter he wrote proposing to her, which is in the family's possession, was quoted by Peter Hinchliff in *Frederick Temple, Archbishop of Canterbury: A Life* [1998], but deserves a wider airing:

My dear Miss Lascelles,
I find that I can come up to London on the 3rd whether there is business to be done or not, which I do not yet know, and I wish to come very much if you would like to see me but I cannot help having some fear that possibly when you find what I mean you will not desire it any more. I have become very fond of you and find that unless I can have you for my own altogether, duty to my own peace of mind and to the work I have to do requires me to keep away from your presence for the charm of it haunts me day and night. I know that you like my society but you may not like it enough to be my wife. Possibly you may even resent my asking you and think it somewhat hard that you cannot enjoy a pleasant friendship with one so much older without bringing on yourself such a solicitation as this. I acknowledge that if this be so I have no right to complain, I am much older than you, I have no wealth to offer you, for I have nothing but what I earn, and what is worse my life and yours are so different it would be unwise to change from yours to mine unless you can give me your very heart. I can only plead your own sweetness, frankness and kindness which made me dream of a happiness such as I have never experienced in my life, and you can give me that happiness if you will. Shall I come and see you on the 3rd - Ah- if you could understand how much depends on your answer.

After that wonderful letter - he was Bishop of Exeter at the time - he still signed,
'*Yours ever, F. Exon:*'

Unfortunately, he tore up the next letter, but she accepts, and the next letter runs:

My dearest Beatrice,
How delightful it is to call you Beatrice - the name fits you so exactly for it means the Blesser, you do bless me my dear, with an exceeding blessing. The sound of that voice, and that delightful smile, the most delightful sunshine I've ever seen, make my life sweeter every time I enjoy them, and every time I remember them, but you are not to be conceited because I say this, because there is no merit in you at all, you cannot help it. Other people do sometimes confer a blessing by their deeds, and sometimes by their words, but you need not do or say anything, you only have to be.

This was the man who to the outside world was thought to be very stern. In some letters he called himself her 'big cat' and wrote letters of pure Lewis Carroll non-sense to his two sons.

He was delighted when a small boot-boy in an hotel woke him in the morning with a knock at the door, having rehearsed carefully the fact that he was to say, 'My Lord' first. In his nervousness, it came from his lips as, 'It is the Lord, my boy.' Frederick was immensely amused too when someone selling him grouse, when he was Archbishop, said, 'Grace, your grouse.' Once, at the Old Palace in Canter-

bury, Archbishop Frederick, at an ordination retreat, was seeing how well his
young clergy visited. He pointed to one
of them and told him to go out of the
room, and come back as if he were visiting him. When he re-entered the
room, he saw the Archbishop of Canterbury lying on the sofa. The young
man plucked up all his courage and
said, 'Ah, there you are, Temple; drunk
again, I see.' The Archbishop leapt up
and said, 'You'll do; you'll do.' Frederick Temple dined out on such stories
and repeated them often, as did his
grandson in later years. And does it really matter if some of the stories got a
bit embellished over the years?

Frederick Temple died in 1902, and
his wife, Beatrice, in 1915. Frederick

Archbishop Frederick Temple with his
sons, Frederick (Freddy's father, on the
Archbishop's right) and William.

and Beatrice had two sons, Frederick Charles and William, born in 1879 and
1881 respectively. Frederick Charles was the father of Freddy Temple.

Frederick and William, later to be Archbishop of Canterbury himself, grew up
together in the Palaces at Exeter, Fulham and Lambeth, and the Old Palace at
Canterbury. The two brothers were very close and remained so until William's
death in 1944. When his father died in 1957, Freddy inherited 679 letters from
William to Frederick, letters he had written from the age of eight until just before
he died. More will be said later about Freddy's own relationship with, recollections of and reflections about, his Uncle William .

Frederick, Freddy's father, went to school at Colet Court, the preparatory
school for St. Paul's, then on to Rugby and Balliol. He did not, however, graduate,
because the Boer War intervened, and he went out to South Africa. After the
Boer War he toyed with the idea of settling in South Africa, but was dissuaded
from this by family pressure. His brother William wrote to him: 'I wonder if you
will really stay out there. I need not record my own or the family's sentiments on
that point, but is it not possible that S. Africa may be nearly full to bursting of people in much the same position as yourself?' .

Instead, encouraged greatly by Lord Kitchener, he returned to England to
study engineering. He served his apprenticeship under James Mansergh, FRS,
between 1901 and 1903, and his first post was as Engineer at the Birmingham
Elan Valley Waterworks until 1905. In that year he went out to India, to a post
with the Military Works Services, from 1905 till 1907. Between then and 1919 he
held a variety of posts with various Works Services in India, before being appoint-

ed Chief Town Engineer of Jamshedpur. Between 1924 and 1932 he was also Administrator of Jamshedpur. After the catastrophic earthquake in Bihar he was appointed Relief Engineer and Supply Officer to the Government of Bihar and Orissa, and oversaw the reconstruction of Bihar. While in India, he served with the India Volunteer Force, the Bihar Light Horse, the Indian Defence Force and the Auxiliary Force (India). He was Lieutenant-colonel, the Officer in Command, of the Chota Nagpur Regiment from 1928 till 1933, and Honorary ADC to the Viceroy of India from 1931 till 1936.

Whilst in India, Colonel Temple gained for himself great respect as a man of probity and commanded enormous respect from his employees for his scrupulous fairness. On June 4th, 1931, the following letter was sent to him:

Highly Honoured Sir,

Early in the dawn of today's lucky day my friend has given to me, to my intoxicating gladness the very pleasant tidings that your benevolent honour has for his disposal a fine job where I may be able to display my real zeal and abilities to their utmost height, so that by the grace of the All Impotent God it may prove beneficial to all connected.

I am belonging to a Holy Brahmin family full of respectability but by some unforeseen pleasures of God it is not prosperous nowadays.

As to my adjustments I appeared for the Matric Examination at Ooty, but failed, the reason for which I shall now describe.

To begin with my writing was illegible, this was due to climatic reasons, for I having come from a warm in a cold climate found my fingers stiff and very disobedient to my wishes.

Further I had received a great shock to my mental system in the shape of the death of my only fond brother. Besides most honoured Sir, I beg to state that I am in very uncomfortable circumstances, being the soul means of support of my fond brother's seven issues consisting of three adults and four adultresses, the latter being the bane of my existence owing to my having to support two of my wives as well as their issues of which by God's misfortunes the feminine gender predominates.

[The succeeding paragraph is so intimately physiological in detail that it has been thought best to omit it!]

My ambition was to pass my B.A. examination, but honoured sir, amidst such above mentioned monstrous and thundering difficulties lying like hideous mountains in my way it was beyond my humble and humane power.

Honoured Sir, if by wonderful good fortune these few humble lines meet with your benign kindness and favourable turn of mind I the poor menial shall ever pray for the long life and prosperity of yourself as well as your honour's posthumous olive branches.

I remain, Honoured Sir, Your obedient servant.

The man was given a job. Colonel Temple had been much amused by the letter and remarked to the Chaplain of Jamshedpur: 'I simply could not refuse such a comical plea.'

Despite being thought by some a man who was a trifle on the staid side, Freddy's father did possess the characteristic Temple brand of humour. He used to exasperate his wife by sending Christmas cards with a picture of one of his newly-built water towers, and on one occasion a reproduction of the patent of which he was proud - for the Temple Automatic Storm Water Separator. When Freddy's mother remonstrated with him, saying that such cards did not actually portray the true message of Christmas, he once said that their friends were 'almost certainly sated with pictures of mangers, portrayals of the baby Jesus with pater and mater, shepherds, angels and the whole Christian gamut of it all; our cards show God in action in the world.' Somewhere in this sentence can be discerned an affinity with the social gospel preached by his brother, William!

On his return to England, Colonel Temple held an appointment with the Ministry of Home Security from 1941 to 1942, and from 1942 to 1946 he was Regional Controller of the Ministry of Fuel and Power. From 1947 to 1949 he was Director of Open-cast Coal Production. On his retirement in 1949 was appointed Commander of the British Empire.

When he was the Garrison Engineer in Calcutta he had married Frances Copleston, daughter of the Bishop of Calcutta and Metropolitan of India, on January 26th 1907, in Calcutta Cathedral. Fortunately Frances did not inherit the scattiness of her mother.

2   Childhood and School

Freddy was born nearly nine years after his parents' marriage, on November 24th, 1916, in Patna, India, a much-wanted boy after three girls, Beatrice, Rose and Edith. One of the first letters of congratulation came from William Temple, then Vicar of St. James's, Piccadilly. He wrote, on November 29th, to his brother, Freddy's father:

We heard this morning of the arrival of a boy. How admirable! I expect you are frightfully pleased. We are!

Two weeks later, he wrote again,

I am the wickedest fellow alive for I have missed the mail and this is the first after the arrival of my nephew. But the news of that event is the best that has come for a long while. I wonder what you will call him. Frances is frightfully pleased to be his god-mother.

And on January 17th,

We are very anxious to know the name of the new infant. Frances particularly wants to know what name she has given to her godson.

In some eagerness, and perhaps exas-peration, he wrote again on the last day of January,

WHAT is the infant's name?

Soon after that, William and Frances Temple were told that the child was to be baptised Frederick Stephen. Both Uncle William and Aunt Frances were godparents.

By this time, Freddy's father was the Civil and Sanitary Engineer in Jamshedpur. He often used to say that his chosen profession brought the Temple family down to ground. There is no

Freddy, aged 18 months.

Freddy's parents, with Beatrice, Rose, Ann and staff, at Jamshedpur. Edith and Freddy were in England.

doubt that, in many ways, Freddy had an extremely privileged upbringing. Photographs of the family in their beautiful home in Jamshedpur show an impressive array of servants, and in later years Freddy Temple recalled vivid memories of riding on his white pony, Cherry. There are many delightful pictures of him sitting astride the pony, which boasted a temperament more wilful than young Freddy's on more than one occasion.

Behind all the privilege, however, life for the young Freddy was not all happy.

Freddy, aged eighteen months, on his pony, Cherry.

He belonged to the age of the upper-class English where the parents only saw the child for about an hour in the evening; Freddy gained the impression that they both thought this was entirely long enough anyway. In his own words, a 'vicious and unpleasant nurse' (ie nanny) dominated his childhood; her true character was quite unknown to Freddy's parents, to whom she was invariably charming. The nurse bullied and mistreated Freddy, and the young boy was given innumerable lines as punishments for quite trivial 'offences'. He was forced to eat everything put in front of him. Although he was the first to admit in later years that this in itself was perhaps no bad thing, what upset him was the way it was done, and the way she 'sneered at me rather than talked to me'. If he simply refused to eat something, it reappeared first at the next meal, set down without a word, and there was 'no opportunity for reasoning or negotiation'; it had to be eaten before anything else. Cold, clammy and wobbly white blancmanges sat watching him on a plate at many a tea table; beyond lay delicious cakes and sandwiches. To the end of his life, Freddy couldn't bear blancmange.

The young Freddy travelled backwards and forwards to England from India with his mother, home each spring and back to Jamshedpur each autumn. As a boy he used to say that the happiest two nights of the year were sitting up in the train compartment travelling across France to join the ship at Marseilles; the train seemed endlessly long, and he recalled with delight the waits at unfamiliar stations, the strange voices and the violent juddering and hissing as the train drew out of the stations, the 'shouting and the clanging and the great big oily wheels.' The smells of Marseilles were 'indescribable, but never forgotten - a mixture of sea and sweat and vegetables and burnt wood.' Wicker baskets were piled high on the quay and he played guessing games with himself as to what lay inside, just as he would play lonely games imagining pictures from the shapes made by the mud spattered on the carriage window. In the streets surrounding the quay at Marseilles he watched, open-mouthed, the local children, who were 'quite squabblesome', playing on the cobbles. (The word 'squabblesome' would undoubtedly not have been recognised by his philologist great-grandfather, Archbishop Trench.) In a school composition, when aged nine, Freddy

Freddy, aged 3, with his grandfather, the Metropolitan of India.

wrote, somewhat precociously and preciously, 'I dread to think what their mothers and fathers would have said if they knew quite how terribly naughty they were.' And as he walked, young Freddy would sometimes catch his toes in the tramlines and would feel the squelching of muddy water as it seeped over his shoes and made strange patterns on his white socks.

Freddy enjoyed thirteen trips going from England to India and back by the age of eight. By his own admission, he was, when about seven or eight, quite arrogant, felt he knew all about travel and was very scornful about adults who were travelling for the first time. He once told his father, 'They simply didn't know what to do at Port Said and what you did in the East properly, and it was a terrible bore having to tell them.' His mother enjoyed or endured nearly fifty voyages on the P & O, leaving each child in England when they were about eight.

Freddy, aged four, in St. Mark's Square,
Venice.

Thus, in the spring of 1925, at the age of eight and a half, Freddy was brought to England and deposited at the prep. school his parents had chosen for him, St. Christopher's, Eastbourne. Unfortunately, the excellent headmaster retired after two terms. Rumour had it that he ran off with the music and art mistress, which, though it sent a frisson of excitement throughout the school, cannot now be verified. Whatever the truth, the school went steadily to pieces after that.

A brief selection of some of Freddy's letters home give a flavour of his life at St. Christopher's. The letters that are reproduced are as he wrote them. When he was still eight he wrote:

Darling mum and dad,
I thank both of you very much for your adorebull letters. I hope your eyes are well again Dad. How I adore your letters I don't known how it is they make me feel joyfull. Little sits next to me in prep: he is one of my nicest boys. And he tips me nearly all his sweets and I tip him a few. Mum darling you are a sweet tart, precious you both are. My places in form are: Latin 1, English 1, Maths 3, French 1. Sweet tarts you are.

Before signing off he concluded with a sentence which is difficult to explain:

We had some football yesterday, I was goalkeeper, I only let one goal throw we lost by four, I am so sorry. I must stop now. Tons love, Fred.

This sentence might go some way towards explaining why he did not come top in Maths.

Later that year he wrote,

Darling Mum and Dad,
Thank you for your adorebull let-

The prep school boy, aged 8

ters. I have a lot to tell you. There was a lecture last Friday. It was about a ship in ice and snow. This ship was going to the north pole. And they had six months of no sun. It was nothing but dark. And the ship got broken up in the end. So they stayed on an island named elephant island precious one. And the captain of the boat went for rescue and came back in too years with 50 people. Then we had four matchs won three lost one the one we lost by four the scores were us 0 them 4. Then we had an entirement last night, on music, it was afforly funny. And we had to join in the corus. TWENTY years on an ice-berge on the oxen high nothing to wear but pjamas, nothing to do but slide, snowballs to eat rather hard to bit. A poler bear to keep me warm at night. My places in form are Latin 3, English 1, Maths 2, French 1.
Tons of love, Fred.

The following year he wrote,

My own darlingest Mum and Dad,
It is heavenly Mr West told me that Dad had telephoned to say he was coming over on Tuesday, with you Mum I hope, come as EARLY as possible, I am dying with excitement; all the masters know it, my places are not good, I am afraid, only I am so excited. Come to lunch. Mr West is sort of head now, Mr Beck has gone away for the present, and he said he might let me off the little work we do that afternoon. It is only Geography and Maths or History and French, nothing important one or the other I am not quite certain. Come, do not put off, both of you MUST come.
My places are Latin 2, English 7, Maths 4, French 6. Very bad, it is all due to excitement. I have been counting the very hours, I forget how many there are now, only you are coming on Tuesday, all the better. Come EARLY. I have been thinking about it all the time, I am dying (I hope that's spelt right) to see you. I am going to try and work really well this week. I can not find your letter, only I do not think there were very many things to answer. There were matches yesterday, I played the one, we lost: I bowled two people and made six. The sermon today was by Mr Browne.
With love, Freddy. Come EARLY.

On his tenth birthday, November 24th, 1926, in a letter thanking his parents for his birthday presents, the young Freddy finished with his first recorded judgement of a sermon: 'Today Mr. Browne gave a very good sermon'; this was followed a few weeks later by his second essay into sermon criticism, 'Mr. West gave a very poor sermon today. With love, Freddy Temple.'
On December 8, 1926, Freddy wrote one of his more desperate letters:

I'm so sorry to say that I had a terribul night it was thunder and litghing (dont know

how to spell it). I'm so sorry to say to that I cried and cried and cried. I tried not to but I did. Matron came into our dorm and said not to bother but why mum you couldnt be there to say that I dont know. Why do you leave me in this awefull place. I have something called a veruka on my toe and it hurts but matron says all I do is make a fuss but I cant sleep because it hurts so much. She called me into the corridor last night because she said I was disturbing the other boys. But I don't think I was for I think I was being quiet but it hurt. I had to stand there for one hour. Why are you lots of miles away. I have to wash in cold water with other boys. I dont exactly wash with them but we have basins in the middle and tooth mugs and they all have other toothpastes. You said my sort was best but they all laugh at mine and they all seem to have the same other sort and say that they have the best so I dont know what to think. I hate it here I really really do. I have to learn to paint tomorrow with a lady who they say has a mustach (wish I could spell that better). They say she gets annoied and tants [taunts?] you if you cant draw and paint. Most of the other boys are going out with their parents this Saturday for its a special day out but I've got to stay here for you are so many miles away. I wish wish wish wish you would come to see me or better still come and take me away.
I love you all precious ones.
F Temple.

Other letters are about games, including such gems as,

On Wednesday there was a match against Temple Grove, which was a draw 3-3. In my last letter I think I told you that the match against Temple Grove on Saturday, which we lost 14-3, they fouled and won unfairly. Well, in this match, Mr. Beck naturally was strict on their fouling and they actually argued with him and called him 'a fat old thing', and when they scored their try, their man was really in touch and their touch judge never put his flag up. We will never play that school again'.

In another he wrote,

Yesterday was the Boxing Comp: I was too heavy to box, so I had to be a second and wave the towel; it is a frightfully tiring job.

During the summer holiday of 1926, Freddy's mother took him to see a Phrenologist in Brighton. Whatever one might think of the 'science' of phrenology, the four page report was, in many respects, uncannily accurate. The report opens thus:

PHRENOLOGICAL DELINEATION OF THE CHARACTER &
CAPACITIES OF MASTER FREDERICK S. TEMPLE, AGE NEARLY
11 YEARS.

*This youth possesses a brain capacity far beyond the range of the average person,
and his head is very distinctive in shape. The frontal or intellectual lobes of the
brain are particularly well represented, giving him good powers of observation, but
especially a thinking, planning and reasoning mind, and he is intuitional, a rather
keen reader of character, and will like to study human nature.*

*He has imagination in a well marked degree; is very cautious - far too cautious;
possesses strongly developed domestic and social affections; an aspiring disposi-
tion; and there is a good moral development. I think he may well enter Holy Orders
- or perhaps study law.*

The Phrenologist had never met Freddy or his mother before; he had no idea of
their background or any ecclesiastical connections.

On the 31st March, 1930, Freddy wrote, 'I was confirmed on Tuesday by Dr.
Bell of Chichester. There were 151 confirmed; about 25 were boys. Matron has
given me such a nice prayer book for my Confirmation. Mr. West also has given us
all a little book called "Communion and Offering".' By all accounts, his Confirmation preparation was a bit 'hit and miss', which may well account in part for the
importance he was to attach in later years to the need for a thorough grounding in
the Christian faith, and not just what he was to call a 'namy-pamby, wishy-washy,
won't it be lovely to be confirmed, dear, and be able to "go up" [ie to the altar rail]
with mum and dad?' He also told the story in later years of a school he visited (well
before he himself was a bishop, where he read a notice, 'The Bishop will be coming to school on the 16th of next month to take a Confirmation service. If you
don't want to be confirmed, please sign below.' Freddy added that all that notice
lacked was the sentence, 'Those confirmed will have a half-day holiday.'

As a child, Freddy suffered from frequent chest infections, especially in the
winter; the very first winter at St. Christopher's he had to leave to return to the
more favourable climate of India. Another year his mother received a call from
the Headmaster to come home as speedily as possible because Freddy had contracted measles, bronchitis and pneumonia and was seriously ill. A dramatic series of telegrams from England to India tell the story of how he very nearly failed to
pull through. All this did nothing to help his studies and he passed into Rugby
lower than he might have done in 1930. (Ill-health continued to dog his footsteps
until he was about sixteen.)

Freddy found life tough at the School House, Rugby, and he was never really
happy there, much to the disappointment of his family, especially his father, who
could not really understand why. Freddy himself laid part of the blame on his parents. A bicycle was essential at Rugby as the playing fields were far out of the

town, and to cycle back quickly after a game was the only way to get a hot 'tosh' (the Rugby word for 'bath') first and thus have more free time. Freddy was one of the only boys whose parents did not at first provide one. After a time he was given a bicycle and had in shame and misery to learn to ride it. While learning, he was surrounded by his taunting peers; Freddy never forgot the humiliation of what he had to suffer as a boy of fourteen; his peers never let him forget either. On one attempt he lost control, shot off the road and got caught in a tree while the bicycle careered on without him. 'A touch of Absalom' said one bystander, as he approached to help him down.

Freddy, with his mother, after his first term at Rugby.

Freddy's first letter home, in September, 1930, started,

We got up at 7-30, then dressed and came down to breakfast at 8. Then at 9 we had to assemble at the West Door of the Chapel. There were three paths leading to it and the middle one was the quickest, so I took it and as I was walking down I noticed that everyone was looking at me very queerly and as I was near the end I walked on; afterwards I realised that that path was only for masters. Then we were shown our places in chapel; then came chapel. After that we went to the Temple Speech Room to have our voices tried; I don't know what he thought of mine. It is very lonely here.

The next day he wrote that he had to go for a walk with another boy called Prideaux - 'and I have to say he seems very stupid.' He then went to the Temple Reading Room 'which is a marvellous place and has a museum above. I do not like it at all here, but I may get to like it.' He also complained about the 'hot milk (sour) which I have to drink at 7am, and breakfast at 8-15am, with vile porridge and, as usual, sour milk.' He continued:

The French master jabbers French hard, then actually expects you to understand it, and some of the people aren't very nice; it is rather horrid to find bits of mouldy grapes chucked in your locker and after a game to find your trousers lying on the floor in a puddle. On Friday afternoon we got off first lesson in honour of Lord Kilbrackon's first visit to the school after his illness. He is Chairman of the Governing Body. On Saturday morning I was invited to breakfast with the Headmaster; it was great fun; Lord Kilbrackon was here under Grandpapa. I must stop my letter now as Prideaux is going round dirtying people's letters.

The first letter of his second term began,

Well, here I am at this awful place. At some moments I feel it is a vile place and at others not so bad. I don't know what it is, but somehow everyone seems to stare at me as if they hadn't seen anything like me before. Here it does not seem to be the correct thing to say ones prayers; so far I have been the only one to get out and say mine. The amount of swearing done here is remarkable; "damn" is an ordinary word, it seems. Mr. Megson is my Maths master; a fat, middle-aged gentleman, but he is very nice (his only drawback is that he is very keen on neatness). Mr. Hardwick takes me for Greek; he is full of common sense and is always trying to make us use ours. Mr. Attwell takes us for Science: he is a dear middle-aged man, tries to be very interesting, but fails slightly. I'm in Mr. Odger's form. If you leave a book behind, you do not have to do many lines but, if the weather is fine, have to roll his lawn for quarter of an hour, but if it is wet (the first case I should think never applies at Rugby) you have to make what he calls 50 spills; you tear up an old piece of paper into 4 inch long strips and fold them in a certain manner so that he can light his pipe with them; you have 48 hours to do them in.

On May 15th, 1931, Freddy wrote:

I always find one forgets all one wants to say unless it is put down immediately and that is why my letters are so short I'm afraid. Yesterday I had my hair cut; the hairdresser sits the whole time (it is rather sweet the way he moves round taking his chair with him). I don't know why he does because he looks quite able-bodied to me. He can only do the sides and just has to make wild snips at the top of one's head. This term in Geography we are doing India. Today has been a pouring wet day. I have discovered my waste paper basket; Spens had sold it to a new boy who wanted one. (There has just been a fag call and I have flung down my pen anyhow and luckily there is no smudge.) He is going to refund the money to the new boy and I am selling my brand new one which I have just bought to the new boy so it is just the same as nothing having happened except the new boy having bought a waste paper basket from the shop. Greek this term is very nice: it is annoying when Greek goes so quickly and P.T. goes so slowly. There are some marvellous 2d. potato crisps at the Stodge now with salt complete. The time is crawling along. Last night some boys were laughing so much over a book that I asked what the book was; I think they must be mad because it was 'All Quiet on the Western Front' which is one of the saddest books out I was always told, and yet to them it seemed as if it was the funniest thing they had ever read. The ten shillings is coming in most useful: I am going to buy a lampshade and get those frames of the drawings of Grandpapa stuck together again and lots of other little oddities. I got a new cap today as my old [one] got torn by a mad boy (he is mad: he came up and tore a large bit out of my cap and now keeps it all wrapped up). That Latin prep I thought I had done badly in I found in fact that I had done well in: so far, touch wood, I am doing well this fortnight, which will please you and it certainly pleases me. We have just had a Corps parade which was just so boring. Most boys like them but I can't see the point at all and think it all very silly. I can't say that sort of thing here though or I'd get jumped upon very speedily. One big Corps person is an oaf and swears foully and I really don't like that and think it is quite unnecessary. Well, that's it, my darling ones. Can't wait to see you again. Altho' I didn't know what to write at the start, I seem to have filled quite a bit of paper, don't I? I hope I haven't made you feel too bored. My French is getting better, I hope.

Three weeks later, Freddy penned the following letter home:

I have been very tortured this week. There is an older boy called [X], who is great fun. I like him a lot and so does everyone. He is very gentle and kind. I think you know his father, who is fairly famous and [X] is a good cricketer too. Suddenly on Tuesday afternoon he said he would like me to go to his den for he wanted to tell me something. Of course I said I would go. He made some tea but hadn't any biscuits: I said not to worry at all. He then looked very embarrassed and red and said, 'Temple, I am very very fond of you.' I didn't know what on earth to say and felt myself very awkward and wanted to run away, but somehow I couldn't because he was in distress and tears rolled off his cheeks. I put my head close to his and said something like, 'Not to worry'. He turned his face to mine and gave me a kiss. The kiss happened so quickly and I let him kiss me. He suddenly stood up and said something like, 'Temple, you must go now because you must despise me.' I didn't know what to do or say, so I went after saying goodnight. I know it's terribly wrong to fall in love with other boys and I really shouldn't ever speak to him again. But I like him so much and surely it's not his fault if he feels like this? He was so kind and upset about it all. I want to be a real friend of his and help him sort this out. Is this what Grandmama Copleston would call 'naïve and simple'? I am confused.

I met [X] on Wednesday morning; he smiled at me and gave me a wink and said he was going to buy some biscuits and would I like to share them? He said if I now hated him he would quite understand and he would have to eat the lot. But I certainly don't hate him. I also don't know what to do.

On June 10th, Freddy wrote:

I still, apparently, keep others awake by coughing all night; I feel sorry for them, though they're not very nice to me about it. The strange thing is that my coughing doesn't seem to wake me up. There must be some explanation.

And again on June 17th:

> *This older boy came up to me on Tuesday and said, 'Temple, I would very much like to hit you in the face.' I was a little confused as to how to respond to this, so just walked on. I do seem to get picked on a bit…. The bad news is that I hear Lord Kilbrackon has had a setback with his health, but the good news is the Stodge has started to sell those 2d. potato crisps again.*

And so, in this sort of vein, the letters continue throughout his time at Rugby. Specially amusing are his rather sharp and penetrating adolescent character sketches of the masters. If some of the masters had managed to intercept some of these letters before they had been posted, they might have learnt a few home truths through the eyes of one of their young charges. Freddy loathed the fagging system, and in his early letters inveighed against the 'awfulness of such a donkeyish way of doing things'. Sixth formers were allowed to beat fags and others. 'Any sixth former', wrote Freddy to his mother, 'can call "fag" at any time of day and all the fags have to run to where the call comes from'. Freddy reckoned that the worst sort of sixth former used to wait till all the young fags were squashed at table in the dining hall and they all had to leap out over the table, knocking over their precious marmalade and jam that had come from home, crash up the stairs where they were having their tea, and make sure they did not arrive last. Recalling these times in later life, Freddy said, 'Going back downstairs I was alright for I was fairly big and tough and all you did was leap on the back of the smallest boy there, who then crashed to the ground and, bruised and tortured, arrived last to do the job. I'm not quite sure that this was what the St. Paul had in mind when he said "Bear ye one another's burdens"'.

Despite the fact that he so heartily disapproved of the fagging system as a fag, this did not stop Freddy from having a fag himself when he reached the top of the school. One of his fags was Hugh Montefiore, later to have a distinguished ministry in the Church, as Vicar of Great St. Mary's, Cambridge, Bishop of Kingston and Bishop of Birmingham.

Life didn't seem all bad, however; some letters were positively cheerful. Freddy played games fairly proficiently, including rugby, tennis and cricket and on the whole enjoyed them, especially cricket, despite the fact that his uncle William, when Headmaster of Repton, had once famously said to the parents of Reptonians: 'Personally, I have always looked on cricket as organised loafing.'

On June 24th, 1934, Freddy wrote:

> *This morning I went out to breakfast with one of the Spens family whose mother had met you in India when I was a year old: we drove out into the country and had breakfast at the first inn that looked nice. We ended up at the Craven Arms in*

Southam. The boy said, 'He's going to be Archbishop', whereupon the mother turned and started telling me all the things she wanted me to do when I was Archbishop and all about her doctrine of Reincarnation. I floundered rather but apparently it was enough to say in a surprised voice, 'Really?' 'Yes, quite', she said when we parted and I rather naughtily threw out, 'The world will be a better place when you and I enter it again.' At that point another Spens turned up with his mother and I was introduced and then the first one said to the second, 'He's going to be Archbishop', to which he got the reply, 'Oh, but that's the height and depth of hopelessness. Let me see, weren't you Hackitt in The Ringer? Of course the only thing for you is the stage. I've never seen such a good performance. Archbishops are fat and stupid.' I decided to keep quiet about my Grandfather and Uncle.'

Freddy's next but one letter home included the following:

A Mr. Hubbard preached an excellent sermon this morning. It <u>was</u> good: such a relief after all the dreary ones from our own masters. It was very amusing too: he told one story about the war when a woman said to him, 'I'm so glad I'm not the Almighty. What an awful fix he must be in with all the cross-praying that must be going on between England and Germany.'

Soon after that, he wrote:

The Corps Inspection was yesterday: an antique general from the Crimaea toddled round our ranks with the usual cortege. It was pouring most of the time but of course it had to be done all the same. There is nothing more fatuous I know of: they are all of the same class, the Royal Tournament and Inspections: all meant to thrill one with the grandeur of the army and its ceremonial. He smelled of whisky but I thought I had better not point this out or I might be responsible for a court martial for him for having had a drink at an inappropriate time, while on duty, and I wouldn't want to wish that on him for he seemed a harmless sort of old buffer (or duffer?). He probably only had it to keep the rain out anyway, in some ways very admirable and far-sighted.

Freddy always claimed to have had few real friends at Rugby. It must have been difficult for him to be a member of the Temple family, with all the family's associations with Rugby, and the other boys' relationships towards him might well have reflected a kind of ambivalence in the way in which he was regarded. What is certainly true is that Freddy was invited to meals with the Headmaster in a way that other boys were not. This could not have failed to lead to a certain jealousy, and on one occasion Freddy wrote home, 'The seat of my trousers is quite worn out with the number of kicks I have received.' It would perhaps have been kinder if he had been treated a little less preferentially. He certainly found being a member of the Temple family hard to cope with. In later years he wrote, about his time at Rugby, that 'the vision of my grandfather and my uncle haunted me throughout my years there; I was always expected to do better than I could.'

Winter holidays during this time were always spent with his grandmother, Edith Copleston, widow of the Metropolitan of India, at her home in Putney; his sister Edith and he (by this time, Beatrice and Rose were back in India) also visited Uncle William (now Archbishop of York) and Aunt Frances regularly and spent very enjoyable Christmas holidays at Bishopthorpe. Uncle William and Aunt Frances gave him a series of Buchan books each Christmas; they were devoured eagerly, and Freddy looked forward to receiving the next.

Grandmama Copleston was an awesome character. Family prayers were held in true Victorian style, with cook, housemaid and parlourmaid gallantly waiting outside the room as long as possible to give the schoolboy a chance to be on time. Mrs. Copleston was a stickler for time-keeping, but Freddy had a winning smile for the servants. Freddy had to learn and recite the collect for the day every Sunday; Edith stood behind Freddy prompting when necessary - although the whole exercise was ludicrously unnecessary, as Grandmama was deaf. At Mattins on Sunday morning at St. John's Church, just across the road, Edith and Freddy sat very close to their grandmother on either side, so that when she fell asleep, as she invariably did, she did not sway from side to side. Freddy found it hard to suppress his giggles, and it did not help his concentration on the sermon at all. They always sat in the same pew and Freddy knew every creak it made. If their grandmother's weight became oppressive, Freddy and Edith perfected a technique for waking her up, by pushing their bottoms against the back of the pew, making a creak just loud enough to rouse her. On one occasion they made themselves very unpopular with other elderly members of the congregation by pushing too hard; the pew made a groaning sound which Freddy said was enough to wake the dead, let alone the living elderly who were enjoying the sermon in their own way.

One of her grandson's tasks was to read *The Times* leader to Mrs. Copleston every day, and most days she asked him to start a game of chess with her; the games did not usually progress very far, as it would not be long before she nodded off and started snoring gently, which in turn made Freddy go into paroxysms of giggles. It was through his grandmother, one of the great formative characters of his childhood, that Freddy learnt to love and admire the elderly. She also encouraged his love of history and his sense of curiosity; if he did not know something, he would not be allowed to rest until he had looked it up in her well-stocked library.

On one occasion, when staying with his grandmother as a boy, Belisha Beacons were introduced, and Mrs. Copleston was uncertain as to what they were. 'I can show you what they're like', said the young Freddy eagerly. He went out of the room and came back with a small pencil he had been given; it was in the form of a Belisha Beacon. His grandmother looked at it and said, 'Oh, I hadn't thought of looking for anything quite so small.' A charming picture comes to mind of roads dotted with tiny Belisha Beacons. Freddy also remembered his mother and himself trying to persuade his grandmother to have a hearing aid. At length they got her to try one out. Young Freddy went into the drawing room to hear the young man say, 'Can you hear, Madam?' 'Yes', she replied, 'I can hear quite well but I do not like the sound of the voice at all.' There was a pause and the young man replied, 'That, Madam, is not the fault of the instrument.'

Freddy's father was only in England every four years and remained a rather aloof, distant and strict figure. Freddy longed for a closer relationship with him. He once plucked up the courage to write to him about a personal problem and ask for some help and advice; for some reason he received no answer, and this hurt Freddy. He wrote, 'I curled up and fought a desperate battle on my own, thinking myself frightful.' It was only as he grew older that he really appreciated the greatness and Christian goodness of his father, his massive discipline and self-control, his affection which could bring him to tears when his wife was on occasions hard to him. He also wrote wonderfully detailed letters every Sunday to each of the children; he even kept a note of which of the children had received which carbon copy so that none of them received the last and faintest copy each week. These superb letters, which Freddy kept all his life, did much to weld and keep the family together when they were apart. They were the foil to his mother's more impulsive and entertaining letters, which were also very good; they were shrewd and asked questions to make the children think about the meaning of life and their place in the world.

It was always a great distress to his father that Rugby never meant as much to Freddy as it did to him. On one occasion when he was in England he visited Freddy at half term. He was an impossible father to take around; he kept diving into the 'dens' (studies) of senior boys when Freddy was quite junior and hauling out pieces of furniture to see if his name was still carved in a certain place. Freddy stood terrified in case the sixth former should appear round the corner. When they were in the country, his parents were not good at taking him out from school. They stayed with a dear but extremely fusty master called Chatwin and his two spinster sisters. (In January, 1932, Freddy wrote in a letter home: 'It is going to be very awkward this term when I want to criticise my form master, Mr. Chatwin, being as he is a friend of my revered papa, but still, if I may say so, very very reverently, he is very boring though I think he tries his little best to be interesting.') Freddy's mother would often just retire to her room to rest in the afternoon, with curtains drawn, and there was nothing for Freddy to do but sit beside her unable even to read because of the darkened room. When he got back to school he used to listen to the exciting things other boys had done with their parents; he was shamed into telling lies about imaginary things that he had enjoyed doing with his own.

At the end of one summer Freddy and John Kisch, one of his few close friends, were the two chosen from Rugby to attend the Duke of York's Camp. The two boys were a little apprehensive as they had never mixed with 'tough working-class boys' and it had been instilled in them that it was most important not to appear snobbish or stand-offish. They were issued with a little book, which ended: 'Camp Rules: One Only: Play The Game'. This stuck in their critical public school nostrils terribly. The boys had to meet in the Royal Mews; they were late so went there by taxi and were driven round twice before they plucked up the courage to get out and pay the taxi driver, feeling that every working-class eye was upon them.

In a letter to his mother, Freddy wrote, 'I started off with a beautiful faux-pas: I saw one boy I was certain I had seen once on a visit to Oxford and dashed up and accosted him. He replied, "Sorry, Hi 'ave never been to Oxford. I'm in Chivers." I recovered and said, "Oh! I hear the jam at the camp is very good".'

Freddy's aristocratic mother was taking no chances and had issued him with a tin of Keating's Powder to ward off fleas; she told him to sprinkle this all round his bed each night, which he solemnly did; the boys either side apparently took it in their stride. When he tried to make conversation with his neighbour on the first evening by asking him what he was reading, the boy gave him a withering look up and down and said, 'Too crude for you, chum', and carried on reading. Later in the letter alluded to previously, Freddy wrote, 'The night was frightful except for me with my extra rug (provided by his mother). I was woken at 5-30 with, "My God, it's cold" and "Crikey, it's freezing", which was all very obvious and tiresome.' He also told his mother that John Kisch was not happy: 'He just does not click with his section; he had one who looked cultured but when John asked him his school, he said, "Portsmouth Grammar".' Doubtless the two of them were looked upon as a couple of prigs by the other boys in their section - not without justification.

The games at the Camp were tough; there was a form of rugby, seemingly with no rules, on hard-baked ground. Freddy soon saw how many people were getting the skin ripped off their arms and sensibly kept well clear. There was a ghastly three mile run in the heat of the day; Freddy came in 220th out of 400, and his diary says he was sick. The Duke of York visited for a night; all the boys had to make a circle round him while he undressed on the beach and then he swam out the furthest any boy had. Freddy bumped into him in the water, much to his delight. The conversation, if there was any, is not recorded. When he got back to the beach he was upbraided by one of the Duke's detectives and told that he was lucky he had not swum quite as far out as the Duke, for it was his (ie the Duke's) prerogative to swim out the furthest. Freddy was not impressed; he told John Kisch that when he was older he would 'counteract such stupidity'. What exactly he meant by this we do not know, though we can guess the tenor of his feelings.

When his mother was in the country, Freddy would, of course, spend his holidays at Damerel, the family home in Sussex. He specially enjoyed playing tennis and entertaining his few close Rugby friends. One friend of Freddy's can recall vividly an afternoon in the summer of 1932 when he and Freddy were 'mucking about with a couple of tennis racquets and a tennis ball that had seen better days'. They were lobbing it at the garage door at Damerel. His boyhood friend recalls:

> *Freddy gave the ball an almighty slam, with the result that the ball bounced into the undergrowth nearby. I expected him to go to retrieve it - but was taken aback to see him walk up to the garage door and come back with, cupped gently in his hands, a Camberwell Beauty butterfly - squashed and quite dead. Freddy had tears in his eyes and kept repeating, 'I didn't mean to hurt you, my dear.' Freddy must have been about fifteen then. I remember thinking at the time that, to my mind, he was being extraordinarily sentimental and silly. In fact, I told him so. Freddy turned to me and said with, what I can now recall as utter conviction, 'God made this little beauty, and I've just destroyed him. May he and God forgive me.' Freddy didn't just say this for effect. He meant it. He then threw his tennis racquet on the drive and said, 'Let's go inside and find some tea; I've no more stomach for games.'*

In the summer holidays Freddy often used to go up to Loch Lomond to stay with another friend, Peter Lumsden, at the family's large house, which boasted the postal address, 'Arden, Dumbartonshire'. This provided for him an insight into a life of luxury which he had not previously known, for although he had lived in a large house in India, money had been tight. A car and chauffeur used to meet him at Glasgow, and there was always a large party staying. He played tennis with balls that were not used more than four times; there was bridge each evening and much grouse shooting. The family had a large launch on the loch and he spent many happy hours on that. He enjoyed all but the grouse shooting. Hamish Lumsden, Peter's brother, recalls how Freddy was always the life and soul of a house party, whether on the tennis court or swimming in the loch. His wife Sheila remembers climbing Ben Lomond with him and others, and how he kept them all going with his wit and laughter. At the end of his second visit, Freddy was taken by the chauffeur to catch the London train from Glasgow. When he arrived there he had an hour to kill before he train left. 'I walked up Sauchiehall Street', Freddy wrote to his Grandmama, 'and met so many people who the papers call "unfortunates". It was so *so* sad. There was I, so very fortunate. Maybe one day I will be able to do something for them.'

Near the end of his time at Rugby, Freddy spent a great deal of his free time acting - a talent he was to exploit to the full at Oxford and later in his life. Amongst other parts, he played La Tremouille in Shaw's *St. Joan* and *The Rugbeian* reported that he was 'amusingly pompous'. He was always cast as the comic and longed to play the tragic. He also directed the School House play in his last year and admitted in his letters home that he was spending 'far too much time doing this - but it's such fun and keeps me sane.'

Freddy was also for a while editor of *The Rugbeian*, the literary supplement to *The Meteor*, Rugby's magazine. (He often used to say in later life that producing

The Rugbeian was good training for the constant grind of producing a parish magazine every month.) In the first edition he edited he ended the editorial thus:

> *And now the Editor is going to prophesy: he feels that this number marks the beginning of a new era in School literature: that laziness will not in future curb the flow of contributions, and that Rugby will no longer consider as an unimportant byproduct a paper which, however feeble are its efforts, is trying and will continue to try its utmost to encourage and propagate the best literary instincts in the School.*

Also in this edition of the magazine was an article (which had been accepted for publication before Freddy became editor) which tells something of how Freddy viewed the beginning of each Rugby term, though from a rather quirky viewpoint. It is headed, 'The School for Parents':

> *"What? No, I'm afraid I can't; I would have loved to but you see, my mother goes back today; yes, Nottingdean are always rather late - Oh! Really! Your father went back yesterday; so did mine. No, I don't take him back; I just put him into the train and he's able to find his way now; he's got four more. Doing quite well, I think. Had an excellent report. Well, you see, mother goes back today, and I shall be thought very bad if I leave her on the last day, and I generally see her back to school, too. She's another year; what? Well, I don't think they do like it their first year, no; the fagging, you know, but luckily she got off that early, as she's in the Knitting Six. What? Oh! that's awfully nice of you to say so - yes, she is rather athletic. I'm hoping she'll get her Darning Blue next term. Yes, well, we must meet next week".*
>
> *Peter Thompson hung up the telephone and ran upstairs. He met Nanny on the way. "Ah, Nanny", he said, "has she everything? You know how forgetful she is. Remembered her darning? Good. You put in a few of my old socks for her to practise on; she'll want to put in a good deal of practice this term". He went through into the Nursery, where her mother was just finishing her tuck-box. "Ah! There you are, mother; now have you got your pocket money, and your Bible and your Prayer Book? Good. And there's a stamped and addressed postcard for you to write tonight. Let me see: I must go sign your Health Certificate; you'll tell the Matron about being one dress short, won't you? I'll send it next week, but it's at the wash - it's the crepe de chine one, isn't it? Yes. Well, mother, these hols have been fun: still I'm sure you'll enjoy this term. Let me see, who is it you share with? Lady Hophman. Ah! Yes, I liked her. Well! I think that's the car. We must be going".*
>
> *Victoria Station was crowded with boys seeing their mothers off. There was a great crowd round the bookstall of boys buying 'Women's Journal' for the mothers on the journey. Peter suddenly met an old friend and got engrossed in conversation. "No, if you ask me, I'm sure they don't mind going back a bit now; schools are not what they used to be, no. Where's mine? Oh! met a particular chum and*

they've gone off to get seats. I hope they remember to keep me a seat, too; well I must be going". As the train went off, there was much talking on the platform. "Mind you come top in the Care-of-the-Baby Class". "Yes! I'll send that stocking: there was nothing else, was there?" "Yes, I'll try to come down at half-term for the stitching match".

The journey to Nottingdean was rather dull for Peter, as most of the mothers were enthusiastically discussing the prospects of the term - except for one new mother, who was disconsolately sucking jujubes in the corner and sobbing into a very wet handkerchief. The rest of the carriage were discussing the time when silly Mrs. Jackson dropped the baby in class that time, and it had squeaked and the Mistress couldn't stop it howling.

At last they arrived in Nottingdean. Peter managed to procure his favourite porter, who was very jovial. "Yes, sir", he said, "this is our best time when all the old ladies are going back to school". They got into a taxi and drove off. At the school they were met by the headmistress. "Ah! dear Mr. Thompson, so glad to see you; how do you do, Mrs. Thompson: glad to be back to your work, I expect? Let me see, yes, you're in No. 2. I expect you'd like to go and unpack while your son and I have a cup of tea and a little chat - run along, there's a dear". Soon the hall was filled with boys and the sound of tea cups, as they sat down to tea and to discuss their mothers. "Mr. Thompson", said the headmistress, "I hope Mrs. Thompson will get on better this term: she's clever, there's no doubt about it. But last term, yes, I'm sorry to have to say so, she was found reading after lights out with a torch. I never asked you, but I hope you will think it right, of course I stopped her games. She was not allowed to play croquet for a week". "Oh! quite correct", said Peter. "Yes, I'll speak to her about it. Ah! there you are, darling; I expect you want to show me something, don't you?" he said, as Mrs. Thompson returned. Together they left the hall and went through the swing doors to the mothers' half. There was pandemonium in there already. Lady Halford was having a quarrel with the Duchess of Eden: the Duchess had by mistake trodden on one of Lady Halford's best woollies, so she had prodded the Duchess with a knitting needle. However, the noise ceased as a son came through and they all returned to their tuck-boxes. Mrs. Thompson and Peter went on until they came to a row of small studies. "Ah! is this yours? Yes, how nice; you will remember to sit back to the light, won't you? Your eyes are not very strong, darling". "Ah! good", said Mrs. Thompson, "Lady Hophman hasn't returned yet: I can bag the best drawers". "Now darling, tell me what else you'll be doing today". "Oh well, at nine there are prayers in hall and lectiones are given out; and then we have to be in bed by ten. And tomorrow we are all allowed breakfast in bed, and then at twelve there is a dancing class. In the afternoon I expect I shall play croquet". "Well, darling", said Peter, "I'm afraid I must be going now or I'll miss my train. But you must come to the station and see me off". At the station Peter bought a penny Nestle, as Mrs. Thompson was rather tearful. "Well, goodbye, darling", he said. "Oh, I nearly forgot, and here's a pen-

ny for the 'bus up to the school. Work hard".

A particular coup in this edition (November, 1934, the hundredth edition) was the following contribution from Uncle William:

A CONGRATULATION

I write in the spirit of the purest avuncular obedience, for I have nothing remotely appropriate to say. But I am an ecclesiastic; and when I reflect that the nephew who makes the demand is the great grandson of one Metropolitan, the grandson of two others, and the nephew of a fourth, there is nothing for it except that I should (in the words addressed by the Chinese Emperor to H.M. King George III 'tremble and obey'.

I, too, have been twice an editor; but one of the periodicals entrusted to my care perished after absorbing the hard-earned savings of many excellent people, at the age (I think) of eight, while the other, after an existence always precarious, passed unnoticed from the world when only six years old. The hundred numbers career of The Rugbeian, therefore, moves not only my admiration but my envy; though I wonder if it was driven to save itself by changing its name; for when I was best acquainted with it, and conducted in it wordy warfare with my senior contemporary, Mr. Chatwin, it had a title more suggestive alike of brilliance and instability than that which now claims for its columns the established dignity and abiding fame of the greatest of English schools.

Whatever coruscations I might have attempted in honour of The Meteor, I can address to The Rugbeian only the tribute of a sober congratulation and the humble good wishes of an admiring friend. WILLIAM EBOR:

Damerel, the family home.

(Freddy added in the editorial, 'His Grace the Archbishop of York appears to have confused us with our Meteoric cousins.')

Freddy wrote a diary throughout his time at Rugby, but by his own admission it was turgid and adolescent, and he destroyed most of it in 1959. Some odd jottings, however, survived. One is a quote, now famous, from Mahatma Gandhi's autobiography, *The Story of my Experiments with Truth*, which had been published in 1925:

I must reduce myself to zero. So long as a man does not, of his own free will, put himself last among his fellow creatures, there is no salvation for him. Ahimsa (non-violent respect for all creatures) is the farthest limit of humility.

The fact that Freddy jotted this down in the first place, and the fact that he did not destroy it in 1959, is perhaps indicative of its importance in his own thought. Throughout his life he often referred to Gandhi in his letters, talks and sermons.

Despite all that he did accomplish, Freddy always felt that he failed at Rugby, a second best. And again, despite the better moments, Freddy did not care for Rugby much, though, paradoxically perhaps, he thought it a good school. His Uncle William once told him that Rugby was an efficient, strict school and that Rugbeians were not nice, but if he wanted anyone to do anything well, then he would ask a Rugbeian. Interestingly, Freddy was to send his own son, Stephen, to Rugby.

Perhaps the last words about Freddy's Rugby days should go to his form master and the Headmaster of Rugby. In Freddy's final school report, his form master wrote that, in his estimation, it would not be in the too-distant future that Freddy would follow his grandparents and uncle in sporting a pair of gaiters. The Headmaster of Rugby capped this by writing that Freddy was more likely to sprout a pair of angel's wings. This comment can, of course, be taken in two ways. But what a distant social world this whole narrative conjures up.

3 Oxford

Following in the footsteps of his grandfather, father and uncle, Freddy went up to Balliol College, Oxford, in October, 1935. This was the opening of a new life for him; after the narrow restraint and underlying grimness of Rugby he found the freedom of the University and the opportunities to learn and to make and enjoy new friends were intoxicating. Many of the friendships he formed there survived until his death.

The Freshmen's Dinner, at which the Master proposed the toast 'Floreat Domus De Balliolo', took place on October 9th. On the middle table, chaired by the President of the Junior Common Room and the Captain of Boats, Freddy Temple sat opposite a young man fresh from Chatham House Grammar School, Broadstairs, E.R.G. Heath. An immediate rapport between the two was struck. Freddy wrote home that he had met 'a man called Heath, who appears extremely musical; we have good conversations and he's fun to be with. I hope we shall remain good friends'. In his autobiography, *The Course of My Life*, Sir Edward Heath wrote, 'Two Balliol contemporaries who became particular friends were George Hood from Newcastle Royal Grammar School, who was later ordained and spent much of his life as a missionary in the Far East, and Freddy Temple, Rugby-educated and the nephew of a future Archbishop of Canterbury, William Temple. Freddy sat opposite me at the freshman's dinner, and we hit it off immediately.'

In another of his letters home, when Freddy had been at Balliol for about a month, he caused his mother a deal of consternation by writing:

I have had a very exciting week, as Tuesday was November 5th. And there are always riots in Oxford then; squibs are let off under policemen's feet and so forth. Bell and I went out to see what we could see and met David Elias [both were friends of Freddy]; we got into the midst of a huge crowd where Lindsay [A.D. Lindsay, Master of Balliol], surrounded by four or five police was getting it rather hot and the police were continually taking men away into quad; when suddenly there was a cry of 'Progs' and everyone ran for their lives; David absolutely shot away and Bell and I followed but we were not fast enough and were each gripped by the seat by the Bulldogs; and then the traditional ultra-politeness followed, 'Sir, the Proctor would speak to you'. Then you go up to the Proctor who doffs his cap and says, 'Sir, are you a member of this University?' and then, 'Would you oblige me with your name and College and return to your rooms immediately?'. It was all very comic, but the comicest [sic] thing about it is that we have not yet been called for; all the others who were caught during that night in this College have been called before the Proctors and fined £1 and 'gated' (not allowed out after nine at night) for a fortnight; it looks as if they must have have lost our names in the scramble of having so many. There is still hope that we will get off which would be rather good. I have been told that it is essential to be 'progged' once while here and so if I get it free, and it is usually an expensive form of entertainment, it will be very pleasant.

Freddy's mother, however, was decidedly not amused, and worried about the incident. She would rather he had not been 'progged' quite so early in his Oxford career, if he had to be 'progged' at all. She decided, however, not to make too big an issue of it, and spent most of the rest of her letter worrying about, and questioning him on, his health. In reply, Freddy wrote:

I like letters full of questions; it gives one something to answer; Grandmama says that a mother's letters should always be half questions; I don't think it need be as sweeping as that, but the principle is good. No 1: the cold: it has almost gone. Sawyer [Freddy's 'scout'] came up to me yesterday and said, "How long are you going to do without a fire, Sir?". I said that I didn't know, so he carried on, "Let me give you this bit of advice: doctor's bill for a chill: £5; coal bill for the term: 30/-; it's worth it". Rather sweet and quite untrue of course, because the way colds are got is going from a stuffy room into the cold air. However, don't worry; I shall have fires when I feel cold. No 2: the blankets: I have enough with the rugs, I think; thanks awfully.

It appears that at many times during his time at Rugby and Oxford, Freddy's mother tried to off-load blankets on him. An Oxford contemporary, Michael Booker, wrote, 'Freddy had the reputation of an ascetic and certainly his rooms were amongst the coldest in Oxford.' Freddy himself reckoned at the time that he felt no desire for a fire and that he worked much better in the colder atmosphere; he then added that it saved him three shillings a week.

Freddy took to Oxford life like a duck to water. His letters home were full of excitement at all the opportunities he was given. He 'tasted' all the societies which attracted his interest most - and joined some, though not as many as he would have liked, for the allowance given him by his father was quite meagre and did not stretch far. Indeed, a constant preoccupation at this time seemed to be his lack of money and the difficulties he faced in making ends meet. He joined the Oxford branch of the League of Nations because he could get to hear worthwhile and famous speakers for 1/6d, with a good lunch thrown in. He contemplated joining the English Club and enthused, in his first letter to his father, about the privilege of sitting at the feet of Herbert Read and Edith Sitwell. He thought, however, that he could not afford the 15/- subscription per annum. He did join the Conservative Association, though he was not impressed with the first meeting, at which the Secretary of State for India spoke. Freddy commented:

He spoke quite well but he was very pompous and fussy and had a very bad set of false teeth. He was speaking on the India Bill and he made one terrible faux pas; he spoke of the Indians as very much inferior and backward; he ought to have known that Oxford is stiff with Indians, and when the time came he was in for it as one after another the poor Indians arose and attacked him with questions.

Freddy read Honour Mods under the classicist, Roger Mynors, for whom he developed a great affection. Mynors set him sixteen lectures a week, which was probably about double those of other disciplines. It didn't take him long to discover that 'few people can lecture well', that most of his lecturers had written books on their subject anyway, and it was more gainful to read these, rather than attend every lecture. Freddy was fond of quoting Stephen Leacock (*My Discovery of England*, 1922): 'Most people tire of a lecture in ten minutes; clever people can do it in five. Sensible people never go to lectures at all.'

In his second week, Freddy had his first tutorial, and he told his parents that Mynors, 'a very tame man', was quite pleased with his prose and unseen. He also had to read an essay (on Sanctions) to the Master; this projected tutorial worried Freddy, and at the last minute he decided it would be politic to expunge all the jokes he had made in the essay. He attended with four others students who, said Freddy, had luckily written poor essays, so his own appeared up to standard. He regretted afterwards that he had left the jokes out, for he found Lindsay 'really quite affable' and he was probably ready for Freddy's humour. George Levack, another Balliol friend, can remember reading essays with Freddy to the Medieval historian, Richard Southern. He said that he always felt that, with a classical and Rugbeian background, Freddy's views and conclusions were much more mature than his own and had a more positive basis in philosophy. He deemed it a pleasure to have shared Freddy's sense of humour and the resulting lightness of tone which he could bring to conflicting theories.

Not all of Freddy's essays were appreciated, however. On February 24th, 1937, he wrote:

I have had to write on 'The Survival of the Fittest', which is really quite an impossible subject unless one is a biologist and a great admirer of Darwin. It took all yesterday to find out anything about it and him before I could manage five sides, which is the bare minimum. I had to read it to Lindsay. It is quite the worst essay I have ever written and before I presented it to the Master I told him I thought it so. He heard it through, sat silent for a whole minute and then said, 'Well, my boy, we are in total agreement for once; it's quite the worst essay I've ever heard.'

A month later, he again wrote:

I had to write an essay on the Coal Industry this week which I think is quite the most fatuous subject there is - and that came across in what I wrote. I don't know what I was thinking of, for it temporarily was completely blotted from my mind that, of course, it is one of the Master's pet hobbies. He was not impressed.

Freddy also had to write an essay for the Master on 'The Royal Family and the Constitution'. The essay does not survive; nor do Lindsay's comments - but it is worth mentioning that Freddy's attitude to the Royal Family at this time was ambivalent. Though certainly not anti-royalist, he simply could not understand the 'enormous fuss' made about them and 'some of the nonsense that people think about them.' Unfortunately, he did not elaborate. Interesting among Freddy's correspondence at this time are the following excerpts from Freddy's letters home, following the death of King George V at Sandringham on January 20th, 1936. They tell us more about Freddy's theology than the Royal Family. On January 24th, he wrote:

All games have been postponed till after the funeral; what a pathetic little party they look in the picture of them standing at the station; I thought it was only the more emotional Continental races that went into such deep mourning with those heavy veils; I suppose they have the advantage of screening the face from the public view but the whole attitude of funerals always strikes me as a little unchristian. If one believes in an after-life, then presumably one thinks that the person is in a better place than he was here on earth, suffering - and if so one ought really to be very glad. Admittedly, some marks of respect should be shown to show the respect one held them in, but the idea of mourning for a long time strikes me as being morbid. I remember thinking how good it was of G'mama, as Daddy told me, being so completely unmorbid and the very day of Uncle Richard's death wanting to listen in to the Derby as they had already arranged to do. As far as I can see mourning is really self-pity, and so a selfish emotion and should be curbed. And the whole idea of lying in state is odd, because most people come with the idea that the King is still there and that they are thus paying their respects to him. But surely they should think as Socrates said, that when they handle his dead body they are not handling him, but that he is far away among the blessed. I read in one paper this morning, 'The crowd was still and silent as he is still and silent now.' That is nonsense if we believe in an after-life at all.

The following day, he wrote: 'How frightful the papers are being about the dead king; I do hope the funeral service will be sensible and that the hymns will be resurrection ones.' And again on January 31st:

I listened in to the funeral which was very impressive though I thought Uncle William was given the worst part of the service, though he read the prayers beautifully; he had that curious prayer about 'how glad we are our brother has departed from

this vile world' which always strikes
me as so curiously worded.

And a fortnight later:

*It was great fun seeing Rose the Sun-
day before last though I thought it
was a little morbid to be still in black
for the Royal Family. I suppose the
clothes have got to be worn out
somehow, but anyhow the whole
theory is wrong.*

At Balliol. Joan's brother, John, is on
Freddy's left, in the centre of the photograph.

Freddy, ever a keen sportsman, made
the most of the facilities provided at
Oxford. He initially played rugby for
the College Second. XV, though he
had set his heart on getting a place in
the first. When he failed to make it into the first XV, he concentrated on squash
and was very soon to develop into a formidable opponent in the court. He played
on occasions for the University. Indeed, sport played a large part in his life
throughout his time at Balliol; in the summer, squash gave way to tennis, at which
he was also no mean player. And he played table tennis for the University. He
developed his keen interest in, and appreciation of, the theatre - a passion that
was to stay with him all his life - and watched plays whenever he could afford to.
The D'Oyly Carte came for three weeks in the summer and he went to every opera; indeed, he went to every single performance of his favourite, *The Gondoliers*,
which to some might have seemed excessive, especially in view of his precarious
pecuniary state.

Freddy met the College Chaplain for the first time at the end of his second
week, and wrote to his parents:

*Did I tell you about my intimate heart-to-heart talk with the college padre on Satur-
day night? Apparently he goes through the College in singles and tries to get to know
the students well; he was quite pleasant but it was all a little too intimate; he had
apparently been impressed by my attendance at chapel, as there are so few who go.
And it is not really surprising as I have never known Holy Communion taken with
less feeling and so much in a drone. I shall in future go to some church in the town,
I think; and the service in the evening is no better; the Master read a sermon; it may
have been from his own pen but the whole effect is lost when it is read. Later in the
term we have to read an essay to him on Sermons and then I think I shall point that
out.*

Unfortunately, no record exists of this encounter.

He decided to try worshipping at St. Aldate's, and wrote home:

> I had an awful experience on Sunday. I went with two others to St. Aldate's for the morning service, but we were put in a pew which had a radiator immediately underneath it and so it was most uncomfortable. When I got back I wrote a letter to the Vicar telling him how horrible it was, and I have had a very charming letter back. He says he had no idea of such a problem and that he will remedy it as soon as possible. It seems amazing that nobody has mentioned it before; one of the men I went with now complains of a small boil on the behind, which I strongly suspect of being a pile.

He decided to give St. Aldate's another chance:

> On Friday I went to the first of Mr. Guinness' addresses at St. Aldate's; I thought it worth giving him a trial as he might have proved very good. He was in fact very bad, but luckily he did not speak long.

He decided to try elsewhere, 'unwilling to cope with bad sermons AND the probability of piles.' Much later in his life he told those on an Ordination Retreat he was conducting in Southwell that 'a disastrous experience at Oxford' had taught him of the importance of thorough preparation of sermons on the part of the clergy; just one ill-prepared and ill-delivered sermon had put him off attending a particular well-known Church for all time. He was probably referring to his unfortunate experience at St. Aldate's. Perhaps this seems a little bit hard on that particular church, but it does underline the maxim that first impressions count.

Freddy, with a group of young friends, made his spiritual home at the University Church of St. Mary the Virgin. He found the intellectual and spiritual content of the sermons 'electrifying' and the devout way in which the services were conducted suited him. The Vicar of St. Mary's, Dick Milford, was an enormous influence in his spiritual development, and he often spoke afterwards of his undying gratitude to him. After the evening service, a group would meet to discuss the sermon and other matters pertaining to the Christian faith. These meetings would sometimes not end till midnight, when Dick Milford would finally call it a day and the students reluctantly went back to their rooms. It was only in later life, when, in the parochial ministry himself, he tried to emulate what he had learned from Milford, that he realised how taxing it must have been for the Vicar of St. Mary's. He could then understand why Dick Milford called it a day at midnight, despite the protestations of the young people present.

The fact that Freddy made his spiritual home at St. Mary's did not preclude his attending other churches to worship. In fact he rejoiced in 'doing the rounds' of many of Oxford's churches. He wrote home, 'I hope this will help make me a well-rounded Christian.'

On April 25th, 1937 he wrote:

I have just been with him to the Church across the way [St. Mary Magdalen]; it was a good service, very high but beautifully sung by the priest. I came away thinking I could actually make my spiritual home there; the Vicar (for I assume it was he) preached well, if a little too fast. He's obviously well-read and I would have appreciated more time to assimilate what he said. There were lots of young men fussing around and dressed up, which I found distracting. However, they gave the impression that they weren't play-acting, but were actually very devout. I'll go back. However, I like doing the rounds; next week I may be a Presbyterian again, or a Methodist. I know in my heart though that I will stick with Milford at St. Mary's - Anglican and such good visiting preachers.

Freddy told his parents that all that he had told them of his activities might well sound as if he'd been doing no academic work. A good deal of work was, however, done in odd minutes and hours, especially between 4pm and 7pm; he had already decided that he could not afford to have tea, so worked instead. His genuine lack of money at this time seems to have mirrored that of his grandfather, Frederick Temple who, as we know, experienced the same sort of problems while at Balliol. His small allowance acted as a check on his activities. Although he quite often complained about his lack of funds (he once wrote home, 'I really am finding the cost of everything terrifying, and sometimes don't know how I can manage'), he admitted in later life that his financial difficulties at Oxford taught him the value of money. At the time, though, he thought his father was being unreasonably un-generous.

He was, however, specially pleased that his relationship with his father on one level seemed to be growing closer: he wrote regularly with wise comments and advice on many points as Freddy mentioned them. In one letter Freddy's father told him that all the reading and learning he was doing was all to the good: 'it must ultimately create something worthwhile.' Freddy replied that he had had interesting confirmation of what his father had said. He had been helping to correct some of the proofs of a poem by one of the Balliol men, who was 'keen on doing great things and sending messages to the world, etcetera.' It was, apparently, a long poem of some forty seven pages, and, wrote Freddy, was 'in modern rhythm, which means that it could have been in prose but would have been poor prose and so has to have the excuse of verse.' He continued:

It says absolutely nothing worth saying and in the end says what has been said over and over again, starting with Horace preaching a return to the rustic life and a little less learning. It is full of lines like, "It is not in the voice of the homosexual nor in the

Cancer Hospital that we find life": all of which was one line, whereas the next line was probably only two words or so. The poor man is trying to get five hundred copies sold; it was impossible to tell him to tear it up and try something else.

In another letter, Freddy's father propounded his views on intercessory prayer. This brought a swift riposte from his undergraduate son:

Very interested in what you said about intercessory prayer but don't agree at all. If you think that just wishing good does any good to anyone but yourself, where does your idea of an all-good and all-knowing God come in? You can't believe he isn't doing all that is possible for that person (it is only when your intercession is able and ready to be backed by action that you make yourself a channel or weapon to be used by the Divine Spirit and so may be of some use): but for that I do feel intercession is idolatrous, i.e. involves a misconception of God. Your second point about being comforted by others' prayers is true but it is NOT a result of prayer but a certain psychological state: what about the atheist for whom you should be praying just as much in that case: tell him you are praying for him, and he will either laugh or be furious. I wish I could believe this was wrong, but I can't; perhaps you can show that it is.

There was still, however, some friction in their relationship. Freddy still felt that he could not be his own man and that his family, especially his father, were pulling strings 'as if I were a puppet'.

In January 1937, he wrote:

One thing I find a bit too trying is that Miss Spooner has written to me; no doubt the old lady is quite too delightful but to have to fit in Daddy's friends as well is a bit difficult; though of course it is very nice of them to ask me at all.

And again, in the summer of 1937:

I have had a summons from Ruth Spooner. I know that Daddy was only being thoughtful and kind in letting her know that I was in Oxford, and I look forward to meeting her. I wish, Daddy, you would realise that I must make my own friends of my own age. I don't mean to be terrible about this, but she sounds quite antique. David [Elias?] says I simply must go and said that if I could arrange for him to go as well, he would try amusingly to turn the conversation round to her father. In this way, he said, we could maybe 'learn a few more sayings'. [Ruth Spooner was the daughter of Spooner, Warden of New College, famed for his 'Spoonerisms'.]

Meanwhile, Freddy's thoughts on pacifism were beginning to clarify in his mind. In the spring of 1938, he wrote:

On Wednesday I went to a brilliant play at the New called 'Red Night'; it was all about the war and the whole theme was the futility of it. It was also very funny, though not in the way that some would appreciate; one of the mildest jokes being where a cockney says to the hero, who is rather poetic, 'Gawd, you're as bad as Keat's "Ode to a Bleeding Nightingale".' And there is a dear little Scot who is always taking guard for the others and when an officer comes along and asks where the proper man is, he says in a plaintive little voice, 'He's gone to the latrines'; all too shock-making. But when we came back from that play I just could not see how Uncle William could think that pacifism was a heresy; the last words in the play are, 'Christ Almighty, what's the bloody use?' And that was the theme through the whole of the play. Not one war has ever been a success. I hope the play goes on in London; it will make the most marvellous propaganda as it is the first play not to make the whole thing out to be very fine.

I have had the most delightful letter from Uncle William asking me to go to York this next vac to spend Holy Week with him. Doubtless we shall have wonderful conversations and disagreements about pacifism.

A week later, he wrote:

I am being severely attacked on all sides about Uncle William's words in the Assembly; bit of a pass when his dim-witted nephew has to carry it all for him. And I find it impossible to argue as I agree with my attackers entirely that the Church position seems to be that of sound common sense but entirely divorced from Christian teaching or ethics. I have had another long letter from Uncle William which I very much appreciated and for which I have thanked, and which on first reading seemed convincing but now I don't think it is; however I shall not continue the discussion as it would take up too much of his time.

Uncle William (and sometimes Aunt Frances) visited Freddy in Oxford fairly frequently. After one such visit from them both, Freddy wrote home, on May 7th, 1938:

It was great fun having Uncle William to tea last week, though he had a bad cold and had to be rather quiet. Aunt Frances' eagle eye took in everything in my room at a glance and I saw her notice the large (it certainly does look formidable) case of beer bottles (which I may say last me nearly the whole term and are better and cheaper than in college). However, she probably thinks that I get through them all in a week and have it constantly restocked. As befits Aunt F, she made sure that I saw that she had seen what she saw; she didn't need to <u>say</u> a thing. Uncle William preached a good and very amusing sermon in the evening at St. Mary's, but I was a little surprised when he descended to mere attacks on political parties, extremely funny though they were.

One of Freddy's greatest delights came from his membership of the Oxford Union. He enjoyed attending the debates, and often made comments in his letters, sometimes bordering on the scurrilous, on the merits of different speakers. At the start of his third year, he wrote to his father telling him that, on perusing the list of Union motions for the term, he thought they were all 'very stupid', and that he could think of nothing original to say on any of them - though he must try and speak for the first time sometime. Seven days later, he wrote again saying that the great event of the week - and he knew this would please his father enormously - was that he had made his first speech:

> *Suddenly, after I had just written to you last week, and said that the motions were very bad, I was seized by a fit of madness and went round to the Union and gave my name in without thinking, and regretted it severely afterwards as I could think of nothing to say.*

The motion was 'That this House has no use for aristocracy'; Freddy gave his name in against the motion. He was not called on to speak till after eleven and thought that everything that could be said had been said. He decided to be quite irrelevant and amusing; the speech seemed to go down well and enlivened a rather sleepy House. He told the House that it was only his great affection for the President which had made him speak, but he was an aristocrat and he had his uses, the chief one of which was that he, as one of the make-up team, had made Freddy up as Alcestis each night of a Balliol Players' tour. The report of the debate in *The Cherwell* had one sentence about each of the late speakers; in Freddy's case it was, 'Mr. Temple was very amusing and complimented the President.' In a letter a few days later to his father, Freddy sent his father a copy of the comment and wrote, 'This is very favourable as they can be very horrid and say, "Mr. X was trying to be witty and failed".' Freddy concluded his letter by writing:

> *Now it will be easier to do it again on other occasions; I am convinced that the only thing to do at that hour of the night is to try and be funny; one must wait until one has been put on to speak much earlier before trying to bring forward cogent arguments and really trying to speak properly.*

In a review of another Union debate, 'That this House considers *The Times* unworthy of its position as the leading English newspaper', the *Isis* reported, 'Mr. F.S. Temple (Balliol) gave a delightful defence of 'The Times', because its crosswords were a great boon to the clergy and because it made such wonderful bonfires'.

Following his successes, Freddy spoke briefly the following week. The *Isis* reported, 'In a class by himself is Mr. F.S. Temple (Balliol), whose all too rare orations are gems of humour.'

Then, on February 10th, 1938, the Question for Debate was 'That the Law is an Ass'. This was moved by the Hon. Hugh Fraser, and opposed by Freddy Temple. The *Cherwell* reported that it was one of the most amusing evenings for a long time, and continued:

> *Mr. F.S. Temple (Balliol) opposed the motion in what must have been the best maiden paper speech for a long time. The law could not be quite an ass, he suggested, since even policemen yielded to the blandishments of his sisters. Mr. Temple next dealt with breach of promise, table manners and the subtlety of the distinction between burglary and house-breaking, with the rule of the road and Trial by Ordeal. It was a good thing that we did not live in ancient times as we should have to build churches to expiate our crimes and this might lead to building congestion. Mr. Temple ended his speech with a reference to Proctorial Authority. He has a quiet and rather charming delivery.*

The *Isis* reported:

> *Opening for the defence, Mr. F.S. Temple (Balliol) said that he was a very law-abiding man. He then gave an explanation of why there were only ten commandments, and quoted the Apocrypha. He then got on to the vital subjects of Breach of Promise of Marriage, Table Manners, Burglary, Belisha Crossings and Trial by Ordeal. If one went back to the old legal system, one would have to build churches to expiate one's wrongs: think of the number that would bring into being today. But the law had progressed, whereas the ass had not. Hence he concluded triumphantly that the law was not an ass, but a good thing and Church of England - all of which was very funny and phrased nicely.*

Another critic said that his speech was characterised by the 'happy phrases' employed, its 'pleasing urbanity, and its complete lack of argument'. His speech was a 'happy, haphazard, ha'penny dip into the bran tub of the forensic life of the "Average Man" - all delivered in a quiet, but assured manner. The style had sequence, and gave the same appearance to his argument. It lost nothing by having none'.

Finally, *The Oxford Magazine*, under the signature 'E.R.G.H.' (Edward Heath), reported :

> *Mr. F.S. Temple (Balliol) opposed the motion. He held up our policemen for admiration, and urged the House to see a psychologist about its unruly passions. He argued that the ass had not developed or progressed for centuries, and was now hardly to be found in this country, except in the army. But the Law was growing and progressing all the time. He quoted to us extracts from his Woolworth educational primers, which had taught him all he knew about etiquette, and then showed himself quite an authority on breach of promise cases. For burglary - the real thing, between the hours of 10pm and 6am - he appeared to have an admiration, but he*

scorned housebreaking - the deed between the hours of 6am and 10pm. He con-
cluded by showing how Mr. Hore-Belisha had helped the law to become more effi-
cient. Mr. Temple has a very pleasant manner of speaking, of the type which kept
the House continually chuckling, rather than intermittently cheering. It is a style
difficult to maintain during a long speech, but Mr. Temple did it very well.

The motion was lost by 151 votes to 64. Freddy was ecstatic.

Freddy did not limit his debating to the Union. In the early summer of 1938, he
wrote:

On Monday I go up to London to speak at the Eight Thirty Club. I am all for taking
every opportunity of speaking one can get; but of course this will only be in the gen-
eral discussion after the paper speakers have spoken. The debate is, 'Wrecked on a
raft in mid-ocean are a bishop, an actor, a judge and a famous cricketer: one of
them has to be thrown over in order that the others may live; who is to go?' I feel I
must see that the bishop is not drowned. Which reminds me that I must stop and go
for a walk before tea when Uncle William and Aunt Frances materialise. I suspect
Uncle William would like to see one or two bishops drowned, but he's far too nice to
say so.

The debate obviously went well, for the following week he told his parents:

What a success the debate was. I was most impressed. There were four speakers,
each of the profession on the raft, and each speaking in his own defence. After that,
anyone could get up and speak. It was all impromptu and just so very funny. Hav-
ing been invited to be present by the Secretary, I felt obliged to speak. I pretended to
have a dream in which I found myself on board the raft with the Bishop of Birming-
ham, John Gielgud and Mr. Duff Cooper; I myself was representing the famous
cricketer. They decided to throw me over, but I disliked the idea and so, being the
strongest, threw them all over except the bishop, who did not resist. So I advised
them not to throw the cricketer over as he was probably the strongest - and drew
two morals from my dream: firstly, complete pacifism and secondly, always to be
on good terms with the strongest side. It seemed to go down well.

Freddy also delighted in his membership of the Balliol Players, a group who went
round the South and West of England after the summer term, producing a Greek
play in English. The Players were a rather select group who continued their existence by self-appointment, purely on the grounds of compatibility and not on any
acting ability; that, if there was any, was to be discovered later. Ashley Raeburn, a
contemporary of Freddy and a life-long friend, who joined the Balliol Players in
1938, recalls the Players as a 'motley and pretty undisciplined crew with little if
any acting talent or experience'. The tours were great fun; the Players usually had

enough cars in which to move around and arranged to meet at the next venue three hours before each performance, when scenery was erected. The stage props and those who could not find room in one of the cars were transported in a pantechnicon rented from a local removing firm with, as Ashley Raeburn says, 'an avuncular driver of infinite tolerance of the way of unruly young students'. Freddy was, he says, 'with his infectious and reverberating laughter, a leading member of this frivolous and enjoyable enterprise'.

Freddy at Oxford.

The Balliol Players performed in some charming spots, including the old quarry pits at Burford, Corfe Castle, Old Sarum, the Old Castle at Sherborne, and Madron Seligman's (a close friend from Balliol) lovely garden in Wimbledon, where as the evening drew on gardeners went round hanging up Chinese lanterns. They also - to ensure a good fee and a large audience - performed at Public Schools, Radley, Malvern, Winchester, Marlborough, Charterhouse, Whitgift and others. Rather incongruously, perhaps, they performed too at Raynes Park County School, perilously near the Kingston by-pass, where, in 1937, in the words of 'The Times' critic, ' … amid the roar of traffic on the by-pass and the hum of aeroplanes in the "Vast Ether", Aeschylus and Euripides disputed their claims to immortality.'

After the play the Players would repair to the nearest pub where thirty large portions of bacon, eggs and sausages had been ordered, and with pints of beer they sang and ate till late in the evening. One close friend remembered that in these gatherings Freddy was always conspicuous by being at the centre of it all; 'where there was light and laughter and sparkle', he said, 'there was Freddy right in the middle. It was always the same. He was breathtakingly fun to be with'. They slept in the strangest of places, ranging from the downright uncomfortable, under hedges, in barns and in haystacks, to the luxurious, like the Drawing Room of the Palace at Chichester, the home of the Bishop of Chichester, where the Bells pampered them with strawberries and cream. It was a wonderful three weeks at the start of the Long Vac.

The first summer, 1936, the Balliol Players performed the *Alcestis of Euripides*. This was the play alluded to in his first Union speech, in which Freddy was cast as the tragic queen, who dies quite early in the play. Not much information now exists about this tour, except that Freddy found it a difficult part to play, made more difficult by a boy at Charterhouse muttering in the front row as he trod lightly in bare feet over the stony gravel of the Headmaster's drive, 'How could Admetus have married a woman with such hammer toes?'

The next year the Players transferred to comedy, and Freddy produced *The Frogs of Aristophanes*, in the translation of Gilbert Murray; Freddy himself took the part of Dionysus, God of the Comic Theatre. Certain alterations were made in the text, after much deliberation and after consultation with Professor Murray, in an effort to improve rather than preserve the comedy. The changes were confined to the topical jokes in which the archaisms were changed into the nearest modern equivalents. For example, there is a joke about an oil-can in the trial scene, in which the two tragic poets, Aeschylus and Euripides, contend for the right to be allowed to return to earth from Hades: the Greeks often used to carry an oil-can with them for washing after exercise and not infrequently lost them. Few, if any, English people make a habit of carrying an oil-can, but their adventures with an umbrella are proverbial. Another diverting touch was the introduction of a replica of one of the early AA signs, giving the distance of Hades to Oxford as over 5,000 miles, to Cambridge as one mile only.

The correspondent who witnessed the performance of 'The Frogs' at the Pump Rooms, Bath, stated that 'the premier honours in a large cast were earned by Mr. F.S. Temple as Dionysus, whose mastery of facial expression was admirable, and who invested the trial scene between the rival poets with its full measure of humour.' The article concluded:

> At the conclusion of the production, Mr. Temple thanked the audience for their appreciative reception, remarking that the Players were more used to out-door presentations. When playing indoors it was more difficult to observe the attitude of their audiences and to decide whether any of their patrons had gone to sleep or left before the play had ended (laughter and applause).

After the performance at Marlborough, the editor of *The Marlburian* wrote,

> Some of the jokes (in 'The Frogs') are dead and some of them we are glad to bury; to preserve the proportions, the producer, F.S. Temple, added a certain amount of comedy to which only the most arid pedant or the excessively patriotic Cantabridgian could object.. Topical allusions were widely and ruthlessly cut; one of the merits of 'The Frogs' from the acting point of view is that this can be done without seriously affecting the plot; no one could object to the substitution of Putney Bridge for the Cerameicus and we all took it as a compliment that Treacle Bolly found a place among the delicacies of Hades.

If Freddy Temple had produced the play in 2000, he would undoubtedly have brought it yet more up-to- date.

There also exists a letter from the Sixth-Form Classical Master at Charterhouse:

> *I write to express my gratitude and appreciation for the performance given by the Balliol Players at Charterhouse last Thursday. It was the first time that I had had the opportunity of seeing the work of your company and I find it difficult to avoid the charge of fulsomeness in speaking of them. It was from the beginning to the end a most delightful performance, full of vigour and fun and the genuine Aristophanic spirit. I would especially like to thank and congratulate Dionysus; I do not see how he could have been improved in any way and I wish I could see him in the part again. I am afraid you must have been very disappointed with the reception given you by the audience. It cannot be denied that the Charterhouse boy is a depressing person to act in front of. It apparently does not occur to him that people like a little applause and encouragement. It may be some consolation to you to know that this is no indication of whether he enjoyed it; I have discussed the production with a great many of the boys and find that they liked it very much indeed. My own form, the VIth, some of whom saw the Cambridge production last year were most enthusiastic. I am also informed that you were dismayed to see some members of the audience with novels open in front of them but the only two I know about were texts of Aristophanes.*

The music for *The Frogs* was written by Edward Heath. The following years, 1938 and 1939, saw performances of *The Acharnians* and *The Birds*, which again received excellent reviews. The music for *The Acharnians* was written by Edward Heath and Walt Rostrow, who was later to be a foreign affairs adviser to President Lyndon Johnson. Roy Jenkins was also a member of the group. In all the newspaper photographs, not only does Freddy look incredibly young, he also always seems to be standing in the centre of the group.

Perhaps above all, it was the delight he found in his friends that characterised his time at Balliol. Many of these friendships continued throughout his life. Mention has already been made of Edward Heath. Sir Edward Heath tells of how it became commonplace for a circle of friends to meet in his rooms shortly after ten in the evening, where over coffee, plum-cake and biscuits they would sit and argue about every conceivable subject. In addition to Freddy Temple (from whom, Sir Edward recalls, he learnt a great deal about religious matters from late night talks at Balliol), they were joined by some of those who had joined the College in 1937: in particular Sir Edward remembers Ashley Raeburn, a refugee from Nazi Germany who afterwards became a civil servant at the Treasury and then went on to work in Shell, Tim Bligh, a science scholar who went on to become Principal Private Secretary to Harold Macmillan at No. 10, and Stephen Verney, later to become Bishop of Repton. Sir Edward Heath remembers Freddy as one who joined wholeheartedly and fiercely in the group's arguments about political and personal morality, and recalls how Freddy would write to his uncle, Willam, at that time the Archbishop of York, to obtain his views on their unresolved doubts. In his autobiography, Sir Edward Heath writes, about William Temple:

> *My Christian faith also provided foundations for my political beliefs. In this, I was influenced by the teachings of William Temple. Temple's impact on my generation was immense. He believed that a fairer society could be built only on moral foundations, with all individuals recognising their duty to help others. Like Lindsay, he was a socialist and, in his wish to redress the balance of power between those who own and those who produce, he sometimes failed to see that some would seek through socialist measures not justice, but power for its own sake. He was, however, the first Anglican leader for decades to set out the Church's teaching in modern terms. He propounded a view of morality which was not preoccupied with sexuality, but which was relevant to the myriad problems besetting the individual in the personal, professional and social spheres.*

In conversation with him, Sir Edward Heath's regard for William Temple was obvious. He commented that things would have been very different for Church and Nation if he had not died so tragically young, and that his *Christianity and Social Order* did more than anything else to bring in the Welfare State. Sir Edward wrote the Foreword to a new edition of this book in 1957. He acknowledged his debt to Freddy in helping to nurture his admiration of this giant of a man and Archbishop.

Amongst the host of friends whose company he enjoyed and valued so much, one of Freddy's closest friendships at Oxford was with John Webb, two years his junior at Balliol, who was later to become Director of the Christian Medical College and Hospital at Vellore and then Professor of Paediatrics at the University of Newcastle. Freddy himself was later to marry John's younger sister, Joan.

Freddy's last year at Balliol was lived out under the threat of war, although he always said that the prospect of war never really loomed very large on the Oxford horizon before 1939. Even then, he and his friends thought about it very little; there had been so many crises in the world each year, and each one they hoped was the last. The rights and wrongs of Munich had been doubtful, but anyhow it had averted war. To those of them who were Balliol men, the fact that the Master felt called to emerge from College life and fight an election in protest against the Munich settlement came as a shock. Were things really so bad? But few people knew the facts of Belsen and Buchenwald then. The Master was not successful.

Freddy concentrated on the last year of the History Schools and all the friends that Oxford gave. In the spring he and a party of friends went down to the Quantocks. On March 16th he drove down with Madron Seligman in his car. In a fragment of diary that still exists, he wrote with a touch of cynicism:

It was a lovely day and with democracies crashing in the East, we sped west and down to Bath and tea in Glastonbury. We arrived at Bincknoller [where they were due to stay] to find Stephen Verney and George Levack already there, both of them Balliol men. Stephen Verney I was to see a great deal of in the next three years. His small body was full of enthusiasm; and his brown eyes in his squirrel-like face were full of sparkle. He had hitchhiked down from his home in Anglesey. George Levack was of a quieter, more languid temperament; he was reading History and writing occasional poetry. Alister Lloyd arrived after supper. Irate, vague, charming and inconsequential. Oliver Coburn [a friend from Rugby days] was there too: a brilliant brain; he was over-bashful and sensitive about his inexperience of practical affairs.

Stephen Verney's memories of this time are amusing:

At a farmhouse, at Bicknoller in Somerset in the spring of 1939, we had a wonderful time. Every day we had to walk through the farmyard with its assortment of butting cattle and barking dogs. On the Sunday morning we went to the Parish Church; it must have been Palm Sunday, for we sang Psalm 22: 'Many oxen are come about me: fat bulls of Basan close me in on every side. They gape upon me with their mouths .... I am poured out like water, and all my bones are out of joint: my heart also in the midst of my body is even like melting wax .... For many dogs are come about me.' We started to giggle, and then we lost control completely, and the astonished vicar watched two pews-full of apparently intelligent young men getting up and stumbling out of his church.

In the evenings after supper they would all wander down to the local inn, drink rather too much cider and play skittles with the village. Freddy wrote, 'We laughed at the slightly vulgar jokes of the publican and felt grown up.' It was for them a wonderful spring, and there in the farm they read, walked in the Quantocks in the afternoon and ate large farm meals of chicken, apple pie and cream. Czechoslovakia had been invaded; the outlook grew worse on the Continent, but most of the group was too immersed in Schools to worry much. Freddy read out at breakfast one morning that his mother had sent a telegram to Chamberlain urging him to introduce conscription. Everyone laughed; Madron Seligman said he would go down to the local Post Office and send a telegram to Chamberlain saying 'Disregard Mrs. Temple's telegram'. They then rolled about laughing at the thought of the Prime Minister saying to his Private Secretary 'I've been told to disregard Mrs. Temple's telegram, but I don't know where it is or what it said, so I don't know what to disregard. Find it.' And then, in their undergraduate imaginings, the whole business of government and international diplomacy came to a grinding halt whilst everybody searched for the relevant piece of paper. None of this close group of friends wanted conscription; Oliver and Freddy were pacifists.

Stephen was then agnostic, humanitarian and pacifist; he was always enthusiastic and keen about what he thought at the time, and 'all that he had previously thought', wrote Freddy, 'was quite wrong.' Freddy reckoned at the time that Madron was too much of a politician to be a pacifist; he was more a realist than most of them. George Levack was going into the Colonial Office, so it did not affect him. Freddy knew that Alister 'would always do the orthodox thing in a charming way.'

Thus the Oxford years came to a golden end.

4   Uncle and Nephew

This is the stage at which something more should be said about Freddy's relationship with, and recollections of, his uncle, William Temple, together with the barest resume of some of William Temple's thoughts and actions that most influenced his nephew.

Mention has already been made of the Christmas holidays Freddy so looked forward to at Bishopthorpe when he was a schoolboy at Rugby. His relationship with his uncle grew yet closer, perhaps in part due to the fact that William and Frances Temple had no children of their own. Freddy always said that William and Frances treated him as their own son. On his holidays at Bishopthorpe, Freddy enjoyed being treated as an adult. His uncle would go up to his bedroom to wish him goodnight, whenever his evening duties permitted, sit on the end of Freddy's bed and talk through everything that he had done during the day. Freddy remembered him saying often (when he was still an early teenager) 'Now, what do you think, Freddy? Do you think I said the right things or not?' If Freddy just said, 'Yes, uncle, I'm sure you did the right thing', his uncle would round on him gently and say, 'But you must tell me why you think I did the right thing, Freddy.' Freddy could remember many occasions when his uncle said to him something like, 'Freddy, your Uncle William is not infallible, despite what you hear some people say'. Freddy could remember him saying this sort of thing 'with a sad, almost wistful, expression in his voice.' He remembered when he was about thirteen his uncle saying, 'Being Archbishop at this time is the most lonely job in the world', and not understanding what he meant. As far as Freddy was concerned, living at Bishopthorpe, surrounded all the time by other important people, was anything but lonely. But he was to learn.

When he was not with his uncle, William (and often Frances) wrote regularly. Freddy cherished all the letters he received from him. He cherished too all the other William Temple correspondence which has survived, and which he inherited. William and Frederick (Freddy's father) used to write to their mother - Freddy's grandmother - every day when at school; she kept every single letter and postcard. Even the postcards which nowadays parents would tear up, saying, 'Why doesn't the wretched boy write a bit more?' become interesting, when one knows that he became a famous Archbishop. One letter simply says, 'My dearest Mother, Absolutely nothing to say; and that being said, good morning. William'. Much to the dismay of the Director of the National Records Office and the Librarian of Lambeth Palace Library, when in later life he was an Archdeacon and Bishop, Freddy used to put some of these letters in an old overnight bag and take them round the diocese of Bristol, delighting in giving talks to groups of folk about them. He disregarded any attempt to make him photocopy the originals.

Fortunately, the letters and documents have survived in remarkably good condition.

William suffered from gout from a very early age, although he was in fact teetotal (and was actually a member of the teetotal society of Rechabites) because like his father he felt that there were certain things that a Christian ought to protest about in the society of the time - though he did recognise that a little drink did not do anyone any harm. This meant that when Freddy, as a teenage boy and undergraduate, used to stay at Bishopthorpe, he was confronted with the rather insipid barley water that was served at meals; alcohol was not provided at Bishopthorpe or, later, at Lambeth. 'Not that that worried me much', wrote Freddy.

What was also thought very revolutionary at the time was a little notice in the bedrooms at Bishopthorpe saying, 'We would ask our guests never to give any tips. All the staff in this house are adequately and properly paid'. These notices were put up by William himself. Freddy said that when he found himself in later life on the Standing Committee of what was in those days the Church Assembly, he found it sad, staying for a meeting when there was a different incumbent at Bishopthorpe, that the practice of tipping had returned. And when some of the members of the Standing Committee were driven by the Archbishop's chauffeur to York Station he, as a rather poor incumbent, managed to be looking the other way, thus allowing richer laity to dig in their pockets.

Freddy remembered his Uncle as having a photographic memory; he read very slowly as his eyesight was poor, but nothing of what he read was ever forgotten, and sometimes when talking with Freddy he would say, 'You'll find the argument best put out by so-and-so; it comes half-way down on the right hand side of a page somewhere in the middle; I think it's about page 104.' He once heard that a young female reporter had lost the shorthand notes of his sermon the day before. Freddy was with him when the Archbishop asked his secretary to ring and say that if she cared to come out in the afternoon to Bishopthorpe he would dictate the sermon again to her; this he did without any notes, and when later she compared it with others who had taken down the first transcript, it was identical.

William Temple had a quick and keen sense of humour. Freddy remembered one day when he and Stanley Baldwin, the Prime Minister, were sitting on a bench at Bishopthorpe, at the place where the Ouse runs through the gardens, past the Palace. The Prime Minister and Archbishop were deep in discussion; Freddy was tidying up some leaves. A barge went by on the Ouse; the bargee looked them both up and down very severely, and then called out, 'I see you're keeping better company today.' Freddy's uncle turned instantly to Baldwin and Freddy heard him say, 'One of us has just received a pretty compliment.' Both Freddy and the Archbishop dissolved into fits of giggles. 'Baldwin smiled wanly', said Freddy.

Another time when on holiday, Freddy was with his uncle in a café having tea when there was another bishop present in the party. A group of people had been looking over at them, and a lady came across to the Archbishop and said, 'Your Grace, we are having an argument; could you please explain to me the difference between a Bishop and an Archbishop?' Freddy's uncle pointed to the curve of his rather big stomach and said, 'There's the Arch', and, pointing at the Bishop, continued, 'and there's the Bishop.'

Once in the United States, when William Temple was trying to be as full of joviality and heartiness as the American bishops tended to be, he was struggling to get out of a low car; the American bishop had got out first and as he was going up the steps to his front door, his dog, called 'Gaiters', came down, with tail wagging, to greet him. The bishop patted him on the head and said, 'Come along, Gaiters.' The Archbishop, who had not seen what was happening, called out, 'I'm coming as quickly as I can.' Although Freddy was not present on this occasion, it was one of the first things that Uncle William told him with glee on his return to this country.

Then again, when Freddy was one day travelling with his uncle in the car to a Confirmation, Brindle, the chauffeur, was uncertain of the way. The Archbishop said, 'You'd better ask, Brindle.' Brindle replied, 'I will enquire, Your Grace.' Uncle William turned to his nephew and said, 'We have just been mightily rebuked.'

Freddy also recalled his uncle being very good at Racing Demon, playing very fast and telling amusing stories all the time. Out of the blue, at dinner one evening, the Archbishop got everybody around the table playing 'My Aunt went to Paris'. The guests, amongst whom were some quite distinguished people, including a Government minister, had in turn to tell the others what the Aunt had bought in Paris, and had to remember what the others had put on her list of purchases. In no time, everyone was in hysterics. The Government Minister (unfortunately, we are not told his name) kept getting the list in the wrong order or omitted some of the purchases. The Archbishop of York looked at him from the end of the table and asked simply, 'And you're meant to be running this country?'

Freddy delighted in telling the story of an incident that occurred in February, 1941. He had fifteen days leave, and spent eleven of them at Bishopthorpe. On the second day Aunt Frances said that Uncle William wanted to talk to him, but he was in his study at the time with 'a member of the Northern aristocracy'; Aunt Frances thought they wouldn't be long together - 'for they're talking about munitions or something - and who can possibly talk about that sort of thing for long?' She suggested that Freddy knocked discreetly and waited outside the study door. 'If you do that, uncle is bound to come out to be relieved, and be relieved'. Freddy did as he was told. His aunt had this sort of effect on him. It was not only the 'member of the Northern aristocracy' in his uncle's study; the Foreign Secretary was there too. The former had been talking about the requisitioning of his family seat and the Foreign Secretary was talking about the progress of the war. Freddy wrote:

When, two minutes later, the two came out, the Foreign Secretary thanked me for the interruption and smiled; the Earl glowered at me. Uncle then called me in;

I told him that the Earl did not seem too pleased; Uncle William said something to the effect that nothing pleased the Earl at the moment. But the Foreign Secretary was a pleasing and pleased man, and thought the war was going well. When I told Aunt Frances that the Foreign Secretary had also been in uncle's study, she said, 'Oh, these wretched politicians seem to get everywhere these days.'

William Temple inherited a family characteristic in that he had an enormous laugh. (An incumbent in the Exeter diocese when Frederick Temple was Bishop of Exeter once wrote that his new Bishop had a very un-episcopal laugh, rather like a braying donkey.) On one occasion, when his uncle was staying at Freddy's family's home in Sussex, Freddy's younger sister, Ann, who was quite small at the time, became bored with the fact that they were all pealing with laughter and Uncle William was laughing the loudest of them all. She piped up, 'Hee, hee, hee' in a ringing voice, at which they all stopped in stunned silence. Later, Freddy's mother said, 'How could you do that, Ann? It was so very rude.' She replied, 'I did it in order to stop you all laughing, and it did.' Freddy inherited this laugh, as all his friends knew all too well.

In the early 1960s, Freddy edited a volume of William Temple's letters (*Some Lambeth Letters*, O.U.P). On one page of the book, Freddy said that some people have wondered at what moment it became the usual custom for ladies not to wear hats in church. In this volume, Freddy includes a letter from Hugh Dalton, the President of the Board of Trade, which shows that these things can happen from rather practical, not grand reasons. On 30th August, 1942, he wrote to the Archbishop:

> *I hope I am not overstepping the boundary line between Church and State in a proposal I want to put before you.*
>
> *Two of our hardest problems at the Board of Trade, in trying to keep the nation adequately clothed, are women's hats and stockings. Hats are bound to become scarcer and scarcer; so much so that we do not even put them on the ration, but hope that women, and men too, will largely give up wearing them. Though there is a better supply of stockings, much labour and material would be saved if more women would go stockingless.*
>
> *But convention yields ground slowly, and it would help me very much if you felt able to announce that women could, without impropriety, come hatless and stockingless to church. I do not, of course, suggest that you should say that I had asked you to make such an announcement. This would not only be inappropriate, but might create prejudice. I observe, however, that many individual churches already show notices that women may attend uncovered, and I therefore hope that you might, perhaps, feel able to take the action that I have suggested.*

On 15th October, the Archbishop replied as follows:

My dear Dalton,

I had the opportunity of discussing with the Bishops the question which you put to me in the summer. We did not think any difficulty could arise in practice concerning women's stockings. It is usually quite impossible to tell whether they are wearing any or not! But it was agreed that I should take steps to put out a statement to the effect that women should not hesitate to come into Church with their heads uncovered and I hope that no bar to their doing so would be found when they came.

Yours sincerely,

William Cantuar:

The following was the statement issued by the Archbishops of Canterbury and York:

Questions are frequently asked in these days concerning the old customary rule that women should not enter a Church building with their heads uncovered. The scriptural authority behind this rule is S. Paul's regulation, but this required that they should be veiled. That has long ago fallen out of use, and after consultation with the Bishops generally, we wish it to be known that no woman or girl should hesitate to enter a Church uncovered, nor should any objection to their doing so be raised.

William Cantuar:

Cyril Ebor:

It is well documented that William Temple was refused ordination at first because of his unwillingness to express literal belief in the Virgin Birth; the Bishop of Oxford turned him down as a candidate. There was, however, a tradition that Archbishops of Canterbury could ordain dons of Oxford Colleges; William was at the time a Fellow of the Queen's College, Oxford. A very discreet, tactful correspondence proceeded between the Archbishop and the Bishop in which the Archbishop said very gently to the Bishop that, though it gave him no pleasure per se to override him, he felt this young man had promise and that possibly his views were not as extreme as he had first implied and expressed. And so Randall Davidson ordained William. The story behind his uncle's ordination meant much to Freddy, and he took infinite pains when he himself was a bishop to be alongside those seeking ordination, especially those who had been heart-broken by decisions made at Selection Conferences.

William Temple's energy was quite phenomenal, and as an undergraduate Freddy used to have tremendous arguments and discussions with him on paper. The Archbishop was leading an incredibly busy and taxing life, both mentally and physically, but he nearly always replied to his nephew's letters by return, in his own hand; his letters were often written on trains. They make fascinating, if a bit wobbly, reading. By his own admission, Freddy was a very precocious undergraduate and felt he knew all the answers, and his uncle gently and firmly, and some-

53

times at tremendous length, put the
other points of view.

One of Freddy's abiding memories
was of a famous mission that the Archbishop of York conducted at the University of Oxford at the beginning of
the thirties when the practice of religion was at a low ebb. The University
Church was packed to the doors for
every address and on the last night
Freddy himself, still a schoolboy at
Rugby, was present; he could remember that one undergraduate hung by his
arms from the balcony throughout the
address - all forty five minutes of it - in
order to hear it. All of these talks, of
course, were delivered without any
notes. Freddy could remember people
telling him when he went up to Oxford
himself that during these talks they

Archbishop William Temple

had experienced the most profound moment of their lives. William Temple was
not a man for gimmicks; he used to stand very still and preached in a very quiet
voice. During the last hymn, 'When I survey the wondrous Cross', he gently
stopped them singing just before the last verse, and asked them to read through
the verse carefully:

> *Were the whole realm of nature mine,*
> *that were an offering far too small;*
> *love so amazing, so divine,*
> *demands my soul, my life, my all.*

He then said, very quietly, 'If you cannot sing that and mean it, don't sing it. If you
are absolutely confident that you can sing it and mean it to the full, sing it loudly.
If there are others of you who long to mean it but feel you often fail and need help
in fulfilling it, sing it very softly.' The packed Church of St. Mary the Virgin almost whispered this last verse - a breath-taking, haunting moment. Many wept.

After the mission, the Archbishop penned the following to his nephew:

> *Thank you for what you said about the Mission. I have written to your Headmas-*
> *ter to thank him for letting you have time with me in Oxford. If what I said meant*
> *something to just one person there then it would have been a success.*
> *Affectly, W. Ebor:*

Freddy always acknowledged his 'incalculable' debt to his Uncle when it came to preaching, and, as will become apparent later, he emulated some of William's practical preaching skills. Freddy also owed a lot to his Uncle's practice of the life of prayer. In the front of one of his prayer books, Freddy wrote something that Uncle William had said about prayer, 'Prayer is not an aid to conduct; conduct tests your prayer'. All through William Temple's books can be found these jewels, put so simply but powerfully: your prayer life and your friendship with God are tested by the sort of person you are.

When his hosts used to ask whether he wanted some time of quiet before a service, Freddy recalled his Uncle telling him that he sometimes told them that he would be grateful if they could provide a good paperback thriller and he would go away and read that. He was a man of great depth of spirituality, and Freddy once questioned him about this remark, obviously thinking it would be more seemly if the Archbishop could be seen kneeling alone in prayer, preparing himself. In reply, the Archbishop simply said that he 'couldn't care a fig' about what others thought; God alone understood how he found it best to prepare himself.

Freddy learnt his politics too from his Uncle. In all his writings William Temple never once said that Christians should necessarily join one or other political party, though he was himself for a long time a member of the Labour Party; he did, however, say that there were certain definite principles that all parties should ensure that they are upholding. He thought, and re-iterated in letters to Freddy, that these principles are based on Man, his dignity, his tragedy and his destiny. The dignity of every human was in being made in the image of God and that was the only thing that really made people equal; otherwise it was perfectly clear that they weren't equal. All have different abilities; some are much more attractive in character than others, so it was only because of the dignity of each human being, the fact that God, through Christ, loves every person, and cares for each one, that this truth held. Then came the tragedy of the Fall, and the ensuing selfishness, which meant that people had to be utterly realistic, William Temple making the profound remark that the job of Government was to devise laws which made man's self-interest in the end work for the best for all human beings. You had to take that into account; you could not just have an idealism that was not based firmly on the ground. Then, the destiny was that of being the children of God; and certain derivative principles followed from that, relating to freedom. Temple stressed strongly how Christ and God respect our freedom absolutely to the utmost, right to the end, and therefore our freedom must be respected. He stressed that democracy cannot be backed because it is the *best* form of government; it is the *least bad*, and there is at least a chance of periodically checking those who are governing. What was almost certain was that all majorities would be wrong. No advance at any time in society has ever come from a majority thinking it a good thing; it has always come by respect for minorities who are pushing things forward. In 1926, in the time of the great depression, he wrote to the major newspapers as Archbishop of York and asked that all Christians who agreed with him write to the Chancellor of the Exchequer, and to their own Member of Parliament, to say that they would rather taxes were raised, or at least not cut, than that the dole should be cut. Enough people did. Baldwin protested violently and asked the Archbishop how he would like it if he offered to teach him how to baptize. Freddy could remember his Uncle showing him the letter, shaking with merriment and saying, 'Look what our dear Stanley's just penned to me.' On another occasion, in the year of the General Strike, when Freddy was out in the garden at Bishopthorpe, Uncle William called him into his study and said, 'Oh dear, poor Stanley really doesn't like episcopal intervention.' He showed Freddy a letter he had just received from Baldwin. The letter asked how the Archbishop would like it if he were to ask for the revision of the Athanasian Creed to be referred to the Iron and Steel Federation.

William Temple was sure that together men and women had the ability to cope with forming a new society and that Christian principles should now go into society as a whole and 'religion' not be something that is 'done' privately in your spare time, and did not impinge on the corporate running of the whole of life. His book *Christianity and Social Order* (1942), which sold thousands of copies in its Penguin edition was, many people believe, a very significant contributory factor to the great Labour victory in 1945 and the foundation of the Welfare State.

William Temple had a unique ability to say profound truths in simple terms that everyone could understand, and this was one reason why he was known as the 'People's Archbishop'. During the War, the B.B.C. broadcast on the radio an incredible programme by today's standards in which the Archbishop spoke every week for a quarter of an hour to the troops, entitled 'The Archbishop speaks to the Forces'. Freddy can remember, when he was in the Syrian desert, seeing mechanics come from out of their cars to stop for a while to listen on their small sets to the Archbishop speaking to them. He toured England with the Cardinal Archbishop of Westminster during the war in the blackout and, despite all the difficulties with the bombing and the lack of petrol, held meeting after meeting, encouraging and giving new spirit to all his listeners; he was brilliant, in a quiet way, at boosting morale.

William Temple did not expect to be appointed to Canterbury because Churchill did not like the line he had been taking on a great number of things, and he wrote to Freddy's father, just before the appointment:

I shall be surprised if just at this moment the 'powers' select me for Canterbury. Some of my recent utterances have not been liked in political circles, and it would be thought that to choose me now is to endorse them. I don't deny I should like to be asked! But if I were, I should have to go; and I do not think I would like the job there as much as the job here. Anyway, it's as it will be. Confidentially, Cosmo [Cosmo

Gordon Lang, the retiring Archbishop of Canterbury] *does want me to follow him and has told me so quite plainly.*

He was of course appointed and moved on there but only had two years before he died. The last letter to his brother had to be a dictated one:

Please forgive me dictating a letter: that attack of gout that Alice [Alice Lascelles, a cousin on his mother's side] *found me recovering from returned before it was quite gone with prodigious violence, and I have now got acute gout in both knees, which, as you can imagine, is quite immobilising. I just wanted to send this as an explanation of why I have not written. Of course it may clear quite quickly as it sometimes does - but at present I am able to make no plans.*

He died just over a month afterwards, on the morning of 26th October, 1944. The whole country was staggered and dismayed at the news of his sudden death and many people said it was the equivalent of the loss of Churchill at that point in the war. Freddy himself, as will be seen later, was devastated.

5 World War Two

Looking back over old diaries, jottings and letters sent and received, it is not easy to detect an exact moment when one could say that Freddy became a pacifist; from Rugby days onwards, thoughts about pacifism flitted in and out of his mind. His was no crisis conversion. Mention was made earlier of the quote from Mahatma Gandhi found among Freddy's papers, jotted down when he was at Rugby. Also found from the same period was the poem 'Waste', by Geoffrey Studdert Kennedy:

> *Waste of Muscle, waste of Brain,*
> *Waste of Patience, waste of Pain,*
> *Waste of Manhood, waste of Wealth,*
> *Waste of Blood, and waste of Tears,*
> *Waste of Youth's most precious years,*
> *Waste of ways the Saints have trod,*
> *Waste of Glory, waste of God,*
> > *War!*

Freddy obviously came to his pacifism from an orthodox upbringing in the Church; this was not the case with so many of his friends at Oxford. In fact, for some, it was the other way round; they found Christianity through pacifism. (An example of this was Stephen Verney, a very close friend through the War and subsequently, who came through pacifism to Christianity and then left the pacifist cause during the war to become a member of the Intelligence Corps, working with the Greek Resistance in Crete. Freddy reckoned Stephen to be 'one of the great Christians of our generation'.) Freddy was of course in close touch with two of the finest exponents of the Christian non-pacifist position of the time, the Master of Balliol, A.D. Lindsay, and his Uncle William. Freddy always had and retained a profound respect for the Christian soldier. He had always been on the right wing of pacifist thought, feeling strongly that far too often pacifists did not consider the best of the other side. Thus, he said in an address to clergy in Portsmouth in the mid-1960s:

> *Just as we ask to be judged by our best, so we should only consider the best and most penetrating of the other side. There was much during the War which was shoddy and weak in the pacifist cause: the neurotic, the mental coward who wanted the spiritual jam while others did the spiritual dirty work for him, the person who was really against everything, the anarchist.*

The Master of Balliol used to conduct an open discussion group once a week in his room and here he expounded much of what came out in the first years of the War as *The Two Moralities*. It was a very important book for Freddy, as, indeed, for many others of his generation. Lindsay's theme of the morality of man's station and its duties and the morality of grace fitted in with Freddy's reading for the History school, and while all the time he saw the logic and necessity of justice backed by force, he became more and more impressed by what Canon Charles Raven (Regius Professor of Divinity at Cambridge and later Master of Christ's College and Vice-Chancellor) was to call 'the survival value of the saints', the power and importance of the morality of grace for those called to it. It seemed to Freddy to be something that started below mental logic and reason and superseded it; people called to the morality of grace were protesters against the imperfect logic of their society. Freddy remembered the Master saying to him once, 'Argue with me and I can counter with you every time and you will never convince me; tell me this you must do and no other; then go out and live your life and I will judge your faith by it'. Over the years that was what, for Freddy, summed up the argument.

It was a tremendous help to his nephew that Uncle William supported Freddy's sticking to his pacifist convictions, although he himself was firmly in support of England going to war. Interestingly - and William Temple often had this sort of tense holding of paradox - he felt that England would only be worth fighting for if there were a large number of conscientious objectors in it. He always thought it important that there be certain people standing for the other point of view. He used to say that there was not a consensus of Christian opinion, that it was through the holding of different opinions that something new was sparked off. He was an enormous help in backing Freddy against his family, who were very strongly opposed to the principles and practice of pacifism, especially his father, a Colonel in the Volunteer Army in India. 'Young men do silly things', wrote Freddy's mother to one of Freddy's elder sisters, 'he'll get over it'. Freddy's sister Edith told him in 1940 that if a German were to parachute into the garden at Damerel she would have to shoot Freddy first, 'for I wouldn't know what you'd do.' She was speaking seriously. In a broadcast on BBC Radio Bristol in the 1980s Freddy said, rather sadly and wistfully: 'My uncle was the only one who saved me from complete rejection by my family.' It was his Uncle's backing that gradually made his family feel that Freddy's position was tenable. The Archbishop told Freddy quite firmly, however, that if he were going to refuse to help the state in its moment of difficulty, he must not expect to receive any of its benefits. Through working that out logically Freddy thought that the only thing that he could do was join the Quaker Friends Ambulance Unit, right in the front line, and receive no pay. It was quite easy for him as a young man, unmarried, but he saw what a tremendous sacrifice some of the married Quakers, and their families, made. There was no invalid pension for those who were wounded; no pension for those families in which someone was killed. His uncle told him that that was the only position that the sincere conscientious objector could take up, and Freddy concurred. William Temple was, in fact, a convinced League of Nations supporter and was certain that if a small amount of force had been used right at the beginning, when Italy invaded Abyssinia or when Germany invaded the Ruhr, war could have been avoided.

As Freddy looked back in later years over his Uncle's letters to him, he found that so many of the points which the Archbishop made then and which Freddy argued against and did not see, with greater experience he learnt to understand. Freddy argued in favour of greater Christian commitment by all who called themselves Christian; that there should be a more clear-cut division between the Christians and those who were not. His Uncle replied that Freddy's argument had that clear-cut line which was so easy in theory but so disastrous and unchristian in practice. Freddy wrote in the 1960s:

Having watched Pacifist reactions of oneself and others during the War and now trying to run a large parish myself, I see the wisdom of that; who will dare to say who is Christian and who is not, when even in one person the light shines strongly in one place and all is darkness close by? Wilberforce worried about the slaves but cared little about industrial conditions in his own country.

Freddy judged that he had always been a bad member of the pacifist cause because he was never able to sign anything which said that God calls all people to be pacifist; he had seen and known men of the deepest Christian insight who had not been so called; he could not call them misguided, for their understanding and discernment of the facts was clear. He saw others of his own generation quite clearly called by God to give up their pacifism at great cost to themselves. Any facile presentation of pacifism made Freddy squirm; it struck him as middle-class, comfortable and unreal. He felt later that much of his and his friends' presentation of it was just like that before the War.

At Munich Freddy wavered but in 1939 he was firmly convinced that he was called to Pacifism. After attendance at a Tribunal, for which references were supplied by Uncle William and A.D. Lindsay, Freddy was registered as a Conscientious Objector. Freddy's appearance before the tribunal was very high profile and was much commented on in the national press, under such headlines as, 'Archbishop's nephew is a Conchie'. The press reports upset Freddy. With some justification, he thought them 'disparaging' - and once again in his life he was frustrated that he was not regarded as his own man, but as the nephew of William Temple. If the reports frustrated Freddy, they exasperated and angered his family. 'What *are* you doing to the name of our family?', wrote one of his sisters.

At first Freddy had a job with Dr. Joe Oldham on the *Christian News Letter*; then came the chance to join the Friends Ambulance Unit. Freddy wrote to his Uncle for advice. The Archbishop urged him to stay with the *News Letter*, using the argument that his past training made him of use there, but not as a stretcher-bearer. He did add, though, that subjective personal reasons might tip the balance the other way. Freddy decided after some time to join the Friends and wrote to tell him. He wrote back that he was delighted and always hoped that that would happen, but in giving advice he always stuck to the objective facts of where someone could be of most use.

The Friends Ambulance Unit brought Freddy into contact with all sorts of pacifism, including that of the birthright Friend. Freddy once commented that at its best nothing could touch it; it had little of reasoned logic in it but was the witness of a complete life. At its worst, it was for the young Quaker as automatic and ill thought-out an action for him to join the Friends Ambulance Unit as for an Etonian to join the Guards. On November 19th, 1939, he wrote from the Training Camp at Birmingham to a friend:

> *The people are very interesting in that they have thought about things a bit in order to be pacifist. Some, a great number in fact, are, I think, really anarchists in principle and do not realise how much they depend on law. There's a great deal of 'the individual getting a direct insight of God' and no need for a Church; they don't realise that their whole idea of God is coloured by tradition and the Church's keeping of that tradition. I let my section go on talking after lights out and we have very interesting discussions: not on the height of Oxford discussions - but very varied ideas delivered rather dogmatically. One man, whose zeal I admire, gets up an hour early in the morning to have a 'quiet time' and tends to wake one. Is that really unselfish and Christian?*
>
> *Today I had a bath at the Manor House, a huge place owned by Dame Elizabeth Cadbury: money no object. Very interesting. I didn't know luxury of that type could be combined with Quakerism.*

It was not long before the Unit were told they were being sent to Finland. Freddy stayed at Bishopthorpe for a while before embarking for Finland in the closing days of February, 1940. In an alliterative letter left by his bedside by Uncle William, Freddy read: 'Farewell, Freddy. Fight the freezing cold if nothing else! I am fearfully proud of my nephew.' Going to Finland gave them all in the eyes of friends and others a tremendous status; the phoney war still held most soldiers in Britain, but the pacifists were straight off the mark. Comforts of every type poured in: twenty-five years later, Freddy was still using up the stock of gloves given him then. They went with their Norwegian passenger boat, the 'SS Bessheim', to Oslo; their journey through Norway brought days of great comfort and feting by local people. Some ambulances broken on the voyage caused delays, but nobody seemed to mind.

Then followed for Freddy a wonderful journey to Stockholm and up the Baltic coasts, stopping each night in the comfort of a good hotel; the Unit was young then and learned prudence and economy later. Freddy's co-driver of Ford ambulance 13 was David Rowlands, who later became a GP in Gloucestershire. He recalls some alarming experiences in the snow, including once when Freddy lost control of the vehicle and they plunged into deep snow up to the windscreen. David continues, 'We cut down fir branches and put down logs in an effort to get out. Freddy was a good companion and we worked well together - but this time we were beaten. A snow plough eventually towed us out.'

Just over a fortnight after that incident, Freddy and David were transporting a refugee family, including an old man, his wife and a young woman with an infant in arms.

Freddy got into a broadside skid and finished up in deep snow, with the ambulance at a perilous angle. The passengers were severely shaken. 'We managed to get them out; the temperature was below zero and it was snowing hard. Another ambulance relieved us of our passengers and we were eventually towed out. In spite of their ordeal the family gave us profound thanks. Freddy apologised in halting Finnish for causing them so much suffering but the old people continued to express their gratitude and threw their arms round his neck. He had a way of endearing himself to so many.'

When he was asked in an interview in the 1980s what most frightened him during the War, he replied without hesitation that it was driving ambulances in snow. In April, 1940, Freddy had written to his parents, 'We drive 100 miles every day; it's shattering; the road is so fiendish, so foul, so hellish.'

Freddy once recalled in an interview how the passenger in the ambulance was always icy cold and wanted the windows shut and all the heating on, whilst the driver, through sheer nervousness and anxiety, would be dripping with sweat, and wanted all the windows open. They had to wear gloves at all times; if they touched anything metal without gloves, their bare hands would immediately stick to the metal.

David Rowlands also recalls the occasion when a number of the party were having a break from their travels and with due reverence entered a Church. David writes, 'I have a vivid memory of Freddy picking out the tune on the organ and in stentorian tones singing, "Little birdie I cried ... a rather tough little worm in your little inside, tit willow, tit willow, tit willow." Wherever Freddy was, laughter was never far away.'

The Finnish war was over by the time Freddy's party arrived in Tornio, but he helped in refugee work there. The novelty interest and variety made that a happy month's work; few gave any deep thought to the tough and heroic families with all their belongings in the back of the ambulances. Freddy felt a bit of a fraud, treating it all as an adventure. He found the Finns congenial. They especially appreciated his effort to learn their language, which was something Freddy did wherever he went. Freddy too had his first experience of a sauna while in Finland. He once recalled how, by decree, the women attendants had to be 'elderly and ugly', so that those having a sauna 'didn't get funny ideas whilst being lashed by twigs to stimulate circulation'. After the sauna the group were expected to go out and roll in the snow, though Freddy tried to avoid this, thinking it a sure way to succumb to a heart attack.

As the Germans advanced, the Unit drove back into Norway and took part in the hurried departure of the troops from Namsos. Half the Unit, including Freddy and David, travelled back to Britain with the British forces on a French warship. This was the first time Freddy had met war. Packed tight in the grossly over-laden holds of the ship, with food soon running out and the bombs coming down in the water beside, Freddy felt the first feelings of fear. David Rowlands remembers vividly seeing him coming up on deck when the ship reached home waters looking severely shaken, having endured the shuddering of the vessel from bomb blasts and the anti-aircraft fire from their own ship, in the confined space below. It did not help that the ship was laden with ammunition and, despite the 'No Smoking' notices, some of the soldiers were so petrified that they lit up anyway.

Paul Roake, another FAU companion who escaped from Namsos on the same ship, recalls Freddy on the quay at Gourock in a white sheepskin (tea cosy) hat on the morning they disembarked from Norway listening to General Carton de Wiatt congratulating them on their escape. Freddy himself recalled that the General (who had only one eye and one arm and was, said Freddy, if the ship had been torpedoed, 'the sort of General who would have swum ashore with his batman in his teeth') emphasised that they had not been driven out, but had merely withdrawn to fight again. Paul Roake commented, 'Freddy wore a very wry smile as well as the hat!'

Back in England, the Unit was sent to serve as orderlies at some of the hospitals. Freddy was at Gloucester, which members of the Unit called their 'Siberia'; conditions were Dickensian and atrocious. Freddy was there during the Dunkirk retreat and came in for some hostility from the troops at the hospital and from the staff, who appeared to go out of their way to humiliate them. The Matron specially was against having pacifists working in the hospital, despising them as 'unpatriotic and spineless'; on another level she assumed that Freddy, who was the leader of the first party in the FAU to take up this work, would corrupt her nurses, especially when she heard it said that FAU stood for Free and Unattached. The Matron's favourites were the VAD nurses; Freddy commented acerbically that these nurses were too 'hoity-toity' to give a bedpan, but they cut 'nice' sandwiches. Matron was desperate to get rid of the Unit, and it required great diplomacy on Freddy's part to win her round. In Paul Roake's words, 'Freddy did a marvellous job in taming the shrew!' Gloucester City Council were also very much against having Conscientious Objectors working in Gloucester, and a vote in the Council decided by only a very narrow majority that the COs should be retained. David Rowlands writes, 'Freddy, along with the rest of us, accepted the humiliation and willingly carried out the most menial tasks. Gradually the Matron came round and actually appreciated the contribution of the FAU'. Richard Wainwright, who was later to become the Member of Parliament for Colne Valley (1966-70 and 1974-87), recalls: 'His [ie Freddy's] constant good humour kept alive our spirits and made us buoyant. Without his friendliness we would have been lost - a true leader indeed.'

In the Unit as a whole in the summer of 1940 there was a general feeling that pacifists should have a message as well as a job; the Unit should think out its meaning and purpose anew. And so, with the radical and sweeping methods of the young, while the bombs were falling in London, a Conference was held on 'What is wrong with the FAU?' The difference between just doing a job well and quietly and trying to think through the pacifist position and live it out was talked about. The upshot was that there was to be a staff meeting regularly of representatives of all sections of the Unit. Two people called Group Leaders were to tour the sections, staying for two or three days with each, and to try to formulate a common Unit mind on the problems of the day. As Freddy was to comment, many years afterwards, 'A great deal of excitement and enthusiasm ended in a Constitution, just as the Life and Liberty Movement ended in the General Assembly [of the World Council of Churches].' A *Unit Chronicle*, to which Freddy contributed, was started under the editorship of a brilliant Balliol man, Stanley Mackintosh (who died an officer in the Army in Burma later in the War). Freddy was appointed one of the two Group Leaders, the other being John Bailey. So after a year in the FAU he found himself, among his duties, back in the same type of job he had avoided at the *News Letter* as being the wrong thing for a young pacifist like himself.

Freddy found it interesting, though, trying to make something of such a conglomerate body as the Unit. He was worried all the time at any signs of the pacifist demanding rights: that seemed quite contrary to the ideal of complete self-sacrifice which must be the basis of any pacifism. But when an organisation got as large as the Unit and involved in so much varied work, he and others wondered more and more if it could be done without a great deal of insistence on rights and working for them. One friend wrote to him,

> I have an uncomfortable feeling that behind our very existence and behind our Unit life, there stands a great deal of emphasis on rights, extending backwards down the whole Quaker tradition, and being strongly maintained for our benefit today. As we sit talking, disparaging this kind of pacifist action and encouraging that kind, there must be a great many forceful people securing the existence of the Unit by all kinds of trafficking in which we ourselves disdain to soil our fingers. I have been wondering whether there is a stronger spiritual life among the less ambitious pacifist Units whose work is simple enough not to require a vast income and a great organisation.

During this time, Freddy lived in London, and so was there for the early part of the

London blitz, in which the FAU did invaluable work. Freddy wrote the following account, entitled *The Night of May 10th, 1941*, for Mackintosh's *Unit Chronicle*:

I left Biddy Phelp's flat at about half past ten; it was now dark and a large and full yellow moon was rising. The siren sounded just as I got into the train at Victoria, but there was no activity at Whitechapel when I arrived at the Hostel. I went upstairs and changed into an old pair of flannel trousers with a hole in them and a polo sweater. We all then 'mustered' in the lounge and David gave me a party of four. He asked us to check the black-out all round the building, which we did. Soon after that the planes began to arrive and bombs began to fall. A telephone message came through from Poplar saying that the hospital had been hit and some of the FAU hurt. Arnold Curtis, Colin Prior and my party were asked to take the ambulances and go and see what we could do. We collected stretchers and bandages and loaded the ambulance. Four of us crowded into the back of the ambulance and waited for Arnold Curtis who was just coming from the Hostel. At that moment we heard incendiaries on their way down; I had visions of one landing in the middle of us through the roof; we would be unable to do anything, as the ambulance door shuts on the outside. They landed just in front of the car and beside it and behind it; they were the exploding type. Dick Harris, the driver, asked if we should do anything about them but I said we must go on as there were plenty more people in the Hostel to deal with them. Commercial Rd had been badly bombed most of the way.

At Poplar, as was natural, there was a certain amount of confusion and none knew exactly where the FAU were. Arnold and I went up the iron fire-escape outside to their ward; we found the door locked, but we climbed in through a broken window; and there we saw that the entire wall of one side of the ward had been stripped away and we looked straight out on to a blazing fire in the next building. All the FAU had moved. Downstairs in the ward below there was a large party rescuing patients from the rubble and helping the others to get away. When we found we were not needed there we went down to one of the main halls and there found John Burtt who was in charge of the Poplar section. All the FAU were safe except the two who were on the roof, but they were now in Outpatients and did not seem very badly hurt; one may have broken some ribs. A moment later, someone hurried up to us and asked if we could help; they had heard breathing through a pile of rubble. We went and examined it but saw that there was nothing we could do except report it.

As bombs and land-mines continued to fall with unceasing regularity very close, the Medical Superintendent decided to evacuate the entire hospital. Then came the long and pathetic job of moving all the old chronics and fractured femurs and pelvises; some of the fractures had only been set that day and were certain to break again on the journey. Pale, terrified faces peered at one through the blankets. When that was over and the nurses had climbed into the ambulances as well, I noticed David Mattingly, a nineteen year old of the Poplar section, looking very white

Freddy at the centre of his FAU section. Stephen Verney sits at his feet.

and faint. He had been very near the wall when it was torn away and was suffering from shock. I sat him down and gave him some water to drink. There was no tea to be made. We took him back to the Hostel when we returned. Just before going he handed his insurance papers to John Burtt and said, "You'll send those to my father if anything happens to me, won't you?". He was very frightened at returning to the Hostel as there were large fires blazing there and it looked as if it was worse there than at Poplar. But we were able to give him food and tea and put him to bed. Driving back along Commercial Rd Dick heard an explosive falling; he stopped the car for a moment, listened, then decided it was going to fall behind us and accelerated fast; it fell in the road just behind us and the blast blew the car forward. All the buildings around the Hostel had been hit and were blazing merrily.

David had plenty of men up and we were allowed to go and rest, on call if wanted. I did not sleep but just listened to the incessant fall of the bombs. The All-Clear went at six; on the roof one could see huge fires still belching up their smoke into a clear summer morning sky. There were streams of people coming out of shelters, who anxiously hurried towards their homes, turned the corner, and then stood dazed as they looked at a pile of rubble. A reporter, watching it too, turned and said to me, "Bloody murder; and what for?".

After nine months of touring the sections and trying to foster a common mind, a task which took him out of London for much of the time, Freddy felt that this was becoming too dangerous a job for him to do, not physically, but mentally and spiritually. He asked to go abroad and was put in charge of a second party to join the Hadfield Spears Hospital Unit, working in the Middle East with the Free French.

On August 28th., 1941, Freddy wrote to his parents:

This voyage is being very tiring as now we are allowed to sleep on deck which is at least a bit better than down in a temperature of 110 which is what it reaches at night down here when the place is full; but on deck it is very hard and people are continually tripping over one and then at 4 in the morning one is woken by the crew washing the deck. I'm sure they only scrub the deck at that stupid time to annoy us [ie the Conscientious Objectors].

The mobile hospital had been set up in 1940, at first with eighty beds, and the surgeons, doctors and pharmacists were officers of the French army. The first impressions made on Freddy were described in an interview in 1995 with Lyn Smith of the Imperial War Museum, who was researching for a book on the Friends Ambulance Unit in the Second World War:

There was this bunch of extraordinary - now they seem very old-fashioned - women drivers of the very cut-glass, upper class voices who thought themselves right above everyone else. A few years ago a very misleading TV programme about the HSU - 'Silk Stockings and Tin Hats' - concentrated wholly on these drivers who made out that it was all a great lark: 'no more caviar and champagne, just bully beef. Like the boys'. They called the really marvellous group of English nurses 'the nannies' in a very derogatory way, although these were hard-working, highly qualified nursing sisters. Then, oh dear, shame, there was us - the FAU - whom the drivers called 'dogs bodies' and treated us likewise.

Freddy found the work immensely satisfying. There was a tremendous need for medical care in Syria and the Lebanon. Malaria was rife, as were eye diseases like trachoma; there was a great deal of dysentery, deficiency diseases and skin infections arising from a mixture of poverty and ignorance. Freddy used to drive out and tell the Bedouin tribes about the clinic at Tel Tamer, and see if they wanted any medical assistance. He recalled that he had to put up with interminable hospitality rites; he had memories of hearing sheep being killed for a great welcoming feast when he arrived and being offered the chief morsels after the sheik had grubbed around in the middle of the sheep with his dirty hands. The most important morsel to offer was the eye, so Freddy became used to eating eyes. He and his companions would charge the wealthy sheiks for medical care to enable them to treat the poor for nothing.

The interview with Lyn Smith gives a flavour of his life in the desert:

One night Stephen [Verney] and I stayed the night with a sheik. He spent the evening picking fleas from the head of one of his small sons and chatted and then went off to sleep and we lay down to sleep. Then I woke up in the middle of the night as a sheep appeared - there being a door in the tent - strolled up to where Stephen was sleeping and then performed right by his head. I have never seen Stephen wake more rapidly. We certainly got very close to the local community there.

One day Dr. Shrijian prescribed three teaspoons of a certain medicine for a patient and told her to come back in a week if she wasn't better. The sheik brought this wife back saying that she was much worse, so the doctor increased the dose to a desertspoon. They had wooden spoons. The next day the sheik came back and said, 'The teaspoons she could manage, but not the desert spoons!' We presumed they had been sawn up and eaten.

The major operation was the one for trachoma where the eyelashes were turned under the eye; the rubbing of the eyelashes through the shrinking of the eye is what causes the blindness. We had to cut a slit in the upper eyelid and then take a sliver of skin from the lower lip and insert that into the eyelid and it turned the eyelashes out. Dr. Shrijian said one day, 'We could get more of these done, Freddy, if you took on the sewing up of the lips', and I agreed. The first patient I had was someone who had quite a large moustache and when I was mopping up the blood I found that I had sewn his lip into his moustache. The doctor looked down without saying anything. So I slit it open and sewed it up again. I would visit the poor man in the hospital each day, asking with trepidation, 'How is your lip?' 'Quite alright, quite alright'. And his lip apparently recovered quite well.

Most of the men wouldn't let their wives be in the operating theatre alone with us. So they would huddle in a corner in their dirty old clothes which made it difficult to get good antiseptic conditions. I remember once there was a poor wife under local anaesthetic; she wasn't badly hurt but just couldn't keep still. So finally we had to say to the husband, 'Could you persuade your wife to keep still?' And the persuasion was to step forward and give her some hearty slaps. Some patients were frightened of beds and you would find them sleeping under, rather than on them.

We'd look out in the morning and see a cortege coming across the desert and wonder what it was. Then you'd realise that the wealthy sheik you had in the hospital was just changing wives. We couldn't provide any cooking, so someone had to do this and after a while he'd feel like a change and the new wife would come in and the old one go back.

We loved living in our little mud house. It was a good, simple way of living.

It was while Freddy was in the desert that Uncle William was appointed Archbishop of Canterbury. Hamilton Mills writes:

I was with Freddy in North Africa when he got news of his uncle William's appointment as Archbishop of Canterbury. Freddy thought some congratulations would be in order. The army post office accepted telegrams, provided they were selected from a set list: 'Happy birthday, mum!', 'Get well soon' or 'Deepest sympathy', and so on. Freddy decided that the most appropriate on offer was 'Good show! Keep it up!', and this was the telegram he sent. I don't know what they thought of it at Lambeth!

On November 16th, 1942, Freddy included the following in a letter to his parents:

I wrote a sketch about the operating room and made it as ruthless and pointed as possible: only possible among the French, who have no false pride. It went down far better than I had expected. Some said it was the funniest thing they had ever seen: the Colonel said, 'A real masterpiece: très très bien, Freddy: je vous remercie infiniment, quoi?' (If you are from the top drawer in France, you throw in the odd 'quoi?' here and there: as you descend the social scale it turns into 'eh?'. But it seems quite universal; why are we not taught it at school?) It was fun doing a little acting again.

In February, 1943, Freddy wrote to his parents that he had 'dug a grease-pit for the car today. I learnt a new Syriac compliment: to anyone working a passer-by must say, "May God give you strength", and the reply is, "May your mother and father go to Paradise". And so as I walk through a village many a pious Assyrian is hoping that you will both go to Paradise. I hope this makes you feel happy!'

In his next letter, at the beginning of March, Freddy wrote:

On Friday evening the nurse rushed in just as were sitting down to supper and said that the little boy who had scurvy badly was bleeding badly again and would bleed to death. And so we rushed down, lit lamps, boiled instruments, and I climbed on to the table and the doctor took some blood from me. Then we went into the dark little wards with their one light and got the boy from a weeping mother. He was a dear little boy who never moved when we told him not to. His veins were very collapsed and the doctor had much difficulty in finding one to put the blood in, but at last he succeeded. It was an impressive sight, the two Assyrian orderlies holding lamps, the doctor bent over the thin arm picking out a vein: Stephen stirring my blood in a bowl to stop it clotting (we had luckily typed the boy's blood in the morning and I was the same class) : I held the boy's hand and talked to him. When we took him back into the ward the weeping mother fell at my feet and said she would sacrifice herself for me! The boy is living at the moment, which is something'.

Freddy went next to Tobruk and the Western desert, where he encountered fighting again. He was pleased to be back in closer contact with the military, though he was depressed by the sheer folly of some of the deaths; he remembered three men dying after drinking disinfectant, thinking it would make them drunk. There was obviously a great lack of water and some people used to wash their clothes in petrol. It just needed a friend to approach smoking for the person to go up in flames,

The clinic at Tel Tamer.

and Freddy remembered treating horrific burns. He also recalled scrubbing amputated arms and hands prior to getting rings off fingers to return to their owners.

Freddy spent the late Autumn and early Winter of 1943 in Cairo, and was able to do a little sightseeing. He spent some time at the Moslem University, where one course involved 15 years study of the Koran. 'You can't help but admire their dedication', wrote Freddy, 'and it's an impressive place; as always my Damascene accent caused much amusement and they all roared with laughter. It is probably much the same as if a Frenchman came to London and spoke broad Lancashire.'

Freddy's natural ability with languages often stood him in good stead. For those who found foreign languages difficult, things like reading a menu could be fraught with difficulties. Nev Coates, a member of Freddy's unit and close friend, wrote, when describing a brief holiday he and Freddy enjoyed together:

> *On the way from Damascus to Hama, we had a brief stop at Homs in a fly-ridden restaurant where the menu was written in Arabic which the waiter translated into very broken French.*
>
> *'Did you enjoy your meal?' asked Freddy afterwards.*
>
> *'Yes. Very good. Why do you ask?'*
>
> *'You ordered sheep's testicles.'*

Nev Coates added that it was 'typical of Freddy's wily humour that he just sat there, saying nothing until I had devoured them all.'

In his next letter home, written at the beginning of November, Freddy wrote:

I have been making a more extensive study of the Copts. I went round quite a number of their churches on Sunday after having attended Mass at one of them. They have a lot of very fine stuff; particularly screens of ebony wood inlaid with ivory. Their crosses are very similar to the Iona crosses and some of their paintings remind me of the early English stuff one sees in England, like the paintings in Chichester. The service was in Coptic which is a mixture of Egyptian and Greek; I recognised quite a number of Greek phrases in it. They all seemed to know their responses well. But it was a weird slow sombre affair; very different from the Cathedral the Sunday before on All Saints' Day, when we sang loudly,

'Ring out Dominions, Voices, Powers,

Virtues, Archangels, Angels Choirs'.

The place was quite full and everyone just shouted; there was a dear little Colonel next to me, rather fat and thick about the neck, who went quite purple toward the end of each verse.

The following week, Freddy wrote:

I'm getting quite an expert on the Coptic Churches. Today I went on a tour run by a Mrs. Devonshire; it starts at the station, every Saturday at three. Any troops who care to come, may. Imagine Aunt Francie in Cairo and you have it. Mrs. Devonshire rolls her rr's in the same way and is about 80 and very Queenly; she has a devoted policeman who takes a chair around for her to sit in, whenever there is a moment's delay. We all piled into garries and then moved off at a stately pace through the narrow streets. I was in the 'royal' vehicle. She got out of her coach with great dignity and slowly mounted the steps of the Mosque with her hand poised à la Trench [a reference to Freddy's great-grandmother], and all the keepers of the Mosque rushed forward and kissed it with great signs of welcome. It was a great sight; she was also very well informed on her subject and only took one round two places very slowly and leisurely. Apparently the old thing does this three times every week; a remarkably good bit of war effort.

Freddy left Cairo on December 8th. On the morning of that day he paid a last visit to one of the mosques and wrote home saying, 'I bumped into the Chiang-Kai Sheks in a Mosque in Cairo. She shows a very pretty leg in a naughtily-cut long dress!'

Freddy went back into the desert to much hard work. In later years he confessed that sheer exhaustion sometimes made him wish to shirk the job, especially 'tedious things like helping severely burned patients to feed when I myself was starving'; he commented that 'some members of the Royal Army Medical Corps did the job so much more Christianly than I did'. In one letter home he wrote:

Here still the same overwhelming amount of work and so time rushes by. Oh! bedpans: can you imagine emptying them in a place with no adequate arrangements for sluicing and rationed water? All our 80 patients have a dose of salts every morning: most of those from the front have not been to the lavatory for days. This usually means two bedpans each of the worst variety. Sorry to be so crude but it is such a dominant feature of our work. That is what 'succouring the wounded' means: I defy anyone to say they like it: it would be physically wrong if they did like such smells: all one can say is that it is a job and someone has to do it. I see why Quakers are so silent: they know that so much social work is unpleasant and they can't really enjoy it; for others the hypocrisy of saying how pleasant it is. I suppose a real saint would enjoy it. But goodness! It is difficult. You go right to the end of a ward at the end of a 12 hour day, a man asks you for a bedpan, back you go, fetch it and paper and then the man next door says, "Can I have a bottle?" Internally you feel like going up in smoke that he didn't ask you when you were down the first time, but instead you smile and say, "A bottle? OK". I feel I am being very insincere, but I manage never to show my feelings. A quiet voice from a New Zealander in bed said the other day, "Have a break; your carburettor won't stand it if you go on at that pace. I can't thank you enough: you are the only one who really looks after us". How glad I am that he does not know how I really feel; I just wish I were saint enough to have done it all genuinely. Really the world is full of hypocrites like me. Whilst here I have been constantly reminded of Father Zossima in The Brothers Karamazov. *Can you remember the piece where Dostoevsky has him say, 'Love in action is a harsh and dreadful thing compared to love in dreams'?*

Freddy confessed to being 'absolutely shaken' by the sheer physical suffering he encountered. It preyed on his mind for many years that sometimes, when an operation in the theatre had not been successful and it was obvious the patient was dying, he would rush him back to the ward in unseemly haste so that he died on the ward, and the ward staff would have to cope with all the work involved. It is obvious from his personal correspondence that Freddy desperately needed a break; he found himself not giving enough attention to 'the little things that mean so much to a patient.'

The following week he wrote:

Some of the patients are delightful: suffering makes the good better and the bad worse. Uncle William is right in saying that we are not to mind about the suffering of the innocent but rather the suffering of the guilty. On the ward one gets such a feeling of being in a situation which is just too big for everyone, a sort of sickness the world must go through. During bad raids it is amusing to see what an almost theatrically steady nerve one has developed: and it is necessary as most of the patients have lost their nerve. Plaster casts are under the bed in no time when a bomb falls.

October 26th 1944 was a shattering day for Freddy, as indeed for many others. He wrote to his father:

At tea today I just heard the abrupt headline news of Uncle William's death. It was brutally sudden and I was stunned. So unexpected. What a tragic loss: quite the worst thing that has happened to England these last five years. There was so much he would have done. For us, who knew him personally, it is unnecessary to speak. Knowing how I feel as a nephew, I realise a bit what you must feel as a brother, and I sympathise. I am going down to the 9 o'clock news to see if they give any further details.

He later asked, 'Why has this happened? Why?' He added, 'But I suspect Uncle William would never have asked this and would give me a very good reason for not doing so. So I won't. But I do'.

A fellow worker with Freddy in the desert says he saw him about ten minutes after hearing the news of his Uncle's death. Freddy, he said, 'looked grey, twenty years older and his eyes looked as thought he had been caught in a particularly violent sandstorm'. When he asked him what on earth was the matter, 'Freddy could only mumble, almost incoherently, "I've just lost my best friend."' When Freddy told one of the French doctors later about his Uncle, the doctor replied gently, "I think your country has too lost its best friend; weep for your country as well, my friend."'

On October 31st, 1944, Freddy wrote:

I sat in the little café which is our Mess and listened to the broadcast of Uncle William's funeral. I was fortunately free and I was glad to be able to follow and share in it that much with you. I can't really reconcile myself to it. I hope the people coming back from leave bring some cuttings. And only two years ago you wrote saying how young and strong he looked when preaching at his Enthronement. It is very baffling why in an age of leaders and great personalities, one of the few really good ones should be taken away so soon. But it must be meant in the end. Listening to the service and thinking of you all made me feel the contrast of this existence with home again very much; on the whole so many people one has to deal with are so sordid in their petty dishonesties and hypocrisies.

Freddy was also becoming jaundiced by the attitude of some members of the Unit with whom he was working, thinking that they were not paying enough attention to the spiritual side of their witness; religious practice went by the board. There had also crept in a lack of 'corporate feeling'. He wrote to Tegla Davies, the Head of the Unit, expressing his misgivings and fears and received the following letter in reply:

Your letter about the visions of the Unit which some of us had in the earlier days made rather humiliating reading. Perhaps we have been aiming at the impossible in

73

taking people with such different ideas and philosophies and ever imagining they could have enough common outlook to make possible the model of which you speak, but if those who call themselves pacifists - men of peace - find it so difficult, under what are in many ways very disadvantageous conditions, to produce an organisation with a message as well as a job, it makes one feel how enormous is the job of bringing the world as a whole to a change of heart.

In July, 1943, Freddy had written to his father:

At the beginning of the war I knew quite well what I wanted to do and was very keen ('felt the call' or something is I believe the trite phrase) to be a cleric. But at the beginning of the war I determined to spend the war years as an ordinary man, with no stamp of an ordinand on me: I thought I would learn more and experience more with my fellow creatures that way. And so I studiously avoided SCMs, meetings for would-be ordinands, etc. etc. out here. Of course I lost as well as gained in that: but I think I've gained more. I've learnt a great deal this War, more particularly since coming abroad: I've learnt a lot about a lot of things but particularly about myself, which hasn't been pleasant. There were moments when things all seemed to slide particularly in the Desert. Then I've had a year in that very isolated spot, Tell Tamer: it has all been wonderful experience. But now I rather wonder and doubt my ability and quality to be a cleric. I still want to be one: at least I see the job properly done with real inspiration is the most important there is. But if I can do that, I don't know at all - and yet I'm sure I could do much better than many of the padres I've seen. So there it is. Maybe things will clarify in the next year or so. My immediate plans are to get my eyes fully cleared.

(For much of the time during his spell in the desert Freddy had had serious problems with his eyes, involving on more than one occasion lengthy stays in hospital.)

On May 26th 1944, Freddy wrote:

I have joined the Ordinands Scheme out here. There is a correspondence course in Lectures. I have been sent a 'Devotional' one as a start. I must say I find it fairly frightful. It talked about preparing oneself to be 'a Father-in-God to the Mothers' Union'! Really! What has happened to such a man's sense of humour? I see Dick Sheppard found his theological college quite intolerable. I feel I may too. Lectures like that one make me think seriously about becoming a Friend and going to their Mission Field. I have filled in innumerable forms. One was given three lines in which to state why one wished to be ordained. I wrote, 'Impossible to reply in the space provided'. This lecture was also full of how a padre must never take a lady even out to lunch, for 'fear the weaker brethren may stumble'. Far from making me feel 'devout', that sort of thing makes me feel quite sick. I showed it to a very fine Quaker, who commented shrewdly, 'Isn't that what the Pharisees thought about Jesus eating with the wine-bibbers, etc.?' I intend anyhow to become an 'Attender' after the war. Friends have 'Members' and 'Attenders': Attenders can be members of other churches but are people considered to be sufficiently in sympathy with Quaker ideals and the Quaker way of life.

Then on the September 8th 1944, en route home at last, he wrote:

In some ways I still don't feel sure about being ordained. All these lectures I have received from BNAF say so much about being sure of your vocation: absolutely vital I can see but what does that mean? I can't talk impassionately about 'winning souls' etc. etc. I see it more as a job more worthwhile than any other: but at the moment so much of ritual and 'order' strikes me as a nuisance and meaning nothing to most people. So much strikes me as an intolerable encumbrance: while the job of making Christianity real to oneself and the ordinary man is so much more important. So many Army padres have just horrified me. Maybe I shouldn't go in for it: but I can talk that over when I get back. At the moment I feel the right thing would be to be ordained and then teach, probably some history. But I've got other things to think about at the moment; we've had a wonderful drive up through the Massif Central. And the welcome: pelted with fruit: grapes, pears, peaches: a peach hard in the cheek is quite painful.

One of Freddy's last letters, before reaching England, ran as follows:

During the last week we have done one of the most unusual and interesting jobs I've done in the war. The Germans in this sector here asked for some medical help to deal with civilian wounded. And so some of us went in. It was very odd and quaint: they un-mined a track on the road. A French car took us to the little frontier village and there we were met by a German staff car and the convoy went on. I was in the Operating Theatre Truck, a huge, wide thing, following directly behind the little staff car: I had been told to follow closely in his tracks because of mines, so it was a bit nerve-racking. I will tell you more about this when I come home. I was one of the first allies into that bit of enemy territory.

This episode was never given any publicity, probably because it was not good wartime propaganda.

There was even humour involved here. The French surgeon, ably abetted and encouraged by Freddy, took to sewing the operation wounds in the shape of the Croix de Lorraine. Freddy, in later years, wrote that he felt 'mildly ashamed' of his part in this, though he could not help but smile at the thought of 'many elderly German tourists sunning themselves on foreign beaches, sporting, probably quite unconscious of the fact, the symbol of the Free French Army on their tummies.'

In conversation with a BBC television crew many years later, Freddy said 'It was a stitch-up in more ways than one!' The producer of the programme said that, 'having delivered this sentence, the Bishop went off into paroxysms of laughter. I suspect he'd told the story before; that was the way he was. Interviewing him for our (serious) programme was such a delight. He touched us all – even our hard-bitten cameramen! – with his sheer sense of fun.'

And so Freddy came back home to leave the Unit and prepare to go to Theological College. He left, in his own words, 'with little changed in the pacifist equipment with which I started, but having had a real experience of myself and of the world.'

6 Towards Ordination

At the end of March, 1945, Freddy finally decided to apply for permission from the Ministry of Labour and National Service to start training at Westcott House, Cambridge, for the ministry of the Church of England. Accordingly, he wrote to the Regional Controller explaining that at the time his sole condition of exemption from military service was full-time work with the Friends Ambulance Unit. He continued his application by saying that, subject to a Selection Conference, he had been accepted for training at Westcott House prior to September 1st 1939, and so he could have gained exemption from military service then, if he had so wished. However, with the outbreak of war he had wished to play a more active and closer part in the relief of suffering and so had joined the Friends Ambulance Unit in November 1939. He set out in detail all that he had been doing during the war. The Principal of Westcott, William Greer, supported his application as did George Bell, Bishop of Chichester, within whose diocese Freddy's family home, Damerel, was situated. The case was heard speedily and successfully at the Fulham Appellate Tribunal in mid-April.

On Tuesday, April 24th 1945, Freddy set off nervously to Warlingham for a Selection Conference, at which his vocation to the Christian ministry would be discussed and tested. By chance, he travelled on the same train as the Secretary and organiser of the Conference, Ken Carey (later to be Principal of Westcott House and Bishop of Edinburgh), who offered him a seat in his taxi up to the House. Warlingham was in the outer London suburbs and was the Diocesan Conference House for the diocese of Southwark. It had a lovely garden, which, on this April day, was a mass of blossom, and Freddy's spirits were high.

Ken Carey and he arrived at the House at 4.30 and as the Bishop of Maidstone, the Chairman of the Conference, had not arrived, he was asked over to eat the Bishop's sandwiches at the Warden's house; this further raised his spirits! Over tea, the Warden, a Canon Armitage, whom Freddy described as 'pleasant and intellectual, if remote', asked him what he was going to do with the rest of his life. Freddy bit back the reply that he thought the next few days should be helping him think deeply about that very question. Otherwise, what was he doing there?

The other candidates, sixteen in all, arrived by five o'clock; they had all particularly been asked to be there no later than five, but to Freddy's dismay - he was not at this time of his life one to sit still doing nothing - nothing was going to happen till half past six and there promised to be one and a half hours when he expected that they would all eye each other, wondering how on earth the other could be there. Freddy sat chatting aimlessly for half an hour with the others, and found most of them 'very shy, gauche and stiff'. Not being able to bear it any longer, he invited a kindred spirit, Andrew Hunkin, son of the Bishop of Truro, for a walk in the garden.

One of the other candidates joined them and walked quietly with them. Freddy and Andrew Hunkin talked about the task of rebuilding the Church in the years following the War. When the quieter one was asked what he thought the priority for the post-war clergy was, he said, 'Oh, just the same as before, I suppose. The War hasn't made all that much difference, has it?' He then noticed a minute spot of mud on his shoes and went inside to wipe it off in case, he told Freddy, he gave the 'wrong impression' to the Selectors.

When the two returned inside, a young cleric came up and asked Freddy to distribute a lot of tiny yellow name labels which everybody had to pin on to their lapels. The writing on them was so small that the thought raced through Freddy's mind that obviously the Holy Spirit was determined on making it difficult for any with poor eyesight and perhaps had decided not to be recommending anyone with myopia on that particular week. He was a bit taken aback by the way that the cleric ('with a collar ten sizes too big and an enormous Adam's apple, which must have made the act of swallowing a major undertaking') assumed that he was doing Freddy a favour in choosing him to distribute the badges. He half expected to be patted on the head and told what a lucky boy he was.

At supper there was a great to-do about the washing up; would the candidates mind helping and would they mind making their beds as well? There would be people in during the day to do the washing-up, but the young cleric said it would give them all 'enormous satisfaction' if they could possibly help with the supper dishes. Coming from the Friends Ambulance Unit, Freddy - a stickler for 'order' at this and perhaps any time - had taken it for granted that there would be an orderly rota made out and that all would join in together to do the chores. The Warden said it would be 'a real act of Christian charity' and the Bishop made some joke about the possibility of 'people not knowing how to make their beds'. In a letter home, Freddy said simply, 'Really! Is it still so much the religion of the upper classes?'

After supper, all the candidates had, in three minutes, to say what they had done during the War. The group listened to a lot of 'bomb-dodging stories and such remarks as "It was an experience that I shall never forget", etc. etc.'. Freddy took all of his allotted three minutes to relate the barest facts, without comment, of his 'War Story'. After Compline he went to bed, feeling very depressed and 'strangely uneasy and restless'. He confided to a friend later that on this first night at Warlingham he feared that if he was to move forward to ordination in the Church of England, he might well turn out as a square peg in a round hole.

For the next three days the candidates attended four services each day: Holy Communion, Matins, Evensong and Intercessions, and Compline and Address. There was a lecture in the morning, followed by questions and discussion; Freddy was further depressed by the way that most of the candidates were so self-satisfied and complacent. One candidate told him that he wanted to be appointed to a country parish where there was easy access to trout fishing. In the afternoon, everyone had a thirty minute personal interview with each of the four selectors. There was another lecture in the evening, and Freddy found it dispiriting and slightly wearing. One of the selectors, a Mr. Allison, Principal of Ridley Hall Theological College, who was of an Evangelical persuasion, was not used to so many services and quietly confessed to Freddy at the end that he was tired and exhausted by it all. 'Well, really!', was Freddy's comment home. Allison was later to become Bishop of Winchester.

All the selectors hinted that Freddy's next step would be Westcott House, though official notification of the result of the Conference would be sent to Greer. Freddy found the Chairman, the Bishop of Maidstone, very 'wise and amenable' and he seemed to think that ultimately teaching would provide a good outlet for his talents; Freddy himself felt much attracted that way. He found it 'staggering' how much of everyone's thought there, except the Bishop's, was 'tied up in the most unreal way' with the Church of England. The continual implications were that the only Christians in the country were the baptized members of the Church of England. Freddy kept on asking about the place of the Free Churches, the Roman Catholic Church and the Society of Friends; the Bishop supported him. The rest were, in Freddy's words, 'a bit bemused by me and could not seem to grasp what I was saying.' After a lecture by Canon Armitage, the group was asked how they would explain the doctrine of the Church as the Sacramental Host of God to the ordinary man. Freddy commented further, 'I surprised people somewhat by saying that it was the very last thing the ordinary man would want to know. And the Bishop who, I think, had been wondering if he ought to disagree with one of his selectors, again agreed with me.' (It transpired that the Bishop had been devoted to Uncle William, who had consecrated him to Jarrow and then took him south when he went to Canterbury.)

Three days after the end of the Conference Freddy received a letter from Ken Carey saying that he had been recommended for training for the Ministry, and could take up his place at the end of July.

On his return from Warlingham, Freddy agitated strongly with the Friends Ambulance Unit to send a team immediately to work in Belsen where they were still desperately short of nursing staff. He volunteered to go himself for three months as he felt it to be an emergency big enough to justify putting off Westcott till the autumn. Enough volunteers were forthcoming, however, and Greer said he really wanted him to start on the 26th July.

Freddy set about planning a VE-day celebration for the Unit or, as he preferred to call it, an 'End of European War Day'. He arranged for some fowl to be delivered from the country and got in some cider, telling his parents that 'this place is frowsty at the best of times, so I want to liven it up for once.' The next week he wrote in very disappointed vein that the Unit did not do anything in the end on VE-night, for too many thought it would send the wrong signals. Freddy saw their point, but felt that they might just have had a small party, for peace, if not for victory - especially as he had gone to the trouble of organising the fowl and cider!

Instead, Freddy went with a few others to Buckingham Palace, where there was a phenomenal crowd. They waited for the Royal Family to appear on the balcony. Despite the crush, the crowd was very good-humoured and orderly, though they had to wait a long time without anything happening, and listened to some of the comments: 'I wouldn't have waited if I'd known the King would be so long.' 'Really it's so unfair keeping us all waiting.' 'I bet they're finishing off their tea.' 'No, they're putting the silver polish on their tiara things.' But they finally appeared; Freddy told his mother that 'the Queen looked very regal in a white evening dress and Margaret Rose in blue; Elizabeth in the hideous uniform of the A.T.S.' He continued, 'Today [May 13th], I saw them ride through on their way to St. Paul's in an open coach. How deplorably platitudinous old Fisher was! Quite unbelievable; and there isn't one in a thousand in the streets who equates military victory with spiritual victory; Uncle William would never have done that'. (About fourteen years later, Freddy was Senior Chaplain to Dr. Fisher; we do not know if he ever mentioned his thoughts of 1945 to him.) Freddy continued:

> *Two more of our POWs have returned; they got back late last night and so took them out for a good meal in Soho. They have some fantastic stories to tell; they saw a good deal of concentration camps and have some photos. One of them I knew in Finland and trust as a good, reliable witness. He has been fairly horrified by the Americans. Near him were captured five SS officers; a German Jew in the American Army asked and got permission from his CO to do what he liked with them. He got them in a field and surrounded them with machine guns and told them that they must come to attention and not move at all; they would be shot if they did. At the end of 24 hours one had been shot; at end of 38, two more; and the last was shot after 51 hours. Understandable and just, you may say; but what a world. This man has also seen an American tank entering a German town, supposed to be surrendered; the children ran after the tank and the Americans gave them sweets. Then suddenly a fanatic fired from a window and shot one of them in the tank; instantly, the tank gun was swung round and all the children were mown down. In such a world benign pronouncements from Canterbury that humanity stands at a higher level than it did before just don't mean anything. Europe as a whole is in chaos and all standards are lower.*

For the next six weeks, Freddy read a great deal in preparation for Westcott, and grew more and more impatient to be settled there. Amongst other reading, he bought Dom Gregory Dix's newly-published 750-page tome, *The Shape of the Liturgy*, which he 'devoured with excitement'. He judged it 'a really scholarly work which does away with much of the sentimentalism of modern Anglo-Catholic thought'. He was particularly interested in reading about how all the various rites and customs had developed. He jotted down: 'An Anglican priest, if he wants to, can have six candles on the altar like some of the Popes in the thirteenth century, five like the twelfth, two like some other, or none like the pre-tenth century and face the congregation - ritual fits the times and wishes of the day and is not sacred in itself.'

Armed with *The Shape of the Liturgy* and a collection of his Uncle William's books, which had remained with Dr. Fisher at the Old Palace in Canterbury until Freddy collected them on June 22nd, he set off for Cambridge. His first letter home, written the day after he arrived at Westcott, did not concentrate on the nitty-gritty of theological college life, but on wider matters:

> *Well, what an election; I find it all rather exhilarating; not that I have that confidence in the Labour party, but it is a sign of the sanity of the British public that they were not taken in by that enormous one-man publicity stunt by Churchill; over 10,000 voted against him even in his own constituency and it is a sign that people are prepared for radical changes; let's only hope that they make a success of it. It is an odd thing, which I remember Uncle William commenting on in a letter to me, that the Oppositions have always made the best peaces in our history. Poor old Liberals; gone right under. I wonder who will be Minister of Fuel and Power* [of particular concern to the Temples because Freddy's father was Director of Open-Cast Mining]; *I suppose Nationalisation will come now.*

After that, he wrote about first impressions of Westcott. He had adequate but rather dark rooms, and on the whole impressions were good. The Principal talked to the new men after supper on the first day. He told them that there were hardly any rules; indeed, other Theological Colleges delighted in a joke about Westcott - that there was a notice in the Chapel saying, 'Members are asked not to smoke in the Chapel on Fridays.' Dressing for College dinner was expected, and the story goes that one student in Freddy's time at Westcott kept a valet in rooms close to the College. Westcott at the time was very much 'middle of the road Anglican.' A story that Freddy told was of the College bursar, who, on being told that an ordinand had experienced a vision of the Blessed Virgin Mary in the College Chapel, replied that that sort of thing 'simply wasn't done at Westcott House.' The newly-arrived were told that no questions would be asked if students did not appear at many of the services of the day, though it would not pass unnoticed. The Principal did not elaborate. Freddy's over-riding impression was of the youthfulness of the staff. His supervisor (tutor) was David Paton, and Freddy took to him immediately, as he did to Greer, the Principal, whom he described as 'realist with a good sense of humour, which will keep the balance as we have the inevitable high ritualists amongst the ordinands.' He decided to opt for learning Hebrew, which he was sure would be comparatively easy, having already mastered Syriac and Arabic during the War.

After he had been there a week, he had tea with Greer, who told him he was keen for Freddy to do the full Theological Tripos at the University. Although it meant that he would have to work much harder, Freddy felt that he could cope and promised to investigate the idea. He had tea with Charles Raven on August 12th, who had no doubt that this was the right way forward for Freddy.

The ordinands were also plunged almost immediately into practical, pastoral training. Freddy wrote:

> *The House runs various shows when up and I have to take a frightful Sunday School this afternoon which is allowed to run riot when taken by the local Vicar during our vacs and then is turned over to us during term. I suppose it's good practice but I think the whole thing pretty useless unless one follows it up and gets to know the children. It is considered a great success if you can get through the service without the whole thing breaking up in pandemonium. Of course really I feel that on a fine Bank Holiday weekend Sunday there should be no Sunday School, but the whole family should be out on the river; but I have not been here long enough to air that sort of view.*

At the end of his first month, Freddy had a real outburst:

> *I am staggered and horrified by the attitude of some people here; Westcott is supposed to be very much in the middle as far as Theological Colleges go; but it is very much higher than I expected. At the extreme we have one man who, I gather (I have not talked to him myself), has no intention of using the Prayer Book when he is ordained but will use some Sarum Missal or something. He will get round his ordination vows by some verbal quibble and feels quite justified in doing so. He continually signs himself and beats his chest in the service, etc. Greer, the Principal, is low church and takes the service very well I think, and is an admirable man. And we also have the Bishop of Tinnevelle on the staff this term, who is a fine man and takes the service well and without fuss. But the Vice-Principal, who comes from Cuddesdon, has all the paraphernalia; innumerable bobbings and signs of the cross and little extra bits put in. And I am considered very low church here. They do seem very silly to me all these old-fashioned parties in the Church. I am all for a bit of ritual which means something to the people taking part, as long as it is patiently explained. But in some places the divorce there seems to be between clerical thought and the laity is colossal; to so many clergy the laity are rather a tiresome body whom they have to tolerate and who must be trained to tolerate all this abstruse stuff, with no explanation whatsoever. Most of the laity are quite at sea with it and just don't come after a time unless the parson has a big enough personality to attract them to his parish in other ways.*

82   The following week he preached his first sermon from Westcott, at a little village,

Dry Drayton. Freddy found the congregation of about a dozen friendly, so, despite the fact that the Principal had vetted the sermon as acceptable and had warned him against making any changes without first consulting him, risked adding one of his jokes about his great-grandfather, Archbishop Trench. He told them the one alluded to earlier about the dinner party at the Deanery at Westminster.

The congregation tittered gently. Spurred on by their response, Freddy thought that he would carry on to tell them another, about his great-grandfather being rather a silent and gloomy man in his more advanced years. While at a dinner party in Dublin, a pretty young lady was sitting on his left. Trench was totally silent throughout the whole meal, and then at the end turned to her and said, 'It's come; it's come. What I have always feared has come.' 'What is that, Your Grace?' 'Paralysis of this leg. I have been pinching it throughout this meal and have felt absolutely nothing.' 'There is no need to worry; it is my leg you have been pinching.' Freddy went on to explain that the story has been told of others, and the family doubted its authenticity. When, several years later, however, there was a controversy in *The Times* about whether this story was really true, an elderly lady replied, 'Indeed, it is; I am the proud possessor of the leg.' Family tradition had been confirmed as history.

Whether it was just family tradition or history, it was certainly nearly Freddy's downfall. The congregation remained straight-faced and disapproving in their pews, and Freddy's characteristic snorts of mirth disappeared rapidly into the stuffy atmosphere. He doubtless compounded his error by saying, before announcing the final hymn, 'We'll sing hymn number 126, and then you can breathe a sigh of relief and get outside to where we would all far rather have been for the last hour, enjoying the evening sunshine.' When Freddy recounted this in later years to a friend, he told him that the experience had taught him something, though he wasn't sure what.

Freddy laid great stress on preaching. One evening, a couple of weeks later, he went with some friends to a church at which one of his fellow students was preaching. Although Freddy thought the content was 'quite good', it was 'barely audible and far too long.' He said at the time that it seemed to be a tradition at Westcott to praise the sermons of others that one has heard, and that it would appear as jealousy if one did not. He found this extremely silly as honest and friendly criticism would be far more helpful. Indeed he gained a reputation at Westcott for being a very severe critic; he went out of his way to tell others that he wanted the same treatment for himself. He wrote at the time that the Principal was an excellent critic; in a friendly way he used to show Freddy how useless some of his sermons were and that it would be better if he were to rip them up and start all over again.

Freddy's admiration for Greer increased daily. The more he came into close contact with him, the more he liked him; he admired above all his sincerity, realism and humour. Unlike many of his lecturers at Oxford, he found Greer's lectures inspiring and thought-provoking. In one of his lectures, Greer told the ordinands that, if they followed the practice of fasting, they were not to make a fuss of it and let people know. According to Freddy, Greer continued, 'How often have I seen the vestry fluttering with cups of tea and buns and the Vicar sitting solemnly and rigidly in the corner, determined that everyone should know that he was fasting until he had taken the High Mass at noon; better eat two beefsteaks than do that; and that's sound Scripture for you too.'

The following week saw Westcott's Quiet Day, of which there was one each term. The Conductor was the Bishop of Sheffield and Freddy was looking forward to the Day, because he had read his 'invigorating' book *The Parson's Job*. But he found the bishop very disappointing. He had a poor delivery and his subject matter was trivial. Freddy knew him to be an extremely lively and vigorous bishop, but to his mind he failed completely to get this across. He wrote to his parents, 'His failure to enliven us will surely teach us all a great deal about preaching, so all was not wasted.' What had been needed, he said, was a 'deeper message expressed more simply and directly, for there is much to learn from directness and simplicity.' Freddy decided too to fast throughout the day. He wrote home, 'I did it quite quietly, but one or two of our valetudinarian High Churchmen, who make a good fuss about getting through without swallowing any of their tooth water, noticed and were a bit shaken.'

And so the first term ended. Freddy wrote, 'This term has certainly flown by and I see more and more what a vast amount there is to learn if one is to do this job at all well, not only the actual theology, but the technical side too.'

When Freddy arrived back at Westcott, he had it confirmed that his supervisor for the Tripos was to be Bishop Stephen Neill at Trinity Hall. Before he started on his work for him, Freddy sat four papers of the General Ordination Examination, two on Doctrine, one on the Prayer Book and one on Morals and Philosophy. He was exempt all the Bible papers. Freddy passed the GOE papers, comfortably but not spectacularly; he hadn't expected for more as he had prepared for the exams in such a short time, and had his eyes set all the time on clearing the way for starting work on the Tripos. In the Tripos, he told his friends that he was going to work flat out for a First, though he would not mind if he did not get one. The valuable thing for him would just be having covered the ground fully. He had doubts as to whether he had the 'best exam type of mind'. Though at Balliol he had been a little disappointed with a Second, since then he had learnt to rate intellectual ability at its proper level: as something of great value, but not everything. He found working for the Tripos 'fascinating', especially the comparative study of the Gospels. He wrote to his father:

> I am astonished how little use of it is made in sermons nowadays. One very seldom gets an expository sermon; I suppose it is because the intellectual standard of the clergy has gone down so much. It is amazing how much our ideas of different stories

in the New Testament are a vague muddle of all the accounts in the Gospels; and it is great fun sorting them out with the different texts, and seeing what was probably added by Matthew or Luke and how it varied. With the usual time lag of thirty years between expert and ordinary opinion there is still a popular feeling that historical criticism has debunked most of the Gospels in a vague way; whereas for a long time scholars have realised that on the contrary they all point to a definite core of fact which can't be explained away.

Freddy continued by saying that he knew that, to many people, this was all 'quite simple stuff', but that he would be 'thrilled beyond measure' if he could, in his future ministry, bring something of the 'sheer excitement' of biblical criticism 'to those whom so many preachers treat like simpletons.'

The College Quiet Days began to mean a great deal to Freddy. He looked forward to them each term, though he confessed that he was very much in the minority as many of the students found them a strain. He fasted, not only because fasting gave the body a rest, but also because he found it made him more 'spiritually alert'. Once he had made the decision to fast, he was relieved not to have to attend silent meals, as he found them 'unnatural and a bit silly'. Apparently, some of the students did their best to make the others laugh at meals, which Freddy found 'juvenile and trying'. He told others that 'there are so many opportunities for laughter at College, and I must confess I go out of my way to find them, but [and this may have sounded a bit priggish and trite to his fellow students] there's a time and place for everything.' Some things were too serious to be taken lightly. He had come the nearest to being incensed when some fellow students deliberately spilt salt on the table and played noughts and crosses in it with the tips of matchsticks throughout the meal.

He had also been dismayed when a handful of the students had poked fun at one Canon Anthony Otter, who had come to conduct a Quiet Day. Canon Otter had been a country parson for fifteen years and had refused many offers of higher jobs in order, in the words of Greer, to 'love the good folk of his parish into the Kingdom'. He was extraordinarily powerful, said Freddy, not so much in what he said as in what he was; a sort of modern George Herbert. He stayed in the College the following day in order to answer questions on the ministry. Freddy commented that 'he was admirable in that he did not mind in the least that the village as a whole did not come to Church; he said that they never have and he didn't think they ever would'. Freddy continued that 'he came down slap on the side of evening Communions as being the only reasonable and right time for farmers. He had heard a nice comment from a Vicar in Bristol, Mervyn Stockwood (later to be a controversial but greatly-loved Bishop of Southwark), who in answer to someone who said that Communion must be taken before breakfast, fasting, said, 'All right: then would you like the Words of Institution changed from "After supper he took the cup" to "Before breakfast he took the cup"?' Soon after this, Freddy wrote home:

I have been sent to a local old people's home quite a lot recently to take services. My first time I hated it, quite hated it. In fact the second time I dreaded going and nearly copped out. The poor dears sit in upright chairs around the room, drooling and dribbling and, I'm sorry to say, smelling high somewhat. I found taking services extremely tiring for I would be reading from the Bible and one lady would, half-way through, take it into her head to shout across the room to someone else and then they'd have a full-blown conversation together, which was both inconsequential and bizarre. Last time it was, 'That young man hasn't combed his hair, has he?' 'Oh, I don't know, I think he has, dear.' 'Well, I don't mind if he has or hasn't. Somebody's been stealing my biscuits.' So unthinking and silly of me, but I felt really very annoyed. Especially as I had combed my hair. But now I've got used to their little ways and foibles I'm ashamed of the way I felt. They don't ask to be there; they don't deserve to be there. I don't know whether they want to be there or not, however. But they are there - some of them because their families simply cannot be bothered with them. I'm on a rota to go there twice a month, though sometimes I pay them a visit in between my rota services and the staff and patients seem to welcome me - although the latter don't sometimes seem to know who I am from one week to the next. Accordingly, I was very upset when Greer asked to see me on Tuesday in his study. He told me that he thought I was becoming too involved with people and that I had to learn to be more 'dispassionate'. 'Otherwise, Freddy', he said, ' you'll collapse under the weight of other people's suffering. I can see it happening'. I was totally put out by this - coming from Greer especially, and told him so. He took what I said squarely on the chin and we talked more before he ended the conversation by apologising for what he was going to say, which was, 'One day, when you're in a parish with ten such similar establishments, you'll know what I mean'. He thought that I'd think that that was condescending. He was right. But I can't be annoyed with him for long. I think Greer is probably a saint.

The following month, a letter home included the following paragraph:

On Friday we had our termly Theological Colleges Union service; this time it was at Wesley House, across the road - the Methodist place. It has an incredible Chapel with a large modern painting which looks like an advertisement for the Agricultural Marketing Board. As you know I am very keen on the idea of Churches getting together; in fact it has to happen if we are to be true to the Gospel. But if we are to work together with the Methodists, we really must teach them something about aesthetics.

86   In his free time, Freddy continued to play squash and tennis regularly and well. He

liked to win and was once rather put out when beaten by Peter Baelz, though he did concede that he shouldn't have taken it so badly, seeing that Baelz was a squash Blue. He enjoyed going to films and seemed to spend much time in cinemas in Cambridge, his choice of films revealing very catholic tastes. His letters home show a great zest for life and great enjoyment in the company of his friends.

In a letter to his father on November 25th 1945, Freddy wrote:

I had a very good birthday [his 29th]; thank you very much for your present, which will be very useful as always. Aunt Frances sent me a nicely bound volume of Arnold's sermons with grandfather's signature, 'F. Exon:', inside; fun to have for historical reasons, but what sermons to dish out to boys. I am sure grandfather was a noble man; if ever I am asked to preach at a public school, however, I, not to mention the staff and the boys, would cringe if I used the same sort of rubbish. Esmond Smith and I went to the cinema yesterday afternoon and saw 'Liebes Melodie'; it was very funny and we laughed loudly a lot, though the rest of the audience were rather glum. Then after supper we went out to a pub and had some beer and then at Esmond's excellent suggestion went along to a café and joined in the dance there; we were not in good clothes at all; I was in Uncle William's odd fitting trousers and a sports coat. But we soon found two very pleasant Norfolk girls who were up in Cambridge and a bit bored so had come to the dance and were very glad to dance; and said they were very glad to see two people who hadn't dressed up at all. It was a good floor and a good band and was quite fun. It stopped at 11 and then we took them home. It is very easy to get out of touch very quickly with the ordinary pleasures of ordinary people; this morning some people looked startled when we told them and feel it is very 'dashing' etc. It is no wonder that the Church is so much out of contact with ordinary life.

On December 17th, Freddy made his first mention, in a letter to his father, of Joan Webb. She was the sister of his closest friend, John, and he had gone from Damerel to Chingford to spend a weekend. Unfortunately, all letters from Freddy to his father for the next four months have been lost, but on April 14th, 1946, he wrote:

It has certainly been an eventful week. I must have startled the family a bit but I think Mum could have picked up indications of what was on from her visit to Cambridge and evenings in London: I'm very glad you were both at Damerel: and I was certain that you would approve of her: she is quite ideal in every way. And she took to all the family too.

Freddy then took Joan to London to meet Aunt Frances for lunch at her flat. 'Aunt Frances was pleasant', Freddy told his father, 'but she overawed Joan a bit as she does so many. Joan, poor, dearest dear, did not know whether she was coming or going after her "interview"'.

Joan Catharine Webb had been born into a middle class, Christian family in Chingford, Essex, on the 3rd of January, 1923, the fourth child of Guy and Elsie Webb, sister to Bunty, John and Michael. Guy Webb designed and manufactured children's clothes; he was proud of the fact that Queen Mary once bought a dress of his design for the young Princess Elizabeth. The family was central to Elsie's life and her strong Christian faith and example were formative influences in the lives of the children. Bunty, after leaving school, worked for a while in her father's offices before marrying Robert Abraham, a designer of scientific instruments, in 1937. John, as we know, was at Balliol with Freddy; he eventually went to Vellore, a Christian Medical College and Hospital, in South India, to set up a paediatric department. On his return to England he became Professor of Paediatrics at the University of Newcastle. He married Alison, another doctor, in 1947. Michael, after St. John's College, Oxford, joined the Indian Army. He was killed in action in 1944.

Joan, the youngest child, went to Queen Anne's School, Caversham, but at the outbreak of war left, at the age of 16. She worked for a while in a factory canteen, an experience she later described as 'quite an eye-opener.' She continued, 'for the first time in my life I had my bottom pinched; I didn't know whether to feel upset or exhilarated.' Joan then worked in a war nursery for bombed-out babies near Byfleet; this was run by the 'Waifs and Strays' charity and subsidised by the American Red Cross. It was hard work, and again a totally new experience for her - 'dealing with nits, runny noses, bugs and scabies.' She herself ended up with scabies. She then wanted to try a new experience, so joined the Land Army. After a month's training near Northampton, where she attended lectures between cleaning out cow sheds, chicken runs and pig styes and looking after sheep, she went to a farm at Girton, near Cambridge, looking after 120 pigs and 40 calves. She followed this with a stint at another farm and well remembers acting as a scarecrow for two days in a field of young beans and other green vegetables.

By this time, however, Joan was becoming restless; if the war went on for a long time, she imagined her brain itself becoming a cabbage. She decided to come out of the Land Army and join the A.T.S., in which she stayed for the next four years. She learned how to operate radar systems in Devizes, eventually becoming a Radar Instructor, as a Lance-Bombardier, attached to the Royal Artillery. She was soon promoted to Sergeant. Her experiences in the Sergeants' Mess were varied; the language was more than florid, and some of it was picked up by Joan, much to her father's grief. After telling him a tale about one of her fellow sergeants taking out his dentures at the end of the first course and wiping them on the tablecloth, her father was very distressed and told her she must get a commission at once. Which she did. After the war she stayed at home for a while and taught in the Sunday School of Chingford Parish Church. This gave her the opportunity to do some serious reading, and she secured a place at Bedford College, the University of London, to read Sociology. She was never to take up her place, however, for, meanwhile, she and Freddy had fallen in love.

Joan had first met Freddy when he came to stay at their family home, 'Amberley', in Chingford, as a guest of her brother, John, before the War. She was fifteen years old and was more interested in sport than young men; she accompanied Freddy and John to the Connaught Club to watch them play tennis and admitted to a fleeting fancy for Freddy's legs. The whole family, Joan recalls, found Freddy fun.

She then heard that Freddy had gone to Finland, back to Gloucester and then to the Middle East. It was not until 1944, while he was still in the desert, that, in her own words, 'I suddenly knew I was going to marry him. Don't ask me how or why; but it was utter conviction.' She continued, 'When he did come home, I knew I would have to play it very cool - for he didn't know, poor chap.' The following year Joan was stationed in London, when a 'phone call came from her mother saying that Freddy was coming to dinner at the family home; would Joan like to join them? 'My heart thudded like a piston, but I remember saying, in an airy sort of way, "I'll try". In reality, I would have gone AWOL if necessary.'

Freddy was just as much fun, and Joan remembers going back to London on the 38E bus with him to Piccadilly Circus, and parting there. She tried not to think too much about him, until, several weeks later, out of the blue, she received a postcard 'of some classical panel or something.' Freddy began the postcard, 'Isn't this recherché?' 'None of us ATS mess knew what recherché meant, so we had to look it up. But we still couldn't fathom what was recherché about it.'

Joan decided to call on Freddy at the Middlesex Hospital, where he was working with the FAU. She walked round and round the hospital five times before plucking up the courage to walk in the main door and ask to see him. Freddy took her upstairs to his room, on the way passing a little room with a sink. He stuck his hand in the sink, whisked it round, explaining to Joan, 'They're my pyjamas; it's the way I wash them.'

Joan recalls that the two of them 'had a lot to say to each other.' After that, they met quite often. They invariably went to 'Chez Auguste', a restaurant in Soho, 'where a decent meal could be had for five bob.' Joan also recalls the time they went to see 'Lady Windermere's Fan' at His Majesty's Theatre. It was the first time she had worn a dress instead of her ATS uniform. 'Freddy said much later that his breath had been taken away.' Soon afterwards he asked Joan to go down to Damarel for a weekend.

Before Joan arrived, Freddy went out into the highways and byways and ditches to pick primroses. He arranged them in vases and a very large bowl - and placed them all over the guest room. Freddy's sister, Edith, recalled in 2002: 'I do think he went, in modern parlance, a bit "over the top."'

Freddy's mother rang her husband in Newcastle: 'I think something's going on down here; can you come down immediately?' He had a responsible job as Director of Open-cast Mining, was immensely busy, but decided to take the first train south. Joan takes up the story:

> *In great fear and trepidation I took the train to Sussex and was met at Haywards Heath station by Freddy. We took a taxi to Damarel. I remember meeting the family and Freddy playing to me some Gilbert and Sullivan on an old gramophone. I remember, too, walking in the garden and the wood. Edith's children were staying there. On Saturday we played croquet with them all afternoon; Freddy was so good at sending all our balls off into the bushes. At one point I felt really miffed at the way he laughed when he'd sent all our croquet balls packing. The thought crossed my mind - fleetingly, I admit, that he might have a vindictive streak in his character.*
>
> *After a perfect dinner on Saturday evening, we sat over coffee. Freddy's father brought out an album of photographs showing all the water towers he had built in India.*
>
> *'My dear', said Freddy's mother, 'I'm sure Joan doesn't really want to look at all of these.'*
>
> *'Oh no', I said, 'I love water towers.' What silly things one says when under pressure.*
>
> *Meanwhile, Freddy fidgetted. Freddy's mother, Gran, and Anne went up to bed. Freddy kept fidgetting. Granfer [Freddy's father] finished the album, clicked something on the side of it and said that he too was going to bed.*
>
> *Freddy and I said goodnight to him and then said, rather peremptorily, I thought, 'We're going out for a walk'. It was dark and about 10pm. He found a coat for me in the cloakroom; I remember it was enormous. He also handed me an enormous pair of gauntlet gloves.*
>
> *As soon as got outside on to the terrace, Freddy started talking. He talked and talked and talked, and told me not to say anything until he had finished. He said that we'd always be on the move and that it would be such a hard life for me and we'd have no money. And then he spluttered, 'Will you marry me?' 'Yes', I said. 'What did you say?' I said 'Yes'. 'You will? You will?' There was absolute amazement on Freddy's part. At the time he was certain that I was not going to marry him.*

The engagement was announced at breakfast. Everyone seemed delighted, though Joan thought that Freddy's mother had been trying to pair her only son off with another young lady, with a double-barrelled name. In the afternoon, Freddy and Joan took a rug to the woods and sat and talked, 'with', in Joan's words, 'the sun dappling through the trees; it was idyllic.' Freddy, however, kept reiterating how much hard work Joan would have to face as the wife of a priest - and kept emphasising how poor they would be financially. 'It was almost as if he were trying to put me off; he was very sweet.' Walking back to the house, Freddy's sister, Ann, rode past on her bicycle; when she had turned the corner, the couple heard her sing out, 'They've got to the garage, hand in hand.' There was great excitement at Damarel that weekend..

Joan, however, had to get back to work and soon Freddy was to return to West-cott. They wrote to each other every day, and Joan was to visit Freddy very regularly in Cambridge. On the first occasion she travelled to Westcott, Joan was very apprehensive. She had no idea at all what to expect - and honestly imagined that she might have to talk to Freddy through a metal grille, as if he were a novice in a monastery. Her fears were only allayed when she saw the Lodge was full of prams. The letters exchanged between the two show them as a couple who were deliriously happy - though Joan admitted in later years that she was at first 'extremely concerned' about the fact that Freddy was a Conscientious Objector. Joan did not understand pacifism, but thought she ought to. She thought, in fact, that she had to. Freddy showed her a copy of Max Warren's *The Cross and the Crisis*. Joan recalls how, one night, reading this book, kneeling in her bedroom, 'I suddenly understood. And wept and wept and wept. Afterwards I felt glorious.'

Life at Westcott continued as busily as ever, with Freddy finishing off his last GOE papers as well as working for the Tripos. He wished he weren't quite as busy, though admitted that the gain in doing the Tripos more than counterbalanced the loss; the loss was the lack of time for general reading and reflection. He realised that he would leave Westcott with 'stacks still to learn', but said the good thing was to realise that and not think that Theological College had equipped him for everything. He was specially pleased in his last year with his room, facing South into the court of the House. He ended his first letter of the last year, 'Greer has got himself engaged which is rather surprising; he said the first night that he thought he had better have some experience of that line of country with so many of us married or engaged.'

In his next letter home, Freddy began:

> At the beginning of the week we had three excellent lectures by a charming Miss Steel, who is Head of Moral Welfare; it does very excellent work; if people knew more about it they would give to it better I am sure; and she gave a good defence of the name. She was most amusing; she started in the Coventry Diocese; at that time it was the Diocesan League for Purity Work and she was the 'Purity Worker', which she found trying. She was most competent and showed what a vast problem the Church now faces in the complete breakdown of all sex standards; and how seldom the clergy deal with it at all. Just recently a vicar had got in the local Moral Welfare worker to talk to his Confirmation Class about sex and introduced her thus, "I would like to introduce Miss Cook; she is going to talk to you on a most interesting subject; she is an expert in it; her subject is 'The Lusts of the Flesh'.

'Another highlight of the term', Freddy wrote, 'was the visit of a very bright and original cleric to talk to us on how to tackle youth in a parish. He was excellent. He told the students, "You must be prepared for the complete contrasts in the young; at one moment entirely serious, at the next quite frivolous, turning cartwheels; you must be prepared to turn a cartwheel in the middle of your Confirmation Class or they will think nothing of you.'" Freddy continued:

> *He also has an excellent idea of Religion through Drama; you work out the bare outlines of a scene and then allocate the various parts and tell them they must write their own speeches. You tell one person he is Paul at Troas; another is a Greek whose religion is Gnosticism; so he must know how to answer Paul when he talks to him. You tell a girl that she is Lydia, the Greek who was converted to Judaism and is now interested in Paul's teaching. And he says you get boys and girls delving into abstruse books on Judaism and early Christianity in a way you never would by direct teaching; and they really learn the stuff in order to play the parts well, and get to know far more about early Christianity and the Gospels than in a thousand Sunday School lessons. It fascinates me as an idea and I am joining one of his courses next term to see how the thing works.*

At the start of the year he also decided to change his supervisor for the Tripos and go to Canon Knox, who would give him more time and academic attention than Bishop Neill. He told his parents that the change would give him more chance of getting a First. On the same day that he received confirmation that Canon Knox would take over his supervision, he received what he called a 'comic' document from De Gaulle, thanking him for having 'rallied the Free French Forces when France was in mortal danger'. He commented that it was 'one of the more comical illogicalities that a whole group of pacifists should have been sent these.'

At this time, Freddy was 'Sheriff', or Senior Student, of Westcott. Amongst other matters he had to decide the ration of coal students must be allowed for each week. This he found a bit tricky as nobody seemed to know whether any more coal would be forthcoming or not. In one letter, he angled for some inside information from his father, the Director of Open-Cast Mining, though it doesn't look as though that was given. Freddy had to preside at the House Meeting, the 'Moot', on Fridays. At his first, he welcomed the new Chaplain and also, through the Principal, Mrs. Greer, at whose wedding Freddy had been present at St. Peter's, Eaton Square, in September. Freddy wrote to his parents that the new Chaplain, Alan Webster, was one of those who used his exemption from service at the beginning of the war and went up to Westcott in 1939 when Freddy could have done. Freddy said that he did not for a moment regret what he did, but he found it strange that Webster came back after four years in a parish to teach his own contemporaries, most of whom had far more experience of the world than he. Freddy assured his parents that he did not say this when welcoming him. He later acknowledged Webster's undoubted gifts and was grateful for the insights that he gained from him. Freddy presided at the Moot with great humour, to the great delight of the other students, who, as one contemporary said, 'were always agog to see what he would come up with next', and carried through most of the business promptly. He told his father that he had 'arranged' most of it as much as possible beforehand; he had persuaded people to propose and second motions quickly, which left no time for the people who like discussion just for discussion's sake. He ended the letter, 'I think there were some students who, when the meeting had ended, had not really realised it had started.'

The following month, Freddy wrote home:

On Wednesday evening Mrs Greer held what she called a 'Musical Evening'; some people of the House played and sang. I felt I must go as Sheriff: it was quite fun, for it did not last long. If I had been Mrs. Greer, I would have termed it an 'Evening' - and left out the word 'Musical'.

As Head of House Freddy was responsible in November 1946 for entertaining the Bishop of Chichester, George Bell, who had been invited to talk at the College. Freddy was enamoured both with him and with what he had to say, though he found what he said about Germany, from which Bell had just returned, depressing. Bell told them that the situation was far worse than it had been a year previously, and was becoming yet worse; food and clothes were short and morale was exceedingly low. Bell was high in the praises of the German Church, which was really trying to teach repentance, which was bitterly resented by many in Germany. Niemöller was going up and down the country saying that six million Jews had been killed in Germany; and that this was a crime for which all were responsible. In a letter to his parents, Freddy continued:

Bishop Bell thought that people should be doing more to help the German Church and recognise them as having been allies from the beginning. They talked of the Liberation, not the Defeat, of Germany; but the German Church now says that Britain was going the right way to kill off all the Germans in her zone. Even as he spoke Britain was deliberately dismantling Germany's industries, even though every senior Army officer he had met was quite certain that there was no possible chance of Germany recovering any sort of war potential in the next fifty years; the destruction was so complete.

Freddy talked with him quite a lot alone, and found him very challenging and approachable. The previous Sunday they had had Fisher at Westcott. Freddy carried his bags up to the guest room. He had then been Archbishop for two years. He turned to Freddy and said, with a charming smile, 'When I meet people for the first time, the first thing I do is to apologise for not being William Temple.' He and Bell were arguably the two most able men on the Episcopal Bench. Fisher, said

Freddy, was 'the better and more hard-bitten administrator; Bell had far more vision and imagination.'

It was about this time that Freddy received, out of the blue, a letter from George Cockin, Bishop of Bristol:

> *This is just to remind you that if you are ever thinking of a possible pitch, there are some quite good specimens of considerable variety in the diocese of Bristol. Nothing would give me more pleasure, dear Freddy, than to collect some of my friends round me again.*

Freddy commented to his parents: 'Isn't that rather nice? I don't know whether it is too soft a part of the world to go to, though; a pity George is not Bishop of Sheffield. They're worst off for curates and the need is greatest.' Freddy did, however, write back to Cockin expressing 'qualified interest' and received a very enthusiastic response saying that he would do everything possible to offer him a position in the diocese, ending his letter with, 'I need hardly say that to have you working here would give me the greatest possible satisfaction.' A while later he wrote again:

> *I should like to suggest that you might come and work in the parish of Stoke Bishop. The Vicar is Canon Worters. He looks like a very wise old toad, and is without question the shrewdest incumbent in the Diocese, and I believe the best trainer of curates. The parish is good residential, with a lot of young people, and you couldn't have a more delightful person to work under. They are wealthy, so that I should have no hesitation in telling them to pay you properly. I can assure you that Worters does not allow their affluence to influence him in the least. I really am offering you about the best job I think I have, and I greatly hope that you may feel drawn to it. If you will let me know, I will put you in touch with Worters.*

A week later, Canon Worters wrote to Freddy:

> *I hear from our Bishop that you are thinking of coming into the Bristol diocese and he has suggested I should get in touch with you with regard to a title. I do not know whether this is a kind of parish that you are seeking but if you are likely to be in this neighbourhood you might like to come and talk things over and see the surroundings. I don't even know whether you are familiar with Bristol, but this is in many ways a most delightful place both as to situation and people, though it has and is rapidly changing as to the type of inhabitants. The population in 1931 was returned as 2297 but it must have pretty well doubled since then - if not more - and over 50 pre-fab houses are now being erected. We were most 'select' but are no longer! Our churchmanship would I suppose be called 'central' - reverence without fuss is perhaps a good description! E.P., Lights and coloured stoles is I believe*

usually put in advertisements. The Vicar (myself) is a bit of a crock with a game leg and a good many things ending in -itis, especially in Jan, Feb and March, but there is a certain amount of life left in the old dog. He is at heart very early Victorian, but tries to become modern on occasions. He has practically no brain, but has managed to bluff the Diocese for some 45 years. We have good morning congregations but rather poor evening ones. There is plenty of work to be done amongst youth and children, particularly the former, and visiting is more than ever essential.

When Freddy went to Bristol to meet him, he wrote that he 'adored' him, and that despite Worters's handicap and ailments he 'worked like a Trojan and gave of himself unsparingly.' However, after a lot of prayer and thought he judged that the parish would not be right for him, on two counts. He was genuinely worried, rightly or wrongly, that he might have to run the parish more than one newly-ordained should, in times when the Vicar was indisposed. ('It's so unfair', he wrote to his father, 'just because my name is Temple I suspect they think that I would cope with flying colours. I've got to learn as much as the next man.') Secondly, he thought he ought to start in what he described in a letter to Sydney Worters, 'a tougher and more varied parish.' Worters wrote back, in a wonderfully gentle letter, that he thought he knew what Freddy meant, but he couldn't help thinking that 'it is just possible that you might start off in such a whirl that you would not have time to process your own soul.' He insisted that he wouldn't try to influence Freddy any more and 'whatever you decide may you be blessed in your work.' Freddy thought and prayed more, but decided, with more than a little regret, to look elsewhere.

He embarked on what he described as his Grand Tour of Parishes whose incumbents were trying to woo him. With Joan accompanying him, he went to look at Bishopswearmouth (Durham), Holbeck (Ripon), St. Helen's (Liverpool), Davenham (Chester), Porchester (Southwell), Arnold (Southwell), and Leamington Spa (Coventry). When the Vicar of Binley (Coventry) heard that Freddy was looking at Leamington, he decided too to enter the stakes and wrote to Freddy, 'I hear you're considering Leamington. Why not just go to Bournemouth and have done with it? There are far more old ladies in bath chairs there. I bet you that there aren't two chaps like Ashcroft and me next door to each other in the whole British Commonwealth of Nations. Perhaps it's just as well, but if you want a hectic life and plenty of fun, here is your chance. Leamington! Gosh!'

Freddy looked at all the parishes, but there were difficulties or drawbacks with all of them, some relating to the accommodation provided, as he would be taking his new bride to start with him. He nearly did not go to look at Davenham, whose Incumbent wrote, 'My set-up is central, safe and middle-stump.' He added, 'I presume you're ex-forces of course.' The Bishop of Chester, too, had ended his letter to him, 'We were among those lucky people who knew your Uncle for many, many years and he has been a guest in our various houses since his early days as Headmaster of Repton until he was Archbishop of this Province'. Much as he had been totally devoted to his Uncle, Freddy wanted to be himself and not just William Temple's nephew.

He visited and re-visited the parish of St. Mary, Arnold, and liked what he saw. He was impressed with the Vicar, Kenneth Leigh-Wood, and thought he would work well with him, and learn much from him. Joan was equally enthusiastic, even though at this stage a house had not been found for them. The Bishop of Southwell, F.R. Barry, was keen to have Freddy in the diocese.

Meanwhile, Freddy was continuing to study for the Tripos. His letters home at this time tell of his working for exceptionally long hours; his parents worried about his health, but he assured them he had the 'Temple stamina', and was still doing all his other Westcott work and playing squash.

On 15th February, 1947, Kenneth Leigh-Wood wrote to Freddy to say that he had had a talk with the diocesan who had asked him to ask Freddy to write to him officially about being ordained to the curacy of St. Mary, Arnold. The Michaelmas Ordination was on September 21st, two days after the beginning of the celebration of St. Mary's Patronal Festival and the 600th Anniversary of the Church, so Freddy would arrive just in time for what Leigh-Wood called 'all these high jinks.' He continued, 'In case you should wonder what we commemorate on September 19th, we do not observe the new calendar for this occasion, and our festival is transferred from September 8th [the Nativity of the Blessed Virgin Mary] to the 19th; all this dates from 1752, and is rather quaint and bound up with local customs of Arnold and all sorts.' In 1752, because of past incorrect calculations with solar time which affected the reckoning connected with the calendar, eleven days had been lost. The 3rd of September was decreed by Parliament to become the 14th September, thereby correcting the calendar. The people of Arnold, however, would have nothing to do with this and still kept to the same day. As far as they were concerned, nothing had happened. Freddy thought this showed a certain 'corporate idiosyncratic independence', and wrote, 'Who couldn't fail to be charmed by such a place?'

Meanwhile, preparations were going ahead for Joan and Freddy's wedding. On the Wednesday evening, they packed for the honeymoon in France, which Freddy had been arranging with something approaching the precision of a military operation, since December. They were going to spend much of it at a chalet owned by Balliol at Chamonix. Then came a disappointment. News came of a rail strike in France, which put paid to all his careful preparations. They had to make alternative arrangements speedily to spend their honeymoon in Ireland.

The wedding day, Friday 13th June, was, according to Joan's diary, 'sunny and perfect'. William Greer, who, it had just been announced, was to be the new Bishop of Manchester, officiated. Stephen Verney was Best Man. Edward Heath wrote a lovely letter, dated 12 July, 1947:

Freddy and Joan's wedding.

My dear Freddy,

 This is just a note to offer you my heartiest congratulations and to wish you both, very sincerely, the greatest happiness in the future. I am sure we all look forward to when the familiar laugh is echoed by a whole Templary of laughter 're-sounding through the groves'.

 Sincerely,

 Teddy.

 P.S. Not knowing whether you are yet a reverend gentleman or not I have left the address as just a gentleman.

 And please forgive the rather aggressive and intemperate notepaper.

[Edward Heath wrote on paper of the Royal Artillery Company.]

At the end of the service, the couple and congregation sang the hymn, 'O Thou who camest from above'. This was the first time the couple had sung this together as man and wife; it was to be sung at all major services in their life together over the next fifty-three years.

 They had tea at the Great Western Hotel, Paddington, before boarding the train to Fishguard, and so on to the ferry. After disembarking, they had a six-hour railway journey without any food, as the train did not have a buffet car. By the time they arrived at their destination, Dun Laoghaire, they were exhausted - and the place looked very dull; they found 'Andorina', their honeymoon accommo-

On honeymoon in Ireland.

dation, very disappointing, especially in their tired, hungry condition. Their bedroom was not ready and there was a telegram waiting for them to say that Freddy had a Second in the Tripos, which was a great disappointment to them, as Freddy had been hoping against hope to follow his grandfather and uncle and getting a First. Joan wrote in her diary, 'It was absolutely devastating - I fought with a lump in my throat and thought that if marriage is like this until you learn greater wisdom, then I must certainly learn a great deal very fast.' Freddy was to admit later that his Second did come as 'a devastating blow, despite the fact that I realised that it was more of a blow to my pride than anything else, that I was not really expecting one [i.e. a First], and had told people that I wouldn't take it badly if I didn't get one.' Behind this sentence ran also the feeling, not for the first or, indeed, the last time in his life, that he had let his family down, especially his late Uncle William. The phrase, 'Consider your Uncle William', was never far from his mind. He did his best not to let it mar the honeymoon, if only for Joan's sake.

The couple did, indeed, have a good time, despite this and far lesser disappointments. On the Sunday, Gordon Pearson, a close friend of Freddy from FAU days, came to see them and took them to tea at his home. They went to a dance at Laragh House, County Wicklow, with which Joan and Freddy fell in love. Despite the fact that it was June, there were great peat fires burning and spectacular views. Increasingly dissatisfied with their honeymoon accommodation, they decided to move there for a while, and spent much time walking and riding in the countryside. They visited and stayed in Dublin, but the weather was inclement and they did not see the fine city at its best. In her diary, Joan described it 'a city of grey and puddles.' The spent some time in Killarney. On the whole, apart from Laragh, they had depressing experiences with accommodation, but did their best to remain cheerful. There only seemed to be one 'honeymoon tiff', to do with the payment of tips. Freddy, greatly influenced by his Uncle William, believed passionately that people should be paid a proper wage for a job and not have to be reliant on tips. He refused to tip anybody, which upset Joan. Her diary says, 'I behaved v. badly and was annoyed with Freddy and walked away.' It was only after Freddy had patiently explained his reasoning that she relented and admitted that 'he was right.'

On their return to England they were greeted by a letter from Leigh-Wood saying, 'I thought you would like to know at once that we have got the house - such as it is! 174 St. Alban's Road. It is only a workman's house, and I sincerely hope you don't have to stay in it too long. Accommodation is: two living rooms and scullery, two bedrooms, large attic, and cellar - rent 9/6 per week.' Freddy wrote immediately to Leigh-Wood, saying they would very much like to come up and see the house, which brought the response, 'I am quite worried about what you will both say when you see the appalling house, but I must repeat it is only temporary, and the PCC will help to put it in order.' Joan wrote in her diary, 'L-W wrote today that it was a horrid little house; it almost sounds as if he is dreading us seeing it. I long to see it - but dread it in case it is v. depressing.' After their visit to Arnold, Freddy wrote to his parents:

The house is far, far better than anything we had expected; apart from the snag of the bathroom and outdoor sanitation it is very good. The rooms are roughly 12 ft square; the attic is a lovely room but we are not going to use it at the moment; it will do admirably for a future nursery (a peep into a yet unopened Vol. 2; sufficient to say that we are doing nothing to prevent it, feeling that there is not likely to be any moment which will really be more suitable than any other). We plan at the moment to move in on Sept 1st which will give us time to distemper the whole house cream; at the moment it has hideous dark wallpapers; but the PCC may do it. The lavatory is W.C. and not E.C. [Water Closet and not Earth Closet], which is a welcome surprise. It is in a row and so should be very warm and the present occupant says it is very dry. Rent collected by the Rent Man (a very important figure in the community and one greatly to be respected) once a fortnight, 9/6 a week. You will certainly be amused when you see it.

7   A Brace of Curacies

On Saturday, August 30th 1947, Joan and Freddy together took possession of 174, St. Albans Road, Arnold. The next two weeks were spent in a whirl of decorating and cleaning, Freddy tackling jobs he had never had to do, or indeed tried to do, before. Instruction books were followed to the letter. Freddy found it all a bit 'tiresome' (an oft-used word of his throughout his life), but persevered, and Joan and he were thrilled with the final result. Freddy was proud that he could re-sash a casement window and confided in a letter to his mother on September 2nd that he had for the first time used a Rawlplug - 'something I hadn't been prepared for at Westcott.' And on September 7th he wrote to his parents:

> *It will be great fun to see you here in a fortnight. Vast improvements have taken place during the week We are both enchanted with our little house now; we go round from room to room purring with satisfaction. I have seldom seen a nicer little drawing room. The lovely full green curtains which Joan bought that day in a second-hand shop in Brighton give it such a good air and the Globe Werniche and mahogany table from Lambeth, and the walnut table from Damarel, all fit so well with the very fine mahogany wardrobe and chest of drawers that John gave us.*

Perhaps it was a bit pretentious of Freddy to call their 12ft x 11ft front room a 'drawing room'.

Freddy's Ordination Retreat at Southwell was conducted by the Reverend John Phillips, Director of Service Ordination Candidates for C.A.C.T.M., the Church's Advisory Council for Training for the Ministry, who also preached at the Ordination in Southwell Minster. Freddy wrote about his Ordination Retreat:

Freddy and Joan's first home together in Arnold.

*I quite liked John Phillips; he has a total lack of pomposity and a genuine unselfcon-
scious humility which is not contrived at all. He told us that we, at the start of our
ministry, are every bit as important as those who have been at it for years - even as
important as our Bishop. I must remember this in my own ministry. Mr. Phillips,
however, smokes rather a disgusting pipe, with foul-smelling shag tobacco. Despite
this, I'm really impressed with him, and will never forget what he said to us; he was
not particularly profound, but I'll remember what he IS. Does that make sense?
Mr. Phillips will never be a bishop or anything like that, but does that really matter?
He's a bit naïve in a way. Maybe that's the secret of his lovableness. I will try to be
as he but shall fail miserably, for his sort of humility comes from not trying.*

(John Phillips was later to be consecrated as Bishop of Portsmouth and was Freddy's Diocesan for most of the 1960s. Freddy wrote to Archbishop Fisher on April
16th, 1961, 'I never thought that John Phillips was what we used to call 'bishop
material'. I think perhaps that, looking back on our time together, one or two
wrong decisions were made about appointments to the Bench, but this was not
one of them.)

The first few weeks after ordination were again spent in a buzz of activity. Aunt
Frances and Mrs. Barry, the wife of the Bishop of Southwell, came to inspect the
house on the Monday morning and stayed to lunch. The new curate and his wife
could have done without their august presence on Freddy's first day at work. Aunt
Frances 'seemed to think it charming and really exclaimed (with delight) at the
sitting room. Mrs. B was horrified by the bath.' In fact, the Bishop seemed to go
out of his way to tell others that he wasn't at all satisfied with Freddy and Joan's
living conditions. At a junior clergy conference, one of the lecturers took Freddy
aside and told him that the Bishop had said that they lived in appalling conditions, in the depths of squalour in the middle of the slums, but with supreme heroism. Freddy replied that, although the house wasn't quite what they had been used
to, they were happy and had tried to make it a welcoming home. He stopped short
of saying that he and Joan followed Jesus Christ who didn't even have a 'two up,
two down' in the back streets of a Nottingham pit village in which to lay his head,
because he thought the lecturer would feel 'a bit put down.'

Parties were arranged for folk to meet the new curate and his wife; the couple
found it all exciting, if tiring. Joan's diary tells that she was immediately 'catapult-
ed into the Young Wives, without a chance to yea or nay'; she found the whole set-
up, as is so often the way with parish organisations, seething with jealousy and
disquiet. She confided to her diary that she so wished there were someone, apart
from Freddy, to whom she could express her thoughts.

Freddy had to do all the things a newly-ordained curate has to do. He was an
assiduous visitor, and on October 11th he was able to write to his parents that he
had been in seventy homes already, despite the fact that for three days he had
been away at the Diocesan Conference at Swanwick. In one letter to his parents

he included a piece of paper on which he had written out some of the funny things that parishioners had said to him. Frustratingly, although the letter survives, the piece of paper does not.

Only a few weeks after Freddy's ordination, William Greer, who had been appointed Bishop of Manchester, asked him to attend his enthronement in Manchester Cathedral as his Chaplain. Leigh-Wood was not too keen on his doing this, thinking, perhaps with some justification, that Freddy ought to settle down into the nitty-gritty of ordinary parish life before accepting invitations such as these. Correspondence shows that a little gentle episcopal persuasion from Russell Barry made him change his mind. The Manchester Cathedral Chapter were none too pleased that their new Bishop had chosen a Chaplain from outside the diocese. Perhaps the last laugh was on them for, as they gleefully pointed out afterwards, and as contemporary newspaper photographs confirm, Freddy carried the crozier the wrong way round, the way it should face when the crozier preceded a Bishop at his funeral. Freddy dined out on this story many, many times, and usually mentioned it when instructing a Chaplain at Confirmations and other occasions, As usual, he would laugh loudly and lengthily, as if it were the first time the story had been told.

Back in his parish, it was Freddy's task, as with many a young curate, to 'do something' with the youth of the parish. 'Doing something' with the youth of Arnold was a bit of a baptism of fire, but his endeavours with Joan laid the foundations for a remarkable

Freddy, two weeks after ordination, as Chaplain to William Greer on his enthronement as Bishop of Manchester.

ministry to the young in his second curacy and, indeed, throughout the rest of his ministry. Freddy, ever a realist, knew that he had somehow to learn to understand their ways. He wrote to his parents, 'They really are very raw material.' Although he had had some experience of the young in youth clubs in Oxford and Cambridge, he found the children of Nottingham 'a different breed altogether'. He quickly got together a group of sixty youth - 'quite lovely children, some of them anyway, but they have no sense at all of responsibility; they will be keen one day and say that they don't feel like it the next, and it's so wearing talking to them for a quarter of an hour, bullying, cajoling, persuading them into doing things. It's really a nervous and exhausting business.' He organised a 'social' and persuaded one of the boys to run it. Freddy wrote, 'He absolutely bullied and flayed them in a quite marvellous way into playing all the games; to get silence he leaped on to a table and jumped on it, which was a bit devastating for noise, but the table stood.' He continued, 'The mothers of these working-class boys spoil them so completely. The same boy who had really done so well I found this evening putting away all the plates quite wet and when I asked if he did that in his own home he said that he did, though he didn't wash up very much. One boy's mother actually brings him breakfast in bed!'

Freddy and Joan saw it as one of their main tasks to expand the horizons of the youth; he invited people to come to talk to them from outside the community. One of the first speakers was Stephen Verney, who captivated his audience with tales of spying in Crete during the War. Freddy said in a letter to one of his sisters, 'There was many a "Cor" and "Coo" and "Blimey".' It was in Arnold, too, that he and Joan first started using drama as a method of teaching; it was good practice for them; they learnt much from their mistakes; what they learnt in Arnold they put into effect in Freddy's second curacy and subsequent ministry. Sunday Schools, Confirmation Classes, Choir football matches on a Saturday ('Really', Freddy wrote, 'the things we clergy are expected to do; and those boys' rules are so very alien to any that I have ever heard of') took up a great deal of his time. On one occasion he invited his diocesan bishop to kick off a match; 'a mistake', wrote Freddy, 'for he fell over and got covered in mud; then, when he got up, he fell over again. Mrs Barry was not amused. The boys were.'

At the end of November, Freddy wrote to his parents:

With the cold weather we now have our bath in front of the drawing room fire. It is rather fun bathing like that, beside the flickering flames of a good fire, although the paraphernalia of having a bath all takes such a time and I shall be glad when we have a bathroom; but that will not be while we are in Arnold.

My darling Joan is the most incredibly loving and supporting wife, as you know. She puts up with these conditions with such zestful good humour. I am so lucky to have her beside me. I have been visiting the houses round here almost all of this week. How the people breed: nine heads at different levels peered at me round the door of one house, and we talked for a good fifteen minutes like that. They never thought of asking me in. Husband was a miner and they had never known a parson call before - and looked at me agape. In the next house there were eight. We are trying to get round the whole parish.

Our telephone is on its way in; it is at present only wires hanging through a hole in the wall. Our contact with the wider world necessitated a new pole being put up in the street. What excitement that provoked in St. Albans Road. There was much twitching of curtains; the more brazen ventured outside and stood and watched. One old man from 168 or 166 stood for a while puffing his pipe and then had the temerity to suggest to the men doing the work that they hadn't put the pole up straight. He compounded his unpopularity by saying that if a job's worth doing, it's worth doing well. He was given short shrift and sullen glares. Joan overheard all this and went over and hugged him. 'What's that for, lass?' he asked. 'Because I think you're lovely', said Joan, 'come and have a cup of tea.' 'No, lass - but thanks all the same: you see, it's my waterworks.' Joan delights in all these encounters and I delight in watching her talk so easily to just about everybody.

Freddy and Joan were just getting into their stride in the parish when the Vicar, at the beginning of December, dropped the 'catastrophic news' that he was leaving the parish in the following April. He had only been there for two years, and Freddy and Joan had only been there for just over two months. Leigh-Wood was to be a missionary teacher in Africa. This news threw Freddy and Joan into turmoil. What of their future? 'Legally', wrote Freddy, 'I only have a contract with Leigh-Wood and it would be terrible to be under a man one disagreed with a lot.' Freddy was not seeking a second curacy as, a few months previously, he had received a letter from the Principal of the Diocesan Theological College in Montreal encouraging him to consider joining the staff after serving his first curacy. By this time there would be a vacancy which, the Principal thought, would be ideal for Freddy to fill. 'It would', he had written, 'be ideal for you and for us, for you would be able to combine teaching with pastoral care of the students.' He ended his letter, 'Please consider this prayerfully; we need someone with your sort of experience of the world and, above all perhaps, vision. Billy Greer and others think you would fit in here admirably.' Freddy and Joan were keen on the idea. Their plans, not for the first or the last time in their life together, were thrown into the melting-pot.

Meanwhile, it had been confirmed that Joan was pregnant. Freddy and she were delighted, despite the qualms Freddy had expressed after his first baptism about the tiresome behaviour of babies. Joan went into the Peel Street Women's Hospital near the end of March. Michael Frederick weighed in at an enormous eleven pounds five and a half ounces soon after noon on 30th March. Although the birth, by Caesarian section, went well, there were complications afterwards, and Joan stayed in hospital for over a month. In her diary she wrote, 'I quite literally faced death and realised how desperately I wanted to live, and how very good God had been to me in giving me all that I have.' She went home on April 29th, and her diary notes, 'Went home. Freddy and I could do nothing but cry - he had cried himself to sleep many nights; I do love him so.'

They could, however, still laugh together. Freddy told her of one of the visits he had made while she was in hospital, and which he repeated in a letter to his parents:

Despite all the worry, I have been able to do a little bit of visiting. I do get told the oddest things; one dear old soul told me to see that Joan did not do too much when she was home and then went on, 'Of course, the trouble with me, Mr. Temple, was all me strength went into me milk; they flowed, Mr. Temple, they absolutely flowed'; here a graphic description with the hands followed as well.

The child was named Michael after Joan's brother, who had died in the War and Frederick after his grandfather and great-grandfather. Some members of the family were upset that he had not been named William after his great-uncle. Freddy wrote to his parents, 'Our next child will have William as a second name, but not even as a first, for we feel that the poor lad will scream with people patting him on the head and saying, "Well, you've got a great name to live up to", and he will feel he is never recognised in his own right.'

On July 3rd, Freddy wrote that Michael might well have inherited the Temple laugh, for he seemed to spend much time 'gurgling with delight in a most charming way.' On September 6th, Freddy again wrote, 'Michael has now got two teeth in the bottom jaw; two gleaming ivory castles as Joan calls the little rough white excrescences in his mouth.'

Joan carried on writing her diary sporadically, but pressure of work meant it was only fitful. She wrote on one occasion, 'Oh dear, it sometimes seems impossible to combine parish and home.' There are gaps in the diary. At the end of one such gap, she wrote the marvellously convoluted sentence, ' I seem to remember that there are several things that I wanted to remember - things that we have talked about rather than done - but as usual this wretched old book has been forgotten for a while and I have forgotten what I wanted to remember.'

Meanwhile, the announcement of a new Vicar of St. Mary's, Arnold, the Reverend Arthur Kirton, was made; he was duly instituted on the last day of May, 1948. Freddy's initial reactions were favourable; although he reckoned that Kirton did not have the drive of Leigh-Wood, he thought they would be able to work amicably together. It is, however, sometimes hard to adjust to the ways of another incumbent, and tensions were soon to show. In a letter home to his parents on June 27th, Freddy wrote:

I am afraid Kirton concentrates too much on I and me; in our prayers at Matins he always starts by saying, "First, let us pray for ourselves". But it is even more important to be unselfish in one's prayers than anywhere else and one should surely end with oneself and not start there? He is being very friendly and pleasant, but has very different ideas about work than LW. His sermons are all very chatty and matey; Joan came back from Evensong rather squirming as he had been talking about Baptism and started, 'When you are born, you are born into the family of your father. I am my father's son. He's there at the back of the Church; there's no hokey-pokey about it.' It was all rather quaint and not very profound; however it is as well that we are together, as our different styles may satisfy more. A pleasant Austrian refugee who comes regularly to Church stopped me after Evensong last week, and said in his broken English, 'You will excuse me, Mr. Temple: I must just

say one word about your preaching; you put so very much into so few words; I am
marvellously satisfied.' Rather nice, and he is an intelligent man too. I am getting
quite a reputation for brevity; but no harm in that I feel; ten to fifteen minutes is
enough if you have had anything to say in it.

It became increasingly obvious that Freddy and Joan ought to look elsewhere. Freddy was invited to apply for the Chaplaincy of St. Luke's College, Exeter, in August. The Principal wanted him, but pointed out that the appointment was made by a Board, and that there were over two hundred applicants, some with Firsts, and many with teaching experience. Freddy was one of six to be shortlisted; the Bishop of Bristol, Cockin, wrote a glowing testimonial, as did the Bishop of Manchester, Greer, and the Bishop of Southwell, Barry. Barry did not want to lose him and counselled against going forward with his application; Greer also counselled against, though Cockin thought it would be a good move. Freddy was in a bit of a quandary, which was resolved when he failed to get appointed.

Freddy was priested in Southwell Minster on September 19th, the Patronal Festival of St. Mary's, Arnold. His most treasured ordination gift was a leather-bound copy of the 1662 Prayer Book. On the title page are the words 'Archbishop of Canterbury', written in Archbishop Frederick Temple's own hand. This has been crossed out. Underneath are the words, again crossed out, 'Bishop of Manchester', written in William Temple's hand. Under that, in Frances Temple's hand, is written: 'This book, which belonged to Frederick Temple, Archbishop of Canterbury and then to William Temple, his son, (successively Bishop of Manchester, Archbishop of York and Archbishop of Canterbury) was given to Frederick Stephen Temple, his grandson, on the day of his ordination to the Priesthood in Southwell Minster - September 19th 1948'.

On the following evening, the local paper reported that the wife of the late Archbishop of Canterbury was guest of honour at the St. Mary's Feast Supper. The humble parishioners of Arnold were generally a bit overawed by Aunt Frances, though one of their number put his arm round her shoulders, squeezed her and said, 'Nice to see you, duck.' Frances froze.

Despite the fact that Freddy had not been long in his first curacy, he and Joan were now ready for a move, and it was soon announced that he was to be curate of Newark Parish Church. The usual round of farewells ensued, and they were given a very handsome leaving present. Although they had only been in Arnold for a comparatively short time, they had certainly made an impact, not only on the parish, but also on the wider community. A farewell message from the local Irish Roman Catholic priest ran, 'I'm awfully sorry to hear you're leaving here. You'll excuse me telling you but you are known as the Glamour Boy round here; so young and handsome and charming. I'm often pulling them up and telling them it's not right to think on their priest so. But they mean it for a compliment. Ah well, it has been nice knowing you; you have been extremely charming.' Freddy and Joan were greatly amused.

The possible move to Newark-on-Trent had been mooted, even before Freddy's priesting, by the Vicar of Newark, the Reverend G.W. Clarkson, with the full approval of the Bishop of Southwell. (Clarkson was afterwards to become Bishop of Pontefract and then the first Dean of the new Guildford Cathedral.) Freddy went to visit George Clarkson on October 1st. He had been apprehensive about Newark because the tradition there was more Catholic than Freddy was accustomed to. His first meeting with Clarkson was a great success on a personal level. After Freddy had left to return to Arnold, Clarkson immediately penned a letter to him:

I believe that some things are better written than said and I think that the firm offer of a new job is one of them. I have seen two of the churchwardens - we run four co-equals in Newark and are very self-conscious both of the fact and of them. The other two are away enjoying themselves and they will duly agree. Though we have had but two gallivanting hours together, I feel we could work happily as a team in Newark and give each other sufficient confidence to make a job of it. I don't suppose you have many delusions about the amount of work that is to be done, nor any doubts about the real source and energy of our ability to tackle it. On essentials we shall agree by mutual consent to the same truth; in other matters we shall, I feel certain, find disagreement to be pleasant, and even constructive, in mutual appreciation. More than that two men can never ask of each other. And now I am becoming pompous - so it shows that this must come to an end with an expression of my hope that you will come here. On my side there is a belief that the Almighty has been ruling out certain devices of my own contriving, so that there should be the right answer at the right time. Certain happenings indicate that the right answer is on the way. But there must always be your opinion to consider too. But whatever happens I shall remember this afternoon as one of the pleasantest in Newark up to now.

Freddy wrote a reply asking for breathing space in which to think and pray about it. Clarkson replied that he wanted 'a pal and a partner in this job', and he believed they could 'make the grade if we gave the Holy Spirit a chance'. He invited him to come and see him and talk further. Freddy wrote to the Bishop of Manchester for advice. Greer replied:

First I would say choose your man rather than the churchmanship. You would need to discuss frankly with Clarkson the whole question of ceremonial. Within limits one should accommodate oneself; the limits are set by doctrinal considerations and by how far you can go without feeling queer and insincere. Teaching needs to be thought of. Would he expect you to press confession with Confirmation candidates? Would he feel it was all right if you and he showed some diversity in matters

107

ceremonial? Is he a martinet and would he regard diversity (within limits) as dis-loyal? If you satisfy yourself on these points, I would go. Sacristy bells and servers are really neither here nor there. It would do you no harm to learn a few High Church practices provided they did not compromise your own sense of integrity. On the evidence given my advice would be to accept, but then I have not all the evidence; so if you refuse let me know and I'll write to you about possibilities here. Just at the moment I don't see any quite so available as the job at Newark. If you get in a tangle about it all, come up here for a night and we'll talk it over. I'll find the fare.

Freddy accepted the post, and two days afterwards had a letter from the Bishop of Southwell:

I saw Greer in London yesterday. He told me that you had been in consultation with him about Newark and that he had advised you to go there, and this morning I heard from Clarkson that you had definitely accepted. I am delighted about this and I am sure you will find it an inspiring place to work, and in Clarkson himself a tower of strength who will give you just the guiding and backing you want for the next year or two. I fully understand the qualms you have felt, but I feel sure there won't really be any strain on your conscience, and that Clarkson will do everything possible to make things easy for you. I am glad to think that when you have moved I shall probably be able to see more of you.

Freddy was to tell a Clergy Conference many years later that the differences in churchmanship between himself and the parish generally had for him been 'a most wonderful experience of spiritual growth; I learned to accept the diversity of the Church of England; more than that, I learned to welcome it. I also learned not to be so insufferably arrogant in my inherited opinions. Others do have a valid point of view. Sometimes. For these insights I am for ever indebted to my Vicar and the long-suffering saints of Newark.'

A wonderfully witty correspondence continued over the next few months between Freddy and Clarkson; it was obvious from the start that the two of them were going to be a match for each other. Although they did not always see eye to eye and Clarkson sometimes exasperated Freddy (and no doubt Freddy exasperated Clarkson), it was the start of a good working relationship and, ultimately, a life-long friendship.

Joan, Freddy and Michael moved to Newark on Joan's 26th birthday, January 3rd 1949.

The terraced house into which they moved, 55 Victoria Street, had a study and Freddy thus described it to his mother as 'really rather palatial when compared to Arnold.' Joan and Freddy were both thrilled with it. He wrote, 'We are in so much comfort here we feel it cannot last.' The Youth Fellowship, known as the Trinity

Guild, was to be Freddy's 'baby'; and when Freddy took it over it was in a state of collapse and, indeed, had been closed. One of his first tasks was to try to breathe new life into it. He also was responsible for the vast and ramified Sunday Schools in the parish; in the diocese at large, the Bishop appointed him a Diocesan Inspector of Schools.

The Trinity Guild was re-started and met on a Thursday evening, and then again in Joan and Freddy's home every Sunday evening after Evensong. A list of the activities provided show a remarkable breadth of content. The young were given, say, fifteen minutes to prepare a subject and then speak on it for three minutes. Some learnt how to speak well; others remained terribly nervous and, in Freddy's words, 'just groaned and dithered'; but there was no doubt that most of them enjoyed these sessions greatly. Freddy invited a varied group of speakers to talk, choosing people who would fire their imaginations and broaden their horizons. Joan and Freddy too brought 'Religion through Drama' to Newark. The Guild became so proficient that the group was invited to go to Swanwick to perform in front of the Manchester Diocesan Clergy Conference which was meeting there. Freddy himself was invited by the bishop to address the Conference and spread 'The Gospel of Religion through Drama'. Clergy from that diocese have testified to how that Conference fired their own imaginations. One former inner-city Manchester incumbent, over fifty years later, has written to say that the fifteen minutes in which Freddy spoke were 'probably the most magical in my ministry.' Another, from a suburb of Manchester, said that Freddy taught him how to get alongside youth in such a way as was 'to transform my whole way of dealing with the young.' For this he was eternally grateful, as, presumably, were the young people themselves.

At meetings of the Trinity Guild, the young would also get to grips with social problems of the day. Freddy and Joan taught the young to think through problems; they were not allowed to hide behind what Freddy was to call 'shoddy responses' to the great social issues of the time. Barry Rogerson, Bishop of Bristol until 2002, was a young member of the Trinity Guild. In an interview he recalled how much he himself was indebted to the 'imaginative nurturing of Freddy', and how Freddy and Joan gave the members of the Guild the 'supreme gift of confidence.' He continued, 'Freddy affirmed us in a remarkable way; he led us to believe in ourselves and believe that we, and what we thought, mattered.' Barry Rogerson reckoned that underlying the recipe for the success of Freddy and Joan's ministry was the fact that 'we rather callow young people were allowed - no, welcomed - into the Temple family home; Freddy and Joan gave us the impression that we weren't just honoured guests, but somehow we belonged there.' He thought that Freddy and Joan must have been absolutely exhausted at the end of an evening with the Guild; Freddy's own letters and fragments from his diary confirm this. Barry Rogerson also said that Joan was considered by the young people to be 'a curate's wife who was extraordinarily colourful and fun' and he reckoned that she sported the first-ever nylon dress - the height of contemporary fashion - to be seen in Newark.

Michael meanwhile was learning to eat on his own; he learnt to put food on his spoon, though it 'took time to find his mouth'; if he didn't connect spoon with mouth after one or two efforts, 'it was fun to flick it on to the floor.'

The normal parish round continued and Freddy dealt with the everyday tasks of a priest. Friends of the time remember that he especially rose to the unexpected, and would spend hours on end with particular people if he thought the occasion demanded. One Sunday he wrote to his parents:

> At 10-15 on Thursday evening, just after I had got in from the Trinity Guild, Mrs. Braithwaite [the Vicar's widowed sister, who lived at the Vicarage] rang up from the Vicarage to say that a man had come there asking for the key of the Church as his wife was dangerously ill after having a baby and he would like to pray there; she was not sure that he was genuine and had sent him along to me. This naturally worried Joan a bit as you never know these days and so after he came at about 10-45 and we went off she rang the police and asked them to keep an eye on the Church; two big genial policemen did come in for a moment and gave one a remarkably secure feeling, saying that they wondered why a light was on at that time; very tactful and good; but the man was quite genuine. He was completely knocked up and had the oddest ideas about God and his dealings; his wife had wanted to go to Church before going into hospital and he had laughed, and he thought that this was God hitting him fair and square for that. He had no belief in any afterlife; said that he was terrified as to what happened to her if she dies. He had never been near a Church for years; however we said some prayers and I walked right home with him. His wife has lived after all the doctors and nurses had given up hope; and of course he is thrilled and seemed to think I worked the magic formula. I only hope I shall be able to use this mood while it lasts and get him firmly attached again to the Church and we can iron out some of his misconceptions. How important it is to be a teacher of Christian hope; I felt I had accomplished something; all day I had been dealing with petty squabbles of folk in Church who thought they were being hard done by for piffling reasons.

In fact, Freddy persevered gently with this man, gave him a lot of time and space, and he and wife were eventually brought to Confirmation and subsequently to a fruitful ministry in the Church.

Life was busy. At the beginning of December, Freddy told his parents that Christmas services at the Parish Church and St Augustine's were: Midnight, 6.30am, 7.15am, 8am, 8.45am, 9.30am, 11am, 12 noon, 2.15pm (children), 3.30pm (baptisms), 5pm (Hospital) and Evensong at 6pm. They were leaving their Christmas dinner till Boxing Day, on which day there were three weddings.

Soon after this, Freddy told Clarkson about a letter from the Bishop of Grahamstown, inviting him to take on an important educational post in his diocese. Freddy had a open mind. Part of him still wanted to go abroad. Joan was keen as well. Clarkson said he thought Freddy ought to do another twelve months in Newark, then go for a large parish job in England before 'the inevitable'. When Freddy asked him what he thought the 'inevitable' was, his incumbent told him, 'A Dominions bishopric for a time, and then a diocesan one in England.'

Whilst at Newark, Bishop Russell Barry appointed Freddy a Diocesan Inspector of Schools, a task Freddy enjoyed greatly, partly because he enjoyed meeting teachers and children and partly because he usually went to all his assignments on his bicycle, giving him, as he wrote to a friend, 'time to be free and to think, as I pedalled madly through the Nottinghamshire countryside - and also it was exhilarating exercise.' After one of his visits to report on a school, he wrote home:

> *The Headmistress is totally and utterly batty and runs her school in such a quaint way. Perhaps battiness is the secret ingredient in being a good headmistress. She certainly commands respect from her other teacher, and I suspect a love from the children. The results are very fair. She keeps her little dog on her desk; when it yaps (usually when it sees a bird outside the window) she throws the board cloth at it. At intervals throughout the day, she chooses the naughtiest child to take it out to (as she says) 'perform'. It's little wonder that every child, about 'performing time', tries to be as naughty as possible.*

In another letter about another school, the last sentence is a gem, 'The children show great interest in all their tasks, though they are let down by their spelling, which is atrosious' (sic).

After a visit to a third school, Freddy wrote:

> *The middle-aged headmistress is a wonderful person. She sports tiny tufts of down above her upper lip, which always seem to catch the sun. I noticed with a mixture of horror and amusement that amongst the pictures on the classroom wall drawn by the children was one of the worthy headmistress sporting a moustache, the splendour of which would have gratified many an R.A.F. officer. She must indeed be a very special person to have allowed that one to be hung.*

Yet another school provided a source of amusement for Freddy. He wrote to his parents:

> *I went to a school on Thursday whose Headmistress had so obviously thoroughly prepared her pupils to say the right thing to the Inspector. I sat in front of the school at a special assembly, and began by asking the children the name of their school. Thirty tiny hands shot up and thirty little tongues cried out, 'Jesus.' I then picked out a little girl and asked her how old she was. The answer: 'Jesus.' At this point I*

decided to tell them a story about a
mother and father who took their little boy to the seaside. At the end of
the story, I asked them the name of
the little boy. Twenty nine little voices shouted out, 'Jesus.' Thankfully,
there was in this Mid-Nottingham-
shire schoolroom one little rebel,
who followed this outburst, rather
demurely I thought, with 'Sillies. It
was George.'

Freddy and Joan with Michael
at Newark.

Freddy continued to throw himself into parish life and enjoyed it. He told a neighbouring incumbent that if he didn't enjoy the ministry, despite the inevitable sad-
nesses, then there was really not much point in carrying on. There were, of course,
amusing happenings; somehow there had to be when Freddy was around. On one
occasion, Freddy was summoned to the Vicarage to see George Clarkson, who
asked him to go round to see one fairly prominent member of the congregation
who had taken to exercising the family dog by tying it to the back of her car and
then proceeding at a stately five miles an hour up the main High Street, totally
oblivious of the mounting traffic behind her. This sort of encounter had not been
covered in Pastoralia seminars at Westcott and Freddy was unsure anyway that it
was the business of the clergy to interfere. Clarkson gave the reply that it gave the
Church a bad image and that the populace would think that all Christians in Newark were as 'vacuously stupid' as she was. Freddy countered this by saying that he
thought that if she should be challenged it should be the Vicar to do so, to which
Clarkson replied that nothing would give him greater pleasure but he did not
want to make himself too unpopular with that particular family as he already had
'a rod hardening in vinegar with which to beat her husband for quite another matter.'

On another occasion, Freddy wrote:

On Thursday a Mr. Cooper who runs a fish and chip shop here talked to the Trinity
Guild about his recent holiday in Holland. At the end I rather wished he had spent
his holiday anywhere but Holland; he made continual references to the 'Ook of
Olland'. Clarkson had just popped in for a minute to give me some leaflets, but he
was entranced and stayed for ten very long minutes and did his best to make me
laugh by mimicking him. A bit cruel, not so much for poor Cooper, who couldn't
hear him, but for me, as I sometimes find it easy to laugh and the Guild would have
wondered what on earth was going on.

Joan entered hospital on March 4th 1950. She was not, again, having an easy time with her pregnancy. Melesina Catharine Carveth was born on March 15th, and on March 20th Freddy wrote to his parents asking for permission to borrow the Temple Christening robe again.

At the beginning of August, William Greer, Bishop of Manchester, offered Freddy a job which he would like him to start in November, the fairly new parish of St. Ambrose, Oldham. In his letter he did not disguise the fact that it was a tough undertaking; it was a new housing estate in a predominantly industrial setting, and there was no Church building, just a rather vast building with a variety of meeting rooms, one of which was almost exclusively used as a Church. Freddy went to visit it the following week. He found it a grim place: 'great cotton mill chimneys reared their heads just by the Vicarage doorstep and no sign of any green for miles around.' He went on to say in a letter to his parents that it was a large parish of 15,000 with a debt of £2000. He was quite clear that it was not the right place as the Vicarage was far too small for their growing family. Joan and he based their pastoral ministry on visiting and using their home as a 'home from home' for everybody; there were no rooms large enough for groups of any size. They thought that it would be impossible to do justice to the parish without being happy in an adequate home base.

On the 7th of October, out of the blue, a Mr. Courage from London asked Freddy if he would be interested in the living of Shenfield in Essex, of which he was the patron. He went to see Courage, who had a vast house in Mayfair. He was greeted at the door by the butler. Freddy said in a letter that he instantly felt a sympathy for Aneurin Bevan - that all this opulence should be made out of the working man's beer. All went well, until Courage said that it was absolutely vital that he meet Joan. A brother who was there said, 'Yes, the PCC insist on that; they want a married man and a wife who will do her full share.' Freddy told them that Joan was ready to do a tremendous amount in the parish, as much as her two small children allowed, and was already doing a great deal at Newark. But they insisted on seeing her. Freddy called it an 'infernal impudence' to insist on interviewing his wife for his job. It would start things off on entirely the wrong footing if there were any sense of obligation concerning what Joan did. He told them he did not want the job. After he had had his say, it was unlikely that it would have been offered him anyway. He commented afterwards, 'Anyway, the parish did not sound at all like our cup of tea: dormitory, very wealthy, wee congregation, vast house, ten bedrooms, enormous garden with a cottage in the grounds.'

This stirred the Bishops of Southwell and Manchester into action. Barry had nothing suitable to offer, but Greer had some suggestions and wanted to see him. Freddy travelled north the following week. Greer asked him to look first at St. Agnes, Birch-in-Rusholme, a fourpenny bus ride from Manchester City Centre. Freddy liked it. He wrote, 'I was very fortunate in that they had just had a funeral so that the churchwarden who is running things during the interregnum was in the Church; a young fellow still studying at the University whom I took to very much and is obviously very keen.' Greer told him that he was the first to be offered it and it was the most important parish in that part of Manchester. Freddy commented that Greer was Irish and was selling him the parish. Barry tried to stall him, saying he hoped something 'big' would crop up soon in Southwell.

Joan and Freddy went up to look together at St. Agnes's at the beginning of November. 'After lunch we went to look at the Church and the Rectory; I felt my first impressions confirmed and liked it more; the church is cosy and friendly and yet holds 600, which is quite enough. The Rectory is bilious in the extreme on the outside and the garden quite devastatingly public; open iron railings round it and it is on the fork of two main roads and a bus stop just outside; but we would lump that. Joan liked the house inside. If Barry has no more counter-moves we shall accept and that will mean another move in mid-January; not the best of times, but there we are. Joan is marvellous the way she accepts these new homes she has got to make in the oddest surroundings.' The following week he accepted the living. Aunt Frances was very thrilled about it and gave it her seal of approval. She continued to act sometimes as if she were still the wife of the Bishop of Manchester. Mrs. Greer was mature and tactful enough to cope with her gracefully.

Three generations: Freddy's father, Freddy and Michael - a photograph taken on Freddy's appointment as Rector of St. Agnes, Manchester.

Michael continued to enthral Freddy. He wrote to his parents, 'Have we told you that Michael's latest is cooking? Whenever Joan goes to the oven it is full of all her cake tins, full of little neat parcels in every one, which are various things cooking. Little Gran is continually having things cooked for her. The other evening he rushed me to the oven and said he had fish and peas there; the door was opened and a head peered in. "No, not done yet. Not at all. Fish takes hours." "Not at all" is a favourite phrase at the moment.' The baby, Mina, was adored by him, as they both were, of course, by their parents. Freddy told his parents proudly, 'Michael loves playing with Mina and she is starting to enjoy having a bit of paper put over her face which she whips off with great gurgles and then Michael puts it on again with roars of delight.' He ends the letter, 'This letter is a bit disjointed as my wife and son are here in the room; my wife is not being a trouble but my son is a considerable distraction all the time.'

There was a lot to do to tie up loose ends in Newark and say farewell. Freddy wrote to his mother, 'As Grandmama [Copleston] used to say, "Marry or die and you are perfect." Leaving a parish is very much for them like the second, and so there are a lot of nice things being said right and left at the moment. It will be a business getting to know an entirely fresh lot of people again; but this time it ought to be for much longer and I will have a real chance to get down to things.'

The Bishop of Southwell wrote:

You are leaving tomorrow, I think, and I must send you a line to say Goodbye. I am dreadfully sorry to lose you and I wish I could have had you in one of our major parishes in this Diocese. But I am grateful to have been allowed to ordain you and to have you here for these few years. If I am still here and if you haven't succumbed to episcopacy 5 years hence perhaps you will come back to us. Meanwhile I hope you will be really happy at Birch and with Willie Greer, and find the work satisfying and fruitful. Let me know how it goes. My love to you and Joan and God bless you both.

Freddy was instituted on January 26th 1951: Aunt Frances embarrassed him by behaving like the Diocesan Bishop's wife.

8   A Parish of his own

The parish of St. Agnes, Birch-in-Rusholme, in the nineteen forties and fifties might be described as working class, genteel in some parts, less so in others, depending on which side of Hamilton Road you lived. Two miles or so from the centre of Manchester, its housing was mostly back to back terraced, with a 'back entry' or 'side entry' dividing the streets and houses. There was also a large council housing estate whose residents had been re-housed there from the most central parts of Manchester. The area was densely populated, served by small shops and only one pub, 'The Anson'. The main Manchester to London railway line ran through part of the parish.

The St. Agnes Church of England Parish School was an 'all-through' school, providing education for pupils aged five to fourteen years. It was not used by parents who had high aspirations for their children or who were perhaps a little anxious about the 'roughness' of some of the children who came from the wrong side of the tracks. It did, however, provide a centre for evening activities associated with the Church during the week and for the Sunday School. Also situated in the parish was the Roman Catholic Church of St. Robert, but those were not the days of ecumenism. John Heywood, who grew up in the parish, recalls that, when he was a child and teenager, he and his brother Ron were discouraged from mixing with the one Roman Catholic family who lived nearby; their mother used to cross to the other side of the road when nearing St. Robert's Church. Their parents used to refer to the Parish Priest as 'Father Rip-Rap', perhaps because his biretta resembled a cheap firework of the same name, popular at the time among the children in the streets of Manchester. Today, the area is populated predominantly by citizens of Asian or Afro-Caribbean ethnicity.

This was the parish that Freddy and Joan now took on. The previous Rector, the Reverend Edwin Bartholomew, had served the parish steadfastly and quietly throughout the war years and subsequently. He had maintained a choir of twelve boys and several contraltos, together with a few men too old for military service. In the post-war years, a Sunday School flourished and the congregation remained stable. There remained, however, much potential, waiting to be tapped.

It was unfortunate that, just after the move, Joan had to go into hospital for a minor operation; the children had to go to stay with Joan's sister and Freddy coped with the first week or two on his own. He wrote that Joan was 'in a three-bed ward in the Royal Infirmary, a most depressing room of utter gloom where the fire is made up with much noise every three hours right through the night. Her companions are the oddest dears who talk in quite incomprehensible broad Lancashire.'

Immediately she was out of hospital, the Vicarage was opened up for the youth of the parish on a Sunday evening. Forty-six young people attended. Freddy told his parents at the end of February that the Vicarage seemed to be full of people all the time, which was 'great fun' for them. (It is not obvious from reading the letter whether it was 'great fun' for the youngsters or for Freddy and Joan; hopefully both.) Anyway, Freddy and Joan reckoned that they provided over fifty more cups of tea every week than they ever did in Newark.

At this time Freddy wrote home to say that William Greer had increased his workload by giving him extra tasks in the sphere of Moral Welfare in the diocese at large. Freddy reckoned that if he were not to sink under the constant pressures, he would have to have a curate and was planning to find one after a tour of the theological colleges in Oxford and Cambridge after Easter. By this time, he had already started producing the first act of St. *Joan* with the Boys' Club.

It took Freddy and Joan time to get used to the grime of the parish. Freddy wrote to his mother, 'This is a sickeningly dirty spot; I suppose the railway makes it more so. I can sit in my study with closed windows and watch in two hours a piece of paper get covered with black spots. And the bus stop outside the garden means that the place is covered with bus tickets. But the people are so very lovely, and that's all that matters.' Freddy and Joan did at times feel they were living in a gold-fish bowl. One morning, as there was a lot to do in the Church, Joan had got up early to do some washing and had hung it up outside on the line. A lady came over to the Church later and said, 'My, Mrs. Temple, I was passing the Rectory and saw you've been busy this morning.' Joan replied, 'I have indeed; I thought I'd get the washing done early.' To which came the reply, 'Yes, you've got seventy-two pieces on the line.' Freddy always used to say that you could learn a lot about people by looking at their washing-lines. One day, while he was still in his first curacy, he was being driven home from some parish 'do'. Two of the ladies in the rear seat were talking about a third lady who had been left by her husband, and they were wondering whether or not he sent her any money. One said, 'I don't think he does, dear'; to which the other replied, 'Oh, my dear, he does: you couldn't clothe two teenage boys in pyjamas unless your husband was sending you money, and I see her washing-line.'

Freddy ended his next letter home, 'Masses of love from us all. Mina is now very great fun and enjoyed her birthday a lot; poor Mike can't see why his has to be a fortnight later; I heard him going upstairs on her birthday saying, "My naughty, naughty presents not come yet." I went to fetch him from a tea the other day and he rather entranced the gathering by saying as he greeted me, "Have you come to fetch me? What a kind Father to fetch me; thank you very much." Did I tell you that I saw him the other day holding Mina by both arms and gazing intently into her face and saying, "You are bery bery sweet"?'

Freddy and Joan had a host of stories to tell about Michael. They often re-counted one of their favourites - an occasion when the youth were coming to the Vicarage for a meeting and Michael had been asked to clear up the playroom.

While he was doing this, the doorbell went - and Mike rushed to open it. On opening it, he asked simply, 'Are you the youth?'. The Bishop of Middleton, Frank Woods, well into middle age and beyond, patted him on the head and said, 'You'll go far, my boy.'

Freddy had sixteen Sick Communions on one day at Eastertide. He wrote that it was a 'bit of a strain and the Epistle and Gospel become a little tedious the sixteenth time in the day; but for these heroic, bed-ridden dears it is something to which they look forward so much and prepare so carefully that one just mustn't shorten it or skimp it in any way'. He had heard of an incumbent in the diocese who had shortened each little bedside service drastically; Freddy just wrote, rather ferociously perhaps, 'How dare he?'

Freddy at this time was reading the newly-published letters of Hensley Henson, Bishop of Durham, which he found most enjoyable. He sent them to his parents to read, with the comment that he had not realised how much not getting the offer of the Archbishopric of York had made Henson dislike Uncle William; it came out most strongly in one letter. (Perhaps Freddy was being a little too defensive here; a reading of Hensley Henson's letters seems to underline the fact that he liked and admired Uncle William, though he did have criticisms of certain aspects of his ministry.) He also commented on what Henson had to say about clergy wives. On April 4th, 1945, Henson had written, 'In my belief, based on the experience of a long ministry, it would be roughly true to say of the married clergy of the Church of England that probably fifty percent were ruined by their wives, and fifty percent were saved.' Freddy commented that at least he could not see how Joan would ever be considered a handicap in his ministry; and so it proved.

Freddy had to go the following month to the local Scouts Association, and wrote,

> The Chairman of the meeting introduced me with a heavy joke: 'I know nothing about Mr. Temple; but I remember a bearded old man who preached at my school, an Archbishop Temple. I also know a film star called Shirley; I don't know if Mr. Temple is related to either of those.' When I said that I was closely connected with the first, though he was not hirsute, and nothing to do with the second, he was really astonished; he really didn't know. That shut him up for the rest of the evening. Did I tell you too that two people whom Mr. Bartholomew apparently failed to smile at in the street had stopped sending in their Freewill Offering envelopes, but have decided to start again and have filled in all last year's as well, so we had a bumper haul in the Sunday collection? But it is appalling that a smile can do so much; I wonder how many I have already cut dead and are stopping because of it? How Our Lord must be grieved when he sees our pettiness.

Within less than four months, Freddy had completed what he called his 'foundation visiting', all members of the Parochial Church Council, all Freewill Offering subscribers, the three hundred and twenty on the Electoral Roll and the sick, of whom there seemed to be a great many. It was time for a break. Joan and he had earlier decided to go to Iona; when one of the boys in the parish heard that they were going to a small island, he said, 'My, you like your holidays quiet, Sir', to which Freddy replied, 'So would you if you lived in this Rectory long; I feel that with the sea between us people can't pop in and out all day.'

Freddy knew and loved Iona well, but on the train to Oban to catch the ferry to Mull he confessed to some misgivings. He wrote in a book of jottings:

How much will be the same? How much will have altered? That is always the dangerous question when one returns to a favourite haunt of years ago; more dangerous still when the gap has been filled with the upheavals and changes of the war; the place might have changed much, but more probable still, I might have changed still more and fail to see the beauty from older disillusioned eyes, fail to enjoy the ruggedness and freshness with the limbs of approaching middle age.

After the holiday, he wrote the following, which deserves to be printed at length, for it tells us much about Freddy:

At the start I was apprehensive. Would things be the same? Would I see things in the same light? Such were my thoughts as the Mull mail boat, 'The Lochinvar', drew near to Craignure, where my wife, my boy and I were to get off on our way to Iona, that enchanted island which I had twice visited before the war in the fantastic leisure of an undergraduate vac, a place of beauty, a place of peace and gaiety. I was free and independent then; now I had others to consider; would they find what I had told them, or had dreams and memories over-coloured reality?

Cameron's small buses were waiting for us on the quayside. We climbed into them and from then onwards time meant little, friendliness and personal attention everything; that had not changed. Slowly we churned our way across Mull; the road has grass and flowers up much of the middle of it; it is steep and uneven, so gears are crashed and changed continuously.

Some people like Mull, the desolation and the grandeur; but for me it is too severe and serves only to stress the contrast with Iona. That is why we had come this way. Many visitors to the island come round Mull in the comfort of the 'King George V', but they miss the contrast; they miss the reward of effort which those who travel through Mull get; it is the difference between climbing the mountain on foot or going up in the railway. The view is not the same to the different eyes at the top. The journey seemed longer; would we never arrive? But this was my first change: now I was worrying if a three-year old would be sick at the end of an all-day journey in this jolting bus, if the demand for the 'pot' could be controlled to the right time and place. But he is well and sternly trained and all in the bus admitted that he had been 'a guid wee bairn.' It had been cloudy as we drove across but the sun came through as we reached the ferry at Fionphort, just as it had on my last visit. There, across the Sound, lay Iona, friendly, smiling softly in the evening sun, surrounded by its unique clear pale green sea covering the white sands.

The hotel had not changed; still the same quiet friendliness, the candles in the bedrooms, with the corncrakes outside to croak you to sleep. At first, like the evacuees at the beginning of the war, we found the silence after Manchester overwhelming. It took time to slow to the tempo of the island; it took time not to fidget in the one shop in the village as the person in front made, deliberately and with complete leisure, her weekly purchases. There was nothing to hurry for.

In place of the complete independence to do what I liked in the past, there was now the joy of seeing others really happy; a little brown body ran in and out of the sea, while his mother sketched and I read. The island seemed quieter than before, as we had come from a noisier place. Hemmed in for the rest of the year by noisy railway lines and bus routes, with people on all sides, our eyes roamed across the sea to the scattered Treshnish islands and back across the sands with not a soul in sight; the only soul we disturbed as we walked about was a seal basking in the sun. Instead of shunting trains, corncrakes filled the air at night and tireless larks in the day, singing in the clear blue sky until their lungs would burst.

No, the War had made no difference to the Island. In the evening we all climbed the one small hill, Dun I, and watched the sun set on what must be one of the most perfect scenes in the world, with the granite rocks of Mull glowing with warmth in the sea behind us.

The Abbey still kept its quiet spell on the place and to itself, without cinema or theatre to compete, drew all the visitors of a Sunday to learn again the true source of all contentment and power.

When we came to leave, I knew that I took away more from Iona than before, in spite of the passing years. The beauty and peace, the friendliness and happiness of the place and people meant more now than when I had first come. The pleasure had been shared with others and as we waved goodbye to friends who saw us off from the jetty early in the morning, I knew that things can grow better, not worse, as time goes on. And that way lies hope in a despairing world.

Freddy's first letter to his parents after the holiday was full of it. He had never felt so refreshed for a long time. But the unrelenting grind of the parish was soon to catch up with him. Only two weeks later he was to write, 'The pace here just can't go on like this; I get no time to read and we totter to bed at midnight to rise for 7.30 again, and we really hardly see each other during the day but for brief meal intervals.' It was about this time that Freddy's letters seemed to concentrate more and more on Michael's health. He seemed constantly to have colds and bronchial problems; Joan and Freddy were worried. Things came to a head in May 1952, when Freddy wrote:

Our doctor is to our mind too vague and just thinks us fussy; but the poor little fellow makes himself sick at nights with it and so we feel we must see a specialist to see if it is adenoids or not; our doctor says he will always be like it in Manchester; so many children are. If that is the case, then I think we should seriously consider moving for his sake; he is so bright and alert, and I don't want him to miss all the early schooling that I did if it can be avoided. It looks as if he may have inherited Uncle William's photographic memory; to watch him do a jigsaw is staggering; he just knows where the pieces go, the second time, in the puzzle; there is no fitting of the colour or the pattern; it is all done in a trice and he knows just where they ought to be. Just when we are thinking like this comes this letter from the Dean of Worcester asking if I am interested in becoming Rector of St. John's, Worcester. I have written to find out more about it; it looks like the big city church and parish of Worcester. There is a curate there; the present man is leaving to become Bishop of Northern Nigeria. It will only be if Michael needs a move that I think we should go as the Clarkes [Freddy's long-awaited and newly-appointed curate] have just moved here and it would be very unfair to them; not to say very bad indeed for the parish when so much has come to life and it is not yet stabilised properly; I fear it would all fall apart if we went.

The summer came; Michael seemed a little better.

Work in the parish went on apace. John Heywood, a teenager at the time, remembers much of this time, as does his brother Ronald. For obvious reasons John's main reminiscences centre around Freddy's work with the younger members of the congregation. He particularly remembered a series of half-hour evening services which Freddy arranged for young people, which focused on the disciples and their different characteristics. Freddy's talk about St. Peter particularly attracted him as he drew attention to the extremes of good and bad in Peter and, indeed, in everybody.

But it was outside the church building that he believes Freddy had the most lasting effect upon him and his friends. Every Sunday after Evensong (following the pattern established in Arnold and Newark), Freddy and Joan would open the doors of their big Edwardian Rectory to the young people from the congregation. This was something they had not experienced before. 30 or 40 young people crowded into the large living room and were provided with mugs of tea at 2d a cup and had a programme of discussions, sometimes light-hearted, sometimes serious. John can recall Freddy arranging for the older ones present to give short talks about their work and his being enthralled with the account which the fireman on the footplate of a steam train gave. Issues were discussed in small groups, and there was a 'fun' atmosphere. 'Clearly', writes John, 'Freddy was making a very real contribution to our wider social education.'

This interest which Freddy had in widening the horizons of the youth was clearly illustrated by his work with the Boys' Club attached to St. Agnes'.

John writes:

I have in front of me a certificate which is dated 10th May, 1952. It has the National Association of Boys' Clubs crest on it and states that I was a member of the team from St. Agnes (Birch) Boys Team that was awarded a certificate in the Regional Arts Festival for Drama. (It was held far distant in a theatre in Blackpool.) But Freddy had not selected a neat little one act play for this group of lads - he directed us in the first act of TS Eliot's 'Murder in the Cathedral' and I was privileged to play Thomas. 'Now is the way clear, now is the meaning plain, temptation shall not come in this kind again ....'; the lines are still with me 50 years later.

John also has a certificate from the same occasion, this time for the category 'Speech - unprepared'. John continues, 'Freddy coached my friends and me in the art of public speaking and no doubt unknowingly prepared me for working life as a school teacher, and would-be politician. I can recall him advising us that it is always easier to attack than to support. The fact that both certificates fell into the 3rd class category is not significant; standards were high. What is significant is that 50 years later I am very much aware of the impact that Freddy made upon me and upon other young men and women in the parish in terms not just of our spiritual development but particularly upon our cultural experience and self-confidence.'

Jack Strong also remembers Freddy well. He was a young man just recently returned from war, and, having been accepted for ordination training by William Greer, was acting temporarily as Rector's Warden at St. Agnes', his home parish. The two of them formed a rapport immediately. He writes, 'On a visit to the Bishop about my own affairs I spoke to Hetley Price, who was then the Bishop's Chaplain, about the appointment. I asked if Freddy was related to William Temple who had been a previous Bishop of Manchester before going on to York. "Didn't you recognise the Laugh?" was the reply. The laugh was Freddy's hallmark. He broke the post-war gloom in a parish which had had an unhappy time over the previous few years.'

Jack Strong relates how Frances Temple was a member of the Anson family, and the parish of St. Agnes contained the Anson estate, a housing estate built after the first world war. He recalls too how William Temple had been responsible for removing the first Rector of the parish who had become senile. The Bishop had been angry with the then churchwardens for not reporting the state of affairs to him; one of these wardens was still living and worshipping in St. Agnes' when Freddy arrived; a delicate situation with which Freddy coped well. Jack says, 'Freddy was good at dealing with difficult situations.' He tells of how Freddy's preaching was 'beamed at an intelligent audience; short, informative sermons delivered without notes. It was a breath of fresh air. Exactly what was needed.' He

continues:

In administration, dealing with the PCC and Managers of the Church Aided School, Freddy proved firm but cheerful. In pastoral care he was wonderful. He and Joan together did such a systematic and thorough visitation of the parish that the congregation increased until the church was packed at most services. It was a gruelling task as the parish population was then reckoned at 15,000 people. The contribution of Joan to this must be emphasised. How she managed to deal with two small children, a house and deal with other parish matters like the Mothers' Union is cause for wonder. The stamina of them both was remarkable.

Ken Gibbons (who was to follow Freddy as Vicar of Portsea in 1970) similarly recalls Freddy's 'amazing gift of preaching.' He heard Freddy preach at St. Agnes' while he was an undergraduate at the University of Manchester, and remembers the church being packed with students and other young people. After the sermon, Freddy answered questions 'simply, humorously, but with immense depth.'

The parish was really beginning to hum with activity, with a sense of purpose and there was an obvious deepening of the spiritual life of the congregation of St. Agnes'. Then, on September 28th, Freddy wrote to his parents:

We have had rather a shattering week. We took Michael down to see a specialist again, and after a thorough examination, and taking into account all the family history, she says she can only honestly recommend a move out of the dirt and damp of Manchester; she thinks he would be quite all right elsewhere. But here he is liable to succumb to chronic bronchitis. Chloromycetin etc. would get him over each attack but not get at the root of the trouble. The other young doctor who sent us to the specialist was most emphatic and thought we had no right to stay. It is tremendously disappointing just as one had got this parish going so well, and so much really starting to show results; all the spade work of the visiting done; my heart just quails at the thought of doing all that again somewhere else. And then a new diocese and getting to know everyone there again. Probably in time we will find that it was meant, but I do rather tremble for the parish which is in the stage of masses of new ones coming to Church and not yet welded in. Greer says that there is no possible shadow of a doubt but that we have made the right decision. Chichester and Bristol are both looking for jobs for me. I suppose it will be another January or February move. What a life.

On October 19th, Freddy again wrote to say that the Bishop of Waikato had invited him to be the Rector of Hamilton, but he and Joan were not sure about moving to New Zealand. Greer rang Freddy to say that the Bishop of Hong Kong had written to ask if he knew of anybody for a special and important job he wanted done there, but he had not mentioned what the job was. The Bishop had written back with Freddy's name and thought it 'might be just the right thing.' Freddy and Joan were, however, unsure of the climate of Hong Kong. They thought the diocese of

Chichester would be the best solution from the point of view of Michael's health, though the Bishop of Southwell had hinted that Newark might be vacant soon, and he would very much like Freddy to go back there as Vicar.

Frustrations and tensions mounted in the household, and occasioned the following outburst from Freddy to his parents on October 27th:

Thank you so much for your letters; especially that one about taking an easy job, Mum darling, and not overworking. Has Aunt Frances been talking about the great strain we are living under? Alas, poor dear, she little knows that the great strain people live under is a visit from her; I know no-one who isn't absolutely deflated after one of her visits. She is so devastatingly out of touch with real life; all that infuriating nonsense about how much better it is for a guest to keep out of the way and not help. You can't reply that Aunt F needs a rest. And then in she would pop at any hour of the evening and say, 'I am ready for a meal now if it is convenient for you, Joan.' And then a non-stop conversation would start about her prison work; meanwhile Michael and Mina, both with colds, were starting to undress ready for bed upstairs; Joan was on her way up; she would have to get the meal and listen with devastating intelligence to all this being poured out; the telephone bell would go, 'Yes, Mrs. Black, that would be lovely if you would make three dozen jars of Lemon Cheese for the Bring and Buy; yes, I could let you have six eggs if you would call. When? Tomorrow morning then.' Back through into the dining room while Aunt F sits and the table is laid around her; the children start calling upstairs, and now come running down with nothing on. Front door goes. 'No, the Rector is not in; come in will you?' Ten minutes spent hearing about the wife's duodenal ulcer with immense gory details. Back to get the dish out for Aunt F and then upstairs to the children. Down to hear a voice from Aunt F, with feet up in the sitting room, saying, 'I have cleared away, but not washed up.' Why on earth not, one wonders? In fact we found the only way not to get really angry was to realise that the whole thing was a bit pathetic; a desperate clinging to old position; a pathetic rushing through to the kitchen to show Joan how large her post was. A pathetic going round the parish functions saying, 'I am your late Bishop's wife', and not realising it is over 20 years since they were here and really very few, alas, at all interested. And yet other sides of her are so very dear, and we liked and enjoyed her visit; but she was the only real strain we were under and we feel quite recovered now.

Freddy and Joan still had no news of a move, and started to regret the fact that they had turned down Worcester. 'I doubt anything as good will come again', wrote Freddy, 'and we have told Greer Hong Kong is out; there is now a possibility of South Africa as well.' The Bishop wrote to say what a big job they had turned down in Hong Kong, and they agreed to reconsider, subject to seeing a specialist who would advise them of whether or not the climate was suitable for Michael.

On the 18th of November, Freddy again wrote to his parents, telling them that the Bishop of Hong Kong had invited him to be the new Dean of Hong Kong, and Freddy had accepted. Freddy wrote:

> *There has been a battle, apparently, between Hong Kong and Aunt F, waged through the Archbishop of Canterbury; really, the impudence of Aunt F. Hong Kong wrote telling Canterbury he had offered me the job and felt it very important and urging him to urge me to accept; he then consulted Aunt F who told him to urge me on all accounts to stay in England and asked the Archbishop to see me. He has now written very nicely saying he personally has no doubt about the great importance of the job of Dean of Hong Kong and is glad of my decision. But why Aunt F should feel she should interfere I don't know.*

Freddy was excited about going to Hong Kong, but was feeling in a turmoil. He wrote to a friend:

> *I crept into St. Agnes on my own last night to get one or two things ready for the morning, and I suppose to be on my own for a while with God and myself, my dearest Church - (isn't it strange how mere bricks and mortar, which I was leaving for the last time, can captivate one so?). Silly really. I felt the most inexpressible sense of loss, but also the feeling I was doing the right thing in leaving them. I love the bricks, I love the muck. I love the dust. I really do. Above all, I love my dear people here. But I love Michael too so very much.*

John Heywood writes:

> *The last occasion I can recall seeing Freddy 'in the flesh' was at his final Evensong in 1953 when he gave the Blessing. For some reason I was aware both of the solemnity of the occasion but also of the privilege of having been touched by his presence in our community. Hong Kong was another world which I was never likely to see! And so it was a happy coincidence that on 18th November, 2001, just a short while after I had been asked to contribute some reminiscences and reflections on Freddy's life as it had impacted on me, my wife Jane and I found ourselves on the Second Sunday before Advent in St. John's Cathedral in Hong Kong at the 9am Sung Eucharist. Every seat was taken; many were standing. For me Freddy was present.*

9   Dean of Hong Kong

The RMS *Canton* sailed from Southampton on February 6th, 1953. Freddy, Joan, Michael and Mina were seen off by members of the family and friends (including Aunt Frances - who 'wept uncharacteristically and rather too copiously', thought Freddy). She was certainly not one for wearing her heart on her sleeve. Although Freddy and Joan felt 'rather wretched' saying their farewells, they were also very excited. Among the passengers on the *Canton* was a friend from Westcott days, Horace Dammers and his wife, Brenda. They were leaving England as Horace was taking up an appointment in India. (Twenty years later, Horace and Freddy were to work closely together in the Bristol Diocese following the former's appointment as Dean of Bristol.) Freddy wrote to his parents saying that, in First Class, there were some 'quite pleasant Chinese and a few nice English, but most are very dull really. I suspect Tourist is much more interesting.' Horace and Brenda were, in fact, in Tourist Class, but this did not stop the foursome meeting regularly. 'It was fun', said Freddy, 'having them on board.'

Life on the voyage rapidly settled into a routine. Joan and Freddy had a lesson in Cantonese every morning, hoping that they would have quite a grounding in the language by the time they arrived in Hong Kong. However, as will be seen later, they found it difficult to make much progress. Freddy also started working on his first sermon, which was to be broadcast on Hong Kong Radio. (He was later to tell his curates, both in Hong Kong and Portsea, that six weeks must be the minimum time spent on preparing every sermon.)

Freddy and Joan also spent much time playing deck sports. When nearing Bombay on February 21st, Freddy wrote to his parents:

> *The Temples have done quite well in the deck sports: Joan has won the Ladies' Singles Deck Tennis and reached the finals of the Mixed Doubles. I have won the Men's Singles Deck Tennis and the Men's Doubles and reached the finals of the table tennis. We also won a Treasure Hunt the other night which was great fun. Michael was a Jester in the Children's Fancy Dress and Mina won a prize for the best under 3 as Wee Willie Winkie, dressed in a nightdress with a little night cap, made of one of my hankies, bedroom slippers and an altar candle; she looked adorable. Tonight is Gala Night. I hope to get 50 menus from the Steward and go as The Menu, in a tunic made from them.*

Another passenger on the *Canton* was Ron Seaborne, who was going to Hong Kong to join the staff of the Commodore-in-Charge as his Assistant Civil Secretary. He has written that his first meeting with Freddy was 'not one of two minds, but one of three hands, for we met on the deck tennis court of the *Canton* where I caught and threw with my right hand whereas Freddy used his left and right hands with equal dexterity. Later in Hong Kong I found by experience that Freddy played table tennis in the same way, changing his bat from hand to hand and playing every ball with a forehand stroke.' He concludes, 'This action typified Freddy's approach to life - there was nothing ever backhand in what he said or did.'

Another correspondent was, with his wife and two children, also on the passenger list of the *Canton*. Peter Williams, now retired and living in Cornwall, went out to Hong Kong to join the Administrative side of the then Colonial Service in the Hong Kong Government. He writes, 'On board the *Canton* daily life provided many opportunities to get to know people, and we soon realised that the Temple family were unusual in their cohesion, love and happiness.'

On February 26th, nearing Penang, Freddy wrote that the *Canton* moored at Colombo, a city with which Freddy fell in love. 'We went to the Cathedral', he wrote, 'and it was a great thrill to see Grandpapa's throne.' Joan and he also visited Bishop's House and were proud to see some 'quite excellent' pictures of Grandpapa and Uncle Ernest hanging on the walls. Having then spent some time with Robin and Henrietta Woods in Singapore (Robin was Archdeacon of Singapore and was later to become Dean of Windsor and Bishop of Worcester; Freddy and he often discussed together the problems of the Church in the Far East, and each was grateful for the other's presence in the same part of the world), Freddy wrote

The youthful Dean of Hong Kong.

on March 11th to say that they had arrived safely in Hong Kong. At the quayside they were greeted by the Bishop and a large gathering of 'worthies and notables'. Freddy wrote that there were reporters everywhere, and innumerable press photographs were taken. 'It all looks like being great fun; I think the opportunities are going to be vast.'

Freddy and Joan found Hong Kong to be a 'breathtakingly beautiful' place. They had heard many much-travelled people say, when they learnt of Freddy's appointment as Dean, that they knew of no place more beautiful; they were captivated and entranced by the hills, the views, the trees, the sea, the islands, the distant mountains and all the activity of the harbour, with the liners, the sampans and the junks, with their graceful sails, all jostling each other on the water. The Dean's House was the oldest in the Colony. It was vast; when Michael Fisher SSF

St. John's Cathedral, Hong Kong.

came to conduct a Mission in the Colony they invited 2,500 to meet him in the house and garden; luckily only 500 came. The rooms were large with high ceilings and big doors, with a big garden too, which was a great luxury in Hong Kong where, in Freddy's words, '2 million people cling to the side of a rock.'

Officially, no more refugees were coming out of China since the Communist take-over, but they still did, and with the birth rate ever rising, it was estimated that there would be three million in the colony within ten years. Water was the main problem; residents depended on the rainfall and by the end of the dry winter were down to four - sometimes three - hours of water a day.

Because of all the refugees, unemployment was a major problem, and so, as always when there is unemployment, labour was very cheap. Buildings shot up rapidly because developers could very easily get as much labour as they needed. Excellent domestic servants could be acquired for £8 a month and a room; and out of that they purchased their own food. Freddy and Joan had a first-rate cook, Ah Kaai, who ran the house and did the shopping; they never knew what they were going to eat at the next meal. He was always cheerful and willing. Ah Hing waited at table and cleaned downstairs and looked after Michael and Mina when Freddy and Joan were out. Ah Haan was the wash-amah; he did all the washing and mending and cleaned upstairs. Ah Ho was a boy who did the polishing, went on errands and brought Michael back from school. When Freddy explained the domestic arrangements to his mother in a letter, he concluded, 'We realise what luxury and ease it must seem to you all at home; our only justification is that we do fill our time completely in other ways.'

On May 16th, 1963, four years after leaving Hong Kong, Joan wrote the following for the *Portsmouth Evening News*, which gives a flavour of one aspect of life in the colony:

Our house was the oldest in Hong Kong. We had to live in it because it went with the job. We loved to live in it because it was spacious and airy, gracious and serene - certainly not quiet, because the constant rattle and bustle, honking and shunting came up from the busy street below, and provided an essentially Hong Kong background even to our most peaceful moments.

From the tall great windows thrown open to the heat and brilliant sunshine we looked out over beautiful flowering plants to a lawn on which stood sentinel three tall palm trees bent by the winds of the typhoons - the Three Old Men, as they were called.

'If anyone wants me I am going shopping: I shall be back in an hour,' I said to Ah Kaai, our cook and the No. 1 on our staff of four. To employ people as servants was almost a Christian duty to help with the fearful unemployment problem.

Our house was large and the job called for much entertaining; we had four servants and they and the gardener, Fa Wong (King of the Flowers) and their families lived in our half basement which opened on to the ground floor on one side of the house. I remember realising one night, as I went to sleep, that the roof sheltered 21 souls.

Out I went into the heat down the steeply sloping drive edged with enormous pots of chrysanthemums, poinsettias or whatever was in season. For a moment, there was the shady relief of some trees, then … into the sun and across the road, hot beneath the thin soles of my sandals, to the steps which took me down to one of the most famous streets in Hong Kong with shops selling embroidery, ivory, and all the other delicate and ingenious merchandise for which the Chinese are famous.

On the steps, I want you to pause with me because it is here, every time I leave our lovely home, that I am assailed with the tension and doubt - almost guilt - which must be the lot of all seeing people in Hong Kong.

There are about 60 steps down to the shops; they are steep, and halfway up they divide, continuing their upward way on each narrow side, but in the centre they form a platform at the back of which is a door, padlocked now, which led to a wartime store.

At first we went as blithely as the heat would let us, up the steps, the children taking one side each at the division and seeing who could race first to the top or who would be impeded by some heavily-laden soul toiling up their side, or a crowd of schoolchildren, or a mother weighed down by a baby on her back and another little one clinging to her black-trousered leg.

After we had been living there a little while we noticed signs of life starting on the platform, pathetic little scraps of hardboard, waterproof paper and suchlike, and gradually against one corner a little structure grew, just tall enough for a man to crawl into and sleep, held together by string and hope.

Along the wall beside, slowly collected the elements of a home: an old enamel bowl, handle-less cup and a toothbrush was the bathroom; a cooking pot or two, and a tiny stove, was the kitchen.

We gazed at it in horror; surely it must be some rather exaggerated exhibit to try to show how some Chinese live, to arouse the pity and anger of more fortunate people, who would be spurred to take action.

One day, as we went down, leaning over the wall inquisitively and half fearfully to see this little show, we saw that the cooking pot was steaming on the stove; and there, amid these pathetic possessions, squatted an elderly man.

In the brilliant heat he squatted, spectacles on nose, a tattered but very clean shirt protecting his thin back from the sun, his black Chinese trousers rolled over the knees, a very 'holey' pair of plimsolls stopping his feet from burning on the hot steps.

He held an old hammer in one hand, and beside him was a tin full of bent nails which he was laboriously hammering into shape. Many passers-by stopped to watch him, but he was utterly engrossed - if we were rude enough to stare that was our affair; he was just getting on with the business of keeping body and soul together.

He had great dignity, this man; he never begged; he seemed to have found an inner calm. He kept himself alive by collecting bent nails from all the building sites and squatting for hours on his platform home, hammering them gently into shape again. Gradually, he collected a broom, bucket and a few other household articles which were neatly stored away - and his little platform was swilled down daily. His life was very public, but he seemed unaware; in the evening he sat, very often reading a book, which was kept in his little shack. When it rained, water streamed down the walls and poured in between his bits of hardboard; next day a few tattered bits were hung out to dry.

If I told you that this had been a man of property in China, owning some wealthy holdings wanted by the Communists, having to abandon even his wife and family and flee to Hong Kong, it only makes it sound more of a tale of fiction; but it is true. What is more important is that he was our next door neighbour, and down the road was another like him; up the hillsides were thousands like him. On the rooftops, in just such hardboard shacks, lived another 6,000.

Joan concluded this article by writing, 'From your houses of warmth, space and comfort, from your tables of enough food, you go shopping past other homes like yours. Can you really feel discontented? Do you still want that little bit more?'

Freddy found his job fascinating; he discovered that life at St. John's Cathedral was very similar to that at a large parish church in England about thirty years previously: it was packed for Matins, cars rolling up to the doors, and everyone dressed smartly. However he was convinced that most who attended were 'genuine' ('but having said that,' he wrote to F.R. Barry, Bishop of Southwell, 'how presumptuous of me even to judge whether or not I think someone's faith is real') and that Cathedral life was reasonably healthy - 'though not nearly as healthy as it should be.' On his first Easter Sunday in Hong Kong, although Matins was packed, there were also five hundred communicants. All the same, 'this is not good enough', Freddy told the Cathedral Council.

At about the same time Freddy wrote a letter to his eldest sister, Beatrice, in the course of which he told her he had been reading some fascinating diaries and accounts of early nineteenth-century clergy. 'Really,' he wrote, 'it's a wonder the Church of England has survived.' Apparently one splendid incumbent hired someone else to take his services and had his butler stand at the door of the Church and offer 'Matins in Church or a glass of beer in the Rectory with the Rector?' He wondered what would happen if he were to give that option to the Cathedral Matins congregation; he thought it would be an interesting little experiment.

The Cathedral choir of about fifty was good. When Gerald Knight, Director of the Royal School of Church Music, visited Hong Kong on a world tour of RSCM affiliated choirs, he wrote to Freddy that St. John's Cathedral Choir was 'probably the best I have heard since leaving England over six weeks ago.' (He did not, however, say how many he had listened to.) One major problem, however, was that the choir was for ever changing; most people stayed in Hong Kong for a comparatively short period of time before returning to England. Continuity was a big difficulty in general: the Cathedral congregation was ever-changing. Freddy found the congregation 'challenging.' 'It is, on the whole,' he wrote to his parents, 'an intelligent and influential congregation of high-up Government and businessmen.'

Soon after he arrived in Hong Kong, Freddy showed how ignorant he was of the quaintly Edwardian nature of life in the Colony when the ADC to the Governor arrived at the Dean's House and said, 'Mr. Dean, there will be a visitor, Lady Gascoigne, staying the weekend at Government House. Please reserve five seats in His Excellency's pew.' 'Five?' Freddy asked: 'His Excellency, Lady Grantham, Lady Gascoigne and yourself. That's four.' The ADC looked at Freddy with a pained expression and said, 'Mr. Dean, His Excellency's hat.' The Colonial Governor's ceremonial hat was of course a topee with enormous plumes and needed a seat to itself.

There was a delightful occasion, fairly near the beginning of Freddy and Joan's time in Hong Kong, when Freddy invited the Archdeacon not only to preach, but also to pronounce the Blessing at the end of the service. It was a hot day. Freddy wrote to his parents,

After this morning's service, Joan and I went back to the Dean's House; for some reason the dear Archdeacon couldn't join us for lunch. We shut the front door, went into the verandah room and both, simultaneously, flung ourselves on chairs   131

and burst out in hysterics. It was very unclerical I suppose. But we were laughing because we had witnessed the most incredible sight when the Archdeacon was giving his blessing. He raised his right hand, made the sign of the cross and pronounced the blessing. Nothing unusual about that, you might think. But meanwhile his left hand was extremely busy with his fan. Both Joan and I tried to practise doing it ourselves, but failed miserably. It's almost a physical impossibility, but he somehow managed it.

A while later, Freddy wrote to his mother, 'The complete change from the kind of life we led in Manchester is a bit bewildering. It's a completely different way of both living and ministry.' Freddy and Joan were invited out to innumerable cocktail and dinner parties; when they first arrived in the colony they found they were invited out almost every night of the week. Freddy and Joan talked seriously together and decided to go ahead with this style of living for six months, at the end of which time they thought the invitations would start drying up anyway. It was not to be. During the whole time they were in Hong Kong, invitations poured in and the drinks flowed. Freddy decided in the end that it would be both churlish and unwise to refuse invitations, as it was one certain way of getting alongside the congregation outside the environs of the Cathedral. Joan put it to Freddy very forcefully one evening that the rich have souls as well as the poor. What, of course, they felt guilty about was the desperate poverty all around them. From a reading of many hundreds of his letters sent from Hong Kong to his family and others it is obvious that Freddy was never at ease with this aspect of the place; but that does not mean he did not enjoy himself at least some of the time. He wrote to his parents, after the family had been in Hong Kong a month or two, 'The social round goes on in its giddy way and I suppose it will never end. We feel as if we're caught up in some Hollywood film, and that we'll wake up sometime to discover it's all a dream.'

On May 4th, Freddy and Joan went to a party at Government House. Afterwards, Freddy wrote to his mother, 'I decided to take the plunge and got into gaiters for the first time. We had no button hook, and so it all had to be done with a kitchen skewer; we giggled a bit and were both quite exhausted by the time both gaiters were on. Joan expressed herself well-pleased with the comely shape of my legs. I'm not so sure.'

On another occasion, in October, Freddy had a Sunday off and he, Joan and the children were invited to a weekend house party by an influential member of the Hong Kong business community and his wife. Freddy wrote home,

An enormous car with chauffeur swirled Joan and the children away on Friday; I came on later after a meeting of the choir. The vast staff tumble over themselves to see that one doesn't lift a finger to put a lump of sugar into coffee or anything quite as exhausting as that. I could not live with it and it is awful in Hong Kong really with the ghastly poverty there is. Enormous rooms are in different colours with bathrooms to match (down to pink lavatory paper which I thought was just too much.) A lovely tennis court is kept in perfect condition; this was mowed, rolled and marked for us in the morning, and then two ball boys appeared for the game, lest we had to stoop down to retrieve the balls.

Soon after, they went to a Ball as guests; it was a vast affair with more than 500 people present; tickets cost $45 without drinks - 'all totally monstrous,' wrote Freddy, 'in a place with such poverty. But I must bide my time. It was very dressy and so I wore my gaiters again, which intrigued people much; it seemed a very proper dress to dance 'Sir Roger and the Lancers'.

In return, of course, it was expected that the Dean and his wife should entertain at home. Indeed, they entertained a lot, though Freddy assured his mother that their standard was very abstemious. They began by holding dinner parties. Although they had a dining table that seated twenty-eight, they felt that, however many such parties they held, it would still take far too long to entertain all those they wished to. They hit on the idea of having of having after-dinner coffee parties. In Freddy's own words to his sister Beatrice, 'We can keep in touch with far more people - and it's far cheaper as they eat so little after a good dinner.' Whenever there was any difficulty in making conversation with some of the rather more nervous Chinese, Freddy would open the cage of their budgerigar, Frances, who would lightly fly around the room making both friends and a good topic of conversation. In this way, Freddy and Joan entertained over thirty people three times a month. After the first of their coffee parties, Freddy and Joan were pleased to receive a rather gushing letter from a Lady Geddes, which included the sentence, 'This is quite the most civilised form of entertaining that goes on in the Colony at the moment; you avoid stuffing your guests with far too large and expensive a dinner and avoid the crush of a large cocktail party; just the right number to talk to and enjoy.' Freddy was amused that Press photographers used to come and roam about all evening at some of their parties, taking photographs of the guests. 'We've come a long way from Arnold, complete with tin bath, dishing out mugs of coffee', wrote Freddy home, 'but we can honestly say that we do so miss those wonderful days; there was something more 'real' about our life then; some of the dear folk we meet here at our parties are a bit like meringues: one crumbling bite, and that's all there is of them and a lot of air; whereas the people of Arnold were like rock buns - far more substance and meat to them when you bite them.' A little bit of a confused sentence - and doubtless his great-grandfather, Archbishop Trench, would have had something to say about Freddy's phraseology - but we get the gist.

Freddy still battled with trying to learn Cantonese, but both he and Joan found it a difficult language. The tone in which one said a word could often totally change its meaning. There were no less than nine ways of saying the same word, the inflection in the speaker's voice giving it different meanings. The Bishop himself, even after twenty-five years as the Diocesan, struggled with the language, and never quite mastered it, though Freddy believed that nobody ever had the courage to tell him that when he said the Lord's Prayer in Cantonese at a service, he invariable began not with 'Our Father, who art in heaven,' but 'Our Pig, who art in heaven'. The Chinese, inscrutable as always, grew accustomed to this and accepted it as a matter of course. Freddy wrote to one of his Balliol friends, 'I reckon I am good at languages, as you know, but Cantonese is quite different from, say, Arabic or Hindustani; this is, I think, the main factor of the almost total barrier between the two communities here: not hostility: the Europeans are friendly and like the Chinese they meet, but they just don't get near the majority. So the two lives and two societies exist together, totally separate.'

We turn to the children. Michael and Mina were happy; in his letters home, Freddy frequently referred to Mina as 'adorable'. Joan started a Nursery School at the Dean's House. There was a great demand for such schools in the Colony. On September 14th, 1953, Joan opened the school for nine children, including Mina, between the ages of three and five, from nine till noon each morning. Freddy backed her to the hilt, though he did express reservations about the workload she was taking on, all on top of the duties she was expected to undertake as the Dean's wife. Freddy and Joan found to their amusement that, with a fee of $45 a month, they had undercut similar schools; the others charged, on average, $75. There was a waiting list for parents anxious to enrol their little ones in the school - this not because the fees were relatively cheap, but rather that there was a certain cachet to be enjoyed in telling others that little Belinda was going to school at the Dean's House. Partly to Freddy's relief, the school only lasted a year; pressure of other work proved too great.

Michael enjoyed himself at the Peak School. The Peak School enjoyed having him. By all accounts he was an unusually mature, caring and bright little boy. He was obviously greatly loved by his teacher. 'I don't think,' she wrote, ten days after he had started school, 'that I have ever met such an outstanding little chap. He's so extraordinarily articulate, immensely humble and loving and cares deeply for the other boys and girls with whom he shares the school. Thank you so much for sending him to us. I have no doubt that Michael, as he grows older, will be making a huge impact on the lives of all those with whom he comes into contact.'

Since moving to Hong Kong, Michael's health had improved immeasurably; the future looked bright. Freddy and Joan could not have been more happy. On the first day of June, 1954, Freddy wrote to his parents: 'Poor little Mike goes in [to hospital] to have his tonsils out on Thursday; he suddenly got enormous glands on the neck and has apparently the largest tonsils the doctor has ever seen on a child. We hope to get him back on Saturday.' Freddy and Joan planned a little party with some of his special friends for that afternoon.

134
The tragedy that followed is perhaps best told by Freddy himself, in letters he

wrote home to his parents. The first letter was written on June 4th; it is postmarked 6pm - so was written sometime in the afternoon.

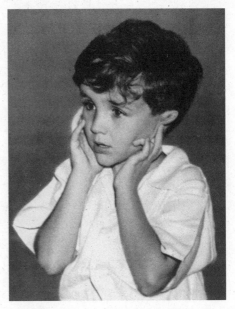

Michael Frederick Temple, Freddy and Joan's son. This was taken at a wedding reception in Hong Kong; Michael had just been told that the best man was about to propose a toast. Expecting a 'bang', he placed his fingers in his ears. This photograph was taken a few months before Michael died.

You will by now have heard that our precious darling Michael left us this morning so desperately suddenly. He had had swollen glands for some time and the doctors found some of that horrid bug Joan had in his throat [Joan had been suffering from a severe infection since Christmas] *and so they urged taking the tonsils out. And he went in so happily yesterday evening, very brave, as thoughtful and unselfish as ever; Mina loathed him going in and said at lunch, 'I think he is going to die.' This morning dear Dorothy Crossley, the charming X-ray person there, rang us at 8.15 to say Michael would be going in next and that he was quite happy and cheerful; we started to worry when at 10 he was still in the theatre, and then again at 10.30. And then at 11 they rang to say he had collapsed under the anaesthetic; they did artificial respiration for two hours, but no good. It is quite unbelievable at the moment; but Joan and I both admit how we had moments when we felt we would not have Michael for very long; there was something so special and so good and unselfish about him; he was almost too good for this world. Joan is being wonderfully brave; far better than I am; and Ann* [Freddy's youngest sister, who was living with them at the time] *is being sweet. Oh the plans; oh the emptiness now without him. But still we must be thankful for six wonderful years. Poor little Mina, so miserable at leaving him there and now alone; it needed such courage for both of us to have her to be with Michael, and Joan was so ill with both of them. How I wish we were not so far away at a time like this.*

June 8

Thank you so much for your letters; oh how I wish we were together just now; I suppose the ache gets less in time, but now we are back in our own house it all seems unbearable at moments. Before answering the absolute mass of letters, I should

135

think already over 300, it is to you we must write so that you can share a little more in it all.

God is very wonderful; he gave us absolute serenity for the service; both were quite dry-eyed and full of faith; and that has been something; many people have written or said they have been tremendously inspired. I was at all services on Sunday and preached at nine and felt a power not my own giving a force to what I said; the Bishop preached well at eleven to a packed church. Joan has been quite incredible; as Ann said, 'Madonna-like' in her calm in public, with an incredible beauty even in the suffering in her face. She suggested, after Mike's body had been brought down into the Bishop's Chapel late at night (there had been some talk of an inquest as he died in the theatre), that we go and see the two doctors and cheer them up, and again with them we were both given an incredible calm and peace; they were shattered and their two wives had been crying; the Bishop seems to have been very struck by us doing that and mentioned it in his sermon.

But when alone we howl together; and then poor little Mina, who has understood completely, says, 'Please don't cry; it makes it so much harder for me not to cry.' She came back from being with friends on Friday and suddenly asked, 'Where's Michael?' We told her he was now with Jesus and she went on playing; and then suddenly turned to us and said, 'It's not true; he hasn't gone to Jesus; I don't like you when you don't tell the truth.' And then rushed upstairs and howled when she realised it was true. But now she says bravely, 'I know Michael is happier now and is with Jesus all the time.' But the agony of bathing only one for Joan and all the toys and all the plans.

Some of the letters are very wonderful and all HK seems to have been stirred; I will get copies done and send them soon by air. The Bishop is going to scatter the ashes at sea this week. Joan is so wonderful, having no regrets now; I can't help gnawing at myself; he was so well; why did we not try something else first, such a happy unselfish little fellow (oh and he had become so good, so breathtakingly understanding this last year). We tucked him up in bed that night at the hospital; very particular to be tucked in both sides; Joan did the one, I did the other; quite brave; only one comment, 'Are they very sharp things they put down your throat?' He had developed the sweetest little nod of the head when saying 'yes.' And so we waved him goodnight.

We heard in the morning that he was quite happy until he went in; and then we rang at ten; still in the theatre; then again at ten thirty; still there, and we were then sick with fear. At eleven came the message that we were to come as quickly as possible; how we prayed then that breath might come back into that little body and heart. Then in came two doctors; Eberle, our own, with face quite distraught, and young George Watson, the surgeon, crying. Joan, quite calm, asked to be led to him, turning to the Matron to ask if he looked all right; there in a little room we turned back a sheet to see that lovely head quite still; I shall never forget Joan kneeling down beside him and saying in a such a gentle, almost reproachful, voice, 'Oh

Pooky (her little nickname for him) darling, must you leave us so soon; can't you come back to us? If I put my hand on you there, couldn't you breathe?' And then she drew back the sheet a little more and looked at those little arms and said, 'Your little bitten nails; I never cured you of that, did I?'

And so we left him; one can believe now that he is so much happier; the gospel of Whit Sunday is tremendous; do read it; I could not believe anything could fit better: 'If ye loved me, ye would rejoice that I go to the Father.' We brought his body down to the Bishop's Chapel that evening, where all was peace and quiet and lovely. Six of the Chinese clergy carried the coffin in and the Cathedral was packed and there was the most profound feeling everywhere. Ann was beside us and such a help in everything. Flowers everywhere and police outriders to escort us to the ferry and over; funny little Mike, how thrilled he must have been by it all; we feel so much of it was not just for us; so many letters say genuinely how much people loved him; little Saint Michael I do genuinely feel. We sang his favourite hymn, 'Onward Christian Soldiers' and then Joan and my favourite hymn, which we had at our wedding and I have at my inductions, 'O Thou who camest from above.' Look it up; very lovely; and we went out singing 'Jesus lives' with great triumph; every candle in the place lit, flowers everywhere, no tolling of bells but triumphant peals, and God helped us to live up to it and it has helped many others apparently; the head of the Hong Kong Bank's wife, as she broke down, leaving Joan, said, 'I'd do anything, absolutely anything, for you both; but then you know all Hong Kong is turning round in circles wondering how to help.' We think so much of you all, having to hear it so suddenly, but no more suddenly than we did; all our love, sympathy and prayers; don't worry for us; Joan can genuinely say now she wouldn't have him back now if she could, as he must be so much happier. I think I can say that too.

June 13: Our wedding anniversary

How we wish we could all be together at this time; there is so much we long to share and I am afraid that hundreds of letters have had to be answered here and so we have not been good about those home. Thank you so much for all yours; what a lovely poem of Grandpapa Trench; it is true: it is the dull ache in the morning that is worst, but we are both getting so much better now; every day more and larger periods of utter serenity and trust flood over one, upheld by all the love and prayers, which does make the agonising gaping void seem less. Alan Eberle, our doctor, came in this morning and comforted us a lot; they took every precaution; ether and oxygen alone were used; he never uses injections for a child; it is .04 percent of cases that collapse like this and they usually have either an enlarged thymus gland or spleen; Michael had been screened and both were perfect; the anaesthetic went perfectly and then suddenly as they put him back on the stretcher to take him to his bed, his heart went; they did everything they could; everything was immediately at hand. The tonsils were quite vast and had they not been taken out, Eberle says he might have choked if they had swollen any more, and if left with that bug in he

137

would slowly become anaemic like Joan and all the bronchial trouble would have started again.

So we feel quite clear humanly everything was done as it should have been, that Michael was allowed to win his place in the next world without pain and so soon because he was so good; letter after letter from different parents say 'He was quite without exception the most charming child I have ever known' and 'He was so lovely and unselfish'. Letters pour in from Manchester and Newark, people devastated and remembering all his little doings and sayings; we will in time make an album of scraps and photos and all his things; a little notebook of all the places I was to take him to see on our leave which he had learnt in history, the New Forest, Hadrian's Wall and Westminster Abbey, etc. But we don't regret for him; such much bigger plans and learning are his now; he is free of time and space and we feel him very close when we are being unselfish. And Mina has been so good this week as if part of him has gone into her; she has been so brave and done her best to cheer us up. People have been wonderful here; I will get more copies of letters done to send you, lovely poems and quotations.

The following day, June 14th, Ann wrote to her mother and father, 'Little Mina has been so sweet, realising absolutely. "Michael is luckier than we are; he can see Jesus all the time" or "I wish Michael were here - he can see us, but it would be nice if we could see him too."'

I am sure Joan and I will be more use now to others; in fact today a young wife with a small baby has just heard that her husband in the Volunteer Air Force has died crashing into the harbour, and she has so little faith, poor thing. Joan and I hope to be absolutely back to normal next week doing everything; this week has been all letters. We are not sure about our holiday; we will have got used to this house without him but it might be a strain always to see that happy little figure running ahead down to the beach and helping Mina down the steps at the bottom. It is difficult to realise what normal life was like before this; but I am sure that with real prayer and trust we can use this to make a greater good than if it had never happened, for that is the heart and meaning of the Cross; for Michael it is all wonderful as long as we are not sad; that can be the only thing to upset the darling; far more even than Mina, he hated to see us sad. And I am sure Joan and I can be of more use now, though I ache for her even more than for myself, the constant little reminders at every turn, especially the sacred evening time when two little figures listened intently to long stories read and then prayers, Michael's always so varied and unselfish.

One mother told us a nice story: 'Did you play with Michael at school today?' 'Yes, but it is very difficult to play with Michael; everyone wants to play with Michael.' His Memorial Home we are going to build to house 17 orphans out near the lovely bay at Taipo Orphanage is doing well; we have 5000 dollars; we shall easily get the six to build the home; I am quite staggered; it is something like £400; it has all come in countless bits from hundreds of folk. Every bit of our love; in many ways it is harder for you as you are not only aching for Michael not being here, but bearing our pain as well and that is so hard. We had a little sob this morning to think in seven years our little son had come and gone on.

June 23

Of course there are periodic shattering moments when the finality of this temporary parting dawns more and more; I suddenly went into the drawing room the other day to find darling Joan sitting on the sofa, tears streaming down her face; she was correcting the Sunday School register, and had just drawn a line right through all the Sundays for the rest of the book; my eye followed back across to the left hand page to the long column of children to find it against 'Michael Temple, The Dean's House.' A column that hadn't a single miss till then. His Memorial Home for Orphans can now be started as the fund stands at 7,500 dollars, nearly £500; the house will look out over the most lovely view in all Hong Kong.

June 29

We have already answered 500 letters personally and also kept everything going here which seems to get more and more as the life of the Cathedral grows all the time. I had a bad bug and spent the day in bed, alone in the Deanery. I had a good day in a way going through all the letters and looking at the photos; a wallow on my own with a good many tears; but comforting in a way. Joan and I still cannot look at the photographs for long. There is one that is exactly as we last saw him when we had waved goodbye and crept back to see what he was doing, and he was just gazing across at the other children in the ward just wondering what to say first.

While on the launch picnic yesterday, Joan and the Solicitor General's wife were changing to bathe in the little cabin; they were silent, and then the wife said, 'It's funny, but I don't see how life can ever be the same in Hong Kong without that wonderful little boy.' Admiral Gladstone, Second in Command in the Far East, writes (he has just returned from a trip and wrote within an hour of return): 'You and I know there is a purpose though it's hard to see what it is. Can it be that Heaven was falling short of its quota of children? For it will be a very sorry place if there are none there.' A new, rather quaint, idea.

Nearly a month has gone now; sometimes one just wonders if it has just been a delicious dream having him at all. We will get some pictures of the Orphanage soon. We feel Michael will be so thrilled to think of seventeen orphans in his own Home with his photo smiling down at them.

In the July edition of the *St. John's Review* (the Cathedral magazine), Freddy wrote the following:

Never in our whole life together have my wife and I been so conscious of the goodness of God as we have been this last month; we have been astonished at the tremendous sympathy, love and prayers that have upheld us not only from countless friends here but also from dear relations and friends in other parishes at home; and there have been moments when we have felt carried up and along in great serenity and trust; and it is those moments which matter and are real, moments when one felt the tremendous power of prayer made on our behalf; it is true that there have been and are many, many moments when human selfishness and self-pity make the dreadful gap in our family an almost unbearable ache and life a misery. And then we realise the tremendous care and devotion of the doctors and nurses; how every care was taken and how much they shared our grief. And we thank God for the gaiety and happiness with which he went into hospital, that he was allowed to slip through the door of death into a closer life with God so easily, possibly because he had learnt already so much unselfishness. For him we must have no regrets; all plans and schemes we human parents had are now in God's hands; and for ourselves we can, in those good moments, see in this the touch of the good and loving God who quite rightly can be very stern. How shallow and trivial men can be unless they know the depths; to preach the Cross in comfort is counterfeit; and we both hope and pray that the stern and loving God will now make us a little more able to help and sustain others in the depths of life, to make words and sympathy more real and to guide others to the foot of the suffering on the Cross where above all we can find the power and goodness and love of God.

A letter written by the Bishop of Hong Kong to Stephen Verney, dated June 23rd, ran as follows:

Forgive my writing.

But - what he is doing in Hong Kong is so incredible in its direct and simple and gallant and gay spirituality - that it is difficult to see the inner spring of it; the exterior is so spontaneous and natural (this refers to before Michael's death - not only after it.)

Could you, without Freddy knowing of course, try to collect the letters he has written to others as he did to you about Michael. I think some of the secret will be in them and perhaps later - when his biography is written - they may show the secret.

Something is happening here at the level of the parish priest in his job - that I'm afraid - to my rebellious heart - seems far far far more significant than Harringay. [The Bishop was making reference to the 1954 Billy Graham Mission.]

He has often spoken of you. I rejoice in this direct contact.

One of the joys of being old is the dearness of the young.

The Good God keep you always.

Percy Smith, was to write in the same vein in 2001:

> Freddy and my time together in Hong Kong was comparatively short, but the one outstanding memory is what I can only call 'the supernatural grace' with which Freddy and Joan accepted the sudden and unexpected death of their young son. This was truly astonishing and an inspiration not only to myself but to everybody who knew them at the time.

Freddy's next letter home was on July 7:

> On Sunday Abbott ['Bunny' Abbott was a prominent member of the congregation.] presented a chalice and paten in memory of Michael. I love using it, but it still seems strange to be someone who has lost a darling little boy. Every time I visit the Matilda [the hospital in which Michael died] I go past the little room to which we were led to see him.

July 14

We find our depression depends almost exactly on how nervously exhausted we both are through continually meeting people and giving out brightness and gaiety all the time. We had 60 people in after Evensong on Sunday. Joan bustled round so brightly among them; then a moment later she disappeared. I went into the darkened drawing room to find her on the sofa, sobbing her heart out with his photo in her hands. Of course we are quite happy about him and know that for him it is such a minute moment before we see him again; he is seeing us all the time. We both know the grief we get now is directly related to weariness and so we shall be much better when we are rested.

Do you know this good illustration we have just discovered in a book I am reading? We have found it most helpful. Perhaps we may come nearest to essential truth about the matter (the earthly end of a human story) by a simple human parable such as this. Imagine a fevered little child in bed in a darkened room. Now try to describe that little child's 'world.' There are the aching limbs, the throbbing head, the pillows and the bedclothes; strange shadows in the darkened room cast by a flickering fire or perhaps a hidden night-light; dim shapes of furniture or pictures on the walls; the rain beating on the window; and outside, black night and the dark unknown. That, and that only, is the child's 'world.' And now imagine that a strange and sudden thing occurs. The electric light is switched on. The shadows vanish, the dim shapes disappear, the old 'world' has passed away; and there sitting watching all the time, close by, is 'Mother.' She had never really gone away, but the child's first thought is, 'She has come.' And with her coming all things have become new. The old world of shadows has gone, swallowed up in the new reality of wonder and love.

The little child is our humanity, fevered and ill at ease, conscious only of dim shadows and flickering lights, of mystery and unintelligible pain, of homelessness and night. And then something happens, something for which we mortals have no name, but the one and only thing which matters - and men become aware of things unseen, of spirit, love, reality and God. He has been there all the time, for Christ is never an absentee.

September 11

Life is very busy and both Joan and I find ourselves psychologically lame now as if a limb had been amputated. One can get about and do the job and live, but it is all more of a business and more exhausting; especially after a busy evening where one has been occupied all the time and one comes back to the quiet house; two children make a noise; one doesn't.

September 20

You must be sad about Geoffrey Taverner [Freddy's parents' Parish Priest in Sussex who had died], but how lovely for him; I found it impossible to pray that he should live when you first let us know as he has always struck me as so indescribably sad and lonely since her death; they must be so very happy again now. It is odd how this intense certainty of Michael's happiness and greater freedom and opportunity now makes one's prayers for people when ill very difficult; for the young and fit certainly one prays that the world may have them for a period longer; but for the lonely and old it is difficult not to want to speed everyone fast through the door into something better.

September 27

I have just come back from the funeral of a 12 day old baby; a very distressing affair as the mother and father were quite hysterical in the Cathedral; there is one little girl aged six and she they brought to the service; I felt so worried for her as she saw her parents like this that directly after the service I went straight up to her and asked her if she would like to come and play with a little girl who had a brother in heaven too; I thought it vital that she get into a sane and happy atmosphere about death. And so we have her up here and have shown her photos of Michael and talked to her about him and Mina has taken her under her wing very well; poor little Mina, taking on the task of consoling bereaved children rather young in life.

December 27

It has been a very full and very tiring Christmas with a Sunday directly afterwards; but it has been better attended than any ever before. Some of it was sheer agony for Joan and me; the two children's services particularly; one never knew how moving certain hymns could be and how much certain things would mean. I feel someone ought to write to the Queen and tell her how many of her people have some sadness at Christmas and she should not just talk of the happiness of family *reunion. That evening we had a party of people who were finding Christmas difficult and as they listened they all became a little sadder; I think she ought to add some little word possibly; it is only when one knows oneself that it is all opened up.*

April 4 (1955)

Mike's birthday was in many ways more difficult almost than when he died as one was so stunned then; but people were very kind. It was of course on Wednesday. I had to teach at the Peak School which was difficult as I came out just as all the parents were collecting up their children. Mina was very sweet and all the way up the bank on her way to school she kept turning round and calling out to Joan, 'Be sure, now, you don't cry while I am at school.' And she had quite firmly decided a few days before that we must not treat it as an ordinary day as she was certain Michael was having the most wonderful birthday in heaven and 'all the angels will be in their party frocks.' This was not decided on without cost to her as Joan discovered too sweetly on the Tuesday night when she had put her to bed; she always buries down under the clothes; and later Joan thought she heard sobs and went out to the landing where her bed is now and turned back the bedclothes to find a very sodden little face not wanting Joan to know that she had been crying but very sad that Michael was not going to have his birthday party here but in heaven.

June 3

We like to think of tomorrow as Michael's 2nd birthday into a great and wonderful life full of excitement and happiness.

It was at this point that a new great joy came to the family: the birth of a second son.

July 15 - the day on which Stephen was born

We hope this is a new start to our life again; Stephen can never be a replacement for darling Michael whom we can never forget any day of our lives; but with another boy the memory can be a happy one and also we feel the saint in the family is gaily and unselfishly in heaven standing for the eternal things in our midst all the time; how happy and thrilled he must be.

When Stephen appeared the surgeon said, 'All Hong Kong rejoices with you today as it wept with you a year ago'.

November 19

Michael's Home at Taipo opened today. It was a wonderful day, though tinged with sadness. We are so proud of our little Mike. I know he'll enjoy looking after his little ones here.

What of the general effect on Hong Kong of Michael's death? It was certainly tremendous and the news made the front-page headline of the *South China Morning Post*, which in itself says much, considering that the Temple family had only been in the Colony for a little over a year. Such was the affection and regard for them, and the impact they had made on the lives of so many. There was a general, genuine, outpouring of grief. Some of the letters and poems received by Freddy and Joan are included in an appendix of this book.

Freddy was to write later that many of the final total of over nine hundred letters received (this does not count the large number of 'In Sympathy' cards, usually sent by people who felt totally inadequate to make comments of their own) were 'simplistic' in their comments - 'but in a funny sort of way they too were a great comfort.' He then made the comment: 'It really didn't matter to Joan or I whether we believed the simplicities expressed; we knew that what they were reaching out to say was well-intentioned. Indeed, it would have been more comforting for us if, on Whit Sunday, R.O. [Bishop Hall] hadn't concentrated quite so much on the element of Chance; somehow it felt to us both, especially Joan, to be a little cruel to express it quite so forcibly at a time when we were both obviously feeling so desperately raw.'

Life had to go on, and Freddy and Joan immediately plunged themselves back into the duties of the Cathedral. From one point of view this was probably the most therapeutic thing for them to do. Freddy and Joan, outwardly, continued to be the perfect host and hostess. They resumed their coffee parties and, at the end of June, a very successful buffet supper for forty five people, mostly generals and diplomats. Joan and Freddy felt a bit impish and thought they would shake them all up a bit, so they made them perform biblical charades afterwards. Freddy wrote home, 'The French Consul was too sweet; he had to do Judas; he looked around his group, looked at one moustached man and told me afterwards, "I looked at him and said, 'Non, positively Non'" - and then he planted a kiss on the cheek of the prettiest young wife there; rather too Gallic, I thought, for the Dean's House.'

When Joan and Freddy arrived in Hong Kong the Sunday School at the Cathedral numbered thirty children. Joan took it over. In May, 1954, Freddy was able to tell the Cathedral Council that the number on roll had risen to 200; in April, 1955 to 240, and by May 1956 numbers had rocketed to over 300. Joan gathered around her a band of excellent, enthusiastic teachers. 'Standards in the Sunday School were high, very high,' wrote one of these, 'and Joan wouldn't allow anything second-rate or slap-dash in our teaching.' She continued, 'I don't want to give the impression that Joan was a martinet or anything like that; she somehow had the knack of carrying us along gently and enthusing us; I don't know how to put it other than that. We loved her so much, just as we all felt she loved us and the children so much. I am one hundred per cent sure that she not only knew each child by name, but knew all about their family circumstances too. We marvelled at her.'

The Sunday School and other Cathedral activities were so successful that the Cathedral Council met and agreed on a new building in the Cathedral compound. In May, 1956, Joan laid the foundation stone of the new hall. It seems from the records that members of the Cathedral Council were, at least ninety-five percent of the time, solidly behind Freddy, and he was for ever grateful for their support and encouragement. The Council was, in fact, a formidable body. Freddy wrote to his parents, after the 1956 Annual Meeting:

As I looked around the new Council I realised what an extremely weighty body of men we have now; the Bishop agreed that, apart from St. Margaret's, Westminster, there is probably not such a weighty Church Council anywhere in the Anglican Communion: Howes, the No 2 in Government, the Deputy Colonial Secretary, the Director of Education, the Director of Medical Services, the Chief Justice, the No 2 of the whole Hong Kong Bank, the Manager of one of the most vast Insurance Companies in the world, the Head of the Consulate of the United States, two Headmasters of schools - and the rest are all heads of big business firms here, each used to running his own show completely and competently. It is pleasing that the Church is holding and attracting such people to give such service.

Enormous Michaelmas Fairs, under the patronage of the Governor of Hong Kong, were held to help raise money. In January, 1954, Joan sent out 750 letters inviting people to join a Working Party. Freddy wrote, 'Heaven knows what we are going to do with them if only a quarter of them come.' People travelled from all over the Colony to be present at St. John's Michaelmas Fairs. The printed programme for the one held on October 1st, 1955, boasted 154 pages.

Pastoral Visiting was always at the top of Freddy's priorities. It was not always a hard slog, as the following letter written to his parents in September, 1953 demonstrates:

I expressed an interest in visiting, with Joan, a project on one of the islands. It turned out to be another of our romantic adventures. At 6 pm on Friday evening a big launch sped into the bay and a young medical missionary leapt ashore. He showed us into armchairs at the front of the launch. We sped away through the evening sunset to a neighbouring island, Hay Ling Chan, which means Isle of Happy Healing: a leper colony is being developed there - a barren island two years ago. There are a profusion of lepers in Hong Kong; about 2,000 untreated. The lepers themselves are building the place. Dr. Fraser, the Superintendent, met us and showed us round: an eager Scot who has such plans: what a wonderful job for him to develop this island. I am reminded of the story of Father Damian of Molokai. We had dinner with them all and then in the dark the launch sped us back; the waves were all luminous with the phosphorescence; sailing boats with their lights gliding by; the lights of Hong Kong in the distance; into our funny little har-

145

bour here. So ended an evening's work. I didn't realise 'work' could be quite so much fun.

One of the highlights at Christmas time was going carol singing. Freddy wrote home that it was not quite like carol singing parties in England, when a group of the faithful, clad in greatcoats and scarves, would walk around the parish attempting to sing carols by the light of inadequate torches, shivering hands holding the carol sheets. He continued,

> Choir Christmas Carol Singing in Hong Kong is just too romantic for words. We get into an enormous launch, about 70 of us. One of the wealthy sees that tremendous quantities of hot food and soft drinks are constantly circulated by waiters in white, and we speed up to each of the Navy ships in port and sing alongside them; a lovely evening, not too cold if one had a greatcoat on, with both the moon and sailors listening, the sailors listening over the side of these grey hulks in the darkness. Sometimes we are invited to climb aboard; and, as we sing, I can see glistening eyes among our listening sailors; doubtless thinking of Christmas at home. They are all so very appreciative. However, on all the American ships they were at the inevitable movies; they have film shows every night. One or two ventured to the rails.

In subsequent years the captains of the US Naval ships were apprised beforehand of the date of the carol singing, and they ensured that no films were shown on that night; what the sailors made of that is not recorded.

Freddy also regularly went to the Naval Mess and beat everyone there soundly at table tennis. 'It gives me considerable status,' he said, 'and they are to be seen in the Cathedral afterwards for some time. The Lord certainly does work in interesting ways.'

During the years that Freddy was Dean, much was done to beautify the Cathedral. Three new stained glass windows were added. Freddy wrote at the time, in the *South China Morning Post*, 'Amidst all the poverty in Hong Kong, people may tut-tut and say that the money should have been spent on the poor. I have every sympathy with such a view. The facts are, however, that the money for the windows was donated; if the money were not to be used for the windows it would not be forthcoming. That was made plain to me. But, more than that, it's important to have these windows. They aid worship. They help give our Cathedral an element of mystery, of the numinous. We meet God in our beloved Cathedral. God deserves to be met in a worthy building. I've no doubt that he wouldn't be in the least bit concerned if we gathered to meet him in a shack - but somehow I think he must surely be pleased that we've actually made a bit of an effort. It also helps *us* too. I don't think I'm alone in thinking how much more helpful it is to meet our God in a place of beauty and, yes, mystery. For that is what God is - both Beauty and Mystery.'

The Hong Kong Bank also provided money for some new bells to be installed. The bells were installed to commemorate the Coronation in 1953. Because of the lack of strength of the Cathedral tower the bells could not be swung but had to be played as carillon. There were advantages in this - the bells could be controlled by a single bell-ringer and hymn tunes, written in an appropriate key, could be played.

Freddy thought it would be a friendly gesture to preface Matins at 11 o'clock with the sound of Big Ben. Following the first occasion on which this was attempted a letter appeared from a Chinese resident in the *South China Morning Post* applauding the idea, but pointing out that the bell ringers had played the Westminster Chimes incorrectly. Freddy asked the bell ringers to listen to the actual sound of Big Ben on the BBC. To their dismay, the Chinese correspondent was proved right; the ringers had got it wrong. 'Keeping face' is very important in dealings with the Chinese. So, they had a problem. How to admit that they had made a mistake, yet not 'lose face'? Freddy was equal to the task. He wrote to the editor of the *South China Morning Post* congratulating the paper's correspondent on spotting that what had been played was not a true rendering of the Westminster Chimes. What *had* been played, however, was a variant of the Westminster Chimes, known as the Pompey Chimes - a version instantly recognisable by the navy. It was a welcome to join in Sunday worship at the Cathedral. After this was published, Freddy sent a memo to his secretary, Miss Remedios, 'Gosh, I got away with that one. Sometimes I seem to live by the skin of my teeth'.

Incidentally, Miss Remedios, Freddy's secretary, could be enormously protective of him. On one occasion Freddy returned to the Dean's House looking very crestfallen; he told her that he had parked his car illegally and been given a parking ticket. Freddy then watched and listened in amazement as his secretary immediately picked up the telephone, rang the Hong Kong Police and demanded to speak to the Chief of Police there and then. 'Do you know what one of your officers has just done?' she asked. 'No, Madam', he replied. 'One of them has just given a parking ticket to the Very Reverend the Dean of Hong Kong. You do not give parking tickets to the Dean of Hong Kong. Don't you realise his mind is on higher things?' The parking ticket was withdrawn.

In the many letters received from people from the time of Freddy's tenure of the Deanery of Hong Kong, two themes often recur: Freddy and Joan's hospitality, pastoral care and 'ministry of encouragement' and Freddy's preaching.

On Noel Ranken's first visit to St. John's he joined the Sunday Evening Fellowship which met regularly after Evensong in the Church Hall. He recalled that both Freddy and his 'elegant' wife Joan gave a wholehearted and warm welcome to all newcomers and immediately ensured that from the very first one met others in the group, made friends and became involved. There were all sorts of activities - shades here of Arnold, Newark and Manchester - some serious, some much less so, but essentially everyone participated; there were no cliques, no groups within groups and no-one ever felt 'left out.'

Noel was enormously taken with Freddy. In his middle thirties, he seemed to him a bit young to be a 'Very Reverend.' He remembered especially his 'shock of unruly hair on that huge dome of a head,' his peals of infectious laughter, his immense enthusiasm for whatever was in hand, be it a game or a serious debate, his wealth of innovative ideas, his talent for theatrical devices, music or verse and most of all, his great ability to motivate and encourage others. Noel writes, 'He was the absolute natural for his job - the right peg in the right hole.'

The following spring, Freddy produced a 'radio' version of Dorothy L. Sayers' 'Man Born to be King.' It was performed in the vestry with loudspeakers in the body of the Cathedral, in two parts during Holy Week. Freddy invited Noel to play the part of Jesus, which he declined - 'not only did I feel totally unworthy but he had the choice of judges, university scholars and clerics of all persuasions - but no, he had decided on me, he wanted to use my voice, and insisted that I do it. Freddy was not a man with whom one would argue. When his mind was made up, nothing could change it.'

Noel recalls that they used to have regular debates at Fellowship meetings at which Freddy was a forceful debater; he would often choose a subject and attempt to reach a conclusion after approaching it from every angle. Noel remembers one such debate in which Freddy held extremely strong views. He had invited comment and discussion on the then topical subject of the reinterpretation and modernisation of the Bible. 'His sheer love of the English language and the beauty of it in the King James Version', wrote Noel, 'was such that he would not contemplate changing a word. His contribution to that debate was the most powerful I have ever heard him give and his reasoning so compelling that he convinced me there and then that these modernisers should never be given credence.' It is interesting to note that, although Freddy always maintained his great love for the King James Version, when the first part (New Testament) of the New English Bible was published in 1961, he was in the forefront of those commending it to the attention of the faithful.

It was particularly thrilling for Noel to spend the Christmas holiday with Joan and Freddy in 1954. 'It was a most joyous time when after the Christmas services were over we had a happy time opening presents and generally doing what every family does on Christmas Day. I treasure to this day my gift from Freddy and Joan, a bound edition of "Other Men's Flowers".' Christmas Dinner was, apparently, a formal affair, held late in the evening to coincide with the broadcast of the Queen's Speech from London. The men were in black ties, the ladies in their finery, the guests being the cream of Colonial Society. There was the G.O.C, General Sir Brian Sugden, the Colonial Secretary, Mr. Robert Black, who would later become Governor successively of both Singapore and Hong Kong, the Chief Justice and other representatives of the professions and the university. Noel writes, 'As an unknown young serviceman, who just happened to be a house-guest, I was put in the unreal position of being equal to all. We listened to the Queen's Speech, drank the loyal toast and then, led by Freddy and Joan, proceeded to play silly party games until well into the night'.

Alan Wright and a friend, John Wackett arrived in Hong Kong in late 1953 as National Servicemen. Hong Kong was a very different part of the world from anywhere they had known before. They were homesick, far from loved ones and were faced with the prospect of nineteen months in an uncongenial military community sustained only by a daily occupation which to both of them was 'utterly tedious and generally loathsome'.

Matters were only comparatively briefly this gloomy. Human beings find pleasure in far less comfortable circumstances and Hong Kong, the colony, was beautiful although socially cruelly unequal. There were cinemas and the world of amateur theatre to enjoy and there were friends to make. 'Nevertheless', wrote Alan, 'central to the process of re-humanising the two young soldiers was the life around St. John's Cathedral, and the Church and family life over which Joan and Freddy Temple presided there.'

Alan continues,

> It is highly inappropriate, in fact, as anybody who knew Freddy and who knows Joan will instantly recognise, to say that this young couple - then in their thirties - presided over - any gathering, for their manner was egalitarian and every person they met or welcomed was accorded, quite properly, equal dignity, and treated as a treasured friend. It is truer to say therefore that they took part in, or shared, the gatherings at the cathedral, but they were certainly inspiring or motivating members of the large groups who met either in the church hall or in their own home at the end of most Evensongs. To begin with, it was their invitations which had enabled the meetings to take place, and once the get-togethers had been launched, the Temples infused them with joy and enriching comedy.

The opportunities for newly arrived expatriates at St. John's Cathedral were not confined to services and the comic and heart-warming events following services. There was also an on-going programme of charity work and, Alan says, there were a lot of plays produced - plays to mirror or celebrate the events of the Christian calendar; or plays, staged in the Cathedral itself, chosen because they had a Christian connection and because they seemed to Freddy and Joan to be works of quality. A group of confident young subalterns, for example, arrived one day from their regiment somewhere in the New Territories to present a very convincing production of T.S. Eliot's 'Murder in the Cathedral.' (When Alan Wright met Freddy many years later and mentioned this moving production to him, the latter recalled the occasion instantly and went on to name the actors who took part.) If a visiting serviceman missed out on this wide range of offered opportunities, then

Freddy, says Alan, 'worked hand-in-glove with a colony-based Christian spy network who scuttled around, popping up everywhere, and keeping a caring look-out for anybody who appeared to be crestfallen.'

Alan continued:

It was a comprehensive service that Freddy provided, and the Temple family offered an informal reinforcement of this spirit of creativity and goodwill. There was usually one member [of the family] around who was willing and keen to join in a conversation: Mina, precocious, intelligent and delightful, was excellent company, and Michael, earnest, concerned and always welcoming, made all visitors feel needed. It is not surprising, then, that the two national servicemen whose experiences in the company of Freddy Temple I have been outlining, felt re-humanised by meeting him, but it has been more important to provide this brief account because the loving process of rehabilitation was extended to literally scores of young people, unwilling servicemen most of them, who were fortunate enough to make contact with the Dean of Hong Kong.

Alan thought that if Joan were asked whether she remembered reacting in this sort of way to the heterogeneous gathering they welcomed to church and home - whether it was Bishop Hall, the Governor of the Colony, visiting thespians Dame Sybil Thorndike and Sir Lewis Casson, Gunner Alan Wright or anybody - she would be puzzled by the question. All were naturally equal as far as the Temples were concerned.

Phillip Ward-Green first met Freddy and Joan in Hong Kong. He was living with his parents between school in Australia and going up to New College, Oxford. He too attended the Sunday evening Fellowship and remembers well 'Joan's exquisite tact, beauty, good humour and firm guidance.' He continued, 'We did all sorts of things, from dancing Scottish reels to writing and performing our own play in the Deanery garden. I remember playing Origen, whose lines in my nervousness I forgot, though I had written them, and had to be prompted from behind a curtain!'

Unfortunately, it has been possible to make contact with only one candidate Freddy prepared for Confirmation whilst in Hong Kong, though there were many hundreds. Many Confirmation candidates had intensive 'crash' courses whilst on their Summer holidays from boarding schools in England. Although Freddy had no wish to usurp the pastoral responsibilities of these children's School Chaplains in England, many parents were adamant that their sons and daughters be prepared for the Sacrament by Freddy himself. Anne Macey-Dane grew up in Hong Kong, where her father, Professor K.E. Priestley, held the Chair of Education at the University. It was Freddy who prepared her for Confirmation and she was twelve or so when attending his classes. She writes, 'I remember them as being very "open-minded" - just what is required today. In essence the Christian message was there, but as young people we were encouraged to think and voice our own thoughts, however simplistic. As I recall we all felt "safe" to do so.'

Much will be said about Freddy's preaching later, but it is worth mentioning here a few points as related by members of the Cathedral in Hong Kong.

Ron Seaborne was present for Freddy's first sermon there and from then on, having previously been very irregular in attendance at Sunday worship, he became a committed member of the Cathedral congregation. Freddy's sermons were for him a 'revelation': always preaching without notes, 'he spoke with such a logical conviction that his congregation hung on to his every word.' Ron said that Freddy could also be forthright and outspoken. On occasions when he felt that the Hong Kong Government had failed the Colony's community in some respect, he did not hesitate to make his views known from the pulpit.

For the Revd Patrick Rain, D.F.C., the effect of Freddy's preaching in the Cathedral stands out in his memory, for it seemed 'effortless' and 'apparently noteless.' Juliet Scholes said that his sermons were memorable for 'stirring the conscience of the congregation.' Brian Hart said that one of the things he most remembers were Freddy's sermons. He added, 'For me they added a new dimension to preaching - e.g he said of Advent that when you saw the Church putting on liturgical purple you knew it meant business.' According to Noel Ranken, Freddy was 'without doubt one of the finest preachers I have ever been privileged to hear, his sermons offering great depth of thought yet within the understanding of all.'

Perhaps some of the last words about Freddy's preaching whilst Dean of Hong Kong should come from Freddy himself. Four days after he arrived at the Cathedral he wrote a letter to his parents saying that preaching to such a congregation might well prove 'more than a little interesting.' The former Dean, Alaric Rose, had stayed on at the Cathedral as a Canon, and preached at one of the services on Freddy's first Sunday. Freddy commented, 'Afterwards people said with bated breath, "Isn't Canon Rose brilliant? We can't understand a word he says"'.

Mention was made earlier of Jimmy Froud. His relationship with Freddy and Joan was of such importance in Hong Kong that more must be said. Jimmy worked for Toc H and was sent to Hong Kong in mid-1952 by Tubby Clayton. He made his spiritual home at St. John's Cathedral at about the same time as Freddy started his ministry as Dean. Oddly, at almost the same time, headquarters in London decided to close the Hong Kong TocH house! Freddy, seeing his potential, immediately challenged him to stay and work from St. John's as a Lay Worker. Bishop Hall (who was a friend of Tubby Clayton) agreed to take on the responsibility for him and to pay him.

Freddy set him to work, visiting people newly-arrived from England, helping out at the Cathedral Office and with the uniformed organisations attached to the Cathedral - in addition to a variety of jobs in and around St. John's.

Jimmy had long felt a vocation to the priesthood; in 1954 he was made Deacon

and the following year was ordained Priest. His training had been undertaken by
Freddy and Canon Alaric Rose. Jimmy writes:

*If it were not for Freddy's patience and composed calmness I would not have been
fit for the Priesthood. He never gave up - day by day, with utmost grace, he would
point out where I went astray and we would laugh together. Never a day went by
without us meeting - in his home and alongside his family - so much so that I practically became a member.*

Until his death in 2004, Jimmy was still very active as a priest in the diocese of
Chelmsford, and was known as 'Visiting Jim.' Freddy would give him lists of people - newcomers to the colony, those whose absence from the Cathedral had been
noticed, the sick and the vulnerable. Jimmy said that Freddy thoroughly enjoyed
visiting people himself, calling on families and challenging them, 'but never leaving without gaining their laughter.' He continued, 'Freddy was a past master and a
great teacher. I still think of him bowling into a house or meeting somebody on
the street - always a cheerful greeting. And then he would listen. He taught me to
be quiet.'

Jimmy continued:

*His preaching was out of this world; it just seemed to flow from him - natural,
earthy and plain, - and yet with a great depth of spirituality. I was not a preacher -
and still I am not; I enclose some of his notes, for which he was famous; how he ever
put up with me, I know not. But I never, ever felt unwanted or hurt; I did try and I
still do.*

*Freddy was a very strong person - always on the go - with a strong faith and a
rather innocent child-like trust. He was very able to speak out boldly and be counted. This didn't bring him enemies or rivals, for Freddy was never confrontational;
logically he would make a point and stick to it. He not only trusted individuals but,
what is more, they knew and I, in particular, knew that he did - never fussing round
or checking. I never ever found that I was being hounded or driven.*

Some of the 'notes' that Jimmy mentioned Freddy penned to him are of interest,
for they tell us much about Freddy's attitude to preaching and ministry. An undated note runs:

*You're naughty: that sermon was quite good, full of ideas, but it could have been
very good. It just wasn't prepared. There were three sermons all going about in it.
You have had ages to prepare this course of three and it just isn't good enough to be
rewriting on the Sunday afternoon. Even if the composition is good, you haven't
time to rehearse delivery, pauses, climax, etc.: a prepared sermon is a little like a
part in a play.*

I can, as you can I know, think of several things which you ought not to have gone to with a sermon unprepared, the party after 'Desert Highway', 'Othello', etc.

Sermons are a sweat: but vital: don't neglect them: there are no born preachers; all [sermons] come from sweat and tears. You definitely could be good. And the day will come when you will have 4 on a Sunday to do in your own parish.

It isn't a question of more reading, but preparing. Why am I not seeing them on Thursdays or earlier nowadays? I had my Lent course all done in January.

Be careful about bringing in 'bloody messes': Jezebel last night - really nothing to do with the Covenant. And you gave us a 'bloody mess' in the two sermons before, so much so that Beatrice [Freddy's eldest sister, who was staying with Joan and Freddy at the time] said after the second, 'I like Mr. Froud and his sermons will be good in time: but he seems to have blood on the brain.'

You could be a good preacher: and ultimately that matters more than meeting folk, etc.: so keep at it hard.

In another undated note, Freddy says:

Frankly, I'm baffled how to help with sermons if I don't see them beforehand. We all need help and we all submit sermons for at least 6 years: 2 in College and 4 ordained to be helped with them.

Last Sunday had all the ideas, but the construction and delivery were just not prepared. There were so many 'possiblys' at the beginning: one sentence, quite short, started with 'possibly' and ended with 'I think'. One sentence had the verb, and then one could count 12 before the object came. It is much better to deliver something which seems dead to you but alive to us. One has to go through this period of working and working at a sermon; when you were submitting them they were 100% better; everyone noticed it.

Anyway here is full warning: your next is May 20th. I would like to see it fully written out by Tuesday, May 15th; then we can really work on it. I am doing my Whitsun sermon now: and hate it, but it will come alive in a week or two.

We have got to keep at sermons: you will ultimately be preaching at least once if not twice a Sunday.

Another undated note runs:

You are now reading and taking the Communion Service much much better in every way, but the one thing to watch now is to read in phrases and pause at the end of phrases. For instance, at 9 yesterday in the Consecration Prayer there were two immense 'ands' - 'who in the same night that he was betrayed took break and ..... long pause .....when he had given thanks he brake it, and .....'.

And yet another (edited):

> *We all feel inadequate for the Priesthood; we all are. But I knew for a long time you were under a strain: being ordained is a strain, much more than any layman knows - and it is a lonely life. It is not just a social service life hotted up: the strain of sermons, if they are to be worthy; the strain of pastoral advice, etc. That is why maybe you should again see how much you do outside the Cathedral specifically? Street Sleepers, Lepers, Barbecues for Missions to Seamen, etc. etc.: all excellent things, but we can only do so much. Especially in the first few years of priesthood we must get enough quiet; I don't think I have said enough about prayer; besides Matins and Evensong, do you get enough quiet? At least half an hour a day to let the mind roam on God: do you deliberately have 2 quiet evenings in a week just to think, not to write an essay, but to let the mind roam as you want? The danger is, as one feels the strain, to want people round all the time; but we have got to be alone with God: not to fill it with the activity of set prayers but with the rest of prayer. God is already doing a great deal through you to help folk: you will be a great priest. Like us all, you are in the early Galilean stage of great popularity: 'Grand chap, Jesus; always everywhere; great crowds'. But inside you know that it is not enough. And the next step was Jesus away alone, often when wanted: inhibiting people who wanted him to do more. Give yourself more time. The deeper, better people will respect you more.*

In 1958, Jimmy decided to return to England to work. It was decided that before he started out in a parish he should attend Cuddesdon Theological College, Oxford, for six months. On February 4th, Freddy wrote (again edited):

> *You won't want more parcels now so I have asked Blackwells to send you at Cuddesdon 'Jesus in his Time': it comes with all our love and gratitude for four great years; it is a book you will always use. Thank you most warmly for everything.*
>
> *Keep a watch on your times of prayer and intercession besides the daily Mass, won't you? Somehow I feel you have an idea I don't like a daily Celebration: I can't imagine why, as apart from Monday I have a daily one. But prayer and intercession will go on in heaven after Sacraments have ceased: and so while Sacraments are a necessary aid, prayer is vital, and more important. So that is my last little note! It is important to pray long for folk.*

So Jimmy Froud left for Cuddesdon. An interesting letter from Jimmy to Freddy and Joan survives amongst Freddy's papers, dated May 21st, 1958. It tells of his life at Cuddesdon:

> *Have now been at Cuddesdon for a month and have done nothing else but read. Knapp-Fisher [the Principal] is excellent, but a little frightening, but of a certain-*

*ty that is good for me. He shows none of your forbearance and love, but has your
fearless courage. He says it, though, instead of writing it - even more devastating.
Have just been reading through some of your notes; they will make very good
teaching points sometime. Your last one says, 'Joan and I naturally want very
much to see you off on Monday and will be very much hurt if we are fobbed off
again as we were last Thursday; it did not need much telephoning to confirm what
we felt, that you knew quite well when you were leaving.' You were quite right, of
course, as you confoundedly always are, but I was dreading the final leave-taking.*

*My hair is dreadfully long, but there was no Joan's 'Jimmy, deeeear …', only a
penetrating glare from the Principal. I must get it cut.*

*Your book has arrived from Blackwells, 'Jesus in His Time'; have started on it
and am enjoying it. Thank you both so much. Have read Gore, Davidson, Lang
and Temple again; Kirk's 'Vision of God' and one on the Dead Sea Scrolls. Have
been studying specially Jeremiah and Romans. In fact it's all been tremendous. I
Celebrate once a week here and take services in the neighbouring villages, which is
a delight. But I must confess I am getting itching feet to be out and about again; this
all seems to bear no relationship with the world, but I'm told by Knapp-Fisher,
'Yes, that's the idea; it's only you and God for the next two months and then you go
out and give what little bit you have learnt to others, and then on occasions come
back for more.' That could have been you talking.*

*All my fondest love to Joan; I do hope she exerts some discipline upon you, that
you do not do too much. At a baptism lecture the other day I was asked to comment. I said with great dignity, 'I was taught with the aid of a Dachshund by Freddy
Temple.' It brought the house down.*

Freddy used to teach his curates the 'mechanics' of baptism using the Temple family's very wriggly family dog, named Friday, in place of a baby. Freddy once commented. 'Although of course I don't believe in re-baptism for Christians, I think
Friday must be the most baptised dog in all Christendom. I don't think he ever
quite understood what was going on at these sessions, but he learned to accept it
all with canine Christian grace, perhaps because he could be sure of a little 'treat'
after he'd sometimes been excessively sprayed with water. I can't remember
which of my curates it was who succeeded in dropping him into the font when he
was being excessively frisky, but we did give him two biscuits after that episode.'

The year before this, Freddy had been given a nine month's leave in England,
leaving the Cathedral in the capable hands of Jimmy Froud, and Freddy, Joan,
Mina and Stephen sailed in February, 1957. They had a good sea trip, and enjoyed
a period of 'winding down.' Once again the Temple family seemed to be more
than successful in deck sports. They were excited about the prospect of seeing
England again and, of course, seeing their families. They were specially looking
forward to showing Stephen off to them for the first time. They were due in England at the beginning of April.

Then came a telegram to say that Freddy's father had suddenly and unexpectedly died. Freddy wrote on the 26th of March,

My own dear darling Mum,

    How much Joan and I long to be with you and think of you all the time. It still seems impossible to believe. The charming Chief Steward brought the telegram while Mina and I were doing school and we sent one off straightaway. We couldn't be more cut off from you apart from prayer, which we use all the time: ten more days till we reach a port and get news and then only a few hours so we must post ours before reading yours. How I wonder how you are. Of course as I think of Daddy my main feeling is one long paean of thanksgiving for a wonderful life of such solid, quiet, unselfish Christian worth - and lovely for him to go without an illness. He longed to die in harness, didn't he? And so he did. He is a wonderful person: a great father: how we shall miss those superb letters, so unselfish in their utter reliability and how unselfish he was in letting you come home to us each summer from India and finding the money for it; I realise that now.

    Joan and I longed to show him, ourselves, Stephen; we know what Mike's going meant and we wanted to show him another perfect Temple grandson. But of course he is enjoying him now. For Daddy, let our thoughts be a great shout of thanksgiving for a life which had such sterling Christian worth and strength. But all we children will be thinking of you: after 50 years the gap will be enormous and will be there all the time, I know, precious one. And poor Ann, and her wedding. I wonder what you will all plan for that. Don't try and do too much or anything: let those who long to do it for you do it all, and try not to worry over details.

    Easter will soon be here with its wonderful message and certainty. Mike's birthday is on Saturday: I like to think of them and Uncle William and the old Archbishop and others together.

    I will come to Lewes as soon as I can after arrival, which is still planned as the 12th. I imagine the service for Daddy being Friday probably; but anyhow you are never out of our thoughts. I know he never expected to see us again when we left: but I had so hoped he was wrong. How grateful we are for showing us such a happy married life.

    All our love and sharing in it all.

    Freddy.

Naturally, Freddy's father's death overshadowed his leave. He and Joan spent much time with his mother and family, with Stephen Verney and other friends and with 'Clarky', his Vicar at Newark, who by now was Bishop of Pontefract.

    Then in a letter dated 27th June, he heard from Geoffrey Fisher, the Archbishop of Canterbury:

I write again just to raise a question to see what might be thought of it. I have had

you in mind ever since I saw you [Freddy had visited him at Lambeth at the beginning of June to talk about matters relating to his Uncle William's estate], *wondering whether before you went back to Hong Kong some suitable opening might occur to put before you. I do now mention Croydon Parish Church. It is one of the great parish churches of England, like Leeds and Rugby, and so on. It is the central church of a great borough of a quarter of a million people. It plays a leading part in the civic life of the place. It ought to have, and generally does have, a wonderfully enthusiastic congregation drawn, not so much from the parish, but from the district round and not least from places like Purley and Sanderstead, which are actually outside the Diocese. There are schools like the two Whitgift Schools, where the Vicar of Croydon traditionally prepares for Confirmation boys who are to be confirmed. It is in fact a great parochial charge. I am sure that the new Vicar would step straight into a great and a golden opportunity.*

I do not know whether you would consider such a task as this; I do not know whether you would consider it possible to desert Hong Kong at comparatively short notice in order to take up work in Croydon before too long. That is the general proposition on which I merely want to know what you would say. If you thought it worth exploring it, I should like to see you again and we would explore it further. On the other hand, you may feel that at this short notice, you would not wish to look into it. Please let me know what you think.

Freddy replied that he felt it his duty to return to Hong Kong, if not for another full four years, for at least two. The Archbishop, in a letter dated July 8th, was obviously disappointed: 'I was immensely attracted by the thought of having you at Croydon, but I fully appreciate what you say'.

The leave for Freddy and his family ended all too quickly, though by the end of it they were looking forward to getting back to Hong Kong and, in Freddy's words, 'to see what messes will have to be cleared up'. There were none. 'They seem,' wrote Freddy, 'to have got on better without me, though the depth and warmth of our reception brought tears to Joan's eyes'. Work carried on at a typically hectic pace.

An interesting letter from Freddy's papers is dated January 12th, 1958 - especially interesting because of what was to happen the following year. It was written to his mother and contained the paragraph:

I suppose people are preparing for the Lambeth Conference now; what a disaster it appears more and more that Fisher is at Canterbury. It seems so clear that he can't brook able men who have different ideas around him. I think the leadership of the Anglican Communion will pass more and more to the Presiding Bishop of America, Sherrill, which may be all to the good. I know our own Bishop wants very much to get passed that the next Lambeth Conference will not be at Lambeth but in some other country with some other Archbishop or Presiding Bishop as Chairman.

It was soon after this that the Bishop, R.O. Hall, went on leave (including attendance at the Lambeth Conference), leaving the diocese for almost a year in the capable hands of Freddy.

In the middle of March, 1958, Freddy was surprised to receive a letter from the Bishop of Newcastle, New South Wales, dated March 6th:

> *May I introduce myself as a very old friend of your father who was a contemporary at Balliol in the rather distant past. I am writing to ask a very daring question. I have tendered my resignation of this Diocese as from September 30th next; my successor is to be elected by Synod when it meets on April 22. Is it conceivable that you would allow yourself to be nominated for the position? You would find the work full of interest and you are young enough to be able to look forward to returning to England after you have given 8 or 10 years' service here. I cannot, of course, guarantee your election, which is entirely in the hands of the Synod, but it would give me personally very great pleasure for the son of so old a friend to succeed me. If you would let me have a line, more or less by return mail, saying whether you are willing to be considered for the position, I should be very grateful.*

Freddy was not at all sure whether he wanted to be Bishop of Newcastle; he hoped to return to England in the not-too-distant future as a Parish Priest. But after a great deal of discussion and prayer with Joan they decided that he should allow his name to go forward, in case it were the prompting of the Holy Spirit, 'but we rather hope it's not'.

And so it proved. In a letter dated April 24th, the Bishop of Newcastle wrote:

> *I am sorry to have to tell you that my nomination of you for the Bishopric of Newcastle was not successful. As I told you in my previous communication, the cry of 'Australia for the Australians' is being increasingly heard and it prevented no more than a minority of my Synod from accepting my recommendation of you. I hope you will not think of this rejection in any sense as a reflection on you. It simply results from the fact that the Diocese hesitates to accept anyone of whom it has no personal knowledge. I think this also is a mistaken one, and I feel that this worked out possibly to the disadvantage of the Diocese by Synod's unwillingness to accept my nomination. I am most grateful to you for allowing your name to go forward and for saying that you would come to us if you had been the choice of the Synod.*

In March, 1959, the Duke of Edinburgh paid an official visit to the Colony. Freddy told his mother that from the moment he stepped off the Britannia, he was 'charming and informal.' Freddy continued,

158   *We saw a lot of him, of course. He also came to the Cathedral on Sunday. I think I*

made myself more than a little unpopular by refusing to reserve seats for the 'high and mighty' of the colony who had never before attended the Cathedral. I did of course reserve seats for the Governor and Lady Black, for they are regular members of our congregation. But others had to take pot luck. The Cathedral was naturally packed, even with numerous extra chairs; some were standing - but none were turned away. The service went well and, as it was Mothering Sunday, the children came in to receive flowers for their mothers. Philip enjoyed this very much, as 282 children filed in past him. I escorted him out at the end, and he said he had enjoyed it very much. And I really think he was being totally sincere. His private secretary wrote a very nice letter afterwards, expressing the Duke's amazement at the number of children at the Cathedral.

Less than a month after that there followed a visit from the Archbishop of Canterbury and Mrs. Fisher. Freddy wrote to his mother:

We had a wonderful four days (April 2-6) when they came through on their way to Japan. The upshot of it all is that we shall be back in England by the middle of August. The Archbishop of Canterbury has asked me to be Senior Chaplain at Lambeth. He hinted that he might make the offer so that we had time to think about it. When he came back through Hong Kong on April 25th for a short stop to refuel the Comet, he first talked to the Bishop at the Airport and then to me and asked me definitely to come. I am to start work there on September 1st.

It will be very strange not to have one's own parish and church, but it sounds an interesting job in quite a different way. I said 'no' to the Archbishop 2 years ago when in England about another job, but there seemed to be no good reason to say 'no' this time. Joan will miss her side of parish life very much, but in London she will be right in the centre to do much for all the Chinese from Hong Kong who are there. There are many, many things we shall miss: the life and bustle of the streets, the wonderful Chinese, the warmth of the people and of the sun.

We will live apparently in a tiny house in Lambeth Palace grounds, but have kindly been told that we can store stuff in the crypt. If ever there was a good moment to leave any job, now is the right time for the Cathedral as the Bishop is just back from leave and both Chaplains are here for at least two more years. The third stained glass window is to be dedicated on Whit Sunday and that completes the restoration of the Cathedral and the main alterations I had in mind when we arrived.

As I say, the Archbishop's visit was a wonderful time. He gave himself so unsparingly to everyone and spoke so amusingly as well every time. We liked Mrs. Fisher very much too and thought her charming. When they returned to refuel there was some problem with Comet and it could not take off again. And so they spent the night with us and went off 24 hours later. This really was quite fortuitous, as we could talk at length about my new responsibilities.

We see no sign of the misgivings expressed only a few months before.

Freddy's old friend and training incumbent, George Clarkson, wrote:

> *No doubt you are being inundated with these things, but I can't refrain from offering to the C of E due congratulations upon having a Temple at Lambeth again. I know nothing of that set-up - never having fallen fair or foul of it - but I am quite sure that, having your enormous capacity for good work and your grand sense of recuperative fun, will do it and him and us incalculable good.*

Edward Heath, who was at the time Lord Privy Seal, penned the following from 12, Downing Street:

> *I am delighted to hear that you are coming to Lambeth. Many congratulations. With Tim Bligh as PS to the PM and you to the Archbishop, the Balliol net appears to be properly re-established. I hope we shall still be here by the time you reach the other side of the river!*

Aunt Frances wrote an enormous six-page letter to Freddy, of which the following is the penultimate paragraph:

> *This is a life which calls for tremendous unselfishness in the wife - as of course there is nothing for her to do at all. On the other hand, she could no doubt do endless things in South London if she were willing - but that is not quite the same thing as being the leader of so much parish work - and I know how much you would miss that too, because you have got such great gifts for personal and evangelistic work, both of you. I'm not sure I would not rather have seen you at Croydon where you could have gone 'all out' as leader of your own show. At Lambeth the Chaplain has unavoidably to keep to a certain extent in the background. But having said all that it seems proper to have a Temple at the Palace again.*

When it was announced in Hong Kong that the Temple family were leaving, there was genuine and heart-felt distress. The *South China Morning Post* made it their front page headline and throughout the paper Freddy and Joan were eulogised. Letters poured in from all over the Colony expressing a sense of disbelief; phrases like 'Hong Kong can never, ever be the same again.' It would be tedious to end this chapter by rehearsing a selection of the masses of letters received, let alone what was said of them in the *South China Morning Post* and on Hong Kong Radio. Let the reader imagine. However, Freddy and Joan were pleased to receive this one from the Governor of Hong Kong, dated April 29th, 1959:

> *I read the announcement this morning with very mixed feelings, and I must confess that the uppermost feeling was one of regret. We shall all miss you and Joan great-*

ly: you have done so much for the Cathedral and for the Community; you have left a strong impression of your personality here and given inspiration and encouragement by your own strong faith and so evident sense of Christian mission and humanity.

I realise, however, that there is another side of this, and I must hasten to add that my better instincts, this morning, made me see it - and I am very glad that your fine work has received this fine recognition and that you will have the chance of working in a wider field and that others will be able to enjoy the fruits of your devoted service. I know if my wife were here she would join me in sending our warmest congratulations to you and our very best wishes for the future to Joan and yourself and to the children.

The Farewell presentation to Freddy and Joan took place in the last week of June. The Bishop presided. He began his speech thus:

A recent letter from England hoped that 'the Archbishop's visit had strengthened the Church.' The writer knew of the act of highway robbery carried out by the Archbishop on his visit. His remark was perhaps meant to be humorous.

I suspect that no one will miss the Dean more than I shall, and that is saying a great deal, as this packed hall can testify. I just cannot put into words how much he has done to help me personally by his restless energy, quick and disciplined ability, and unhesitating willingness to do every kind of difficult and monotonous work behind the scenes, and to do it quickly and well.

We shall get our revenge on the Archbishop. September is still the typhoon season. When 'Typhoon Freddy' reaches Lambeth they will not know what has hit them. For the Dean is the only priest I have ever met who has a mind even quicker than the Archbishop's own. He is also, if such a thing is possible, a greater glutton for work than the Archbishop.

The remainder of his speech was fairly lengthy, but the last paragraphs give a flavour of it:

I think my first letter to the Temples spoke of the need of young parents for help in teaching their children about God. I had no idea then of the genius of Joan Temple for Sunday School work. Her name on the Foundation Stone of the new Cathedral Hall will be a continual reminder to us of what this astonishing team of two have done amongst us.

We thank God for their coming to us, for what they have done amongst us - not least the 'living sermon' they proclaimed when Michael died; and we will pray continually for God's blessing on them in the difficult and wearisome job at Lambeth which they have so willingly undertaken as a duty to be done for the sake of the whole Church.

161

His Excellency the Governor then spoke on behalf of the Colony. He began by saying that almost invariably he was told he *had to* make a speech, but this was an occasion when he had asked if he might say a word. He continued to pay a warm tribute to the influence of both Freddy and Joan in the Colony as a whole; he spoke of them as having stamped the impress of their personalities on the whole community of Hong Kong and over an area very much wider than that which the Christian community circumscribed. Secondly, the Governor said that he would like to speak as a member of the congregation, and amongst other things he spoke of the way Freddy had always been prepared to do himself whatever he had asked of others. Thirdly, he chose to speak as a personal friend and said what a source of strength the Temples had been to Lady Black and himself, and how very much they would miss him.

The Presentation was made on behalf of the Cathedral by Colonel H. Owen Hughes. In a yet more lengthy speech than his bishop's, he began:

> *Naturally we feel sad at losing them - that is but part of the frailty of human nature - but sadness shall not be the keynote of this gathering. We are proud that our Dean and nobody else has been selected for this important office which will provide scope for his undoubted talents and which we feel sure he will fill with distinction. I think we can claim credit for his success in Hong Kong since we are the raw material on which he has had to work. By any standards we must be deemed interesting material, so varied that we are hard to define and hard to work - may I say we are a conglomerate amalgam of many races softened by dough? I speak feelingly and gratefully as Treasurer of the Cathedral for the benign influence of this commodity which is so important in the fashioning of our edifice and which has been so generously available during this period. As a craftsman Freddy Temple has shown great skill in the technique of easing dough out of amalgam and applying it to the best advantage.*
>
> *But it will not be for his work on the material side that he will be best remembered, great though this is. Individually we recall words and acts of kindness and guidance, of comfort and of challenge in our domestic affairs, and collectively he has kept before our eyes the whole duty of man. I suggest that he has been a faithful interpreter of that Dragoman to whom he referred in his address last Sunday. He has told us that the Dragoman wants us to come along this way and that he has arranged a resting place for us at the end of the road. How often, listening to his sermons, and realising how wicked other men are, has a fiery dart, a winged word, struck home where we feel it most, so that we have said, 'He is aiming at me.'*

Soon afterwards, Freddy, Joan and the children sailed back to the United Kingdom, feeling, in Freddy's own words, 'that strange mix of desperate sadness at leaving, but joyous anticipation of what the future offers.'

10 Lambeth

As Freddy, Joan and the family steamed into the King George V Dock in London, the first person they saw was Jimmy Froud pacing the dockside; he had come to meet them and help them with their luggage. Freddy and Joan were very moved by this gesture; 'somehow', wrote Joan at the time, 'it made us feel at home.' They went straight to Lambeth Palace. The Archbishop and Mrs. Fisher were away and had lent them their own flat in the Palace while they prepared their tiny cottage in the grounds.

When they had been there a couple of days, Freddy received a letter from the Archbishop:

> *I have heard little reports of you from my wife's sister, Miss Forman - now, I gather, you are 'on the bridge' at Lambeth, I hope it will be the beginning of a happy voyage for us both - though certainly through squally weather. My greetings to your wife and the children. I will ask no questions and expect none from you about anything until I get back!*

Freddy and Joan found the first week or two grim in the extreme; the little furniture they had was very dirty after six years in storage; the house was none too clean, as it had been empty for quite a while. They realised how spoilt they had always been in the past, serving in parishes where there was no shortage of people to help in every way. They found they had to buy a great deal and that London prices were very expensive. (Freddy's stipend as Archbishop's Chaplain was less than half of what it was as Dean of Hong Kong.) Freddy wrote in November, 'We often wondered why we had ever left Hong Kong.'

However, their depression was short-lived. Mina gained a place at Christ's Hospital at Hertford; Stephen went to a small school just over the bridge in Westminster, and after his fifth birthday started at Archbishop Tait School, next door to the Palace. The family had full use of the lovely, vast gardens of the Palace; the Lambeth Palace Librarian, Dr. Bill, and his wife had two small children as well, and Stephen and young Richard Bill used to go off into the wilds of the garden af-

The Senior Chaplain to Archbishop Fisher, with his son, Stephen.

ter school quite happily and safely; the garden was completely walled, with no traffic. Joan became quite used to Stephen returning for meals absolutely filthy; there were some marvellous rubbish dumps and bonfire heaps in which to play.

Joan became Chairman of the London branch of the Hong Kong Diocesan Association and Freddy joined the Asia Christian Colleges Council. They were both determined to keep their links with the Far East. Joan wrote in June 1960 to her friends and relations, 'Thank you all who have written to us so magnificently - you cannot know the joy that your letters bring and how the Hong Kong ones waft us so willingly back to the sights, smells and sounds of that beloved place.'

Freddy wrote, after eight weeks at the Palace, that he was enjoying his job very much; on Sundays he was pleased that he was usually free to preach where asked, as the Domestic Chaplain usually accompanied the Archbishop. He did, however, miss not having his own church for which he was personally responsible, and hankered after the Sunday crowds at St. John's Cathedral, Hong Kong.

Freddy also had the time to edit a collection of letters written by William Temple during his short time as Archbishop of Canterbury. Although completed while Freddy was still at Lambeth, the Oxford University Press did not publish them, under the title, *Some Lambeth Letters*, until April 1963. The collection was to receive some excellent reviews and, slightly to Freddy's surprise, for he thought that the price set by the publisher was 'far too high', the book sold well and was immediately to be found on many a clerical and lay bookshelf. Michael Ramsey (then Archbishop of York and soon to move, like William Temple, to Canterbury) wrote a particularly appreciative letter.

Freddy remembered that one of the very first things Archbishop Fisher impressed on him was the need to treat the Press with care. Press relationships over forty years ago were perhaps less fraught with possible pitfalls than they are today; but wariness was still necessary. Freddy remembered the Archbishop telling him a cautionary tale about a visit he made in the early 1950s to the United States of America. As soon as the ship, the *Queen Elizabeth*, had docked, reporters by the dozen jostled to interview him. Geoffrey Fisher always prided himself on his ability to parry awkward questions: he was supremely good at thinking on his feet. It was not long before a teaser was tossed his way. 'Your Grace, do you intend to visit any night clubs while you are in New York?' Fisher thought he dealt with that one quite well; he was not, however, very pleased when he opened the papers the next morning. The report began, 'The very first question the Archbishop of Canterbury asked on his arrival yesterday was, "Are there any night clubs in New York?"'

This story whiffs a little of the apocryphal - though Freddy would tell it as if it were definite fact; and it may well have been. It certainly made an impression on him. He boasted gently at the end of his time at Lambeth that he was not aware of having once embarrassed the Archbishop in his relationships with the Press.

Perhaps the best way to give an impression of Freddy's time at Lambeth would be to quote from something he wrote at the end of his time there. He wrote in the

North End Review, the Parish Magazine for St. Mark's Church, North End, Portsmouth:

> *In a parish a vicar can go to see his people or they can come to see him; he can advise them, guide them, rebuke them and care for them face to face. So he is Pastor, or shepherd to them. An Archbishop does just the same, but has to do it by letter, for his parish is the whole world and his care the care of all the churches. And yet when the same pastoral work is done by post, people call it administration and often maintain that it is not spiritual or pastoral.*
>
> *The Archbishop of Canterbury must do his 'caring' for people mainly by letter, for only thus can he have time to choose and deal with those problems with which he alone can deal; every day at 8.30am (there are Celebrations of Holy Communion at 8am in the Palace Chapel on Thursdays and Saints' Days) the three members of his personal staff open, sort and read the mail. This takes until 9.15 when Matins is said and then at 9.30 the Archbishop joins his staff to consider the day's post. There will be two piles of letters, diocesan and general. The diocesan pile concerns all the affairs of the Canterbury diocese; parishes wanting new vicars, confirmation arrangements, men wanting to be ordained, and often simple pastoral problems from people in Kent. In the other pile there will be letters from all parts of the world, a missionary bishop wanting advice about some point in his diocesan constitution, an African Bishop asking for guidance, some point about the World Council of Churches, a Peer writing about some important debate in the House of Lords, the questions to be asked in some television programme, the Agenda of Convocation and so on. There will be some straightforward ones which chaplains can best refer back to the bishops of the dioceses concerned who can then get a local incumbent to visit the writer.*
>
> *No problem is left unanswered; anyone with a serious difficulty will get a fully considered reply, stern and candid if necessary. A heavy and incessant mail is the background to the Archbishop's work; most ordinary men would be crushed by it. There is many a week-end, when the Archbishop is not in his diocese, when he has to retire to his study and dictate into a dictaphone for much of Sunday, apart of course from services. The secretaries are used to finding sixteen dictaphone belts waiting for them on a Monday morning; one belt takes a good secretary two and a half hours' typing, so you can imagine the number of letters thus answered. And yet some call this 'being bogged down in paper and administration'; it is the way an Archbishop can care for his people and help them.*
>
> *Within this framework of relentless mail the Archbishop sees people on every type of church and state business, presides at Church Assembly and Convocation and enjoys himself best when in a Kent country church taking a Confirmation. He has also travelled widely, giving himself completely to each and every person he has met in every continent. He has done much for Reunion: the title given him by the Armenian Patriarch in Istanbul, 'The Supreme Hyphen', because he brings*

churches and people together, is one the Archbishop treasures much.

He has been the great Carer for churches and people, bringing a gay and heroic endurance coupled with a brilliant logical and practical mind to every problem presented to him, not hesitating to go into the smallest detail of any tangle in order to help. It would always be easier for any Archbishop to appear more in public shedding friendliness and goodwill around him, but back at Lambeth would be piling up more and more letters asking for guidance and advice, through which the Archbishop can give much greater and more solid, if less conspicuous, help to Christians and the Church. We should all thank God for the relentless and brilliant devotion to every side of his daily work that Archbishop Fisher has shown.

The Archbishop wrote many of his own letters and then expected the two Chaplains and Robert Beloe (the Lay Secretary, who had recently joined the Lambeth staff to the newly created post of Lay Secretary to the Archbishop, after a very distinguished time as Chief Education Officer for Surrey) to vet them and stop any that they thought ought not to go. The comments below, by Freddy, relate to a very fierce letter that Fisher had written to Dr. Verwoerd, Prime Minister of South Africa (the Archbishop called his Chaplains and Lay Secretary his 'three dragons'):

Dragon FST would be happier if this didn't go on the basis of what you have upheld so often: South Africa is another Province of the Anglican Communion and you only do what the Archbishop and Bishops of that Province recommend and ask; also at this moment when you are involved with Church negotiations with de Blank [Archbishop of Johannesburg], it might be better not to write. I took the liberty of showing it to Bishop Bayne [the newly-appointed Executive Secretary of the Anglican Communion] who would hope it was not sent, as if a word of it got out to de Blank, it would make his (Bayne's) mission inordinately more difficult. Bishop Bayne feels that an eirenic kite could be flown here in something you say rather than a letter like this.

The Archbishop destroyed his letter to Verwoerd.

On Freddy's retirement as Bishop of Malmesbury in 1983, Robert Beloe reminisced in a note about Lambeth days:

Do you remember doing 'Letters' every morning? After Matins, you, Michael Adie [the Archbishop's Domestic Chaplain] and I would face Archbishop Fisher across the table, and he would tease out, by arguing with us, what he would do about any letter. And then he would dictate to Priscilla Lethbridge [the Archbishop's Private Secretary]. Sometimes the letter dictated would be very different from what we thought we had decided. Fortunately, Priscilla could not always type all his letters the same day, and she had a way of occasionally showing us a letter which she had not had time to prepare for the Archbishop's signature.

He decided, against the advice which we had daringly offered, to write to President Eisenhower and Mr. Khrushchev telling them to be good boys and get on together. We thought this would be a mistake and suggested that the Russian monks who had just been to Lambeth might not survive their return to Russia if this letter were sent.

The Archbishop was at his most belligerent - 'Anyhow, martyrdom is a very good thing,' he said. We stuck to our guns and begged him not to send the letter. Silence followed and then we proceeded to the next business.

Next morning he showed his greatness. Taking me by the lapel, as he would, he said, 'It's all right. I haven't sent that letter, but, of course, I was right to want to send it.'

One of Freddy's first 'big occasions' was his attendance with the Archbishop at the marriage of Princess Margaret and Anthony Armstrong-Jones in 1960. Freddy wrote a detailed account of it for his family. In a letter to his mother, he asked her to keep it totally confidential within the family, 'not to leave it lying around, and certainly not to be sent by post'. Twenty years later, however, Freddy began sharing his impressions when he talked to groups about his time at Lambeth, so it may be said to be in the public domain. He wrote:

The rehearsal was at 4.45pm on Thursday the 5th [the day before the wedding]; at least that was when the Dean [of Westminster] asked the Archbishop to be there. As the Archbishop was already at a meeting in Church House the other two chaplains walked over with me: Michael Adie, the Domestic Chaplain and John Satterthwaite, the Secretary of the Council of Inter-Church Relations, who is always brought in on these affairs when the Archbishop wants three chaplains. And he wanted as many as possible this time in his strange historical private war with the Abbey over ritual and precedence. The new Dean, Eric Abbott, was as determined as any of his predecessors to uphold the Abbey's position of being 'A Royal Peculiar' in which the Archbishop has no place of right or any jurisdiction at all. The order of ceremonial really went too far and just referred to 'The Visiting Prelates'; the Archbishop is not a Prelate but a Primate. Full details were given of every other procession but no mention at all of the Archbishop's small procession, which consisted of the former Bishop of Norwich, Dr. Herbert, as Clerk of the Closet, and the Bishop of London, as Dean of the Chapels Royal.

We arrived to find that the rehearsal had been going on for a long time already and strange young men were standing in for stranger foreign royalty the next day. The Archbishop arrived and we were taken up to our seats in the Sacrarium; Michael Adie in front with the Primatial Cross and John and myself behind. The Queen, the Queen Mother and Prince Charles arrived next and then came the Princess with the Duke and the bridesmaids behind.

Immediately the Queen looked agitated and started making gestures to the Princess which she did not at first understand; then she tumbled to it and turned to Princess Anne who had come up from the back of the bridesmaids and symbolically handed her the bouquet. In fact the Queen throughout the rehearsal and the wedding seemed like any other mother to be much more concerned with how Princess Anne got on as bridesmaid than about anything else. The Princess was firm and quite definite in what she wanted to do and not do; the Archbishop was firmly asked not to say, 'Follow me' when we went up the altar; she had rehearsed; she knew and they would follow. Meanwhile the two Queens had been in earnest discussion and then the Queen said, "Yes, they are much too close together", and down the steps she went to string out the bridesmaids much more apart. The Duke watched the rehearsal amused and then said to the Archbishop, "Surely you've married them now; there will be no need to come back tomorrow". We went through into the Confessor's Chapel to see where the registers would be signed. As always the Queen rather stern and quite at ease not worrying a bit who was there, but the Queen Mother being very consciously gracious and charming, speaking to everyone, fussing with stole or fur all the time. The Queen has much the nicer face of the two sisters; Margaret's is striking but not charming.

The evening was warm and fine; Joan and I went round the Mall and saw the crowds getting ready for the night. Some mothers with quite young children bedded down by the pavement.

The morning was equally fine and sunny. Mrs. Fisher and Mrs. Ramsey (the Archbishop of York was in Africa) went off in Ebor's car: Mrs. Fisher in her usual mistaken pastel shades which do nothing to relieve the grey grimness of the Forman moods. Mrs. Irvine had already taken Bishop Bayne and his family off to their seats. They had boldly asked for seats and got them; this had not been approved of at Lambeth at all.

We left at 10.45 with a police outrider. Joan had mustered nine folk to watch round our set. She took some photos before we left. We did not pass through much crowd on our way into Dean's Yard where we went the back way into Jerusalem Chamber and there robed with the two Bishops. We heard the noise of the Queen's arrival and then at 11.17 a verger came for us. Earlier the Dean had come in and told the Archbishop that he and the Chapter would have just escorted the Queen to her seat and they would like to bow to His Grace as he passed. Would he please acknowledge that bow with a bow in return? "Ah no", said the Primate, "because I shall not have bowed to the Queen; when I am in full procession into church behind my cross I do not acknowledge the secular Head and so I can't bow to you afterwards". Quite illogical, as the last time in the Abbey he had bowed on going in to the Queen Mother and the Duke at the Mountbatten funeral. This I pointed out; but he was not going to bow to anyone today. After all, why be Archbishop if you cannot be illogical? So out the Dean went to tell his Chapter they would get no Primatial bow in return to theirs.

So off we went; all the chairs had been turned lengthways to the aisles and so everyone got much longer views of the processions and then could look at the television screens opposite. On up the nave over great-grandfather's tomb and into the choir. How frail and old Winston Churchill now looks; sad to see the lion of the war like that. Up into the Sacrarium where the Queen was still standing until the Archbishop had passed, no bows, and then we sat and waited for the bride. The Countess of Ross, the bridegroom's mother, was a very striking figure but terribly nervous and embarrassed all the time. Alexandra looked as usual the most delightful of the royal party. The fanfare of trumpets rang out and up comes the bride; the false chignon of hair was I thought a great mistake; it took away from the charming simplicity of the dress and introduced a totally false note of artificial sophistication. The service went well; the Dean's voice is rather high and feminine (I can never forget the frightful Quiet Day he took for us at Westcott just after the War on the theme of the 'Enlarged Heart of Jesus'; just back from the War we all writhed under this) but he read well. I knew my sole task would be caring for the Archbishop's spectacles if he wanted to take them off, and to hold his book when he wrapped their hands in his stole. To my relief he decided to leave his glasses on his seat and I had just to hold the book. At the end of the service we moved through to sign the registers. Even there, royal kisses were very sedate between mother and daughter and the two sisters; cheeks delicately to cheeks with great care about the makeup and the Queen had to get out her bag and touch herself up again with great care. The bridegroom's parents stood discreetly to one side and the Queen proffered a hand to the Countess who curtsied low; but it was the briefest of words. Princess Anne gazed intently at us three in blue and turned to her mother and said, "Who are those three men in blue?" We did not hear the reply.

Back we went to our seats with great ceremonial. The Abbey procession was marshalled and the Dean and his Chapter went out. Then a long pause so that everyone should have a good view and then the bridegroom and bride, followed by Princess Anne. As they passed the Queen, the Princess dropped a very low and stately curtsy while the groom bowed and then the little Princess curtsied to her mother. Then out went the Queen followed by the Royalty; one watched the wave of curtsying and bowing as she moved down. Meanwhile the Archbishop and his little entourage looked quite lost up in the Sacrarium as all the lesser royal cousins down to Abel Smiths etc. went out; by then most folk thought all was over and had sat again and started talking. I'm glad to say they rose again as the Archbishop moved except for Winston who had stood for the Royalty and was not going to rise again. But the Archbishop's exit was most unseemly and undignified, left till so late. However it had all gone well and everyone seemed happy.

We got back at one to find them all glued to the television with Joan having no idea it was lunchtime and I had invited the Bishop of Coventry in. But in her usual wonderful way a good meal was ready within ten minutes.

Freddy later elaborated on the part of the service the Princess objected to - the Archbishop saying, 'Follow me'. The Archbishop replied, 'I always do'. The Dean saw that the Princess was upset about this, came forward and told the Archbishop that Her Royal Highness was worried that the very sensitive microphones would pick that up and broadcast it to the world. The Archbishop replied that that wouldn't matter; it would be a nice family touch. No more was said, but that night Freddy was on telephone duty at Lambeth and a message came through from Clarence House, 'Would you please tell the Archbishop that Her Royal Highness is fully instructed in the wedding service and asks that he does not say 'Follow me'. Freddy knocked at the Archbishop's study door, went in; the Archbishop was reading. 'What is it, Freddy?' Freddy gave him the message. The Archbishop thought for a moment and then said, 'Silly girl. All right, then, I won't.' They surmised that the Princess did not want anyone to hear anybody, even the Archbishop of Canterbury, tell her what to do.

Freddy appeared to enjoy his contacts with the Royal Family; he found Princess Alexandra the 'most charming.' He continued, 'I talked with her a lot at Prince Andrew's baptism; she is such an interesting, thoughtful and considerate person, with a delightful sparkle. At Andrew's baptism, the Palace drawing room was like a rough sea with people curtseying up and down as Royals talked to them and other Royals talked to the Queen. The Queen Mother wanted to kiss some non-Royal and did not know whether to catch her on the way down or as she was coming up.'

On November 13th, Freddy wrote to his mother:

> *How bad I have been about writing, but Lady Chatterley and Rome have absolutely swamped us in paper, and it has been Church Assembly week as well so I have been returning about six to answer eighty or more letters.*

John Robinson, Bishop of Woolwich, had given evidence on behalf of Penguin Books in favour of the publication of D.H. Lawrence's *Lady Chatterley's Lover*. The point at issue was whether the book constituted an obscene publication according to the law; if so its publication was illegal. Lambeth was overwhelmed with letters and telephone calls protesting against the Bishop. The *Lady Chatterley's Lover* case was one of the few occasions when Freddy found himself in a difficult position vis à vis the Archbishop. The Archbishop of Canterbury upbraided the Bishop of Woolwich for getting involved and actually admitted that he had not read the book and had little intention of doing so. Freddy had read the book and thought it 'extraordinarily moving'. He admired John Robinson for making such a public defence of it. But Freddy had to toe the Lambeth line, which he found 'difficult in the extreme'.

The following Sunday Freddy was due to preach at Windsor. Freddy wrote to his mother:

On Sunday, all three of us, Joan, Stephen and I, drove to Windsor and went to the Chaplain's House and then to the chapel which is in the grounds of Royal Lodge.

The preacher sits in the Sanctuary and so looks straight into the Royal Box on the other side. They were all there: Queen, Prince Philip, Anne, Queen Mum and some guests; they drive up in their own cars and go in by a special door into their box; the Chaplain and I had to bow when going to our places but nothing else. I preached on the Sermon on the Mount as it was their Patronal Festival for All Saints. The little church was quite full of folk off the Estate. After the service the Royals, as they seem to be called, came round and shook hands and talked; Joan was introduced and they shook hands with Stephen. The Queen Mum was very sweet about the sermon and said how very much they had all enjoyed it. The Queen was rather reticent and shy; Philip chatted about Hong Kong. They had the King of Norway coming to lunch in the Castle so we were not invited back to drinks in Royal Lodge as often happens. We had lunch with the Chaplain and his wife and then went off to Bradfield. [Freddy was preaching at Bradfield College at Evensong; the Headmaster was his cousin, Anthony Chevenix-Trench, later to be Headmaster of Eton.]

Last Wednesday the Archbishop and Mrs. Fisher had dinner at Buckingham Palace and both the Archbishop and Mrs. Fisher very nicely told us how first the Queen Mother had come to them and said what an 'excellent' sermon they had last Sunday and Mrs. Fisher said she went on and on about it; 'most remarkable', said Mrs. Fisher. Then the Queen came up and mentioned it too. And later Prince Philip came up and said, 'We had an excellent sermon from your "what's-it" last Sunday', unable to remember the words Senior Chaplain. So that was all rather gratifying.

Freddy was to recall later that when preaching at Windsor Chapel, the small church in the grounds which was the particular care of the Queen Mother, he and Joan learnt that the Queen and Prince Philip did not like the enormous stand and Prayer Book that King George VI had given his wife and felt it spoilt the chapel; they had asked the chaplain to ask the Queen Mother if it could be put away as she had not used it for a long time. The Queen felt that she could not ask her mother but asked the chaplain to do so. Freddy noticed on that Sunday morning that when it came to the psalm the Queen Mother opened the enormous Prayer Book and found the psalms and was clearly using the Prayer Book! Elizabeth and Philip gave each other a nudge and realised they could do no more about it.

The major event during Freddy's time as Senior Chaplain, and, indeed, perhaps the major event of Fisher's primacy, was his visit to Pope John XXIII, which followed his pilgrimage to the Holy Land and visit to the Orthodox Patriarch in Istanbul.

Freddy was responsible for the following Press Release on All Saints' Day, November 1st, 1960:

It is announced from Lambeth Palace that the Archbishop of Canterbury plans to leave London on November 22nd for Jerusalem where he will be the guest of the Anglican Archbishop in Jerusalem, the Most Reverend Campbell MacInnes. His Grace will visit the Holy Places and call on the Orthodox Patriarch of Jerusalem and heads of other Churches in the Middle East, expressing in person the close friendship which has long existed between Anglican and Eastern Churches.

On the way back the Archbishop hopes it will prove possible for him to call at Istanbul to visit His All Holiness Athenagoras I, Oecumenical Patriarch of the Orthodox Church. After Istanbul the Archbishop of Canterbury proposes to spend a few days in Rome in the course of which he will pay a courtesy visit to His Holiness Pope John XXIII. The Archbishop will return to this country on December 3rd.

During the past 50 years the Church of England has increasingly come into friendly relationship with other Churches. Foremost among these have been the Church of Scotland and the Free Churches in the United Kingdom with their sister Churches overseas, the Protestant Churches of Europe, and the Orthodox and other Eastern Churches, with whom there is a long tradition of friendship.

All these Churches are members of the World Council of Churches whose Central Committee met at St. Andrews this summer. At this meeting there were members from the Roman Catholic Church. The Archbishop of Canterbury who attended stated recently in his Diocesan Notes:

The pace is quickening. We must enter into unity of spirit with Baptists, Congregationalists, Methodists, Presbyterians and even Roman Catholics. We all know that we must get together and learn to like to be together before we can seriously grow together. And, as was said on good authority at St. Andrews, the attitude in Rome itself to this movement towards unity of spirit and understanding is changing rapidly. Where there was ignorance and suspicion, there is now increasing sympathetic interest, and in some quarters a manifest desire (if I may so put it) to enter into the spirit of this movement to see what God can teach us all through it. A clear sign of this is that the Pope has set up a new piece of Church organisation - a new Secretariat for the Unity of Christians, of which Cardinal Bea is leader and Monsignor Willebrands (who was present at St. Andrews as an observer) is secretary. Such a permanent organ of the Roman Catholic Church established for the very purpose of maintaining and increasing contact with non-Roman Churches is indeed another sign of the times, and full of godly promise.

It is in the light of what he has written that the Archbishop desires in the spirit of courtesy and friendship among Christians to visit the Oecumenical Patriarch and the Pope on his way home from Jerusalem.

Throughout the tour the Archbishop will be accompanied by the Reverend Fre-

derick S. Temple (Senior Chaplain) and the Reverend John R. Satterthwaite (General Secretary of the Church of England Council on Inter-Church Relations).

Lambeth Palace was inundated with letters to the Archbishop. Sadly, though many of them congratulated Fisher on making this initiative, many of them protested strongly about the projected meeting with the Pope. Quite a few were extremely vitriolic in tone. Freddy was responsible for answering all of them and said that, for the first and only time during his period as Senior Chaplain, he had to resort to issuing a general, rather than personal, reply. To everyone who wrote to the Archbishop, Freddy replied:

> The Archbishop of Canterbury asks me to acknowledge your letter about his visit to Istanbul and Rome. He has read it with care; but as he cannot answer letters on this subject personally he asks me to send you a copy of what he said recently to his Diocesan Conference on the subject, and this I enclose.
>
> He is grateful to those who sent encouragement. He is sorry not to have had the chance of talking things out with those who criticised or condemned his journey. He trusts that all alike will be stimulated by this event to more sincere and earnest use of the words from the Prayer for the Church Militant:
>
> 'Beseeching thee to inspire continually the Universal Church with the spirit of truth, unity and concord: and grant that all they that do confess thy holy name may agree in the truth of thy Holy Word and live in unity and godly love.'

Freddy was asked by the editor of the *Church Times* to write an 'intimate account' of the journey. The following was published on December 9th, 1960. It is a long piece, but is included as it stands, for it describes a momentous occasion in the history of the Church of England, written by one who was actually there. The editor wrote to Freddy on December 6th:

> I am delighted with your article. It is all I had hoped for, and more. As I read it I found myself instinctively muttering, with distant memories in mind of our 'Copy' system at Rugby, 'Show this to the Headmaster' - but that would have another meaning today! I really am extremely grateful to you for what will be the best thing in this week's CT by far.

The article reads:

> Each place that I visited with the Archbishop made its own distinct impact.
>
> In Jerusalem the division of the Church hits you hard. The pre-war scaffolding outside the Church of the Holy Sepulchre still stands, as no agreement can be reached between the Churches concerned as to who should pay for what. Eight for-

mal calls in one day on heads of different Churches, eight glasses of liqueur, eight chocolates and eight cups of Turkish coffee could not fail to impress on the mind and the digestion that the Church was divided.

Jerusalem revealed Good Friday; but it also showed us Easter Day. The welcome in St. George's Cathedral immediately after the Archbishop arrived was simple, yet unusual and moving. In purple cassock the Archbishop in Jerusalem led the Archbishop of Canterbury into the Cathedral through the cloisters, preceded by the kawas dressed in fez and girt with sword beating the ground in front of him, the relic of a custom from Ottoman days.

Inside the Cathedral was a wonderful galaxy of varied ecclesiastical dress, of every Christian community. A well-trained English Roman Catholic reporter did not come inside the Cathedral for the prayers of welcome, and could not believe it when he saw the French 'White Fathers' and the Franciscans coming out at the end, having prayed with us and received the Archbishop's blessing.

As we came out, all the kawases of all the Heads of Churches joined together, and to a thunderous beating of the ground we returned through the cloisters to the Archbishop's house. Throughout the time in Jerusalem the Latins, as the Roman Catholics are there called, went out of their way to be as friendly and welcoming as any other Church, asking the Archbishop to pray with them at their altars and many kneeling to kiss his ring.

This was no quiet personal pilgrimage that most English folk would like to make. Only in the vast Temple area was there quiet and peace as we were shown round by the Sheikh in his fez; a quiet broken by an American lady in slacks addressing her companion, 'Say, which is the Archbishop? The one with the fez?'

But in Bethlehem and the Church of the Holy Sepulchre vast crowds in great enthusiasm and friendship engulfed the Archbishop, three monks of different denominations seized each arm, and he was swept from place to place through a sea of folk, often passing me almost air-borne by the vigorous and eager welcome.

The Archbishop accepted this completely, and was most moved by it. He knelt with Greek, Latin and Armenian at their altars, rising from one and saying to a young Franciscan who gripped a third of his arm as he rushed along: 'I am the only one of you who is equally happy at all three altars.' He knelt by the star in the grotto of the Nativity with its inscription in Latin, 'Here Jesus Christ was born of the Virgin Mary 1720.'

He was led to the altar of St. Jerome, and, on being told that Jerome had translated the Bible, the Archbishop replied, 'The work of translation still goes on', and knelt in prayer. 'There', he said as he rose, 'that was a prayer for all translators.'

Jerusalem showed Easter Day as well as Good Friday; the growing unity of spirit to conquer division was there, and burst for the moment into flower during the Archbishop's visit.

The political division runs deeper still. In Jerusalem at night there is a narrow strip of rubble and damaged houses in darkness dividing the lights of Jordan and Israel. *Neither side refers to the other. The Jordan papers said the Archbishop would visit occupied territory on the Sunday afternoon.*

No Arab congregation could sing easily the Benedictus, 'Blessed be the Lord God of Israel', nor some of the psalm, 'If the Lord had not been on our side, now may Israel say.' On both sides you refer to 'the other side.' At tea in Israel Canon Jones's little girls had smart shoes of which they were clearly proud. I commented on them. 'They are other-side shoes,' they said.

In Jerusalem one felt the divisions in the Church could and were beginning to be conquered; and here one saw the quiet, steady, reconciling work of the Archbishop in Jerusalem and his staff. But as yet there appeared only darkness over the political divide.

It was strange to be met at Istanbul by a group of men in dark suits and black ties, with only the Anglican chaplain and one other in dog-collars. After Christian Lebanon, where the power and place of the Church is openly recognised, we were in a land where the Church had lived for centuries under alien and often hostile government; even now, only the head of a Church may appear in clerical dress in the streets. It was hard to realise that these men in black ties were Patriarchs of the Church, soon to reappear in all the magnificent robes of the Orthodox liturgy.

The Patriarchal Cathedral is small and restricted, in a slum district, a strange successor to the bare and now cold magnificence of Sancta Sophia; but here in the Phanar one felt was a Church which had been true to the gospel throughout centuries of suffering and persecution, drawing strength from the magnificence of its powerful liturgy.

The service on St. Andrew's Day, their patron saint, lasted three hours; the Archbishop joined it after the first hour, the Church and its galleries were crammed with men and women, all standing. His All Holiness the Ecumenical Patriarch is a magnificent giant of a man, with kind and tender eyes, a deep resonant voice, and a flowing white beard. At the end of the liturgy he came down to his throne and stood opposite the Archbishop, who was in the royal throne on the other side of the choir.

Having made formal speeches of welcome and reply they descended and embraced each other, and the Patriarch gave the Archbishop a jewelled encolpion. At the luncheon afterwards the Archbishop gave the Patriarch a silver alms-dish inscribed with the arms of Canterbury and words commemorating the visit; His Grace also gave the Ecumenical Patriarch the Lambeth cross, very rarely given and only to those who have worked conspicuously for the Ecumenical Movement.

Here was a Church rich in warmth and affection, and with long experience of suffering and humble witness, ready to reach out to even closer relations with the Anglican Church. Already in Istanbul, as a sign of such contacts, was Noel Vincent, one in a line of Anglican ordinands who was spending a year studying at the seminary of Halki on an island in the Bosphorus. It is very good to know that a future Ridley Hall man is coming to grips with Orthodoxy.

Also in Istanbul was the Rev. David Harding, teaching with the Armenians. The Archbishop called on the Armenian Patriarch; they talked of the visit of the Supreme Catholicos to England, and the Patriarch said, 'But you, Your Grace, are the Supreme Hyphen, because you bring people and Churches together.' 'The Supreme Hyphen,' the Archbishop laughed, 'I appreciate that title very much.'

In the Vatican we were back in the cautious and exact diplomacy of the West. All was friendly and cordial, if slightly nervous in the lower official circles; the protocol of five hundred years ago could not be remembered, nor did it quite fit.

I felt as if I was in some royal palace of two hundred years back, as we went up in the Vatican lift and walked through room after room, each with its own guards in different uniform. Those expert in such details told us that this was an unexpected sign of courtesy, as the guards had been called back from their Advent retreat exercises.

We turned the corner and went on through more rooms, all of whose doors were wide open, another subtle mark of welcome, the expert diplomats noticed, until a door opened and there was the welcoming figure of the Pope in white and the Archbishop went in. We waited outside in an ante-room.

As the minutes ticked by the chamberlains assured us this was most unusual, and a sure sign of an unusually friendly conversation. The hour's interview was apparently something of a record. The chaplains were summoned in, the Archbishop presented his gift of the Coronation service: the Pope had already given his gift of some volumes of his addresses. We were presented with medals, there was a little conversation, and we left.

The Press were all behind in the Piazza which divides the Vatican City from Rome, but there were small groups of well-wishers who raised their hats and clapped, as the Archbishop drove through St. Peter's Square. As the Archbishop has repeatedly said, nothing definite was meant to result from the meeting; but a good example of friendly conversation may be followed.

This account has deliberately left out many details of fact which have already been told elsewhere. The Press reporters who followed the Archbishop through his tour were most friendly, courteous and understanding the entire time; their affection and admiration for him by the end was considerable. Our hosts in each place deserve an entire article of grateful praises for all they did.

Possibly the whole trip can be summed up best in one of the shorter unsigned letters which the Archbishop received which applies not only to Rome but to Jerusalem and Istanbul. 'Dear Primitive, I think to pay a visit to his Holiness Pop John is a great thinck for Unity.'

Freddy was also to write later to his family:

As the Archbishop and I were going to the Cathedral [in Istanbul] for the big service, there were a mass of patriarchs there. The Archbishop turned to me and said,

In Jerusalem with Archbishop Fisher and other senior ecclesiastics.   Freddy prepares to take a different view.

'Freddy, you will tell me whether I kiss twice or three times, won't you?' And so as we approached each Patriarch according to his status and dignity, I would whisper. 'Twice, Your Grace' or 'Three times, Your Grace'. Freddy admitted afterwards, though not to the Archbishop, that he was not sure about two of the Patriarchs, so he simply guessed.

In an aide-mémoire, written two days after his return from Rome, Freddy wrote that the Archbishop, on leaving the Pope, 'slumped in the back seat of his car' and said to Freddy: 'We have just met a man of such simplicity and sheer goodness. I felt a Presence surrounding him and knew he was walking very close with God.' Those, according to Freddy, were his exact words; he had jotted them down on a piece of paper almost immediately. The Archbishop had then told Freddy how little affected the Pope was by all the pageantry around him; he was quite content to let them get on with it, if that's the sort of thing they enjoyed - and as long as it kept them happy, so be it. Freddy emphasised that this was just the gist of what the Pope had said, and the Archbishop was not quoting him verbatim.

Freddy and Joan's relationship was so close that even if only away for a night, Freddy would invariably find time to scribble her a letter. On this trip, which Freddy found 'absolutely exhausting', he still found time to write to her at some considerable length These letters, between husband and wife, are obviously very personal, so I have edited them heavily. The following are quotations from different letters sent from Jerusalem and Beirut. Freddy did not write a letter to Joan from Rome, but sent a telegram.

(From Jerusalem)

It was so lovely to have you at the airport, especially as Miss Forman [Ro-samund Fisher's sister] had been so catty in the car. 'Where's your hat?' 'None ever fits.' 'So swollen-headed. I thought so.' Said not really with a smile. Mrs. Fisher tried to retrieve the situation.

[Throughout his time at Lambeth Freddy found it hard to cope with Miss Forman: he talked or wrote more than once about her 'grim moods' and the fact that she 'always seems to want to get in a dig at me.' Close friends say he was genuinely upset and bewildered by her attitude.]

This is a nice big house. [The Archbishop's party was staying in St. George's Close.] *Big rooms, lovely crisp fine cool weather with blue skies: everyone with overseas friendliness. And great bowls of varied fruit. Why did we leave Hong Kong?*

There has been no moment yet to do anything for oneself. When the Archbishop rests and goes to sleep John and I deal with the press, etc. Today we went first to the Dome of the Rock, then to the Church of the Holy Sepulchre where there was a to-tal and complete scrum of friendly welcome. When we went to the actual tomb, a band played 'God Save the Queen'!

(From Beirut)

We had a good flight and then with police outriders swirled in great state through the town, two Archbishops in one car, another behind and John [Satterthwaite] and I in the third Cadillac. I couldn't do this for long; it has little of the Gospel in it.

Jim Woodhouse and his wife, Sarah, who had a flat in the Footman's Tower at Lambeth Palace, were good friends during these years. Jim taught at Westminster School, afterwards becoming Head Master of Rugby School and later of Lancing College.

Jim Woodhouse writes:

At Lambeth Freddy and Joan were a breath of fresh air, and we grew to love them very dearly. I can't put my finger on any special episode; it was simply a joy and privilege to be his friend. Freddy, with his infinite kindness, humanity and sense of fun, was perhaps the best advertisement for the Christian faith that one could ever imagine. We both felt, and still feel, deeply enriched by having known him so well.

Sarah Woodhouse writes,

Here are two pictures of Freddy which have stayed in my mind so clearly for 40 years that I never think of them without smiling again and again. They show his extraordinary capacity for quick and accurate judgement of a situation and his gift for instant and appropriate action.

On both occasions I was returning to Lambeth Palace with our two very young sons in a pram. Having rung the bell at the main entrance to be let in by the gateman through a side door, an immensely tall, wild-eyed man with long black hair forced his way in behind me before he could be questioned. Shouting, 'I'm God. I've got to see the Archbishop,' he pushed past the gateman and set off across the wide courtyard. I followed on his heels knowing that Freddy, as the Archbishop's Chaplain, would have been telephoned quickly to intercept him.

Freddy appeared within seconds and confronted this wild figure, his head barely reaching the man's shoulders. 'Sir, can I help you?' 'Yes,' roared the intruder, 'I'm God. Take me to the Archbishop. At once!'

'I don't believe you're God,' replied Freddy, completely relaxed and with a big smile. 'I'm sure God wouldn't shout!' Silence fell. I waited a few yards behind. 'We'll whisper then,' growled the giant, and Freddy steered him away through an arch into the gardens for a long and amicable whispered discussion together before feeding him back through the main gate again into the Lambeth Road. He was obviously quite contented with the respect and affection he had been given. Perhaps he had even come to believe that Freddy was His Grace. Mission accomplished.

The second occasion concerns Princess Margaret, before her marriage to Anthony Armstrong-Jones. Sarah writes:

Two photographers from a tabloid newspaper had set up watch outside the main gates of Lambeth Palace, guessing that she would eventually make a private visit to talk to the Archbishop. They were right. An afternoon came when a lone figure, in dark glasses and a scarf, was seen arriving at the gates in a taxi. As I reached for the bell to be admitted myself as well as to save the taxi driver from getting out of his cab - I noticed quick movements in the Lambeth Parish churchyard beside me and saw two men scrambling up on to the back roof of the church, right against the great wall surrounding the Palace grounds. As I walked in I then saw them beginning to lower themselves and their cameras over the wall into the courtyard. I quickly reported this to the gateman and again he rang Freddy on the emergency line.

An unbelievable scene then unfolded right in front of me. The taxi was driving slowly towards the Archbishop who was waiting on the steps to greet the Princess. As the taxi drew up and stopped the two men started to run very fast indeed to position themselves on either side and get their scoop photographs. Before the taxi door had been opened, before the Archbishop had stepped forward and before the photographers had covered more than 30 yards, Freddy appeared like a small black wizard. His speed was so great and his shoes were so quiet that they never knew what was coming up behind them. Never have two rugger tackles been executed in such quick succession nor with more devastating effect.

Both men were flattened, the wind knocked out of them. Both cameras were smashed. Immediately Freddy had them on their feet, back to the main gate and

out into the street before Princess Margaret or the Archbishop had noticed any-
thing amiss at all.

I still find it hard to believe that Freddy managed that with his cassock to his an-
kles. He must have been amazing at the game as a boy at Rugby School.

Freddy had a wealth of stories to tell about his time at Lambeth. One that he often repeated was of the occasion when Mrs. Fisher gave a tea party to welcome the Baynes family when they arrived at Lambeth. Freddy was sitting beside her when she turned to Lydia, a teenage daughter, and said, 'Come and sit beside me, Lydia. Now what will you be doing this summer during your holiday?' 'Oh gee,' said Lydia, 'I guess just bumming round Europe.' 'Oh,' said Mrs. Fisher looking very grey and erect, 'interesting.'

Once at a big service at St. Paul's when the Archbishop's procession had to pro-ceed round the church twice, for some reason Archbishop Fisher popped into his stall after the first time round and Freddy suddenly found himself, carrying the Primatial Cross, going round at the end of a long procession with no Archbishop with him, but he just solemnly went on and someone at the end said how nice it was to have a cross bringing up the rear of the procession, though he said he felt extraordinarily silly.

May 17th 1961 saw one of the final appearances of the Archbishop and his Senior Chaplain together, at the Consecration, in the presence of Her Majesty the Queen, of Guildford Cathedral, the first Anglican Cathedral to be built on a new site in the South of England since the Reformation, the architect of which was Sir Edward Maufe. Freddy could remember the day vividly. He, the Archbish-op, the Dean, the new Bishop of Guildford, George Reindorp, and a whole bevy of the episcopal bench were all waiting for the Royal Family to arrive. George Rein-dorp had been given an enormous mitre made by Lady Maufe, the wife of the ar-chitect, which had the word *Guildford* emblazoned on the front. The Bishop of London, Henry Montgomery-Campbell, peered at it and said, 'Yes, I like your hat; when you're lost, people will know where to return you.' Those who knew Freddy's own sense of humour can imagine his reaction. He said it was the nearest he came to disgracing himself in his two years at Lambeth.

He had another story to tell about Montgomery-Campbell. One day, when opening the letters at Lambeth, Freddy found one from a priest in Notting Hill, in the diocese of London, asking whether the Archbishop could tell him anything about the new experimental services for cremation. The priest wrote that he had received the following one-line reply from his diocesan, but it was not much help. 'Yes indeed, there is an experimental service for cremation and I have already sug-gested a number of names.' Freddy wrote to a friend, 'That was a difficult one; I had to compose a letter explaining things without in any way seeming to go be-hind the Bishop of London's back. But did I giggle! I think my reply was masterly, but dear Priscilla thought I was too flippant and I suspect she toned it down.'

Montgomery-Campbell was indeed the sort of man who spawns anecdotes about himself and Freddy delighted in telling the following in the autumn of 1959. Apparently the Bishop had to decline an invitation to speak at a dinner because he was already booked for a Confirmation, so he was asked by the organiser of the dinner if he could recommend a wit who could be guaranteed to make an entertaining speech. The Bishop replied that he did not know a wit but he had in his diocese several half-wits and wondered if two of them would do instead. Freddy said that, though Geoffrey Fisher was often totally exasperated by Montgomery-Campbell, on this occasion he simply roared with laughter and asked him how many other diocesan bishops would say the same if they dared. Freddy said that he 'kept studiously silent, but smiled dutifully.' Freddy wrote to his mother in November, 'The Bishop of London is driving His Grace to distraction.'

William Purcell wrote a life of the Archbishop while Dr. Fisher was still alive and asked for Freddy's help. Freddy replied that he loved and respected him too much and so he would not, as he would have to be quite frank about some things, which the Archbishop might find hurtful. When he met the Archbishop afterwards, on holiday, Dr. Fisher said, 'I hear you would not take part in the biography.' 'No, Your Grace,' Freddy replied. 'Quite right,' he said, 'you know me much too well.'

The Archbishop told Freddy in confidence in the autumn of 1960 that he intended to retire in 1961. Freddy was a little taken aback, for he himself was seriously thinking of moving on. He was desperate to get back to parish life, both for his own sake and for that of Joan, whose capabilities and qualities he thought were being wasted at Lambeth; but it looked as though he would have to stay at Lambeth for a year more at least to help the new Archbishop settle in. Freddy put it to the Archbishop that it might be as well to move at the same time as the Archbishop himself, thus allowing the Archbishop's successor to choose his own man, but Fisher would have none of it. The Archbishop told him that, although he could not insist on his staying at Lambeth, he would be doing the Church a great disservice if he left.

On December 23rd, Freddy received an unofficial approach asking whether he would be interested in becoming Vicar of Leeds Parish Church. Freddy certainly would and wrote in some trepidation to the Archbishop, who was staying at the Old Palace in Canterbury for Christmas. He thought he knew the Archbishop well enough to be sure that he would receive no encouragement. But the Archbishop seemed to have had a change of heart. On St. Stephen's Day, December 26th, Fisher wrote to Freddy:

Oddly enough, the Bishop of Portsmouth wrote to me the other day, with Portsea in mind. I said that you were not available for a move in 1961 - thinking of course of my own movements!

But Leeds Parish Church is quite different. If that came your way, you ought most certainly to go to it: and anyway, Lambeth would not come to an end - it never does!

And now you have put this to me, I begin to repent about what I said to Portsmouth - and will gladly write to unsay it if you wish me to.

On January 2nd, 1961, Freddy received the following from the Bishop of Portsmouth:

I think I am right in believing that your Lord and Master has mentioned an enquiry I made of him before Christmas as to your availability at this juncture. He replied then, as you perhaps know, saying, more or less, 'hands off', but since then I have heard from him withdrawing his previous letter and saying I would be free to approach you.

The possibility is St. Mary's, Portsea; the patrons are Winchester College and they rather left it to me to do the soundings. I wonder whether you feel this is a job which you might be ready to think of?

I do not imagine there is need for me to say a great deal about the past history of the parish. Much more, it is a question of thinking of it today and in the future. It is still the vast great set-up that it always was, with the Parish Church, five Mission Churches, Clergy House and at the moment six curates. Inevitably it tends to be looking over its shoulder at the past, and Wally Smith, who is leaving at the end of January after 15 years there, has done a wonderful job in re-establishing the parish after the ravages of war, and in putting the finances on a good solid basis.

What it needs now is someone who is going to think positively about the way the parish can best be serving the community in the future, and who is going to able to build up some of the weak spots as well as cope with and train a fairly large staff.

It is probably silly to try to put on paper all that can be said about the parish, and far and away the best thing would be if you felt at all that this was a possibility, that you and perhaps your wife would come down and maybe spend a night with us and go into the whole thing with greater care.

Freddy was in a quandary. In the words of the Bishop of Pontefract, Freddy's Vicar while at Newark, 'What a dilemma! Leeds or Portsea! Fancy these two wonderful opportunities coming up at the same time, and poor you having to decide.' Freddy's papers show there was no shortage of contradictory advice. Half of his correspondents, including F.R. Barry, thought Leeds would be the best place to go; half, including Aunt Frances, thought the challenge of Portsea would best suit him. (Aunt Frances actually wrote an extremely long and detailed letter giving comprehensive, detailed and accurate facts, as well as opinions, about both parishes, demonstrating that somehow she still had her finger on the pulse of the life of the Church of England to a remarkable degree.) Letters were despatched almost daily from Lambeth to Leeds and Lambeth to Portsmouth and vice-versa.

After a lot of heart-searching and thought, Freddy and Joan decided that they would like to go to Portsea, and told others of his decision. On January 25th, Freddy received a letter from the Bishop of Portsmouth, whose first paragraph read:

What absolutely gorgeous news. I had Bishop Anthony Bloom staying the night, and when I opened my letter at breakfast I let out such a yell of delight that he said, 'That sounds like good news!' I really am simply thrilled, and again say how much I look forward to having you with us here.

The Churchwarden of Leeds Parish Church was gracious:

Thank you for your letter of the 26th inst., indicating that you have decided to accept the living of Portsea. How thoughtless of them to have approached you at the present time! Obviously we must accept your decision, though I personally had looked forward very much to seeing you here ..... I do hope you and your wife will be immensely happy at Portsea.

Meanwhile, on January 17th, the announcement had been made from Downing Street that Archbishop Fisher was the retire on May 31st. Within two days, a further announcement was made, on the afternoon of Thursday, January 19th, that Michael Ramsey was to be translated from York to Canterbury. Fisher thought he ought to pave the way with Ramsey by writing himself to him about Freddy's imminent departure, and suggested that Freddy should follow this up the next day with a letter of his own. Freddy wrote:

First, may I congratulate you on your translation and assure you along with countless others of our prayers. My wife and I do hope you will both enjoy life as much here as you did in York.

I understand the Archbishop of Canterbury has written to you about me. With his leave and knowledge I have accepted the living of Portsea, which becomes vacant at the end of this month, and if you are agreeable would like to tell the Bishop of Portsmouth I was free to be instituted any time after May 31st. It seems the best moment to make the break. I am very sorry to be leaving just as Your Grace arrives, but with Robert Beloe and Simon Ridley [who succeeded Michael Adie as the Archbishop's Domestic Chaplain] here the machinery of Lambeth can run perfectly smoothly; for a year Michael Adie ran it alone. So I do not feel so badly about it. In fact, one of the problems about the Senior Chaplain's work now that Beloe has come, is that it is not more than a half-time job except at exceptional moments like the Rome visit; and these do not occur often!! I have profitably filled my time with many other interests and much preaching up and down the country when not wanted by the Archbishop.

> Robert Beloe and I are of course at your disposal if you wish at any time to discuss with us any points about the running of the Lambeth office.

Freddy received the following from Ramsey by return:

> My very grateful thanks for your kind letter and welcome.
>
> We are very sad at the thought of leaving York; but, with so much encouragement and so many prayers, we think we are going to be happy in the new task.
>
> Thank you so much for writing about your personal matter. I shall miss you if you go; but my advice to you is that you should not feel any call to stay longer than is wanted by your obligations to the present Archbishop. The presence of Robert Beloe at Lambeth as a 'continuity man' makes all the difference. So, so far as in me lies, please feel free to take on the charge at Portsea whenever suits best.
>
> My warmest good wishes for most happy work there.

Freddy wrote to his friend, Bishop Frank West, in May, 1961:

> I have thoroughly enjoyed my two years here at the centre of Church life and administration, but am equally enormously glad it is to be for no longer. One could not work for such a tremendously energetic, extremely administratively efficient and brilliant analytical mind as the Archbishop's without learning a great amount and profiting a great deal. I am personally very fond of him too, with his great rugged honesty and humility. Some people think our move is due to the Archbishop's; it is not; it was coming up anyhow. When offering me this job in Hong Kong he said I was to move as soon as the right job came up in England, and there could not be a better job than Vicar of Portsea, formidable though it is in many ways. Joan will have 14 women's organisations to be interested in; each church has its own council and the Parochial Council has 120 members! But the setting is thrilling; this vast and rather lovely Victorian Cathedral-like place of worship, seating 2,000, right in the middle of thousands of folk, with Vicarage and Clergy House just opposite. It only rests now to see how God wants the fire already burning well in parts to spread and the whole place become ablaze.

'Atticus' wrote in the *Sunday Times* on February 12th:

> NEXT BUT ONE?
> They are always tipping the next Prime Minister but five. I feel like tipping the next Archbishop of Canterbury but one, and I give you the Rev. Freddy Temple, Dr. Fisher's senior Chaplain at Lambeth Palace. He has been preferred to the Rectorship of Portsea, the key parish in the Anglican Church, with a cure of 40,000 souls, a stipend of £1,350 and seven curates. It has always been thought of as a spiritual launching-pad, and former incumbents include Archbishops Lang and

Garbett, and five sitting Bishops.

Temple is in his forties and is the only top cleric in the Church of England who wears brown shoes (with the possible exception of the Metropolitan of India). The Chair of St. Augustine must look like a piece of household furniture to him, for his uncle William sat in it, also his grandfather Frederick. But Freddy Temple doesn't hanker after the high places: he spent six years as Dean of Hong Kong, and no cleric with his eye on a Bishopric takes an overseas posting if he can help it. It is pleasant to think that brown shoes and selflessness are not bars to promotion.

11   Portsea

The distinguished history of, and work undertaken in, the parish of St. Mary, Portsea, has been well documented elsewhere (including *The Work of a Great Parish* by Cyril Garbett (1915) and, more recently, *Consecrated to Prayer: A Centenary History of St. Mary's, Portsea, 1889-1989*, published by the Vicar, Churchwardens and Parochial Church Council of St. Mary's, Portsea, 1989). Nevertheless, a brief résumé of the history of the parish might help put into perspective the task to which Freddy was called.

The present Parish Church was consecrated in October 1889, during the incumbency of Canon Edgar Jacob, who had become Vicar of Portsea in 1878. He came to a rather run-down and unwieldy parish and saw at once both the problems and possibilities of his task. He soon gathered round him a staff of nine clergy and built four Mission Halls, and filled what had been an almost empty Church, to an extent where an enlargement or replacement was considered necessary.

The Rt. Hon W.H. Smith, the son of the founder of W.H. Smith and Son, was Secretary to the Treasury and Leader of the House of Commons at the time. Amongst previous positions he had held was that of First Lord of the Admiralty. As First Lord, he had appreciated the nation's responsibility for the spiritual welfare of Britain's greatest naval port. When Canon Jacob's project came to his notice, he made a magnificent monetary donation, which made possible the construction of a noble Parish Church.

In 1895, Canon Jacob was appointed Bishop of Newcastle and, from 1903 till 1920, the year of his death, was Bishop of St. Albans. Anxiety was expressed as to whether any man could carry on the great work now that the founder of the modern parish had gone. A few months later, all fears were set at rest when Cosmo Gordon Lang, Vicar of St. Mary the Virgin, Oxford, and Fellow and Dean of Divinity at Magdalen College, was appointed as Canon Jacob's successor. 'Mr. Lang's acceptance of Portsea is a great relief to me,' wrote the new Bishop of Newcastle to a friend shortly after his successor had been announced. 'He will probably be a Bishop one day. He wants to carry things on, I think, on similar lines to myself.'

Few, however, dreamed that one day the young Vicar of Portsea would be Archbishop of Canterbury or that a newly-ordained curate, C.F. Garbett, who joined Lang's staff in 1899, would one day be Archbishop of York. Not least of the achievements of Lang was to increase his staff of clergy to sixteen. In 1901 Lang left Portsea to be Suffragan Bishop of Stepney; in 1908 he became Archbishop of York and twenty years later was translated to Canterbury.

His successor at Portsea was Canon Bernard Wilson, Rector of Bethnal Green. Wilson greatly endeared himself to his parishioners, not least because of his genius for pastoral visiting. He was an incredibly hard worker, and it is said that the strain was too much for him. He died suddenly in 1909. (There is a postcard above my desk as I write, showing vast crowds, many deep, lining the streets at his funeral.)

Wilson's successor was Cyril Garbett, who was already on the staff. He was in an unrivalled position to be acquainted with the needs, problems and complex administration of the huge parish, and by his energy, insight and eloquence proved himself a worthy successor. After ten years as Vicar of Portsea, Garbett was appointed Bishop of Southwark, was translated to the See of Winchester in 1932, and in 1942 succeeded Freddy's uncle William as Archbishop of York.

The Chancel and High Altar of St. Mary, Portsea.

The great work of the first four Vicars was consolidated by Canon Lovel Southam (1919-28), who became Canon of Chester Cathedral; the Reverend Geoffrey Lunt (1928-35), who became Bishop of Ripon in 1935 and Bishop of Salisbury in 1945; Canon H.C. Robins (1935-44) who became Dean of Salisbury; and Canon Walter Smith (1944-61), who had the task of rebuilding and reorganising a parish that had suffered greatly as a result of the War. He tried to do it along the lines of previous Vicars. Christopher Chessun (Curate of St. Mary's 1987-89, and now Bishop of Woolwich) writes in *Consecrated to Prayer*:

> However as the days of Canon Smith's incumbency drew to a close, it became increasingly clear that although his work to build up the faith and spiritual life of the parish had borne much fruit, the creaking framework of a large staff and plant with limited financial resources was no longer possible to sustain, and no longer met the needs of the modern parish.

This was the inheritance to which Freddy was called.

Freddy was instituted as Vicar on July 9th, 1961. He wrote to his family and friends that the vast Parish Church was 'absolutely packed'. On meeting many of his new parishioners immediately after the service, Freddy realised immediately the enormous pride that the parish had in its past history - and also made him recall what John Phillips, Bishop of Portsmouth, had said to him when they were discussing the possibility of Freddy going to Portsea - that the parish needed adapting and bringing into the 1960s. However, there were signs that parish pride in so distinguished a recent history might make necessary changes far from welcome.

Amongst the many friends, relations and parishioners who attended the Institution was, of course, Aunt Frances, who could remember being allowed to stay for a night at the Clergy House when Garbett was Vicar. The Clergy House was very much a bachelor establishment and, said Aunt Frances, it was a rare privilege being allowed to stay, given a little grudgingly. Dr. Alan Don, former Dean of Westminster, was also present. Alan Don always said that he owed a great deal to St. Mary's, Portsea, for as a young man he was cycling round the parish with the then Vicar, Canon Bernard Wilson, when the latter turned to him and said, out of the blue, that he ought to be ordained. Until then he had never considered ordination, and from that moment the direction of his life was changed. Alan Don also remembered a rather less happy occasion when, as Senior Chaplain to Archbishop Lang, he returned with the Archbishop to St. Mary's, where Lang was preaching. He leant the Primatial Cross against a wall; halfway through the service he watched it slide to the floor, resulting in quite serious damage to the Cross. After Freddy's Institution, Alan Don wrote to Freddy:

> I am so glad to have had the opportunity of seeing you installed yesterday evening in the place adorned in days gone by a great succession of Vicars - Jacob, Lang, Wilson, Garbett, Lunt, etc. I thought of them shedding their benediction upon you, as you entered upon the great heritage they had bequeathed to you. I do hope you and your wife will be happy with your fine team of curates.
>
> I shall not live to see you mounting the ladder of preferment until you succeed your grandfather and uncle on the throne of St. Augustine. But I trust that when the time comes, the Prime Minister of the day will not break the family entail. In the meantime, may you do great things for the Lord.
>
> PS I can forgive you for wearing your Cambridge hood inside out - but if you were to do it with an Oxford hood I should protest!

Freddy was a graduate of both Oxford and Cambridge, and used to wear whichever hood took his fancy. Obviously on this occasion he had been a bit slipshod when robing. (When he was Dean of Hong Kong, Freddy always used to wear the hood of the University of the winning crew on the Sunday after the Boat Race - so if any of the congregation had not heard the result of the Race, they only had to look at the way he was dressed.)

Geoffrey Fisher (by now Lord Fisher of Lambeth) had hoped to 'creep into the Church without making a fuss and sit at the back.' He did not materialise, and three days later wrote to Freddy:

> I missed the day of your Institution, I'm sorry to say. But now I have begun to recover consciousness and spaciousness, I write to send you both our prayers and

best wishes as you embark on this great work. Really I have not stopped to realise what was coming to you - so challenging and so much a task after your own heart. That you should be called to it justifies my bringing you home as I did - a breather at Lambeth (and its breathlessness) before putting your shoulder to this great wheel. I hope you will enjoy it in proportion as it exhausts you! God prosper you in it. We are still revelling in the joy of nothingness! And resent a week of engagements before us. Our love to you both.

Almost as soon as he started work as Vicar, Freddy was in for a shock. He had been assured by the Bishop that he would find the finances of the parish in a sound condition, and this too, is what the former Vicar, Canon Walter Smith, had told him. Two days after his Institution he was able to obtain the accounts for the first time. The parish was, in fact, over £8,000 in debt, an enormous sum in 1961 for a poor parish with few, if any, wealthy parishioners. Writing to his family in November, Freddy said, 'Prosperous England has left Portsmouth on one side; the naval dockyard dominates the place and pays very low wages indeed, so low that a mother cannot afford the shilling school lunch if she has several children, but brings them home and gives them baked beans or something like that.' In *Consecrated to Prayer*, in which Freddy wrote a couple of pages, he said he 'felt quite sick and longed to pack my bags and go.' Money had been switched from various other accounts, including the organ restoration fund; a legacy for beautifying the inside of the Parish Church had been switched to the ordinary account, as had £1,000 from the Restoration Fund. Freddy wrote in a private aide-mémoire, 'This really is a scandalous situation and shows that archdeacons and bishops should ask many more questions to know how parishes are doing.' However, the debt proved a blessing in the end as it was the one thing that stirred a 'complacent parish' (Freddy's own words) into doing something drastic. He found six small congregations all turned in on themselves, not seeming to bother about anyone else.

Freddy had to spend the first few months of his time as Vicar going round the various churches preparing them for the closure of three. The staff of nine (which included two deaconesses) seemed, in Freddy's words, to be 'astonished to think that such a thing could possibly happen; most, though not all, of them were very conservative.' But the parish was not only in debt, it was running further into debt. Just a week or two before Freddy had arrived a piece of the tower of the Parish Church had fallen in and straightaway the parish had to spend £1,800 on putting things right. The parishioners simply did not know what a parlous state the finances were in. It was as much a shock for them as it was for Freddy. Or was it?

David Richards, formerly a Reader in the diocese of Chichester, whose father-in-law was Churchwarden of St. Boniface Mission as well as being Treasurer of the main Parochial Church Council, could well remember an Annual General Meeting at St. Mary's, probably in 1958, when his father-in-law warned the gathering that financial disaster was looming. David stood and supported what he said (his father-in-law was ex-Inland Revenue and David was an ex-Royal Army Pay Corps auditor). 'Nobody listened', said David, 'or if they did, could not cope with what was said. The then Vicar was so bound up in the history of the place (we all loved him by the way), that the prospect of radical change was beyond him. Freddy came and bit the bullet and did what was necessary. What Freddy did took courage, but he carried it through with his characteristic loving-kindness. The Church of England moves very slowly to adapt to new needs and different priorities, but we must thank God for people like Freddy who had vision and would cast out into the deep, whilst never losing sight of those for whom they had pastoral responsibility.'

The Archdeacon of Portsmouth, Freddy told his friends at the time, was virtually no help at all, and quietly tossed the ball back to him whenever he asked him for any advice or suggestions. The Bishop, however, 'weighed in' right from the beginning and was masterly at the meeting when he announced the closure of St. Stephen's, St. Mary's Mission and St. Boniface's. Freddy wrote in his diary of the events at the time, 'I have never seen the iron hand in the velvet glove so deftly used. They all went out from the meeting liking him and feeling friendly, and yet realising they must accept the situation.' Freddy was very anxious as to how many of the former Mission Church members would leave entirely. In the end it transpired that at least seventy-five percent, heart-broken as many were, started worshipping either in one of the remaining churches of the parish or in other churches nearer to their homes. 'There are, however', wrote Freddy, 'still a few sad and sullen hearts.' In 1964, Freddy was able to write, 'That first year brought tremendous new life to the Parish Church, where things were at their worst, and as I look round now I see that all the new vigour and life from the newly-appointed church officers comes from the old closed missions.'

The staff had to be reduced from nine to five. The old famous Clergy House had to go. It was running with only four or five clergy in it, with a full-time housekeeper, a full-time daily cook and two cleaners. 'They were', said Freddy, 'living in a state and style totally unsuitable for equipping them for parish work in England afterwards.' A small terraced house, 156 Church Road, was bought, just over the road from the Vicarage.

In February 1964, Freddy was invited by the editor of the *Church Times*, in the light of the recently published *Paul Report* on the future strategy of the Church, to write about 'The problems of a big town parish'. The article was published on March 1st. The editorial of the *Church Times* for that day runs:

Both the writer and the parish which he describes in our article this week on the Church in a town parish carry names famous in the modern history of the Church of England. Not that this is the only reason why we asked the Rev. Frederick Temple, Vicar of Portsea, to write about this subject, now so prominently before the public by virtue of the Leslie Paul Report. He has as realistic experience as any in-

cumbent today of the challenge to the Church in those formidable conurbations of which the Report has much to say.

The chief impression left by this article is of the paradox in which the Church in a large town finds itself caught. It is sadly true that it is out of touch with the great majority of the population. At the same time, an incumbent who means business finds himself and his staff in such demand that the problem is not at all that he rots away in miserable frustration, but that, on the contrary, he has more work to do than he knows how to cope with. And it is all thoroughly worthwhile work. Adults in increasing numbers seeking confirmation, men and women of every sort wanting pastoral help, marriages drifting towards the rocks demanding rescue, the bereaved in need of comfort - all this and much more, as described by Mr. Temple, mounts up to an endless claim on the time of priests who rightly see that through such opportunities they have a marvellous chance to fulfil their ministry.

Two things stand out a mile from this picture. One is the need for more clergy; no amount of ingenious 'redeployment' will make two priests out of one. And the other is the need to train and make more use of the laity - a need only equalled by the extreme practical difficulty of meeting it.

The article itself was very warmly received by, amongst others, archbishops, bishops, clergy, heads of Theological Colleges, the laity and academics alike. Michael Ramsey wrote: 'Thank you for the article, "Problems of the big town parish"; it is a supremely constructive little document, so much common sense packed into so few words.' The Bishop of Lichfield sent a note saying that it was 'the most heartwarming article I have read for many a long time and should serve as a great encouragement to ordinands.' The Vicar of a large parish in Toxteth, Liverpool, wrote the following: 'I feel that here's someone who really understands our problems.' Peter Walker, Principal of Westcott House, wrote, 'So many thanks for today's *Church Times*. This cheerful and level encouragement is just what the boys here want. It was enthralling, and masterly.' William van Straubenzee MP wrote, 'With your vast experience, you know when something has been a success. There is no need to assure you that your article following up on the Paul Report has made a profound impression on many. The comments I have received about it would undoubtedly turn your head.'

Canon Charles Smyth (who, incidentally, in 1959 published the biography of one of Freddy's predecessors at Portsea, Cyril Forster Garbett) wrote from Corpus Christi College, Cambridge: 'May I be allowed to thank you for your article on the Paul Report in the current issue of the *Church Times*? It is an extremely valuable contribution to the Honest-to-Paul Debate (which is doing us all so much good); and I have reason to be personally grateful to you, because you have given me exactly what I wanted for some lectures that I am giving on the Evolution of the English Clergy. So I hope you won't mind my quoting you?' He continued (and it is worth quoting, for it places what Freddy wrote in a wider historical context):

What you have said links up with Martin Thornton (whom I am also quoting). In case this won't bore you, the thesis of my first lecture is that the fundamental Continuity of the Church of England is a continuity of Pastoral Care. In the 14th century, there was a spate of manuals on pastoral guidance and direction for the instruction of the parish priests (like Chaucer's 'Poor Parson of a Town'). The 16th Century was the Golden Age of 'Practical Divinity' or Casuistical Divinity in the C of E, and the concern with 'cases of conscience' (eg George Herbert: 'Country Parson') - which had an interesting sequel in the religious societies at the end of the 17th and beginning of the 18th century. Then this was largely submerged by a century of ethical preaching in broad general terms (influence of Abp Tillotson), followed by the doctrinal preaching of the Evangelicals. Spiritual direction was revived by the Tractarians, but almost exclusively through the confessional. Now, in our own day, the task of pastoral guidance is coming into its own again, and the vicar's study is taking on something of the character of a clinic. And it is at this point that I rest myself on the authority of Fr. Martin Thornton and the Vicar of Portsea!

The full article, published almost forty years ago, read as follows:

Eric James, the newly appointed full-time director of Parish and People, told us in the Church Times of February 7 that there is one fact he will keep ever before him: 'the massive irrelevance of the Church of England as it is to most people, that is, to the majority of the people of our land.'

This is a fact of which all of us in any big town parish of manual workers are continually aware. But the other side of this coin is that the few clergy in such parishes find themselves more than relevant enough to the people of their parish or city. This is exciting, stimulating, frustrating and exhausting. For the one over-all problem, the one over-all opportunity in any parish, is to find out how best to make known the love, forgiveness and power of God. And, as I see it, every plan must always be entirely flexible and sensitive to new occasions and suited to the men in the team. These in a large staff are, inevitably, constantly changing. No deacon ever fits the hole the last man left. The whole team has to adjust, and the balance of work shifts and alters.

So everything in a big town parish consisting mainly of manual and technically trained men depends at this moment entirely on the clergy - what they are, what they plan to do and leave undone. In Portsea nearly all doctors, all teachers, all social workers, all people of the professions and of administrative ability, live outside the parish. They 'come in' to their work. So Leslie Paul's second recommendation of a pastoral advisory committee is difficult to implement as such, though we work together individually with doctors and teachers.

Very few of our numerous excellent laity have any idea of what God wants the

Church to be and do; we clergy, too, are groping our way amongst the many exciting ideas being thrown up on all sides. Meanwhile there are signs of that 'religious revival of a deep and subtle type' of which Martin Thornton speaks in English Spirituality. 'A profound and secret groping after real religion among the faithful and a more thoughtful attitude towards the Christian Faith by a significant minority outside or on the fringe of the Church.' We have signs of this here; far more adults are considering confirmation. There are seven different groups meeting during the week at various hours of afternoon or evening and being taught and discussing the Faith with a view to confirmation; small groups, most of them past the age of mass classes of boys and girls 'being done' because mother and father wish it.

More people are coming to their clergy when in need; I find a marked difference to ten years ago. And I do not think this is just because one is older, for all my younger colleagues find the same. For six months after arrival as a deacon a man can plan his day; but from then on, if he is any good at all, his day will be planned for him by the sheer necessities awaiting him, of which prayer and study are of course part. I can hardly ever leave my vicarage; more and more people, not regular churchgoers, are coming to the clergy for help with marriage problems or family problems (such as a child who has started to cheat or steal); or there comes the middle-aged man who suddenly finds his life empty in spite of a happy home, wife and children, and wonders why.

A small Marriage Guidance Council is swamped at the moment as, quite rightly, the standard for counsellors is kept so high and so many prospective candidates are turned down and, if one passes on a marriage problem, it may be three weeks before a couple can possibly be seen, so one must listen and help meanwhile. Even to pass a person on to the appropriate trained person - probabtion, moral welfare, children's department - all takes much time. Far more of even a young clergyman's time is now taken up with serious pastoral problems.

Meanwhile the Church, or the clergy at least, have been rediscovered as useful in social service. This is good, and it is right that we should work together in close co-operation with all the statutory bodies and that the Church's voice should be heard and its influence felt on all levels in a city's concern for people as a whole. We all now know our probation officers, health visitors and workers in clinics in our parishes. The young clergy are asked if they will take a problem boy into their youth group and, together with the probation officer, consider the care of that family.

Lord Mayors summon us all to meetings in the Guildhall to plan old people's welfare throughout the city. It is easy to feel gratified, but the laity should be doing this work; and it is often an easy escape for a priest who wants to see more positive results to keep his morale up. Also it can divert us from our long-term task of building up an understanding of what the Church should be.

As a constant background there is the permanent need of people who come for the Occasional Offices. Because everyone likes a clergyman at their funeral service and likes to be visited and helped at the time of a bereavement, let us not decry this as a mere formality. There can be no time of greater need for such people than when there has been a death in the home. This parish had sixty-six funerals last month, and it is interesting that more people are asking to have a service in church than were a year or two ago.

Because a large number of young people still want to be married in church (thirty-three for March), let us not deplore this as purely formal, but use it. Anyone taking marriage classes for the engaged will know how eagerly, at that moment at least, they long for help and guidance. Large numbers of parents attending baptism classes offer great opportunities to reach more homes.

In this parish, if we could cope adequately with the demand for the Occasional Offices, we should be pleased; here is our outreach handed to us without any searching. But we have also, together with the laity, to learn again what the Church should be doing. And it does seem that the technically trained man in some manual craft is only ready at the moment to lead in his own technique. Is this why business firms now take 'Arts' men for management training?

This reluctance may be the mark of real humility; only the man really knowledgeable and skilful in something knows how little he understands about anything else. So there are very few indeed who are general leaders of men or youth. The electrician will instruct all who want to learn electricity, the painter those who want to learn painting; yet very few as yet take general positions of leadership. And only slowly are we clergy realising that they should; we have just started getting well-established communicants to take a part in the confirmation training of the young.

Leslie Paul recommends a 'lay pastorate'; this will take a very long time to form in such a parish as this. A great deal of unorganised, really Christian lay visiting goes on, but no one recognises it as 'the Church'; only when a dog collar arrives is 'the Church' visiting, and the best laity are still very shy about doing anything in any way official on behalf of the Church pastorally. After two years' hammering at the need for regular lay visiting, two men in a parish of forty thousand have really understood the need and satisfaction of doing this, and are now doing a tremendous job. It is a tiny beginning.

We speak of the Church's involvement with people where they are. Should one expect men who are skilled craftsmen - doing their job well during the week but waiting to be told what to do, making no big administrative decision - to change suddenly in their work for the church and make large, responsible, administrative decisions? To get this takes a long time of gentle understanding and working together between clergy and people. It is coming slowly, and very good, realistic and honest the decisions are, when made - often not what the clergy would have decided themselves.

This parish has benefited and suffered much from its former vast team of clergy. The benefits are clear, that the pastoral care of each devoted priest brings and keeps more faithful within the fold. We reap the fruit of wonderful work done in the past, particularly now in the innumerable homes of the house-bound and bedridden faithful who receive Communion once a month and whose prayers are the power-plant of the whole life of the place. But the better a large clerical team is, the keener esprit de corps it has, makes greater the divide between the clergy and the laity. The disadvantage in the past of a large staff of clergy has been that, with a very few exceptions, hardly any of the laity have understood what membership of the Church should mean beyond the privilege of prayer, receiving Communion, and being entitled to the attentions of the professional young clergy from time to time, especially when ill.

It was only when three churches had to be closed and sold, and the staff cut from ten to six, that some of the laity really began to understand. For an effective understanding members of the laity should join with the clergy at staff meetings; but how to do this in a parish where hardly any man can ask for time off inside his working hours? Each evening is full either with discussion groups, confirmation classes, visiting urgent cases or necessary organisations for the young.

The city tries hard to meet the needs of the young in many ways, but there is not enough for them to do of an evening, so there is need for the Church to provide for and guide the young, who in their turn form the backbone of much of what the Church can do. But, as yet, few of the laymen are ready to be general leaders of such youth organisations; it rests with the clergy to initiate, inspire and guide.

All this has been written without much special reference to the Paul Report, but the Paul Report has prompted a fresh analysis. I entirely agree that every town freehold should become a ten-year leasehold. It would be impossible to be doing this job really well enough after ten years.

It is an exciting if bewildering time to staff a big, down-town industrial parish. We see the Church still as irrelevant as ever to the mass of folk, but we also find ourselves in greater demand than ever. People want us and what the Church can give through us in the crises of their lives - birth, marriage, death and sickness; here is a great and overwhelming opportunity which could take all our time. More are coming for personal help at a quiet, deep level; if we are to teach men to pray, we must above all keep our own friendship with God in repair.

In social service the Church is being noticed and welcomed again, but, until the ordinary layman is ready to take his part here, are the clergy to say no? We work in Councils of Churches and discuss with Methodists and encourage others to do so; we read Leslie Paul, The Crucible of Love, Honest to God, reports of the Toronto Congress, of Anglican-Methodist Conversations, of the Vatican Council. As the Principal of Westcott House says in his last letter, 'There is so much to form a mind on, so desperately little of the cool hour for reflection before we must deliver ourselves.'

And so, to me, the most helpful book of the past year has been the slender reprint of Max Warren's Master of Time, to help each one of us, 'not to be the slave of Time but a servant of Time's Master.'

Aunt Frances, after reading the article, put her sixpenny-worth in with the words, 'I liked what you wrote, Freddy. Just what your uncle William would have said.' There's no record of how Freddy reacted to this, but it was probably with an element of pride, though tinged with the feeling that what he had written was what *he* thought. It seems that so many people, not least his aunt, were trying to make Freddy out as a sort of re-incarnation of William Temple; because uncle William had died so comparatively young, it was up to Freddy to carry on his work. This continued to place pressure on him.

It had been rumoured in 1960 that Freddy was to succeed Edmund Morgan as Bishop of Truro, but that Fisher thought he was not yet ready for a diocese. This information has come from three independent sources, though there's no documentation. Correspondence does exist, however, which shows that Freddy was being 'very seriously considered' in 1964 as the successor to his friend and mentor, Russell Barry, Bishop of Southwell. Although Freddy had only been at Portsea for three years, many felt that his job was done. Correspondence, however, peters out. Whether Freddy himself pulled out or the powers that be thought it not an opportune moment to make him a diocesan bishop, is uncertain.

On June 19th 1964, Freddy wrote some notes, for whom it is not clear, about his first three years at Portsea:

> *It was a great job to know where my work should lie - whether I should do more in the city as leading incumbent: I am Chairman of the Council of Churches and on the Executive Committee of the city's Council of Social Services. But then if I do too much there or in the diocese as Chairman of the Council for Social Work (the old Moral Welfare) then it appears that I am leaving too much of the regular pastoral work of the parish to the others. I would like to stand for Convocation and Church Assembly but this would mean being away the inside of another five weeks and I doubt whether this is really possible or feasible. This whole parish depends the whole time on rounding people up and chasing them up if they are flagging in any way, as they still expect this from the days when they were spoilt with a vast number of young clergy at their beck and call. The most exciting thing to happen is that at long last a small group of the laity are waking up to taking their responsibilities seriously; we are having a parish meeting in July to see what should happen and how we should go about this. This again may be the start of great new things here.*

Freddy did, however, allow his name forward for Convocation. His election manifesto, published in November of that year ran:

> *I have been persuaded by some clergy in Portsmouth to stand as a candidate for the coming election as proctors in Convocation. I do so because I consider the business in front of the coming Convocation and Church Assembly to be amongst the most important the Church of England has had to deal with for a very long time. And in*

spite of the fact that there is more than enough to do in a parish I think one must be ready to undertake this work if it is clear people want one to do so. During my two years as senior chaplain at Lambeth under Archbishop Fisher, as he then was, I felt that Convocation did not have sufficient ordinary parish priests from the busy town parishes. There were a large number of 'ex-officio' members, deans, archdeacons, etc., and a large number of clergy from the country, or small parishes, where quite naturally there was more chance of them having time to spare for this work, but not many to represent the large town parish and its needs. My experience since ordination just after the war, for what it is worth, has been:

A curacy in a mining parish on the edge of Nottingham followed by another curacy in a Midland country town, Newark; then vicar of a suburb of Manchester, between Manchester and Stockport; six years as Dean of Hong Kong and then two years helping the Archbishop at the centre of the Anglican Communion before coming to Portsmouth.

I consider there is a great need for radical thought on all sides of the Church's life, worship and work. Liturgical Reform is vital but it is most important that it is not to be done only by experts with no knowledge, for instance, of how a new Baptism service may go down with the ordinary family who comes to offer their child for baptism with little or no experience of the Church. The Paul Report cannot just be shelved in innumerable committees and commissions. There is need for change in appointment of clergy and general grouping of our parishes. Here in Portsmouth we know how stimulating a really co-operative partnership with other churches can be, both in worship and in working together for the city; Anglican/Methodist Conversations and further Reunion proposals must be encouraged. I am convinced that some form of Synodical Government of the Church is necessary, so that we can stop the cumbersome arrangement of four Houses of Convocation and three Houses of Church Assembly, all having to make decisions on any major matter. All that the Toronto Congress and M.R.I. stands for I consider vitally important. If you want me to serve I will do my best to try and further sensible and radical reform, but will always have in mind the needs of the ordinary parish, its clergy and its laity; and so try and see that such decisions are based firmly and realistically on the ground and combine both patience, insight and perseverance.

If elected, I would try to be available to answer questions and speak to Church Councils about the central work of the Church.

Freddy was elected as a Proctor in the Canterbury Convocation, which meant that he was also a member of the Church Assembly. From that, he was asked to put his name forward for the Standing Committee and was elected; and from there the Archbishop of York asked him to fill a vacancy on the small General Purposes Committee, a group of about eight or ten, meeting under the Chairmanship of the Archbishop of York, to plan the business and work of the Church Assembly and make suggestions to the Standing Committee. 'This is very interesting,' wrote Freddy at the time, 'as there is a great deal of most important work in front of the Church of England in the next few years if we can guide it smartly and skilfully along the right lines. But this all takes a great deal of time and there are many frustrations. There is so much happening or coming to the boil at the same time - the reforms in liturgy, re-union movements, the reform of the parson's freehold and the whole parish system. But I am delighted to be doing this as it gives me a wider vision than being bogged down in a vast parish and the train journeys to London and back give one peace of mind to think and read.'

As well as his work on the Church Assembly, Freddy was also on the Editorial Advisory Board of *Theology*, and a member of CRAC - the Central Religious Advisory Committee of the BBC. CRAC consisted of distinguished members of all the major churches - and was, incidentally, presided over for several years by Cyril Garbett, one of Freddy's predecessors at Portsea. Freddy wrote to one of his sisters two months after his appointment, and after attending his first meeting in London, 'I fear that, wherever I go, however far from Portsmouth, the Ghost of Garbett haunts me.'

Freddy was also appointed a member of the Commission on Church-State Relations. In sitting on this distinguished Commission, he was following in the footsteps of his uncle William, who had sat on a previous Commission. The Commission on Church-State Relations on which Freddy sat, chaired by Owen Chadwick, grasped the nettle of the basic faults of the Establishment as preceding Commissions had failed to do. In 1970 it made two recommendations of considerable importance. The first was that General Synod (as the stronger successor to the Assembly), and not Parliament, should henceforth be the final authority in matters of worship and doctrine. The second was that bishops should no longer be selected by the Prime Minister but by a committee or college representing both the diocese and the wider Church. It held that these recommendations did not require disestablishment. They were finally accepted in substance (the Prime Minister's role in bishop-making has not been wholly removed but whittled down to choosing between two names selected by the Church).

The Report rejected disestablishment (though three members of its Commission submitted a minority report in favour). The majority view was that bishops should still be appointed by the Crown while the selection process should essentially become the work of a permanent Church electoral board; half the members of the commission wished to exclude the Prime Minister, representing the Crown, from the process altogether; the other half wished to retain his or her role of ultimate choice within a short list, believing that, for legal reasons relating to the Bishops' membership of the House of Lords, without this the Church's establishment could not continue.

Freddy was in great demand for contributing epilogues on Southern Television; one of the producers at the time wrote that they were 'probably the most inspirational epilogues I have had the good fortune to be involved with.' Freddy also wrote regular, short, pithy 'thoughts' for the *Portsmouth Evening News*. If one looks through the newspaper cuttings from the Sixties, it seems as though hardly a day went past without there being some article about, or some mention of, an event at St. Mary's, which the paper often alluded to as 'that vibrant parish'. However, Freddy was not prepared for the consequences arising after the *Portsmouth Evening News* had picked up on an article he had written in *Forward*, the parish magazine.

The administration of Public Baptism as performed in the parish of Portsea is 'in some ways a scandal'. And who should make such a forceful accusation but the Vicar of Portsea, the Rev. F.S. Temple.

Writing in his letter to the parish, the Rev. Temple says: A service at four o'clock on a Sunday afternoon when the Church is empty apart from friends and members of the families of those who are being baptised is nothing more than private Baptism performed in Church.

The Prayer Book firmly tells us that 'it is desirable where possible that Baptism should be administered upon Sundays and other holy days when the most number of people come together'.

And yet here we have got into the complacent habit of disregarding that and having it as a quiet little service when new members are admitted into our Church every week with all the tremendous responsibilities that parents and godparents take upon themselves on behalf of the children.

We tried when I first came to get the Mothers' Union to take on the visiting of the Baptism families, but after a few months that failed through lack of interest and enthusiasm, and now it is the younger members attached to the new Eight o'clock Club [1] who do this work. Some of them are not very closely connected with the Church yet, and receive very little encouragement from the regular congregation in this instance.

On the whole we admit our new members in a scandalously casual manner and take very little interest and concern in them afterwards. They will not take their vows and promises seriously unless they see that the Christian family in this place really cares seriously for each new member admitted into its ranks.

I feel really convinced that as the Church put one of the two great Sacraments back into its proper place in the last century (the Sacrament of Holy Communion) so now it is our job to reinstate the other great Sacrament of Baptism.

We are fortunate enough that people still want their babies baptised. They still come in large numbers to the Parish Church to ask for this.
I am convinced that we have got to put this service back in its right place in the middle of public worship.

---

[1] Joan had started this in 1963, and it had been an immense success in bringing younger women from the parish together.

Freddy was dismayed by what he called 'the howls of protest' throughout the city, mostly from people who were, in his own words, 'ill-instructed or nil-instructed' either in the Christian faith or in the Church and its worship. One correspondent wrote simply (the spelling and punctuation, or rather, lack of punctuation, are as it was written): 'Who do you think you are to tell us when we can have our babies cristend god almity or something its the likes of you who bring the church a bad name didn't jesus say suffer little babs to come to me'. This particular letter caused Freddy more amusement than dismay - but he was certainly upset by some of the letters received from more literate citizens of Portsmouth. He told his Parochial Church Council at their next meeting that he was bewildered by the furore he had caused, adding that what he was advocating was really nothing new. He was further bewildered by the fact that many of his PCC did not back him in what he said.

Freddy saw all too clearly that it was vital to get new life and vigour into the parish and he gathered around him a team of young clergy. By the end of 1964, he was wondering whether he had made a rod for his own back, and wrote, 'Now there is a team of young curates who possibly are almost too volatile in that they spark each other up and find it difficult to live peacefully together for very long. But at least there is a new vigour and life back and religion is interesting in Portsea once more.'

In *Consecrated to Prayer*, Freddy wrote:

It would be invidious to single out any of the many clergy who served in the sixties. With a new deacon arriving every year, it meant the parish could never fall asleep. In the heady Sixties, most deacons fresh from Theological Colleges wanted to question everything that happened and to suggest changes. But one realised how, over the years, the Holy Spirit had trained the laity to help in making Portsea a good training parish. Every curate was able to find his 'widow in Israel' where he could get special titbits and pour out his heart. And the 'widow' would sometimes let the vicar know discreetly if all was not well.

In addition to and alongside matters of pastoral strategy, there were the more personal aspects of pastoral life. In a letter to a friend, Freddy wrote, 'We love entertaining here and the people seem to think it very nice that they are welcomed at the Vicarage and made to feel welcome. Which they are - welcome *and* made to feel it.' Indeed, many of Freddy's parishioners made comments like, 'The Vicarage had a warm, caring atmosphere'; 'you got the feeling you were loved'; 'in a funny sort of way we all thought we were part of their family'; 'difficult to describe, but somehow they made us feel that every one of us was important and we could go to the Vicarage whenever we wanted'; 'Freddy and Joan always seemed to have time for us, even though they were so busy that we worried about them sometimes'. These are all comments similar to those made by others throughout the course of

Freddy and Joan's joint ministry of care, whether in Nottinghamshire, Manchester or Hong Kong.

Freddy himself delighted in telling his stories about life at the Vicarage. Some of the following three may sound more than a little patronising, but they are included because Freddy rehearsed them so often. At one time he had a very scatter-brained secretary and did not realise how certain ecclesiastical words were way beyond her. Freddy always tried to commend newly married couples who were moving away to the vicar of the parish where they were going and one day he dictated a letter to his secretary, Erica, saying that he had married a couple who would be living in such and such a place which he thought might be in such and such a parish and ended by saying that if this were not the case, please forgive him for troubling him and pass it on to the appropriate incumbent. It returned on Freddy's desk, with the final words, '. . . please pass to the next incompetent.' He decided not to change it but just put an asterisk beside it and a note at the bottom saying, 'This is what my young secretary thinks of us all.'

Joan and Freddy had a very good cleaner and helper who, amongst other things, cleaned Freddy's study. One year, after they had been on holiday to Florence, they brought back a photograph of Michelangelo's *David*. Freddy went into his study one day and saw her back bristling somewhat as she dusted the framed photograph, and asked, 'What is the matter, Mrs. Vaughan?' She replied, 'Well, Vicar, I must be frank and say I never expected to find this sort of photograph in a vicar's study.' Freddy told her that it was just one of the finest bits of sculpture in the world.

On another occasion, one of his parishioners had an aunt from Newcastle-upon-Tyne staying with him at his flat. She was duly invited to tea at the Vicarage, and Freddy asked her whether she was enjoying her holiday. She replied that she was having a wonderful time and the day before had gone over to the Isle of Wight. The new Thorneycroft hovercraft service had only just begun to make regular journeys across to the Island. Freddy asked whether she had liked what she had seen of the Island. She replied in the affirmative, and added, in a broad 'Geordie' accent, 'but the most exciting thing was that we crossed the water on a new hoover.'

In June, 1966, after five years at Portsea, Freddy wrote, again exactly for whose benefit it is not clear:

> It is very difficult to feel that we are not getting into a rut. The administration of this place takes up most of my time. One has to keep an eye on everything. Numbers at Church have gone down a little bit, but not very much and this is to be expected with the number of houses being pulled down, and people being re-housed elsewhere. Though I am enjoying Church Assembly and Convocation work, I also feel I need a new stimulus and interest to get me fired again with vitality. Next year is the 800th anniversary of the parish and we are planning big events throughout

the year and hope that it will be a tonic for the place.

The major event of the anniversary celebrations was undoubtedly a series of Ecumenical Lent Lectures. After Freddy had announced these, he wrote, 'inevitably some of our dearest and most faithful Anglicans are already muttering that the Vicar is not going to have a proper Lent course when the few get together for real devotion, but is inviting such a lot of outsiders. What patience and good humour the Good Lord must have as he watches all this.' (On Freddy's first Good Friday in Portsea, in 1962, the parish held a joint procession with the Methodists. One of the most regular and devout members of the congregation said, when Freddy told her that they were uniting with the Methodists for this, 'Good Lord, what do we want to bother with them for?')

The course started with Michael Ramsey, the Archbishop of Canterbury, on Ash Wednesday evening. Freddy wrote:

I achieved one ambition in this vast church, which was to have it packed to the doors with people sitting all round the altars, all along the sanctuary rails, on the font and standing in solid ranks from half-way back. I always remember Uncle William's great mission at Oxford when St Mary's, Oxford, which is a much smaller church than this, was packed in a similar way. The Archbishop came with Mrs. Ramsey and their chaplain, John Andrew, and were quite delightful staying at the vicarage overnight. The Archbishop had sitting round him in the sanctuary some of the more colourful of our boys with long hair and strange clothes and he asked afterwards who the borstal-like collection were; I was able to reply, 'Just members of the congregation, Your Grace.'

His sermon was quite memorable in every way; we then withdrew for a few minutes and he came back and sat in a chair at the Chancel steps and people asked questions for the next hour. I had been warned that people would not do this in such a vast crowd, but after a few minutes the atmosphere was as friendly, relaxed and warm as if we had been sitting in the Vicarage drawing room. He was superb in answering the questions, repeating them in a clearer and more succinct form than the questioner had put it, and then giving a very clear, weighty and yet sympathetic and sensitive answer to each question. A Baptist Pastor who found himself standing in the crowd at the back beside the Roman Catholic Bishop of Portsmouth wrote and told me that if he had been told by someone a few years ago that he would have been singing Cwm Rhondda standing beside the Roman Catholic Bishop, hidden behind a pillar of St. Mary's, listening to the Archbishop of Canterbury, he would never have believed it.

We had similar enormous crowds each week with the church packed to the doors. Cars were everywhere outside the church. One passing driver was heard to say, 'What on earth can they be doing at St Mary's on a weeknight evening to draw so many people? They must be playing bingo.'

Other speakers during Lent were the President of the Methodist Conference, the Roman Catholic Bishop of Portsmouth, the Director of Christian Aid, Janet Lacey ('It was the first time', said Freddy, 'that I had ever led a handbag from the Sanctuary to the pulpit'), Eric James, Director of 'Parish and People' and Canon Residentiary of Southwark Cathedral (he stepped in for John Robinson, Bishop of Woolwich, who was unwell), and Bishop R.O. Hall of Hong Kong, whom Freddy described as 'that Anglican spiritual giant of the Pacific'.

The Vicar of Portsea with Joan Ramsey, wife of the Archbishop of Canterbury.

Much else happened during this Octo-centenary year (Freddy referred to it as 'a happy time of many high jinks'), including a Flower Festival in the summer, when 'over 17000 people shuffled through the church in two and a half days in one immense queue.'

It was, however, the nitty-gritty of parish life that most appealed to Freddy. The post-war baby boom had now become marriageable and St. Mary's became one of the largest 'wedding factories' (Freddy's own words) in the South of England, the staff often officiating at the marriages of eight to ten couples every Saturday, one wedding every half-hour. Freddy never asked any member of staff to take more than five weddings running. Most of those who married were under twenty, and large schools of marriage preparation were held on two or three days of each month. The choirboys loved the weddings: they were paid well! Sunday afternoons saw multiple baptisms, invariably with ten or more babies - and there were often, especially in the winter, four funerals a day. Freddy was always very keen, like any true pastor, to follow up the opportunities of the Occasional Offices.

With Aunt Frances in the Fratton Road, Portsmouth.

Patrick Mitchell (later to become

Dean of Wells, then Dean of Windsor) was Vicar of St. James's, Milton, in Portsmouth, for most of the time Freddy was at St. Mary's, the two parishes being adjacent. He writes of Freddy's time at Portsea:

> *My regular contact was over the Big Three Lunches, attended by the incumbents of St. Mary's, St. James' and St. Mark's (Peter May). At that time we each had four curates, which was a great come-down for St. Mary's, which once had 16 curates under Lang. When we three attended Rural Deanery Chapter meetings with our curates, we accounted for 15 clergymen (some deacons). Other poor incumbents mostly struggled alone.*
>
> *We certainly held Freddy in some awe, realising his links with two Archbishops of Canterbury, his experience in Hong Kong and elsewhere, and his time at Lambeth. He also edited some Temple correspondence. At the same time, we felt sorry for him because he inherited a somewhat diminished tradition in Portsea. Wally Smith, his predecessor, was thought to have let the side down by not becoming a bishop! He also sold the Clergy House in which 'all those wonderful young curates' had lived in some splendour as bachelors. Freddy used to tell us that there used to be a maid in cap and apron who rang a bell through the hatch when the 'young men's' tea was ready. In Freddy's time, the Clergy House became an undertaker's home of rest! Senior parishioners thought that was the end of the world.*
>
> *I remember Freddy, too, as a notable preacher. He was a compulsively hard worker in writing, visiting and training his curates.*

Tony Winterbotham served his title curacy at St. Mary's, arriving there in 1957. By the time Freddy was instituted he was Priest-in-Charge of the St. Mary's Mission Church in the Fratton Road, only a stone's throw from the Parish Church. Tony, who retired in 1991 as Chaplain and Head of Religious Education at Portsmouth Grammar School, and who died in 2004, wrote:

> *Freddy's impact at the Parish Church was immediate. I don't think the congregation had ever experienced such preaching. He would stand in the pulpit without the suggestion of a script and hold the congregation spellbound. I wanted to say that he held them in the palm of his hands. His predecessor, Canon Walter Smith, had always been against the use of microphones and amplifiers, and Freddy certainly didn't need them.*

Tony Winterbotham also recalled that the staff used to go across to the Vicarage for coffee after the weekly staff meeting, and how Freddy was highly amused to hear that previously the curates had to go in by the kitchen door. He remembered how Joan and he made the Vicarage a very happy place. He concludes:

> *I certainly gained a great deal from his leadership and pastoral care. He always*

seemed to have all the time in the world to listen to any problem, and that is some-
thing I have tried to copy in my own dealings with others.

One of my firmest memories of him was of his telling his curates not to get 'too
involved' with folk who came to the door. By 'folk', he meant people who came to
the door, asking for money. He told us to send them straight up to the Reception
Centre, about half a mile away, up St. Mary's Road. I think he was just trying to
protect us - for we all knew that, if anyone came to his front door at the Vicarage, he
would open his pocket. I remember Freddy reminding me once of a line from
Blake: 'Then cherish pity, lest you drive an angel from your door.'

Freddy could be quite strongly critical of others, and be open in his views. On
my rare visits in the later years of his life I greatly enjoyed his outspoken comments,
particularly about the Church of England. The word 'shrewd' again comes to
mind. His very clear and quick mind could sometimes be disguised by his almost
stuttering speech. I will always remember him as an astute leader, a generous
friend, and a Christian who demonstrated his faith in all his relationships. I could
not have wished for a finer incumbent under whom to serve; it was such a very
great privilege.

Roger Legg arrived in Portsea in 1966. He particularly recalls the weekly staff
meetings, by this time being held at Freddy and Joan's home. Roger appreciated
the fact that Freddy 'made time for us as a group of then young rebels'. The *Times*
crossword was finished off over coffee after the meeting, unless the gardener had
done it already; he was better, said Roger, than any of them. Roger continues:

Freddy was a very, very able preacher and clear too, no mean feat in Portsea. He
was not an aggressive up-front person. Rather I guess the nervous laugh gave a lot
away. He took in my view a lot of flak from the PCC at St. Mary's. A lot of it was
just terribly hurtful and gratuitous rudeness.

I remember I used to think he was terribly wobbly on theological questions. This
was in part because he was so hugely clever that he could envisage 1,000 approach-
es to the question all at once.

He was engaged in committees away from the parish. This meant that Ted
[Kendall] at St. Wilfred's and myself at St. Faith's had almost total free rein. It felt
just like being the parish priest with one's own PCC, etc. He had the ability to del-
egate, let you get on with it, and not bother to look over our shoulders. A great en-
courager! He was way ahead of his time then.

I felt that if ever a man served a tough 'curacy' for his bishopric, it was Freddy.
I honour him for that.

Norman Attrill writes:

In 1968, as a late ordinand, I was looking for a parish which would accept me when, by a great stroke of good fortune for me, my theological college received an enquiry from Freddy. He said he was looking for a curate of about his own age, and at least to that extent I fitted the bill exactly. Elizabeth [Norman's wife] and I drove down to Portsmouth and enjoyed an evening of hilarious entertainment as our introduction to the famous parish of St. Mary, Portsea. That was the beginning of a period in which plenty of hard work was combined with enormous fun. Thirty years on, I am still tremendously glad that I was allowed to start my ministry among the people of that parish, and grateful for the discovery of the healing powers of Freddy's gusts of huge laughter - surely signs of the life-giving breath of the Holy Spirit.

Roger Royle, later a well-known broadcaster, observed:

Coping with curates has never been easy. For the Vicar of Portsea it was well nigh a nightmare, especially when he was saddled with two such people as Alun Glyn Jones and Roger Royle. Checking their sermons, suffering their Harvest Supper extravaganzas and coping with their comments at Tuesday Staff Meetings were all part of the rich pattern of life. However it wasn't all work.

There was also the Christmas Staff Party; an evening of relaxation in what was otherwise a highly pressurised time. Well, that was what it was meant to be. On one occasion the end result was slightly different. Back in the early Sixties, Chinese restaurants were not as commonplace as they are today, but because of Freddy and Joan's Hong Kong experience they thought that a Chinese Christmas Dinner would be just that little bit more unusual. How right they were.

Freddy, because of his deep Incarnational theology, always tried to be at one with the people he was with. So he tried to speak to the staff of the restaurant in Cantonese, or was it Mandarin? The look on the faces of the staff was one of blank amazement. They may have come from Chinese stock but the only language they knew was Pompey English. Having failed to communicate, Freddy was still determined to identify with the people. So when the meal arrived, chopsticks were ordered for one and all. While Joan and Freddy were well equipped and prepared to deal with these delicate instruments, the rest of us found that we were getting very little to eat and so had to resort to spoon and fork. Had it not been the Season of Goodwill, Freddy and Joan might have found this latest exhibition of incompetence by two of his curates difficult to deal with. However they were able to grin and bear it. After all, by this time they had ceased to be surprised by the antics of either Alun or Roger. It is also sad to have to report that the behaviour of only one of these erstwhile curates has improved over the intervening years.

The evening of Monday, 7th October, 1968, was a moment that changed the direction and course of Freddy's ministry, an evening which initially caused both Joan and Freddy acute distress and despair - the start of a few months of what Freddy himself described as 'a time of descent into Hell.'

A good deal of Freddy's time was spent in trying to help those who came to him, in confidence, in need and trouble of every kind. He always felt how difficult it was, from the security of a very happy home and Vicarage, really to understand why people are what they are and what makes them act as they do. As we know, at the beginning of the War in 1939, he could have been exempt from military service (as theological college students were exempt), but he felt he wanted to experience the War as an ordinary man, so he served throughout as a hospital orderly in the Friends' Ambulance Unit. When in Hong Kong, Joan and he, from the comforts of the Dean's House, made special efforts to go into all the shacks and tenement parts of Hong Kong to get some insight into how folk lived. Freddy always felt it part of the living out of the Christian faith to try to understand people's backgrounds and, so far as possible, to obtain the necessary knowledge about them. He could often be seen sitting on a bench in St. Mary's Churchyard, talking to 'down-and-outs'. Two of his former curates can still vividly remember him saying on more than one occasion, 'When you go out in our streets, be courteous to all. Treat every person as if they were Christ himself'. Freddy was greatly influenced throughout his ministry by the poem 'Indifference' by Geoffrey Studdert Kennedy:

When Jesus came to Golgotha they hanged Him on a tree,
The drave great nails through hands and feet, and made a Calvary;
They crowned Him with a crown of thorns, red were His wounds and deep,
For those were crude and cruel days, and human flesh was cheap.

When Jesus came to Birmingham they simply passed him by,
They never hurt a haïr of Him, they only let Him die;
For men had grown more tender, and they would not give Him pain,
They only just passed down the street, and left Him in the rain.

Still Jesus cried, 'Forgive them, for they know not what they do,'
And still it rained the wintry rain that drenched Him through and through;
The crowds went home and left the streets without a soul to see,
And Jesus crouched against a wall and cried for Calvary.

At this time, Freddy was much influenced by Father Borelli (a priest who worked with the outcasts of Naples). Freddy had read and re-read a book about him, *Children of the Sun*, by Morris West. Father Joe Williamson, who worked with the prostitutes of London's East End, was another 'hero' of Freddy's, as, surprisingly perhaps, in view of the differences in churchmanship, were some of the Anglo-Catholic slum priests of the nineteenth century, including Fr. Dolling of St. Agatha's, Landport, the adjoining parish to St. Mary, Portsea.

Sometimes while in Portsmouth he had tried to help homosexuals who had come to him for advice about their problems. He wrote at the time, 'They are usually very lonely. I have often felt unable fully to understand them, especially as I am happily married and in a nice home. I therefore felt that, if I once knew, for myself, the sordid atmosphere involved in loitering in a men's public lavatory, I might go some way towards understanding a little better, and as a result have more genuine sympathy.' At this particular time, Freddy had had more homosexuals consulting him than had been usual and their problems had been pressing on his mind.

On the evening of October 7th, Freddy attended a meeting at St. Wilfrid's Church. It was mainly concerned with petty details of church activity, such as the number of card tables needed for a whist drive. Freddy left the meeting a little depressed, and felt the need, before going home, to remind himself that the Christian Faith was more than card tables. He had, previously that day, been told that there was a type of homosexual person who frequented a certain public lavatory. On impulse, Freddy went to see for himself what was going on.

Freddy was arrested by two police officers, taken to the local police station and charged with 'soliciting for immoral purposes.' Joan and Freddy were shattered and in deep despair.

Because of the precariousness of his plight, Freddy opted for trial by jury. The trial date was set for November 26th at the Portsmouth Quarter Sessions. The renowned Jeremy Hutchinson, QC (later to become Lord Hutchinson of Lullington) was briefed to defend him. It became obvious during the trial that the two police officers involved had colluded back at the police station and had fabricated in their notebooks implausible and identical evidence. Hutchinson managed to demonstrate the police officers' lies; he called Robert Beloe, the Archbishop of Canterbury's lay secretary, as a character witness; he said he believed Freddy to be 'incapable of lying'. The Recorder was obviously appalled by the police evidence and summed up for an acquittal. Anyone reading the large file on the case, including the transcripts of all the court proceedings, will surely conclude that Freddy was innocent of the charge. And so it proved. He was acquitted by the jury. Unusually, most of the considerable costs of the case were awarded against the police.

The *Portsmouth Evening News* carried a leading article, which ran:

When there is a wave of car thefts in a community, the police are expected to take vigorous action to prevent crime, or to bring offenders to justice. The more zealously they go about these and similar duties, the more likely it is that, while securing convictions, they may also cause some inconvenience to innocent members of the public. The reasonably-minded citizen who is stopped late at night while driving his car, and is politely questioned by a policeman, may feel a little put out, but will quickly realise that the officer is only doing his duty. While few of us actually enjoy being pulled up in this way when on our lawful occasions, we recognise that the police may be justified in thinking that we are acting suspiciously, or may have their own reasons for questioning us.

This kind of incident can happen to almost everyone. Usually an innocent person has little difficulty in clearing up the misunderstanding, and it is soon forgotten. But there are other cases, in that twilight of law enforcement concerned with what is variously described as morality or vice, which are in quite a different category. This is highly unpleasant work for police officers, but it is a dangerous quagmire for the ordinary citizen. There has been a spate of these cases in recent months in Portsmouth, and a letter in this page reflects public concern. [2]

Police intervention in matters of public morality is always strewn with hazards, and a very heavy responsibility rests with those concerned in law enforcement. Too vigorously pursued, a clean-up campaign can take on the character of persecution of innocent and guilty alike. Any keenness to secure convictions has to be set against the methods that have to be employed to obtain proofs. It is a most unsavoury business. Innocent, frightened people may get caught up in a sordid situation in which they see their world crumbling around them The police, it must be conceded, are placed in an unenviable position in carrying out their duties, but like the Press, they also wield tremendous power: the power to mar permanently the reputation of anyone accused. Such power must be used with the utmost restraint and wisdom. Mistakes can be disastrous both for the private citizen and for the public image of the police.

In the weeks leading up to the trial, and during the trial itself, Freddy read *On Science, Necessity and the Love of God* by Simone Weil. He underlined the sentences: 'Human beings are so made that the ones who do the crushing feel nothing; it is the person crushed who feels what is happening. Unless one has placed oneself on the side of the oppressed, to feel with them, one cannot understand.'

Letters and telegrams flooded in to the Vicarage. Lord Fisher of Lambeth sent a telegram, as soon as the verdict was announced, 'God is in His heaven. All's right with the world. Love to all. Archbishop and Rosamund Fisher.' Lord Fisher's successor as Archbishop, Michael Ramsey, wrote:

You have seldom been out of my thoughts in these days of strain, and I have been trying to pray for you, and now how deeply [word indecipherable] I am that it is over. You will know more than ever how solidly your own folk were with you, and that is a quite unshaken rock.

Derek Worlock, Roman Catholic Bishop of Portsmouth, and afterwards Archbishop of Liverpool, penned the following:

---

[2] The letter referred to was from a former Metropolitan Police officer, alluding to the overzealousness of some police officers in trying to raise their tally of convictions in cases such as Freddy's.

I have not wanted to write before because I did not wish to run the risk of letting you feel that you had the burden of everyone's eyes on you. But I spoke to your Bishop John and offered Mass for you last Tuesday. Now that most of the ordeal is over I wanted just to send you this line of friendship and sympathy - and congratulations on your courage in going through with it all. May God sustain you and your family.

F.R. Barry wrote a long letter, beginning with 'Alleluia!' and finishing with 'Of course I never had any doubt about *you*; but was apprehensive about the jury', a subject also mentioned by Mary Eastwood, a member of the staff at Lambeth Palace, who, amongst other things, said, 'What a relief it was to hear the news this afternoon. I would have lost all faith in British justice if it had been otherwise, but having done jury service myself last year, I realise what awful errors of judgement *could* arise.'

Of the masses of letters received, many of them referred to Joan and Freddy's courage throughout the ordeal, and what an inspiration it was to them. Many could not believe the way in which Freddy and Joan continued throughout to care for their parishioners during the weeks of waiting for the trial. The weeping went on behind the closed doors of the Vicarage.

As a result of deftness by Michael de la Noy, Press Secretary to the Archbishop of Canterbury, and despite the extensive coverage of the trial in the *Portsmouth Evening News*, not a word was mentioned in the national press. Michael de la Noy was quite adamant that there was 'absolutely nothing in these allegations, otherwise I wouldn't have pulled out all the stops for him - and I wasn't at the time feeling particularly enamoured with either the Archbishop or his friends.' De la Noy continued, 'Having said that, Freddy Temple was just incredibly stupid in what he did; he displayed absolutely no judgement or perhaps the judgement of a very tired man. Portsea must have knocked the stuffing and a bit of the sense out of him.'

Just before this traumatic incident in Freddy's ministry, it was confidently expected that Freddy was going to succeed Leonard Wilson as Bishop of Birmingham. Michael Ramsey was still keen for him to go to Birmingham, though other weighty people were not and Harold Wilson, the Prime Minister, had misgivings. The arguments were two-fold: first, that if Freddy, however well-intentioned he was, could make such an act of misjudgement once - he himself wrote at the time that his action was 'excessively foolish' - would he not perhaps misjudge other situations as a diocesan Bishop? Secondly, if the appointment were announced so close to the time of the trial, some of the national press were bound to delve into his background, and it would be almost certain that that they would get wind of the trial and go to print, causing further distress to Joan, Freddy and the family. It was probably inevitable that he was not offered the bishopric of Birmingham.

Freddy himself only rarely alluded to the case, and then only to very few of his closest friends; it had hurt him too much. If a television programme came on involving the police (like 'Z Cars', very popular at the time), he would immediately get out of his chair and leave the room, upset, sometimes in tears.

Some of Freddy's correspondence of the time, however, is revealing. In June 1969, the case of a young man who had a similar brush with the law was brought to his attention. He did not know the man in question, but the circumstances of his case were similar, though not exactly so. On June 10th, Freddy wrote:

I hope you will not mind a complete stranger writing to you. But I do not feel in any way a stranger but a close friend as my cousin, Lady Sandys, has written to me in complete confidence about the great ordeal you are going through. I went through the same fire last Autumn when, in trying to help and understand someone who was coming to me for advice, I went to the spot from which he told me he could not keep away, a public lavatory, to try and understand a bit more and also to show him that I cared enough to do this, and was quickly picked up by the police; from then on, the most staggering charges were brought. In the end, after Magistrates Court and then a month's delay and three days in Quarter Sessions, I was completely cleared and charges were awarded against the police. But I do sympathise and bleed for you as I know what an ordeal it is, although I hope you are finding how wonderful ordinary human nature is and how everyone who knows you respects and trusts you.

I am not quite sure whether you have had the ordeal of the Magistrates Court. I hope you have, as I think this is quite the worst, where one sits in that box all day and just hears the filth poured out against one with no one making any reply. But you are so wise to go on to Quarter Sessions. I know I would be a condemned man now if it had stopped there, because it needed a really good QC to tear the evidence against one into shreds and show it up for what it was. I expect you have got a really good barrister but I do hope you realise, along with your family and friends, what a colossal cost the whole thing may be. In the end, mine came to well over a thousand pounds, but the police had to pay most of this.

I do not know how much the facts of Christianity help you or not. If they do, I hope you will realise anew how wonderful it is that God has been before us all in every trouble that we may have. He too was unjustly accused. You and I at least have some loyal friends and family around us who trust and believe. His friends fled at the critical moment. If you are locked up for periods of the trial as I was, it is again a comfort in one's cell to realise that He too had all this and more happen to Him; at least the police do not spit on one or beat one for sport now. Holy Week, the Trial and Good Friday have taken on a totally new meaning for me and helped me to realise afresh how God is in every conceivable wretched situation that arises; in His case, of course, He was condemned unjustly as well, and so He is in any situation that may arise for anyone.

Joan, my wife, and I will be thinking of you daily in our hearts and prayers dur-

211

ing the next few weeks and if there is any way in which we can help, do not hesitate to let us know. If it is any consolation, it is quite incredible and appalling how many people there are in this sort of plight, and how many we have found ourselves trying to help, especially since we have been through this furnace ourselves. If you can, try to hold on to the fact that undeserved suffering especially, is ultimately always tremendously enriching to life and helps us in the future to help other people far, far more than we can ever realise.

(The young man was, at his trial, later acquitted.)

This memoir has deliberately spent time on the issue of Freddy's trial for a variety of reasons. First, those who hitherto knew nothing of this incident in Freddy and Joan's life and ministry together will doubtless be shocked. But any 'Life' must be rigorous, and unpleasant incidents should not be swept under the carpet. It may be that some will think it unfortunate that something that happened well over thirty years ago should be brought out into the open. Having said that, I have read a mass of personal and private material about the case, and have come to the conclusion that the whole tragic affair can only redound to Freddy's credit, and to that of Joan who, typically, was a rock to which Freddy could, and did, cling.

Secondly, many people have indeed over the years heard garbled rumours about the case; as everyone knows, rumour feeds on rumour and stories doing the rounds get elaborated, so that tales being repeated simply do no justice to the facts.

Thirdly, the *Independent* newspaper on December 8th, 2000, added a fairly long piece about the trial to Jeffrey Maples' obituary of Freddy - fairly sympathetic, but perhaps unnecessary. Many, since the publication of that piece, have raised questions about what actually happened.

Finally, perhaps this account might go some way towards answering the question why Freddy did not rise further in the ecclesiastical hierarchy, as was widely expected. Many people have written, asking just that question.

Meanwhile, Freddy and Joan simply got on with caring deeply for the people of Portsea, with what Jeffrey Maples called 'infectious enthusiasm and renewed dynamism.' Freddy, with characteristic good humour and more than a touch of humility, wrote, 'The Good Lord obviously wants me to stay here, but I hope it's only his short term plan.'

And so it proved. On October 14th, 1969, Freddy received a letter from Oliver Tomkins, Bishop of Bristol, asking him whether he would be willing to consider the possibility of succeeding Cyril Bowles (who had been appointed Bishop of Derby) as Archdeacon of Swindon. Oliver Tomkins said that he had spoken to the Bishop of Portsmouth and the Archbishop of Canterbury, who had both given him their blessing in making an approach.

Bishop Oliver and Freddy arranged two appointments: the first, a meeting on the 22nd October, at the Athenaeum. The second was a weekend stay at Bishop's

House, Bristol, on the 25th - 26th October, for Freddy to meet some of the members of the Bishop's Staff. On the Monday morning, Bishop Oliver wrote formally offering Freddy the post. The Bishop of Malmesbury, Jim Bishop, and the Archdeacon of Bristol, Leslie Williams, 'share my hope that you would be willing to be Archdeacon of Swindon; they both welcome the thought.'

Freddy wrote back, accepting 'with great gratitude and diffidence and looking forward with eagerness to the future.' Two days later, however, Freddy received a telephone call, followed by a letter, saying that Oliver Tomkins and John Hewitt, the Prime Minister's Appointment's Secretary, had 'only just tumbled to the fact that the post of Archdeacon was not the Bishop of Bristol's to offer.' The appointment of Archdeacon of Swindon was a Crown appointment, by reason of the fact that Cyril Bowles was going to a bishopric. He was told, however, not to worry overmuch, as the Crown almost always followed the Bishop's recommendation. Freddy replied to the effect that from the beginning he thought this was the case, from what he remembered from his time at Lambeth, but had kept quiet for he did not want to be considered a 'know-all' and 'being personally involved, I felt it not for me to question whether I was being appointed right!' Her Majesty approved the appointment a few days later.

Freddy wrote a very long personal letter to the Bishop of Portsmouth, expressing his deep gratitude for having given him the opportunity to be Vicar of St. Mary, Portsea, and saying that he was certain that the time had come when the parish ought to have 'a new look and vigour given to it.' Amongst other things in the letter, Freddy pointed out that his successor as Vicar of Portsea would not find a debt of £8,000, but instead over £20,000 invested with the Charity Commissioners and £4,000 invested with the Central Board of Finance.

After Freddy had accepted the Archdeaconry of Swindon, but before the news was released, he was approached by members of the Board of Christian Aid (including David Paton and Robin Woods) asking if were willing to have his name put forward to succeed Janet Lacey as Director. Although there were certain attractions about the job, Freddy and Joan had made up their minds that they wanted to go to Swindon.

In his final letter to the parish in *Forward*, Freddy wrote,

If I were asked to single out one great important change in the Parish compared with eight years ago, I would say it was that we do not spend nearly as much time looking over our shoulders, thinking what a great Parish this has been in the past; we now look mainly to the future and realise that we are just a big Parish with very many problems and opportunities.

In a letter he was to write, in September, 1970, to his successor, Kenneth Gibbons, Freddy said:

Just a line to say how much Joan and I will be remembering you and your family next week as you take up your ministry in Fratton Road and wish you every bless-ing. It is an enormous job with colossal responsibilities and needs tremendous vital-ity and resilience, not only to keep the present structure going and alive but also to adapt and change it; but they are wonderful folk who go along with one, adapt and change whenever they find it necessary and are convinced of the need. You at least will not have to close three churches on arrival as I did, though the role of St. Faith's I felt still needed much thought.

Of course your role as a counsellor, friend and helper of the whole area is limit-less; I found most of my time inevitably got taken up just in the folk who came to the door for long talks.

Anyhow we do hope that you will be very happy and that the moments of vision, reward and deep satisfaction will well outweigh the permanent relentless pressure of jobs to be done and people to be helped.

Clergy traditionally take the inside of a week off soon after Christmas, but it was typical of Freddy's pastoral concern and care that he did not do so after his last Christmas in Portsea, just before moving to Swindon. He wrote in a notebook, 'This winter has shot a great number more into Eternity and there are several oth-ers clearly awaiting their count-down.' Some clergy wives would have com-plained, or been exasperated by the fact that Freddy cancelled his holiday plans because of the needs of the parish. He wrote just before Christmas to his wider family that he had to stay in Portsmouth 'for many pillars of the Church are dying, and I would not dream of being away; I know you'll be disappointed that we won't see you, but there is no option. Some of these dear folk have given their lives for their Church; what's the inside of a week compared with that?' Joan entirely con-curred.

Freddy was later to write, 'As I was waiting for the funeral of one real faithful old spinster who had been everything in the Church for a very long time and so the Church was fairly crowded, fire engines appeared, ringing bells, and swirled in [the Church gate] almost crashing into the hearse. I was thinking how strange and how charming; I wondered what connection she had with the fire brigade. But someone had seen smoke coming out of the top of the tower and, instead of asking me about it, had immediately rung the fire brigade; it was merely a damp morning making the boiler smoke a little at the top. But the dear deceased - how she must be thrilled to think that she caused so much excitement at her own funeral; she had a tiresome life in some ways, and deserved this little boost at her farewell.'

Freddy's heart was always in the parochial ministry. He loved his people; they in turn loved him.

12 Archdeacon of Swindon

Freddy was instituted as Archdeacon of Swindon, and collated and installed as Honorary Canon Diocesan, on January 30th, 1970. In a letter to his extended family the day before, he wrote, 'By the way, for those of you inexpert in the ridiculous niceties of ecclesiastical trifles, tomorrow I age rather rapidly and become "The Venerable" as an Archdeacon. Use the title or don't; it's up to you.' He continued, 'I fear that the title Archdeacon of Swindon doesn't have much of a ring to it; on holiday a few years back, Joan and I met the Archdeacon of the Aegean. Now there's a title to conjure with.'

Freddy and Joan knew little of North Wiltshire. Freddy claimed in jest to be a little apprehensive about moving there after reading the following, written by John Aubrey, circa 1680:

> *The indiginae speak drawling: they are phlegmatique, skin pale and livid, slow and dull, heavy in spirit they feed chiefly on milkee meates which cool their brains too much and hurts their inventions. Their circumstances make them melancholy, contemplative and malicious.*

But in Freddy's first letter to his extended family after becoming Archdeacon, he wrote: 'To be paid to drive round North Wilts is a marvellous job. We had no idea it was so beautiful; then we have the Cotswolds to the north, Oxford close at hand, the Marlborough Downs to the south - and Stratford is within easy striking distance. Could one ask for more? There is also a good, fast train service to London.'

Freddy wrote to a friend, after he had been in post for five months:

> *Oliver [Tomkins] is a marvellous person to work with and under as he is so very good at sharing decisions and information with his staff. Copies of all letters concerned with anything one is doing are always sent to one and so I never feel jumped and always know when talking to one of the clergy what he has said to them. He also has a wonderful able mind*

The Archdeacon of Swindon.

and balanced judgement for all the many problems that arise. He and Ursula do a phenomenal amount of entertaining and this keeps them in touch with the diocese a great deal, and I know is enormously appreciated. Joan and I do as much as we can, but it can sometimes be quite expensive. We are certainly not a Trollopian Archidiaconal family.

This last sentence is a reference to Freddy's having been amused, when re-reading Anthony Trollope's *Clergymen of the Church of England*, by the following passage in the chapter, 'The Archdeacon':

A poor archdeacon, an archdeacon who did not keep a curate or two, an archdeacon who could not give a dinner and put a special bottle of wine upon the table, an archdeacon who did not keep a carriage, or at least a one-horse chaise, an archdeacon without a manservant, or a banker's account, would be nowhere - if I may so speak - in an English diocese. Such a one could not hold up his head among churchwardens, or enquire as to church repairs with any touch of proper authority.

The Archdeacon of Swindon was the only diocesan official to live at the eastern end of the diocese, which made Freddy's job slightly different and more varied than that of many an Archdeacon. Communications between the parishes at the Swindon end became all the more important, 'as we in Swindon, a growing, self-confident town, never think of Bristol, except ecclesiastically', wrote Freddy. He lived nearer to three other Cathedral cities than to his own - Salisbury, Oxford and Gloucester. Freddy counted himself lucky and soon found himself very much an advocate of smaller dioceses. He thought the Archdeaconry of Swindon would make an ideal diocese, just the right size to get to know the clergy and leading laity really well - 'and be round again before they felt they had been forgotten.'

Joan enjoyed their house, 'Morwena', although it was smaller than Portsea Vicarage. She wrote: 'Our house is on the site of a Roman villa and quarry and at first we had high hopes of finding a super Roman pavement; however, when the Archaeological Society dug down, they found, after pumping off the water, the quarry floor - alas, no pavement. So now our rhubarb thrives above the spring.' Freddy thought the house pleasant, 'in a nice quiet part of Swindon'. He had been pleasantly surprised by the quietness, for the next door neighbours, a bank manager and his wife, had said the traffic was heavy. Freddy and Joan noticed only about one car an hour go by - certainly very different from Fratton Road, Portsmouth. 'I hope', wrote Freddy, 'the good man is better at counting money than vehicular traffic.'

Freddy wrote, 'On balance, I am tremendously impressed by the clergy I have the privilege of trying to serve and help; good, dedicated cheerful families quietly and simply doing a great work in good heart. Some rest on their oars; usually the noisier, frothier ones. And they think we don't see through them.'

He continued, 'The church is very much more alive and vigorous than many a paper would have one believe. I sometimes go round parishes unannounced, so see things just as they are. Any other organisation would be thrilled to have the plant, numbers and deployment of committed regular members that the Church has.'

Freddy thought he detected growing signs, in 1970, that there might be a return of religious interest, especially among the young and more thoughtful; the middle-aged liked their comforts and material things. Whether the interest would grow into commitment or not depended on how resilient and adaptable the Church would be.

In 1972, he wrote:

I was lucky enough to be one of the diocesan representatives to the Church Leaders Conference in Birmingham, where 500 of us gathered. There were some brilliant lectures and two of the theologians there , Dr. Ian Ramsey, Bishop of Durham, (how tragic his death is) and Professor Torrance, assured us that the climate of opinion amongst scholars in the sciences as well as theology was far more congenial to metaphysics and theology than it had been for many years; there was always a time-lag before this feeling seeped down into the thinking of the ordinary man, but they foresaw a much more congenial atmosphere of thought to all things religious in ten to fifteen years time. There are signs that the younger clergy, of whatever churchmanship, are more confident and ready to talk about mission and evangelism than they have been.

John Ware arrived in the diocese of Bristol from Sheffield in 1968, with his wife, Phillada, and their three children. John became Rector of Liddington and the Bishop of Bristol's Social and Industrial Chaplain in Swindon; this was an ecumenical ministry throughout the Bristol diocese working in local settings at the interface between society, industry and the churches.

He recalls how Swindon at that time was entering the second phase of its change from a nineteenth-century railway town to a twentieth century manufacturing and commercial centre. In the 1950s the huge Great Western Railway Works had begun a long process of gradual closure and many of the skilled workforce had been re-employed in new factories connected with motor-car manufacturing and engineering. In an attempt to foster more jobs Swindon Borough Council was encouraging people to move to Swindon, especially from overcrowded London boroughs. Large new Council estates had been built from the mid-fifties onwards on the northern and eastern sides of the town. A huge western development was about to be started to accommodate a new population of over 25,000 people.

In all these new areas new churches had been built by the main Christian denominations. The vision of the Bishop of Bristol was that, in all new areas especially, churches should work together in formalised Areas of Ecumenical Experiment. In early 1968 he had invited the Reverend Derek Palmer, who had spearheaded notable ecumenical work in the huge new estate of Hartcliffe in South Bristol, to become Vicar of Christ Church, Swindon. Derek soon established the first formal Area of Ecumenical Experiment in England. So the stage was being set for Swindon to become an important town for the development of ecumenical strategies of work between the main Christian denominations. When Cyril Bowles, the Archdeacon of Swindon, was appointed Bishop of Derby in 1970, it was important that his successor should be a man of ecumenical vision and sensitivity who could, at the same time as helping the churches work together, also enable them to play a key role in supporting the Borough to deepen the sense of local civic pride in Swindon as an emerging new community.

John Ware writes:

It seemed to many of us that Freddy, when he arrived, could not be bettered to lead us in the way ahead. He immediately impressed us all as a person who cared for us as individuals and who had a vision for the mission and ministry of the churches in the 'new' Swindon. From my point of view, as an Industrial and Social Chaplain, it was evident at once that he inherited his Uncle William's concern for issues of social justice and care.

On July 14th 1972, the Swindon *Evening Advertiser* published the following article:

It was the television cameras that really surprised the Venerable Freddy Temple, Archdeacon of Swindon. He never imagined when he joined a deputation which included trade unionists and an MP to lobby Westminster about the shut-down of the Swindon railway works, he was creating 'news.' 'But the cameramen were there at the station waiting for a shot of this strange-looking thing, an archdeacon,' he said, full of good humour.

Mr. Temple, or the Ven. Freddy, as one feels like calling him, is most people's image of a country vicar, grey-haired, and smiling and perhaps slightly otherworldly. It is a picture he dispels almost as soon as he allows it to form. When he uses phrases like industrial shake-out, it vanishes completely. He looked pained when I suggested to him that when a town is faced with growing unemployment and sackings it is unusual for an Archdeacon to join the workers and politicians whizzing up to Westminster to lobby the Government.

'What a question to put to a Temple,' he said.

He was referring to his uncle William Temple, Archbishop of Canterbury in the 1940s who went further than most churchmen towards making ecclesiastical social conscience a political reality.

'I went to London to express concern that so many skilled men are going to be

218

put out of work in a year's time, and that they will have very little chance of finding employment. Our problem is that we do not have sufficient skilled engineering jobs to give them. We are going over to computers and warehouses. If industry is going to have shake-outs it must remember that it is human beings that are being shaken out,' he said.

He said it in the matter of fact way of a man who sees a problem and grasps an opportunity for action. Archdeacons I have heard of in the past have been a little more remote than this.

Mr. Temple describes his job as communications man between the diocese and the parishes. He foresees human problems in the parishes when the railway works are closed, such as skilled fitters finding it hard to learn new skills or maybe finding it harder, especially financially, to move where work is. He said that as far as the deputation led by Swindon MP Mr. David Stoddart was concerned, he played a supporting role.

The Archdeacon lives in a large detached house in Mill Lane, Westlecot Road, he describes as his tied cottage, which is wholly typical of him. There trade union-ists, industrial managers and others have been meeting for some time under the auspices of the Swindon Council of Churches to discuss Swindon's unemploy-ment. He is convinced there is nothing spectacular about an archdeacon taking this sort of lead in the community.

'In this diocese we are very aware of such issues, and the work of the Rev. John Ware, the industrial chaplain, is a supreme example,' he said.

But then Mr. Temple has always found himself in the thick of things.

During the war he worked with a Quaker ambulance team with the Free French Forces. And he was senior chaplain to Dr. Geoffrey Fisher, when he made his memorable trip to meet Pope John.

One thing is sure. He will find his work equally cut out in the industrial field.

John Ware further recalls the great support Freddy gave during his period as Arch-deacon to a group who were seeking to found in Swindon a branch of what at that time was known as the National Association for Mental Health. There had been a growing concern locally for the care in the community of people with chronic conditions of mental ill health and over the amount of time lost from work for rea-sons of mental, rather than physical, illness. There was a great ignorance in the community in general about mental health, and it was felt among local psychia-trists and mental health officers, as well as welfare officers in industry, that the establishment of a Swindon branch of the National Association for Mental Health could make an important and continuing contribution to meeting the needs of the mentally ill in the community. In 1971, at a Public Meeting in Swin-don College, with Freddy in the Chair, the Swindon branch of the NAMH was launched. It continues to this day, now called MIND. John asserts that without Freddy's contacts and support, and his ability to hold together a wide spectrum of people in one vision, it could not have got off the ground.

Freddy was fascinated by the state of the Church at the time. He was convinced that there were clear signs that the country was starting to enter a new religious age: the hippy dropouts in their search for mystic cults were all wild symptoms of it, as was the 'Jesus Movement'. Freddy was impressed by the 'incredible amount of talking and getting into groups for discussion and prayer that goes on at Rugby amongst boys, as we learn from Stephen [Freddy and Joan's son].' He was greatly impressed by the fact that many Anglican religious orders seemed to be having no difficulty in attracting enough novices - indeed by the fact that some even had waiting lists. Whether the 'new age' would be Christian was, thought Freddy, another matter; it all depended on how flexible and alive the institutional Church would be. In 1976 he was to write in the same vein, 'Stephen Verney has just written a very good book called *Into the New Age* in which, from his experience as a Missioner attached to St. George's, Windsor, he feels we are really coming near the dawn of a re-birth and, like the garden at the moment, there are no large signs of this but just innumerable little things popping up everywhere.'

Freddy was asked by the editor of the Swindon *Evening Advertiser* to write about the future of the church in the Swindon area in the 70s. On September 19th, 1972 the following appeared:

A visit to any natural history museum teaches one a great deal. Those vast prehistoric animals with their tusks and enormous armour plating on their backs must once have seemed invincible upon the earth. But now they have all gone, and it is a small, unprotected animal, man, that dominates the world over all others; and he too will only do so if he remains intelligent, sensitive, flexible and light; we all know the dangers of overweight.

Any reading of history teaches the same thing. The knight in armour ended up so heavy that he had to be hoisted on to his charger and he was defeated by the swift lightness of the arrow and gunshot. The big battleships gave way to the small aeroplane. The Maginot Line was useless against the flexible, mobile Panzer divisions.

So there is no reason why people should get discouraged or surprised if the Church (and I mean throughout all the churches) like every other institution, in reorganising and adapting itself in the 70s, has to shed some weight.

If Christians would stop being discouraged they could again realise how strong the Church still is in England; and in the world at large there are places where it is growing fast, like Central Africa and South America.

Each Sunday I go round to a different parish and find a band of dedicated folk carrying on their Christian witness in each place; any other serious organisation or political party would be thrilled if it had the numbers, plant and deployment that the Church still has.

But the Christian army must move where the battle and need is; in the main the

parochial system was devised for a static agricultural community living and work-

ing in the same place. Now large numbers spend the greater part of their waking hours away from home, in the place where they work; and so chaplains for industry and industrial mission will become more important. As society becomes more specialised and involved so clergy for that particular branch of life become needed, like education, hospital work and youth work. The need to serve people in these spheres may well mean more men being withdrawn from tiny parishes where he motor car has made it possible to combine with others.

We are ready to travel some way for most other things of importance, why not for religion? It would mean a few more thousands have a chance to learn of Christian truth instead of one man continuing to care for a hundred or two in one place when another could care for them as well. Still far too many clergy are placed where the churches are, not where people are. There will certainly be changes in deployment. The Christian army will also be an allied army, all denominations working more and more together as we so happily do in Swindon. What are technically called 'areas of ecumenical experiment' will become more and more important. Old Town and East Swindon are good examples of such areas.

We can expect fewer men being ordained in the next ten years. There are many reasons for this, one being that young Christians realise that you can now serve God fully in any occupation and that it is a special vocation to be ordained; when I grew up it was the main opening for most committed Christians to consider first. But there are signs of more men offering for ordination and it would need only a small swing in the general social attitude to belief for this to grow again.

Inflation makes adequate payment of the clergy a major problem. No one wants the clergy rich, but none should want them permanently worried by real poverty, as some are. It will become more common for the clergyman or minister's wife to work when the children are no longer young, partly because most women are now trained for some job and partly because the clergyman's family will not be able to afford not to have her work.

But far more important than these institutional changes will be a shedding of weight in matters of worship and belief. This is a time of reformation, so there will be continual variety and as always in a time of reformation a return to simpler, more basic matters of belief. Godspell, Jesus Christ Superstar and the Jesus People show how much the figure of Jesus haunts and attracts this generation; it is no good just to protest that these are inadequate portrayals. Christians have to be open to anything that might lead others to a greater understanding of Christ and show him forth in their lives. There will be great variety in all our worship; there always has been.

Freddy loved addressing groups of secondary schoolchildren and would accept as many invitations as his diary allowed. He caused a little stir when speaking at Warneford School, Highworth, prize-giving on November 16th, 1972. There were one or two raised eyebrows amongst parents and staff. He told the story (which he had borrowed from Bishop Cuthbert Bardsley when addressing the troops in Hong Kong, while Freddy was Dean) of a lady who was going by train from Cheltenham. She saw a dog tied up on the platform, yapping away and no one paying any attention to it. The dog was still there at night when she returned, so she went up to a porter and said, 'Why haven't you done something about that dog?' The porter replied, 'Madam, *you* don't know where he is going. *I* don't know where he is going and *he* doesn't, because he has been and gone and chewed his bleedin' label.' Understandably, the children loved it. Freddy went on to say that Britain was in much the same state as that dog: 'Many of us are unsure where we are going. Don't be discouraged by middle-aged moaners; you are as fine a generation as there has been. I suspect it could well be *you* who will very soon be teaching *us* the way forward.'

Joan and Freddy enjoyed very much being at Almondsbury (the Bristol Diocesan Conference House) for the South West Ecumenical Congress in the spring of 1973. Freddy wrote to his family:

We had at Almondsbury Archbishop Anthony Bloom who was a marvellous person to talk to privately. He had such a deep strength of repose and also on the Saturday evening after a whole day of other meetings and conferences kept us all enthralled in a cold Bristol Cathedral from 10pm until midnight in quiet and meditation. Lord Longford was also at Almondsbury. He is a quiet character, charming, but as vague and unmechanical as I'd always thought him to be - quite out of touch with the practical needs of ordinary life. He had not brought anything to shave with and in the end I had to lend him a razor with a new blade - and he did not even bother to clean these after he had used them and I had to collect them from his room all full of his own hairs. This seems strange in a man who has written a book on 'Humility'. Rosemary Haughton, the RC mother of ten, who has just adopted two more. She is very taken at the moment with the latest form of psychoanalytical talk called transactional analysis; we all act either as a child, a parent or sometimes as a mature adult. How to get us more often being free adults is the thing. She put it over well, and people liked it. She paid Joan an unconscious compliment at the end, saying, 'I have always grown up with the firm belief that all priests should be celibate. Now I begin to see the point of married clergy; she then asked Joan, 'Can you see any point in a celibate clergy?' The big meeting in the Colston Hall with the Archbishop and Cardinal Suenens was a great success.

Freddy's favourite moment was when Cardinal Suenens was talking about the danger of the Christian faith becoming an abstract philosophy. He told a story which was currently doing the rounds in Belgium of Jesus walking along the street with a theologian. 'And who do you say I am?' asked Jesus of the theologian. The reply came, 'You are the eschatological ground of our being.' 'I am WHAT?' exclaimed Jesus.

Many of the clergy of the diocese of Bristol and their families used to spend the inside of a week every year at Lee Abbey, for a period of prayer, recreation, learning and discussion. Freddy and Joan loved these occasions. In May 1971, Freddy wrote to his family:

We had a very good clergy school on prayer; John Townroe; very good indeed as he combined good psychiatry with prayer. If you have any really violent emotions which you know you ought not to feel, don't just repress them; this in the end makes for a buttoned-up, rather pharisaical character and often leads in the end to acute depression. How true, I felt, of some in their fifties wagging their fingers at the world and seeing nothing good. The one place Townroe says we should toss these emotions is Godward; this is part of the cross that he accepts us as we are, and we should admit what we are to Him and not pretend otherwise. In fact Townroe often recommended, when counselling, that folk do something innocently violent like smashing milk bottles in the backyard or tearing up waste paper, saying a prayer the while. Then slowly a peace returns and quite a new sensitivity to prayer; quite a new line to me; we had one young curate who is a brilliant cartoonist and after this lecture on the board was a delightful sketch of a wife bending over her husband, who had his head in his hands. 'But, dear, I thought you were over your deep depression'. 'I was till this bill arrived from United Diaries: £25 for broken bottles.'

The Temple family, as well as being very closely-knit, have always shared the same aspirations and have invariably been outward-looking. It is obvious from reading so much of what Freddy wrote in the years he was in Swindon that he was profoundly proud, not only of what Joan was accomplishing, but also of how Mina and Stephen were living their lives, and the contribution that they themselves were making to society. It is for this reason that I reproduce two articles from the Swindon *Evening Advertiser* relating to the family:

Two things in particular upset Joan Temple. The first: middle-aged prejudice against the young. The second: social prejudice against ex-prisoners. The kind of prejudice which makes some women who buy tickets for dress shows in aid of charities refuse to buy them if the show is in aid of Lyddington Bridge, the Croft Road Hostel for ex-prisoners and other men in need of help.

Mrs. Joan Temple talked about it at the house her husband, the Ven. Freddy Temple, once described as their tied cottage, Morwena in Mill Lane, Swindon. 'The need for support is fairly desperate,' she said. 'I'm not even asking them to go and shake the men at Lyddington Bridge by the hand. This kind of prejudice is awfully sad. The men are nice, ordinary men who have perhaps not had enough support, have had grave disadvantages in their upbringing and life has treated them in a difficult manner.'

Her interest in the welfare of ex-prisoners and their families dates from the days when her husband was vicar of a parish in Portsmouth. 'Men of the road' were frequent callers at the Vicarage, seeking help.

Mrs. Temple became an after-care voluntary worker, co-operating with probation officers and visiting prisoners' families. She still does this work in Swindon, as well as helping to run Lyddington Bridge. 'Sometimes it's a question of helping them through crises and sometimes just of being there so they know they can telephone you if something frightful happens.'

It's hardly surprising the Temples are champions of youth. They have a daughter, Mina, who is 23, and an 18 year-old son, Stephen. Their first son died at the age of six in Hong Kong, where from 1953 to 1959 the Ven. Freddy Temple was Dean.

Mina, a Durham University graduate, has been doing social work as a play organiser in Belfast and is soon to start a similar job with the Charterhouse Settlement in Southwark.

'She is named after her great-grandmother, who hangs in our hall - painted by Romney,' smiled Joan Temple.

Stephen is between school and university and has a Church Missionary Society youth service job, teaching in Kenya. 'He won a travelling scholarship and is loving it,' said his mother. 'It upsets me greatly when people attack the young generation. I have enormous admiration for the young. They are far more tolerant and kind, far more socially aware than we were. There is great hope for the future if only stuffy middle-age doesn't sit on top of them.'

She regrets that by getting their priorities out of order, many parents are throwing away the chance to be their children's friends. 'I am very old-fashioned in a way about mothers out at work. People want so many things there is a danger of putting the children second and this is why you get this terrible teenager-parental gap.' In Portsmouth, where they had 40,000 people in the parish, she and her husband saw the damage caused to large numbers of latch-key children.

'I try to go everywhere I can with my husband,' said Mrs. Temple. 'Most Sundays he is preaching in two different places, and there are also week-night things that I enjoy going to with him. Freddy calls himself an ordained driver. We cover an enormous mileage.'

They met when she was 16 and he was at Balliol College, Oxford, with her brother. 'Freddy came to stay with us and I liked him, but I didn't think any more about it. Then the war came and he went abroad and without having seen him again, half-way through I knew I was going to marry him. The poor man didn't really stand a chance.'

They married in 1947 and have always regarded Mr. Temple's job as a partnership. 'We have always talked about our ordination, our curacy and so on,' she said. 'I haven't a single clergyman on my side of the family, which is probably a good thing, because his is absolutely littered with bishops and archbishops on both sides and I bring us down to earth with a bump.'

Mrs. Temple confesses to being not terribly interested in cooking or household chores. 'But I like the home to look welcoming and cheerful when people come and I like them to be able to enjoy a nice meal - simple, but nice.' She and her husband enjoy entertaining but if they are giving a small dinner party they have to plan it months ahead, because life is now so busy.

One of the latest things to occupy her time is the Volunteer Bureau, a kind of central clearing house which in the last few months has provided more than 100 volunteers workers for organisations in the Swindon area.

Joan had been asked by the Council of Social Service to form a Volunteer Service Bureau, which took up a great deal of her time, as did her work with Lyddington Bridge. Freddy commented at the time, 'One of the great dangers I see in the next decade is a possible right wing backlash which could irrationally sweep all liberal and progressive policies of reform in this sphere out of the window. It's so important that Joan does this work, though it means that for a while she has less time to accompany me to engagements. But when she can, she does, which is marvellous as together we can serve the diocese in a better way than singly. Both of us pick up on different things when talking to people.'

After Mina had graduated from Durham, Joan wrote, 'We had a 'phone call from her saying that she had got a job, just what she wanted, in Belfast. Freddy and I gulped and said, "How lovely".'

The Swindon *Evening Advertiser* published the following:

Amid the turmoil of troubled Belfast a lone Swindon woman extends a hand of hope to a despairing people. She has lived through a nightmare three months - which has seen the introduction of internment, ceaseless bomb attacks, the murder of British soldiers and Irish civilians - nursing a tireless aim. Every day Miss Mina Temple, community worker and graduate in sociology and anthropology, strives to bring a semblance of ordinary community life to a torn and bleeding area of East Belfast.

Enjoying a brief four-day respite at her parents' home in Mill Lane, Swindon, Mina, daughter of the Archdeacon of Swindon, the Ven. Frederick Temple, will return to the people who have gradually grown to accept an all too obvious 'Englishwoman'. She returns to a country which both attracts and frightens her - a country which she says is 'balancing on the brink of civil war.'

Mina, 23, graduated from Durham University in June. Almost immediately she was in Belfast as a community worker for the Christian Movement for Peace. At first she had the companionship of 11 other graduates and together they worked on an adventure playground scheme. But the others were recalled to England just before internment was announced and Mina was left alone, without a base, operating from her digs.

And then began weeks of hard, relentless work. Days of tramping the streets

225

from 9am to 11.30pm. trying to gain the confidence and friendship of people who had suspected her motives. 'They feel with explosion or murder that their city and country is being destroyed', she said. 'They are very bitter. They feel England doesn't understand and has entirely neglected them. With every death of a soldier they are terribly upset - especially about how people in England regard them.'

Mina operates in an area which has been docile in comparison with the Shankhill Road and Falls Road area. 'But when internment was introduced six factories nearby were set on fire. One could hear shooting in the nearby Catholic area. Any Catholics who lived in my area had been burned out. The men formed into vigilante groups and patrolled the area every night,' she said. 'It was possible to cut the atmosphere with a knife. Children could sense when there was going to be an explosion and cry. Their mothers, with nerves tense from the constant battering they received, would shout at them.'

But in the last month Mina has got herself accepted. She has managed to set up a play school in 'a dirty old church hall.'

'The women themselves are going to run it twice a week to start with, but we hope to build from there. And we run a youth club in the same premises. The teenagers are only too anxious to make a success of it.'

Mina returns to Belfast today to the people who have learned to accept her. She expects to stay for at least a year. 'Most of all I want them to realise that there is something to build for. I want to take their minds off the political situation and get them trained on ordinary, everyday things.'

Freddy claimed never to have been more surprised than when Oliver Tomkins asked Joan and him to stay behind the evening Jim Free, a priest in the diocese who was at the time very sick, was anointed in the Chapel - towards the end of February 1973. Bishop Oliver handed Freddy a letter asking him if he would accept nomination to succeed Jim Bishop as Bishop of Malmesbury:

I greatly hope that you will accept nomination to The Crown as successor to Jim as Bishop of Malmesbury.

The reasons I would put on record are these, which I gave to the Archbishop and to John Hewitt:-

1) Since there is likely to be a very short period between Jim's resignation and my own, his successor will need to play in my successor.

2) For my successor's sake, the new Suffragan should therefore be of established esteem in this diocese so that his continuance here would be welcome whether or no he was eventually called elsewhere.

3) In view of the immense development of Swindon in the next decade, there ought obviously to be a diocesan leader fully conversant with that area. As Archdeacon you have already achieved a great deal of that, but to have the status of Suffragan Bishop would fortify even more the sense in Swindon that they have a responsible churchman at hand to consult.

4) At the same time, by virtue of various previous diocesan responsibilities, you are already well-known to almost all the clergy and to a high proportion of the lay people, not only in the Swindon Archdeaconry but in Bristol as well.

Quite apart from all that, I have learned greatly to value your wisdom and insight in all the sort of things which I have relied on Jim to help me with.

The only hesitation which anybody has had was whether the Portsmouth Police Court publicity would be an embarrassment. I have taken pains to ensure that the Prime Minister would accept your name at the top of the list without hesitation. But it is I think for you to face the possibility - which I would consider to be very remote - that the muck-raking press might drag it up because of the sensational possibilities inherent in joining the name of Temple with the office of Bishop!

Freddy replied,

Thank you for your letter and for the conversation with its most unexpected proposal. Uncle William's clear advice makes the answer quite plain; he always said that the responsibility of choice for a job, whether good or bad, rested entirely with the choosers not the chosen. The man selected has only to decide whether he would like to try the job and do his best to do it well. So after discussion with Joan it is with great feelings of inadequacy and with gratitude, for we are so happy here in the diocese and would love to go on serving you and it, that I am ready to accept nomination to The Crown as successor to Jim as Bishop of Malmesbury.

I feel that if you, the Archbishop and the Prime Minister are ready to accept the risk for the Church of any adverse publicity it would be quite wrong for me not to accept that risk too.

Bishop Oliver wrote from the Athenaeum:

I can't go to bed tonight without sending a line to say how happy I am at your answer! I know it will give great happiness in the diocese - but it is also a great joy to me. You and Joan have done such a wonderful pastoral work in the diocese already - and now I shall have the joy of working with you the more closely. I do not know just how long I ought to stay on, but for however long it proves to be, I shall have a colleague I love and trust and admire - and someone whom I cannot imagine the successor who would not be glad to 'inherit'. Love to you both.

When the announcement came, Freddy and Joan received, literally, hundreds of letters, and they were very touched that so many of the clergy seemed so pleased. Freddy wrote, 'Lady Fisher is giving me Archbishop Fisher's enthronement cope and mitre; will they fit? It's a big question. I should think I could have a bit added at the bottom of the cope if necessary; all those things are so vastly expensive. I have Uncle William's pectoral cross which is lovely; and his ring. But the latter might not be suitable. I was on the look-out for a real shepherd's crook and then was given one, which was lovely too.'

A few weeks before Freddy's consecration, he wrote:

Every Christmas we have had a Ginger Wine and Mince Pie party for the clergy of the Archdeaconry plus the wives and for all retired folk. We're now preparing for this. As Archdeacon this has meant invitations to about 220, though fortunately only about 120 were able to come and between 6pm and 9pm the house did not get too crammed. As Bishop, it will be considerably more. But what fun! A Nigerian, a Belgian and a Persian and three Chinese are coming for Christmas. Quite a number of overseas students must stay in a dull and empty college over Christmas because they have nowhere to go and nobody invites them. This is always fun although this year I have again realised how things may suddenly go wrong even when one does things from the best will in the world. You will remember that two years ago a Nigerian to whom we were all kind in Portsmouth in 1961 - by having him in the Clergy House and having him to Christmas Dinner - decided to take out a writ against two of the clergy, the local doctor and me accusing us of trying to poison him and then later to abscond with his wife and various other things. He himself then absconded, but has left us with legal fees of £800 - £200 each. We don't know where he is. It is just one of the hazards of trying to help - but on the whole one gets infinitely more benefit from helping people of other races than problems. It is startling to realise that anyone can pop up anywhere in the country with the most frivolous of charges - and then it can cost this amount to clear oneself in defence.

Three days before his consecration, Freddy again wrote:

It had been an enormous change and refreshment to leave St. Mary, Portsea, for the job here. St. Mary's was too big and too relentless a job to be really enjoyable. One never knew what crises were coming around the corner. There were great highlights like the Octo Centenary Year with all the marvellous meetings and services. It was full of faithful and devoted parish folk, but it was a time of tremendous change and inevitable retrenchment and so was a great strain. I gather Kenneth Gibbons, my successor, has been doing very well and built things up again. Gibbons has a remarkable ability to gather around him curates whose obvious gifts complement those of the others. They seem a very able bunch. I have enjoyed being Archdeacon of Swindon very much, although I do not think I have been a really good Archdeacon and was probably not firm enough with some of the clergy.

Obviously a new Archdeacon of Swindon had to be found. Bishop Oliver Tomkins had a possible choice of three. Two were unknown to Freddy, but he told Bishop Oliver that he would not be happy with the third. He told the bishop that the priest in question would 'relish being near the centre of attention and would delight in the baubles and trifles of being Archdeacon.' Freddy threw his own suggestion into the ring, Canon Jeffrey Maples, Vicar of St. James', Milton, Portsmouth. Amongst other posts he had held had been those of Director of Education for the diocese of Lincoln, Canon Residentiary and Chancellor of Salisbury Cathedral and Director of the Bible Reading Fellowship. But more important than any of these, said Freddy, was his 'deep compassion for his fellow man: he understands what it is like to be Vicar of a large parish and would be able to come alongside the clergy of our diocese, very much as a servant.' Freddy was delighted when Jeffrey was appointed, and looked forward to working closely with him again.

13   Bishop of Malmesbury

Joan wrote an entry in her diary at the time of Freddy's Consecration, which deserves to be printed in full. She begins her account when the family arrive at Lambeth on the afternoon of Saturday, October 31st, 1973:

In we went; the Archbishop was half-way up the front stairs; he bent forward smiling and, with hands raised, exclaimed 'Ah, the Freddies, the Freddies. Welcome home!' - which gave me a nice warm glow. Joan Ramsey was very welcoming and charming and we had tea with her in front of the fire in the drawing room. She then showed us to our rooms; she had put us in Cranmer's Tower because, she said, 'you will not get lost, as the others might.' Freddy went off to his interview with the Archbishop, and Mina, Steve and I chatted in Steve's room about the difference between the Student Christian Movement and the Oxford Inter-Collegiate Christian Union. Mina thought Steve fairly evangelical and said that the students who live at the Settlement where she works were smug and always making reference to the Bible. Mina talked on about how narrow the Durham Inter-Collegiate Christian Union had been and how unrelated to the outside world. Joan Ramsey joined us for a time.

After that we met others in the hall and went into Evensong. We sat in little huddles of families - the Deakins, the Browns, the Temples and the Tiarks. [Robert Deakin and David Brown were to be consecrated with Freddy; Geoffrey Tiarks was Senior Chaplain to the Archbishop.] In the Chapel I regret that Steve and I nearly disgraced ourselves. Steve had never before heard the awful-dry-un-intelligible-intoning-that-habitual-readers-of-the-daily-offices sometimes adopt, and he was so astonished - and then giggly. The tension going, I became the same; I kept thinking how ghastly to be the wife of someone to be consecrated the next day, and yet be near giggles in the presence of his Archbishop; thinking thus almost made me near bursting point. I have never done so much - I hope disguised! - shaking without bursting.

While we were having sherry in the drawing room afterwards, Steve expressed various doubts which I did not feel I could answer. 'I'll ask the Archbishop to speak to you', I said - and at some moment later while talking to him, I said, 'I wish you would have a word with Stephen, Your Grace; he seems in a great muddle about things.' He took my arm and in his earnest sort of way said, 'I will, Joan, I'll get hold of him; I'd like that very much.'

Over coffee in the drawing room after dinner, I saw the Archbishop grab Stephen and steer him firmly across the room to a sofa in a corner; they had quite a chat. Later, Steve said he had been most helpful. 'I should hope he would be', said Mina, 'after all you did have the top notch man on his own subject.'

The next day, after reaching St. Paul's, we went to our seats in the second row;

Outside St. Paul's Cathedral after Freddy's consecration: All Saints' Day, 1973. From left to right: David Brown, Bishop of Guildford; John Andrew, chaplain; The Archbishop; Freddy Temple, Bishop of Malmesbury; Robert Deakin, Bishop of Tewkesbury.

the first row was reserved for the Bishops. I had quite forgotten the grandeur and beauty, the space and proportion of St. Paul's. This great Cathedral filled with people, many of whom had come great distances to be with us. I felt profoundly moved - and I thought of Michael and all the countless folk who must be with us from the other side. Singing 'O Thou who camest from above', to 'Hereford' - which has been our signature tune since we had it at our wedding - was a lumpy-in-the-throat moment. Another one was when David Brown was being presented to the Archbishop; Freddy stood at the side awaiting his turn. On one side stood dear Russell Barry, very frail and ethereal-looking - very old now and unearthly; he made Freddy deacon in Southwell on the Feast of St. Matthew, 21st September 1947, ordained him priest on 19th September 1948, and was a very good friend to us in the early years and through the years. On the other side stood dear Oliver - a staunch solid rock of a man who has believed in Freddy always and put his belief into action. Really a splendid pair to stand between before going to kneel in front of the Archbishop and being engulfed in this sea of purple-robed figures with blessing hands under the magnificent dome. Incidentally, it was the 32nd anniversary of Russell Barry's ordination by Uncle William.

As we followed the Bishops out down the centre aisle, the Cathedral seemed to be full of our friends; there was really scarcely a row without a loving, familiar face to smile at and I felt moved and blessed anew by so much love and caring. We greeted many, many folk at the back - people from every phase in our life.

We had lunch with family and friends at a nearby Jo Lyons Restaurant, and eventually drove back on the M4 to Swindon - me sitting beside the new Bishop of Malmesbury.

Freddy added to Joan's account:

It was a wonderful occasion; Robert Deakin was consecrated Bishop of Tewkesbury and David Brown Bishop of Guildford. We feel specially drawn to each other. David Edwards preached a magnificent sermon. It was lovely having Oliver and Russell Barry presenting me. Tucked in a vestry were little men from Wippells, and in my case Gieves [Ecclesiastical Outfitters], who kept popping up to help us new bishops put on the new kit in various stages as we came in and out during the service. A bit fussy, but being amused by them helped ease the tension. In fact I giggled a bit, which put Robert [Deakin] off, but he soon recovered his equilibrium.

Freddy also added, 'I had not expected the sheer hard pressure on the head at the moment of Consecration; quite hard work keeping one's head up; so a real feeling of weighty responsibility being put on one. I hope that, with God's help, I can live up to the (rather unfair) expectations people have of me.'

In his Commonplace Book, Freddy wrote - dated the day of his Consecration: 'We bishops must be distinguished from the people and others by our learning, not by our dress; by our life, not by our robes; by purity of heart, not by eloquence.' This was a quote from Pope Caelestius in AD 425, who was rebuking bishops in the south of France for being 'overbearing'.

In the second week of January, 1974, Freddy again wrote, perhaps feeling rather jaded, some words of Bishop Gregory of Nazianzus, written c.382: 'If I must speak the truth, I am of a mind to shun every assemblage of bishops, because I have never seen a good end of a synod nor remedy of evils, but rather the addition of them. There are always contentions and strivings for domination (I do not think I am using too strong language) beyond description.'

Freddy had toyed (apparently for a few minutes only) with the idea of signing himself, +Frederick Malmesbury, but did not need much persuasion from Joan to decide to sign +Freddy Malmesbury. Jim Bishop, Freddy's predecessor, had signed +Leofric Malmesbury and Freddy thought that if he signed +Freddy it would be 'like going from the sublime to the ridiculous.' Some people, indeed, thought that signing himself +Freddy lacked a certain gravitas, and there was, apparently, a certain amount of adverse comment amongst those who had nothing better to do than comment adversely. Perhaps he stretched things a bit when writing sometimes to the clergy and bearing in mind the fact that he was constantly driving from Swindon to Bristol and back on the motorway, he signed himself +*Freddy M4*. Freddy himself wrote in 1974 that he thought it caused a bit of amusement - 'though I do understand from one Rural Dean in Bristol that a group of clergy in his Chapter think I am demeaning my office.' Bryan Jones, a former Vicar of St. Matthew's, Moorfields, Bristol, commented, 'When Freddy told us he wanted to be known as *Bishop Freddy*, I must confess that to my working class ears that sounded a shade like something from Noel Coward or P.G. Wodehouse - but we soon got used to it. I suppose "Fred" was too cloth cap, and "Frederick" too top hat.' Freddy's own explanation was more prosaic: 'Saves ink,' he said.

Within eight days of his Consecration, Freddy wrote to his family:

Even though we are a small diocese, I've already become more of a remote figure, which is unutterably sad. I know that in a way I must in some sense be 'apart', but it promises to be a little lonely. All I ask is that people be themselves with me, and together we help each other along as the pilgrim people of God. No wonder Uncle William used to say to me that he felt the loneliest man in the world.

Soon afterwards he wrote again about the town of Malmsbury itself:

I have been researching into my See and have been fascinated to find what an intriguing place it is. Could you place the first air crash in history? One of the monks, called Elmer, made himself a glider in 1000 AD and dived off the West Tower of the Abbey and covered more than a furlong in active flight but then, 'agitated by the violence of the wind and the swirling of the air, as well as awareness of his rashness, fell and broke his legs and was lame ever after.' He wanted to try again, but the Abbot refused to allow it; he did, however, live to a ripe old age. Aldhelm himself was a charming Saint who, besides being a great scholar, when he found people would not listen to his sermons slipped out with his lyre and caught them on the bridge at the bottom of the street, sang to them and then led the procession back to the Abbey. We are the most ancient borough in England but, alas, had to give up that title with local government reorganisation even though we petitioned the Queen to be allowed to keep it. Athelstan is buried at Malmesbury; we are not quite sure exactly where he is, but he's thought to be in the thriving vegetable garden of the adjoining Abbey House. Thomas Hobbes, the great philosopher, was a son of the Vicarage. I have learnt that Russians coming to Malmesbury are always astonished that we have no plaque up to him as he was a great political collectivist philosopher and thought very much about monolithic states - and so is much honoured in Communist countries. His father, the Vicar, was a drunkard and a great card player and used to go to sleep in the services and call out the cards. Nancy Hanks, the mother of Abraham Lincoln, worshipped in the Abbey as did the forebears of George Washington. So, it's quite a place for its small size.

When the news of Freddy's appointment as Bishop of Malmesbury had been made, one of his correspondents had said that he was so pleased that Freddy was to be Bishop of Malmesbury, 'but do you honestly think that in such a small town you'll have very much to do?' Freddy dined out on this letter many a time.

Soon after his Consecration, Freddy wrote to his family that if he and Joan were in any way to keep in touch and contact with people in the various parishes and get to know them, it would mean not only visiting them but also hosting 'small parties of 16 to 20' people at 'Morwena' - otherwise the 'communications barrier would build up.' 'It is nice', he wrote, 'to have it firmly laid down in the New Testament that a Bishop must be given to hospitality.' He continued:

Joan has indulged in a deep freeze which is marvellous as it means she can get ready for parties a long time in advance and even be out with me most of the day provided that the dishes are unfreezing in the morning. Joan comes visiting with me as often as she can now that I am a Bishop. We think some clergy wives relate better to one of their own sex, and are more likely to bare their souls with her rather than me. Many of the clergy wives are the unsung heroines of the Church. Vicarage children need support and care too; theirs can be a strange, 'different' sort of life to that led by many of their friends. We're often immensely pleased and, in a funny sort of way, humbled, when we arrive unannounced at a Vicarage and seem to be genuinely welcomed - though what's said afterwards we don't know. We were immensely amused when we went to a Vicarage on the outskirts of Bristol a few weeks ago to be greeted by the seven year old son of the house; he opened the door, looked at us for about a second, left us standing on the doorstep and we heard him rush into the house shouting, 'Mummy, Daddy, it's Fred and Joany.'

Freddy (and Joan) were perhaps most at home when visiting clergy and their families in their homes. 'They had this remarkable ability', wrote one parish priest, 'of just fitting in. We never dreaded their visits; indeed, we all thoroughly looked forward to them.'

John Poarch remembers seeing Freddy sitting on the floor and showing his children card tricks, and them Freddy washing up after a meal and filling the sink and almost the entire kitchen with soap suds. Barry Trotter recalls that Freddy came to a confirmation at his church of St John the Baptist, Frenchay, and after they'd had lunch he and Joan insisted on washing the dishes while the 'home team' put them away. Two months later, when Barry had moved to St Mary's Henbury, Freddy went to confirm at a service that had been already arranged so, instead of formally inviting them to lunch, Barry asked if they would like to come and wash the dishes in a different kitchen. Philip Hughes said it was fun to have Freddy and Joan to a meal at the Vicarage; all their three children were bathed at various times by Joan. Freddy had the great gift of making himself at home and putting other people at ease. On one visit, at tea with the family, their small son,

Richard, had been told by his parents to take his feet off the chair. This was met with a sulky refusal, and was threatening to move rapidly to an embarrassing impasse between parents and child. Freddy quickly defused the situation by putting his feet on his own chair, and in a mock-sulky voice declaring that *he* did not want to put *his* feet down. Philip continued, 'This took the wind out of Richard's sails, who agreed to put his feet down if Freddy did. The other two children looked on with eyes as big as saucers.'

John Ware writes that Freddy's personality and humanity were epitomised for many by his famous and unforgettable laugh:

> *In any meeting it was a signal that he was present and there were not a few gatherings where the tension was taken out of situations by his ability to laugh. It liberated us to see other points of view that sometimes our very own commitment prevented us from appreciating. A great memory relating to his laugh in our own family life came from a few years later. Freddy had been consecrated Bishop of Malmesbury in 1973. I had moved to Bristol in 1974 to lead the Social and Industrial Ministry in the diocese. At the beginning of 1979 he asked to come to our home to speak with Phillada and me about a possible move to other work. By then our fourth child, Daniel, had arrived. He was about three years old and was a natural mimic. He made an immediate hit with Freddy and responded to him by mimicking his laugh. Each time Freddy laughed, Daniel laughed more loudly, which made Freddy laugh even louder, to which Daniel responded even more ... and so on. It was an occasion never to be forgotten by us!*

Confirmations took up a large part of Freddy's time; he confirmed about fifty times a year. He found them an 'enormous privilege and opportunity' and wrote to a friend. 'I only hope I shall never go stale on them.'

Freddy often had two Confirmations in one day. Joan usually went with him, though he told her that he would fully understand if she finally rebelled against a continual diet of Confirmations. What usually happened on a Confirmation Sunday was that Freddy and Joan left the house soon after 8a.m., 'as one needs to arrive at least three quarters of an hour before the service. Forty five minutes is necessary if one is to have any time quiet in prayer before the service starts.' Freddy continues in a letter to his family:

> *After the service, we go around meeting people, the candidates and their families, and then if possible have an informal meeting with the Parochial Church Council, at which they are free to ask any questions or make any comment they like to me; some very interesting discussions follow. Usually after that there is lunch at the Vicarage; Joan tells me I sometimes misbehave myself dreadfully with the Vicarage children and get them over-excited and then, after the washing-up, in her own words, 'you just swan out of the Vicarage leaving the poor parents to pick up the*

*pieces!' Still, they enjoy it, and I enjoy it. We rarely go home in the afternoon, in-
stead using the time to visit a few of the retired and sick clergy. The whole thing
starts off again in the evening in another parish and we get home about 11pm.
These are fascinating and enjoyable days but we both return quite exhausted with
having tried to take in and attend to as many people as possible, and also appear
bright and interested all the time. On one occasion recently I was more tired than
usual, but received scant sympathy from Joan. 'It's your own fault, darling; you
shouldn't have spent so long on your hands and knees pretending to be a crocodile
with young Jonathan under the dining room table.' We had a really good day on
Sunday; we enjoyed all the lovely hurly-burly of a big town parish. In the evening
we had the added excitement of a little cub scout being violently sick all down the
aisle after the sermon. I didn't think my sermon that bad.*

The essence of Freddy's pastoral episcopate can perhaps best be illustrated and
appreciated by liberal use of letters received, letters (and copies) sent and surviv-
ing entries from his diaries. Before they went to visit a parish, Freddy and Joan
would always do their homework. Many were greatly impressed by the depth of
knowledge they showed, not only of the Vicarage family, but also of the parish.
However, on at least one occasion Freddy came unstuck. One priest has written
that Freddy said to a colleague of his at the end of a visit: 'Well, keep up the good
work, and I'm always interested to hear about what you're doing in the parish
magazine.' The correspondent continued, 'I am not sure whether the priest in
question had the heart to tell him, or kept quiet about the fact that they didn't
have a parish magazine.' John Poarch remembers Freddy writing to praise the letters he had written in his parish magazine. It was only later that he discovered that
a member of the congregation had written to the bishop to complain about them.

In a letter to his family in 1974, Freddy wrote:

*I went with Joan to a housing estate parish on the outskirts of Bristol last weekend.
We had a wonderful time; the parish priest is so committed to the area and people;
he makes us feel very humble. Not, I hasten to add, deliberately. While Joan went
to see a retired couple in sheltered housing, I went to see a delightful couple - a blind
husband - in another part of the parish, and took them Communion. Before our
little service I asked them whether we should be praying for anyone special; their
response was, 'Please, Bishop, pray for Frank, who's not doing too well.' We
prayed for Frank during our service. After the service, I enquired gently about
Frank - ie who he is, how he was, etc. 'Well, Bishop Freddy, Frank's our goldfish;
we've had him two years; he's always been so lively and fun.' ('Yes', said husband,
'he even used to wink at Laura through the glass.') 'Bishop', chipped in the wife,
'would you please bless him?' 'Well, let's go and see him,' I said. I was taken
through to their front room and introduced to a goldfish bowl full of very murky
water. No wonder the poor thing was ailing. I told her that I really would adore a*

cup of tea, and then I'd bless Frank. While she was out, I told her husband that I had been drinking tea or coffee all day and would like to go to the lavatory. Just a teeny white lie. Knowing that he couldn't see what I was doing, I took the goldfish bowl with me, spilt the brown and rather sludgy water down the sink and refilled the bowl. Took bowl, Frank and fresh water back to the living room. Our tea came. I blessed the fish, but not without being asked, 'Would you awfully mind, Bishop Freddy, if you blessed him as "Francis" and not Frank?' I didn't ask why; by this time I was just too bemused. It would be fitting to be able to say that all ended happily ever after; I don't know whether or not it did.

I remember that one of my curates at Portsea (I think it was Roger [Royle]) was once called in to a home to bless somebody's budgerigar. Obligingly, he went. He was, however, never forgiven, for, in his prayer, he referred to the budgie as a canary. 'Don't they teach you anything about birds at college these days?', asked Mrs. Walters, rather witheringly. I'm thankful I'm not a theological college principal.

Another letter included the paragraph:

Since visiting a parish in the Clifton deanery and meeting a lady newly bereaved, I've been thinking a lot about guilt and bereavement. This dear soul made no bones about the fact that her marriage had been difficult - incredibly difficult. Her husband had been a bully and had beaten her more than once physically - and, just as bad, had cowed her into a sort of submission by constant drips of sarcasm. She admitted that she, for the last twenty years, had been afraid of him and certainly any love for him had long since evaporated. However she was being buffeted about by the intensity and strangeness of her feelings since he died. Relief, yes - but also an overpowering sense of guilt - not about the fact that she could have done more to improve their marriage, but simply guilt that she felt this relief at his death. There are an increasing number of books about bereavement on the market at the moment, but I've yet to find one that addresses this problem adequately. I would like to make a study of it myself. Perhaps I will have to wait till I retire.

Freddy was obviously shocked by a visit to another parish:

Joan and I visited a parish in Swindon yesterday and went to see a home communicant in a parish to give her communion. The Vicar said he wouldn't come because he was preparing his parish news sheet. I thought this strange, but let it go. I took the whole service but was taken off balance when she cried afterwards and said it was the most wonderful thing that had happened to her. When I gently questioned her, she said that her Vicar came in the door, said the Lord's Prayer, gave her the Sacrament and left. This, I think, is scandalous. I mentioned it to the Vicar afterwards, and he remarked, 'Oh don't listen to her; she hardly ever came to church anyway.' Oh dear! No wonder so many are alienated from the church.

I went back to see the lady later in the afternoon, because I felt the church had let her down. She kept her key hanging out of the letterbox, so I knew I could gain entry. She was sitting in her armchair - the same one from which she took communion. She had had an accident; she had wanted to go the lavatory and was waiting for her daughter to come, but the daughter was late. I cleaned her up - and waited for her daughter, who came about ten minutes later. I went back to the Vicarage, told the Vicar what had happened - and all he could say was that she was 'attention-seeking'. I think I was close to blowing my top. Most of the priests in our diocese are marvellous - some exceptionally so - but just one or two don't seem to have a clue.

After another visit, Freddy wrote:

Books seem to be getting more and more expensive these days - and the latest ones just don't seem to be appearing on clerical shelves. I know this, because if I'm talking to somebody in his study I have a surreptitious look when the Vicar leaves the room to get something to boost my caffeine level - which I did during the course of a parish visit last Saturday. I wonder whether we could work out a deanery system, say, of lending and borrowing each others' reading material. I don't know how it would work - perhaps unworkable. That's always assuming, of course, that it's expense and not idleness that prevents some from reading worthy things. I mentioned this at a Deanery Chapter meeting the other day and it went down like a damp squib. Afterwards I asked one of the clergy present why he thought this was - and his reply horrified, and continues to horrify, me: 'Well, Bishop, if you're doing your job properly, you don't have time for reading.' What ARE they teaching in theological colleges these days? I do so hope that this was a one-off response and his fellow clergy don't think the same. Strange, because Oliver and I have always considered this priest to be a cut above average.

Again, in a similar vein:

I mentioned to a priest in the diocese the other day when I was visiting his parish that I had been with Joan to see the film E.T. and that he really ought to see it, for though not billed as such it is deeply theological. Response? 'I don't know where you find the time to go the cinema, Bishop; I certainly can't.' Incidentally, I'm extremely suspect of those who claim never to have time to watch television. There are even one or two in the diocese who don't own television sets as a matter of what they call 'principle'. 99% of such people's parishioners own and watch television, and many have their opinions formed, rightly or wrongly, from what they watch. I think even the soap operas can teach much, especially about human relationships. When I mentioned this to the worthy, redoubtable Mrs. X the other day, she just said 'Oh', in a pitch too high. A very disapproving 'Oh' - or perhaps a genuinely

puzzled 'Oh'. How COULD a bishop enjoy such pap AND admit to enjoying it?
I wonder whether we'll get invited there to tea again?

Bryan Jones observed that in his visits Freddy was never the 'prelate' in the pejorative sense; rather, 'he came alongside people of all backgrounds and seemed at ease with them - and, I think, they with him. He often appeared as a kind of Christian 'Children's Hour' uncle - jolly, but underneath it all, caring and wise. Perhaps, like the apostle Barnabas, he was basically simply "a good man."'

Melvyn Matthews, wrote that Freddy was assiduous in visiting clergy newly arrived in the Diocese:

> I remember he came to see us just a day or so after we had moved into St Paul's Vicarage. There were boxes everywhere. That very same morning they'd been very surprised by the unannounced arrival of an ex-student from Kenya, where Melvyn had been teaching in the University four years previously, together with his wife and very small baby. Freddy thought this was wonderful and he and Joan sat on boxes in the kitchen. Freddy's laugh was so loud that the baby began to cry and the mother didn't know what to do. It was so characteristic of his totally spontaneous and joyful existence.
>
> The other memory of him is at a Stewardship Supper in the parish when he spoke about giving as a sort of seed sowing; he then produced a packet of seeds from his pocket and threw the seeds all over the gathered crowd, laughing all the time.

Anthony Balmforth, formerly Archdeacon of Bristol, remembered that when the Bishop was conducting an Institution it was almost traditional that Freddy and Joan would be invited to a light supper at the Vicarage before the service - an excellent way of knowing how they were settling down to a new Vicarage, and to make their acquaintance if they came from another diocese. His wife, Eileen, and he were also sometimes invited. He well remembers one occasion. The new Incumbent had three rumbustious little boys. During supper they were aware of some activity under the table. Later on, during the service, as the Bishop processed down the aisle he left in his wake a collection of jam tart crumbs from the turn-ups of his trousers. The boys had carefully filled his turn-ups.

Meanwhile, Freddy and Oliver made a good team. It is so obvious from reading their correspondence that there was a very deep love and respect for each other. 1975 was dominated by the retirement of Oliver Tomkins. Freddy looked after the diocese for some months. He wrote to his family:

> I am Chairman of the Vacancy-in-See Committee which meets to state the type of bishop we would like; we can also suggest names and names of those we would not like. The Vacancy-in-See Committee meets next month when we put in our description of the Archangel Gabriel as the type of Bishop we want next. Then the

Prime Minister's Patronage Secretary will wander all over the diocese consulting people - and, of course, if you consult enough people the advice cancels out and you can do exactly what you wanted to do in the first place. Clever stuff.

While he was looking after the diocese, Freddy wrote in *Three Crowns*, the diocesan newsletter, in November 1975:

'Tubby' Clayton, the famous founder of Toc H, had a limitless supply of postcards that he used to distribute wherever he went in his latter years. One of my favourites is, 'My mind is made up. Do not confuse me with facts.' In these days of change and uncertainty I would hope that every Christian and every Church member would pay particular heed to this. In so many situations no-one is sure of what God is calling us to do as the next step and the only thing is to have open, sincere, informed discussion and consultation together. It would be a great help in all our planning for the future as we try to shape the Diocese for mission if we could all believe that no other member of the Christian family is being either deliberately silly or deliberately wicked and selfish. As a Suffragan I see one of my main jobs as being that of keeping lines of communication open and friendly between parishes and the diocesan centre and it is always sad if one finds that people have, on the smallest evidence and facts, already made up their minds about something, because it is then much more difficult to open the discussion up again when further facts are produced. We shall all need much grace, unselfishness and integrity both individually, in our parishes and in the diocese, if we are going to let God the Holy Spirit show us clearly what He would have us do.

At the end of November, Freddy wrote to his family:

Our new bishop is Canon John Tinsley, Professor of Theology at Leeds. This surprised all the ecclesiastical gossips and was a name not known at all in the South West. He is a brilliant academic theologian who has lived the greater part of his life in academic University circles. We have met him and his wife and like them very much. I think he will be a very warm and friendly person but I sympathise for someone having to start from scratch in all the complications of parish life as it is now being reorganised, but the able brain will manage this quickly no doubt. It will be interesting to see what changes and what differences he makes. Joan and I have always been the people to move on before and it will be strange to be in the position of the ordinary layman when they get a new Vicar, having been devoted to the last one - difficult, I am sure, not to say, 'but the last Vicar did it like this.' We shall have then to remember how infuriating we found that remark and how, in the end, it made one want to do things quite differently. All in all I think John Tinsley's appointment is very much an inspired one. He seems very humble; humility is something in short supply amongst the present bench of diocesan bishops. Marjorie is a *delight; quiet, kind, caring. A good team, we think.*

Tragically, John Tinsley's wife died soon after they moved to Bristol. Freddy wrote to his family:

> We and the whole diocese bleed for dear John on Marjorie's death. He's coping cou-
> rageously, though Joan and I wish he wouldn't bottle things up quite so much. If
> only he'd talk about her a bit. But he doesn't. He seems to be entering a shell of his
> own making. We think he's terribly, terribly lonely now. Oh, how I wish we could
> help. Being bishop is inevitably a lonely job; we feel for John so much and wish we
> could be nearer at hand to help.

John Ware wrote of this time:

> In 1975 Bishop Oliver retired as Diocesan. He and Freddy had been a marvellous
> team and they obviously had a great deal of mutual respect, which was clear for all
> to see. Freddy had the task of preparing the diocese for its new Bishop. The new
> Bishop came from a mainly academic background in the north of England. He
> brought great gifts as a thinker and teacher. It contrasted with Freddy's experience
> as part of a great ecclesiastical family with experience of work in parishes in this
> country and overseas and as Senior Chaplain to the patrician Archbishop of Can-
> terbury, Geoffrey Fisher. John and Freddy were two very different people, and
> that they managed to coalesce into an effective episcopal team is a measure of the
> stature of both of them. The demands on Freddy in particular as the 'continuity'
> man were particularly great and the more so because within weeks of coming to the
> diocese, Margery, the new Bishop's wife, was diagnosed with terminal cancer.
> Freddy not only had to induct his new senior colleague into his new role, but also to
> support him and the diocese as it came to terms with the fact that its new Bishop was
> a man living in the deepening shadows of grief. It was a situation that called upon
> all Freddy's experience and tact as an administrator, priest and pastor. That the
> diocese was able to respond so caringly to Bishop John's personal situation was in
> no small measure due to Freddy's graciousness, wisdom and sensitivity. Those of
> us who were fairly close to both men realise just how much we owe to Freddy's gen-
> tle touch on the diocesan tiller at that time.

Pastorally, Freddy seemed to understand the clergy in the diocese, whatever their churchmanship. He had to take a bit of flak on more than one occasion, both from the extreme Catholic and the extreme Evangelical wings of the Church. In the summer of 1978, he wrote:

> I know some of the more extreme Catholic clergy of the diocese don't believe this,
> but I really do feel at home in their churches. I love the sense of mystery. They

would perhaps be surprised at how much I have been influenced by the Orthodox tradition. What, however, I find it hard to cope with are the eyes raised to the church roof when I do something not quite right. I'm all for 'order', but not at the expense of prayerfulness. I sometimes feel that all eyes are upon me just waiting to pounce if I get something wrong. Still, I get by - though it does actually hurt me a little when I catch out of the corner of my eye my brother priests sniggering at something I have done or failed to do. I can't help thinking, at times like these, of the words of Oscar Wilde [The Critic as Artist: 1891]: *'Religion is the fashionable substitute for belief.' Perhaps - even probably - that is a terribly unfair thing to write. But I do so abhor Anglo-Catholic gossip and bitchiness.*

Much earlier, in June, 1974, Freddy had written:

I enjoyed my first Pontifical High Mass; fortunately there was a deacon and sub-deacon each side of me and the Bishop is treated as virtually senile and told everything he must do: 'Mitre: take it off and give it to me'; 'Incense: bless it and cense the altar.' I still find it difficult to grasp that when I hear the words 'My Lord', the person speaking may mean me. There's a certain type of simpering churchman who punctuates every sentence with 'My Lord'.

In another letter to his family, Freddy wrote:

An extremely Anglo Catholic parish has asked me to install two relics when consecrating a new altar; the Bishop and I had to have a long discussion about this, and take advice, and we have decided that this cannot really be sanctioned and is illegal in the Church of England. The young priest - a good man who is doing very well - will be very disappointed as he has already got these relics, one of which is certified in Latin as part of the flesh of Pius X and the other is part of the ashes of St. Theresa of Lisieux's first coffin and part of the ashes of her body. Although I find it alien and strange what some priests like to get up to, I really am sorry to have to take a stand like this. I understand that such things as relics are a real help to devotion to some people; I do so hope that they will not think that I am simply being awkward because I do not go along with this sort of thing. I will never forget seeing three old, careworn ladies in the Holy Land kneeling down and kissing - oh so reverently - the relics of somebody or other with such abandoned devotion and love. It was most moving.

In a letter written to Bishop Frank West, Freddy included the paragraph:

I sometimes worry, quite irrationally, that I'm thought by the Anglo-Catholic parishes in the diocese as 'not Catholic' and 'not quite pukkah.' I went to a parish in Swindon on Sunday last and had been asked to lead the intercessions after the ser-

mon. I was a bit taken aback to be informed by the incumbent that he 'would understand if you don't want to follow our custom of praying for the dead.' The dear man, actually, was trying to be thoughtful and accommodating, and in a way I appreciated what he said. However, there aren't many bishops who are so keen on praying for the dead - or asking the dead to pray for them. I do both. The Christian faith, otherwise, is a nonsense. We're all bound together, in heaven and on earth - in the Communion of Saints. I have even been known to shoot an arrow prayer to St. Bernardine of Siena for a bit of help with a particular sermon; I suppose that would be construed as praying to the saints.

In yet another letter, written a fortnight later, Freddy wrote, again to Frank West:

The extreme Evangelical wing in the diocese is causing us concern; one or two of our younger clergy have been quite, quite silly in what they've written in their parish magazines and in what they have said at meetings. They seem to think that they have everything 'sewn up.' What John and I find most disturbing is an anti-homosexual lobby emanating from them. Little do they know that the best pastoral concern and care can come from some, though necessarily not all, of these priests. In my naughty moments, I can't but help agreeing with Katherine Whitehorn, who wrote recently in the Observer, 'Why do born-again people so often make you wish they'd never been born the first time?'

And again, a while later:

Questions of sexuality have again reared their ugly heads recently. People make such absurd assumptions about homosexual priests - eg they're not 'safe' with boys in the Youth Fellowship or whatever. Maybe this IS true in a minority of cases, but it's just as fatuous to say to say that a heterosexual priest places girls in danger in similar circumstances. I'm sure that many of the great slum priests of the last century were homosexual by inclination. Just as I'm equally sure that they'd be the very last people to abuse their position of trust. And the same goes for today. When, I wonder, will the Church get this whole question right? Or are we frightened of losing the money of the faithful? If that's the case, then God will eventually call us to account.

Bryan Jones wrote that Freddy had a certain sense of delight - naïve, really - in things which tickled his fancy. He once invited him to preach at his Patronal Festival Evensong at St. Matthew, Moorfields. St. Matthew's servers were meticulous about ceremonial (though not at all fussy); this dated back to Mervyn Stockwood's incumbency. So Bryan informed Freddy that when it came to the procession, he should remain facing the altar and not turn to join the servers until the head server ('a kind of ecclesiastical Jeeves who ensured that all went well') 243 said, 'Right, my Lord'. Freddy followed all this to the letter, and afterwards was completely amused and delighted and went round telling everybody how he had had to remain motionless until he had received his orders. 'His delight', said Bryan, 'was somehow charmingly childlike.'

Fred Fuller tells a delightful story about a small boy server - either at St. Mark's or St. Luke's, Swindon - who brought forward Freddy's mitre before pronouncing the blessing. Freddy bowed his head, and said to the small boy, 'I'll put it on now'. The boy misheard him, and, thinking Freddy had said 'Put it on now', he did just that - but not on Freddy's head, but on his own. One can imagine the merriment this caused, not least to Freddy.

Kenneth Clark writes that when he was Vicar of St Mary Redcliffe Freddy would always arrive in good time, always warm and friendly, chatting to servers, wardens and choir members before the service and putting everyone at their ease, and equally relaxed with confirmation candidates and their families after the service. He continued:

> *During worship he was impressive and dignified but never stuffy or pompous. I imagine every priest in the diocese at that time will remember how he began his sermons. He would go into the pulpit during the preceding hymn and, when everyone had sat down, would say nothing but look round the church (be it St. Mary Redcliffe or a small country church) slowly and deliberately, a commanding figure who, without a word spoken, would instil silence and expectancy, catch the eye of just about everyone present, and end all the shuffling and settling-down noises common in most congregations - and when we were reverent and still, Freddy would preach the Word.*

Bryan Jones underlined this, when he wrote, 'Another thing I liked about Freddy was the way he would wait and look round the church before beginning to preach, to ensure everybody was listening. And yet, interestingly, this never came across as 'You've got to pay attention - after all I am the Bishop'. No, it came across as, 'God's word is very important; too important for you not to pay attention.'

Philip Hughes was one of many who mentioned the fact that Freddy always preached without notes, though he said there were certain hallmarks which became familiar to those who heard him from time to time. He invariably began, 'What a wonderful day to be confirmed, the festival of X' or 'the 22nd Sunday after Trinity,' and then, using the readings, explain why. There were various mix-and-match elements endlessly combined with new variations.

Bryan Barnes remembers well that when Bishop Freddy instituted him to the living of St. Mary's, Fishponds, Bristol, on the Saturday evening before Advent 3, 1975, when the theme was 'Ministers and Stewards of the Mysteries of God', Freddy told the congregation that 'steward' came from the old word 'stywarden'. 'I was duly humoured', he writes, 'but the congregation were bemused and maybe none too flattered.'

Wyndham Thomas, Senior Lecturer in Music at the University of Bristol, writes:

I met Bishop Freddy on only one occasion but my memories of him are as fresh now as the impression I gained then. He was conducting a Confirmation service at Bristol Cathedral and he started his sermon in a most dramatic way, leaning over the pulpit and extending his palms to the candidates as he declaimed the single word, 'Hands!'. Needless to say, he immediately commanded our undivided attention as he continued to enlarge on the symbolism of giving and receiving, of work and recreation, of holding and healing. My family and I were overwhelmed by this astonishing combination of rhetoric and compassion. In the true sense, this was a life-enriching experience. After being introduced to Freddy, he talked to my newly-confirmed son, who asked about the practice of prayer. His reply was as simple as the question: 'The Lord's Prayer is a good way to start; just make yourself available ('Here I am Lord'); and always read your Bible.' I am still astonished that a single meeting should have created such an effect - there are biblical analogies, of course.

Anthony Balmforth also underlines the fact that 'it was in the pulpit that Freddy came into his own.' He continues:

My wife tells me that from the mass of sermons she has been forced to listen to she has gleaned very few pearls of lasting wisdom but one of them from Freddy rings in her ears to this very day. Freddy was preaching in Bristol Cathedral and the general theme was 'Loving thy neighbour as thyself', and where did we start? He leaned right over the pulpit, fixed the congregation with a very intense stare and asked, 'Do you keep your friendships in good repair? Do you answer those letters, make those visits and make those telephone calls?' The questions hung in the air while the congregation digested them guiltily. There is no doubt that Freddy could have answered his own questions with a resounding YES. He was a born Pastor. And what more could you ask of your Bishop?

Martin Howell says that whenever Freddy came to a Confirmation, or to preach on some special occasion, he would ask him if there was anything he needed to say to the congregation. 'People will often take it from the Bishop when they won't accept it from the Vicar', he would say. Martin continues:

His sermons and talks were simple thoughts and illustrations which were easy to remember. One of his favourites was talking about the 'black sheep' of the family who were traditionally treated with scorn. But, he said, he found them very cuddly and warm. He was very fond of 'black sheep'.

George and Pattie Mitchell remember well an occasion when Freddy was preaching on the text, 'Hold fast to that which is good', and how he illustrated this by telling the congregation of an occasion when he was Dean of Hong Kong, when there was a service in which children had been invited to illustrate the text, 'Hold fast to that which is good'. One little girl, to illustrate this particular text, came down the aisle, one hand holding her mother's hand, the other holding tightly to a large lollipop.'

Brian Dickson's abiding memory is of Freddy's own prayer of blessing for unconfirmed children at the altar rail: 'The Lord Jesus bless you and make you his friend'. 'I still use this form of blessing', he writes, 'and often remember him as I do so.'

Owen Barraclough recalls how Joan and Freddy entertained regularly and held great Christmas parties. 'We drank quantities of ginger wine, and a trip to their loo was an experience; the walls were covered in homilies, jokes and newspaper cuttings.' (When Archbishop Coggan stayed with Freddy and Joan at Portsea Vicarage, he wrote a delightful 'bread and butter' letter, ending with the words, 'Next time I come, and go to the lavatory, I'll make sure I take my spectacles up there with me, for I suspect the walls made interesting reading.')

Ray Harris talks about the social evenings organised by Joan and Freddy:

They invited people from all walks of life - Local Government, Education, Voluntary Organisations as well as clergy and lay people from Anglican and other Churches. At one of these I was telling two companions of my sense of grievance at the local newspaper which I asserted had misrepresented me on more than one occasion. Recently I had been made to look naïve and foolish but as the episode concerned a family which was named I could not reply. I said that since then when I received a telephone call from the newspaper I always thought of the saying, 'He who sups with the devil must use a long spoon.' One of my hearers said, 'The Editor's over there.' Alas, I did not have Freddy's courage and directness to tackle him face to face.

Freddy and Joan reached out to all faiths and none. The social evenings were just one way by which they gave the Church in Swindon a credible and outgoing image.

Jack House, who engagingly described Freddy as: 'A People's Prelate, Perceptive Pastor and Passionate Prophet', adds to this theme:

An evening at Freddy and Joan's Swindon home where the numerous invitees included the local Conservative parliamentary candidate (a public school master) and a Labour Party branch chairperson (a comprehensive schoolteacher) was a delight; and by dint of regular orchestrations of movement on Freddy's part everyone was given the opportunity to engage with him and with each other.

To more serious matters. Derek Palmer wrote, 'It was always difficult to feel in Swindon that we were part of the Bristol Diocese until Freddy came. He became the first Bishop actually to live at this end of the Diocese, and although he was Bishop of Malmesbury, Freddy soon became the Bishop of Swindon in all but name.' He continued:

> *In Milton Keynes there is now the nearest thing that we have to an Ecumenical Bishop - he is known as the Ecumenical Moderator - but the origin of the idea came from Swindon and from Freddy.*
>
> *He was not just the Anglican Bishop but the Bishop of everyone in the town. All the other Church leaders lived forty miles away, and until Freddy came that was true of the Anglicans. It was a great shame that his successor went back on this, and it is good that the present Bishop is in fact Bishop of Swindon. A true recognition of the work that Freddy began.*
>
> *It was an exciting time to be in Swindon as the rapid development began and the old GWR works died and the new electrical industries took over. There was an unrivalled opportunity for the Churches not only to establish their own growth, but to play a major part in the whole development of the town.*
>
> *That we were able to do so was largely thanks to Freddy (and Joan, of course, as so often we saw them as a team). The importance of him being and living in the middle of all the development, rather than visiting from outside, was tremendous and he brought all his enthusiasm and standing to his work. The fact that he had a famous family name was of some importance, but we soon came to value his friendship and leadership for himself.*
>
> *Soon after he arrived we decided to set up the Swindon Church Commission and he chaired this body which spent a whole year examining the ways in which the Churches could work together both in the old parts of the town, and in the new ones now building. Under his leadership we visited many other places to gain wider understanding and the report when it finally came changed the face of the town and its Churches. We set up a central ecumenical team at the centre of the town, and seven existing or future Areas of Ecumenical Experiment (LEPs) as they were then called.*
>
> *Of these no less than five came into existence and others have come since. I remember well when the Anglican-Methodist talks failed for the second time, and with Freddy we felt let down by the Church of England. It was a dark day for almost all of us in Swindon.*

The respect with which he was held in ecumenical circles can be judged from a letter sent by John Matthews, the Pastor of Swindon's Baptist Tabernacle, at the time of Freddy's appointment as Bishop of Malmesbury. He wrote to Oliver Tomkins, on behalf of all the Free Churches:

I am writing on behalf of the ministers of the Central Churches in Swindon concerning the announcement that Freddy Temple is to be the next Bishop of Malmesbury. Of course we are delighted for him and for you and the diocese.

However it does create something of a crisis for us here and we gave some attention to it at our staff meeting yesterday. We are aware that no group should become over-dependent on one person nor should any person consider himself indispensable ; we do not wish to over-state our case, but the fact remains that Freddy has been more than significant in the development of our scheme here and we do not wish to lose him.

We were pleased to hear, therefore, that there is a possibility of his staying in Swindon, and my colleagues asked me to write to say that were this to be possible it would give us all considerable satisfaction. What Freddy has accomplished in our situation and in the town generally has not just been because he is Archdeacon but because he is the person he is and has identified with the town in the way he has. A number of important schemes would be set back if we had to build up new relationships from scratch with someone who had no knowledge either of the background or the personalities involved in them.

I hope you will not mind us writing what is, from your point of view, an impertinent letter, but we wanted your Council to know our opinion and thus to express our hope that Freddy will be allowed to remain in the town. I may add that I was at a lunch of social workers yesterday, and they are not usually a profession that speaks in such terms, yet they were expressing exactly the same feelings - in their case it concerned Joan as much as Freddy.

Owen Barraclough writes:

The fact that Bishop Freddy lived in Swindon made us feel we mattered as part of the Bristol family. But even more importantly, the local authorities and other local church leaders were able to learn to trust the Church of England at a time when the whole area was changing and expanding phenomenally. The Area Churches Main Committee was a direct result and with the active help of the Reverend Andrew Hake, the Social Development Officer for the Borough of Thamesdown (he was to play a vital part in the writing of the Archbishop's Report Faith in the City*) all the growth in the Borough was carefully planned. The social facilities were thought about at the earliest stage of building and churches were provided for on an ecumenical basis. This was largely due to Bishop Freddy's leadership and to this day the same procedures are followed by the new Borough of Swindon.*

Jim Free continues:

My closest contacts with him were in connection with the Diocesan Council for Unity and Mission (as it was then called) of which he was Chairman and I was

Secretary. *Parallel to that, and spawned partly by DCUM, there was the Bristol Regional Sponsoring Body which he chaired along with the Chairman of the Methodist District. This was no sinecure and he proved his genuine concern for ecumenical advance by taking part in all the varied works of the Regional Sponsoring Body. These included visits to Local Ecumenical Projects, where he was always supportive, together with the Ecumenical Theological Group, which addressed the theological questions thrown up by work in the LEPs. All the Churches involved in LEPs in the Bristol Diocese were represented on this group, including the Roman Catholic Church.*

Kenneth Clark writes:

It was only after I had become Archdeacon of Swindon that I came to realise the place that Freddy occupied in the Church life, ecumenically, of Swindon itself. The town was looked to, along with Milton Keynes, as a front-runner in inter-Church co-operation nationally, and there had been consideration locally of having an 'Ecumenical Bishop' for Swindon. In the end it came to nothing because local enthusiasm was too far ahead of where the Churches nationally had got with regard to orders of ministry. I personally think that the idea caught on in Swindon itself in the later '70s and early '80s because many people saw Freddy himself as fulfilling that role - such was his influence among the Churches of the town.

There were already instruments of ecumenical co-operation, mostly working well, in place when I became archdeacon. The Swindon Council of Churches was probably the least effective; so many of the tasks that such a council would expect to undertake elsewhere were, in Swindon, done by ecumenical bodies, such as the Sponsoring Body which looked after the LEPs and the Churches Main Committee which related to the Borough Council of those days on matters such as the expansion of Swindon and sites for new churches in the Western Development - on behalf of all the parent Church bodies, including the Roman Catholic Diocese of Clifton.

Dorothy Leith, who had worked from the Central (Ecumenical) Church in Swindon, adds:

He exercised the authority and power of a Bishop in a very humble way. He reminded us again and again that God was involved in every part of human life, involved in partnership with us. And this meant our partnership with the local authority, partnership of clergy and laity, partnership between Churches of every denomination. He was never blinded by denominational ties. He did not expect us to be blinkered by our denominational blinkers either.

John Ware writes:

One of Freddy's great pastoral gifts was the ability to 'tell the truth in love'. He never fobbed you off with half-truth or fudge if you went to him for counsel. He never told you what to do, but enabled you to conclude what would be the best way forward - and even if he disagreed with you he never left you feeling that he was rejecting you. Even if the net result of the counselling was that you had to admit that you had been wrong about something, you always left his presence feeling affirmed. Because he had no illusions about human nature he was never cynical, but always totally down to earth. He knew that real love meant taking reality as it was, and if that meant that sometimes he had to be hard to himself or to others, he never baulked at it. When the rigid Anglo-Catholicism of St. Mark's parish meant that the ecumenical plans for the centre of Swindon New Town in the 1970s had to develop without the involvement of the main Anglican parish, Freddy's powers of diplomacy and pastoral care meant the new town centre United Church came into being without resentment or recrimination either from St. Mark's or from the new United Church congregation.

It was not, however, always quite as straightforward as that. Rex Hurrell, formerly Vicar of St. Mark's and Team Rector of the Parish of Swindon New Town, wrote:

This notion [of Local Ecumenical Projects, etc.] was not shared agreeably by everyone, especially by those of a 'Catholic' persuasion. There was fear that the catholicity of the Church was endangered by too close a cohabitation with nonconformists, who had never been too keen on bishops and preferred to express their theology from the Reformation from which they had sprung. This placed much emphasis on the Bible as being the agreeable Word of God, but less emphasis on the Sacraments, the way that God chose to work out his Incarnation in the Church of today.

When a Local Ecumenical Project was proposed for Central Swindon the nonconformists, Baptists, Church of Christ, Methodists, Congregationalists and Presbyterians, agreed that it was a way to proceed - but the Roman Catholic Church, the Moravians and the Salvation Army dissented. So also did the Church of England Parish of St. Mark, Swindon. This was a decision that alarmed the Diocese of Bristol, as there was no Local Ecumenical Project in the Diocese that did not have a Church of England presence. Indeed, there was much concern expressed that, if the Church of England was not involved, it could not in any way be party to ecumenical discussions. The Vicar of Saint Mark's at the time discussed the matter with his Church Council, but they were adamant that they did not want the parish to go down that route, especially as it involved 'shared ministry'; this meant that non-episcopally ordained ministers could be called upon to celebrate the Eucharist. That was anathema, as the Catholic wing of the Church expressed the strong view that the sacraments were only regular if celebrated by an episcopally ordained clergyman. That was the position of the Church of England and was the cause of the rejection of many unity schemes of the 1960/1970s.

Of course, the non-conformists must have felt a sense of rejection as well as disappointment at this decision of Saint Mark's. However, there seemed to be no understanding of the feelings of Saint Mark's people; no-one seemed to allow the people of St. Mark's to have a conscience in these matters. And the Bishop of Malmesbury positively sided with the non-conformists and, in consultation with the Diocesan authorities, came up with a scheme that merely infuriated the people of St. Mark's - thus, sadly, setting back the ecumenical cause. An Industrial Chaplain was to be appointed in Swindon full-time - and it was agreed that the person appointed would be based with the Local Ecumenical Project in the centre of Swindon - thus hoping to give the project the Anglican presence that had been denied them.

The Vicar of Saint Mark's was furious, and the people were affronted that their views should be treated in so cavalier a fashion. The Vicar of Saint Mark's, therefore, inhibited the newly-appointed Industrial Chaplain from exercising a priestly ministry in his parish. Thus, although the Centre Local Ecumenical Project had an Anglican presence, he was impotent to offer any kind of Anglican sacramental ministry. The said Vicar of Saint Mark's was preferred to a position in the United States of America - and a new priest appointed. While keeping to the spirit of the previous inhibition, he allowed the Industrial Chaplain to exercise any ministry that the new Vicar was happy to perform himself in non-conformist congregations. That meant no Sacramental services - but that he could lead/preach at Services of the Word. That eased matters a little.

In a follow-up telephone call to clarify one or two things in his letter, Rex Hurrell told me that in no way was he trying to detract from 'what will obviously - and quite rightly - be the main tenor of your book: that Bishop Freddy was a remarkable man.' He continued, 'Freddy wasn't exactly my sort of a good Catholic - but he did his best to understand Catholic ways; I don't mean that to sound condescending. Frankly, whenever he came to Saint Mark's - perhaps the most extreme parish in the Diocese - you'd think he'd been brought up there. Bishop Freddy was probably one of the kindest and most sensitive bishops I have ever had the privilege of meeting - and doing battle with!'

In the autumn of 1981, Freddy himself wrote to his extended family:

Slowly and laboriously a scheme goes forward for a shared Church and Area of Ecumenical Experiment in the middle of Swindon, but as always at any change there are nice, good people who are terrified and produce every sort of reaction and reason against it. Here mission and ecumenism go hand in hand and now more than half Swindon live in ecumenical parishes where nearly all is done in common and Swindon has now come up with the idea of an Ecumenical Bishop for all the

Churches; it has come from the Baptists of all people. Like any new idea it seems illogical and impossible but slowly it may seep through the stone-like quality of some minds and finally bear fruit.. It won't do so while I'm here but I like to feel that I have had some part in fertilising the whole scheme.

In the summer of the following year, Freddy again wrote:

A very popular Methodist Minister, Derryck Evans, who has been here nine years and done a tremendous amount in the centre of the town in all sorts of spheres is leaving and there was a great farewell and I was asked to go and sum it all up and take the final prayers. I thought what a marvellous sign of co-operation and confidence this is because 10 or 12 years ago no Free Church would have thought ever of asking an Anglican bishop to take such a prominent part in such a prominent Free Church event.

Freddy took a full and active part in the life of the Borough. Lord Joffe of Liddington recalls first meeting Freddy when a group were setting up the Thamesdown Community Trust, a Trust the objective of which was to solicit donations from the Swindon business community and affluent residents for the support of the voluntary sector in Swindon. He writes:

We were looking for a Chairman to provide credibility and confidence in the Trust and decided that Freddy would be the one person in Thamesdown who would meet our criteria. I approached Freddy whom I had not previously met and he willingly accepted the invitation despite his already heavy workload.

Freddy turned out to be an excellent and conscientious Chair who held us together during the difficult formative stages of the Trust. He chaired our meetings with skill, informality and good humour.

During the five years he was Chairman, I got to know Freddy and Joan reasonably well. I had not previously had anything to do with a Bishop so when I first approached Freddy it was with considerable awe. However with his relaxed informality, humility and friendly good humour, he immediately put me at my ease and it was a real pleasure to work with him and get to know him. Freddy came from a line of legendary Archbishops but he never sought to bask in their limelight. He was his own man and by any measure a great man.

Politics loomed large in Freddy's thinking. He would, however, always consider carefully when and when not to weigh in publicly with his thoughts in matters of local politics; his interventions were invariably taken notice of and well received, as is evident from letters he received from the local Member of Parliament and the Editor of the Swindon *Evening Advertiser*. In July 1981 Freddy wrote to his extended family:

We have had a march in Swindon for racial justice and peace which I and other Church leaders encouraged and organised with the MP, but I had to be at a big Readers' Licensing Service and so only Joan could go - and the wretched paper said, 'The Bishop of Malmesbury sent his wife instead.' The Guardian of course picked this up in its 'Naked Ape' column but did not pick up my letter which I instantly wrote to the local paper saying that I never sent my wife to anything, but we worked as a partnership entirely equally. Which the paper published quite prominently as well. All went off quite peacefully and it encouraged the young black Britons to feel that sober, middle-class England really does support them at least here in Swindon. Possibly some of the Government will start to realise that it is worth listening to the Bishops and Church leaders of the big towns and cities who have been saying for years that unless something further was done about the frustration and despair in the inner cities these sorts of riots would happen. It is fortunate that there seems to have been so little actual racial violence among them and the police are stressing this - although in Southall the skinheads certainly came in to attack the blacks. But how marvellous the result at Warrington was because some of us felt that it really was almost too difficult a seat for [Roy] Jenkins to fight, particularly with his difficulty with his r's. Woy of Wawwington was too easy for people to mimic. But Woy certainly did have a great success and one hopes the new [Social Democrat] party will go from strength to strength.

More evidence of Freddy's thought comes from two other letters Freddy wrote to the family at the time:

What a problem poor Mrs. Thatcher has to make herself appear less desperately suburban and middle class on the television - if she is not going to drive the Conservative Party into being the party of the far right and one that has no care about the really poor and needy in the community. Alas, the first signs are not good in the way that she has got rid of the four on the left in the last Shadow Cabinet - but one must wish her well at the start, even though I personally think she may polarise the country into groups even more than ever.

This letter obviously drew a reaction from his family, for the following month Freddy wrote:

What I said about Mrs. Thatcher has been so misunderstood that I must make reply. I did not say it was a bad thing to be middle class or suburban. But it will be a very bad thing if Mrs. Thatcher makes the party appear just that: it will polarise politics, which is always a pity and tends to make each party more extreme when it gets into power. Of course many middle class and working class folk are full of good causes and generosity. (Percentage-wise, though, I still find that the manual workers give more, usually, than their counterparts.) But politically I would hope that the Conservative Party would care more for the needy and not less; they abolished the Development and Aid Ministry.

I find many TUC officials thoughtful, careful and anxious to do their best, but knowing they can't educate their members by confrontation. Len Murray is a fine Christian, a Methodist lay preacher. I'd willingly vote Conservative if Ian Macleod were alive and more willingly vote Labour if Roy Jenkins were to get in as Prime Minister. A good Balliol man, of course, of my vintage - as is Denis Healey!

In one of his letters to the Bristol diocese, Freddy wrote:

This month the General Synod will debate 'The Church and the Bomb'. I agree with the young man who said how thrilling it was at last to have the Church produce a report which concerned everyone, instead of being always only interested in our own ecclesiastical affairs. I hope parishes will get a copy of the report, read it, pass it round and discuss it.

There are alas a large number of church folk who read little church history and assume the Church is concerned only with individual conduct and that it has exercised little political influence and ought to exercise none: this is thought to be self-evident and entirely reasonable and that only 'trendy extremists' question it. It is in fact a very modern, very English view. For Jesus himself as a Jew there was no distinction between 'church and state'. His first sermon in Nazareth based on the year of Jubilee goes back to Leviticus and land legislation on a colossal scale. He preached a 'Kingdom' gospel with tremendous emphasis on the poor and needy. The Church has followed him and always 'interfered in politics'. A doctrine of a just price, how much to charge for things, a doctrine of usury, how much interest can be raised, the abolition of the slave trade and slavery, the Factory Acts, were all political economic 'interference', based on Christian principles. So we must not be misled into thinking we are not meant to consider 'the Bomb' as Christians, but only as English citizens. The report will help us with fundamental guidelines. Then we may end up as unilateralists, multilateralists, or only for 'clean' weapons as against 'dirty, nuclear or germ' - or as complete pacifists.

Amongst letters kept by Freddy is one from an incumbent in the diocese along the lines of 'keep religion out of politics'. Unfortunately, no copy of a reply exists - and the priest in question has long since died. We can imagine the stance Freddy took. He may well have been quite fierce - for a more recent letter from a priest reads:

Although I loved Bishop Freddy - and how many clergy can say that of their bishops? - I was taken aback by one occasion at a Deanery Synod. A very quiet, withdrawn, under-confident brother priest dared to say, during the course of a discussion, that he thought the Church had better things to do than meddle in the sphere of politics. It was the only time I ever saw Bishop Freddy close to losing his *cool; it was not particularly edifying. The poor man did not deserve being rounded on by our Suffragan, and I must admit that I felt very sorry for the priest who had made the remark. Having said that - and this is only surmise - I can imagine Bishop Freddy writing to him afterwards to apologise. Maybe he did. Maybe he didn't.*

One of Freddy's greatest delights and interests was in the care and nurture of ordinands and newly-ordained clergy. On 26th April 1974, Freddy wrote:

I am just back from a three day ACCM Conference at which we were deciding how many of the sixteen candidates were suitable for ordination. It is always a most interesting and lively time, but I find it drains me completely and leaves me quite shattered with exhaustion for a while afterwards, as one has to be so attentive and sensitive interviewing them all the time.

John Poarch, a former Director of Ordinands for the diocese of Bristol, continues on this theme:

My main reflection concerns Freddy and a man who offered for ordination. This man was prayerful, sensitive and caring. I thought he had the makings of a good priest. With his permission I consulted Freddy and Freddy was positive about him (as were other people in the assessment process) and so we sent him off to a Selection Conference. But he was not recommended for training and I ask myself why Freddy got this one wrong - as I did myself of course - because I always felt he was a shrewd judge of people. Forty or fifty years ago this man would have sailed through the selection process, and yet the explanation is not that Freddy had failed to keep up with more recent ABM developments - one of the impressive things about him was the way he kept up to date. Could it have been that he tended to err on the side of generosity? He told me once that it is always the lay selectors at a Conference who are most rigorous; the clergy there remember how they scraped through and want to give candidates the benefit of the doubt. But I don't think this was the explanation either. I think rather his encouragement of this man was an expression of his own simplicity and grasp of essentials. This man was a man who loved God and loved people and who should therefore have the makings of a good priest. I am not saying that the Church's more sophisticated way of looking at selection is a mistake. I am saying, however, that if in the midst of our sophistication we give insufficient weight to the essentials, we shall get things horribly wrong.

After one Selection Conference, Freddy could not sleep for two nights, worrying about whether or he and his fellow Selectors had made the right decision in suggesting that the ministry was not what God had in mind for one candidate. 'I have been assaulted by niggling doubts about the recommendation we have made about one particular young man', he wrote to a friend, 'so much so that I think we must re-assess. He came over as a little wishy-washy at his interviews, but thinking since about some of the things he said, I think we got him wrong. Why do we have to make decisions at the end of a Conference when we're all mentally and physically exhausted? I must talk to my fellow Selectors this evening on the telephone.' No record exists of any conversations Freddy might have had with them, but two days later he, as Chairman of the Selectors, received a letter from the young man's sponsoring diocesan bishop, in which he expressed a 'certain disquiet and surprise' about the recommendation. It was ultimately decided that the young man should proceed to theological college, at which his worth was recognised. After a curacy he became a University Chaplain before returning to parochial life, and is now sought after as a Spiritual Director.

Like most, if not all, bishops, Freddy regarded ordinations as awesome experiences, and wrote to a fellow bishop, Frank West, in 1982; 'I still tingle with excitement when I lay hands on the heads of those whom God has chosen to call; oh, what a privilege!' And then, a few sentences later, a note of humility: 'I know that most of them, with God's help, will be so much more worthy than me.' This certainly was not a false humility, for Freddy, throughout his ministry, had periods when he was vividly conscious of his own shortcomings, and at times considered himself unworthy of his calling. In five of his letters, written to different people between 1974 and 1981, he used the same sentence, or one very similar: 'If people only realised how fragile a Christian I am at times, when I feel too tired to say my prayers, when I am uncharitable, they would want nothing to do with me.'

In the spring of 1978, Freddy wrote:

We hear such a lot these days about four letter words. This last week I've had my mind concentrated on a five letter word. I saw X this morning [an Assistant Curate in his second year of priesthood]. *He's worked himself into quite a state about his doubts. He's a very open individual and mentioned what he perceived as his 'crumbling faith' to his Incumbent. He was devastated, understandably, by the response. Although he can't remember Y's* [the Incumbent] *exact words he said the gist of them expressed horror and he was told in no uncertain terms that on no account must his doubts ever be made public to the congregation - or 'you'll be finished, lad; these things must be kept to oneself'. Y then proceeded to tell him that he saw him as having an outstanding 'career' in the Church which would be jeopardised if he let his doubts take hold. 'Keep them to yourself, lad, get on with your job and just forget they're there.' Oh dear. Where do we go from here? X is one of the most pastoral, gifted, caring young priests in the diocese. I wish his incumbent were endowed with similar qualities. I think David* [Isitt] *is the one person who can help, though David has such a lot on his plate. All this talk of 'jeopardising careers' borders on the obscene. Anyway, John* [Tinsley], *David and I must try to love him through what I perceive as a healthy experience for any good priest.*

Freddy also thoroughly enjoyed his contacts with the young. Early in 1979, he included in a letter to his family:

I met this 14 year old lad at Commonweal [a Swindon secondary school] the other day; he lives just around the corner, in Goddard Avenue. Rather a quaint young man, madly keen about landscape gardening. He offered to come with his younger sister to help with our garden at 'Morwena', for he wasn't allowed loose in his own garden, which was very much the domain of his mother. I said that we didn't really need a landscape gardener, but he could always come to do a few odds and ends. His idea was that he could position angels ('like they have on graves, Bishop') all round the garden. He reckoned that 'a Bishop's garden should look holy'. The thought of it! I'd look out of the bedroom window every morning and be convinced that the good Lord had called me to my eternal resting place during the night. I think I'd rather use the space for parsnips.

In January 1980, Freddy preached at Stowe School. The following day he spent a morning in a local Swindon comprehensive school, going round the forms answering questions. He wrote:

The alertness, the friendliness and the outgoing character of pupils and staff was in sharp contrast to the stiff upper class lips of Stowe. I spoke to 150 twelve and thirteen year olds, and answered their questions. Some were trivial, some very penetrating. A small boy said, 'Please Bishop was it very difficult to learn to balance the mitre on your head?' Later on, when I had talked about pastoral care and the counselling a bishop has to do, this twelve year old piped up, 'And where Bishop do you go when you have problems?' I had lunch with the sixth form and found myself sitting next to an ardently keen Manchester United supporter; so we discussed the team in great depth, much to the amusement of the rest of the table. I find it very contrived when some new bishops say, for the media, that they support such and such a team and suspect some are merely saying it in the hope they'll be thought to be 'with it'. However, I do enjoy soccer at the top level and I find it an enormous help to be able to talk at least about one team knowledgeably. I said how excellent I thought it was that Sexton bought Wilkins twelve months ago and how well he opens up the game from mid-field. The boys at the table were agog. Swindon actually are doing rather excitingly well so far this season, both in the League and in the Cup.

In May, 1980, Freddy wrote:

Today coming home I gave two punk boys a lift; hair waxed with brown boot polish and curled and dyed strange colours; ear-rings dripping about the place; looking very odd, but quite mild and pleasant to talk to. It is of course more a philosophy

257

*and way of life than rock and its predecessors. There is a clergy son very much in-
volved in it, much to his parents' embarrassment.*

In July of the same year he again wrote to his family:

*I picked up a hitchhiker on my way back from Bristol four nights ago, I suppose
about 10 o'clock, just outside Bristol. He was a lovely, gentle boy - intelligent too.
He said he had a place at Keele* [University] *in October, but meanwhile was in
and out of jobs. I had to pull in at Leigh Delamere* [a service station on the M4]
*for petrol and asked him whether he wanted anything to eat. He said he was OK,
but somehow I sensed he was hungry. When we got to Swindon I put my cards on
the table and told him that I was actually the Bishop of Malmesbury and Joan and
I would love to give him a meal. He didn't need much persuasion. Dearest Joan
took it all in her stride. She was in the middle of watching a play on the television
but, without a moment's hesitation, she got up and said 'How lovely to see you;
let's go and find some bacon and eggs; I think somewhere we've got some sausages
too.' The dear boy tucked in and seemed so grateful. Joan asked him, seeing as it
was so late, if he'd like a bed for the night and continue on his travels tomorrow. He
declined, saying that he ought to be on the way to London, so I drove him to junc-
tion 15 of the M4, where he expected to get a lift. The lovely thing is that a letter
arrived from him two days ago, addressed to 'The Bishop of Malmsey, The Palace,
Swindon'. He wrote, 'Thanks so very, very much for all you and your wife did for
me on Wednesday night. I was so hungry and tired and would have stayed the night
but I didn't want to be a burden. I haven't had much to do with faith before, or the
Christian religion, but after what you did for me I can't help thinking there must be
something in it. I hope that one day I can repay your kindness. I don't know my
permanent address at the moment, but as soon as I do, I'll let you have it.'*
[Unfortunately, no record of his having sent an address exists. When I questioned Joan about it, she said, rather airily, 'It happened all the time. You
have to look after these young people. Which one are you talking about?']

In February, 1981, Freddy wrote:

*I drove to Bristol with Joan to confirm in a parish off the Wells Road. We picked up
a charming hitch-hiker on the way. He is in his second year at Exeter reading English. He himself was confirmed by one of my predecessors as Bishop of Malmesbury, Ivor Watkins, when he was Bishop of Guildford. He said that it meant
nothing to him, at the time or later. He only went forward to Confirmation because his parents expected it of him. 'As far as I'm concerned, Bishop, it's all a load
of nonsense - but I don't expect you to agree with me.' We were so sorry that we had
to drop him off in the centre of Bristol; we would love to have had a discussion with
him. I hope that somebody, somewhere, will get hold of him one day and talk seri-*

ously about the faith. Meanwhile, I have put his name in my intercession book and will pray for him every day.

Both Freddy and Joan for many years shared an interest in prison visiting and prisoner rehabilitation. In June 1981 Freddy wrote:

We called on a friend in Winchester prison: alas, all had seemed as if things were going well when he was last out, but he never told the girl he got friendly with or her family that he had a record and she rejected him when she learnt - and he then went berserk again and now has four years to do; not another friend in the world as his family have long ago rejected him; a sex case, and so locked up twenty-three hours of the day, two or three to a cell meant for one and having to have all meals in their cells. Locked up for their own protection as there is this strange prison law almost that you harm and intimidate any sex case, whereas others of violence etc. can be looked up to. Quite what he does when he comes out in four years' time I don't know; we have his few belongings in our loft at 'Morwena' at the moment.

And later the same year he wrote:

I preached at a local prison then went round the cells talking to the men. In the present economic climate little will be done, but I wish that men on remand, many of whom will be found to be innocent, did not have to spend several weeks two or three to a small cell. One young man in for life, first offence, found his wife sleeping with another woman; then went with his wife to burn the caravan where the other woman was thought to be sleeping; the caravan was burnt and no one hurt but the young man (illiterate; he has now learnt to read) got life and the wife is free and divorcing him; seems very strange.

Stephen Fry, in his autobiography, *Moab Is My Washpot*, has a wonderful story:

The Bishop of Malmesbury came to visit one Wednesday. A group of us was selected to sit round him in a circle while he asked us to speak frankly about prison conditions and how we were being treated and what we thought of ourselves. There were screws standing against the walls, eyeing the ceiling and we all knew better than to complain. All except Fry, of course.
'I would like to draw your lordship's attention to one thing that has been bothering me,' I said. 'It is, I fear, a very grave matter and the source of aggravation and discomfort to many of us here.'
There was a hissing in of breath from the others and a meaningful clearing of the throat from one of the senior screws.
'Please,' said the Bishop, 'please feel free.'
'I am sure,' I said, 'that Her Majesty has many calls on her time and cannot be

expected to know everything that goes on in her name within the walls of institutions such as this.'

'No indeed,' agreed the Bishop, blinking slightly.

'However, I must urge you to draw her attention to the quality of the soap available in our bathrooms.'

'The soap?'

'The soap, my lord Bishop. It lathers not, neither does it float; it doesn't smell nice, it doesn't even clean you. The best that can be said for it, I am afraid, is that it keeps you company in the bath.'

This was from an old Morecambe and Wise book I had bought years ago at Uppingham.

The Bishop burst out laughing, and the screws dutifully joined in with smiles, shaking their heads at the jollity of it all.

'If your lordship will undertake to make urgent representation in the right quarters?'

'Certainly, certainly! Um, may I ask you, young man, I know this is not good prison form and you really don't have to answer, but may I ask you none the less, … what, ah, are you in for?'

'Oh the usual,' I said carelessly. 'Churchmen.'

'I beg your pardon?'

The senseless slaughter of clerics. I murdered four minor canons, two archdeacons, a curate and a suffragan bishop in a trail of bloody carnage that raged from Norwich to Hexham last year. Surely you read about it in the Church Times, my lord? I think it made the third page of the late racing extra.'

'All right, now. That's enough of that, Fry.'

'Yes, sir. I'm sorry, Bishop, you must forgive my freakish humours. In here we laugh that we may not weep. It was theft I'm afraid, my lord. Plain old credit card fraud.'

'Oh. Oh, I see.'

In 1979, Freddy became Chairman of the Governors of Bristol Cathedral School. Almost immediately David Jewell, the headmaster, became headmaster of Repton. Christopher Martin, from Westminster School, was appointed headmaster. He writes:

When I joined Bristol Cathedral School in 1979 as a very jejune Headmaster, Freddy was my Chairman of Governors. Having had the courage to appoint me, an inexperienced person, to the post, he then set about supporting me to the hilt with characteristic zeal and enthusiasm. From the outset, he encouraged me to be bold. The conventional view of a headmaster's stance is of one who sits on the fence but with both ears to the ground, an uncomfortable position at the best of times. Freddy would have none of this. 'Christopher, go out on a limb. That's where the *fruit is. The only thing that does not change is that everything changes.'*

All our conversations together in those heady days were imbued with a sense of adventure and of course with high, irresistible good humour. None of this changed when some seriously bad news arrived in my first term from the Dean and Chapter. Not without justice, the Dean wanted to explore the possibility of a commercial rent for the buildings occupied by the school. The financial outcomes looked, for a while, very worrying. Ownership was the issue. Who owned what? The school or the Cathedral? The questions were not easily resolved and Freddy, poor man, was thrust into the middle of some tricky negotiations which took more of his precious time than he could really spare. But he never complained. On the contrary, he always breezed in for those fraught meetings with that marvellously mischievous glitter in his eye which always indicated to me that he was about to join battle with his fellow clerics with real enjoyment. Beaming from ear to ear, he once whispered at one of those meetings in a stage whisper audible right round the room, 'It isn't for nothing that Bishops move diagonally on a chessboard.' With Freddy on our side in such affable but pugnacious mood, I knew we could not lose, and we didn't.

But of course it was his laugh for which I, among many others no doubt, will always remember him most vividly, that extraordinary bellowing laugh, so steeped in gaiety and glee, which shook vigorously both the rafters and those sheltering under them. Very often it was his own jokes that gave him most pleasure, and I recall a sermon to the school in the Cathedral when he laughed delightedly at some splendid reference he had made, and immediately had 500 people rocking with laughter with him. It was truly infectious. The ghosts of the Augustinian monks of the original foundation must have been hugging themselves with delight. For who could remain unaffected by such love of life and indeed by such obvious affection for his fellow men?

Yet with all his self-deprecating guile and wisdom, Freddy never lost sight of the essentials. He and I, among others, were at one point asked to contribute lunch time sermons in a series entitled 'The most important thing in life.' My title was so complex and unmemorable that even I cannot remember it. Freddy's was simply 'People.' I learned a lot from that.

I loved him especially when he was being naughty about someone we both knew. He was far too shrewd to be gulled into thinking everyone was equally deserving of appreciation. While I never heard him judge anyone harshly as a person, some of one's less impressive characteristics often invited his critical appraisal, though even then he was never ungenerous. He was, for instance, simultaneously amused by and scornful of all pomposity and laboured holiness and once confided in me, speaking of an outwardly devout worshipper, 'St. Peter's going to have a hard time welcoming her.'

It was a constant delight to work with him and to share the thrills and spills of the remarkable Cathedral school with a man of such experience and humanity. Everything we did together reeked of fun, even the serious bits. When we started a weekly

261

lecture series for the sixth form, which I believe still runs, Freddy gave the opening presentation, and it seemed natural to name the series the Temple Talks as a result. It was a tiny gesture to a man who was deeply loved by all of us in the school who encountered him. I miss him greatly still.

Freddy could also be teasingly provocative. He was invited to address a meeting of Headteachers at Almondsbury Conference House in the summer of 1978, and began his talk:

Thank you so much for inviting me to be with you. You may think that this morning the dear old Bishop is being 'funny', as in 'funny', or is being 'funny' as in 'funny', but funnily enough he is being serious and doesn't consider what he is to say 'funny' in any sense of that word. For I take as my text some words sung by Pink Floyd, the tune to which you undoubtedly hum in your baths every morning before you set out with eager anticipation to your respective schools. The words are:

'We don't need no education.
We don't need no thought control.
No dark sarcasm in the classroom.
Teacher, leave those kids alone! All in all it's just another brick in the wall.
All in all, you're just another brick in the wall.'

One of the Headteachers present recalls that there was a general shuffling of pedagogic bottoms on chairs.

I wish I'd taken full notes of what he said. Some of the group were distinctly uneasy listening to him; for others his talk was a liberating experience. He dared us to think seriously about what we were doing in our schools, about what right we had to do what we were doing, about the meaning of 'authority', about why and how we taught as we did, about the rights of children. I came away, as did some others, feeling that we had been sitting at the feet of a prophet; others missed the point completely and murmured, rather lamely, things like, 'I'd like to see him say such things if he had a school to run smoothly.'

Freddy's pastoral care for the clergy and their family was renowned. Brian Carne wrote: 'In my forty years of ministry, no other bishop had the same interest in and care and concern for his clergy and their families. Gill remembers vividly the line of nappies parting in the yard as Freddy came round to the back door to see how we were.'

Anthony Balmforth wrote about an experience of his:

I always remember one morning when we had a Pastoral Committee at Church

House in Bristol. It was the time when the so-called Sheffield cuts in the numbers of clergy were to be implemented. Members of the Pastoral Committee had varied and various ways of doing this - to say the least. It had been a fairly difficult meeting and, of course, the Archdeacons took most of the flak. When I got home, Eileen looked a little down and asked how things had gone. I then discovered that Freddy had telephoned her and told her to handle me with kid gloves as I had had a difficult meeting and been on the receiving end of much disquiet. What thoughtfulness and kindness and care lay behind that action. And it wasn't just an isolated case, either.

Roger Clifton had an affectionate link with Freddy because he was the first person Freddy ordained (as deacon in Winterbourne Parish Church in December 1973) after his consecration and the last person he inducted (as Rector of Colerne and North Wraxall in 1983) before his retirement.

Our eldest son was born with a serious heart problem, and my wife and I always remember being at the clergy school at Lee Abbey in 1981, when Ben was about eighteen months old, a month or two before he was scheduled for major surgery. The community laid on a special healing service for Ben and another child who had cystic fibrosis. It was a moving occasion, and the Temples took part - Joan sat at the back and cried quietly through most of the service. She was very conscious of the loss of their own son, and perhaps because of this always took a very sympathetic interest in Ben. I remember how Joan used to refer to their family; I once asked how many children they had and she said, 'Three: two here and one in heaven.'

Philip Cousins writes:

Early in 1976, Freddy and Joan earned a very special place in our hearts. I suffered a nervous breakdown within a month of my institution and the Temples became a tower of strength to my wife. Being in a mental hospital, I was largely unaware of this at the time, but Janet will give you the personal angle on this very traumatic period of our marriage.

Janet Cousins continues:

We lived in Addis Ababa, Ethiopia, for eight years before going to Bristol in late 1975. We had lived under curfew for eighteen months. There were armed guards at our children's school, the banks, post offices, hospitals, etc.; tanks occasionally parked on the church car park. Although we were not directly involved, the 'Creeping Coup' affected us in many ways. The Church, St. Matthew's, was full to overflowing every Sunday. 'It is such a haven of security', somebody once said to me. Yes, it was, but Philip paid the price when we returned to the UK. While still abroad, no-one wanted to know us and there was this added insecurity of pending homelessness because no job, overshadowing our last few months in Addis Ababa. This was an added burden.

However, Oliver Tomkins had met us on two occasions when he had visited Addis Ababa and he offered Philip St. Peter's, Henleaze, just after we arrived back in the UK. We were given a very warm welcome by the parish, but sadly by the end of December Philip had completely shut off from me, the children and the parish. My world stopped too! However, the parish rallied round and I received much love and support. Freddy was on the 'phone immediately; and for the next three months either Freddy or Joan telephoned every week and called in often to see me.

On one occasion, when I was coping with a distraught mother-in-law as well as daily visits to Philip, Freddy said to me, 'The tunnel is very dark at the moment, but there is light at the end. You are going to be able to help many people because of this experience.' How right he was. Later in our time at Henleaze Philip became Rural Dean, and the Rural Deans' wives were asked to deliver invitations to the Clergy Wives meetings. I was able to do this and was amazed at the loneliness of many of the wives who invited me in. No wonder Freddy and Joan asked us to deliver their letters personally. On one occasion, I rang the doorbell and, on seeing me, the wife concerned burst into tears. On returning home I telephoned Freddy and his immediate response was, 'I did know there were problems, but not that they had reached that stage. I'll be there tomorrow.' And he was.

In their concern for clergy families, Freddy and Joan would just 'drop in': 'We don't mind if you have your hair in curlers; we just wanted to check that all is well with you all.'

Angela Pain writes, on behalf of herself and her husband Michael:

The lives of Bishop Freddy and of Joan Temple were certainly one of the formative influences on us, especially during the 1970s. As we look back to those youthful days we recall that this was a decade of struggle for 'women's liberation' from the traditional pattern of previous generations. I remember an article in The Times by the then Bishop of Bradford's wife, Ruth Hook, with the striking headline, 'Bishop's wife finds such mutuality in marriage that Women's Lib is by-passed.'

Michael had been overcoming, with great courage, the difficulty of a stammer which made leading worship and indeed conversation itself quite a draining experience - especially the 'big' occasions like visits from the Bishop. However, Michael, like Freddy, was a warm and sociable person and a 'natural' for parish life. I think Freddy and Joan's caring warmth and sparkle of good humour encouraged me, the rather diffident vicar's wife. They showed me a 'bigger' more mature attitude - and I started to realise that I was allowed to be myself. As I saw Joan writing letters in the car as she accompanied Freddy everywhere, I realised that she too had a rich inner life and the freedom that 'mutuality in marriage' brings. They were less conventional and infinitely more interesting than most of the 'senior clergy' I knew.

Our 'Christmas association' continued down the years until the end of Bishop Freddy's life, maintaining the link when we left the Bristol diocese for Guildford in 1978. The remarkable 'Temple Christmas Letter' would always arrive at the beginning of December; eventually their letter came to mark the beginning of the Advent and Christmas season in a special way. Their openness had a formative effect on our Christmas correspondence with friends in former parishes - encouraged to communicate not only the year's events and family news, but also something of our thoughts and hopes. Their free comments on political matters were liberating and shattered 'establishment' norms of those years

Ray Harris writes:

Adrienne and I had had a difficult time with the vicarage cracking and becoming uninhabitable. I had resisted attempts to move me away and we found a temporary home at Upper Stratton. I think I had just been given added responsibility in the deanery when I received the offer of a parish near Bristol. It seemed to me like one more ploy to get me out of St. Barnabas', Swindon so that it could be rubbed off the map. It made a nonsense of the deanery appointment and I felt undermined and angry. I went to see Bishop Freddy ready for a fight. I said I thought he had better pray before we started as I felt very angry. He did so, earnestly and loudly in his own inimitable way and I told him of my darker suspicions and feelings. There was no fight. He received my criticisms and absorbed all my anger and gave me reassurance and encouragement.

I would say that he loved the truth. He didn't flinch from speaking the truth when it was difficult and he wanted people to speak the truth to him. He received it in love.

Hugh Farlie wrote the following:

A colleague in Bristol once referred to me as an 'effervescent bumbler', which I thought was jolly unfair - though I do admit that I bounce around a bit and sometimes don't get very far. Bishop Freddy and Joan Temple had the remarkable ability to know intuitively when the effervescence was hiding a deep hurt inside. I knew, as with no other bishop and spouse before or since that I could always be 'open' with them and that they would be totally non-judgmental with me. I remember so vividly a time when they made me feel good - so good - simply by recognising somehow (don't ask me how!) that I wasn't feeling as bright as the picture I presented to the world outside. In a strange, magical, wonderful way, I always felt 'safe' in their company, and that nothing I said would shock them. The love and care they gave me - and I know they did the same for others - was unconditional. I can never thank them enough. Having said that, their care and love was absolutely unsentimental; when I did something silly, something of which Freddy disapproved, he invariably let me know in no uncertain terms. And I can remember one occasion when Joan put her hand on my arm and said simply, 'Silly old Hugh; how are we going to cope with this?' And then she hugged me. I think Joan realised that hugs from bishops' wives meant a lot to poor old bachelors like me. And hugs from bishops too. The two made such difference to my ministry in Knowle West. When I finally reach heaven - and hopefully that won't be for many a year yet! - and meet Freddy again, there will, I imagine, be renewed gales of laughter, coupled with salutary comments on how I should conduct myself in my new sphere of existence. It will be good to know that Freddy will be on hand as mentor and friend.

Four months after writing this, Hugh died suddenly and unexpectedly.

A very moving letter from a former parish priest in the diocese runs:

I was at my wit's end. I'd not lost interest in my parish, but I'd somehow - it's very difficult to explain - lost all energy to do the work, to try new things, even to love my people. I was desperate and thought nobody would understand. I confided in a fellow priest. He took it on himself to see Bishop Freddy about me. I was furious. I was spitting blood. I was ashamed. I wanted to crawl into a little hole and lose myself in it for ever and just sleep for a long, long time. Perhaps even for ever. Bishop Freddy came to see me unannounced. I didn't know where to put myself. This is the end, I thought. Two hours later, after much talk and - yes, even a bit of laughter - I felt so much incredibly stronger. At the end, he asked me, very unselfconsciously, to kneel on the carpet in my study. He laid his hands on me, probably very gently, but I felt as if I was being pushed into the ground - again hard to explain. When I got up I was crying, crying tears of sheer joy. It was an experience that meant even more than my ordination, though heaven knows that meant a lot. He saved my ministry and gave me such confidence. I can never be grateful enough that on that day he made all things new for me.

Alwyn Jones remembers how Freddy took such care of those who were unmarried and he, with other correspondents, recalled how much less lonely he felt after a visit from Freddy and Joan. Another priest wrote, 'The two of them just seemed to have an instinctive rapport with those who were struggling with their "aloneness". It was uncanny; whenever I bade them farewell at the end of the Vicarage drive, I went back into the house, which had, three hours before, seemed such a lonely, forbidding place - and I could have done cartwheels in the hall.' Another bachelor priest wrote, ' The Bishop and Joan often used to say, "If you feel on your own and want to talk, you *must* ring, day or night - even the middle of the night." What other bishop or bishop's wife would say that?'

Another priest, whose wife had died three years previously, has written:

The Bishop of Malmesbury and Joan Temple told me once to ring them any time of day or even night if I felt things were hard to bear. I remember one terrible night when I couldn't sleep and things kept churning over in my mind that I felt a desperate urge to ring them. I was too frightened to, because I didn't know what response I would get and wondered whether what they had said was merely said out of politeness. At about 5am I'd reached the end of my tether and felt at a totally low, low ebb. I took the plunge. I telephoned 'Morwena', wondering who would answer and whether I'd receive an episcopal telling-off. It was Joan who answered the 'phone; I told her I was feeling wretched and then burst into tears. What did she say? 'Darling, we've been expecting this call for absolutely ages; why did you leave it so long? Listen, the birds are singing outside. Can you hear them? You've probably got more in your garden than we have here. Get yourself together, keep listening to the birds and drive over here. Can you manage that? Or shall we come to you?' I assured her that I could manage to drive over, but wasn't going to because it would only inconvenience them to have a wreck on their doorstep. 'If you don't come', she said, 'we'll be upset ourselves, for I'm just off downstairs to put the kettle on and get a bit of breakfast ready for three. See you in about half an hour - and do keep listening to the birds. They're heralding the start of another of God's new days.' I remember her words exactly. I had a quick face-lick, as if in a dream, and couldn't help thinking how stupid a person I was being, but there seemed to be no going back. I drove into Swindon. I arrived at 'Morwena' to find the Bishop in the garden, watching a bee on a flower. He smiled at me and said that we humans weren't the only ones of God's creation to start work early. After an hour with my bishop and his wife I felt strangely renewed and went home feeling exhilarated, so much so, in fact, that I nearly had a collision with another car on the road out of Swindon. I remember that either the Bishop or Joan Temple made contact with me by telephone virtually every day for the next month or two. Just knowing they were there for somebody as pathetic as me made all the difference in my life. I never realised that episcopal families could be like that.'

Many people have mentioned how meetings in which Freddy was involved, were always business-like, but carried on with a certain lightness of touch, and not a little merriment. Some of those present remember a particularly turgid meeting at 'Morwena' in early 1982. Under discussion was the subject of Sunday Schools and the problems of communication between Incumbents and their Sunday School superintendents. One of those present was Hugh Thomson-Glover. 'And do you have similar problems, Hugh?' asked Freddy. Hugh, who had a deliciously laid-back, matter-of-fact way of expressing himself, looked up from a doodle he was finishing on his agenda and said, rather languidly, 'No, Bishop; you see, I sleep with my Sunday School superintendent.' Freddy knew that Hugh's Sunday School superintendent at Sherston was none other than his wife, Geraldine, but the rest of the group did not. There was a moment's slightly awkward silence, to be broken by peals of laughter from Freddy. 'I think they call that "pillow talk",

Hugh.' The rest of the gathering looked yet more mystified. At the end of the meeting, Freddy took the secretary aside and told him that he *must* put what Hugh had said in the minutes - 'and we'll see whether the Bishop really does read all the nonsense we send him.'

One priest remembers well a meeting of the Horfield deanery chapter in the late 1970s. One of the clergy was complaining to Freddy about some things that had happened at the cathedral. Freddy said, immediately, 'Yes it's all reminiscent of the story of Sidney Smith.' [Canon of St. Paul's, 1771-1845.] 'I beg your pardon, Bishop?' 'Well', said Freddy, 'it was proposed that St Paul's be surrounded by a wooden pavement. Sidney Smith agreed, and added, "Let the dean and canons lay their heads together and the thing will be done."' Freddy, said the correspondent, was a 'master of the quick riposte - indeed, like Sidney Smith. Members of the chapter were in stitches.'

Bryan Jones writes:

Freddy had a humility about him. I remember being at a clergy meeting when one of the brethren really was quite rude to him. At this distance I don't recall the exact details, but it was something to the effect that if only the Bishop was as theologically knowledgeable as the speaker, then all would be crystal clear. It was discourteous in the extreme, not to say arrogant. Freddy simply took it on the chin.

Amongst letters sent to clergy at various times are the following. Most of Freddy's letters were short and many left something to be desired grammatically. In some, words simply tumbled on to the page. His punctuation was maverick and some of his spelling mistakes were delightful. With some, however, he took enormous pains. These longer ones show his immense pastoral care and sensitivity. Why he kept copies of some and destroyed others is a matter for conjecture. Joan thought it possible that at some stage he planned some sort of book on pastoral care himself - though she did not know of any specific plans - and it certainly reached no more than an embryonic stage.

Freddy wrote to a parish priest in Bristol:

Something that never fails to upset and annoy me is when somebody says, 'Bishop, you're looking so grey and tired.' Mind your own business, I think. Having said that, I'm probably going to upset you now - for you are looking worn out. When I spoke to you briefly after the Chapter Meeting last night I was worried. For you didn't quite seem 'with it', and did indeed look very grey and pre-occupied. Is everything OK? If there is something worrying you, please trust me enough to tell me. Whatever it is, the last thing I'll be in the world is judgmental. I suspect you could do with a bit of a break. I have details of a holiday cottage on the north coast of Cornwall, which you could go to totally free of charge for a fortnight - and you could take a friend of your own choice with you. I don't think it would be a good idea to go alone. There are enough priests in the Stapleton deanery to look after your parish. How about it? Or am I stepping out of line? +Freddy Malmesbury.

A retired priest from Bristol forwarded to me the following letter he received from Freddy in March, 1979. 'It made me feel good', he said. He continued, 'All my life I have been a bit of a shrinking violet; I'm painfully shy - and at times I thought I really ought to quit the ministry before I was too much of a hindrance. I had totally lost confidence in myself and my abilities; Bishop Temple's letter gave me renewed hope and confidence; perhaps I was not a total failure after all.' Freddy's letter ran:

> *I understand that you are getting depressed about the lack of young people in your church and that all attempts at starting a youth club or fellowship have failed. I have heard further that your PCC don't think you're doing your job if you don't have a thriving youth club. Piffle!*
>
> *Bishop John and I know that you are a wonderful pastor; we know too that you are greatly loved by the non-churchgoing folk in your parish and area. We also realise that you are quite shy. I hope you don't mind my saying that? Perhaps running a youth club simply isn't your forte. If the PCC are so desperate to have one, let them run one themselves.*
>
> *Your greatest contribution to the forwarding of the Kingdom in your area of Bristol will be to carry on doing as you are, we understand, doing: i.e. loving, greeting and talking to everybody, young or old or in-between, you meet on the pavements of your parish. We know you find even doing this a bit of a trial, and we are full of admiration for the dogged way in which you accomplish this. Be assured that the people you minister to appreciate it greatly as well. I suspect that if you talk to the young people in the streets, if ever they really want help or counsel in the future, you might well be the first person they'll think of contacting. Far more important than running a youth club just for the sake of it.*
>
> *Joan and I are going to be away for five days from Tuesday. When we return, we'll give you a ring; perhaps you'd like to come to Morwena for tea or something and we can discuss it further? Meanwhile, be assured of our daily prayers.*

To another priest he wrote:

> *After our all-too-brief talk after Synod yesterday about your feeling 'useless' and 'undervalued' and 'not doing enough' I have thought about you a lot and said many prayers. In thirty minutes I'm driving down to Hampshire to conduct a three-day retreat - but I thought I must write to you before I go - though without an original thought, I fear. I quote instead some inspirational words (no - not Steiner Rice!) by Monica Furlong. She was speaking to a diocesan conference in, I think, Manchester or Liverpool - or somewhere up there. The words speak to me and I*

hope they will speak to you - and keep you going until I get back and we can have a chat:

'At this particular time there is perhaps a strong temptation among some members of the clergy to adopt a social worker act, to take refuge behind one of the comforting and reassuring masks which others in the helping professions are lucky enough to be able to wear. At least these roles are something which the world can understand.

I am clear what I want of the clergy. I want them to be people who can by their own happiness and contentment challenge my ideas about status, about success, about money, and so teach me to live independently of such drugs. I want them to be people who can dare, as I do not dare, and as few of my contemporaries dare, to refuse to work flat out (since work is an even more subtle drug than status), to refuse to compete with me in strenuousness. I want them to be people who are secure enough in the value of what they are doing to have time to read, to sit and think, and face the emptiness and possible depression which often attack people when they do not keep the surface of their mind occupied. I want them to be people who have faced this kind of loneliness and discovered how fruitful it is, as I want them to be people who have faced the problem of prayer. I want them to be people who can sit still without feeling guilty, and from whom I can learn some tranquillity in a society which has almost lost the art.'

Another priest treasures a letter he received from Freddy in 1979:

I cannot thank you enough for being so open with me about your feelings of solitude. Alas, it's something so many have to bear. Do you know Roger McGough's poem. 'Vinegar'? Whenever I read it, it cuts me to the quick - for Joan and I know there are so many good and faithful priests just like you. It goes:

sometimes
I feel like a priest
in a fish and chip queue
quietly thinking
as the vinegar runs through
how nice it would be
to buy supper for two.

Although it probably doesn't help to be told that there are many in exactly the same position as you, I hope it might help to know that you are daily surrounded with our love and prayers. If ever you feel like screaming and shouting, just give us a ring, and we will cosset you.

Freddy wrote the following letter, in July, 1979, to a priest whose wife had died three months previously, and who was, inevitably and understandably, feeling very 'raw' and lonely:

This will probably - almost certainly - sound pathetic - but I can remember, two or three years ago, Joan and I had tickets for the theatre in Bath. On the day, Joan wasn't at all well - so I went on my own - and had the MOST miserable time. The play was good, I'm sure; but I couldn't enjoy it because there was no Joan beside me to share in the enjoyment. Oh, my dear, how very pathetic of me to give such a trivial example. Yours is the far greater sorrow. Mine lasted three hours. You and Margaret had been married for 43 years; I can't begin to feel your pain and distress. Earthly partings are such hell. We must simply cling to the assured fact that we and our loved ones will be re-united in God's presence and will - and I don't mean to sound flippant at all - do cartwheels in the presence of the Almighty when we all meet again. I can't wait to see our son, Michael again - and see how he has progressed in holiness. If he has! Nor can Joan. Having said that, it's going to be very difficult for both Joan and I when the two of us will eventually be separated physically on earth; tears, naturally, will flow - however much we know that we'll meet again - and meet in the presence of Mike and so many of our dearest family and friends.

Be assured that Margaret is with you NOW, surrounding you with her love - and looks forward to welcoming you back to her.

Joan sends so much love. Come and see us sometime in the next couple of days; Joan will give you a ring in case you're too shy in taking up the offer. I can't promise to be here personally - though I'll do my best. Whether it's only Joan or both of us, you'll be loved and looked after.

After a meeting of clergy, Freddy had been 'button-holed' by one of the group members, who received the following letter the next day:

To live through the death of faith is a terrifying thing. Not believing in a loving God - or even non-belief in God at all - is just so numbing. My dear, we all go through it. We've all gone through it. I include myself.

Don't sit in your study and agonise about it all on your own. Come and see me. Or I'll come and see you. I only say the former because it might be better for you to get out of the house. Tell me exactly what's going through your mind. I know I'm your bishop - but a bishop is also a friend. I find it strange - and very disheartening - that so many treat their bishops as if they were superhuman, people who don't understand what it means to be human. I'm human. You're human. No difference.

Ring later. If you don't, I will. Joan says perhaps we could go for a walk on the Ridgeway or wherever; I think you enjoy a brisk walk? If I have been misinformed and the thought of it fills you with horror, we can always stay here at 'Morwena' and drink tea!

By the way, do you know the following, by Wilson Mizner? 'I respect faith, but doubt is what gives you an education.' Also, meditate on the following offering from Oscar Wilde's The Importance of Being Earnest *(which you undoubtedly know already): 'I hope you have not been leading a double life, pretending to be wicked and being really good all the time. That would be hypocrisy.' And, while I'm in full flow, a last one from Evelyn Waugh's* Decline and Fall: *'There is a species of person called a "Modern Churchman" who draws the full salary of a beneficed clergyman and need not commit himself to any religious belief.' I certainly do not include you as one of their number.*

Another priest received the following:

Your Rural Dean has told me that you are feeling a bit low at the moment and feeling that, after working in city environments, you think you do not fit into the mould of being a country Wiltshire Vicar - and that you're beating your head against a brick wall in your rural ministry, people don't listen to a word you're saying - and that you don't really understand country ways anyway.

I understand; and we must talk. I'll give you a ring in the next 48 hrs. Meanwhile, something to amuse you; hopefully, it may make you laugh - or at least smile.

In 1646, I think it was, an old journal tells of one who was employed by a country incumbent with the express object of keeping people from falling asleep in church.

'Allen Brydges hath bin chose to wake the sleepers in meeting, and being much proud of his place, must need have a fox-tail fixed to the end of a long staff, wherewith it may brush the faces of them that will have naps in time of discourse; likewise a sharpe thorne, wherewith he may prick such as be most sounde.'

It would seem that Allen Brydges was not a man who shirked his duty, for the diary tells of how one man was so suddenly woken up by the 'thorne' that he knocked his head against the wall, causing him to swear aloud.'

We may picture the perplexity of Mr. Brydges, however, when his austere gaze fell on the women members of the congregation. Were they asleep or not? It was hard to tell, for 'they may sometimes sleep and none know it by reason of their enormous bonnets. The minister does pleasantly say from the pulpit he does seem to be preaching to stacks of straw, with men jutting here and there between them.'

For this unpleasant task of waking sleeping churchgoers, the 'Sluggard Waker', as he was known, would receive something like ten shillings a year. His instructions were not merely to wake up those who had gone to sleep but to watch for the first sign of a nod. This was a signal for a sharp rap on the head of the nodder.

I hope this raised a little smile to keep you going till we meet - which, I promise, will be very soon.

Another incumbent wrote to say that he was having 'immense and long-standing problems' with his Parochial Church Council. He received the following reply from Freddy:

Thank you for your cri-de-coeur about your PCC. I fully understand. So many colleagues in the parochial ministry are saying the same sort of thing. Now I'm a very democratic person (well, I like to think I am!), and am totally for the idea of a Parochial Church Council. So important. I think the problem lies, in many parishes, that it's simply the wrong sort of person who puts himself or herself up for election. Such people come to meetings with scarcely hidden agendas and, frankly, do untold damage to the mission of the Church (and untold damage to the nerves and equilibrium of their incumbents!). In my own parishes I used to have people who strutted around the stage of a meeting, solely intent on blocking. They used to have no idea of the issues at stake, but thought they did. Many clergy have wept on my shoulders since. And - though perhaps I shouldn't be saying this, for it's a judgement I can't really substantiate - so many have little or no idea of the Christian faith. They want to perpetuate their Church as a sort of cosy social club. I'm not of course saying that all PCCs are like this; there are many people of sterling worth and value sitting on our Councils in the diocese, and many are the unsung heroes and heroines of the Church, and can themselves teach their incumbents things. I suspect that all such people are those whose lives are soaked in common sense and prayer. I do so sympathise and feel for you. But don't give up hope. I suspect the Lord can work through petty and silly people, though it does make His mission that little bit harder! Give me a ring and we'll talk about it properly and try to get a bit of perspective. If I haven't heard from you within 48 hours, I'll ring you myself and order you up to 'Morwena'; that would teach you to moan to your bishop! I know Joan would want to send her love and the assurance of her prayers. I think you know that you have mine.

There seem to have been one or two problems with some Sunday Schools in the late 1970s, prompting Freddy to write to one incumbent:

Sunday Schools are just so important; so important, in fact, that it's best not to have them unless you have 100 percent faith in your teachers. Last year I sat in on a Sunday School lesson in a parish Joan and I were visiting. The teacher's profession was, in fact, a teacher, so I assume she had a modicum of intelligence; she held a post in a very important department in a local Comprehensive School. I squirmed all the way through. Joyce Grenfell at her best. Or worst. It seemed the whole half-hour hinged on a discussion of 'above the bright blue sky', and whether the blue in question was azure, cerulean, cobalt, navy, sapphire, turquoise or ultramarine. And this to a class of nine 11 year olds or thereabouts. I suspect she lost nine for the Kingdom in that thirty minutes: surely a record. I felt myself very blue afterwards.

To another Freddy wrote:

> *Some Sunday School teachers will have a lot to answer for when, on meeting their Maker, they are shown how they have absolutely ruined their children's spiritual development. But having said that, and I don't mean to sound too heavy-handed, it's your fault as well; you can't expect the teachers to get it right if you don't put effort into preparing them - and I really think it is necessary to have a preparation class every week. Then you'll know what they are being taught, and how. I agree that so many children are let down, handicapped by their teachers, whose own religion hasn't yet got past the fluffy-lamb-gentle-Jesus-meek-and-mild-above-the-bright-blue-sky nonsense. If the Sunday School teacher isn't prepared to accept the discipline of being taught himself or herself, then it would really be far better to shut the Sunday School down.*

The following was written to an incumbent in November 1980, demonstrating a certain humility:

> *I'm so sorry I was a bit ratty with you last evening; you didn't and don't deserve episcopal rattiness! I was more than a little put out by the blinkered attitude of the previous speaker at the meeting, and when you stood up to speak, knowing you are a close friend of [X], I thought you were only going to underline what he had said, and didn't really listen to you properly. It was only when driving back home that I realised that I had got it all wrong. My apologies. In my defence, I can only plead that I was feeling pretty wretched; my angina was playing up - and, in fact, I was feeling physically sick. Having said that, it's no excuse for my ill temper, and I do so apologise.*

Freddy, in his letters, was often impish. A delightful correspondence exists between him and the Duchess of Beaufort. In 1977, the Duchess wrote to thank Freddy for his Christmas greetings. She told him that she had been very touched initially by the fact that Freddy had included a kiss for her in his signature - until her husband, the Duke, pointed out to her that it was an episcopal cross, and not a personal kiss. Freddy wrote back to Badminton by return, and signed his letter '++Freddy Malmesbury', adding as a postscript that the second cross was indeed a personal one.

Another letters reads:

> *I don't think this is too much to worry about, but I must investigate. I have received a letter from one of your parishioners (a regular churchgoer) to complain that you tend to 'use intemperate language in the pulpit.' She didn't elaborate - so I am left to speculate. Do you swear in the pulpit? Do you dare to use the word 'God'? Please give me a ring, for I'm dying to know what lies behind this. In fact, I am agog. So many good wishes.*

In an address he gave to clergy of a deanery in the diocese of Bath and Wells in 1980, Freddy said:

I'm terrified that one day, in the midst of a Confirmation, I'll simply stop and say, 'Hey, spare a thought for the Bishop; he's human too; don't, please, please, put him on a pedestal. And don't subject dear Joan to be on a pedestal too. We're on a journey together. Joan has her problems; and I have mine.' But I can't say it. Our people just wouldn't understand. And who could blame them? They've been brainwashed into thinking that the Church and bishops have all the answers; the Church might like to think she has, but the bishops certainly have not. Some of them like to think they have; perhaps they don't think. I wish I could be more certain about everything. I wish I could love my clergy more. I try to. God knows what a life they sometimes have in our parishes. Sometimes I just want to be out in the garden at 'Morwena', my house in Swindon, and be myself for a while. When they ring, I go out. Lovingly sometimes, dutifully on others, prodded by Joan on others. When I get to their Vicarages and see what a tangled mess I'm presented with, I weep - and usually weep with them and invariably with their wives - for theirs, perhaps, is the stronger sorrow.

It usually breaks down to the fact that the Vicar feels undervalued - or thinks himself to be so. Parishioners can sometimes be so very cruel.

Freddy expanded on this in a letter to his extended family:

I got back to Swindon very tired from Bristol at about 11pm. We had a good meeting; Christopher [Martin] was on top form, and we laughed a lot. I was greeted by Joan saying that Mrs Y had rung in some distress; her poor dear husband has been drinking again. Apparently he'd gone out into the street and fallen over and had to be picked up by one of his parishioners. Joan asked whether I really had to go. Couldn't his Rural Dean, a good friend of his, go? I think she just wanted me to be home for a bit. There was no way I couldn't go, tired as I was. When I got there, the Vicarage front door was open, which I found disturbing. Mrs Y was out in the garden, weeping copiously. I asked where Y was; she told me that he'd tried to go to bed, but had fallen down at the top of the stairs. I went up; the poor dear had banged his face and cut himself. I went to the loo and got some paper and did my best to clean him up; he was so very far gone that he didn't wake up. I thought for a minute that he might have gone, but checked his pulse. I rang J [a GP trusted by Bishop Freddy, and, incidentally, a Moslem], who was round in eight minutes. He did all the usual blood pressure checks and a few others, said they were fine, though there was a bit of fibrillation of the heart, he thought. 'I could get him into the Princess Margaret Hospital within five minutes, Bishop, but I'm not sure it would be right. If people see an ambulance arriving, they'll put two and two together and make far more than four. I'll ring P [his wife] and perhaps you can ring

Joan, and we'll together sit with him until all's well. Tomorrow will be the time to get appointments sorted out.

This dear, dear man was, and is, so understanding. I thank God for him. Oh, why do we expect our brother clergy to do so much? This latest episode only started because someone in the parish had been beastly to him.

And, on a similar theme:

Life is just a bit busy at the moment; dearest Joan and I are quite tired. But however tired she is, Joan is just so wonderful with others, putting me to shame. We had what dear Ursula [Ursula Tomkins, wife of the Bishop of Bristol] always calls a 'coded message' about one of our clergy in the middle of the diocese. My secretary answered the call from Bishop's House; she said that of course the bishop would rearrange his (ie my) diary) - and went about doing it herself. I told Joan that I was exhausted, and I really couldn't manage to get to see him till the evening. Joan went through the roof. 'You think you're tired, Freddy? Just think what he's going through. We've got to go immediately.' I felt suitably chastened and agreed and felt ashamed with myself. We drove through Chippenham and on to his Vicarage. When we got there, we parked in the drive; the front door of the Vicarage was open, which was disconcerting. Joan was first there and 'coo-eed'. There was no answer. We went though the house and out the back door. Joan locked the front door behind her; it was a Yale. Poor, dear man was slumped in a deckchair, with a half-empty bottle of what I think was gin beside him. Joan went into the kitchen, found a kettle and made three mugs of coffee. She brought them out on a tray she'd found. Somehow she'd found some ginger biscuits too. All this time, dear X was still asleep. Joan woke him with a very tender kiss. 'Don't worry, dearest one, we're here to be with you.' He woke with a start and didn't (I think) even realise where he was. He then said, 'Good gracious, it's Mrs Temple.' He then saw me, and became agitated and said 'I'm sorry, Bishop, but I'm not doing very well at the moment.' I gave him a hug. He relaxed. Poor, dear man - he really ought to be loved each and every day; he has no self-esteem and a horrendous PCC. What worse combination. Joan said that we couldn't leave him there; we bundled him into the car after finding keys to the Vicarage front and back doors. And took him back to 'Morwena'. At about 10pm we had a call from his churchwarden, saying that he hadn't turned up for a PCC meeting. I was a bit short with him, and said that if I were X I wouldn't turn up myself. There was a bit of blustering on his part. He said something like, 'You're taking the Vicar's side.' I replied that I was taking God's side. A bit of a put-down, and I felt a tad ashamed afterwards. I rang him later to apologise if I'd been brusque; he said he understood I must have been under pressure to say what I did - 'but I'm prepared to forget it this one time.' I had to bite my tongue. Until it bled.

276   A rather bizarre letter to Freddy in the autumn of 1979 reads:

I write because I need to talk to you about our Vicar. I have been empowered by the Parochial Church Council. Can we mutually arrange a time to meet?

Our Vicar is just being very strange at the moment. The other day he went visiting, apparently had a cup of tea and then, sitting down on the sofa, he went to sleep. My informant tells me that he slept on the sofa for three or so hours and she and her husband didn't know where to put themselves.

To this, Freddy replied:

Thank you so much for your letter Of course it would be good to meet. My secretary will ring in the next few days giving you possible dates and times.

Meanwhile, do not, please, be too judgmental about your Vicar. He's going through what for him is a frightening time. Until I see you, I ask you to hold him and cherish him; he's been an excellent parish priest in the past - and will, if we all work together, be just as excellent in the future. Anyway, he obviously needed his sleep.

One young priest must have choked on his breakfast cereal on opening the following letter from his bishop:

It has been brought to my attention that you referred to me in a recent meeting of your deanery synod as 'an amiable old fool'. Amiable - I hope so. Old - certainly. But fool? Well, maybe, but a fool for Christ's sake! I'm sure you meant what you said in a loving way, but I only write because some of those present were a little put out by what you said, and have shopped you! So watch your rear! Let me say that I wasn't really put out to hear this; and woe betide the bishop who doesn't listen to what the grass roots are saying. Perhaps I am - but I somehow hope that when the good Lord calls me home, my fellow travellers on earth won't use that as an epitaph.

This comes with my very best wishes; I think what you're doing [in the parish] is an inspiration to very many of us and I hear so many good reports.

To a priest in his second curacy he wrote, after overhearing a conversation at a Lee Abbey Clergy Conference:

You're doing sterling work in your parish; I hear excellent reports from your Vicar and from so many of the parishioners of [X]. Thank you so much for all the care and attention you lavish on those you are called to serve.

I was, however, a little disappointed to overhear a conversation over lunch with some of your colleagues. You, on your part, may be a little disappointed in me in that I was eavesdropping. It appeared to me that you were quite vitriolic in some of the things you said about the folk in the Old Peoples' Home over which your Vicar

277

has given you pastoral supervision. I know as well as anyone how tiresome the eld-
erly in such places can be. But I really can't condone such words as 'moronic', or
phrases like 'What a waste of my time having to go to them every week.'

I hope this doesn't to you sound terribly pious, but all these folk have been made
in the image of God. They deserve respect and they need a great deal of pastoral,
sensitive care. You said that one particular lady was 'loopy' and that you didn't
know why you bothered. 'Loopiness' may come to you and I one day. I'm probably
closer to it than you.

I've been reading the poems of Roger McGough recently; many of them mean
much to me. Have you read him? One, which I would like to reproduce for you to
meditate on, is called 'Sad Aunt Madge':

As the cold winter evenings drew near
Aunt Madge used to put extra blankets
over the furniture, to keep it warm and cosy.
Mussolini was her lover, and life
was an outoffocus rosy-tinted spectacle.

But neurological experts
with kind blueeyes
and gentle voices
small white hands
and large Rolls Royces
said that electric shock treatment
should do the trick
itdid...

today after 15 years of therapeutic tears
and an awful lot of ratepayers' shillings
down the hospital meter
sad Aunt Madge
no longer tucks up the furniture
before kissing it goodnight
and admits
that her affair with Mussolini
clearly was not right
particularly in the light
of her recently announced engagement
to the late pope.

McGough was almost certainly making a different point/s to mine - but I still
think, in the context in which I am writing to you, that 'Sad Aunt Madge' might be

useful in your thoughts, meditation and prayers.

Anyway, your bishop has had his say; think about what I've said and, more important, pray about it. But don't dwell on it; don't think you've been 'told off'. I'm only trying to be helpful and to make you an even better priest than you already are.

Another correspondent says that he had 'worked himself a stew' with some of the pronouncements of his Rural Dean while the latter had been giving out notices at the beginning of one of his Chapter Meetings. He continues:

I realise, now that I am a little more mature in the ministry, that perhaps it was a little forward of me, but I blasted off a letter to Bishop Freddy saying how silly and stubborn my Rural Dean was on this and many other matters. By return came a long and courteous reply from the Bishop, saying in effect that he had noted my concerns but that I must try to learn to appreciate the points of view of others even if I disagreed violently with them. I felt suitably chastened - but then, and this was typical of Bishop Freddy, he added a postscript, asking me whether I was aware of the following saying of his uncle, Archbishop William Temple: 'It is not the ape, nor the tiger in man that I fear: it is the donkey.' Marvellously supportive of his Rural Dean - but just a hint at the end that I might not have got it all wrong.

A priest from the diocese of Chelmsford, who had attended a Retreat led by Freddy at Pleshey, was and is, 'eternally grateful to Bishop Temple.' He wrote:

'I was then quite a raw priest in my first incumbency, desperate to get things moving in my parish - and, in the process, coming up against a great deal of opposition. At the Retreat there was space for us to talk to, and share problems with, the Conductor. I poured my heart out to Bishop Temple. I cannot now recall anything he said at the time. However, two days later there arrived a letter from him, which I have cherished and would like to quote in full:

'I hope you don't mind my writing to you following our conversation at Pleshey. I got your address from your diocesan office. I am a little uneasy and concerned about you. Rush! Rush! Rush! My dear - I think you're too much in a hurry! If you want to rip up this letter, you're welcome to do it now - though I hope you'll read it through.'

Richard Benson, SSJE, the founder of the Society of St. John the Evangelist, wrote the following: 'There is nothing Divine about hurry, and nothing hurried about the Divine.'

Have you read any Fenelon? If not, I would recommend him. He once wrote to a French Duke: 'I want to help you to find how to live a very full, yet a leisurely life.' (The italics are mine.)

Learn to relax - and let God take over. You have so much to offer the Church and, far more importantly, God; don't let freneticism get in your way.

If you'd like to come back to me on this, you'll be welcome to do so; you'll be replying to a fellow pilgrim Christian and not to a bishop!

This letter ties in well with one written by John Neale, a former Bishop of Ramsbury:

I invited Freddy to talk to a Day Conference of parish clergy in Devizes. He had such a winsome style and warned them against giving the impression that they were dashing from one event to the next and were perpetually busy. I recall his own words now: 'When people approach you with the words, "You must be very much in demand; so how are you managing: are you terribly tired?"' I smile calmly and say, 'Oh, I've never felt more relaxed in my life!'

Although Freddy could absorb criticism directed towards him, he was always immensely protective of Joan. Any criticism of her not only upset him, but also angered him. On one occasion he wrote to an incumbent in the Bristol diocese:

I was very upset that your Sunday School leader was so horribly rude to Joan yesterday. Joan was only trying, very gently, to point out ways in which the young Sunday School teacher concerned could have improved the lesson she was teaching and make it more suitable for eight year olds. She said what she said from the very best of motives and with a lot of love. The way in which your Sunday School leader rounded on her was unacceptable. I ask that you show this letter to her. I am profoundly disturbed and my wife is still deeply upset.

+FS Malmesbury

(It was on very rare occasions that Freddy signed himself thus.)

Freddy followed this letter up, dated the same day, with a more personal one:

I'm so sorry I had to write as I did; I thought I had to write formally. And, yes, I did and do feel angry. Forgive me. I know of course that it wasn't your fault and that you had no idea what had gone on. Having said that, I think you ought to look closely and carefully at your Sunday School and its leadership. We have a good team in the diocese who will do anything to help.

Just a little word of advice, which of course you can take or leave! Don't let someone like that walk all over you. We gained the impression that that was exactly what she was attempting to do. Your predecessor had exactly the same problems.

We hear so many good reports of what you are doing in your parish; thank you so much for expending yourself as you do. Joan sends her love.

+Freddy Malmesbury

280   A letter to his extended family runs:

We have had an awful tragedy in the Cathedral: a chorister, aged 11, accidentally strangled himself playing with his tie on a door-handle before going to bed. The parents thought it strangely quiet and went up to say goodnight and found him. Such a nice police father and teacher mother.

Fran Vickery, the boy's mother, has written, many years after the event:

We first met Bishop Freddy when John and Paula [Fran's husband and daughter] were confirmed at St. Martin's, Knowle. He spent a long time chatting with John, so long, in fact, that others were intrigued at this in-depth, long, very serious conversation - and then amazed when we revealed the subject - football! Local mainly, but touching on National and International games. Of course in those halcyon footballing days both Bristol City and Swindon were fielding good strong teams. I think this reveals Bishop Freddy's extraordinary 'ordinariness' - if you know what I mean. Later on he confirmed Jonathan, then the following year came to his funeral.

Fran and John had received a letter from Freddy, which they cherished:

Joan, my wife, and I have been feeling so desperately for you both and have you in our prayers constantly. We have delayed writing till now as we know the pain and grief gets worse for a long time I'm afraid, and most people don't realise this. We had a son die totally suddenly aged 6, a mistake in the anaesthetic for a simple tonsils op, and so we do know a bit what you're going through. It is something we never 'get over' but adjust to in time and, believe me, difficult though you'll find this at the moment to believe, God will be right with you in the suffering and in the end will use you all the more, because it is the people who've been through deep tragedy who can really help others later. God did not plan it I'm sure: almighty Love allows us all immense freedom and he has not got all the future planned to a detail, but he is in it all if we turn to him, bearing and sharing it all with us, as shown on the Cross. Don't be too brave and stiff upper lip: have a good howl together: we did and do now and then, even though it's nearly 30 years since our Michael left us. Tears are God-given and beneficial. You are in for a very difficult time now as letters stop and silly folk start thinking you are 'getting over it' and talk about everything but him, while you long to talk about him.

With such affectionate sympathy from us both.

Fran continues:

He and Joan were immensely supportive at this time; Freddy spoke to us movingly about their son, Michael. It was of great help and comfort to us in those first few agonising years. 19 years on, it is easier to understand how he could still feel and communicate so emotionally. The pain never goes away, but it becomes manageable, though, as Freddy commented, 'there are still occasions when the tears fall with no warning.'

Two short vignettes give a taste of another side of Freddy's life and ministry; both form parts of different letters to his extended family:

The Loss Adjusters dinner was a fascinating glimpse into a totally different world of commerce. I'm so grateful to Gordon Edwards from Sherston for inviting me. But - my, these people do themselves well. It was a very lush hotel. I noticed that my bedroom cost £50 without breakfast; the breakfast was £3 for Continental, £5 for English. My bedroom had colour television and its own bathroom etc. and all the different Loss Adjuster companies had booked suites in which they gave limitless drinks before the meal; then there was a good meal and then afterwards everyone retreated to their suites again for more limitless drinks on their firms. I asked some of the younger ones if this was all on their firm and they said, 'Oh yes; we couldn't afford it otherwise.' Some had come down from Edinburgh and said, 'It's really so simple, Bishop, by air - and only costs £93 return.' I cannot really believe that good business depends on such luxury and it makes me understand a bit more why Arthur Scargill wants a really big wage for miners. But then I am a Liberal and want an Incomes Policy right across the board for everyone, as Uncle William used to want as well.

Secondly:

We went to the Lord Mayor's dinner for the Archbishops and Bishops yesterday. It was quite incongruous leaving the concrete jungle of the Borough of Southwark in full evening dress for the Mansion House. Most of the Bishops were all dressed in bits that have been handed down by others. Mine is a combination of Archbishop Fisher and Bishop Ussher-Wilson. [A former Bishop of the Upper Nile.] I must be careful when sitting down, as I wouldn't want the seams of my 'fancy dress' to split in such august company. Joan thinks I had better never risk having it cleaned as it might disintegrate completely. There is the nice story of Leonard Wilson at Birmingham, when his cummerbund came off and the Queen Mother picked it up and asked if it was his. 'Yes, Ma'am', he replied, and she said, 'How interesting, as inside it has "Bishop of St. Albans 1904".'

By way of summary, the following letter was received from David Isitt:

Verity and I were deeply fond of Freddy and continue to value Joan's friendship very highly. Freddy would always provide good support and sometimes (more importantly) a crisp corrective when we found ourselves floundering in the shallows of cathedral and diocesan affairs. They restored one's sense of balance. He had such good sense, and generally sound judgement, and could see the trivialities for what they were. I suppose this was because his own ministry was based on the best sort of spiritual discipline - not that he was given to talking about this - which gave integrity to his own way of life. I think he was a naturally affectionate man who usually managed to stop short of sentimentality. He and Joan were certainly at their very best in dealing with awkward people and with people in emotional difficulties. I guess this was because having lost one of their own children they had found themselves vulnerable; and people to whom they ministered were quick to realise that they were not simply being sympathetic but could understand them in a rather remarkable way. Professionally, he was excellent with the junior clergy and with NSMs and their families. It was in this context that I usually saw him.

His sense of humour, of course, won people's hearts - for the most part - though that great rumbustious laugh could sometimes grate on the ear. He was certainly more sensitive to the nuances of life (and art, and theatre, and literature) than his rather assured manner might have suggested. Personally I enjoyed his puckishness and his occasionally indiscreet, sometimes even malicious observations. He could be very shrewd.

He enjoyed the fun of clerical life in a way that was engaging for those who shared it but could be off-putting to those who didn't. After all, he belonged to an ecclesiastical inner circle. Not that he was a snob. Far from it. But he didn't always appreciate those who came from elsewhere. I believe this had one unfortunate effect in the latter part of his life. He had been, I understand, a great admirer of Oliver Tomkins and his style of episcopate. John Tinsley was a very different person and worked in a rather different way. Many of us were devoted to him and found him inspirational, but I think it must be said that Freddy didn't, and this made it difficult for him to give quite the whole-hearted support that the in-coming bishop would have welcomed. I never heard any word of criticism from John Tinsley in this respect, but it was sad that there seemed to be an unnecessary coolness between two such warm-hearted men.

David Isitt's letter has been included in full. Perhaps the final sentence will cause one or two raised eyebrows. Two other correspondents raised the same issue. The relationship between Bishop Oliver and Freddy had been exceptionally close; they were like brothers and felt enormous affection for each other - so it must have been difficult for Freddy when Bishop Oliver left and Bishop John arrived. Coupled with that, Freddy and John Tinsley were from totally different backgrounds.

Amongst Freddy's papers, however, are countless letters between Freddy and John and vice versa. Without exception, all are far more than merely civil; many of them border on the affectionate. In letters to his family and others, we have statements like, 'Bishop John, though not an Oliver, is such a dear'; 'I think John has got it wrong, but he does everything from the best will in the world, and I respect him greatly'; 'Bishop John can be so frustrating, but I can't be annoyed with him for long'; 'Oh dear, I don't think I would have tackled it his way'; 'John's put his foot in it again; how on earth can I bale him out?' 'John's just made himself sound a bit silly on the radio, talking about the future of the church. I doubt anyone understood a word of what he said.' 'He accepts speaking engagements for the best of motives - but he's so busy that he sometimes can't come up with the goods.' In a letter to a fellow Suffragan Bishop in February 1979, Freddy wrote:

> *I fear I have been having some more terrible thoughts about John T. He doesn't deserve them. He does his best - and his best is good - and he is good. He would be mortified if he could visit the workings of my mind. I'm ashamed to confess that at times I have been just so reserved towards him. The Lord knows why this is, and I know too - though I find it hard to acknowledge. I know this diocese through and through - and everything screams at me that I would do things differently. How utterly pathetic. If people knew just how pathetic I am, they would want nothing at all to do with me. Some people have picked up on my feelings, which have at times been unforgiveable - specially when he is such a good, kind, able and - yes - holy man.*

On a Sunday afternoon in the spring of 1982, Freddy and Joan chatted about their future. Freddy was not well; he wrote to his sister, Edith, that he felt lethargic. Things came to a head when Bishop John was laid low with a virus and Freddy had to drive to Bristol for a Confirmation. He said that, half an hour before setting out, he felt 'wretched and completely drained.' On Joan's insistence he rang round to what he called some 'tame Bishops' to see if they could take his place. Unfortunately, all of them were otherwise occupied. The Incumbent concerned was alerted to the fact that Freddy was not well and probably would not stay too long after the Confirmation. Freddy was sweating profusely when he arrived and asked if he could sit down in a chair in the sacristy. The incumbent wrote:

> *I shoved the servers elsewhere and Bishop Freddy slumped in the chair and appeared to be nodding off. I recall saying to him, about five minutes before the service was to begin, that if he were OK it might be time to get himself together. All I can say now is that he was immediately 'electrified'. He said that he would sign the confirmands' books after the service, so 'let's go!' I have never, ever heard such a brilliant sermon in my life, or a service taken with such love and care. When I whispered the candidates' names to him, he laid hands on them, confirmed them - and then put his hands under their chins, looked them straight in the eye, and said to each one, prefacing it with their Christian name, 'God's got work for you to do; get on and do it.' After the service, Freddy signed the books and was the life and soul of the party. Meanwhile Joan, though casting anxious glances at Bishop Freddy, was her usual self, listening, loving. Wherever she goes she makes people feel better.*

Joan recalls that she was worried about Freddy driving home. 'We made it, however, had a mug of coffee and went to bed. Freddy was absolutely whacked. Before he went to his bed he said, 'We did it, but I can't see us doing it for much longer'.

In preparation for their retirement, Freddy and Joan had recently bought a small terraced cottage in the neighbouring town of Wootton Bassett. The time was approaching for them to move into it. It was not long before the official announcement was made that Freddy was to retire a little earlier than many had expected. One correspondent wrote, 'The announcement seemed to so many, clergy and laity alike, like the end of an era - and a golden one at that. I think it would be true to say that there was a profound sadness throughout the diocese, a sadness shared by everyone.' Freddy fulfilled his more immediate engagements; Bishop John and he re-allocated others. It was not long before his successor was announced - Peter Firth, a Senior Producer of Religious Programmes with the BBC. Freddy wrote in May, 1983:

> *Peter Firth will I think make a good bishop - an inspired choice of John's - though this end of the diocese is very sad that he is going to continue living in his own house in Bristol, because no matter how much you sally forth to the other end of the diocese you do not get the same feel, nor do people deep down psychologically feel you belong in the same way as if you lived and slept in an area. But this, of course, I am not saying outside family circles as the bishop and he made the decision apparently on his appointment and it is publicly no concern of Joan and mine - but we are hearing a good deal of rumbling.*

Peter Firth himself did not actually dislike the prospect of living in Swindon, but understandably did not feel it fair on Felicity, his wife, to uproot - as she lectured at the University of Bristol. Once before, when Peter had been an incumbent in the diocese of Manchester, she had given up a fulfilling position to move to Bristol. Peter Firth argued that it was time that her needs should be taken into consideration - the basis of which argument, in fact, would probably have found favour with Freddy.

Although both Freddy and Joan were sad to contemplate retirement, there was for them also an element of excitement. In the summer of 1983, Freddy wrote to his extended family:

> *I have taken over to the cottage some 2500 books or so in driblets; I am now quite well known along that old little part of Wootton Bassett and they have never seen so many books pouring into one of those houses. But it is starting to make the cottage warm and alive. We will never have to decorate again as there will be not an inch of wall space visible with books and pictures everywhere. I suppose it's all really rather fun.*

Freddy and Joan's diocesan farewell presentation took place in Chippenham, in the centre of the diocese, in early Autumn, 1983. Bishop John Tinsley began his farewell address thus:

I find it very difficult to try and compass words which will be sufficient to try and express our appreciation for all that Freddy and Joan have given to this diocese. Very difficult first because Freddy is a unique person among the bishops. What other English bishop - what other bishop anywhere - has washed General Charles de Gaulle? [This was when Freddy was a hospital orderly in Beirut.] *It must have been an exceptionally long task. And I often wonder why the General didn't admit Freddy as one of the Companions of the Order of the Lib(er)ation.*

Then of course Freddy has a unique laugh. So much so that I've been tempted to add a line to Browning's famous poem ....., which goes something like this: Freddy laughs; 'God's in his heaven and all's well in the world' - because whenever I arrive at a meeting and hear Freddy's laughter, I know we can now begin with confidence. And that all is well. But it's a laugh also which I think indicates a ready ear and eye for the pompous and the absurd.

It's right of course in any general remarks about Freddy to begin in this light-hearted way. Because Freddy and Joan have obviously enjoyed their time among us and enjoyed their time with us. And we're going to miss so badly the cheerful presence which they've brought to so many during their time here. And in the diocese we're going to miss them on a number of counts. We're going to miss Freddy, a beloved pastor, clearly one for whom the welfare of clergy and people was the first concern. And Freddy and Joan were a real partnership in this, as they went about together so often throughout the diocese.

Bishop John continued to talk about this unique partnership, about the outstanding contribution Freddy had made in his support of ecumenical relations in the diocese and about his stimulating preaching. He ended by striking a personal note:

I'm losing a trusted and wise colleague to whom I've never turned in vain for advice - and, frequently it's been necessary, for warning. And a very willing colleague always ready to expend himself on more work, so much so that I've hesitated to ask Freddy to do things because I knew he would say 'yes'. Above all, we're saying farewell to a real friend and I use the simple phrase now, because I can think of no other, a 'good man', without whom the diocese can never be the same. Freddy and Joan, then, a real partnership in ministry - thank you both for being what you are and blessings on you both for the future as you enter the next, and I hope splendid, phase in your lives in retirement. Thank you for all you've been to us.

In reply, Freddy said:

Through all the loving, warm farewells that we've had I've found that afterwards I've always had to say a prayer for the speakers - praying that they might be forgiven for the times that they've erred from the strict truth, and any extravagances - and I'm afraid that the same prayer is necessary tonight. And then of course with it has had to go another prayer - that Joan and I might be forgiven for enjoying it all.

But thank you, dear Bishop John, for all that you've so extravagantly said. Thank you all for the incredibly generous presents which we shall value enormously and use some of it in getting a great deal done to our garden that's in chaos at the moment; we shall be able to get help for that. And thank you all who've arranged this evening so wonderfully. But a thanks above all to the Diocese for the wonderful thirteen years of our ministry together, and I say 'our' because ours has been quite deliberately from the beginning a shared ministry.

We felt privately and quietly that if the Church is right in saying that marriage makes one one flesh it doesn't really matter that hands are only laid on one head at ordination. And so we quite deliberately got married some months before ordination and that was at a time when it was not the right thing to do. 'Young man, you mustn't take on two vocations!' And so, just for a moment at the beginning, for the only time publicly, I want to pay tribute to the other half of the shared ministry, which has always been more flexible and more varied than mine, because it had to do quite different things in each place, and take up whatever was necessary and lacking. For instance, in Hong Kong we found only thirty young people in the Sunday School. Joan took over the Sunday School and left behind, at the end of six years, four hundred children and eighty teachers.

And besides all her partnership with me in the diocese there were many things she did in Swindon. We arrived to find that Lent Lunches and Hunger Lunches were hardly known, so for three or four years they were organised in our house, with between 100 and 120 coming each week; this immediately allowed her, at one wholesale Cash and Carry place, to have a card as 'Ecclesiastical Caterer'. Now these lunches are scattered all round Swindon and are quite established and normal. There's a Volunteer Bureau that started from minute beginnings in our house, now professionally organised and established. The Church of England Children's Society within six years saw £54,000 raised. And an ex-offenders' hostel that's now expanded to three houses. And besides that, of course, the major pastoral side of our ministry: as we went down the motorway, it would be she who would tell me, 'Now remember, John was doing 'A' Levels the last time we went there. Mary had had trouble with her foot ...' and so on. And it was made very clear to me what part she played when I arrived without her in one parish and a deaconess said, 'Is Mrs. Temple with you this evening?' And I said, 'No, I'm afraid she couldn't come.' 'That's a great pity, Bishop, because she has her own ministry that in no way can you possibly fulfil.' And so, tonight, I'm glad to pay tribute to the other half of the shared ministry.

But then, many people have asked us, 'Haven't you missed having a parish of your own?' And we haven't, because you've all made us so welcome everywhere. And there's always been the great excitement of the infinite variety of the worship throughout the Diocese. Take for instance the giving of the Peace - there's every variety in this Diocese. There are parishes one might call 'The Daily Telegraph White Highlands', where it's not quite 'English' to touch anyone in church, and certainly not 'Public School'. And then, in the middle, there was that marvellously diplomatic parish where a majority wanted physical contact but a sizeable majority did not. And so they had a 'no-go' area. There was one aisle in which was written in large invisible capitals, 'No Touching Here'. Apparently it worked without any fuss and the capitals were able to come down. Then at the other end of the scale those wonderful parishes where each time they pass the Peace they re-enact Match of the Day. And a few years ago, when hair was longer (and more hairy), there were those parishes where hairy and bearded clergy hurled themselves at everyone in sight. I think it must have been one of these parishes that two churchwardens had experienced when I asked them, 'Do you have physical contact at the Peace?' 'We do, Bishop. But please, no heavy petting!'

But far more seriously than that, we'd like to thank particularly those parishes that had us for weekends - those marvellous weekends spent with you. And I think above all, far more than the big services, far more than the meetings with the young or with the PCC, we remember dividing and separating on the Saturday afternoon and visiting the house-bound and sick and seeing their wonderful example of sensitivity, courage, patience, love and caring. And we'd take away from those parishes little treasures and jewels of Christian love. And we're enormously grateful to you for that.

And then of course I must say that we're most grateful to both Bishops with whom and under whom we have served. Bishop Oliver - that wonderful quality of listening leadership which, you remember, he could always describe so humorously. I remember once, in the old Church Assembly, lurking as I was then as Senior Chaplain to Archbishop Fisher behind his chair, waiting to do his bidding, a new Bishop of Bristol got up and started by saying, 'Having taken up the usual episcopal position of sitting on the fence with both ears close to the ground ...' -and I knew there was something special about this man. Then he had that lovely quality too of managing somehow to remain friends with people with whom he completely disagreed. I treasure the copy of one letter sent to an incumbent firmly telling him not to do something he wanted to do. It ended, 'This will disappoint you, because there's such a lovely streak of anarchy in you.' Who could be cross after that?

And then Bishop John. Well I tried in the Cathedral to say what we felt so deeply personally about him and that I personally, and Joan as well, have learnt so much from his own personal example of quiet courage and realism in his job. And we've learned and take away and value that enormously. And then his tolerance in having to accept his close staff who weren't of his own choosing. All of you incumbents know how you really feel that the parish is yours when all the people you've chosen are in place, however much you liked the others. Well, Bishop John has had to take a lot of us for a long time and his tolerance and patience and acceptance of each other as we are has been something wonderful.

So then to the clergy. Our privilege has been to have been made such close friends of all of you in the vicarages and rectories and clergy families of the Diocese. And though we're as human as any other profession, and there are a few of us who have hearts of gold but are possibly wooden from the neck up, on the whole the Diocese is incredibly well served by its clergy and it's been a privilege to have been welcomed right into your midst and to be made such friends - and we do thank you and value that enormously.

And if asked finally to say what was the major thing I feel from these years together, it is that Eternity is be going to be such fun, because in spite of all the suffering and misery in the world, clearly God must have such humour and such love to have created such quaint, strange creatures as human beings. I've many illustrations I could give of that, but I'll end with just four.

Two from when I was Archdeacon. One of the first things I had to do was to arrange an Institution in a country parish where the church and the manor house were together and the village was some way away and the lady of the house offered us rooms for the clergy to robe in. I arrived early as Archdeacon and she said, 'There are two rooms I've made ready.' And I said, 'Thank you very much. We'll put the clergy in there, and the Bishop and the Rural Dean and the new Incumbent and I will stay in here.' And she said, 'Oh dear, will I be in the way?' And so I said, 'Not at all. We only have some swearing to do.' Without a flicker of a smile on her face she said, 'Oh dear, I'm used to "bloody", but nothing much worse.' I assured her that I didn't think an oath to the Queen would shock her too much.

And then, one time, with the Archdeacon's Visitation, I was worried about whether there were sufficient fire precautions in the church and two of those lovely farmer churchwardens, who always bring Archdeacons firmly down to ground if they're being fussy and bureaucratic, gave two lovely answers. I asked one question: 'Does your church have sufficient fire-fighting equipment?' Reply: 'Yes. Lake by church.' The next question was, 'Are these re-filled and serviced regularly?' Answer: 'Level of lake appears to remain constant.'

And then just two from having been Suffragan Bishop. Some dear incumbents give bishops marvellously annotated service sheets. In one team parish where I was led in in marvellous style by eight churchwardens, the instructions then said, 'Proceed to chair. Turn and bow to dispose of eight churchwardens.' It's not always as easy as that.

And finally. After having preached one evening out in the country at a deanery festival we were taking coffee outside on the grass and two elderly ladies came up to me and said, 'We loved the sermon. It took us back years and years and years. You see, in our parish we have modern ones.' As I was trying to digest that, another person came up to me with a rapturous look in her eye and said, 'I loved the sermon. So simple. Nothing clever about you.' I was grateful for that, because the greatest preacher I've ever heard and ever had the privilege to serve under was Bishop Hall of Hong Kong. He had a tremendous ability to put profound things in a simple way. I asked him once what aids he had to do that and he said, 'Well, there's one prayer I use every time I mount the pulpit - "Lord God, who made me simple, make me simpler yet".' It's a prayer that I've taken on from him.

And so, thanking you all for the marvellous times that we've had in the Diocese, Joan's and my prayer will be that in our pilgrimage together we'll go on searching for those simple profound truths of God shown in Christ.

After the Farewell, Freddy wrote to his family:

We have been living in a marvellous warmth of love, affection, friendship and farewell after farewell, which has been moving but also rather sad. Now we are back to reality and ready to start the new chapter of our life which, once we have got settled in, will be very exciting I think, and great fun. We are already known in Wootton Bassett and folk in The Barton are quite intrigued to be having a retired bishop amongst them. We shall of course be close to friends. The job will be knowing what things to say 'no' to, as already I am being asked to do this and that.

I begin to feel that one must add one more phrase to Grandmama's great comment: 'Marry or die and you are perfect' ought to read: 'Marry, die or retire and you are perfect.' A wise old saint once said about these occasions: 'They do not do you too much spiritual harm if you do not inhale too deeply.' It is rather nice that we are still with an address connected with Malmesbury Abbey as The Barton was the granary part of the monastery in the Middle Ages.

14 Retirement

Incumbents, when they retire, usually go to live somewhere away from their old parishes so that they do not tread on the toes of their successors; in a similar way, when a bishop retires he, again usually, finds a place to live in another diocese. Freddy and Joan loved Swindon and had many friends there, so they had looked for a house within striking distance of their friends. The town of Wootton Bassett, though close to Swindon, lies in the diocese of Salisbury; Freddy and Joan liked the picturesque and bustling town and, importantly, felt they would be at home worshipping in the Parish Church of St. Bartholomew. Accordingly, a year or two before they retired, they had set about looking for a convenient house. On meeting one estate agent, Freddy told him that he and Joan were looking for somewhere small, convenient for the shops and for the Parish Church. The estate agent looked Freddy up and down and then said, 'Is it a terminal house you'll be looking for?' Freddy, being Freddy, dined out on this story many a time; he told the estate agent that perhaps he and Joan would call whatever place they found, 'Terminal Cottage'.

Bede Cooper, who was Vicar of Wootton Bassett when Freddy and Joan moved there, writes:

Yes, we in Wootton Bassett had heard of him. After all, he only lived a few miles down the road, across the M4, that modern boundary between two ancient Dioceses - Bristol and Salisbury. We had read about him in the Swindon Evening Advertiser *and in the* Wiltshire Gazette and Herald. *The local gossip was in overdrive.*

'Have you heard? The Bishop of Malmesbury is coming to live here!'

'No! Where?'

'Down in the Barton.'

'Surely not! That's too small for a Bishop and his wife.'

Such exchanges were probably going on all over the parish. There was a feeling of incredulity. Bishops were rare creatures. Even as clergy, you only saw them very occasionally; down in the Cathedral at Ordinations, or at the Maundy Thursday Eucharist; and every three years at Summer School; and most stressful of all, at a Parish Confirmation when one greeted them with a dry mouth, shook their hand with your sweating palm; bags under your eyes from a sleepless night beforehand, and finding yourself saying as they drove back South, 'Thank heaven that's over!' But now a living, breathing wearer of the purple and pectoral cross was to come among us permanently! Would he queue in Roper's for cod and chips? Or at the checkout in Gateways? Heavens, of course he would probably come to church and worship regularly on Sundays! For a Bishop to come once a year was bad enough for a parish priest, but to have one around all the time would clearly add to this priest's already silvering hair, and increase the furrows on his once serene and young brow.

Well, Bishop Freddy and his beloved Joan did eventually move in. On Tuesday 18th October 1983, 7 The Barton, was taken over. So much stuff was carried inside that little house. Clearly it must have had elastic walls; how else was it possible? All those books, and the splendid furniture, and books, and the pictures, and books, and the statuary, and books, and all those plants, and books. But in it all went somehow. And so it became Freddy and Joan's home - with museum-like overtones. For Freddy took such delight in showing those interested, as I was, the letters and papers and documents to do with Archbishop Frederick Temple; history remembered came alive in that house as one listened to him spellbound, and pored over sepia photographs and the copperplate letters and documents.

The first letter Freddy wrote to his family from Wootton Bassett included the paragraph:

It is lovely to get time to read at leisure again and also gently to go at the garden. I know that this might sound a little trite, but we feel very close to God in the garden, as if in some way we are co-operating with Him in his design for the world. I haven't explained this well, but it's far different from romanticism and would need a theological mini-treatise, which you would undoubtedly find hard to digest along with your Cornflakes. So I'll leave it at that. But if you would like me to expand, I will. I assure you it's not Patience Strong pap.

Although he enjoyed pottering in the garden, Freddy would be the last person to describe himself as an accomplished gardener. He tended to go for instant results, as exemplified by the fact that at the beginning of each growing season, he would go to a garden centre, buy a pot plant or two, put the plants in the garden and stand back, satisfied with what he called 'instant colour'. Not many people know that he was a Vice-President of the Sweet Pea Society; how exactly he obtained this illustrious honour is lost in the mists of time - and is yet more confusing as Freddy was not particularly fond of sweet peas anyway. He would far prefer to grow parsnips. He regarded his Vice-Presidency as 'a bit of a giggle really', but reckoned it would 'look good on my CV.' Freddy's love for creation did not, however, extend to dandelions, which were dug out of the garden and lawn relentlessly and ruthlessly, with a zeal bordering on the fanatical. Joan's approach to gardening was more gentle and methodical; and she talked to her plants.

Freddy was certainly not, however, to allow himself to vegetate in his retirement. Within a fortnight of settling into their new home, he wrote to his family:

Yesterday I chaired an interesting meeting of the Howard League for Penal Reform, but alas you never get many people at them: not a popular subject these days

- but could, amongst other things, save so much money if we came anywhere near
most European countries in what they do as alternative forms of punishment.

By the end of the year, he was able to tell his family that he had broadcast a great
deal on the local Great Western Radio, whose studios were about eight minutes
walk away. One of the presenters on GWR recalled how, whenever Freddy was on
air, many who worked on the station used to stop what they were doing to listen to
him. 'When the Bishop was in the studio', he said, 'there was an uncanny silence
in the building, the only time during a frenetic day.' He also mentioned how fortunate it was that each studio was well sound-proofed because 'when the Bishop was
waiting to do his bit, invariably there was some serious discussion in the adjoining
studio. It would have been unfortunate, to say the least, if the episcopal laugh had
been heard during, say, an intense interview on capital punishment.'

By this time, too, Freddy was also doing valuable work as 'Consultant' to the
Melksham Team Ministry, was being called on for Confirmations in the diocese of
Salisbury, and preached regularly at the Parish Church. He was also in demand as
a retreat conductor. Mary Oakley recalled an occasion when in retirement he led
a weekend retreat at Glastonbury. One woman told Freddy how worried she was
when administering the chalice - as she was a bit shaky at times and afraid of spill-
ing the wine. Freddy's immediate reply, 'Our Lord's blood was spilt for us.' Mary
said that she remembered gasping on hearing Freddy say this, not because she disapproved of what he had said, but because she had never before thought of it like
that. She continued, 'It was, too, the quiet, simple, gentle and immediate way in
which Bishop Freddy made the remark. Incidentally, I tried so hard to persuade
him to record or write down his talks to us - but to no avail. They would have made
such a wonderful gift for a Confirmation candidate as they were the most practical and telling series of addresses I had ever heard - simple, yet profound. That was
one of his many gifts, combined with his gift of words and drama.' Mary herself
was somebody of immense depth of spirituality - and in her own life helped many
others on their spiritual journey.

A retreat Freddy conducted in 1989 was again attended by Mary Oakley, who
remembered that Freddy ended one session by saying that Canon David Isitt had
left the diocese of Bristol for Cambridge a few years previously, and that he had
never forgotten David Isitt's speech at the farewell party. Freddy apparently had a
tape of the occasion and had copied bits down for his own use. 'It made such an
impression on us all', wrote Mary, 'that we asked for copies for ourselves. I would
like to share it with you as an example of the sort of thing that really moved Freddy.' The piece in question was:

I'm told that the Eskimos have a number of strange characteristics. Some of them
not to be mentioned in a place like this. But one thing about their language, appar-
ently, is that they have no word to express joy or pleasure. Not strange when you

think how limiting it must be to live in an igloo. So when the British and Foreign Bible Society came to translate the New Testament into Eskimo, they had a problem. What were you to do with a phrase like, 'There is joy in heaven over one sinner that repenteth'? You can't translate it into Eskimo. But, if you are an Eskimo, there is one very concrete expression of joy and pleasure which you witness every day - when the Husky dogs come home and are unfastened from their sleds. And therefore, when you read your Eskimo New Testament, you will find the agreeable text, 'There is much wagging of tails in heaven over one sinner who repents.'

You have to translate your enthusiasms, your insights, for your neighbour to understand them and for your neighbour to share in them. The translation of ideas is what is sometimes called the educational process. And if you are trying to do it, then you're living in an igloo of the most depressing kind. You may have all the right ideas - about the Christian Faith or about the right way to live - and you may have understood that religion for the Christian is a matter of repentance and forgiveness and joy in heaven. But if there are not real tails wagging in your vicinity, you haven't even started.

Freddy, wrote Mary Oakley, said that those two hundred and fifty words spoke more to him than many a weighty tome on evangelism had ever done.

At the beginning of January 1984 Freddy ended a letter to his family, 'A Happy New Year to us all if that cowboy across the Atlantic can be restrained from seeing everything in terms of cowboy films with goodies and baddies all the time.' By Easter he had been able to tell them that he had been getting more involved with the fair votes campaign. Freddy had been becoming more and more convinced that Britain must have proportional representation if the country was to have stable government - a government which, in his view, was not as extreme as the two main parties of the time. It was not long before he was asked to be President of the North Wilts campaign.

John Baker, the Bishop of Salisbury, at this time asked Freddy to become available as a counsellor and 'listening ear' for clergy wives in any difficulty as they needed someone outside the diocesan structure whom they could consult in confidence: they were so often apprehensive of going to other clergy for fear of letting down their husbands.

Freddy wrote to his family at about this time:

I have joined Probus; I imagine the name is the idea that all of us worthy retired men are so upright and full of probity. It is a good way of meeting folk, but the talks so far have been fairly awful old men's nostalgia for a rosy past that they feel no longer exists - and they are totally out of this world in that they ask two wives to come and do coffee for them at the start of the meeting; no women's meeting would ask husbands to come out and do that. I don't, however, mean to sound churlish about Probus; a wonderful, caring and mostly intelligent group of lovely people. I have made many good friends.

At Easter, he wrote to his family:

> *I've had a letter from the Bishop of Chelmsford, asking me if I would consider being a Consultant to the Harlow Team Ministry. He said that he wanted someone 'of great stature in the Church' to do this. I preened myself for a while (as I was probably meant to do). Joan and I talked it over. Why retire, if you don't retire? I thanked Bishop John and pleaded angina! The task was later offered to Canon Robertson, the retired General Secretary of the United Society for the Propagation of the Gospel.*

By this time, Freddy's Aunt Frances, widow of Archbishop William, had become more and more frail. In March 1983, Freddy had written, 'We found Aunt Frances very bright when we saw her, but almost tearful when we left; it is such a dull existence just being in that bed in that small room: when one thinks of the wonders ahead for her, she must long to go on.' Aunt Frances died soon after Easter, 1984. Freddy wrote to his family in May, 'How lovely it is about Aunt Frances: to think she is reunited with her William and so many others, and the tedious confinement of these last years is over. How much she has learnt through them; she has become a very much nicer, more patient and humble person than she was. We will, however, miss her so much.' Although Freddy often felt frustrated and annoyed by Aunt Frances, who at times seemed to think it her mission in life to mould him into being a 'second William', an underlying deep affection was always there - and her death was, in Freddy's own words, a 'destabilising time'. He also said, 'I have had to make some psychological adjustments.' It is a pity he did not expand on this last sentence. He did add later, though, 'I owe so very much to the love and care and understanding that Frances and William showered on me, especially Uncle William at a time of my life when I was working out exactly who I was and where I was going - and despite the fact that Aunt Frances' showerings of affection felt like being hit by a veritable pluvial deluge.'

Freddy in retirement indulged himself in reading, thinking, talking and writing about politics. Perhaps he was never happier than when reading political biography. In May 1984 he wrote to his family:

> *I find the miners' dispute very difficult to understand; I see the very sober and balanced Archbishop of York has come out saying that it is probably even economically wrong to be closing any pit before it is worked out, as once closed a pit is seldom ever opened again. And we shall in the next century need all the coal we have when oil and gas run out. And then of course it does shatter the whole life of some communities when a pit closes; we learnt when in a mining community how balanced and sane a lot they usually are. I hope it can get resolved before too much harm is*

done to too many. *It is always sad when it comes to a dispute that it has to be someone as extreme as Scargill to fight some of the good points on the miners' side.*

In December of the following year, Freddy was again to write:

*It was excellent that the Government made such wild and stupid comments about
the very mild Church report on inner cities; it really says nothing most reasonable
people would not agree with. But Tebbitt and others have made it a best seller and it
is reprinting fast. It's not often that the present Government have been so helpful
and accommodating to the Church.*

Two months later he regaled his family in a letter with:

*We have been enjoying 'Yes, Minister' very much on TV and there were times last
month when, the programme coming just after the News, one was not quite sure
what was fact and what was fiction, as both were dealing with quite fantastic
events.*

In May of the same year he was asked by the Dean of Durham Cathedral to preach
a series of Lectures on 'Politics and the Church'. Freddy's comment was interesting:

*I suspect Peter [Baelz] wants me to follow the Uncle William line and do a bit of
'blasting off'. I would be quite good saying a few hard words about Thatcher - but
is it worth it? Is 'blasting off' the way to save my soul?*

A year later, in April 1987, he again wrote:

The Times *and the* Sunday Times *have become less reliable since Murdoch took
them to Wapping. It is the reason the* Independent *is doing quite well, refugees
from the* Times, *though the* Times *letters and death columns hold the loyalty of a
lot of folk. Nearly all papers are biased in reporting: one of the worst is the* Daily
Telegraph *because it is so subtly invidious. One tiny personal example is of a
friend who was very annoyed when I became a bishop to read the comment in the*
Daily Telegraph, *'...quite inevitable with his pedigree' - and then implying that it
was solely nepotism of an old-fashioned type. The* Guardian *is always openly critical of any government, and one knows where each writer stands and can allow for
it. Uncle William once preached a marvellous sermon on prayer at a boys' school
but ended by saying that sometimes God does not want you praying or thinking
about him, but getting on with the job. Headline next morning, in I think the* Telegraph *or* News Chronicle, *'Archbishop tells boys to forget God'.*

A year later he was again to write:

I have been talking with John [Webb]. All conscientious doctors are politically radical, very worried about the state of the NHS and how to cope. We used to be proud of a national service we as individuals, responsibly together as a society, asked our government for. Government is not 'them'; it is us. The Government must organise and plan so that everyone when in real medical need can be treated and not have 2 or 3 year delays. Government is us and as Christians we have a right and duty to say how we would like our money spent, on the NHS or tax relief. The really sick are not scroungers doing nothing. There is no way that individuals can contribute to see how more operations can be performed. But the Church is also saying 'loud and clear' that we all must individually help our neighbours. Take the Hospice movement, springing up all over the country - nearly all Christian-inspired and financed entirely voluntarily. We can't now go away in either March or September as Joan alone has so many boxes to collect and count from modest income folk here; she alone hands in £1000 a year and there are collectors everywhere.

The next month, Freddy was to write:

What is happening? I never expected to live to hear a Prime Minister say publicly, 'There is no such thing as society: only individual men and women.' I wonder if she ever goes to Communion and hears about us all being limbs of one body, interdependent.

In July 1991 he observed:

I dedicated a new window to Thomas Becket in Box, a village in the Bristol diocese, this month. The majority of St. Thomas' churches in England are to Becket rather than Didymus. I enjoyed being able to start by saying that I felt a close kinship with Thomas Becket being closely related to two Archbishops of whom the Government of the day could well have said, 'Who will rid me of this turbulent priest?' Remembering the uproar before Frederick was consecrated to Exeter, immense petitions against it, and William and Baldwin over the miners' strike amongst other things.

Freddy also, in retirement, commented freely on the affairs and personalities of the Church of England.

He wrote in July 1984 after the fire at York Minster:

It is very sad about York Minster - but how few folk can have heard David Jenkins or read the script of what he said, and only heard the headline or what they wanted to hear. *The cleric who protested from the lectern admitted that he had not heard him speak or read any script, but just what he had seen in the papers. David is a passionate believer in the Incarnation and stated that he believed in Christ as God and Man, and a passionate believer in the Resurrection. But of course once headlines are out it doesn't matter what you say afterwards; some will not listen. It is interesting for us Temples to remember the violent outcry against Frederick's appointment to Exeter; I have all the letters between Gladstone and grandpapa about this and the petitions from clergy and others. And also interesting to remember that Bishop Strong refused William ordination because he did not like the way William said he believed in the Virgin Birth; it was only the tact and diplomacy of Randall Davidson who, as Archbishop, was allowed to ordain Oxbridge dons that got William ordained at all. Uncle William I remember once told me that during a concert at the Queens Hall the Virgin Birth became clearer to him: I wish I had asked what bit of music. As for the Resurrection, St. Paul in 1 Corinthians 15 makes it quite clear that any spiritual body will be quite different from a physical body; Christ's clearly was: he could walk with close disciples all the way to Emmaus and not be recognised; he comes through closed doors and disappears again; this was all David was saying when he said he did not believe it was a normal physical resurrection.*

As for signs at York: I do believe in some signs, but not in a God who would do that; it does not fit with the sign of the cross. As Habgood said, it takes us right back to the God of the Old Testament Christ came to wean us from. A scruffy young man on the Robin Day question programme said, when this came up, that he would not believe in Christianity when some of its followers believed in a God who would destroy a beautiful old building because one bishop believed certain things.

It is interesting that David has been head of the William Temple Foundation for so long and has had the same tribulations as the two Temples had.

In 1991, he wrote:

One of the most exciting and wonderful things that has happened in the Church recently is the appointment of Jim Thompson, the quite marvellous Bishop of Stepney, as Bishop of Bath and Wells. I just hope that Jim can cope with the mainly rural diocese of Bath and Wells after the wonderful things he has been doing in London. Of course, it's well known that Thatcher couldn't abide him; he really should have followed Hugh [Montefiore] in Birmingham, but the blessed Margaret blocked the appointment. With Jim Thompson at Bath and Wells and John Baker at Salisbury, the South West has two men of outstanding calibre.

We're so lucky in those two. All over the country there have been some mediocre appointments in recent years; I can think of quite a few parish priests in the Church of England who would make absolutely marvellous bishops - kind, loving, caring, intelligent and, most important, spiritual. When is the Church going to get it right? What on earth would Christ say if he were to pop in at General Synod? But that's another matter.

I first remember Jim when he was a student at Emmanuel, Cambridge: he came with his chaplain and a group of students to St. Mary's, Portsea, to learn about parish life; Joan adored him from the start. The other students seemed to her to be a bit 'stand-offish', but they were probably just shy. When they arrived, Joan hadn't finished measuring the study floor for a new carpet; Jim recognised her problem immediately, got down on his knees, did it for her. Joan hadn't finished the meal for them and suggested they go into the drawing room to have a drink. They went. But Jim followed her into the kitchen, and, without being obtrusive, helped.

I thought at the time that he was a wonderful person, but I also thought that in a strange way he was vulnerable. He has sad eyes despite their warmth. Has he, I wonder, suffered? At the same time, also, I knew he was a definite for a bishopric. Strange thought, really. Bob [Runcie] knew it too. After Jim had done a title curacy in East London, he whisked him back to Cuddesdon as Chaplain, where he was justifiably loved by the ordinands.

I've only met Jim once since - but was so impressed with the way he seemed to exude common sense and spirituality, and I won't forget that he was always interested in what I had to say; he used to fix me with a warm gaze, very twinkly, humorous eyes - thank God for making people like Jim. He's going to be a very good Bishop of Bath and Wells. I spoke to Robert [Runcie] at Synod the other day and told him what I thought; he fixed me with his watery eyes and said, 'Thank God he's been recognised at last; you're right; he is wonderful.'

Freddy was sad when, in 1993, John Baker announced his retirement as Bishop of Salisbury - 'I felt in some ways', he wrote to his family, 'as I did when Oliver retired from Bristol, though obviously our relationship, as diocesan and poor old retired bishop, wasn't quite the same.' He continued, 'I wonder what the Holy Spirit is cooking up for our next one?' It was not long before he was able to write:

We've now got a new Bishop in Salisbury, David Stancliffe. He was formerly Provost of Portsmouth - and did a magnificent job there; he has made the Cathedral a holy place and, with much rebuilding and sensitive re-ordering, a spiritual centre of which the City of Portsmouth should be proud. I knew David's father a bit; he was Dean of Winchester and a magnificent preacher: I've borrowed one or two ideas of his myself! In fact, on one occasion, I was an unashamed plagiarist! We served together on one or two committees in London. I knew David slightly before he went to Portsmouth, for he was Chaplain of Clifton College in Bristol. Bishop John will be hard to follow, but if anyone can, I think perhaps David Stancliffe can. His forte is liturgy; but his sights don't stop there. He, like John, will be very much a pastoral bishop. He will care for his clergy and get the most out of them - though I suspect he won't suffer fools gladly. I wonder whether he's going to suffer an old fuddy-duddy like me?

Other letters that Freddy wrote about members of the bench of bishops and others who enjoyed a high profile in the Church of England are not quite as complimentary. With observations like, 'X is now a dignitary, which I suspect is what he has been after since he was first made deacon and - oh dear! - doesn't he stand on it!', some of his comments make entertaining reading. His letters are reminiscent perhaps of those written by his grandfather, Bishop Copleston, in retirement to his friends Mandell Creighton, Henry Scott Holland and Edward Talbot: *The Times* obituarist wrote that he sometimes used 'delightful freedom' in describing others! Some of Freddy's letters were not quite as gentle as those of his grandfather.

Meanwhile, about Freddy and Joan's day-to-day life in Wootton Bassett, Bede Cooper writes:

No.7 was, above all, a home where we found we were always so warmly welcomed. Bishop Temple was also 'Freddy', who so easily and naturally became one's friend. The door of his heart as well as of his home was wide open to us. We went there for supper parties, enjoying a glass in the go-down as the sun cast its evening light across the Dauntsey Vale; for Bible Study; and the knitters for the Children's Society went there with their needles and knitted and nattered; or you could go and just talk with someone who listened and shared and advised and, above all, affirmed you. You always felt lifted up when you had been in his wise presence.

Oh yes - and those Lent hunger lunches; what soups Joan made! People flocked down to the Barton on those Fridays, then would slip into a subsequent conversation, 'When I was having lunch with the Bishop......'. The elastic walls of no.7 took in all and sundry. Every chair was used and every stool; some declared, as arthritic joints protested, 'No really, I am very happy to sit on the floor'; others much preferred sitting on the stairs; while others actually went into the Bishop's bedchamber (oh yes they did) and supped their soup whilst sitting on his bed. That was the preferred place, for then one was able to slip into a subsequent conversation: 'When I was in the Bishop's bedroom....'

When not entertaining at home, you might see them off on some adventure; or perhaps it was only a shopping trip? Well, that too was an adventure as they sallied forth in their Renault 4, with Freddy swathed in his Dr Who scarf in the passenger seat and Joan at the helm as they pitched and swayed along, attracting the admiring (who said apprehensive?) glances of pedestrians from the safety of the pavement.

Not just was it fun to have the Temples at the bottom of Wood Street, but it was so very good that they took such an active part in parish life; helping to hold the fort when I went on my summer holidays; on the panel of an 'Any Questions'; saying the Office as part of the ministry team; spiritual director to one of my colleagues; and someone to whom I could turn in any time of uncertainty and from whom help and advice and prayer and love was never ever withheld, but given so gently and abundantly.

Above all, we will remember him for his preaching. I know not how many sermons have been delivered from that Elizabethan pulpit in St Bartholomew and All Saints Church, but there can have been few, if any, preachers like Bishop Freddy Temple. He would climb into it; he would stand there; the hymn would end; the congregation would sit; he would look slowly around, and into, the congregation; people hardly dared to breathe; his Adam's apple would move; then the beautifully modulated voice would start; gently, or fiercely, and always with magisterial conviction; without a note he said what he wanted to say and what needed to be said; he could also speak with his exquisite hands; and then there would be that explosion of laughter!

One correspondent recalls vividly hearing Freddy preach at the beginning of Lent in Wootton Bassett. Freddy had told them that when he was Bishop of Malmesbury he 'devoured' as many Vicar's Letters as he could manage without getting indigestion. He was surprised by the number of letters which suggested that fasting or giving up things was out-of-date and without purpose. Freddy disagreed. 'I remember well what Freddy said next', he wrote. 'He paused for effect and said, in a sort of stage croak, "The stuffed belly seldom sees visions."' He also recalled Freddy telling them from the pulpit that when somebody told him what he or she had given up for Lent and went on to ask him what *he* had given up, the temptation to answer 'putting up with little prigs like you' was almost too great.

Bede Cooper mentioned Freddy's 'Dr. Who' scarf, which might seem a small matter. But many correspondents have mentioned Freddy's scarves; almost as many as have mentioned his laugh. Indeed, long scarves seemed to have been one of Freddy's trademarks over the years. One former Portsea parishioner said that Freddy would often, in winter at least, arrive on the doorstep, 'looking a bit like an Egyptian mummy, wearing at least ten foot of scarf, coiled round his neck like a cobra.' Of his time as Bishop of Malmesbury, Kenneth Clark wrote, 'A vivid memory, when Freddy arrived at Bishop's Staff meetings, remains of Freddy unwinding what seemed to be miles of woollen scarf after he had removed his overcoat on entering Bishop's House; Joan told me that such scarves were the height of fashion in pre-war Oxford when Freddy was at Balliol, and that he retained his taste for them throughout his life.' A resident of Wootton Bassett made the observation, 'When walking along the High Street I was often accosted by what appeared at first sight to be a walking scarf.'

In 1987, Bede Cooper left to become Rector of Wilton. For a variety of reasons, a year or two later Freddy and Joan began to worship at St. Mary's Parish Church, Calne. Alan Woods, the Dean of Gibraltar, was then Vicar of Calne; he writes of this time:

There were difficulties within the parish of Wootton Bassett. Freddy's loyalty to the parochial system, and in particular to his own parish, made sure he continued to worship there. After a long while he felt he could no longer do so and came to make Calne his spiritual home. This was appreciated by the Calne clergy as there was among us a man of great wisdom and understanding who never tried to interfere, but was always willing to give words of support and advice when asked. He would maintain that his principal ministry was one of encouragement and with various younger, and older clergy in the Calne set-up he ensured that this ministry was fulfilled amongst us all. He never outwardly criticised a sermon, for example, but would always find something good to comment on before he told you how to improve it.

During the Calne period, the time came when Freddy had been ordained Bishop for 20 years. Freddy, as was quite normal, did not want to make a fuss - but the parish, led by the clergy, felt it really should be noted. Bringing Joan in on the planning she too felt it was good to do something, so with her connivance we started to set things up. And when arrangements had got pretty well down the line we were able to tell Freddy what was happening and it was then too late for him to say no. His main worry was his eye-sight and not being able to celebrate the Eucharist properly. When we talked to him we discovered that if the prayers he was going to lead on his own were written in large script in very black ink he could actually read them. (This was before computer enlargement was common-place.) This happened and a wonderful Eucharist took place with many of his clergy and other friends present and playing a part. I hope my memory serves me right that the preacher on this occasion was his great friend and past colleague, Archdeacon Jeffrey Maples. A wonderful party continued afterwards in the church.

The text of Jeffrey Maples's sermon, preached on All Saints' Day 1993 in St. Mary's Parish Church, Calne, deserves to be printed in full:

Blessed are the pure in heart: for they shall see God (Matthew 5.8)

Three men were waiting outside a closed door. After twenty minutes one became rather restive. The normal length of a private audience with the Pope was twenty minutes, said his Chamberlain. For the place was the Vatican on December 2nd 1960. Beyond the closed door was Archbishop Geoffrey Fisher and Pope John XXIII. Two great leaders of world Christianity were engaged in private conversation, aided by an interpreter - the first meeting between an Archbishop of Canterbury and the Pope for over 500 years.

After nearly an hour the Archbishop asked if he could introduce his Chaplains, the Reverend Freddy Temple, whose twenty years of ministry as a bishop we celebrate tonight, and the Reverend John Satterthwaite, later to become Anglican Bishop in Europe. To him the Archbishop dictated an account of the meeting. Pope John had told him that he was most happy as a pastor and disliked ambition. He had been very surprised to be elected Pope. From his ordination as priest he had tried to have three guides for his own spiritual life. First, a love and desire to serve others *always; second, to accept cheerfully whatever was sent; and third, to wish for less more and more.*

Two themes emerge from this encounter - unity and holiness; themes closely linked. The future bishop confronted here some of the problems of Church Unity: how to repair the divisions of the last thousand years of Church history which gravely hamper the spread of the Christian Faith in this and other countries. With the Archbishop he had already visited the leaders of the Churches in Jerusalem, Beirut and Istanbul. The visit to Rome brought about a new atmosphere in Church relations. So it is not surprising that much of Bishop Freddy's ministry in the Bristol diocese concerned pioneering ecumenical work. Even though progress has been slow, Our Lord tells us that the peace makers will enjoy the blessing of being called 'Sons of God'.

In too many Anglican parishes these issues seem remote. We have learned to live with our differences and to ignore Our Lord's desire that his followers should be one. Nevertheless, by the mercy of God, the life of our Church goes on. There must have been a deeply felt contrast between the future bishop's life as Dean of Hong Kong or at Lambeth as Senior Chaplain to the Archbishop, and his next post as Vicar of St. Mary, Portsea. There he experienced at first hand what he once described as 'the problems and opportunities of a vast urban area.' No one had told him that one of the most famous parishes in England, nursery of two Archbishops, was in fact deeply in debt and could only be rescued by the personally costly and deeply unpopular decision to close some of the daughter churches. In Portsea a series of curates were to owe their vision of ministry to their Vicar. Rumour had it that preaching duties were assigned six months in advance, when preparation was expected to begin. The Vicar always preached without a note.

In time the parishioners became possessive and resented the hours their Vicar was expected to spend on the affairs of the wider Church. These included the Church and State Commission, which led to reduced control by the State in the appointment of the Church's bishops and freedom for the Church of England to order its worship, as illustrated by the Alternative Service Book. Happy indeed were those who had hungered and thirsted to see right prevail in this particular matter.

The Church's mission has to be adapted to local circumstances. If it was right to contract in Portsmouth, it was necessary to expand in Swindon, as the one-time railway town developed new industry, resulting in a growing population. As Archdeacon of Swindon, and later Bishop of Malmesbury, Bishop Freddy shared in guiding the Church's response. The Swindon Area Main Churches Committee and its Joint Working Party with the Borough offered scope for working out the ecumenical principle that 'the Churches should act together in all matters, except those in which deep differences compel them to act separately.' So it came about that the new church building in Dorcan, provided with Anglican money, was shared in use by Methodists and Roman Catholics; and the first church in the western development at Toothill, built with Methodist money, was opened by a Roman

Catholic priest and dedicated by Bishop Freddy in a service which included contributions by Baptist and United Reformed Church leaders, and a sermon by the Methodist District Chairman. More was to come. Popularly known as the Bishop of the M4, Bishop Freddy had to convince the diocesan authorities in Bristol that a new town the size of Salisbury was being built on the west side of Swindon - and would need churches and clergy. The Lydiards Ecumenical Team Ministry was one result. How blessed are those of a gentle spirit: they shall see their projects carried out.

But the Bristol diocese, unlike this one of Salisbury, does not have Area Bishops - and the M4 was the route to much pastoral activity: visiting, preaching, confirming in Bristol and beyond, as in the numerous smaller towns and villages in between. This work has continued in retirement on both sides of the diocesan boundary. Perhaps this ministry in parishes will be the deepest source of satisfaction of this bishop and the best remembered by others - for people are remembered long after the plans and projects which demanded so much effort. John XXIII was not the only bishop to be most happy as a pastor. I understand that one of the most dog-eared books in Bishop Freddy's extensive library is Journal of a Soul, the record of John XXIII's growth in holiness.

For is it not the primary role of a bishop to help people to recognise their need of God - in the words of the Gospel tonight - and so qualify for the Kingdom of Heaven? Or in other language to be a leader and shepherd of God's people? The first reading tonight, from the current service for the Consecration of Bishops, spoke of the gifts of the Spirit needed by leaders of God's people from ancient times and recognised by the Laying on of Hands. The second, from the Prayer Book order for the same purpose, provided what we might call a check-list for a leader's qualities. It would be too embarrassing for us all to go through it in detail, but some phrases might be noted. For example: husband of one wife. Bishop Freddy would be the first to acknowledge the support of Joan in numerous stressful situations, as well as in the task of hospitality, gratefully experienced by many in Arnold, Newark, Manchester, Hong Kong, Lambeth, Portsea, Swindon and Wootton Bassett.

Together they have also experienced the consolation promised to those who mourn. And again, in the words of tonight's Gospel for All Saints' Day, it may often fall to a bishop to have to adopt an unpopular decision on social and political issues and to suffer persecution for the cause of right. At the same time he is to have a good reputation with the outside world - as many in the public life of Swindon could testify he did.

Consider what is the purpose of all this work - this striving after unity, managing change. Chairing meetings and conferences on such topics as Stewardship, Family Life, Missionary Outreach, Youth Work and Education, travelling, preaching, counselling. Surely it is to promote the way of life with which Christ challenges us in the Gospel. Are we among those who hunger and thirst to see right prevail, who have ceased to be satisfied with ourselves, who seek to build constructive relation-

*ships, to be generous in our judgements, to care for those in need, to treat others
with understanding? These attitudes took Jesus to the Cross and the Resurrection
which we celebrate in every Eucharist. The Gospel tonight stresses expectation
and hope, confidence in a Kingdom which always lies ahead, whether already in
this life or beyond. As a lady of ninety-three said to me a few days ago, 'I am always
looking forward; never back'. The Church exists to proclaim the vision of the
Kingdom and attract people to accept it. So the bishop in Confirmation prays for
each individual, that they may daily increase in God's Holy Spirit more and more
until they come to his everlasting kingdom.*

*'O Lord, we are now in the evening of our life', wrote Pope John XXIII in
1957; 'I am in my 76th year. Life is a great gift from our heavenly Father. Old
age, likewise. A great gift of the Lord's must be for me a source of tranquil, inner
joy; a reason for trusting day by day in the Lord Himself, to whom I am now turned
as a child turns to his father's open arms'.*

*Blessed are those whose hearts are pure, the single-hearted in service of God and
man; they shall see God. So we prayed earlier in this service, 'Cleanse the thoughts
of our hearts by the inspiration of your Holy Spirit'. We thank God for a ministry
directed to advancing the claims of God's Kingdom and the work of his Spirit in
many human lives. For the goal of all this endeavour is the vision of God. Blessed
are those whose hearts are pure: they shall see God.*

Madeleine Evans has contributed the following about Freddy and his time in
Calne:

*I was always aware of his support for the ministry of women in the Church and was
grateful for his interest in me. I came to Calne as a deacon and it was while I was
there, after nearly eight years in the diaconate, that the moment came for me to be
priested. There was no doubt in my mind that I wanted Freddy to be one of the bishops who would assist at my ordination. To my delight he agreed. The Vicar, Alan
Woods, helped Bishop Freddy on to the rostrum where the ordination was to take
place and stood by his side as the bishops laid their hands on my head. It was a wonderful moment for me and I am sure that Freddy was glad to have had a hand in the
first ordination of women to the priesthood.*

*Not many weeks later I discovered that I had cancer and the overwhelming sup-
port I received from Joan and Freddy among my many other friends was wonderful. I was cosseted around with prayer - and Freddy and Joan were great
'pray-ers'. They delighted in belonging to a parish prayer and study group and their
presence was much appreciated. Freddy always put his many gifts at the disposal of
the parish.*

*It was a real joy to me when Freddy agreed, with the Bishop of Salisbury's per-
mission, to confirm an old man who was dying in his own home. Freddy insisted on
his full episcopal robes to make it an occasion - and he was right, for the widow nev-*

er forgot how wonderful it all was. With his usual consideration Freddy insisted that I should celebrate the Eucharist, and we all shared in John's first communion at the side of his wife, who had been a regular communicant for years. From then until John's death Freddy and Joan kept in touch with them - and thereafter with the widow. You can imagine what that meant to them both. This was not to be the last of Freddy's confirmations, for a little later he also confirmed another older lady in church at a weekday service and gave her all the happiness she had been missing in her regular church attendance over the years. She was grateful also for his kindness and understanding of her timidity and shyness, which had kept her outside the sacramental life of the Church for so long.

Some time later Freddy produced a prayer for the parish to use and it was fascinating to discover that he had summed up the people in Calne, and felt that the particular phrase about complacency was important:

'Lord God of love, open our minds and hearts to your creative power and give us the sensitivity to see you at work in this world. May your love cleanse and strengthen us. May it shine in our homes and in the community. May your love renew the Church in Calne and free us from all complacency in belief and practice. Give us a fresh vision of your glory; and a new understanding of your power, that under your guidance and with your strength, we may extend your Kingdom in this place and throughout the world; in the name of Jesus Christ your Son, our Lord. Amen.'

Madeleine later concludes her observations thus:

As life goes on, perhaps we all become more outspoken about the things we see going on around us, and Freddy was no exception to this rule. I suspect that this was one of his qualities or faults (depending on how you see it) always - but it became more pronounced as the years were added to his life. Sometimes he put his foot in it and told someone what he really thought when they were busy pouring forth their opinion to him. It caused hurt at the time, but often needed saying. Perhaps he forgot that what a bishop says carries a good deal of weight, and he was certainly sorry when people were over-sensitive to his words: they were never meant unkindly, but were an attempt to get at the truth.

We were so blessed in Calne by the presence of Freddy and Joan in our congregation: for their obvious spiritual life, their kindness and love which they shared with so many. They were a wonderful team and drew strength from one another.

At about the same time as Freddy and Joan moved their place of worship to St. Mary's, Calne, Peter Giles was ordained priest in St. Bartholomew's, Wootton Bassett. Freddy agreed to preach at the ordination. Peter writes:

My abiding memory of that sermon is the picture Freddy painted of priesthood as a call to the role of servant to God's people. His own life and ministry epitomised

such a role. In the context of extreme tensions within the parish at the time, his ser-
mon was brave, challenging and controversial. I sensed that Freddy was never one
to hold back from saying in public what he believed in his heart and I came to realise
later what the open expression of his pacifist views during the second world war
must have cost him personally.

Peter continues:

Although humble himself, Freddy was quick to use any opportunity to give value to
others. It would have been so easy for his wife Joan to have lived in his shadow and
I suspect he would have disapproved of her being introduced as 'the Bishop's wife'.
I remember an occasion when Freddy was introducing Joan. With a twinkle in his
eye, he said, 'May I introduce you to Joan, who is a person in her own right!' Al-
though I cannot recall, I suspect Freddy might well after such a remark have dis-
solved into those gales of laughter with which all who knew him would have been
familiar. I have quoted this particular remark on more than one occasion in wed-
ding addresses, when emphasising the importance of newly-married couples giving
value to each other's individuality within their union.

The problem arose of Freddy's increasingly poor eyesight. Freddy himself had
written to his family in May, 1986:

My eyes have gone wrong. I went to see if I needed new glasses and the optician did
a test to see if I had pressure in the eyeballs; he got very excited and said he must ring
my doctor, kept telling me there was 'absolutely nothing to worry about' so often
that I knew there was; he told me to see my doctor the next day, and Dr. Bliss, who
is very good and straightforward, told me I had glaucoma, and arranged for me to
see a specialist in Swindon. I hope he can halt its progress.

In October of the same year he wrote again:

It looks as though glaucoma can be hereditary. Grandfather Frederick had bad
sight: even when he was Bishop of London he had sometimes to be helped down-
stairs; but ahead and upwards he saw quite well - and continued to write 4000 let-
ters a year in his own hand.

His comments about his sight grew a little more poignant. One day in 1989, after
he visited Kingston Lacey with Joan, he wrote, 'It was so full of interest, but all the
blinds were half-down in all rooms, so I found it *very* dark indeed and difficult for
my eyes. But I enjoy hearing others rhapsodise.'

Again, he wrote in November1991, 'I am taking a Confirmation on Sunday in
Bristol; the bishop has a burst peptic ulcer, poor fellow. I can still hit a head and

know the Confirmation bits by heart, so if people warn me of steps, all is well. But the eyes get steadily worse.'

In October 1996 Freddy wrote simply, 'My eyes get worse, so I write by faith!' The following year, in November, he told his family, rather sadly, that the letter he was writing was the second attempt. 'The first attempt, Joan has just told me, I have written all over the table!' Although he ended that sentence with an exclamation mark, there can be little doubt that he found his increasing blindness difficult to come to terms with.

Later in the same year, Freddy wrote:

We were invited to a party at a country parish near here on Friday; the Rector was celebrating the twenty-fifth anniversary of his ordination and I had been invited to preach. After the service we adjourned to the Village Hall, a rather old and rusty tin hut, for 'eats', which I must say were very good. Then came a presentation of, I think, a fairly substantial book token. And then some speeches. The Rural Dean spoke adequately, as Rural Deans tend to do, and a fellow student of the Rector from Cuddesdon days spoke quite brilliantly. And then one of the churchwardens was called upon to give a speech. Well! What fun! He was a delightful Wiltshire nonagenarian. His speech MUST have been ghost-written. It included the word 'panache' three or four times. The dear man kept pronouncing the word 'panache' as 'panic'. So he said things like, 'Everything our Rector does is done with panic' and 'The Rector is so full of panic.' If Christopher [Martin] had been there we would have been beside ourselves with merriment and would undoubtedly have disgraced ourselves. Without Christopher's encouragement I just managed to hold myself in check. This sort of thing makes some days so brightly jewelled ; I thank God that, though my eyes grow dim, my hearing has not been taken from me.

Amazingly, while his sight was deteriorating rapidly, Freddy lived life to the full. As Kenneth Clark observed, 'Everybody admired the way both Freddy and Joan coped with increasing blindness and disability. Joan learnt to drive and they went regularly to the theatre; she would explain what was going on. She also read to him every day, and they welcomed visitors, thus keeping closely in touch with all that was going on. They had a European banner over their doorway; they did not hide their politics.'

At about the time of his diagnosis, he wrote to his family:

We had a visit to the Barbican to see A Comedy of Errors last week. Degree-giving was going on in one hall and we saw a young male punk, single cox-comb of purple and blue hair on his head: in hood and gown he really looked rather splendid. His mother looked as though she was sucking a lemon. Father in blue pinstripe suit, was nervously toying all the time with a superb set of gold cuff-links. Good luck to the boy. How I love the freshness and exuberance of the young.

The Bishop
of Malmesbury,
on- and off-duty.

Freddy and Mina concentrating on a game during Freddy's retirement.

Freddy and Stephen enjoying some family photographs after Freddy's retirement.

Freddy and Joan loved having the time to go on extended holidays - in this country and abroad. Freddy invariably wrote a diary of each one. Although they continued to take holidays when Freddy's sight was failing, the description following is of their 1985 holiday, while his sight was reasonably healthy:

We have had a wonderful time driving some 1700 miles or so through France; it is so wide and open and empty in the west of France that it is no strain to drive at all. It was great fun to get back amongst the French and to use the language. We would buy our picnic lunch of baguette or brioche, cheese and trois jolies tranches du jambon; how surprised they would be in Swindon if I were to ask for pretty slices of ham - but I heard it in front of me one day in a shop and it always got us more interest and better slices thereafter. This would be followed by peaches, melon and other fruit. Each day we chose some lovely spot for lunch, nearly always in brilliant sun and heat.

We drove down through Tours and then on to Le Puy, staying there a night; the cathedral and cloisters there are very good. And we found the Virgin was dressed in different clothes for the season of the year, as the Buddha was in Bangkok; she was a black virgin like that of Rocamadour which we saw last time in the Dordogne.

Each evening we parked the car and then usually Stephen and I went in search of rooms, either Relais Routiers hotels - transport cafés in England, but the French lorry driver demands a really good meal and a clean room for very little - or one star. We were astonished and delighted to find that still the French don't plan ahead and, even in August in a busy place, if you stop before 4.30pm you get in quite easily and for very little; though by evening they all have their 'Complet' signs in place.

On from Le Puy to the Gorges du Tarn, staying at La Malène for a night and taking the boat through the wonderful gorge and then a taxi back. Then on to Avignon, which we loved; full of gentle, long-haired young making their metal jewellery and giving the place so much colour and vitality. The famous bridge is not up to much and involves a long climb up in the heat. The papal palace was good and full of good stuff. There we saw rather a pleasant country circus.

From there to Nîmes via the famous Roman bridge which we walked over. It always distresses me that the clever Romans never tumbled to the fact that water will rise again to any point not quite as high as its source; it would have saved all those massive aqueducts.

The reason of course for the cheapness of the French hotels is that there can be no trade union of workers and they work flat out from early morn till about 11 at night; we found always the same one on duty for the petit déjeuner as was rushing quickly and efficiently between masses of tables at night. Meals take a long time as there are usually only one or two to serve a full restaurant - and so many small courses all freshly served on new plates. Again we were struck by the discipline and quietness of the typical French country family; small children, black-ringed with tiredness, sat up at meals, being angelic as Mama and Papa quaffed the vin and ate the pain; Joan has seen so many fat youngish men and women that she has come back resolved to slim some more.

From Arles we drove into the Camargue which has been discovered in a big way and was packed out; a disappointment - though I was interested to see there signs that Christian youth were taking action and trying to stir folk about the long hours and abysmal pay of the saisonniers, the holiday workers. From Arles to Narbonne, which had not a great deal except a wonderful long letter from Mina waiting at the Poste Restante; a great delight and thrill. From there to Carcassonne - though commercialised, still very fine and striking. What a quiet race the French have become; a restaurant full of French and hardly anything can be heard; a park is the same. A package tour of Germans arrived and the noise was terrific. It is surprising they don't find it odd to talk so loud when a war memorial nearby lists those civilians 'fusilées'. I found the French very friendly; one dinner companion said, 'Il faut jamais oublier que l'Angleterre a sauvé le monde tout seul en quarante.'

From Carcassonne we started back, stopping last Sunday at Albi, which is quite fantastic; what a cathedral; each of those statues is so perfect and yet no one knows the name of any of the artists, just that they were Burgundian. And yet how awful that the Cathedral was built as a fortress to crush the Albigensians, who were in some ways the heralds of the Reformation. It has always been a part of history I have enjoyed. The Son et Lumière in the evening of course slanted everything on the side of the Church. At Carcassonne we also saw a perfectly lovely Flemish pietà. We had a superb meal in our Relais Routiers there. On the next day to Edward I's little town of Montpazier with its walls and covered streets and arches; very attractive. Then up to the Loire to a chateau we had not visited, Saumur. We also looked in on the Abbey of Fontevrault on the way, where some Plantagenet kings are buried; we apparently now and then try to get them back to Westminster Abbey, but the French say that as they were Dukes of Anjou this is where they should be. The extraordinary kitchen there is good evidence for the need of the Reformation; so many cupolas each with a chimney so that, we were told, seven different patisseries could be prepared for the Abbess at the same time!

I ought to have mentioned that we were in Albi for the evening service and somewhat astonished and charmed to be told near the beginning by a youngish French priest that the fact that we had all come from the cooling refreshment of our own houses into the heat of the afternoon, be we habitués of the Cathedral or tourists, was, we could rest assured, giving the Virgin great satisfaction. Then the reading was announced - from the writings of St. Bernard who, we were told, 'was a specialist on the Virgin', and would be from one of his famous sermons against the Albigensians. At this, the other two Temples, whose French is not so strong, asked if we could leave.

At Saumur we saw something I had not met before - a rather charming figure of

St. Anne holding the Virgin her arms, who in turn was holding Christ in hers. From there to Avranches so that we could visit Mont St. Michel; packed out, though we went early, as we had heard they had 7,000 visitors a day. The few monks there now make speedometers; rather charming monastic work. And so home.

One of Freddy and Joan's last trips abroad was in 1996. Alan Woods writes:

As Freddy and Joan were personal friends as well, when I was appointed to be Chancellor of St Paul's Anglican Cathedral in Valetta they dropped the hint that they would like to visit. They came out to us in May 1996 and not surprisingly made a great impression on the congregation which as always included many visitors. One of these spoke to Freddy at the airport as they were leaving and said he was the person Freddy had mentioned in his sermon. Freddy had been talking about the difficulty sometimes in coming to worship in one's own community if you have not been a churchgoer and how much easier it is sometimes to go somewhere whilst on holiday. Freddy also stressed the point that one needed the courage to move into one's own home community and perhaps the holiday worship could be that spur. This same visitor on a subsequent visit to Malta said that he was now worshipping regularly and preparing for confirmation.

1997 was a specially happy year for Freddy and Joan: they celebrated their Golden Wedding. Friends from all periods of their life together flocked to Wootton Bassett for different parties. In addition to family, amongst others present were Freddy's Balliol friends, Ashley Raeburn, Stephen Verney, Madron Seligman and Edward Heath, and friends extending through the years right up to the latest friends they had made in Wootton Bassett. There were many, many messages of congratulation, amongst them one from Edward Heath, which summed up the feelings of many:

Warmest congratulations to you both on your 50th Wedding Anniversary.
Together you have enjoyed a wonderfully full life, the crowning mark of which has been service - service to God, to the Church and to others.
We all owe you a deep debt of gratitude for your contribution over so many years to the welfare of all your parishioners, diocesan members and friends.
Thank you, again and again and again. Ever yours, Ted.

However, as people were preparing for the new Millennium, many of their friends were distressed to hear the following from Joan:

After seeing a consultant and various tests we learned that Freddy has cancer of the prostate and, after a fall, his left leg ceased to bear him and he became unable to

311

walk; we learned again how kind people are when troubles beset us - we have had endless kind and unselfish acts and offers given to us. One neighbour comes most days, morning and afternoon, to help Freddy walk with the zimmer across from his chair to the hall into his bedroom, turning zimmerly at the end wall and back again; through John's perseverance and Freddy's great effort he can now do this without a rest! When trying to transfer Freddy from chair to wheelchair or bed he lands on the floor in the middle. Many friends are ready to come running, literally, night or day to the rescue.

So now you know the sort of fun we have! In a bleak mood one can feel on a treadmill of deprivation and loneliness - then you look at the newspaper and feel how sinful you are! Or we have a visit from our wonderful, kind doctor and feel secure.

On one occasion Freddy, in the middle of the night, fell on the stairs. Joan could not lift him and, rather than disturb friends, decided to dial 999 for the fire brigade. A fire engine appeared rapidly and, in Joan's own words, 'four or five strapping young men emerged.' She continued, 'I felt a little bit silly, but they, the dears, seemed to think it the most natural thing in the world to be lifting an old bishop into bed in the early hours of the morning. They were so gentle and kind - and there was much laughter, from them and Freddy.'

On November 4th 2000, Freddy was to send his last letter to his extended family:

Joan and a friend have spent a long time looking at various nursing homes for respite care. They have chosen one as the best and it waits on the husband of the partnership who run it, to tell us when there is a vacancy. They hope this will be soon. So it looks as if all the worry of so many relations about getting Joan a breather with me in respite care, is moving. I shall feel so much less guilty when I hear on the 'phone that something is going to happen.

Freddy settled in comfortably at Ashdowne House. Joan, of course, visited regularly. Roy Blake wrote of a visit he made:

When I heard from an ex-churchwarden of St. Mary's that Freddy was ill and in a Purton nursing home, one I used to visit regularly and to which I took the Blessed Sacrament, I decided that, although I had kept away from my old village as much as possible, I was sure my successor would not mind me paying a visit. I went over that evening, and found him in a small, narrow room, sitting in a small chair, listening to a tape of a politician's memoirs. I have an idea it was R.A. Butler. His head was down, and for a while he said very little and rarely looked up. But when I said that although I didn't go to Bristol often nowadays, I had just returned from a visit and that everyone - knowing that I came from the Swindon area - had asked,

'How is Freddy?' and sent their love, his head came up and he asked to be remembered on my next visit. He smiled. I'm so glad I was able to tell him how much people cared for him. And I shall always remember the way he looked up and smiled. I left a birthday card with him, on which I wrote, 'To the best of all bishops'. And so he was. Together with Bishop Oliver.

Then came the news by telephone - followed up with a letter - that many of his friends had been half expecting for a while. Joan wrote:

Our darling Freddy collapsed and died on 26th November, 2000. We are so grateful to God that he does not have to suffer any more: he had been wonderfully patient in a no-life situation. It is just so glorious to know that he can now see, walk - run even! - and respond with talk and laughter and love with Michael and all the dear others there.

At Christmas, 2001, Joan was to write:

You may well remember that last year our Christmas letter had an enclosure telling that Freddy had collapsed and died on Sunday 26 November. Most of you knew that his health had been failing for some time but even so his death was quite a shock. All through October and November our life was really quite full and busy - we had many friends in pairs to coffee and phone calls from family and friends. People had been worried about me so it was decided that Freddy would go into a nursing home for a fortnight for me to have a rest. Margot Butler and I chose Ashdowne House at Purton, a village nearby, out of those we went to see. Freddy and I went in the afternoon of Monday 20 November, were welcomed to Ashdowne House and Freddy settled into his room. Each day I visited all the afternoon; mostly we went up to his room. On Friday 24 November it was his 84th birthday and sherry lightened the afternoon for everyone, and a beautiful cake, inscribed in icing 'Best wishes, Bishop Freddy', was carried in by the cook who had made it.

On Saturday Stephen arrived and we stayed with Freddy all afternoon and into the evening, when others came. Freddy knew that this arrangement was only for a fortnight and, though we did not care for bidding each other goodnight, he had settled well. On Sunday we were just about to pack up the car, as we were going to visit Freddy for an hour and then drive to Stephen's flat in Balham for me to stay till Thursday when I would be back to visit Freddy and bring him home on Saturday. But the 'phone went from Ashdowne House; Freddy had collapsed. He was being dressed and laughing and chatting, but as the nurse got him up from the bed he collapsed on to her. We said we would meet them at Princess Margaret Hospital in Swindon.

At the hospital we waited and waited; four ambulances came, but no Freddy. Finally Stephen went to the car to phone Ashdowne House and I sat on the seat

313

outside Casualty saying, 'Lord, please take him - go, Freddy, go.' Freddy and I had talked together many times and I had told him not to hold on for us - we would manage somehow. Stephen came back; Freddy had been too ill to move, but they were now getting him into the ambulance. He arrived and we were taken through straightaway to the 'Resus' room. It was like an emergency scene from 'Casualty' - a group all round the bed and a lady doctor gently using a hand-pump. Freddy's arm slid off and I held his hand. I said, 'I don't really want you to do this.' They went on in silence. 'I really mean I don't want you to do this - he is 84, blind, has angina, cancer of the prostate and cannot walk or stand on his own; this is a no-life for him.' The staff nurse, a Canadian, had her back to us but said, 'We are hearing you.' The doctor looked all round the group and they nodded; she stopped pumping and gently put it down. We were led to the Relatives Room opposite and sat close together on a sofa. The doctor knelt beside us and said, 'It was very good that you said that; we have to go on trying, but when we know how the relatives feel it is a great help to us.' Staff Nurse also came in and said some kind words. Later, after a police sergeant had filled in a form, we were left on our own. Suddenly, out of the corner window which showed a little bit of sky, we saw a bright piece of rainbow and we both knew that it was all right with Freddy; he was on his way. Three times we saw the rainbow - the last as we drove away from the crematorium; it was not raining, but there was a marvellous arch of rainbow in the sky between the trees - it was wonderfully, marvellously comforting. A lovely message!

Freddy's funeral service, at Kingsdown Crematorium, Swindon, was simple and unpretentious, led by Jeffrey Maples (who gave the address), Peter Giles, the Rural Dean of Calne and Bob Kenway, the Vicar of Calne. Other bishops and clergy sat in the congregation. Freddy's body lay in a coffin made of cardboard. A few days later, Freddy's ashes were scattered in the garden of their 'terminal cottage', a beautiful garden in the creation of which Freddy had played a great part, and in which he delighted. It was a simple ceremony, with few present. Prayers and the Committal were said by his nephew, Rupert Hoare - a former Bishop of Dudley who had recently become Dean of Liverpool.

In the following February, a moving Service of Thanksgiving took place in Bristol Cathedral. The Cathedral was full. The address was given by Ken Preston, a priest in the diocese of Bristol, and a close friend of Freddy and Joan. He said from the pulpit:

This is not a sermon - I am just going to talk about Freddy. I am going to give you a text none the less, because I work on the principle that if you give people a good text, then if the rest of what you have to say is rubbish, they have got at least one thing worth remembering and taking away with them.

My text is from the Acts of the Apostles: 'He was a good man, full of faith and of the Holy Spirit.' In Acts those words are said about Barnabas but I reckon they could be well applied to someone else who is not very far away from our thoughts at the present time.

But I'd like to begin with Shakespeare. Freddy was a great theatregoer, a regular at Stratford and Bath, and so it seems appropriate to begin with a quotation from Shakespeare. It is from Julius Caesar. At Caesar's funeral Mark Antony says, 'My heart is in the coffin there with Caesar.' If this were Freddy's funeral, which it is not, and his coffin were here, which it is not, I expect we would all be saying 'My heart is in the coffin there with Freddy', such affection and love did we have and still have for him. Except for one thing. Freddy would not be in that coffin. Whatever was in that coffin it wouldn't be Freddy; he would be already risen, as he is, and in that new life, the resurrection life.

When Freddy preached at my wife's funeral eight years ago he said, 'Don't think of January the sixth as the day Mary died; think of it as her birthday, her heavenly birthday.' So we don't think of the twenty-sixth of November as the day Freddy died; we think of it as his birthday, his heavenly birthday. And this is his birthday party, a celebration of his life and a thanksgiving to God for all that he has given to us through Freddy's ministry and personality.

So where is Freddy now? I ask this question quite deliberately because I want to give the answer that I heard Freddy give to similar questions on many occasions. He used to say, 'The next life, the resurrection life, isn't up there or out there; it isn't a long way away, it's all around us. We are living in the midst of it. We can't see it because we're not in it. When we are in it we shall see it. Until then it is all around us.' So where is Freddy now? He's very near to us.

And what is Freddy doing now? Again I ask this question quite deliberately so that I can give the answer that I heard Freddy give. Freddy used to preach and talk about that lesson from St. John 14 that we have just heard read: 'There are many dwelling places in my Father's house. If there were not I should have told you. I am going now to prepare a place for you, and after I have gone and prepared you a place, I shall return to take you with me; so that where I am you may be too.' I don't think Freddy would have gone along with the translation 'many dwelling places'; he would have preferred 'many rooms', providing that you thought of them as rooms in an inn or lodging-house where you stayed for a night or two before going on further. He thought the Lord was likening himself to the dragoman of those days. In those days if a nobleman was going on a journey the dragoman would go on ahead, find the lodging-place for the night and return to conduct the traveller to the place where he was to lodge. So what is Freddy doing now? I think from Freddy's teaching we may think of him as travelling on in his pilgrimage from stage to stage, growing in love and holiness until he comes to that perfection to which the Master is calling all of us. I think we may assume, too, that Freddy is praying for us. He was a man of prayer in this life and there is no reason to suppose that he will be any different wherever he is. And if there is any way in which those in that life can help us in this, then I think we may assume that he is doing his designated task.

Freddy. How can I put Freddy into words? Of course I can't. I doubt if anyone could, not even the Bard himself. How, for example, can I put into words that warmth - you all know what I mean by that - that warmth of personality that made you feel when you were with him that you were the most important person in the world to him. It's all right, Joan dear, and Mina and Stephen, we all know that you, together with Michael, were the most important people to him - and if any of you don't know the reference to Michael, Michael was their eldest child who died in Hong Kong at the age of six and was always and still is as much a part of that family as he ever was. But Freddy had that great gift of making us feel as important to him as you - and that is a wonderful gift. And while I am on the subject, we all saw that great love that you had for Freddy - and it was not surprising because it was love, for love. The love you had for one another was wonderful; no, I am not going to use that word; I am going to use one that Freddy used sometimes to describe things: marvellous. I can hear him saying it now - marvellous - the love you had for one another was marvellous and an example and inspiration to us all.

And then there was Freddy's humour. So many people have spoken to me of Freddy's sense of humour. One friend of his said that Freddy could make an ordinary story sound hilarious. And then there was that laugh. An organist said to me, 'I was sitting at the organ on a day when Freddy was coming and I heard that laugh and I thought "Freddy's here" - and I felt the better for it.' That was another of Freddy's qualities - he made you feel better; he affirmed you. But to come back to Freddy's sense of humour. Freddy had the true sense of humour, the sense of humour that enables you to laugh at yourself. I remember Freddy telling me of an occasion when he had been preaching. Two women came and spoke to him. Their comments were obviously meant to be compliments but Freddy turned them round as a joke against himself. He said, 'I was standing at the back of the church and a woman came up to me and said, "Thank you for that sermon; so plain, so simple; nothing clever about you."' Freddy continued, 'I was just digesting that when another came up and said, "Thank you for that sermon; it took me back years and years; you see, in this church we have modern sermons."'

Someone said to me that although Freddy was so kind and gentle and loving, yet he was no pushover. He was very shrewd in the best sense of that word; he could see the point at issue in anything; he could see through shams, whether of persons or ideas. And when occasion demanded he could rebuke. I can remember only one occasion when I received a rebuke from Freddy, and that rebuke was so full of love and kindness that it was all the more penetrating. The best way I can describe it is by ripping some words out of their context in the book of Revelation and altering the meaning somewhat. Freddy's rebuke was the wrath of a lamb.

Freddy came of a great ecclesiastical family. I remember him saying that there were six archbishops in his family, but Joan says that it was four, and I suppose I must accept her version - though at lunch time I raised the question with one of Freddy's sisters. In the end the consensus was that there were five. But four or five

Freddy concentrating on the crossword in the garden of their retirement home in Wootton Bassett. The M4, with which Freddy enjoyed a love/hate relationship, runs through the valley in the middle distance.

Freddy and Joan in retirement relaxation at Avebury.

Freddy and Joan relaxing at Bowood during retirement.

archbishops in a family is not bad, though, is it? Together with several bishops of various sorts thrown in for good measure. But, as someone said to me, although he came of such a great family it never made him stuck up or proud. Freddy had a great humility about him.

Some ten years ago Freddy's health began to fail. First he began to lose his sight. In the end he became totally blind. But before that and while he could still preach, because of his little sight he had to walk about very gingerly and had to be led in unfamiliar places. This made him look so frail that when he was going up into the pulpit you were frightened to cough in case he fell out of it. He usually prefaced a sermon by saying, 'I'm all right below the eyes.' On one occasion - though not when he was preaching - I said to him, 'Freddy, I'm more interested in what you're like above the eyes.' I think he then changed to saying just that - and, above the eyes, he was as brilliant as ever. I said that, going up into the pulpit, Freddy looked so frail, but as soon as he began to preach he was electric - he was electric! Listening to a sermon by Freddy was an experience - you felt that he was not only communicating the love of God; he was living it.

As well as going blind, Freddy developed a heart condition and suffered from angina; he had difficulty in walking and he had cancer of the prostate and all the side effects that go with that. But Freddy never complained; he endured it all with great courage and fortitude and cheerfulness. And he never talked about his ailments. To find out anything I used to have to drag out of him how he was. I used to say, 'Come on, Freddy, I want to know how you are bit by bit; I want an organ recital.' You could say about Freddy that he bore the worst of things and made the best of things.

I said at the beginning that Freddy was a great theatregoer. He was old enough to remember the old Music Hall. Whether he ever went or not I don't know, but he would certainly be acquainted with the standard opening gambit of the old stand-up comedian: 'A funny thing happened to me on the way to the theatre this evening.' Well, I can imagine Freddy arriving in that new life, on the next stage of his journey, arriving there, on that Sunday morning, looking around him and saying, 'A funny thing happened to me on the way here today.'

Bede Cooper's earlier observations ended:

Oh, what a laugh he had! Can you not hear it still? Does it not ring round the very courts of heaven? I give thanks to God that this Bishop came and made his home among us; that he encouraged us and inspired us and helped us on our way; on the way that brings us, in the end, into the presence of the loving, forgiving and most merciful God and Father of us all.

At Freddy's Thanksgiving Service we all sang the hymn, which had been sung at Freddy and Joan's wedding, at Freddy's ordination, and at a host of other significant occasions during Freddy and Joan's fifty-two years of married life:

O Thou who camest from above,
The pure celestial fire to impart,
Kindle a flame of sacred love
On the mean altar of my heart.

There let it for thy glory burn
With inextinguishable blaze,
And trembling to its source return
In humble prayer, and fervent praise.

Jesus, confirm my heart's desire
To work, and speak, and think for thee;
Still let me guard the holy fire,
And still stir up thy gift in me.

Ready for all thy perfect will,
My acts of faith and love repeat,
Till death thy endless mercies seal,
And make my sacrifice complete.

Many think that Freddy was joining in the singing too.

appendix i   Sermons and Addresses

Many people were greatly influenced by Freddy's preaching; in the words of one correspondent, 'Bishop Temple exercised the remarkable gift of profound preaching, couched in terms of deep simplicity.' A number of them have mentioned that they would appreciate reading a selection of his sermons. The great problem, however, is that Freddy almost always preached without notes. One of the few occasions on which he preached from notes was at a service to mark the opening of a legal year at which, in Freddy's words, 'there was more than a spattering of judges, barristers, solicitors and other ne'er-do-wells and I certainly did not want to be served with writs afterwards because I had injudiciously slandered anyone.'

No sermons survive prior to Freddy's tenure of the Deanery of Hong Kong. The *South China Morning Post*, however, kept an old-fashioned tape recorder in the vestry at the Cathedral and taped most of his sermons and subsequently printed many of them in the columns of the paper. Dr. Alec Vidler, in the late 1950s, suggested that a selection of these sermons be published; a choice of twenty was made and the sermons were edited. The project then, however, ground to a halt. The eight sermons printed below are a representative selection of the twenty.

The epilogues delivered on Associated Rediffusion Television are printed as delivered. No other sermons or addresses survive from Freddy's Lambeth or Portsea days. The sermons printed from the time when Freddy was Archdeacon and Bishop have been edited from tapes made at the time, acquired from a variety of sources, as was the memorial service address which he delivered in his retirement.

Nothwithstanding the difficulties over material, I was also more than a little apprehensive as to how the sermons would read in cold print. The words do not quite capture the way that the sermons or addresses were delivered: the occasional long silence between sentences; the sudden change of voice tone; the sort of stage whisper - to be followed by a gleeful exclamation; the searching look in Freddy's eyes. Freddy never lost his acting touch. For those who knew him well, the rather cold words can be read with these thoughts and images in mind - something more difficult for those who never heard him preach.

It is a pity that none of his sermons delivered at public schools can be put on paper. Word must have got round the Headmasters' Conference that it would be worthwhile to invite Freddy to preach, for his papers contain many letters from Head Masters testifying to how much the sermons were appreciated by both staff and boys. Many of these letters were not just the sort of perfunctory thank-you letter that one would expect a Head Master to dictate to his secretary on Monday morning. The letters teased out things that Freddy had said and included comments made by both boys and staff. What I found interesting was that, although Freddy religiously followed the biblical readings for the day, the texts of sermons delivered at public schools were invariably not biblical. Some bordered on the cynical; some were downright cynical. Perhaps Freddy thought this was an essential element in talking to teen-age boys of the mid-twentieth century. I suspect too that Freddy must have employed a modicum of ingenuity in order to get the two - the text and the biblical readings - to complement and elucidate each other. The contribution from his uncle, William Temple, to the list below is the most orthodox!

I let out an Archimedean cry of delight when I stumbled across the following list of 'texts' or opening sentences Freddy had used when speaking to boys at public schools at various times during his ministry:

(1) *A crank is a small instrument that causes revolution.* [E.H. Schumacher, after saying that he did not mind being labelled a crank.]

(2) *Christian, noun: One who believes that the New Testament is a divinely inspired book admirably suited to the spiritual need of his neighbour.* [Ambrose Bierce: *The Devil's Dictionary.*]

(3) *Parsons always seem to be specially horrified about things like sunbathing and naked bodies. They do not mind poverty and misery and cruelty to animals nearly as much.* [Susan Ertz.]

(4) *If Jesus were to come today, people would not even crucify him. They would ask him to dinner, hear what he had to say and make fun of him.* [Thomas Carlyle.]

(5) *Say what you like about the Ten Commandments, you must always come back to the pleasant fact that there are only ten of them.* [H.L. Mencken: *Sententiae.*]

(6) *Men of simple understanding, little inquisitive and little instructed, make good Christians.* [Michel de Montaigne: *Essays.*]

(7) *The most serious doubt that has been thrown on the authenticity of the biblical miracles is the fact that most of the witnesses in regard to them were fishermen.* [Alan Binstead: *Pitcher's Progress.*]

(8) *I went to the Garden of Love,*
And saw what I never had seen.
A Chapel was built in the midst,
Where I used to play on the green.

And the gates of this Chapel were shut,
And 'Thou shalt not' writ over the door,
So I turned to the Garden of Love,
That so many sweet flowers bore,

And I saw it was filled with graves,
And tomb-stones where flowers should be:
And Priests in black gowns were walking their rounds,
And binding with briars my joys and desires. [William Blake.]

(9) *I am greater than the stars for I know that they are up there and they do not know that I am down here.* [William Temple.]

(10) *People may say what they like about the decay of Christianity: the religious system that produced green Chartreuse can never really die.* [Saki (H.H. Munro): *Reginald on Christmas Presents.*]

(11) *Sunday, bloody Sunday.* [Penelope Gilliatt; film title]

(12) *An elderly cockney man and wife were in bed when the air-raid sirens sounded.*
Husband : 'Down to the shelter; quick.'
Wife: 'Let me just get my teeth.'
Husband: 'They're dropping bombs, not bloody sandwiches.'

[Reputedly a joke told him by one of his successors as the Archbishop of Canterbury's Chaplain; used by Freddy as an introduction to a Remembrance Day sermon.]

It is certainly intriguing to think how Freddy developed his themes.

Sermons and Addresses: 1953-1989

Preached at S. John's Cathedral, Hong Kong

Remembrance Sunday 1953

Every year as this Sunday comes round we come face to face with the problem of peace, the problem of how we human beings can live together without killing each other every few years; and it is frightening and humbling to realise how little progress we make. It is easy to forget it: to get so busy in our private lives that we never look up to gauge our wider responsibilities: as easy to do that out here as it is in England; or if we do try and face the situation we swing from one extreme to another.

It is interesting to notice how differently men reacted at the end of one war to another: in the twenties it was a common thing for ordinary church folk to be supporters of the League of Nations in more than vague goodwill. Money was raised; meetings were held at which its principles were taught and understood; Christians toured the country speaking, convinced that support of the League was vital to any Christian belief: the success or failure of the League became synonymous to some with the success or failure of the Church. There was eagerness and there was optimism: the ideals were so good that surely everyone would follow them automatically. And so when difficulties came, the disillusionment was complete: and after the failure of the League, England slipped into one of her worst periods of foreign policy and looked for scapegoats elsewhere. And yet her Foreign Secretaries were sincere Christians: it was because they had not a sound public opinion behind them. And so came, in Churchill's phrase, 'the unnecessary war.'

At the end of the 2nd War opinion had swung to the other extreme: 'once bitten', now they would be cautious and realistic: what good could come, they thought, from the United Nations; it was just a meeting place for disputes and wrangles. Amongst groups of ordinary Church folk little interest was raised: meetings drew pitiful numbers compared with the League of Nations meetings. All these international ideals were of no use, was the common thought: we all had enough to do living our own private lives as best we could. And so, without much heed, the world was allowed to go on its way: and here we are today, most of us not daring to look up too much for fear of what we may see.

Of course there was much good in both points of view. At the end of the First War, there was a real vision of God's Kingdom on earth: a real longing for a reign of peace - and many Christians worked hard and long for it. But it was shallow and not realistic enough: men did not realise how small a part reason plays in human affairs: to assert with the mind that a thing should be done is not to get any distance on the road to doing it. The selfishness, the laziness, the lack of energy to want the things that make for peace, was all underestimated: under cover of grandiose schemes and ideas, men forgot their own selfishness, their own sin.

After the Second War, most men realised that we had to start much further back, much deeper down: that was good: that to draw up plans and schemes did not touch the root of evil. And it is marked how much of a swing there is in England away from the social gospel of the twenties and thirties to a deep personal religion of commitment to God: a new understanding that the quality of individual life is all important; without that, the most ideal scheme will founder. But with this new understanding went a cynicism which saw little hope in working for any collective ideal: a cynicism which ceased to bother much about the other person. And so the United Nations Organisation and international foreign policy seems to be just what our cynicism expects: and Christians do not take an active and informed part in it - and we are denying the power and activity of the Holy Spirit at work in history, waiting and longing eagerly for our co-operation.

As Christians we ought to have been on the lookout not to step into these two faults. The fault of over-impatience and easy optimism with which the ordinary person starts a new organisation and expects everyone to take to it immediately. It starts with a great spurt and then withers away wen it meets real indifference and real difficulties: it lacks guts and lacks depth of ground for its roots, like the sower's seed.

It is equally wrong to keep out in disillusionment and leave it all to others: that was the fault of Luther. He told his followers that a Christian must obey the State and do all it commands, as long as State does not interfere with what a Christian believes - well described as the faithful housewife who implicitly obeys her husband all over the house, but woe betide him if he comes into the kitchen. And so in Germany they largely abdicated politics and left it to secular control. In the main, Christian opinion is doing the same today.

If we had known our own doctrine well enough, we would have realised that man can live by God's laws, but not in his own power; we would have welcomed the greatness of the ideals and gone all out for them - but would have known the original sin within us all and been ready for the difficulties and problems of it all, and that it is only with the power of the Holy Spirit that we can hope to live in that harmony with others and make those organisations work which are framed to that end. It is for us to go wholeheartedly into all the organisations which aim to improve man's condition, national and international: for we who are Christians can give that stability, that lasting power to them; because we do not rest our hopes only in this world; we do not expect full success to any human venture: we know too much about the frailty of man for that: we do see the vital necessity of improving the conditions under which men can live as Christians now and prepare for eternal life. We shall be ready for all the upsets and struggles of human men trying to live as Christians and work together: and far from discouraging us each time they happen we shall turn in greater dependence to God to over-ride our jarring, fractious wills - and then God can use us. We must not stand aside: the solution is an international one: world famine or world war are the crucial prob- lems facing anyone under fifty. And they are the old problems: can men unite and learn to live together? It is the problem Demosthenes had with the city states of Greece: the same problem the nations of Europe had and now the continents of the world face: can men will the things that make for peace? That is the question: not, why do men want war? No-one seriously does: but not enough of us really will and work for the things of peace: and it does mean hard work and thought: to un- derstand our fellow man and to recognise in him, wherever he is, in Russia, Eng- land, China, Japan or Hong Kong, someone of infinite value in God's eyes, whatever his present state; of the same infinite value as ourselves, and to help each other to realise our true value. And by ourselves we can't do that: indiffer- ence, personal dislikes, are always raising barriers between us; and then slowly but surely the world drifts in private life, in public life to a state of war: only under the shadow of the Cross can we get enough love and understanding to start that task, because only then do we realise how much understanding God lavishes on you and me. Only then can we be worthy of the great opportunity bought for us by those who died. And in this city what a witness the Church should make to the fact that every single individual is of infinite worth to God, is a member of His family and each one of us has continually to understand and care for each other. To live and act indifferent to that fact is to make for war, however charming your private life may be. No prayer for peace will be of value until it is backed by a life of striving for peace and understanding with all men, particularly with all living close by us, by loving our neighbours as ourselves.

Christmas Day 1953

Today marks the difference between Christianity and all other religions. If any-one in simpering tones suggests to you that after all, all religions are the same, aren't they, and why do we not let everyone believe what they like, point to Christmas Day. There, right at a certain moment in history we see that God acted and came to us as a human baby. God acted; not God commands that you do this or not do that. Other great religions have their prophets who tell people what God demands; no other says that God acted. That is why today is our great day of hope and happiness; if God is only outside the world, telling us through great men what to do, then we shall be miserable however good we may be; we shall only live a life of heroic despair; for we can only flounder if we are left to ourselves. And the more we discover and understand of the world, the more dangerous our flounder-ing becomes.

Today is important not because of what it tells us about Jesus but because of what it tells us about God; if Jesus is not God himself then today is no more impor-tant than thousands of other birthdays of great men. That is why the Gospel for today is from St. John's Gospel, not just the simple narrative of the event but the interpretation of the event, for that is what is important. 'All things were made by Him and without Him was not anything made that was made.' The world was made by Him. Let none approach the baby in the crib with patronage in the heart or condescension; let no one say how nice for the children and neglect the crib himself; for it is God Almighty the maker of the stars and atomic power who lies there trusting in our care and love. So great is his love and goodness that he has come and still comes so; that is a cause for wonder and happiness for us; it is also a cause for awe and fear, for it means that God is not someone remote and far away; he has come right into our lives, right into the most trivial details of everyday ex-istence; he has shown his 'big-ness' in little things.

And like anything great that God offers, we can either accept Christmas for what it is, God's coming to us as one of us, or neglect it as a charming fable, as a charming interlude from reality. If we accept it, then we see how great we are meant to be; he came as a baby, as a human being, for there was no greater way he could come. He did not come as cloud or thunder or lightning; he came as man. Nothing is as great as a person; human character is the highest thing we know. Is your character the highest thing your friends know? God expects it to be; and like a real friend he will not cease to try to make it so. He came into his own; we are God's if we would let him take us and mould us every day. He came in trust, right into the heart of dirt and evil and suffering; do you shun those things, shut your eyes to them - or do you go out to redeem them and conquer them? He came in such trust; nothing could be more trusting than a new-born baby, completely de-pendent on the help of others; if God trusts so, how tremendous is your responsi-bility in everything you do.

It means that God cares for every side of life, be you Government administrator, teacher, soldier, lawyer, artist, housewife, factory worker, servant, farmer - whatever it may be. With all His power, God in his love trusts and expects the best; and is ready to go to any lengths to get the best. 'Let there be light; and there was light.' So easy did God find it to create the world. But to win men to their best, through penitence which is greater than innocence, *that* demanded Christmas with all its neglect, all its squalor, and all the love and devotion of Mary. Even at the start Mary for all her happiness must have realised a little what terrible ordeals her baby boy was going to go through; what a hideous gift myrrh was; to be reminded of his death at the start.

The Saints who follow straight after Christmas Day show us a little what that facing of the world means; you will notice in your prayer book that the three Saints' Days which follow Christmas are put in amongst the other Sundays of the Christian year, not tucked away amongst the saints. For they tell us how we must observe Christmas and understand it. St. Stephen tomorrow: the first martyr, stoned to death. A sharp warning to any who have here on Christmas Day not meaning business; not realising that Christianity means courage. Love and understanding of the faith mean little without a foundation of sheer guts to see them through.

St. Stephen is followed by St. John: plain courage is no use - even villains have that - unless it is informed by a lifetime of love and loyal service to Christ like John's; a love and loyalty that transforms the character as it transformed John from the impetuous young man with the mother who spoilt him into the disciple who could write the Fourth Gospel. So do not come to Christmas unless you are ready for God to change your character for the better; that may mean giving up many failings you rather enjoy, many weaknesses you have got accustomed to.

Following courage and love comes the slaughter of the Innocents: for just those two qualities are needed if we are to understand the tremendous suffering of the innocent that goes on; the hideous evil in the world caused so often by the reaction of bad men to good things. It was God's coming that caused the slaughter of those boys; nothing else. If Jesus had not come all those mothers would not have been weeping like Rachel for her children; Christmas caused just that; Christmas faces just that.

And so if your observance of Christmas is genuine, it must mean business. It is not a child's festival; it needs courage, and a patient love and understanding of a lifetime of loyal service to Christ; only then can we hope to fathom the chaos and misery of this world. Only then will Christmas be real to us now, as it was at the beginning. Only then shall we really understand that God came into our life alongside it, to face it with us. Only then can we wish each other a really happy Christmas.that goes on; the hideous evil in the world caused so often by the reaction of bad men to good things.

Easter Day 1955

'And they said nothing to anyone; for they were afraid.' So ends the earliest historical account we have in the Gospels of the Resurrection; St. Mark's Gospel originally ended there, with the women running away frightened by what they had seen of the empty tomb and the young man inside in white. 'They said nothing; for they were afraid.' It has been well said that this text should be up in every parson's study as a warning against glib speaking on the great themes of God. And here in the Resurrection we touch God's power and majesty at its greatest; this conquest of death, the inevitable crisis facing each one of us. It is no wonder that the women were afraid; there is in the Easter story a great and deep joy and strength, but only for those who have had their own complacency and self-sufficiency shaken to the utmost.. There must be no fitting in of the Easter story to the mental furniture of this world; it belongs solely to God and the next, to show us that we belong in the end there as well.

It is a great pity in a way that Easter comes in the spring, as so often the Resurrection is whittled down to the re-birth of nature in spring, which is then going to die again in the autumn. Christ rose to die no more - Christ who claimed to be God, whom the respectable people in the world has killed because they were unable to fit him in with their small scheme of life without his disturbing it too much and too radically.

Pilate represented the good government of Rome; a good government indeed - such a good Public Works department with its roads and buildings, up-to-date sanitation for the time; such an excellent record of peace through its army and police. But the good men responsible for government at the time could not bother with him; administrators must be practical and have little time for abstract moral and theological ideas. 'What is Truth?', they ask - and seldom stay for an answer.

The religious leaders of the time could not fit him into their rigid scheme of ethics and worship; his trust in man's freedom seemed too dangerous to them and his claims were too big; it was sad, but one man must die for the people. The cultural leaders in the Sadducees did not want him disturbing their plan of quiet absorption of all that was best in Greek and Roman thought by the Jews; he threatened to disturb their educational programme. And the common people, who had hoped that he would give them what they wanted, had cheered loudly on Sunday and turned to curses and shouting on Friday; and his close friends, his friends who had been with him for three whole years, were shattered and fled. No wonder the women were afraid when they found that he had not been conquered by death; he had been victorious. All his claims were true; where would they all stand with him now? They who had all failed him so badly.

It is surprising how often the word 'fear' comes in the New Testament; it is a salutary corrective to the charming, polite Public School picture of a Jesus just teaching good manners and ethics. 'Fear not', say the angels right at the start, when first God's power bursts in a new way into the world. The man called Legion is healed and the keepers of swine nearby are so panic-struck that their fear is conveyed to the swine, who rush down the slope and are drowned. So the neighbours, coming out to see the man now sober, are frightened by this sign of God's power and ask Jesus to leave. Jesus comes across the stormy seas of life to his disciples, walking on the water - and they cry out with fear. Peter, James and John seem him transfigured on the mountain as he sees what God's purpose for him is - and the glory of his radiance frightens them. He tells them that the Son of Man must suffer - and they were afraid to ask him what he meant. He strides up to Jerusalem in front of them, and they follow behind - afraid. Those are a few of many examples; and all through we find Jesus saying, 'Be not afraid; fear not.' His coming brought with it fear, for it shook men's small and shallow security - the security of paddling on the shore. He told them to be real men and launch out into the deep.

The opposite of faith is not a mental agnosticism, but fear in all its forms; fear of insecurity, fear of being discovered for what one really is, fear of sickness, fear of death. And God came in Christ to win us from those fears, to trust and surrender to him. In Christ he was ready to go to any length to do that, and on Easter Day God vindicated his power and his goodness and his love. But, at first, to frightened disciples who had not been able before to trust in him when they saw him giving himself up; when they could not believe that God could still win. To frightened disciples, then, God's power must have seemed overwhelming; they could not believe that his forgiveness could still have them back. And so he moves amongst them saying, 'Fear not: peace be with you' - a peace which comes when you know you have enough resources for the tasks in hand. We have peace of mind when we know we have enough behind us for the jobs we have to; we only panic when we feel unprepared and uncertain what may come. Christ comes at Easter with such assurances; but he only comes to those who have been shaken to the utmost; to those who have realised to the full that they have failed. He did not appear to any but his frightened and scattered disciples: it would be no use for him to come to those who had not been shaken - as they still believed they could manage on their own, and so were in no position to accept what he could offer; they did not see their need. Only to those who knew their need could he come in the certain historical fact of Easter, and say that God is always victorious in the end in his own way. Trust in him and you need have no fear; whatever the sin and suffering in this world, it is already conquered; you have only the mopping up operations to complete; trust and be at peace.

So he comes to us. But we cannot receive that assurance and that certainty unless we see how completely our own ideas and plans for our own salvation, and the world's, have failed., until we know what the fear of the Lord is - what it means to face the power and glory of God. Until we have known that, we cannot know the peace of God. But when we do, we can come just as those first disciples did and humbly confess our failure and desertion; and then be sent out with all the power of his resurrection, full of peace and confidence to live and work as he did. He   *327* came unto his own; and his own received him not; but as many as received him, to them he gave the right to become children of God. The right to become children of God on the same terms as did; through facing the reality of the world, not avoiding it.

Harvest Festival 1955

Christianity is the most realistic and practical of all religions, the most material. You have only to look at the references to bread in the New Testament, and follow them through, to get a clear-cut miniature of the Christian attitude to material things.

Jesus was a workman, not an intellectual, or a rich man who had no need to work for his living. Nor was he a prophet or priest who lived on the gifts of others. God came a s a workman into the world, to bring the great good news of his love and care for all men. To do that he worked quietly and unknown for thirty of his thirty three years here.

After his baptism he goes into the desert to think out his mission, how to carry it through. And the first temptation is to do with bread; give hungry people enough to eat and they will follow. Give men the elementary needs to live; stop starvation and they will follow. It must have been very tempting. But he rejected it as a way to win men to God.

But he did not reject the need for bread in its right place. In his model prayer it comes after the petitions of God's Kingdom and the hallowing of his name; only then can the need for material things take its right and proper place. And the model he gives is, 'Give us this day our daily bread.' Give us each day our daily needs; needs, not luxuries; we are not to pray for extras, for luxuries. And it is 'daily', not monthly or yearly; we are not to ask for the certainty of this year's daily needs but to be confident enough will come for each day. Too often we pray and live for the certainty of years of comfort and security.

Our daily needs have their place in God's strategy but not our yearly comforts. When the five thousand are in the desert Christ is concerned to feed them. He can use the prudent generosity of the lad with five loaves and two small fishes, prudent because he had remembered to bring his lunch with him; if he had forgotten, God could not have fed those crowds. Generous, because he was not concerned about his own lunch but ready to give and share what he had. Christ the Workman delights in hard work and prudence, with a readiness to share when there is need. He takes the loaves and gives thanks, so certain that God can use that offering and then through his disciples feed the crowd - through his disciples, not directly himself, he uses men to distribute the fair shares of his material blessings. The feeding of the poor is our concern and must not be left to God alone. And then when the feast is over, Christ gathers up all the crumbs, so much does he dislike any waste or squandering of his material bounty.

After that meal, the crowd wanted to make him King, and he slips away from them up into the hills to be alone with God, to recover his balance and his poise. He will not be made king for that reason. He will never allow us to make Him King in our hearts if it is only in order that we have sufficient material things that we want him there. God is continually slipping through our grasp when we claim him for that reason alone.

And the next day he tries to teach them the right place of material things. 'Ye seek me not because ye saw signs but because ye ate of the loaves. Work not for the food that perisheth but for the food which abideth unto eternal life which the Son of Man shall give you.' To work for just material things is to work for something that dies and brings no satisfaction. But then Jesus adds that the living bread which he will give for the world is his flesh. At that, many of his disciples grumbled and murmured that it was a hard saying - and left him. He alienated many would-be followers by what he said. Why did he do it? Because he wanted to be sure that our devotion to him and worship of him should not just be vague and airy; a sentimental choosing of those bits of the gospel we like; a following of the spirit to worship when we feel like it and where we like. We all know that type of person. Christian devotion was to be pinned down to a specific act of his and a specific time, to be centred on his death for us, for you cannot eat flesh unless the person die. And there is nothing sentimental about death; it is hard and realistic and is the acme of self-sacrifice. We are to receive that type of living bread, the bread of complete self-sacrifice, taking into ourselves all the power of Christ's life given in his death and resurrection. Our worship must be centred in that definite act of self-giving. And so it is at the heart of the Communion service. There we offer up our material work in the bread, the symbol of our activity during the week, to have it broken by Christ, who is host at his own table - broken for two reason: first, it must be broken because it is not adequate or good enough unless purged of all self-complacency before Christ can use it as the means by which he comes back to us; secondly, it must be broken to be shared. We cannot keep it all intact. Then the broken and shared Christ can use it as his own instrument to come back to us as living bread, eternal bread.

Such are some of the thoughts to guide us at Harvest Festival time. God understands and delights in our hard work and care in gathering in the good fruits of his earth: he is concerned that each man has what he needs. But that is not the real bread for which to labour: we are to work for the bread of life which can only be won by joining in God's self-sacrifice to the limit; from that comes the bread eternal for life eternal. And so we have to keep that God-given balance which the church always finds so difficult; the right concern over material things. At times the Church and Christians with their social gospel have been over-concerned about bread, and asked God to succumb to the first temptation and tried to make him King to give them material things. At other times Christians have forgotten our Lord's concern with the thousands. He did not say, 'I am only interested in teaching: it is no concern of God what you eat.' But he took the prudent offering of the boy and used his Church to distribute God's bounty to those in need. Here in Hong Kong there are clearly thousands in need. Are you offering all you have for God to use and bless? Or are you keeping it back, frightened there may not be enough left, wanting to keep it intact? But if your offering is to become a 'living' one full of God's power, it must be broken in pieces for God to use and to share with everyone. Only so can all our material things be instruments of real eternal life.

St. Barbara's Day (Patron Saint of the Royal Artillery) 1955: Gunners' Service

Very little is known about St. Barbara. We know that she was young, very beautiful and had a jealous father who kept her locked in a tower for fear lest a young man should come and marry her and so take her away from him. There in her solitary tower she studied the wonder of the sky and earth and, through the servants who brought her food, she heard of the great Christian teacher Origen, who later sent her one of his disciples, disguised as a doctor, who converted her to Christianity; her father was so angry with her that he denounced her to the Roman Government; the Consul, Martian, tried to get her to renounce her faith and worship the Emperor. When she refused, her father with his own hands cut her head off; then immediately fire and lightning consumed him and the Consul, Martian, completely. A strange story and one doesn't know how much of it we are to believe: but with certain important lessons to be learnt from it.

St. Barbara is little known; we know very little else about her except her goodness - and yet here you all are, because of her, assembled in this Cathedral today, because of the goodness of a young girl. Her father and others who lived with her, far more important at the time, we have forgotten; but her we remember. Her courage too we remember, standing firmly for what she believed right no matter what the consequences; no compromise at all. It was such a little matter to bow before the Emperor's image and cast the necessary incense on the shrine. She had but to do this and live; and still she could have been a Christian in her heart; but she was going to have no compromise at all. How many of us stand firm always for what we know is right when it is so much simpler to keep quiet? When something dishonest is being done by those around us? When something untrue is being said? When something foul is discussed? It is ultimately the good and brave people who change the world; not the proud, the powerful or the wealthy.

The other thing we learn from her life is that finally all the powers of the world are under the control of God's goodness and are meant to be used for his purposes. In that rough story of the thunderbolt killing her father is the truth that goodness is finally vindicated because it is what God wills; we see that supremely on the Cross where Jesus died for what was God's will; no compromise with him either; courage to go right through to the end; he refused the anaesthetic of wine mingled with myrrh to deaden his pain; he saw all his friends desert him; supreme goodness died there, but God vindicated it by raising him on Easter Day. At moments we find it difficult to believe that the forces of the world are under any control; as we wait for a typhoon; as we see what tremendous powers scientists find in the atom; the power for good and evil to be found in injections; used either for healing or to distort the brain in the concentration camp. Terrific powers to be used in the world; for good or evil. Surely the discovery of atomic power was planned by God to coincide with the discovery by men that half the world is starving and that new means must be discovered to feed and clothe the millions of undernourished and homeless folk. It is a sign of the chaos and misery of the world that at the first all the research and wealth of the world has to be put into finding ways to use that power for destruction.

You may soon be using atomic artillery; and in the present state of the world you have the duty and privilege to be called to guard and defend the better from the worse; but whether the better will not become worse depends finally and completely on the personal lives of each one of us; the goodness of the man behind the gun is in the end more powerful than the power inside the gun. That is the main thing I want to say to you today; every time you do what is right, and stop what is wrong being said and done, you are exercising a power far greater than atomic power; for you are allying yourself with the heart of God's power as shown in Jesus; in the end it has more effect. It is the only thing which changes the world; the powerful, the proud, the wealthy, the dishonest may rule for a time, but in the end it is the good and the Christian who are remembered - whose ideas and influence have most power.

We are all getting ready for Christmas. The lesson of Christmas is that if we do not want God to come in with us, if we are too busy with our own preparations, then we do not stop God - but he will go elsewhere; his purpose will go on. Hardly anyone knew when they turned away a tired man and a pregnant woman they were turning away God Almighty; but God showed his power by coming as a help-less baby; so much did he trust you and me; so confident was he that in the end goodness would triumph even if it meant the suffering on the Cross first.

So on this St. Barbara's Day we can take heart that in the end it is our own per-sonal lives that matter, that are the really powerful things in the world; much more powerful than any gun you may have to fire. Because the good influence of your life will last long after the explosion from your gun has gone. If you wonder how one life can have so much effect, let me remind you of a story told in a recent number of the Colony's paper, 'Outlook'. At a big military tattoo suddenly all the lights were put out and a voice in the darkness asked everyone in that vast audi-ence to strike a match. It was a strange request but slowly, one by one, laughing, people complied; here a light was struck and there; and then in a few minutes the whole arena was brilliantly and adequately lit. 'Thank you', said the voice, 'you see that by individual efforts of each person, darkness is turned into light.' And the show went on.

Ordination 1955

No clergyman forgets the Gospel set for his Ordination day. You who are being ordained this evening are fortunate. You have a very suitable Gospel, the story of the healing of the nobleman's son, the story which St. John puts second in his series of seven signs or miracles to show the characteristics of a Christian life. This story illustrates the one quality needed, faith; all other qualities of intellect and character are useful extras, but faith is the one vital need. Most scholars think the story is another version of the healing of the centurion's servant which St. Matthew gives us, the centurion of whom Jesus said, 'He had not found so great faith, no not in Israel.' The centurion's faith had three main characteristics. They are not more important than each other; rather they are facets or sides to the jewel of faith, each equally important and all related to each other. But we must look at them individually.

The centurion was humble, obedient and he expected things to happen. Humble because he would not allow Jesus to come under his roof. That is a cardinal quality of faith, humbleness in front of God; we are not told that the centurion was humble in front of his fellow men with the mock humility which would not take responsibility. But faced with Christ he knew he was nothing; that must be the keynote of any ordained person's life, complete humility before God. God has to work through us and we must be nothing. You will find it very, very difficult, as we all do. The more gifted you are, the more successful you are, the more difficult it becomes; our very keenness to do the job well makes it so hard not to bring our own personality between our people and God. It is true that God is humble enough to use our weak characters to draw men to Him through us; but we must always be a ladder or path, not a fence at which men stop. We must be humble enough to know that the winning of any man to Himself is His doing and never ours, something that will happen in his own good time and not before. The longer one has in the ministry, the more one finds oneself completely baffled as to what finally turns a man to Christ or what keeps him away; humanly you may have tried everything in the way of reason, friendship and sympathy, with no result. Then something wins a man over and you realise that it has been none of your doing. There are deep recesses in the characters of each of us which only God and sincere prayer can touch. Only our humbleness before God will stop our energy and abilities becoming fussy, over-worked and self-centred. So we must safeguard our times of prayer, when all our work and plans are offered up to God for judgement, correction, guidance and strength. We are nothing before God. God is so good and so great that nothing can be too good or carefully prepared for his service and worship. This brings us to the second quality of the centurion.

He was obedient, recognising in Jesus someone under a greater authority than he was, 'I am a man under authority also.' We are under authority; we must be obedient and careful in very little things. We who traffic daily in spiritual things can so easily become slipshod and slovenly in our ways. We all know the vicar who is the loudest talker in his own church. You must be obedient in your life of prayer. Enthusiasm and goodwill may carry a layman a long way in his prayers; but it will not last any priest long who has himself to talk and teach of Christ. The journey in prayer becomes more arduous, not less. Christ is always moving on, demanding more of us - and we soon find if we are not scrupulously obedient in all the little details of our prayer life that he has gone on and we are left talking about Him second-hand. And what a travesty of preaching that is, however much it is decked up in scholarship and academic knowledge. Little will go permanently wrong if we are always obedient in prayer, in moments of dryness at least clinging to our rule of saying the Daily Offices. From an obedience in prayer will come a life of Christian freshness and vitality which will not be self-concerned and which will automatically show an obedience to God in daily living.

And if we are humble in our nothingness before God and obedient to his calling, we shall always be expecting God to do great things. No one with any vision of God's power and creative activity can become bored or automatic in his dealings with men. We must always expect God to act; no ministry without such an expectancy has a cutting edge or challenge to it. Never preach without expecting God to convert someone, possibly only because of the weakness of your words. I know of one man converted when the Provost of Southwell got into the pulpit of Southwell Minster before a packed congregation and said with considerable embarrassment, 'I am sorry there will be no sermon; in my prayers just now it became clear that what I had prepared is totally unworthy and inadequate. We will now sing the next hymn.' The Provost was a man of spiritual depth and humility; he was certainly not lazy, intellectually or otherwise, and he had definitely spent much time preparing his sermon; he certainly had not simply omitted to prepare anything. All his sermons in the past had been engaging and challenging. In the afternoon, in his confusion, he received a note from a man who had been there, 'That was the greatest sermon you have ever preached' - and one more layman is now actively winning men to Christ. Never preach without expecting God in his great humility to use even you. Never visit without prayer of expectant hope as you ring the bell or knock on the door.

We have all known God use the simple visiting card slipped through the door when no one is at home. Never let any part of your parish life become dull or monotonous. Jesus took the ordinary things of life and lit them with new meaning and hope to show men how God is at work amongst us. We can do the same. We shall *expect* if we are always obedient in giving time and care to our conversations to God, when we realise afresh every day his grandeur and goodness and kneel again, amazed that he has called us to this close service for Him; but we need have no fear. He who chose the stable and the criminal's death can make use of you and me, and *will* make use of us if our minds are turned always to him and never to ourselves.

Dedication of the new stained glass window and Lady Chapel 1958

To dedicate a new stained glass window and Lady Chapel on the same day is an exciting event. Anything that beautifies the House of God and makes our worship more worthy is always of great spiritual value. And if at any time any of us feel that 'this money were better used for the poor', we must always remember that it was Judas who made that comment and our Lord himself had only praise and love for the woman who broke the alabaster cruse of ointment over his feet in an offering of pure worship of love, because of course it is true that the two go hand in hand together. An untidy and ill kept church never means a parish alive and active in the place and in caring for the poor.

A tidy and beautifully kept church where people are moved to give gifts for its enrichment and its beauty is always one in which you will find more and more people being ready to spread his Kingdom and show his care and love for all in that place. I am sure it is no coincidence that this year when we have made so many alterations to the Cathedral, more people have given well and generously to St. James' Settlement and more people have offered of their time and their service to the church's work elsewhere in the Colony.

We are grateful to God for this gift of the former members of Holy Trinity Cathedral, Shanghai, and it reminds us that Christians are still using that Cathedral in conditions of much greater difficulty than we have in using ours here. Are you praying for them? Are you just writing them off, as people living in a Communist country, saying that there is no church, there is no hope for Christians? We should be praying specially for our Chinese Christians and friends, we who are near them, and can understand them and appreciate the trials and difficulties through which they have to go. Pray that they may be guided to do right and what is best for their country, that they may stand firm in all the fundamentals of their faith, that they may help in the end to win China for God.

And now for the window itself, which as I see it has a humbling and yet awe-inspiring message for all of us, depicting as it does three of the simple scenes from Christ's life, the Nativity, the Baptism and the Ascension. The message that those three scenes tell us is that God the Creator, the maker of all the world, the God of the Heavens, the God of the beauty of the sky and sea, the God of the atom, the God of all power and might, trusts and cares for all of us human beings and uses the simple ordinary things of life to show his power and his glory and to win us slowly and patiently to Him. So at the right appointed time He was born of a simple peasant girl in Bethlehem. He did not come in a great visit of power and state with special privileges, with a lot of preparation and publicity beforehand. He came as no special VIP with special labels and parking place, special accommodation reserved, but he was found in a refugee squatter hut, found first too by simple shepherds, who arrived and found what they needed - what we all need, you and I - a Saviour from ourselves, a Saviour from the meanness and pettiness that we know is in ourselves, the Saviour who will stop us being death to ourselves if left to ourselves. They, the simple people, found him first. It was long afterwards that the clever and intelligent, who had to travel far to reach him, with their gifts of all the problems of government and rule in the world - the gift of gold; the gift of all their intellectual wrestling with the problem of suffering - the gift of myrrh; the gift of all their philosophical thinking on the meaning and purpose of the world - the gift of frankincense. The educated and intellectuals have always a longer journey to come to God than the simple and the unlettered, but when they arrive they will find the same simple new born babe - and then they will need the purity, the simplicity of heart, to realise *that* is what they have come to worship, and not mind that the shepherds were there first. God came into the world as a small baby, totally helpless, needing all our service and trust and loyalty to him, realising that the best way to win people to him was to be in a position where they had to offer him service. To stand above people, always able to offer them money, service, advice and guidance, is not the way to win them to you - but if you can strip yourself of that and get in a position where you need help from them, then real friendship and loyalty results. This is what God has done for us at Christmas time.

Then on the other side of the window is the baptism, where Jesus, the only Son of God, comes down to be baptised by his cousin, John the Baptist. John the Baptist is startled to see him coming and says, so truly, that it is he who should be baptised by Him, rather than Jesus should come to him for baptism. It would have been so easy for Jesus to feel that he had no need of this simple, ordinary service which other people were going through; that he was above that - he was cleverer, better than the ordinary run of people and did not need to come to this service of baptism. It is so easy for us to feel that we do not need the regular, simple discipline that the Church has offered throughout the ages, to be above the ordinary run of men that we can worship God in the fields, on the golf course and the beach, wherever else we feel we would like to be on a Sunday; that we do not need to pin ourselves down to some regular discipline of worship. It is in submitting himself to the *ordinary* things that *ordinary* people are doing, that Jesus as a man gets the full realisation of his mission from God. This he described in the way that the disciples will understand, for the Jew always thought of the Spirit of God as something gentle and brooding like a dove; he always thought of God the Father as a cloud concealing the glory of God, because there is nothing human that can worthily portray God until Christ himself had arrived. So He comes out and tells his disciples that he saw the heavens open and the dove descending upon him and God speaking to him and giving him his commission. This is another illustration that God himself has used the ordinary things that ordinary human men can devise, to help them to a better and more Godly life.

In the middle we have the Ascension. Christ has lived with his disciples on earth, gone through all the passion and agony of Holy Week, died as a criminal on the Cross, risen again, and is now showing his disciples, again in a way they would understand, that he is returning to the eternal realm of God the Father. Were He living now, when we know the world is not flat and that Heaven is not a place above us, no doubt he would have used some other form of Ascension - but Christ, the good teacher, always taught in a way that people would understand at that time. Now if we have worked hard in Hong Kong for some special cause, some special work, and we were leaving for good, we should have done our best to see that it was endowed with money, that there was a good headquarters from which it could work, some imposing modern building opened by some celebrity in the place, with constitutions and rules, so that our wishes could be carried on. We would have done our best to see that there would be a good treasurer, a good secretary and a good committee, on whom we knew we could count. Christ, as he returns to God the Father, leaves none of these things, only a small band of eleven disciples, simple fishermen, none of them startlingly brilliant or very well educated. Many may know of the nice legend which says that Christ, as he returned to Heaven, talked with Gabriel about his time on earth, and Gabriel asked him what means he had left to see that his work was carried on; did he leave some strong society, some institutions, some good foundation on which it could be built? And Christ pointed down to his eleven disciples and Gabriel said, 'But if they should fail?' Jesus replied, 'They will not fail; I have no other plan.'

So that window tells us that the God of the Trinity, God the Creator, God the Almighty of all Heaven and Earth, the God of Jesus Christ, the perfect man who lived and gave himself for us unto death, and rose again, the God of the Holy Spirit who inspires all poets, all harmony in musicians, all beauty in painters, who leads all men in their search for truth, that this very God never neglects or despises ordinary human means of human people for doing things. It is there that we are to see the King of Glory revealed; there, if our eyes are not blinded with self-interest and self-concern, we shall find his Kingdom being carried forward, in the squatter hut, in all places where people are caring for the poor, in all places where all men are simply and loyally trying to follow Him. We shall learn too that he did not despise the ordinary, simple rules of obedience to the church of his time that John the Baptist devised, to bring men to God and join in with them - and through them learn of God's power and commission to Him. And we shall learn through the Ascension that, to us and to us alone, is committed the task of furthering God's Kingdom, and that his promise is that he would be with us for ever more.

So we move from there through into the Lady Chapel, the anonymous gift of a most constant and loyal worshipper of this Cathedral for many years, that now there will be a quiet place of withdrawal, for the many who use this Cathedral on week days to say their own prayers, free from the bustle of this noisy city, a small quiet place of beauty for the daily services, on which the spiritual energy and life of this city depends so much. Here, every day, are prayers offered up, for all the life and work of this city, for the life and work of the Church and nations of the world. Here, where two or three are gathered together, Christ is in the midst of them and answering their prayers. It is rightly named in honour of the Virgin Mary who, like all good mothers, slowly withdraws from the centre of the scene, and learns and accepts what God her Son has to teach her. From her deep understanding of what the agony of the Cross means to God, and must have meant to her as she watched her Son die there, from the glory and victory of Easter Day, she was able, when she was taken home by John, to change that impetuous, wilful young disciple into the man who could write the wonderful beauty and depth of the fourth Gospel; here again today we learn that it is in the quiet depths and silences of your heart and mine that God's power and glory must shine forth and his Kingdom be furthered.

So we thank God today, not only for these gifts, but for the message that they tell us - that you and I are never deserted by Him, that he is interested in all that we do; he expects our obedience to all the little things of Christian life and worship, and will use them to show his power and his glory to us; that he commits his Kingdom to us now, with the promise of His presence with us forever.

Farewell Sermon 1959

When it comes to a farewell sermon there are so many things that one would like to say, but in the end one falls back on a few simple fundamental points which one has tried to stress during one's ministry in a place.

So I take two texts: one a comment about the disciples from the Acts of the Apostles, 'They took note of them that they had been with Jesus', and the other from Jesus' words in the Upper Room, recorded by St. John in Chapter Fourteen, 'In my Father's House are many resting places; if it were not so would I have told you that I go to prepare a place for you? I will come again and receive you unto myself, that where I am, ye may be also.'

They took note of them that they had been with Jesus. Friends of Christ: that is the wonderful high privilege to which you and I have been called by Christ, not servants but friends, with all the intimacy, affection, knowledge and understanding of deep friendship so that Christ in the end lives in us and we look out on to the world with his eyes and love. We are not only to obey but to become like. The mind of Christ is to dwell in us. And from that will come a personal quality of life, entirely recognisable when you see it, yet unable to be pinned down into categories and watertight compartments - but as free and powerful as the wind blowing where it listeth. The man of the spirit of Christ will use all the well-worn means of the Church but not be tied by them. And from this quality of life will arise a real and living family of the Church and from that, a society and community which more and more reflects the care and compassion of Christ wanting the best for each one of us.

There are many ways of defining or describing the friend of Christ, or the man with the mind of Christ, such as showing is care, his compassion, his self-giving - but primarily the man of Christ has a depth, a new dimension which the natural secular man never has. Two men can be just as charming, just as pleasant, until suddenly some crisis makes you realise that the charm of one is shallow and trivial and solely directed to its owner's ultimate gain and good; the other has a depth and calm, a sureness and certainty which nothing ruffles; its roots are not here in shallow soil but in the rich loam of conviction that God reigns.

There was a description in the weekly English paper, the *Spectator*, a few weeks back by a man who had just been round Auschwitz again, the site of a Nazi concentration camp. He said what impressed him was 'the filth of enormous littleness, the malice of mean little minds. In the finish the impression is that of small-scale meanness multiplied by millions but remaining small.' The power and yet the pettiness and little-ness of evil and malice; the meanness that cannot care in a big way; the pettiness of envy and slights harboured and fostered. The narrowness of the small mind that can see no way but his own. Have you not often been surprised at other people's pettiness, at the sudden smallness of good people in some sphere of life they have not let God enter and control; the little things that upset and disturb - as no doubt others are surprised at our own smallness; and maybe with the grace of God we are ourselves sometimes staggered at our own pettiness and triviality.

The depth and power of the friend of Christ: it is the new dimension which makes all the difference to all our living, all our plans. For this we must see there is always time for prayer, not necessarily for long prayer but for the reality of prayer, for worship together, which must be expressed in Christian service both in our actual jobs and in our free time. There must be Christian stewardship of all our resources, of our time, our money; oh, the amount the Anglican Church could expand and develop here if we gave anything like a tenth of our income; at the moment there is not the money to pay more full-time clergy of the Chinese parishes on even the pittance they get. There must be stewardship of our time, our money, our interests and abilities.

But all this may be dead to you at the moment, your prayers, your worship, your giving, even your work which once was aglow with Christian enthusiasm and meaning. Then I would remind you of the other text, 'In my Father's House are many resting places.' The Greek word there means hotels or inns; Jesus is comparing himself with the guide or dragoman who went ahead of the wealthy traveller to warn those at the next inn to prepare and get ready; you could not ring up and reserve accommodation. So the guide went ahead - and then, when the travellers arrived, a bath could be provided, a meal was ready while the animals were rested and changed. Jesus is our spiritual guide through life and our life is a continual movement from resting place to resting place along the route; you cannot stand still long in the world of the spirit. Even the first resting place is within the Father's House. If you find that hard to understand, a resting place inside the house, it is only because we have such small and mean ideas on houses. If you have been over Versailles or Blenheim then you will be right glad of resting places en route. Even the first step taken on the Christian road is within the Father's care, love

and joy; Christ is here at the resting place; even if it only be the first step of penitence at the last minute, like the dying man on the cross. Then suddenly, it may be
overnight, or slowly, it dawns that all your Christian life and belief has become
empty and dead; there may be some like that here today or listening in. You would
not be here if someone had not led you by the hand, if you had not recognised
Christ in your life by your side to give it meaning. Then it all became dead and
empty; Christ has gone ahead to get the next place ready for you. Now all depends
on each one of us making the next move making the next move and seeing what
the next step to stir ourselves may be; it is unpleasant to have to get up and move
out again into the dusty hot road of spiritual life, especially the older we get - but
move we must; otherwise we may stay in some advanced resting place of the
House of God, knowing all the answers, all the theory of worship and prayer - but
Christ will have moved on and our lives will be flat, empty and dead: and we will
be left like all people left to themselves without God, worthless and trivial. And
that is the tragedy sometimes found in the Church: the Christian soul which has
ceased to travel, ceased to move forward. Then, on the other hand, there is the
new believer who radiates the joy and friendship of Christ discovered in the first
resting place of the Christian journey. As soon as we go out again on the road,
Christ comes back as he promises, to lead us on - that where he is, we may be also.
And that is the sole purpose and meaning of life; that man should be with God, his
maker and creator. A purpose which will absorb all our time here, not only to understand with the mind, but in every part of our being - which will show itself not
only individually but also together in the type of society and community we create. Sin and the devil have made and make the task of great difficulty; but we are
assured of the continual patience and love of God, always turning back for us, if
we make that first response, each time to get started again; a response to be made
in prayer, worship and conduct - and then together with God we can all go forward, each leading others by the hand into the same Joy.

Five Epilogues on Associated Rediffusion Television: 1961.
Associated Rediffusion's Press Release, put out by the producer, ran:

> *This week's Epilogues are to be given by the Rev Frederick Temple, Senior Chap-
> lain to the Archbishop of Canterbury. 'My theme for the week will be Christ as
> Friendship', Mr. Temple told me. 'This is of fundamental importance: to meet
> God as a friend and leader. The more people who see my theme that way, the easier
> it will be for them to approach the Church.'*
>
> *Mr. Temple, a nephew of the late Archbishop of Canterbury, Dr. William
> Temple, tells me that this is his first appearance on television, although he has given
> radio epilogues in Hong Kong.*
>
> *'I shall not be trying to make my talks a substitute for attending Church,' he
> said. 'They will be merely a method of leading people towards Christianity.'*

No. I

I want to tell you the true story about a boy, the only child in an unhappy home. He knew from an early age he was not wanted; he was bright and quick and realised this. So he started by being difficult; then he broke things, then he stole. He was testing to see if there was anyone who was ready to take any real interest in him. Then he became violent and finally he became dangerous and had to be put in a padded cell in a mental home.

At this hospital a young Christian doctor made a special study of his case and one day said to a friend of mine, 'Of course the problem with X is that we can never spend long enough with him. The doctors are all too busy and they always go in with someone else and leave the door open. That is no good; the boy is too quick not to spot that and he just becomes more violent. I have been in alone shutting the door behind me, but of course leaving it unlocked; but after a time I have always got the wind up and edged behind a table or a chair nearer the door and then I know it is no good.' That young doctor went on, 'I am convinced that the only cure for that young man is for someone to go in unarmed and have the door locked behind him and to stay in there until the boy kills him without doing anything to resist. Then in the remorse and realisation that someone has really cared for him right to the end, his cure will begin; but of course there is no man you can ask to do that.' No *man*; but it is just what we Christians believe God has done in the world.

You have only to open your newspaper any morning and read the headlines of troubles in the Congo, in Laos, of police hunts for murderers of young girls in England, to see that our world is very much like the cell of that young man, full of people who mistrust each other and don't really believe anyone cares very much. Christians believe that God did not just send gifts to the world, or instructions, but came into the world through a door that was locked on the outside, the door of birth, and stayed just as long as man would have him. But man, then as now, was so full of mistrust, suspicion and fear that God was put to death and showed his love like that. But the story doesn't end there. Christians also believe that three days later Jesus rose again; so God proved that nothing in the end defeats his love and care for us.

If only we could all get hold of that truth and live it out in the world. No matter how gloomy the news looks tomorrow morning in the papers, no matter how nasty and horrid you know in your heart you have been today to people round you, how fundamentally selfish and self-seeking we know we each are, or how horrid we think other folk have been to us, God cares completely for each one of us and enters the mad suspicious cell of our life; he has come to stay as long as we want him and even if by our actions and thoughts we try to kill him, nothing can conquer his love ever and he is always ready for us to turn to him and live happily in his friendship under his guidance. Take that thought to bed with you tonight. Goodnight.

No. II

If you are planning to meet your best friend, you arrange the meeting carefully. You plan a time when you are free, and if possible a convenient and pleasant place where you can enjoy each other's company. You don't say, 'Well now, I would very much like us to meet; I like you very much but I am always terribly busy; if you would like to hang about all day and wait till last thing at night just before I go to sleep I might be able to give you a moment or two, but I shall anyhow do all the talking.' But many of us do treat God in just that way when we say our prayers. Christianity is friendship with a person and you cannot get to know a person unless you spend time with them regularly.

To say our prayers last thing at night is a very good thing when we are children; when we have had our bath and are all clean and quiet we are ready to listen and pay attention. We continue that habit when we are grown up but on the whole I think it is a very bad thing indeed. We are usually very tired and unable to concentrate very well. Then to make matters worse we leave what is often the one warm room in the house, go upstairs to a cold bedroom, then to make matters still worse we undress, get into cold pyjamas and then, with our teeth positively chattering with cold and tiredness, we try to say our prayers. In meeting a friend we would not say, 'Now let me see; yes, let's meet where we shall both be thoroughly cold and uncomfortable and not enjoy it at all.'

I think this point, of how and when we say our prayers, is most important because our religion should be an exciting friendship with a person and all the reading and learning about that friend will not take the place of meeting him and knowing him ourselves. So many good, honest and decent folk give up their religion rather sadly and unhappily when they find their prayers mean nothing to them and then everything starts to slide.

So I want to suggest that if you don't find saying your prayers easy, or have given up, see if you could find three or four minutes at some time earlier in the day when you could sit quietly and think about God, listen to him and talk to him. If you are a housewife it may be that after you have seen your husband off to work and the children to school, there are a few minutes when you just sit and look at the paper before starting the day; you could use that for your prayers. If you are a man or woman out at work there may be a moment after you have come in, either before your evening meal or after it, when you have a few minutes before you start on the evening's occupation. Plan it as you would plan meeting a friend. Don't leave it until you are really too tired.

But if you do find last thing at night the only quiet, peaceful moment of the day, why not say your prayers by the fireside in the warmth and comfort of your living-room? There is nothing particularly religious or holy about being cold and uncomfortable in your bedroom. I know several husbands and wives who have started again having a time of friendship with God by quietly using the last few minutes by their firesides together in their own comfy chairs before going upstairs to bed. Goodnight.

No. III

I have been talking this week about Christianity being above all a meeting with God as a personal friend, a friend who cares for us no matter what we may do or say. Last night we thought about where and when we should meet our friends. Tonight I want to think about what we do and say when we meet. We all know the type of person who does all the talking when we meet them; so that we leave them exhausted and say, 'I didn't get a chance to put in a word edgeways,' or 'I wanted to help so-and-so but they never gave me a chance to say anything; they were so wrapped up in themselves that they would not have listened even if I had got a chance to put a word in somewhere.' Such people are crashing bores and there are plenty of them in the world.

Many of us are crashing bores in our prayers and conversation with God. It is as if a friend came up to us in the street and said, 'Hello; thank you for what you did yesterday; I am sorry I did that today; please help me to get this and have that and don't let the other happen; help this person and that one and all those I love; goodbye' - and off the friend went. If the same friend did that every day for years we would very soon get bored, lose patience and feel this was not a real friendship at all; it was all one-sided. Fortunately, God does not get bored and lose patience with us because that is what most of us are like in our prayers; we do all the talking and do not let God have a chance to get a word in edgeways. Plan your prayers as you would a meeting with a friend; when we meet, we put out our hand and say, 'How do you do?' and if we are polite we wait for an answer. The first thing then is to say, 'How do you do?' to God in our prayers; by sitting or kneeling quietly and thinking about him; this we can do in different ways; most people do it by opening their Bible and reading a short passage, thinking about it and letting it sink into their minds; or as someone has said, letting a short passage dissolve like a lozenge in one's thoughts. In that way God can often tell us something about ourselves and make clear something we ought to do or not do. But don't be worried if you do not feel God tells you anything the first few times you try this; it may be that he has nothing special to say, or it may be that if you have been doing all the talking in the past you are not a very good listener; if we are great talkers then we find it hard to listen well.

After saying, 'How do you do?' to our friend we thank him for anything special he has done for us since we last met. It is good to thank God for all the good things of our lives early in our prayers; a wise old bishop once told a class of small boys to use all their fingers to thank God every night, to find ten things to thank God for. A small boy came back proudly in a week's time to say he used all his toes as well; he had found twenty things to thank God for.

After thanks, we then would say sorry for what we had failed to do: 'By the way, I forgot to post that letter you gave me' or 'to give that message' or whatever it might be. So next we say sorry to God for what we have failed to do for him.

If we start like that with, 'How do you do?', 'Thank you' and 'Sorry', then we can go on as we like asking help for our friends and ourselves, for guidance and direction. If you are not doing this already, try it for a few minutes each day. It can be the most exciting friendship in the world. Goodnight.

No. IV

I have been speaking this week about Christianity as friendship with God as a person and what we can do when we meet our friends. But someone may easily say, 'I can get along quite well without your friend, thank you; I know what an influence and happiness a friend can bring, but I am quite content as I am and I do not need him.'

I want to answer that with a story, a true story. A parson was going round a hospital on the East coast of America where there were a lot of sailors who had been saved from a torpedoed ship. Some had been killed; some had drowned, for it was in the middle of a stormy, cold winter night that the torpedoing took place. Others were just shocked and needed a rest. There was one young fellow there who was not physically hurt but was in misery. The parson talked with him. 'I just can't get it out of my head,' the sailor said, 'that night. You see, there wasn't time to throw over enough rafts for all of us. Those of us who were strong swimmers and had our life-belts got to the rafts first and clung on; men fought to get near the rafts, and others clung on behind on to our backs; but then after a time the cold and stormy waves were too much for them and they slid off one's back into the sea and were drowned; some with cries and some quite silently.' The boy turned in his bed. 'I can't sleep; I keep feeling those hands slowly sliding down my back and feel dreadful that I am alive.'

The parson tried to comfort him: 'That was not your fault, son; it was only natural what you did; it was only human nature that you should try and save yourself as everyone else here did.' 'Oh, no,' said the sailor, 'I am quite different from everyone here.' 'How is that?' asked the parson. 'Well, you see, as soon as we were hit, I rushed up on to deck in a panic and then realised too late I had not got my life-belt. I did not know what I was going to do and must have looked pretty white with fear when I saw one of the padres standing near; he looked for a moment and then without a word he took off his lifejacket and put it on me saying, 'Here you are: over you go,' and I jumped over. I had never met him nor ever known him, yet he did that for me. I had heard him say that having God as your friend helps you to be different. I can never be the same; having met that sort of thing I know it isn't really natural to be selfish although it may be normal.'

A great friend can influence us for good or bad; all of us who are parents watch anxiously to see what sort of friends our children make, knowing the effect they can have on them. So with God as our friend he can influence us and change us more than we can ever imagine. As we see that we make time for our friendship with him every day, we shall find that the prayers that we say change. You will re-member the Prodigal Son in the story starts by saying to his father, 'Give me my part of my inheritance.' Give me; that is our first selfish prayer, our first normal, selfish wish - like that sailor's wish to be saved and cling to the raft. But at the end of the story the Prodigal Son 'comes to himself' and realises what he is missing as a real man; he returns home and say, 'Make me as one of your hired servants.' The prayer is now, 'Make me.' 'Give me' changes to 'Make me' as we trust ourselves to God as our friend to make us into real men as God would have us be. Goodnight.

No. V

All this week I have been talking about Christianity being friendship with God as a person. We know what a difference a great friendship makes; we are never the same again after we have met a great person whom we admire and respect. We have been jogging along quite contentedly before the meeting with this person, thinking we are quite happy and making quite a success of life in a quiet, self-re-specting way, and then suddenly we are shown new possibilities in ourselves, work that we ought to be doing.

This knowing a person is quite different to knowing about a person. We can all describe some people but we know it is quite different from really knowing a per-son as a friend; this can only be done with sympathy and loyal understanding. The same is true with our friendship with God. We have all met the Christian, some-times alas even the person who thinks he knows all about God and can talk about him, but in his life shows he hasn't really met him as a friend.

I want to illustrate what I mean with a story. A famous actress once gave a party to which she invited all her stage friends; it was a very grand affair at her house in the country, and to it came all these grand famous theatre folk. But the actress was also a keen Christian and a good member of her local church when she was there, and so she invited along as well the quiet little country vicar of the place. It was a wonderful party with good food and wine, talk and much laughter. Then, after dinner, everyone was asked to do one turn to entertain the others. Opera singers sang, pianists played, acrobats did some turns; one famous actor recited the twen-ty-third psalm, 'The Lord is my Shepherd; therefore can I lack nothing.' He recit-ed it beautifully and everyone applauded and said they had never heard it recited so well. Then suddenly someone saw the little parson in the corner, trying to make himself small in the hope that no-one would ask him to do something. 'Come along,' they said, 'You mustn't be left out; you must do something.' 'Oh, no,' he said, 'Please not, there is nothing I could possibly do; I'd much rather not.' By this time everyone was watching him and more people said, 'Yes, there must be something you can do; recite something; you must know something by heart.' And he was pushed and pulled, in a friendly fashion, into the middle of the room; there was only one thing he knew well by heart, the twenty-third psalm, the very psalm that had already been so exquisitely recited. His reciting would seem terrible in comparison; but everyone was quiet now and there was nothing for it but to begin. However he was a very good, humble and great Christian who loved his Master and cared for his people all his life; this psalm expressed all his love. So without any of the training or superb diction of the actor, he started and poured all his life's love of God into the saying of that psalm. A profound silence filled the room and everyone was much too moved at the end to speak for a minute after he stopped. And then suddenly everyone started talking again.

Later in the evening the actor slipped across to the window where the parson was sitting and said, 'The difference between us is that I know all about how to say that psalm, but you know the shepherd.' Goodnight.

Diocesan Choirs Service: Bristol Cathedral, 1975

It's always a great pleasure and privilege to talk to members of choirs because every one of you, from the youngest and smallest to the oldest, from the smallest country parish choir to the Cathedral choir, you are all - all of you - very important people. Christianity, we know and believe, is the truth about the world. It's not just an extra option that people can choose if they wish or don't wish to. We believe that God - a short three letter word to describe the power that made and controls the world and has given us our purpose and meaning in life - has shown what he's like in Jesus Christ, that he has asked such tremendous things of each one of us - again from the youngest to the oldest - and expects so much from each one of us that if we're honest we know we can't manage it on our own, that we can't live up to those standards without his help, and, thank heaven, he has also shown by his life and death and rising again on Easter Day that we don't have to do it on our own, that he is continually giving himself to every one in the world at every time, no matter what circumstances they're in or when they lived, how uneducated they are, how well educated, how poor or how rich, that he's always doing this wonderful thing.

And that is what worship is about. It's offering all the worth-ship of life to God. Worship is to fill the mind with the truth of God, to enlarge the imagination with the beauty of God, to strengthen the will with the purpose and energy of God, to flood the heart with the love and forgiveness of God. And you can't do that on your own. And that's why people - Christians - want to come together in song and prayer and offer this to God. And so all of us clergy and all of you in choirs, are tremendously important. Every act of worship - it doesn't matter how many or few there are in the congregation - every act of worship is very important. And how much depends not only on how well you can sing, but how ready and willing you are to lead the prayers, by your manner, by your devotion, by the sign - and this can be true again of the youngest - that this means something real to you. And so every time we come into church for a service, what you are and what I and other clergy do, is vitally important.

We are all of us marked men and women. Having been a bishop now for two years, I agree wholeheartedly with the remark my uncle William, the Archbishop of Canterbury, made to me once as a boy: 'I know exactly what sort of service I'm going to get from the atmosphere in the vestry beforehand.' It doesn't need necessarily to be very drilled and disciplined, but if everyone is bustling about trying to find things at the last minute, if there's one catty, gossipy choirman or choirwoman, if there's some boy or girl squabbling or fighting with each other, that's going to be reflected in the type of service there's going to be inside the church itself. It's still ideally true that if you want a worthy act of worship nothing should happen in any chancel a quarter of an hour before any service starts. Everything should be ready, so that there's a sense of effortless peace and people assembling for the service can have time to be quiet, and recollect what they are going to do. This is vitally important. I can't tell you anything about the musical side of it; you have your choirmasters and choirmistresses to tell you that. But it is this disciplined other side that is equally vital. It doesn't matter how much of the service is said or sung. But the way prayers are answered with a meaningful 'Amen', the way people are reverent and quiet, not gazing about, not chatting - all this is vital. And you are doing a marvellous job in leading the worship of this diocese and this country. You are proclaiming all the time the truth about the world. You're not just doing something tiresome or extra or something you rather like doing because you like the singing. You're doing the crucial thing that's necessary for everyone, to understand that they can't live a really full life without coming to God for his help and his forgiveness. You are giving a public service, as much a public service as the gas or electricity boards; by coming to church you are witnessing that this is the Truth.

The last time I spoke at this service I remember I pointed out how Evensong is a wonderful drama or play about God's acts in history, starting with the hymn that they used to sing - the psalm. And then a story about God's acts in the Old Testament, narrowing down to the Virgin Mary and the Magnificat, with Christ's coming - and then a story about Jesus or comment on his life from the Epistles. Then the Nunc Dimittis, thanking God again for what we've heard and understood. And then proclaiming it all in the Creed. Evensong is a wonderful structure like that. But equally true is the main service you go to, the Holy Communion or Eucharist - that there, in this wonderful way, God Almighty we believe is giving himself completely to everyone who comes and eats the bread and drinks the wine. What a wonderful thing that is. If only people could really understand it. You may know the story of the man in prison who was told about the Communion Service. When he was told this he said, 'If you Christians really believed that, you would crawl miles on your knees to receive it.' Well then, how vital that as people come up to Communion there is not a single little choirboy, choirgirl, man or woman, talking with anyone else. No-one gazing about, no-one trying to spot who's in the congregation. We are all marked people. People are either attracted to Christianity or put off by it, not by what they hear but by what they see in other Christians' lives. Let it never be, as, alas, it was once said about one clergyman, 'I cannot hear what you say, because it screams what you are.' What your life is screams and drowns what you try to say. And so God bless you in all that you are trying to do and remember that it doesn't matter how small at any time the worshipping community is; stretch your imagination wider and realise that the Church throughout the world is growing. And still on a Sunday morning more people are at worship than doing any other serious thing through the week. If only we Christians would stop moaning and realise that with our plant, our deployment, our loyal family of Christians everywhere, we have more manpower than any other serious organisation in the country. Let's take that to heart.

Maybe it's a bit difficult for any who have not been abroad, but for those of us who have, we can think, as I can, having been Dean of Hong Kong, of the choir in, say, Singapore Cathedral early at 8 o'clock tomorrow morning, in their time, leading a packed Cathedral in their Eucharist. And Hong Kong Cathedral an hour and a half later. Christians in China, either secretly or openly, singing and worshipping God. In Japan; throughout Africa, where the Church is growing by leaps and bounds. You belong to one of the largest societies in the world; I trust you'll all be worthy members of it. And realise what great things you are doing when you sing well, when you lead the worship well in prayer and praise, not only for God and for your church, but for every single man and woman in this country. They may not heed it at times, but you are always bringing them back to the point that this is what they need. Because this is what you publicly proclaim *you* need. And this is the most important thing that we all need to remember. So when you are doing it well, one of the great joys for you when you've died and got over to the other side, may be to find someone saying, 'I was brought to know God through the way you sang, through the way you prayed.' I hope to God there will be no-one who will say, 'Well, I was totally put off because of your cattiness, your gossip through the village or through the town or the way you behaved so often in your worship. I could not believe that if it only meant this to you, there was anything in it.' So we thank God for what he has called us to do, to proclaim his Truth, his Beauty, his Energy, his Love and his Goodness.

The Prodigal Son: St. Gregory, Horfield, 1980
We are all so familiar nowadays with the parables but still the problem for most of us is that we generally have vaguely heard them rather often and got used to them. And the best way of getting the most out of any story of Jesus is to stand in turn with each character in that story. So let's place ourselves with the younger son. He has everything he wants in his father's house. We know he has a loving, generous father, so why does he want any more?

Now you do not get your portion of what belongs to your parents - your inheritance - until your parents have died. So what the son is saying is, 'I do not want any

347

more obligations towards you, father. I want to take it that you are dead.' Do you know anyone like that? Anyone who treats God as dead? Nowadays we ourselves do not want to recognise that God is alive. Maybe the son, too, like any good teenager, was hoping for a row; he hoped possibly that his father would explode and say, 'No you are not; I am still alive. You are jolly well going to do as I ask.' To his surprise, this God, this father, is so generous that he straightaway gives it all. 'Give me', says the son - and of course it is given and will always be given. And then off he goes. Then he finds that all these wonderful things - the sun, the air, light, health, friendship - all become quite different when you are away from the father's house. You start to feel no real satisfaction in it any longer - and you devour it, eat it, consume it more and more until it has all gone. And then comes that wonderful phrase, 'When he came to himself.' Most of the great phrases of the Bible are very short, using words of only one syllable. You remember in the story of the Good Samaritan, 'He came where he was.' That sums up the whole Christian story: God coming where we are. The Prodigal Son came to himself, became a real man. We only come to ourselves when we realise our need for God; we are restless till then. And back goes the Prodigal Son; and then his prayer changes, and what a wonderful change it is: from 'Give me' to 'Make me.' You can really tell how Christian you have become when your prayers change from 'Give me' to 'Make me.' No longer is it, 'Give, God, give: let me have this; let me have that', but 'Make me' - and make me just as one of your hired servants. I just want to serve you in any way you are willing to have me. That is the only really necessary Christian prayer. For any of you who are parents, you can tell how Christian you have become if your prayers have changed from, 'Give them' to 'Make them.' It is quite difficult - and I know that as a parent - to become really unselfish in your prayers for your children. We can become fairly unselfish in our prayers for ourselves, but it is a different thing when we have to change from 'Give them' to 'Please, God, just use them, make them servants of yours.' That is what we can learn from the younger son.

Then let us stand by the older son - always ready to serve his father, but unable to realise what joy, what a miracle it was, when that father was ready to welcome back, and the love there was when that son returned. That was what was wrong with the older son: he did not realise that forgiveness is always a miracle. None of us are worthy of anything, if it were not for God's love. Forgiveness is not a rubber band that always stretches however much we ask of it. If we think it is like that it will suddenly snap, and we will find that it is no longer there. Forgiveness is always a miracle. Then you notice that that son is not ready to extend the forgiveness that God is always showing him to his brother - that brother becomes 'Your son who has returned.' How often as parents, even if joking sometimes, have you said to your wife or husband when one of the children has been difficult, 'Can't you manage your daughter?' or 'Can't you manage your son?' For that brother he becomes 'your son.' In effect, he says, 'I do not want to have anything to do with him.' However much we stay within the father's house, if we cannot realise that love and forgiveness are the essence of the whole thing, we have a lot to learn; we have a lot to realise. God, too, is not saying, 'How mean and selfish you are.' He just turns and says, 'Can you not see that I want to have the fatted calf? That I want to get out the best robes for him?' God will always go on being so astonishingly loving.

Then we look at the father; and the father is God himself in that story. He will always answer your prayers whenever you ask them - and that is what is so terrifying; because if they are selfish they will be answered. If we do say, 'Give me; I want to go away from you; I want to be on my own; I want to reckon you are dead', sadly and reluctantly God will see us go away into the far country. But then he is always pacing on the rooftop, waiting for us to come back. That younger son does not have to come back to a firmly closed front door, ring the doorbell and wonder what sort of reception he is going to have. The father runs to meet him; that means even more in the Middle East. Most middle-aged men do not look particularly dignified when they are running fast and I am no exception. The father, however, runs to meet his son. He does not mind what other people are thinking; how they are looking on. The father 'fell upon him.' He did not say, 'So, son, you have come back, have you? Are you really going to behave?' And he put on him the best robe, and placed a ring on his finger. All of us who are married know what putting a ring on a finger means - the trust, the love, the commitment, the confidence. It meant even more in a country where very few people could write, because the ring had your seal. How amazing that this son, as soon he got home, is given the father's ring so that he could go off straight away and say, 'Yes. That is a document of his; I will sign it for him.' Such trust. The robe and the ring take him straight back into every place without any grudging in any way. And still the Father runs an enormous distance to meet us. Interpret the Cross, always, by the parable. The distance God runs to meet us is the distance running to be born, to live, to be spat on, to die - and to rise again.

I end with a story of how far God runs to meet us. At the end of the last war, in a Jewish concentration camp, the German officers of the camp, the Nazis, decided they must have some reprisals. They decided they would kill two men and a boy, by hanging them. The men died immediately; but the boy's weight was not enough. He hung there, still alive, dying. The prisoners were marched slowly up and down past that slowly dying boy. One of the Jews, as he marched past, turned to another and said, 'Where is God now?' His friend turned and said, 'He is there, dying and suffering for us all in that boy.' That is the distance the father is continually running to meet and to serve and to love.

Patronal Festival: St. Peter, Chippenham, 1982

'Go tell his disciples and Peter ...': that was the message that the women brought back from the tomb; so we are told in St. Mark's Gospel when they found it empty. And I want to stress those two words, 'and Peter.' It is quite astonishing really that Peter, who denied Our Lord so terribly just at the critical moment is especially remembered. Have you ever done or said anything to anyone that you have bitterly regretted, and have not even had the chance to make amends? Something that you have said or done or could have done - and then that person has died. You wish terribly that you had had a chance to make it up, to apologise, to make amends. A little bit of advice I remember my mother once gave me and I give it to all of you, of whatever age you are: never leave anyone in anger, particularly anyone you love, without restoring the relationship. For you never know whether you will have a lifetime bitterly regretting it, not having made amends. Peter himself must have been in total despair. When you think of all the tremendous promises and boasts he had made - that he was going to be the person who would never deny him, that he was ready to draw his sword when the fight was really on. Like so many of us who feel that something big is demanded, something tremendous, something that people would notice - yes, we would be really Christian then. But cold, frightened, tired, crouching by that fire, suddenly a servant girl went up to him and said, 'You are one of them, are you not? I recognise you by your accent. You come from the North, a Galilean. And so often when caught unawares, with a sneer, something quite small, we make that first denial. Then there comes another, a bit stronger. Then a total downright denial that he knows the man - and then Jesus coming out and looking on him, and Peter going away into the dark and weeping bitterly.

Whatever form you think that that angel or messenger of God - for that is what angels are - came to the women when they suddenly realised that the tomb was empty, God Almighty, the Creator of the world, the vastness of the universe, the Creator of the atom, the Creator of the vast space of time, who has shown himself in Christ, who has this purpose for the world, could so easily have sent the message, 'Tell the disciples.' But a special individual is added, 'and Peter.' This vast, massive programme that the Almighty God has in mind includes you and you and you. And you. Every single one of us, whatever age we are, however young, however old. We are not just dots in a vast mass. There is a special concern particularly for those of us who dither, for those of us who often fail. Is not that wonderful? Peter makes more mistakes almost than any other person in the Gospel - but he is at least ready to come out candidly and stand up and say what he feels. And as we know, that is a turning point in the whole story of he Gospel - when he is ready to say, 'You are the Christ.' You are the person we have been waiting for. And on that sort of affirmation, that sort of statement that each of us can make, that is the sort of rock on which Christ will build his Church. And when you make that sort of statement, either openly or just by your life and what you are doing, you are then given the most wonderful thing. Each of us here, the youngest scout, the youngest choirboy, the oldest person, is handed the Keys of Heaven, the keys of eternity. You are then handed the key which means you are then someone who, if you use that statement, allow God to use it in you, can unlock and go into a most marvellous new world, a world of unselfishness, of love, of beauty, of truth, of goodness. And leave outside selfishness, self-assertion, contempt, mistrust.

To all of us here, on St. Peter's Day particularly, if we are ready to say to Jesus, 'Yes, you are the person we have been expecting; we will try to follow you', he straightaway says, 'Then here are the keys.' We then have the opportunity of unlocking that door and letting people in - the people you eat with, the people you meet in form in school, the teacher, the neighbour at home, the friend at work - and letting them in to this marvellous Christian world. Or we have the opportunity of keeping the door locked and saying, 'No, I keep this key for myself. I am not going to let you in. I am going to keep this key all to myself, and no-one else is going to have it.'

If you think to yourself, 'All this is far too grand for me', then remember how often Peter made mistakes. Just after the passage which we have read this evening, we remember that Jesus goes on to say that he is going to suffer; this is the way he is going to bring in the Kingdom. And dear Peter, instantly, cannot bear it. 'Be it far from you, Lord.' So, after having called him 'the Rock', suddenly Peter is failing so much that even Jesus had to say, 'Get thee behind me, Satan.' As so often happens, temptation comes from our friends, comes from our loved ones, comes from those near and dear to us, who are not ready to demand the best of us. Very rarely does temptation come in the form of a hostile enemy saying, 'Ha ha, will you do this?' We can all resist it then. It comes subtly in the form of some friend saying, 'No, you owe it to yourself, dear. Do not do it', or 'Really, you ought to be frightfully upset that so-and-so said this to you.' That is the way temptation comes. And Peter then was trying to tempt God from his course - and yet Jesus and God himself is ready to return to him.

You remember that Peter could not bear the thought of God himself kneeling to wash his feet. One of the first things we Christians have to do is not think proudly all the time. 'What service can I offer to God?' Let God offer service to you. Let God, in whatever way he wants, kneel and wash your dirty, smelly feet. Maybe some dirty and smelly bit of your character and life. And to cleanse it - and so free it. Then, as he show, we become totally part of him. And we are told especially that after the Resurrection there was a special appearance to Peter. We are not told much about it, because a very discreet veil is drawn over it. It must have been a wonderful appearance. One can just imagine what Peter must have felt as Our Lord appeared specially to him. And then there comes that lovely time by the shore when Jesus gently, with such good humour, mocks Peter. 'Peter, do you really love me?' Peter answered with a lesser word, 'Lord, you know I am your friend.' And then he said, 'Peter do you really love me?' 'Lord, I am your friend.' And then

Peter drops to the lower word, 'Peter, are you really my friend?' And poor Peter, all he can do is say, in effect, "Lord, you know everything; I just have to put myself into your hands. I cannot trust myself any more. I entrust myself to you.' And each time, Peter is given a greater job to do for God.

So tonight, on St. Peter's Festival, remember that all we are asked to do is to be ready, by our lives, to say, 'Yes, we do try to follow; we do try to realise that you are the Christ.' And then to each of us is given those keys, either to unlock or stop people going into, this wonderful Christian life of goodness, truth, love and service. Even though we will constantly fail like Peter, if we are genuinely sorry, God himself has a special message, a special thing he wants each of us to do for him. And, if we let him, then we can all be a Rock on which he can build.

Confirmation: Bristol Cathedral, 1983

'I will give you the keys of the Kingdom': words that Jesus said to Peter just after he had made his first public statement that he believed that Jesus was from God, was the special person sent by God. In one sense it might be called Peter's Confirmation. And that is what God is offering all those of you being confirmed today: the keys of the Kingdom. When you are offered keys, when you get the keys of the house, it is a moment when your parents trust you, give you a new sense of responsibility and a new freedom, to come and go as you will. When we get offered the keys of the car of someone else it is a sign of trust, responsibility and freedom. And that is what Confirmation is about. Today God is saying that to all of you, and it is an astonishing thing to say, and we often do not believe that God really is so trusting, so free. Most of us are suspicious with each other; most of us parents are not ready to let be and let go early enough, and just be there with love, support and guidance. But God is very trusting; God has given us tremendous freedom. He is saying that he does trust, that he is always there to help - and that he has been right through, right to the end in the Cross and that nothing will ever defeat his love. There is nothing that you and I can ever do which in the end will defeat his love. It may cost him dear: the Cross cost him dear. And with your freedom, when you step into that car, if you are not responsible, if you have not learnt how to drive, you are free to do a great number of people a great deal of damage. God does not keep us all on puppet strings all the time, but is there, trusting.

Also realise that he expects and demands, asks from you the very best. That is his trust. There are going to be certain things in the world that will never get done if you do not do them. There will be certain things that will happen in the world that will never happen if you are not all that you could and should be. And that's what the judgement will be when we get into the next world, not a judge hearing evidence, but just the very quality of what we are will come out then. And there will be - alas - a whole lot of people who will bear the marks of our missed opportunities. We hope also that there will be many people who will be able to say, 'Do you remember when you did this, or when you did not say that, or when you smiled, or when you were like that? You helped me so much.' It's far more likely from what we are, quite unconsciously and without effort, just by what we are as people, that we will be opening with our keys the doors of that Kingdom. There could be no greater thing given to any Christian - and what I am saying applies to everyone confirmed here. We have in us each day the chance of opening the door of the Kingdom of God and letting other people come in to all that love, all that goodness, all that forgiveness, all that idealism, all that truth, all that courage, all the great spiritual things of life. And as Our Lord goes on to tell Peter, it is just a matter of fact: 'Those whose sins you forgive are forgiven; those whose sins you retain are retained.' That does not mean going around pronouncing forgiveness. If you are the sort of person who, when people in your company suddenly feel released, suddenly have a new vision of life, a new purpose, a new goal, then they are released from the sins of their own selfishness, the sin of being enclosed, possibly going just for money, going just for their family, going possibly just for their reputation, being bound by material things - and are suddenly released into a totally new aspect. But - alas - if you have lost your keys and you do not know where to find them, then it may be that other people are not finding that and are still being bound in their own selfishness, in their own narrowness. So, it is a tremendous trust, a tremendous responsibility. That is why you have all been prepared for Confirmation, for this commitment; that is why we need to go on realising that we are people 'on the way.' Christians were first called 'People of the Way.' You do not stop en route.

I drive continually down from Swindon to Bristol and I think how odd it would be if along the motorway I suddenly found little clumps of Christians saying, 'I have stopped here.' In a sense the clergy are rather like motorway police, trying to keep people moving: to help them when they break down, but also to keep them moving. I hope there are no older, middle-aged Christians here who have stopped en route, who have just stopped at their Confirmation; who have lost the keys of their car and do not know how to move on. And have now got rusty and do not know what to do. But God is always there with his messengers, with people of all types, who can come alongside, help and get you moving again.

So, there's that responsibility and there's a tremendous freedom. God will not bully; God will not specially protect. In fact he tells you that on that journey there will be suffering - but it will be worthwhile because he will always be with you, right through to the end. On that journey we take up our Cross and follow. That is the wonderful adventure into which forty of us are being called today. As you say that you trust in him, God is saying that he gives you the keys of the Kingdom, and he asks you to be people who will always let people in to this wonder, this beauty. He trusts you, and it is tremendously responsible. He will give you this trust at such cost - the cost of permanently being someone who bears as much of the suffering of the world as he did when hanging on the Cross. But it is worthwhile, he says, because every single person here is of such enormous value. He is not going to bully; he is not going to cosset.

I would say also one final word to those of you who come to support the candidates with your presence and your prayers. God bless you, all those of you who have those keys and are still opening that door, still trying to follow all the time, still letting other people in. But if there is anyone here who is really rather casual, whose religion has become somewhat conformist, who likes now and the, as it were, to get near the door of that Kingdom, give it a nod and ring the front doorbell now and then - you have certainly lost your keys. If it all seems to have become rather dull, rather tame, I tell you that you still have a colossal responsibility - and especially if you are in any way connected with anyone being confirmed today. It will depend very much on what you are, what you are like, as to whether they are able to follow and they are able to keep this up. It will depend on how much mum, dad, uncle, aunt, granny, grandpa, godparent, older brother, older sister, are giving that example - or whether it has been something that has just been chucked outside sometime afterwards, after school or later on - and that people are still being bound in their own petty materialism and selfishness and concerns for themselves. Today again, will you take up the invitation that God gives you, of trust, responsibility and freedom, as he gives us all the keys of his Kingdom.

Mothers' Union Diocesan Festival: Bristol Cathedral, 1983

Sometimes, when a young couple fall in love, we say, 'Well, I cannot imagine what he sees in *her*'; and some parents say, too, 'I cannot imagine why she has chosen *him*.' But love opens the possibilities and the potential in other people. So it makes me certain that our God is true and a God of love that here, right at the heart of a very human institution, is the truth about the Christian Gospel - that we are accepted just as we are by God - and we have to realise our own weaknesses and not try to conceal them from him. And yet that he has great longings for us to give of our best, which is far greater than we can ever imagine, and also that in a happy home there is great patience with all the weaknesses of each other. And a great forbearance. And yet a great strength and a great guidance. And this is love at its best.

In the Mothers' Union you have always to keep this balance between what I would call conviction and compassion. As you stand for ideals there is a danger that you become narrow and rather deplore people who cannot keep up to this standard - and then just look back to the past with longing and tutting and wondering why things are not better than they were. Or one becomes so liberal and, as people might say, permissive, that you are ready to welcome everyone in all the time. The tension always between Christian ideals and Christian forgiveness is a very difficult one to hold. You are at work in your homes and all that the Mothers' Union tries to do and one hopes in the parishes, in all the solid little things of life. And as I tried to say in the Mothers' Union sermon some time back Our Lord helps us and you are to find meditation really so much easier than a lot of other people.

Just to remind you for instance about salt. - that it brings the best out of people, it preserves goodness; it is no use if it stands on the edge of the plate. It is only any use if it gets right into the middle of the stew of the world; and it never receives any thanks. I have yet to know any meal at the end of which people have got up and said, 'Thank you so much; the salt was perfect.' But it may have been just the right amount of salt that made that right. And yet all these things sometimes go wrong in a Mothers' Union; 'Well, I think if the Vicar does not show more appreciation than that I am not going to do much more about it. He seems just to expect us to go on and on doing these things; if we are not to be recognised a bit more ....' Familiar? We have to get a balance between doing regularly all the things that are needed; to realise that an organisation like this that has been going a long time is now, as it were, a well-set channel of God's grace. It was Max Warren who once, in giving advice to young missionaries going out abroad talked first to the young ones and said, 'If you find the middle-aged ones out there a little staid, a little set in their ways, realise that it may be that the channel of their grace has now got dug and recognise what water, what grace, is flowing through it. It may also have got a bit silted up and need a bit of cleaning. It will not be, after a time, as it were, bubbling out so much all over the place, effervescently.' And then to the older ones he would say, 'When you get this young one coming out who seems to have such bounding ideas, realise that this is the start of the fountain gushing. And you are feeling all the time, "Ah well, we have to channel this and get it going in certain ways to make sure it is effective, so that it really does water the ground all about - otherwise, it will get lost in a lot of early enthusiasm that goes no further."'

If you in the Mothers' Union can also all the time be rekindling your vision of what the Church is about, you have a key job in the parishes, particularly in England in the next ten or twenty years, when the Church is going to change more enormously than you can have any idea. And your job will be to alert to what God wants and very often it will be the older ones amongst you will be more sensitive and alert. It was Simeon and Anna who spotted the young child coming into the Temple. I found in my parishes that it was not necessarily the young or the middle-aged; it was the really deeply spiritual, the deeply sensitive and alert, who spotted the need for change. Very often it was the grey-haired members of the parishes who said to me, 'You are right, Vicar; that does need altering and changing. I cannot battle with you on the Parochial Church Council about it, but I will pray about it and support you to the hilt.' Remember too that Simeon said, when he saw this baby, 'This child is set for the fall and rise of many.' Very wise to have 'fall' first; what an astonishing thing that was, was it not? What would be said now in a parish if a young mother brought her child for baptism and the vicar said, 'Mmm: this child is set for the fall of many; he is going to cause a lot of trouble - and a sword is going to go through your heart too.' You can imagine: 'Well, do you know what he said? Not going *there* again. Really. Do you think he is alright?'

If you go and look at those old museums in London it is those big cumbersome beasts that used to people the earth who have died and gone. Man and things smaller and more alert and more mobile have lived in the end. So, I plead with you all: do not keep hankering back to the days when there was a parish here, a parish there. Because all that is going to change. And do not think that you are going to get away unscathed in the future, as we cut down on the clergy. (I am having a lovely time in these last six months of mine in this diocese because I can say a whole lot of things and then go.) Do not think you are going to get away without cutting down on buildings, because you are going to kill your clergy otherwise. You tend just to think that you can have fewer and fewer full-time clergy and still have them running round the same number of buildings. It is worth realising, for instance, that we look at the Roman Catholic Church and think it quite strong. In Bristol I think there are nineteen Roman Catholic parishes; in Swindon there are four. One of the great strengths of them is that they are able to start from fewer bases. The good Lord is always in charge and so on you depends a great deal whether what is the right thing to happen in the future gets a vision and a push or gets hindered. When Joan went to one of the Mothers' Union branches in one of our parishes (I will not say which), the Diocesan President said, 'I am sorry you have to take over that branch; it is like moving through thick mud.' That was rather severe and it managed to change after a time - but I hope there is no branch represented here about which anyone would say that it is like moving through thick mud. And why? Because they were all looking back to a golden past.

So, God bless you in what you are going to be doing in the future, right at the heart of things, all the nitty gritty, all the simple things that have to be done time and time again. Have a vision of what can be done outside the home and through-out the world. Realise that you are continually on the move. Remember that the first Christians in the New Testament were called, 'People of the Way.' The peo-ple on the road. As you know, I spend most of my life on the M4 and call myself the Bishop of the Motorway. I signed myself the other day, '+Freddy M4' in a letter to one of the clergy and was delighted to receive a letter back, signed 'John A420.' I think, as I drive down the motorway how strange it would be if one met groups of Christians dotted here and there, saying, 'We are stopping here. This is where a very nice Vicar who left us twenty years ago got us - and we are not budging from there. And you can possibly look on those who have been called to full-time of-fice, both in Church and Mothers' Union, as a form of motorway police, to help you when things go wrong, but above all to keep you on the move. And then you need to travel light. I am sure we will all need to travel light: to cut down on what we feel we need in 'plant'. Try too to develop all the time a feeling of serenity amidst all the changes going on around you. A great simplicity is what is needed in outlook and ways of doing things. Then you will have a vision; then you will be pure in heart. Never forget that the word 'sincere' is a Latin word meaning 'with-out wax.' You will just have no make-up, no mask and it will then be so much eas-ier to see God.

Thanksgiving Service for David Kinder: St. Bartholomew, Wootton Bassett
The passing on into the next world of a young husband and a young father is always heart-rending for those who are left behind. Having had a father and a son myself who went on just as unexpectedly, I know that well. There may be some who will try to give comfort by saying that it is God's plan that somehow, somewhere, sometime, we will know the reason why. I do not believe that. I could not believe in a God who treated us as puppets, pulling us on a string here and a string there, according to some pre-arranged plan. That's not the God whom I see revealed in Jesus, a God of infinite love and caring, who made us free to become real people able to respond to his love and working with him. God's world is far too big, far too mysterious, far too complex, as any scientist will know. And life is far too wonderful in all its ideals and aspirations, far too deep - and as the tragedies of the last year have shown us, far too fragile in its beauty - to be something played at like puppets on a string.

So there are no easy, trite answers to give. But I do know, as I know that Linda knows, that God is with us in every experience of life, and through the deepest pain and suffering we turn and hold his hand. He will take us through that and beyond it to a richer and fuller understanding of life and its purpose. This we know from Jesus' own misery and pain and desolation on the Cross, followed by the certain victory of love on Easter Day. I do not know David well - and I use the present tense quite deliberately, because I'm certain that David is even more alive now than he was before - and as that lovely reading reminded us, the room next door is very close, the walls are very thin, and the door is unlocked. But I do know of his very happy, loving family life. I do know of that frank, open friendliness of the true Yorkshireman, the man from God's own county. And I do know of that passionate dedication to his teaching. I do know of the devastation that the news caused in the school and the love and respect in which he was held; that the swimming gala arranged for the day did not take place because of what happened. And I know that he was keen on PE, not merely in order to rear and train competitive young men and women, but because of the team spirit, unselfishness and co-operation that this brought out. And like the true Yorkshireman that he is, he was ready to speak out about what he believed.

A few years ago the *Daily Telegraph* ran an article bemoaning the fact that competitiveness was seeming to take a low place in English schools. And David wrote an answer criticising what had been written; and drew quite a hostile mail because of it. His dedication was constant right to the end of his life here. When he woke in pain in the middle of the night, thinking it was just some major digestive disorder, but he knew that he couldn't go to school that day, at 4 a.m. he got up, wrote a full page of A4 to the number 2 of his department, saying what he would like to happen to his classes that day. And it ended, 'Sorry to land you with this. David.' And so that is why Linda, Simon Penny and Sorrel and all the family want this to be a Thanksgiving Day for all that David is, has been, and is giving now.

A great-grandfather of mine, a poet, once said that those whom we really love closely in a family are God's 'lent jewels' - lent to us for a time - and then we hand them back into God's sake keeping. And so today, with deep sadness but proud thanksgiving Linda and her family are handing back to God a very precious 'lent jewel'. David is not 'lost'; how I wish people wouldn't use that word about people who have been bereaved. David is handed back - and a fortnight ago he celebrated his heavenly birthday. If everyone who has been bereaved would think of the day their loved one passed on as a heavenly birthday, how much better it would be. And so today, with great thanksgiving, but an understanding of the sorrow and the grief, we celebrate David's heavenly birthday, this precious jewel handed back into God's safe keeping - and surround Linda and her family with all our love, all our affection, all our prayers.

Evangelism: Address to Clergy, Lee Abbey, 1972

To start with, may I say that if you were rather dismayed when you saw my name kicking tonight off, you could not have been as dismayed as I was. But this is the fault of the working party and I am just an obedient person who does what he is told. I felt that we are going to have a lot of experts, over the next few days, and we are going to consider the techniques and the modern methods of Evangelism - and that the important thing tonight was to get back to the very simple fundamentals of biblical evangelism - of our Good News. And so what I am going to say may well be (and this is where one is rather nervous with fellow clergy) very platitudinous to a great many of you. But at least they are important to me. And you know this tip, do you not? That when you're listening to a devastatingly dull sermon, it is worth remembering that at least it must be meaning something to the man who is delivering it. And try and see what that 'something' is. And this may well apply this evening; these are the things I have to keep reminding myself about.

My texts are nearly all visual. Firstly, there are over 90 in this room. Look at your neighbour. 'God created man in his own image; in his own image created he him.' If you do not feel that what you are looking at is particularly God-like, then I suggest that you think of any of your heroes in whatever sphere you are attracted - whether it is Beethoven composing his symphonies, Yehudi Menuhin on the violin. If it is in movement, think of Nureyev or Fonteyn. If you're an addict of 'Match of the Day' late on a Saturday evening and arrive bleary-eyed at the altar at 8a.m. the following morning, think of your favourite footballer; for me it's George Best on form, moving down the pitch for Manchester United to score his goals. Or if it's courage, think of Oates or the nun who quietly stepped into line in the concentration camp, letting the sobbing, frightened Jewish girl out. Whatever specially attracts you, realise again the wonder and greatness of man and what human beings can be and do at their best.

The next text I suppose could be said to be the setting of this Abbey and the drive here to it: 'God saw that it was good.' One of the strange joys of being Arch-deacon of Swindon is that I have enormous times of being on my own, driving my car. I have never had so much time of quiet and meditation on my own in any post so far. For the first time after more than twenty years of ministry, I find that I am again looking at nature - and looking at the road at times too. Looking at nature again and realising, for instance, how wonderful the sky is so often, and how beautiful. The shapes of trees, especially in the winter, 'bare ruined choirs, where late the sweet birds sang.' And so my first simple point is that evangelism is about God in his fullness. It is not about the Church; it is not about moral pollution; it's not about Christ first. It is about God in the fullness of the Trinity. We do a great disservice when and if we try to take people straight to Christ; it has to be first of all the wonder of God's whole creation, as Creator and God in his fullness.

The next text, as it were, is on the wrists of nearly all of us - our watches. Time. Redeeming the Time. We need evangelists - and we are all primarily evangelists - to make sure we have time to enter the Kingdom as a little child, to have the wonder, expectancy, excitement - and being still, knowing that 'I am God.' But so often that is just done in a very drab and often rather un-beautiful sanctuary or vestry or church. Find time to do this elsewhere, outside - where we can really recapture the wonder of the small child and the excitement; there must be time to do this, time to be quiet. And we do not get a mastery of time until we realise that we are creatures of time and that everything that we offer to God will inevitably, as creatures, be incomplete and imperfect. One great lesson that Joan, my wife, and I learnt from one of the many curates under whom we have been privileged to serve was from one at the Cathedral in Hong Kong. He was for ever 'hectic' and rushed, and this got us down so much that we decided we would cut out the word 'hectic' from our vocabulary. And believe me - although it is an awful example of one-upmanship and showmanship in a way - when people say that they expect you are busy, you say, 'No, no; not at all; I've plenty of time' - it does make a difference. It does make for a much greater calmness in the end because one can deliberately cut out the feeling that time is on top of us and to accept, in redeeming the time, that we are creatures of God and that we are not gods in control of time.

From there we move on to looking at the extraordinary life of Christ, the Window on God. 'Sir, we would see Jesus.' 'Except a grain of wheat fall into the ground and die.' I have here some seeds picked up from home; I am far too mean and parsimonious to undo the packet. Seeds are all little things - and how much there is a stress in the New Testament and in Christ's teaching on the tiny stuff, on the vulnerability of all that God does. God, the foolish sower; how they must have laughed as Jesus started that parable. No economical, poor Palestinian farmer would scatter seed over the dry soil, over the rocks and stone. He would want to be sure that he put it into some place where it would grow. We would all get worried if our wives came in and said, 'I have bought some seeds, darling, and I have scattered them down the drive, where I know the cars will come.' We would say, 'My dear, you have overdone it, you know.' And this is the sort of thing that God is for ever overdoing; the tiny seed, the tiny vulnerability of all that God does. The start of evangelism is always this little thing, a little beginning - with limited means and the likelihood that a great deal will always be lost: this is God's method. Yet we continually say, 'Well, I have tried' - especially when we get grey-haired and the arteries of the imagination start to harden - 'I have tried that, and it does not work.' Always realise the incredible generosity of God and the vulnerability and the timing of the thing. This goes on in so many ways: the candle or the light burning that will inevitably give itself out - or the oil needing replenishment all the time. There is always the burning out of the evangelist. At the heart of every Christian parish there is a dying priest. That is something we tend to forget: that nowadays this will be the key in terms of spiritual success. So it is a burning up, a vulnerability, something tiny and small, something that may never be large, yeast in the leaven getting lost in it all; so you cannot say, 'Well, what is the result of it all in the end?' It has got lost in the middle - the way the Holy Spirit so often works. You cannot track it down and say, 'That is the result of it, the result of his working', because it is like yeast or it is like just the distinctive flavour that salt gives to the whole. It is the pearl in the field - and you have to buy all the muck of the field as well to get the pearl, something tiny in the midst of it all.

o the next simple and obvious point then is the smallness, the vulnerability, the dying, the death. Then the most extraordinary part of it all - the ordinariness of the tools: wood, hammer, nails, hands: the stage props of the divine drama. A DIY kit that everyone has, so that there is never any need to think we need something very special, very expensive, very clever. The very tools that Jesus used throughout the hidden part of his life as a carpenter are then used here passively on him for the supreme moment of the gospel. Then the example given the night before: again, very simple. The 'texts' here are knees, towel, soap, water, hands, feet. God is often down here kneeling, doing the job that so often Christians feel they cannot do - or are too proud, too tired, too weary to do - that it is again something not very special; and it is something that will have to be done time and time again. And returning to that point about time: 'He knew that his hour had come.' And yet how slowly he moved: that tense, taut moment when he girds himself with the towel, gets the bowl of water. You cannot walk very fast if you are carrying a bowl of water. Already Judas has gone out to do quickly what he has to do. At the fifty-ninth minute of the eleventh hour the link is forged that is the supreme link for Christians through history; very startling, that: right at this very last moment. Then it is that this very simple act has been done: the washing of the feet - followed by the very simple act of the bread and the wine. Not something great, ornate or precious that can be kept forever, but something that is quite ordinary, something that will grow mouldy if it is not used: something that has to be broken and eaten straightaway - and so must be absorbed and used. The Christian religion is not something that you look at, discuss and consider; you participate right in it; you have to get right into the doing of it. So, we have the very simple point of the ordinariness of the tools and the fact that God is in control of time in an extraordinarily leisured way, right to the end, and can wait until this very last minute almost before making this very simple link and connection for us all through time.

Then, as we go on, we learn that failure, by the world's standards, is part of true evangelism: failure and nothing that can be said or done. The very weakness gets more and more, so that he has to remain silent. And pain: pain is part of the perfect scene, and we believe the Cross to be part of the perfect scene. We need not be frightened of pain or think that there is something wrong or degrading or God-forsaken about it. Desolation and despair are part of that scene. Although it's not there as a 'text', any one of us who has been in the East, will know that part of that scene are those terrible flies. I remember once when I was in an Arab village as a medical orderly during the war, before I was ordained, the awful scenes: there would be a mass of flies on the ground, and suddenly there would be a stirring - and there was a baby underneath. The flies were there sucking on the moisture and the eyes and every part of the body. And as Christ was strung on the Cross, with the sweat and the blood, part as it were of the evangelism must have been the flies and the awfulness of not being able to get rid of them. Yet in that moment that we would feel was a moment to get through as fast as we could, come the two supreme prayers: the model of what prayer should not be and the model of the perfect prayer. 'If thou art the Christ, save thyself and us.' Instead it should be, 'Give thyself to us to the end.' The other brief and supreme prayer was 'Jesus, remember me', uttered by the only person to call Our Lord by his first name throughout the Gospel, because only penitence creates real intimacy. Then comes the wonderful answer we know so well: it is not a case of, 'Well, wait, I would like to see whether you are going to do better', but 'Today, thou shalt be with me.' That is the only prayer we need to pray. God can be working in these moments of complete desolation, confined by the nails and the pain and the dying, towards this true evangelism - that point of winning people to him.

Finally, the extraordinary thing that he came back to the group who failed him. That is quite extraordinary. Surely, if you or I were making a new start after Resurrection, we would say, 'Well, they failed; they are out. I will start with another group.' But God is ready to come back time and time and time again to those who have failed him: part of the glory is the marks of the self-sacrifice and the only link between this world and the next, apparently, the only means by which he is recognised, are those marks of self-sacrifice. The disciples are frightened. They do not recognise him, even if he walks to Emmaus with them - until there is the breaking of the bread. This is part of the glory; the glory of Christ risen is not with the self-sacrifice cleared out of the way - a sort of 'That is over and done with, and now I am stupendous, without any of the marks of it.' The marks of the self-sacrifice are part of the glory.

So there, very briefly and simply, are certain points I would feel I would want to have at the back of my mind about evangelism. It is about God in his fullness - and come back to that always as you think of Christ and his suffering and weakness. This is the nature of the God of the atom, the God of the beauty of the world, the God of power. We need to give ourselves time to realise this - that we are creatures of time, not masters of it. Then, as we turn to Christ, the tiny vulnerability of all evangelism at the beginning - and the readiness for this to be so and for a great amount of it to appear to be lost and appear to be in vain. Then the ordinariness of it all, the simple, ordinary tools. And how even right to the last minute the most supremely simple acts can be of complete importance: the washing of the feet, and so on through the suffering and the death, even using those last minutes of dying for this wonderful example of prayer and what prayer is about. And the return to the people who have failed, showing them that they are pardoned and forgiven and that the marks of the self-sacrifice are part of the eternal glory.

appendix ii Correspondence

between Freddy Temple and Stephen Verney
on theology and pacifism, April 1939 - July 1941

SEV to FST 2.4.39

Quite a successful hitch-hike. I got clear of Newport by 10.15 and got a pillion ride on a motor cycle to Usk, a lorry to Monmouth and another to Hereford, where I arrived about 12.30 and had bread and cheese. Then two private cars to Leominster, a car and a lorry to Ludlow (2.45), two lorries to Wellington (4.30) and a lorry and a car to Chester (5.45). Then, as my knee was hurting a bit, I took a train and got home for 7s.9d. Really with that hitch-hike and those two days in the Rhondda I have seen my own class as they look from 'underneath', and it's an odious sight. The way we despise and condemn and slight and sweat the working class is nauseous enough, but then on top of that we're so worthless in ourselves, so simpering and spineless, so callow and lax, that we're not fit to be masters in the best ordered society, but like some poisonous parasitic growth we ought to be lopped off and burned. I positively shudder now to meet these painted puppets and wasp-waist dowagers. We're all so unnatural and neurotic and dishonest with one another. It's rude to look another person between the eyes, anything that's open-hearted is 'not done', we can't laugh, or feel, or love; we're rotten and we call it culture. Now I suppose I'm being intolerant again, but to our own opinions, we rich, when it leads in effect to the persecution of our betters? Poor saps that we are!

I am more frightened than I like to confess. It's all this unsound doctrine of yours about Christ and the Church and surrender; I'm terrified it might prove sound. Now I'm quite prepared to accept Christ as the son of God, though I think it unlikely. I could at a pinch accept the leadership of the Church, abhorrent as it would be. But if there's one thing above all others which I *cannot* do, it is to surrender myself for any reason to anything ever. And yet that's just what I'm beginning to see the necessity of. I see it like this. If God is the first cause of everything, and if we are just attributes of him, all this setting up of ourselves, and all this striving after anarchy is just selfishness. It is cutting ourselves off from the limitless power that is behind us. Every increase in my own individuality is just another fetter, another barrier between me and God. Experience bears this out all along the line, and right behind experience, deep down with that longing to love and be loved, there is another longing, to be overwhelmed by the majesty of God, and to be ground underfoot by him, and to reach perfect happiness as his slave.

But, but, BUT - where or what is God? I get almost petulant here. If I've gone so far as to admit, against the grain, that I might be right in surrendering to him, why the devil doesn't he show me what he is? I can't surrender to nothing; if it were a 'well informed circle', that would be enough. And if it were what you think it is, a father who is love, and who was crucified for us at Golgotha, then I think I should swoon with delight, and go delirious with happiness. But the whole idea is fantastic, and yet it's gripping me by the throat, and I'm afraid of it. Last night we discussed the nature of God, sitting in the moonlight that streamed down over Snowdon and across the Menai Straits, and he was there in the silence. That I know, and that is the only thing I know about him, that he is there where silence is. Beyond that, everything is painful and uncertain.

FST to SEV 5.4.39.
Thank you very much indeed for your letter which contained great signs of your having read Newman (that subtle flattering touch!). I have given you a special file all to yourself among my letters which I can assure you is a high honour, instead of putting your letters among 'Oxford: various 1939'.

I'm glad you got back so easily. I went straight back to London. I went round to Ashley Raeburn's and we went for a long and very fast walk, with him talking, as he does, very bitterly and earnestly about Germany: we discussed pacifism which is very difficult for him as some of his uncles have been in camps and now committed suicide; and he told me that he had discussed it with you. It is dreadful the way 'the faithful' are falling away: Oliver has been to a Liberal rally and feels less sure. Tom Sadler has given it up too. But I am becoming more and more deeply convinced. Have you read Joad's 'Why War?', one of the latest Penguin Specials? Good - and he puts all the intellectual arguments about force and justice clearly. I feel quite satisfied now: Joad and a little religious conviction make a solid pacifist I think.

I have also been reading more about English Imperialism between 1895 and 1905: oh! it made me so angry; I had to fling down the book and go out for a bit. We wanted to divide up the Portuguese Empire and establish military control over Spain in order to keep France quiet in the colonies. And then at the Hague Conference of 1898, this is what the British delegate said to someone - or at least was reported to have said: 'The sole principle he admitted was that might was right and he had made it quite clear that in the event of war he should regard any agreements that might be concluded at the Hague as null and void, if they were opposed in any way to the political and military interests of his country'. Well!

I agree with what you say about the 'upper classes' to a great extent. I don't mind the unnaturalness at all though: I think the game of polite conversation etc. is most amusing and it would be dull to drop it. I hope you can bear rather a long extract from an excellent book by Renier, a foreigner, on 'The English: Are they Human?':

Now it would appear that conversation from which all that is personal and all that
is brilliant has been banned must be extremely dull and unimaginative. Must not

the conversation of the English Upper Class be unutterably boring? That is where the subtle and adaptable genius of the nation plays its part. The Englishman is a being of delicate shades and distinctions. Behind his serene face and reserved manner he hides the reactions of an appreciative mind. He may not utter them directly, but he loves to pour himself out by implication. Oh! the strange charm of two English people seeking one another and finding one another through the barrier of conventional talk! No brutal searchlight as between Continentals, to set out the other person in clear-cut outline. There is a pleasant game without set rules; thoughts are thrown out that dance like fairies on the thrilling air of a hot summer's noon, meeting and joining hands for a dance that defies the laws of gravity. An illusion to a half-forgotten admission, a hint that is thrown out, caught up without seeming effort, memories that rustle, dulled chords that faintly vibrate. Echoes re-echo, minds open and admit a new notion which is silently stored up. It is the greatest and finest game the English play - and do they even know that it exists?

He is referring only to the Upper Class. But I agree with you on the whole that we are rotten.

How good about your coming round to surrender etc! I think it is vital: personally, I go even further and don't allow even a limited free-will. Then of course you say, as you have in the past, 'How can there be any condemnation etc. and judgement?' I refer then to Brunner and his article resulting in, 'I ought but I cannot', which I do think sums up the case entirely. Predestination does not of course lead to inactivity: on seeing the good (by that I mean seeing with one's whole soul and being) one just must do it: but that one should see it at all or want to see it, is all due to God: without him nothing can be done and ever will be done if we strive by ourselves. SURRENDER is the cry all along the line. And if God is love and love is best as I'm certain it is when redeeming, all is satisfactory. I agree that the theory that God was crucified is fantastic: I wish more people would realise when they mumble the Creed that they are then speaking more fantastic stuff than they do all the rest of the week.

I agree with you about silence but feel God there just as much in noise, especially in the sea and wind. I'm sure that, along with the personal love side, it is vital to emphasise the awe-inspiring, almost catastrophic, side of God as shown in Nature.

SEV to FST 29.5.39

I don't really know whether I ought to write you this letter or not, but you led me so far up the garden path that perhaps you would like to know what I found at the top. Well, it was something like this.

For about 18 months, I suppose, ever since I came up to Oxford and began to think, I have found Christianity very difficult to swallow. You know what I thought - it was superstitious and anthropomorphic; Freud would have a lot to say about it; it was a projection of man's own personality and limitations upon the incomprehensible eternity of God, and so on. So I made an excursus into Yoga, and that seemed to satisfy the need for mysticism; there I did seem to find a peace that passeth all understanding, and there my mind did seem to come to rest upon the eternal values. I see now how disgusting it was that a mind of 19 should come to rest, and I suppose the finality of the whole thing was what made me feel uneasy about it all the time. Anyway, when I became acquainted with you it was the beginning of a lot of trouble. Philosophy was conjuring up for me tremendous conceptions of a cosmic order, with God as the source, and with all creation as his attributes. But it was all static; it was the 'well-informed circle' of Bicknoller, something to be worshipped perhaps, but nothing that could respond. (How like Newman's 'Apologia' this is getting. But wait a moment.) Then in the Vac I was arguing with a cousin, and all in a flash God had become vitality. This must have been the beginning of the end, for at the beginning of this term I tried to write that paper about the 'Divinity of Christ'. I was working very hard at it, reasoning about it, mastering it, proud of it, but uneasy that if God was the source of all vitality I must surrender myself to him. And after I had read it and discussed it and thought a bit more about it, I came to an intellectual decision that I would surrender to God. That was just a week ago. What has happened this last week is not yet clear, but one thing I know, that if I am to describe it I must cut out the word 'I', or at least define it as God working in me. For what happened passed beyond my control. Really, do you think it ought to be put on paper? But I'm sure I could never tell you otherwise, and you'll understand and fill in the gaps.

The general confession last Sunday shook me. I had never realised before quite what it meant. I'd always thought that on the whole I wasn't quite as bad as that, and that pretty comfortable quarters must be a-building for me up there. But suddenly I confessed some sins, and forgiveness didn't come. I surrendered to God, rather condescendingly, and he just didn't seem to be interested. That was a nasty jar. The next day I tried again; I even prayed on my knees, and all the time the sense of my sin grew, and there was no forgiveness. Then I did begin to understand that my whole life had been based on pride and selfishness, how nothing that I had ever done had been of any value. You know, Freddy, that was awful, because even what had seemed good acts I now saw had just been self-gratification, in an effort at self-perfection and the rewards I knew would follow on that. I was just helpless, because any activity that sprang from myself I now saw was useless and I couldn't find a substitute. Do you remember that on Monday night you told me that surrender wasn't just accepted gratefully by God, but that he waited until it was complete? Well, on Tuesday, I set about making it complete, or rather I just ceased from all activity, and layer upon layer of selfishness, all the things I most cherished, just peeled off me, all the things I had most loved, and hardest of all, my friends had to go. And then, it was on Wednesday morning, for a moment there was nothing between me and God; for a moment life stopped; there was nothing left to support me, and I fell, fell into the arms of Christ. It's ridiculous to talk like this, but it *was* ridiculous, for suddenly he said to me, 'Blessed are the poor in spirit, for theirs is the kingdom of heaven'; and then I believed. There it was in my Greek Testament, 'Blessed are they who are beggars in spirit: for theirs is the Kingdom of Heaven; blessed are they that mourn, for the Holy Spirit shall come to comfort them. Blessed are the meek; blessed are they which do hunger and thirst after righteousness; blessed are the merciful, the pure in heart, the peacemakers'. Yes, of course, not blessed are the Greats men, blessed are the secretaries of musical societies, blessed are those who have individuality of character.

Good Lord, I am a poor sap! Fancy having been blind for twenty years. And now I know what happened when Christian threw off his burden, and though it is still terribly hard to believe that Christ is the son of God, it is harder not to. When the self dies, then, and only then, does it become possible to believe, and then all the laws of reason and of philosophy are superseded. All sorts of problems are resolved; there are all sorts of new avenues to be explored and new stones to be turned. And the perpetually humiliating thing is that I cannot myself explore them or turn them, but only if God thinks fit to give me grace can I even go forward again.

There's much I've left out, all the passages in the Bible that suddenly have fresh meaning, all the new light that is pouring in from all round; but it's no use trying because I don't understand it yet.

I must stop before I bore you with what you must feel to be platitudes. That's another humiliating thing! But don't forget, there's more joy in heaven over me at this moment than over 99 yous!

SEV to FST 3.9.39

I have just heard the Prime Minister and Richard Bishop has left the house. He comes from George Davis in South Wales. George Davis is president of the Welsh Pacifist Association and is forming a corps of pacifists to work on auxiliary fire work or ambulance work in S. Wales. He is a friend of the Commissioner for that Special Area and is sure that he can obtain from him permission for the Corps to work there under civil and not military control. This is probably a unique privilege that we should not obtain in other parts of the country. Consequently I am in on this, subject only to your being in on it too. The snag is that it is Wales, and not London; it is hard to work in a country of which you don't feel a part, but we can't pick and choose. I hope that S. Wales may be the rallying point for English pacifism and that from there we may be able to send units to London or abroad. Do come. If you were there, particularly, and others to whom I am writing, we might really be able to form a society under George Davis that could preserve the things we care about and perhaps be the nursery for the builders of the future. I have worried a lot about pacifism during the last weeks. I agree with you now that it is hard to go against the church. But the church is divided. Its pronouncements about war do not cover modern war and many prominent churchmen are pacifist, including the Bishop of Birmingham and I think perhaps the Pope. These arguments satisfy me that, where I feel the personal call so strong the other way, I should obey it. We shall not be deserting our country, but I hope serving her physically and spiritually with all our might.

It might be that there will be a University Ambulance Corps. Would you rather join that? On the whole I should vote for S. Wales, since it would not be class distinct and would provide a field for a lot of other work while we were not being bombed! They seem to think that Cardiff etc. will be a dangerous area.

FST to SEV 11.9.39

George Davis is a great attraction in Wales. The Master [of Balliol, A.D. Lindsay] also said I 'couldn't do better' than go with him: that is very strong advice I feel from such a man. George Davis says I could be of great help at Maes-yr-haf at the moment. So I feel I may go down there and wait till something more important in London is needed. I wish I knew what to do!

SEV to FST 12.9.39

London looks like being more efficient, more immediate, more dangerous, more at the heart of the war where the pacifist influence is most needed. But Wales is under the guidance of the finest leader and would probably give us work of a more valuable nature. We should be fighting poverty quite as much as air raids, I imagine; and thus perhaps fitting ourselves better for the peace-making.

London and abroad! For a country bumpkin like me that is a prospect full of glamour and heroism. If I am to face up squarely to this war I think I should spend a time working in and behind the trenches. And yet of course these are silly emotional reasons. What we should do is go where the best work is to be done, and damn the glamour.

You see I am as puzzled as you are. I have written for particulars of the London unit, and shall write perhaps to George Davis. If you are going anyhow to Maes yr Haf, you can find out how their plans are progressing and if it looks like being useful work. If not, let's go to London.

FST to SEV 15.9.39

I feel we must end up together and we seem to be equally puzzled as to what to do and feel the same. I will write more later. At the moment I am working at a Citizen's Advice Bureau in the mornings: all types of work and fascinating!

SEV to FST 15.9.39

'Who is my neighbour?' Luke 10.29. Answer: The brother of George Davis. He has received a letter from George implying that nothing is being done in S. Wales direct and that the best thing is to apply to the P.P.U. [Peace Pledge Union] He also mentions this Quaker ambulance, organised by Arnold Rowntree (whom I know). His brother is writing to Arnold to ask if non-Quakers will be admitted. Meanwhile he advises the P.P.U.

This seems also what George advises in his letter to me. So I am sending my name in to the P.P.U. on the form you sent me. Will you do so direct?

On the whole I'm glad. It relieves us of the moral compulsion to go to S. Wales and opens up all sorts of more exciting, if less righteous, avenues! I am in the middle of a Red Cross course in first aid, but I expect we shall get sent to some training centre. Shall you still go to Maes yr Haf? George hinted in the letter I forwarded that you would probably rather do ambulance. Long letter from George Levack; he has given up pacifism.

FST to SEV 18.9.39

How frantic it is to decide and how all one's letters seem to cross! I have sent in my name direct to the P.P.U. It was very difficult to know what to do about Maes-yr-haf: it would have been terrific to have worked with them and I heard this morning that they could have me and would be glad if I came. But I feel it was only good as a waiting place while watching developments in ambulancing etc. I don't think I should have been happy there for the duration; possibly this was moral cowardice but I would have felt everyone saying, 'Young man: why isn't he doing something more active?' I hope we will land up together; I said on my paper I would like to go with you! As they have over 1000 names we might otherwise have landed up, one on the land in Cumberland or somewhere and one in France. But we will have to take what comes.

I have joined the Anglican Pacifist Fellowship and am very much excited by their pamphlet written by Evelyn Underhill, whose vast book on 'Mysticism' I have just finished. I am in almost entire agreement with it and I had no idea that such a body of opinion was being created in the Church. Write for it - 'The Church and War' - and join it if you agree. You would indeed be fully in the Orthodox lap then! It is much better and greater than the P.P.U. doctrines.

Yes, I have had a long letter from George as well: I knew he would not keep to his pacifism after a letter from him in July. Russell Acheson has given it up too, but it is surprising how many people have written saying that they hope one sticks to it and how many, when one tells them outright, respect it.

I have not done any Red Cross as yet; I shall do that when definitely allotted to it. I feel I must do a great deal of reading still and I think 'Federal Union' is a vitally important idea to spread. I see no hope for a good peace without it. I have sent out a great number of pamphlets and some people are interested. Do you belong? If not, why?

I had a very harrowing day on Saturday. My sister Rose went off to India on the 'Strathmore' to be married. There was a full-dress family goodbye and it was too much. She went out with another friend going to be married, who also had her family there. And the two little brides stood at the window of the train, waving and smiling gallantly with tears streaming down their faces: very sad and touching. We don't even know if the boat had a convoy.

My work at the Bureau is great fun. One is taken by it to weirdest and dirtiest little streets and houses, behind all of which the great struggles of body and soul are being fought.

SEV to FST 21.9.39

Well, Freddy, I've written to all your societies, Anglican Fellowships and Federal Unions. They all sound terribly right and I shall shortly be an ardent member of them all.

I have written too to Birmingham. Stanley Davis (brother of George) has heard that they have 300 applicants, and room in their training camp for 60. Friends get first choice. Friends of Friends will also be accepted. Are you a friend of a Friend? You are at least the friend of a friend of a Friend.

My sister Marjorie visited the P.P.U. in London yesterday on my behalf. They seemed doubtful of starting on ambulance work for many moons, since it would have to be under the Government and at the moment the Government has a full complement of medical workers. The Quaker thing looks more promising and ever so much more attractive. Like you, I should far rather join the Quakers - but even the Quaker unit would probably not be ready for us much this side of Christmas. The P.P.U. suggested I should come to London and do the sort of work you are on. That is one alternative for filling in the gap. The other is to go back to Oxford for next term. The Master wants to know at once and I have promised to tell him by the middle of next week. Will you advise me? I should like to start straight away training, if it were possible, so as to be qualified by the time the air raids come. But I don't think it worth hanging about doing odd jobs when there is the chance of reading Plato in Trinity. (Do you believe it? Balliol men are being housed in bloody Trinity!) So unless the Quakers say, 'come at once', or you say that there's a really important job which I ought to be doing in London, I think I'll go up in October. I could always come down again in a hurry if anything offered.

What horrid things family partings are. We had a sort of one this week. Eight children were all at home, perhaps some of them for the last time. 4 sons of military age, and 2 daughters in it as well this time. It must be ugly for parents. Ralph is in Oxford, getting put into the army, and Hugh took the oath in Liverpool yesterday. If they kill him, I don't know but that I should run amok. Though what's the use then? We shall all have worked harder to prevent this, and we must work harder again to end it for ever. As you say, a lot of people respect one's views, and there is no sign of white feathers. We'll break those swords into ploughshares yet!

FST to SEV 22.9.39

I can't really advise you well because I don't think it is a matter of duty but inclination. Both at Oxford working at Plato and in London at a Bureau you would be doing work of vital importance. And so now I can only give the reasons why I would choose London and not Oxford if I were in your position.

I think those who go back to Oxford have a very difficult time, especially if they have enjoyed Oxford in the past. And the whole place will be *so* different and will be heavy with the atmosphere of its happier past. Most of your age group will be away too. And then for one term only? Will you be able to settle down to Plato just for one term? It would be different if you meant to do it for a year. Would you like that? When all your family are doing other work?

I don't *want* to deter you but you must face these questions and answer them: and you mustn't go if you can't answer them to yourself satisfactorily.

I have decided life is infinitely sad! Today's moving thought! And I'm glad: I find a 'divine melancholy' pleasant and quite amusing!

SEV to FST 26.9.39

Here is my reply from the Quakers. It looks as though they would like to accept us at a later camp if we liked to apply.

Did you hear the Quaker sermon over the wireless on Sunday? He interpreted 'whose service is perfect freedom' as meaning that we should stand up and speak to God face to face as free men, not grovel in front of him like slaves. Now that seems to me very revealing and explains that uneasy feeling that we both had at Maes yr haf that the Quakers lack something; their humility was somehow proud and their gentleness hard. Because, I think, they have omitted John the Baptist. John came to prepare the way for the Lord, by preaching the baptism of repentance for the forgiveness of sins. Christ himself lays very little emphasis, except at the beginning, on repentance. He goes on to preach the positive gospel of love. The Quakers, it seems to me, live the gospel of love, but not based on a life that has forgiveness. They take Christ's precepts and commandments, and obey them. But they are beginning too high. That's where the Church is so good, the Church to which they don't belong. It realises the psychology of men better than the Quakers, understands that very few of them are yet level with the first milepost, repentance, and so lays emphasis on it and puts it right in the forefront. That is the Church's weakness as well as its strength. By harping on repentance it gets a reputation for 'doctrine' as opposed to 'good works'. But of course its weakness is only the weakness of its critics. If they would hurry up and repent, and clear away the obstacles of their own selfishness, then the Church could begin to build in them the kingdom of love.

Do you agree with any of that? I think I myself have just about understood what John the B was meaning and am beginning to explore the possibilities of Christianity itself, for it is now for the first time possible for me to understand it. And it's a fascinating and most necessary exploration. Perhaps it's cheating to bring in Oxford here; I had meant to keep it for the next paragraph, but really the problem is all one. Theology and philosophy for me mean very much the same thing; only theology takes on where philosophy leaves off. But I must learn all that philosophy can teach me first, and to give up learning now seems to me a pity, not so much because I should lose my education, as because (I think I'm honest in saying this) it would block the road by which I seem most likely to come to a knowledge of God. I couldn't study thoroughly by myself. I was trying last night to understand Epicureanism and its consequences and really felt hot and choked, as with frustrated sexual desire. I simply long to understand why it all is, and where we are going; not 'long' in the sense of 'it would be nice to know', but long and desire with my whole self, as though I were pregnant with a knowledge that is beating and hammering to be born. I don't feel ready to live yet. I'm three years younger than you, remember, and though I want to fashion my life towards the same end as you, I don't see the way through so clearly yet. I'm right in the middle of a whirlpool of questions and unless I solve them I can't see myself being much use in active work. That's why even one term at Oxford would be so invaluable.

And now the chief reason for going up. Prof. Collingwood has offered to tutor me, in spite of war. I know that he could teach me to think. He has an amazing clarity of mind, a clarity that seems itself to have become a source of light, and to illuminate the dark corners of our own sluggish brain. And if I could think straight, I should be doubly effective. So that's my 'Apologia' for going up.

Yet I feel uncomfortable about it. As you say the work in London would be 'pedestrian'. I can see a certain venom light up your eye as you write that word. You know quite well that what I hate, and what I need, is pedestrian work; and having taken it on yourself, you see my failing all the more clearly. I also feel that I may have let you down in our bargain to work together. Have I? The long and short is that I am writing today to the Master to ask if I can come up, and be tutored by Collingwood, until I am needed for Pacifist work, and that, when I am wanted, we must work together.

FST to SEV 29.9.39

I am very glad indeed that you are going back to Oxford: I wanted to make quite certain that you were doing right and so weighted the other side as heavily as I could. I saw your letter to John when you said that you were giving up Oxford and did not want to go back now; I wanted to be sure that you had not forgotten the reasons you put forward then.

I agree with what you say about the Quakers; repentance and surrender are the vitally important things. I have reached a very odd stage of thought, Stephen: one to which I have been coming for some time - that of the 'essential paradox'. I have a firm conviction of determinism: I can do absolutely nothing without God's help. And yet I have an equally firm belief in good and bad and right and wrong. I see it clearly myself and yet can't explain it to others. Then again, to be really happy one must be continually discontented with oneself. To live fully one must die to one's self daily, and that is a painful process. To make the most of life one must realise the essential tragedy of selfishness and the stupendous task of redemption and all the suffering involved. To enjoy and love one's friends fully is to be continually in pain at parting from them. Christianity itself is paradoxical enough: the Cross is its supreme instance: a crucified criminal deserted by all: in bodily pain, 'I thirst'; in mental anguish, 'My God, my God, why hast thou forsaken me?' Yet it is here that men 'fall down and worship'. It is just that love and unselfishness are supremely worthwhile. Why? One can give no answer but one's life - and that may influence some. Doctrine and reasoning are only of use to those who have an inclination to believe. Do you agree?

What are your views on intercession? I find it very difficult indeed to relate to an Almighty and all-Good God. In fact at the moment I like almost silent prayer, just a sinking back into, as it were, the arms of God: I find it needs intense mental concentration but when attained it is like floating on a powerful stream. One has only to think of humanity and all the moral struggles being fought out in each soul, and then the universe and nature, to grovel in abject humility before the God who controls it all.

Have you read 'the Uncle' on St. John [William Temple's *Readings in St. John's Gospel*, 1939]? Do if you can; I really do think it is very good indeed and each page gives one so much to think about. Yesterday I walked on Wimbledon Common and it was a perfect evening: England in Autumn: a soft wind blowing and just that touch of wistfulness which makes anything perfect. It is the time of year when all the country seems to understand one fully and the trees say, 'Yes, we realise: you needn't tell us'. I saw

> 'The light that never was by sea or land
> The consecration and the poet's dream.'

My bureau work continues to be interesting. How poor people are! What a fight we have got, Stephen, both with ourselves and others, to get the world any better.

FST to SEV 11.10.39
I wonder when you return to Oxford? Anyhow, I write this to speed you on your way for a successful term.

I had dinner with Ashley last night. He and his family have suffered so much - and that's what always upsets me most about pacifism. It's terrifying the standard we have set ourselves in accepting it, Stephen: quite terrifying and I think impossible without long periods of prayer (or will be later as one plunges more and more into the fight).

SEV to FST 17.10.39
It was kind of you to have that letter waiting for me.

Oxford is mutilated, but still alive. We are all packed into Trinity, but fortunately I have got into a room with Madron, who is a delightful companion. There is little private life to be lived and little solitude and time for quiet thinking. It is rather a time when the whole environment is stimulating you to action and argument; discussions are much less academic; the old problems are suddenly real.

I wish I were a better person. As you say, one needs long periods of prayer, in which to gather one's failures together and marshal them like troops for a new battle, and to let the grace of God take possession and work through one. I find it hard to believe that I am a good enough person to be a pacifist, and yet in times of prayer a great strength does come, and a great confidence, and I feel that, though I am only a man, if I ask him, God through Christ will give me power to transcend my own mortality. And so I am going on with it.

SEV to FST 22.10.39

I feel too tired, and consequently depressed, to trust my own judgement at the moment. Pacifism is terribly hard again; it seems to crush all the life out of me by the demands it makes. I long to throw it all up, to let the burden of idealism slip from my shoulders and find some relief in a tangible fight against Hitlerism, ideal enough in its way, and with the support of millions of my countrymen, and my own reason. But something else (Love incarnate carrying a cross?) fascinates me so that I must go on. Even as I write I see my own mistake. What is it that 'the Uncle' says about not struggling? I'm trying to carry the whole weight of pacifism, and the implications of its witness, on my own shoulders. Idiot!

FST to SEV 26.10.39

I had my interview last Friday with Cadbury at the Penn Club. There were about 10 of us, of all sizes and shapes. Cadbury saw us all together at first and said he hoped we realised that ambulance work was not heroic rescue of the dying so much as the continual emptying of the bed-pans of those who have diarrhoea! He then saw us alone and sifted us according to our convictions. I started the usual about it being one aspect of a whole type of life and he put down his pen, turned to the other man there and said I ought to write his speeches for him!

Anyhow, we got on well and he said he would probably take me in the next camp. I feel uneasy about this, Stephen, but I felt, as I feel now, that it would have been selfish and ungrateful if I had said then, 'Oh! but I have a great friend etc.' I do feel it is right for me to take whichever camp I am offered, Stephen. And I feel sure if we weren't at the same camp we would connect up in France all right. I do hope I haven't let you down.

I have had since then a most exciting offer to work on the Christian News Letter run by Dr. Oldham [J.H. Oldham, leading ecumenical campaigner]: this may be *the* thing of the war as regards the Church. He has got working for him 'the Uncle', Lindsay, Milford, Eliot, Cockin, Barry, Toynbee, Tawney, Dorothy Say-

ers, Niebuhr and all the greatest brains. They are going to deal with present problems in the light of Christianity. It will be a thrilling newsletter each week. I had
tea in the Athenaeum with Oldham and he offered me a job on the editorial staff.
It was very tempting - but wrong for me I know. It would be shielding behind pacifism. However he needs help very much as the demand for it is far larger than he
had expected, and so I am going to work with him till wanted by Cadbury.

Pacifism is, as you say, useless if one struggles alone. My view of it is now entirely that of 'the Uncle' I think - that it is a call to certain people and demands higher
standards all round. Well, that is terrifying and stimulating, Stephen. It means
God has picked on us among others for the task, while utterly unworthy for it.
One can only grovel before such an offer and ask for help to carry it out. One's
belief that one has been chosen for this course is so arrogant that one must be incredibly humble.

I have come to the conclusion that the one supreme problem for theology is
that of evil and reconciling it with omnipotence. And there is no intellectual
proof. Only life and example can show that redeeming love is the best thing the
world knows, better than a love that has no redeeming to do.

SEV to FST 29.10.39

What a mark you seem to have made in high places! It's a tremendous honour to
have been asked to join Oldham and you're the right man for them. You'd do it
well and enjoy it. But I'm glad for your own sake you refused. Emptying bed-pans
will be a better training for taking orders, because you are already rooted and
grounded in the Church, and more ecclesiastical work would only be labouring
the point. What a good thing too about Cadbury. Of course you couldn't have said
anything about me; it would have sounded most ungracious. But if you are definitely to join their next camp, I'm not sure that I won't make another effort on my
own to get accepted. George Davis might help.

I have reached, I think, the crisis of pacifism. Since the war has already begun,
I believe that pacifism is politically *wrong*. It will make a German victory more
likely and a German victory would mean a disastrous peace treaty. Whatever we
may think about the fruits of war, there is no doubt that a British peace would be
more Christian than a German peace. An arbitrated peace would be best of all,
but that doesn't affect the issue. The hard fact remains that pacifism, when the
issue of war is in the balance, is making a Nazi peace treaty more likely; so that by
following Christ we seem to be stabbing him in the back.

'The Uncle' would say, 'Be realists. God has given you a mind; use it. He means
his work to be done by human minds, subject to his will, but nevertheless subject
to their own limitations. Man must work for God on his own level and, understanding that human affairs evolve according to laws of this visible world, he must
work within those laws himself if he is to help mankind forward.'

That seems to me to be a very Christian and common sense point of view. Our only answer can be to accept it for the majority of men, and to agree that unless the majority accepted it there would be anarchy. (Anarchy must lead in a generation to general warfare, tyranny, etc.) But we must add, 'We believe that for those who are pure in heart there is another way, to transcend human evolution by being carriers of the direct power of God. This is an amoral doctrine, or supra-moral, perhaps. If it were general it would lead to anarchy, and in fact it never will be general, for we do not believe in the Millennium. But we do believe that a few have a direct duty to witness to God and damn the consequences, and have the right to stand aside from earthly battles, to be protected physically by others, while they fight a spiritual battle. They are to be the pure flames of the gospel, burning relentlessly and without any regard for consequence. Others may scheme and puzzle and hammer out the world's course. These few are there to keep alive the light and the warmth of love, and that alone is their duty.'

It is only in this belief that I can now justify my pacifism, and that is why I think I must have reached the crisis. Because it means either I join up in the armies of England and the armies of the Church and, accepting my destiny as a man, fight for the cause of Christ as my reason and my moral sense demand, or I claim, which is manifestly ridiculous, to be one of those chosen few, the pure in heart. Yet is it quite ridiculous? For I believe that the power to purify my heart can be given, and will be given if I can live that life of 'daily dying'. Therefore the complete surrender of my life, and the unconditional pledge to serve God with all my powers, are the only conditions on which I can remain a pacifist. I seem to have reached the Master's position and, finding myself anything but a saint, am perturbed.

FST to SEV 1.11.39

I agree about pacifism being *politically* wrong. (I underline the other word to you.) But we are not 'stabbing Christ in the back': the Christian's duty I feel is to live a life of love and lead others to do the same, and I'm sure it is not fruitless even if there are no *political* good results. Christ's rebuke to Peter, as Underhill says, is I think the answer to that. I do see the Master's point of view very strongly and did at one time hold it: even then I think we should go on being pacifist. Of course we are not 'pure in heart', but that power can be given. But now I am tending to swing back to Raven and Underhill's view. Raven wrote a terrific letter to the News Letter (I deal with all the letters, sorting out what I think will interest Oldham) saying that he thought that all the collaborators [i.e. with the Government] belonged to the Old Order and were mature before 1910 and did not understand the new outlook. I think there is much in that. Doesn't the Master's and 'the Uncle's' view involve too great an identification of Church and State, the blunder of the Church since Constantine? England is *not* Christian. To be un-Christian does not stop a person being charming, but there is, or ought to be, a radical difference between them. One is God-centred and one self-centred. Should Christianity only be for the few at the moment who feel called? Has it not always been thinking it has too wide a membership? Has the time come to break away from the State, reduce and purify membership, and then start out again into the world winning over individuals and working fully in the world, living up to absolute standards? Does this involve pacifism as well? I don't know as yet, but I think so. Anyhow, on the orthodox view too I think pacifism is justified, especially yours: I wouldn't say that if I didn't mean it, and I know you well.

Do you see 'Christian Pacifist'? A very good article by Underhill this week about peace in the soul: 'Though on the surface it may be rough weather, twenty fathoms down it is quite calm'. That is what one should aim at. 'The peace of God does not mean indifference to sins and sufferings. It can co-exist with the sharpest pain, the utmost agony of compassion. It is peace bought at a great price: the peace of the Cross, of absolute acceptance, utter abandonment to God, a peace inseparable from sacrifice. The true pacifist is a redeemer and must accept with joy the redeemer's lot. He too is self-offered without condition for the peace of the world.'

[At this time, Freddy and Stephen joined the Friends Ambulance Unit, went to Finland, and were then taken home through Norway with the British army.]

SEV to FST 26.5.40
Has the question not now become, 'Are we justified in trading on our consciences any longer?' Trading it is; that I realised as soon as I began contemplating the R.A.M.C. as an alternative. Our lot is so much pleasanter. We must be careful of masochism, but we must be even more careful of self-indulgence. Let's admit, then, that a good 25% of our horror of war is horror of discipline and discomfort and all the difficulties that will be obstacles to the Christian life, such as environment, bullying sergeant-majors, ignorant officers, and the purposes of violence and destruction towards which we shall be directing our energies.

But these things cannot be urged as conscientious objection. In so far as war makes the Christian life harder, it's only a challenge. Does it make the Christian life impossible? No, we've admitted it doesn't. We've further admitted that the war has to be fought by a Christian country and that universal pacifism would be a disaster. What is left? The idea of a prophetic minority. The idea of a special call, and faith that must follow. So long as Britain's winning, by all means be a prophet of the new era that victory is to herald in. While we're on the up and up, let's be one step ahead.

But when once we start slipping down, what was a step ahead will become a step behind. If pacifism is in any way a Christian judgement in the realm of *politics*, then pacifism in face of a German victory is just utopian, out of the picture. It will be just a feeble clutching at a receding raft. For Nazism, I do believe, is leagued with Satan. We can excuse it, but we can't shut our eyes to it. Their victory will mean a dark age.

Our only loophole, then, is if pacifism refuses to face the fact of politics and,

377

laying down the duties of citizenship, offers itself and, if necessary, its nation, as martyrs to the naked ideal of love. That sounds well. But are we right to be hopeless optimists? Your uncle would quote Browning:

> *This low man, adding one to one, his hundred's soon hit*
> *That high man, aiming at a million, misses an unit.*

We shall 'miss an unit' and, what's more, register a minus score in the age of emotional paganism that will ensue.

FST to SEV 29.5.40

Stephen, I hope I see you soon to talk. I hope you will stay in the F.A.U. For one thing you would do nothing in the army for weeks, months, years! But that is not a real argument. I see nothing to make one change over from our pacifism. I can now only give my own views as my attack is very personal and may not do for you. I have considered it and am prepared to see the Nazis in England, in Damarel, in Balliol. I think I must be prepared to let all the embodiments of values I have go under rather than violate them by fighting them: the values will not go under. The Cross is the supreme example. And England is not the only hope of the world. There is China and India. I feel I can do best by trying to keep on the Christian goal of perfect love, failing hopelessly all the time of course, and not minding really seeing those things one loves go: the Master was so good on that a fortnight ago. If the Nazis win, we will be in a unique position as some of the few Christians who have kept out of the struggle: we would be offering a protest to the Nazis in the same way as the German Christians now in a concentration camp. And if England wins, we can help to keep Christianity apart from the national struggle and level to which it is already sinking. These new events have not shaken my pacifism, but made me more humble about how I have failed in the other respects.

Well, that may be of no use to you, Stephen, and you may feel you must go. Home has been difficult: I disagree on so much now and though it seldom comes above the surface, there is never complete calm. Have you read 'Good God', a new Penguin? Rather good. The Uncle has written a good article called 'Theology Today', which admits that all his past stuff is out-of-date and agrees much more with what we, or at least I, feel.

SEV to FST 31.5.40

You don't mind if the Nazis strut in Damarel and Balliol. I do. Not because they are foreigners, or revolutionaries, or imperialists or pan-Germany, but because they are anti-Christian and anti everything that is necessary for the foundation of Christianity; I mean chiefly Reason. Other wars have been waged between rival imperialists, but always between rival Christians. I am speaking now of the wars of the last century, from which we have deduced the futility and wickedness of wars.

These have not touched the eternal values. Whoever has won, the Church has gone on, and universities have been honoured. So we thought it best to put our pride in our pocket and, realising how wicked a thing fighting was, and how nothing of Christian value worth speaking about was won or lost, to repudiate all war and take our stand on pacifism.

This time I believe something more is at stake. I believe that Fascism is a symptom of a deadly plague, of which other symptoms are D.H. Lawrence, football pools and the Oxford Group (so called). I believe that this plague is contracted by people who find the world too difficult for them and who are afraid or too lazy to make a concentrated intellectual effort to understand it. It breaks out in the form of emotionalism, following on the abandonment of reason. This emotionalism saps the vitality of truth, gnaws at the roots of civilisation and, reaching a climax of lunatic hysteria, throws a fit and passes out. We are now infected by this plague, while in the Nazis it has reached its secondary stage. Our only hope is a strong inoculation of theology. I use that word because it combines the gospels with an intellectual effort. Such an inoculation might save us. As for the Nazis, no prophylactics can save them. They are tossing already in the throes of the fever and if their lives and ours are not to be lost together, we must put them firmly to bed, and nurse them.

FST to SEV 3.6.40

I have just read your letter a second time. I have now come right down on the side of the F.A.U. My protest is I realise in a sense illogical, but remember the Cross was 'foolishness' to the Greeks! The Master says all protests are illogical. I don't agree that millions have a Christian dislike of war. Hardly a million I feel have any idea of Christianity. I don't see what we should do at the moment as an alternative to the war but that is because Christian pacifism is in such a minority still - but it does not make it any the less right.

All Christians I feel should be hopeless optimists: they believe in a God who just before he went to a degrading crucifixion, was deserted by all friends and his God; we believe in a God who at that moment said, 'Be of good cheer; I have overcome the world.' We must cling on to it even more in defeat, I feel. Were all the early Christians wrong? Were all martyrs wrong? I don't mind a dark age too much; as a historian I know there were really no such times. Rome was rotten when she fell. London is rotten and may fall now. I hope selfishly that we win, but I think that a new age will in the end be more difficult to start if it has to be grafted on to this one. I feel we must, and will have more and more to become, 'voices crying': stern denunciations are not going to come from the Church and should come from somewhere.

What decides me and has always decided me is that were I to accept your reasons and fight, afterwards when I was asked if I was a Christian, then why did I fight? Then I know down in my heart I couldn't answer. I just wouldn't be true to something which I must follow and which I have tried to subject to reason.

SEV to FST 6.6.40

Brandon writes that you are in a frightful hospital in Gloster. Is this true? He asks if I'd like to join you, and of course I said I'd like nothing better.

Souls are saved by hearing the gospel. The question for me becomes, 'Will the Nazi victory make it impossible, or even very difficult, for men to hear and receive the gospel?' It may do. 'Education' is at the moment my great difficulty. If our children are to be brought up under the Nazi educational system, then will they emerge from it as Christians? If not, oughtn't we to fight now for what liberty is left in England and, when the German war is over, go on fighting with all Christian austerity and sacrifice, for a better England?

FST to SEV 8.6.40

Yes! I am in a hideous hospital here! At least it is 10 hours *very* hard work a day amid the military wounded. The place is grossly understaffed and we run round all day doing all and sundry, emptying pig swills and then doing an important dressing, wash up and then give an enema. Do come here as soon as possible.

'Souls are saved by hearing the gospel' - and seeing men live by it. So then, you must ask whether you can really live by it and take part in war. The Nazi educational system *will not* triumph if there are enough Christian lives in opposition to it. Rome had to recognise the early Christians. Individuals *do* change systems.

SEV to FST 3.9.40

We joined the F.A.U. because we could not pass by on the other side while humanity lay suffering. First it was Finland, then Norway, then Gloucester. We came to each in answer to a need, expressed or unexpressed; and when those first two needs disappeared, we disappeared with them. Now there is a need in the East and I am of the opinion that we should go in answer to it.

All that could hold us would be Gloucester's need, and Dr. Cookson made it fairly clear this morning that he *could* dispense with us and that now would be a convenient moment to do so.

In that case, if we stay, it will only be to bear witness to our creed by humbling ourselves to the most menial service; and I believe that such a deliberate humility would be selfishness and inverted pride.

What we must set before our minds is not *our* witness or *our* influence or *our* survival in distinct units and sections, with rights and privileges and a dignity of our own. What we must do is to take a bird's eye view of England and, considering ourselves only as instruments for the relief of suffering, search out where we can be of the best service.

I should be surprised if we found that a few convalescents in Gloucester claimed our final attention. Three months ago they were the Dunkirk casualties, but many bombs have fallen since Dunkirk.

So I recommend that you give notice to Dr. Cookson tomorrow, that you co-operate with him in finding alternative employment and that directly this is available we pack up our baggage and move East.

FST to SEV 8.9.40

I have been reading some more of 'War and Peace'. How good all the different love scenes are between Peter and Helen, Maria and Anatole, and Sonia and Nicholas. There is a very good bit where Maria is praying and a voice says to her, 'Ask nothing for yourself, seek nothing, do not worry yourself and envy no one; the future must remain hidden but when it comes, it must find you ready for whatever it may bring.'

I am becoming enthralled with the idea that the whole world is one vast example of original sin; the flea has fallen and so has the mosquito; it would be fun to write out Genesis for the flea and also imagine in what form religion and atonement have come to them. You might work that out while you are at home. I have also been reading 'Good God' again. Laurence Housman is all wrong in his idea of God being primarily immanent and not transcendent.

FST to SEV 7.10.40

About Gloucester. Don't rush things.

FST to SEV 14.10.40

I can't decide about China. Is it a form of escape? Ought we to stay here and battle and wrestle with people who have the wrong idea and outlook? Don't we see a bit more than some? Or is that arrogant? Hasn't pacifism of our type a great part to play here soon? I don't know; I may argue the other way tomorrow. I have written to the Uncle to ask him.

SEV to FST 29.10.40

Before we volunteer for China, and before leaders are appointed, an urgent question must be asked.

What was wrong with the Finnish expedition and how can we avoid the same mistakes in China? I believe the root of the trouble was that we were a British Ambulance Unit and not a Friends Ambulance Unit. We went in the spirit of adventure and not in the spirit of Christ. Individuals did their best, but the Unit had no corporate Christian standards and made no corporate pacifist witness. Amongst the relatively primitive and bellicose people of Finland this was a pity, but no more. In China it would have been a calamity.

For a party of young British adventurers to come gallivanting down the Burma road, full of self-importance and thinking themselves entitled to the gratitude of the inhabitants, would be an insult to Chinese civilisation. That is the spirit in which we crossed from Haparanda to Tornio and it must not happen again.

We must enter China in a spirit of deep humility, conscious of the privilege of serving her and learning from her. We must understand that the Chinese despise soldiers and adventurers, and if we have any example worth setting before *her* wisdom and *her* patience, it can only be Christian charity.

Therefore, if anyone is volunteering for China just because he wants ambulance work, I appeal to him to wait until work develops in Europe or the Near East.

SEV to FST 11.11.40

I wrote to Hugh asking him if I should go to China. He wrote back from Sandhurst a long and interesting letter, the gist of which is as follows.

We, he says, are spending these years of our lives killing Germans and Italians. We are forgetting all the lessons - of civil life, how to live together, how to treat other people, what does and what doesn't matter. Your job is to keep alive the stream of civilisation and to go on experimenting in Christian living. You must do it here in England. We don't want to hear after the war that you made a successful experiment in Christian communal living in China. That would be easy enough. But what we do want, and want desperately, is to be told after the war that you went through it all with us here in England, and stuck fast to your Christianity and proved that in Modern Europe Christianity has something to say.

It was a moving letter. Written very simply and from the heart. An appeal to us not to desert them now that things have got so desperate. Already, I think, some folk are beginning to look to us and after the war it will be thousands more. The appeal of China is largely that we want something new, something adventurous in the spirit, if not directly in the flesh. And here at home, among the millions that cast us out, there are already ones or twos, perhaps tens or hundreds, who are appealing to us out of their despair for this very newness that we are going to look for in China. We have the newness, and if we only had enough faith we would stand by it here.

I'm feeling, you see, that we oughtn't to go, feeling it now rather strongly after Hugh's letter. That appeal seemed to me to be God's own message that if we are faithful he will use us here as his instruments. You may have heard other voices! Let me know.

FST to SEV 12.11.40

About China: if you still think the Unit should send people there, I think we ought to be prepared to go. The Unit as a whole will go on in England living or trying to live as Christians, but we may have a minute part to play in China. I have definitely decided to volunteer, deciding to leave it to the Unit to say whether I am better suited to work here or in China. And I must leave it to others to decide that: it would be arrogant and impossible to say oneself. Will you do the same? One must look at it from the Unit as a whole and *not* think where we personally can do best. One could argue that we should go to China: by our education more likely to learn from them than others. Or we may feel more suited to work here, seeing perhaps a little further than the others as to what the Unit should do and be. But we would go to Greece if asked, wouldn't we? Or Egypt? We have a part to play in a whole, not an individual part. We must leave it to others to decide where they would have us go, as long as we agree that it is right that some people go there. That is how I feel at the moment. I can assure you the appeal of China is not for me newness. I do not in a way like the idea at all! But I see I may be meant to go there.

FST to SEV 14.11.40

I hear you now feel doubtful about a Unit going to China at all and may want to try and stop it. Stanley may have exaggerated this. I have several reasons why I hope you won't do that.

(a) A minor one: the entire Unit has had a great deal of time to decide if it did not want to send a Unit to China. I think a former staff meeting accepted it. It would be *a very serious step indeed* now to ask the Unit to go back on its policy when we have made agreements with so many committees.

(b) But that must not weigh if you really feel the Unit ought not to go. I feel very strongly that it ought and that we will never be able to work really well in England if as a Unit we do not give our support to China. We will have become selfish and self-centred. We can teach Europe that Christianity is more than a domestic concern of Europe. I do still hope you are volunteering and leaving it to the Unit to decide: I feel I must say this, though selfishly I hope very much you don't go as I think I shall be staying. I leave it in the hands of the others.

SEV to FST 14.11.40

Creative imagination must be an asset to the editor of the Chronicle, yet even fantasy should be but the embroidery of fact. The suggestion that I am preparing to sabotage the Chinese convoy is fantastic in an illegitimate sense, since such an activity would have no ground, content nor motive related to any fact whatsoever, nor could the suggestion have been begotten or conceived by intercourse between any fact and the aforesaid imagination. No. It is a case of parthenogenesis, fathered upon Stanley's innocent mind by a spirit; and whether a demon or an angel it is not for me to guess. I am only the poor Joseph of the transaction, responsible under the law. Does it perhaps follow that I should take up the child and flee with it into Egypt? And what part do you take in this nativity play? Why, the ass, of course!

No. No. No. I was not conscious of exaggerating during Stanley's visit. Indeed, his mastery of the art shamed me into reasonableness and I remember saying nothing about China except that I did not *want* to go. But I see now that Christian discipline must be exercised and that we must bear what witness is given to us. God is unlikely to be depending upon you or me for any essential fulfilment of his

383

purpose, and if the leaders are real Christian people, then they will choose men with a due sense of responsibility. I don't know whether to be glad or sorry that you are definitely staying, and that because I have not set my mind on either course.

FST to SEV 19.11.40

I am honoured to play ass to your Joseph! Latest developments up to date: for you alone as being my strictest confidant. I may be leading the *Sudan* convoy: a mobile hospital Unit, providing the male staff, working with the Free French forces; probably a great deal of work and just what we have trained for. I did not volunteer for it but it is where people want me to go, so I will - and would enjoy it.

SEV to FST 20.3.41

Enclosed is a copy of a letter from Uncle Ebor. I asked him about the 'dangerous and insidious force for evil', and whether good works really were good without Christ.

Oldham's supplement, 'Predicament', Feb 26th, raises the same question. It is really the question of transcendence and immanence, and Oldham says he thinks this is the burning question of our generation. It is startling that we should all be coming to this same conclusion at the same moment. The Spirit is troubling us all to think out this same problem and the answer cannot be far off. The Uncle puts it beautifully clearly from the intellectual point of view. Emotionally, as we agreed on Robin Wood's hill, the answer lies in a personal friendship with Christ and personal loyalty to Him. The Uncle is leading up to that, though he doesn't actually say it.

I am thinking of joining up! No, that isn't an exaggeration, but I must talk to you about pacifism.

Copy of the letter from William Temple to Stephen Verney
  Bishopsthorpe
  York
  March 17, 1941

My dear Stephen,

I am horrified to see that your letter is dated Feb 28, and look at the date of this! I do apologise. Life is a whirlpool just now. And my secretary has been ill so that I had to write a lot of my official letters by hand.

Your position is a restatement of Article 13 (among the 39) and the same problem arises. If a pious pagan - e.g. Socrates - acts in accordance with a right conscience, is this action at the command of Christ? It *is* at the command of the Logos - or may be.

I always want to start from John 1,9 (R.V.): The light lightens every man. Yet only in the historic Christ does it shine fully. Therefore only in conscious response to Him can we be sure of walking in the true light. Elsewhere there is always doubt and usually - perhaps always - some positive error - (a) because of defect in the medium through which the Light reaches us (b) because of distortion in our own perception or reception of the Light.

The mind becomes what it feeds on; we become what we see - or contemplate. Hence 'Whatsoever things …. think on (i.e. occupy your minds with) these things.' Times of concentrated remembrance of God and review of life in His presence are necessary to Spiritual growth; without these we shall stick where we are, doing and even being *some* good, but with an admixture of bad that vitiates it.

Do your 'Friends' think they are perfect; if not, how do they propose to advance towards perfection? Is it by the effort of their *ex-hypothesi* imperfect will?

I am afraid this won't help much, but it is the best I can offer.

I wish you would come here again.

Yours affectly,

(signed) William Ebor.

(Article 13. Of works before Justification.
Works done before the grace of Christ, and the inspiration of his Spirit, are not pleasant to God, forasmuch as they spring not of faith in Jesus Christ, neither do they make men meet to receive grace, or (as the School-authors say) deserve grace of congruity: yea rather, for that they are not done as God hath willed and commanded them to be done, we doubt not but they have the nature of sin.)

SEV to FST 24.3.41

The question is this. Can the grace of God break its way into the heart that is steeled against it?

I don't believe it can. Ignorance, for example, seems to be an absolute barrier. Psycho-analysis has shown me that you may pray till you drop to be filled with love towards your fellow men, but if you are all the while harbouring a secret hate, it will avail you nothing. You must understand your hate, and then the love of God will annihilate it. And as you are always pointing out, Christianity is foolishness to those who are not ready to receive it. It would be a waste of time to go and talk about redemption to Hitler. You would first have to convince him of the necessity for redemption by pointing out to him the error of his own way.

What I am saying is this, that John the Baptist had to come before Christ. A change of heart and mind must precede the preaching of the Kingdom.

And so what of pacifism? In face of Nazi barbarity we are preaching the Kingdom. Now you must allow me that the Nazis need a change of heart and mind before they can possibly understand the teaching of Christ. You must also allow me, with your uncle, that we stand for freedom, which is a necessary environment for Christianity. And what is our excuse for refusing to fight for the necessary environment of Christianity against the Nazi barbarity? Only that it is not Christ's way of fighting.

But may it not be John the Baptist's way? And are the Germans not at the moment in that condition of mind where they might listen to John, but would only laugh at Christ?

We can go on preaching Christ to free people, but tyrants and their dupes have to be brought to their senses first. And the only way to bring Hitler to his senses, at any rate by means at our disposal (and why should we not help God?), seems to be by defeating him in battle.

I must discuss this with you face to face, because you will never understand what I am driving at through a letter. If I am right, then I must join up. I won't decide anything before Easter - so come then, and we will decide the matter.

FST to SEV 28.3.41

Your letter is almost identical with the letter of last June you wrote to me. The only difference is that last June I agreed slightly with you: I don't at all now and am a convinced pacifist. I should have thought you would be after 'The Cross and the Crisis'. You must read 'Christian Pacifism Re-examined': it answers all the Niebuhrs and Uncles in the world. Pacifism will not alone solve all the difficulties but don't become militarist just because it solves the few problems; doesn't militarism leave many others unsolved? About John the Baptist, I don't think war and a call to repentance are analogies: war does not bring about a change of heart. You are merely succumbing to the 3rd temptation (and in Lent too!!?!). And anyhow I don't think John the Baptist is of universal significance.

Did Christ fulfil the historic role of Messiah? Did he fight for Christianity or for monotheism? A change of heart is needed, yes - but it can only come if Christians now in the world are full of a real, powerful redemptive love. That is why at the moment all Christians I feel should be denying themselves, should be curbing their own selfish expression, so that they will really be filled with love. Then possibly one or two hearts will be changed, but 'the Kingdom is like a grain of mustard seed'. We must not want quick results.

Christians should I feel now deliberately choose the ascetic, self-denying life in order to redeem the world: later, in a few million years possibly, the full Christian life, yes. But not now: it is just selfish. Christ's life was not particularly beautiful or full: he *deliberately* chose poverty: he deliberately chose a Cross.

So, you see I don't feel you have any reason whatsoever for joining up!?

SEV to FST 1.4.41

My mind becomes clearer by writing, so I will try and pen you an answer, though we shall never discuss this question profitably until we meet.

'Pacifism', you say, 'will not alone solve all the difficulties, but don't become militarist just because it solves the few problems pacifism doesn't.'

I would answer that Christianity, if it is the revelation of God, does solve all problems; and therefore that pacifism must be an incomplete interpretation of Christianity. My own doubts arise out of a greater stress on the immanence of God. If God were only transcendent then it would be right to abase yourself before him, to make a complete surrender and to ask him to use you as a channel for his omnipotent power. You would not bother about consequences.

And in so far as he is transcendent, this is the right attitude to adopt.

But we agree that this is not the whole picture. God works also through the nature of man. He is immanent in our instincts, and in our talents and powers. If we would worship this God, it must be by our own activity, harnessed always to the vision of his transcendence, but nevertheless through the heart and soul and mind and strength which are his human expressions. And it is just in this combination of immanence and transcendence that Christianity is unique. If you were a Buddhist, I would agree that you should 'choose the ascetic, self-denying life.' But Christ came to give life *more* abundantly, not less. Asceticism is like martyrdom. Don't run around looking for it, but take it cheerfully if it comes. I don't agree that 'Christians should be denying themselves, should be curbing their own selfish expression so that will really be filled with love'. They won't really be filled with love. If you resist evil, and try to crush it, you only give it a new impetus. If you deliberately curb your wish to relax into an armchair, you will never be *happy* in a slum, though you may stick it. But stones can stick it; Christians must be happy. To overcome evil, you must first of all understand it.

And this is where pacifism comes in. 'Resist not evil' means resist not evil in your self, but understand it and overcome it with good. But this does not mean resist not evil in other people. The German doctrines are evil. The only way the Germans can overcome that evil in themselves is by understanding it, and then overcoming it with good.

This good will be Christ; but before the Nazis can overcome the evil of fascism, they must be made to understand it. The best way to enable them to understand it is to keep alive freedom in England, and to shock them into an awareness of their own stupidity. This will be done best and quickest by a military defeat.

Then, after a military defeat, when they are humbled and ready to repent, will be the moment to love them and suffer for them. Christ loves and suffers eternally for us, but only those who have repented can feel the power of the Cross. Remember that to the Jews it was a stumbling block, and to the Germans today it is foolishness. So I believe that John the Baptist *was* of universal significance.

I don't want to fall into the third temptation. Britain must not rule over all the nations of the world. But may she not be God's instrument in bringing them to repentance? May she not be John the Baptist, yes, with all her faults? And then Christ will come again to hearts ready to receive him.

This is my puzzle. You must help me solve it at Easter.

FST to SEV 4.4.41

I agree that we will never solve this until we meet but nevertheless here is a bit of an answer. Remember that Christ, who had God Immanent in him to a greater degree than anyone else, nevertheless humbled himself and made himself a channel of divine power; it was only thus that he went to the Cross. He did deliberately choose it; if he had wanted to help God in human ways he would not have done so - but just gone off elsewhere and spread the Gospel further afield. Peter wanted to help Christ but was told to put up his sword. We must not decide what God's purpose is or how we will bring it about. Self-denial does give life more abundantly and one is happier when practising it; real happiness is not to be found in giving in to the baser instincts of sloth and ease. Was Christ's life particularly happy in the sense of full and comfortable?

Then of course the other place where I disagree is in your saying that a military defeat does shock people into an awareness of their stupidity and make them humble; that is never the reading of history and there is no reason to suppose it will be true this time. The Cross will continue to be foolishness to thousands for years to come, but one cannot force people to recognise it. Are you wanting quick results? Are you not like Peter wanting to decide what is God's purpose?

SEV to FST 14.4.41

The future is so very uncertain in so many ways that I can hardly tell yet what course of action I shall be taking in the next few months. Perhaps the war will be over, and the Germans in London. Perhaps we will be with the F.A.U. in Greece or Turkey. Perhaps I shall be in the R.A.F.! Who can tell?

FST to SEV 11.5.41

If you really feel you must join up, you want to be moved from Gloucester to London for a bit, and experience a heavy raid - and see if you feel you could inflict it on others. Last night was terrific. I enclose a copy of a bit of my letter home: egotistical, not well written, but it may interest you. I find I do not mind raids at all now: there are so many people obviously more terrified than oneself that one can be fully occupied in cheering them while working.

FST to SEV 24.6.41

This weekend there has been a call for fifteen more men to join the Hadfield-Spears Unit in Palestine. I have been asked to go in charge of them; I think now that it will be the right thing, though it would have been wrong last time. You have been chosen for the party as well; this was not done for any personal friendship reasons; I insisted on that and said that we never wanted that to stand above other more important considerations; but most people agree, including yourself, that it would be good for you to have a move anyhow fairly soon; this is certainly a bit rushed - but this is the convoy on which you can be of most use; you enjoy the French and you know and are respected by most of the people out there. And so we all feel it is right that you should go.

It will mean moving very fast; we may sail in a fortnight's time and there will be all the equipment to get and various injections to have. It will be an interesting party; it has worked out that everyone is pretty compatible and has one person they know really well. We will be a combination of all sorts, including an artist and a well-known actor; I am a little frightened of these two as they are much older. Nik writes that there is an olive grove at the bottom of their compound and they pick fruit by the sackful daily. Nik also says the whole outfit has the atmosphere of a Crazy Gang cum circus. It sounds amusing.

FST to SEV 3.7.41

I intend to learn French and Arabic on the way out but am not taking many books otherwise: I shall take 'War and Peace' and some Dostoevsky and then do a very thorough study of the Bible in all its parts. I think one wants some good periodicals sent out; the 'News Letter' can be sent out; what about 'Theology'? It might be a good plan to have that sent out as well. I don't think I shall take any Greek, especially if you are taking the 'Iliad' or 'Odyssey'.

See you next week and together we will sally forth; as you put on the book you gave me at the end of the Training Camp, 'Hobgoblin nor foul fiend'.

appendix iii Letters from Father to Son 1964-1996

Whenever Freddy's son, Stephen, was away - be it at school, Oxford or when working abroad, the two would keep in touch by letter. When in adulthood Stephen was in Britain, but not at home, father and son kept in contact by telephone. Stephen collected an enormous pile of letters his father had sent him over the years, of which the following extracts are typical.

The first letter was written after Stephen had left home for the first time, at the age of eight, to go to his prep school.

29.4.64
Darling Stephen,
   How I long to know what dorm was like; who do you sleep next to? Is he nice? What form will you be in? Is the master nice? Who do you sit beside? We shall miss you *so so* much, but remember how much we love you. But I am sure when you settle in, it will be fun and exciting. We are so proud of you and remember what I said about your prayers, and Bible-reading.

1.5.64
We are longing for your first letter and to know what you do. Can you send us a time-table so that we can look and say, 'Ah, he is doing this or that'. We will miss you *so* much. Ma is over at Grandpa's today, hearing Uncle John speak at Storrington, so I am alone. I am changing my calendars as you are not here to do them.

6.5.64
How I wish I could be a fly on the wall in your bedroom or classroom and just *see* you and hear you to know how it is all going. A week gone by, and only a fortnight till we come for Sports Day.

8.5.64
We are LONGING for your next letter: *do* please make it a nice *long* chatty one; it would be so unselfish and kind. Tell us what you are doing in work: who is your form master and do you like him? Can you copy out the work time-table? Have you any friends? How is cricket? When do you go to bed? When do you get up? Please answer some of these. Ma misses you so much: so do I. Clean your teeth well; and remember your prayers.

1.11.65
   Je suis trés heureux d'entendre que tu es plus content et que tout va bien. Nous

arriverons jeudi le onzième à deux heures après-midi. A bientôt.

Ton père qui t'adore beaucoup.

26.1.67

Don't forget God at school; he is there to be your friend.

13.6.67

A lovely letter. But *don't* become someone who talks and fools about in games: they are really being very selfish and spoiling it for others. You really could be good at games, you know; you don't really try. Also not too much Monopoly - it really gets you nowhere and you are in a position to set an example in the school and *not* be led. Remember, really hard work is vital this next year or I might not be able to afford a Public School for you without a scholarship. Ma and I are doing without £300 a year to give you a good education; we are not spending it for a craze on Monopoly. We could be having a lovely holiday abroad instead. But we feel sure you will use it properly by trying hard *at everything*; don't be someone who just mucks about. Our wedding anniversary today; Ste [Stephen] is one of our delights.

19.6.67

I am so glad you are starting to think really hard about religion and God. This is a very good thing to do. Here are some points to think about and then we can continue either in letters or at home, as you will have lots more questions I am sure.

We cannot prove there is a God; nor can anyone prove there is not. But then all the best things in life cannot be proved. When Ma and I married we could not prove we would go on loving each other or that we did love each other; we took it on trust. You cannot prove love, unselfishness or any other ideal; you can just see certain actions, and argue from that - and horrid people can always argue that something unselfish was really done for selfish reasons.

But you are a keen historian and as a good historian you must notice that the religious sense is one that man has always had; it is one of the main facts of history. Then you must notice that vast numbers of the cleverest men have been believers in God and followed him in one form or another. It is not true that it is only silly or simple folk who believe in God. Then as you read history you will find most of the best men who have had the greatest effect on folk have been religious men: Francis of Assisi, Wilberforce, Scott, Buddha, Socrates, etc. Then as you look at life, you will see that the greatest ideals are those of love, truth, courage, unselfishness, beauty, etc.; and you can't think of those except as being shown forth in people. It is most unlikely that just an impersonal force could of its own create these ideals.

Then look at the life of Jesus; the Resurrection is a historical fact as certain as that William the Conqueror landed in England. The gospels have been most critically examined and the teaching, death and rising again of Jesus is a hard, certain fact of history. So at least we must take this into account as possibly being true. So many people like to dismiss it. But if it is true, then it will make a difference to the whole of our lives and how we live.

If it is true, then we try and follow what Jesus says and he tells us to be friends of his, of God as shown in him. So prayers should be a time, not of a lot of talking set prayers to him, but quietly thinking about him and letting him talk to us in our consciences, through reading about what he said and did. Don't be put off Christianity by the dullness of school or church services or set prayers; the best people are slowly trying to change all that. You are quite right: prayers don't have to be long, but if you really love someone then you see that you listen to them and talk to them regularly; you have to meet and listen and talk to be friends; it is selfish not to do so.

I'll explain more about Communion to you in the holidays; it is a very simple way of doing what Jesus said, of gathering as friends to have a meal and eat and drink something, remembering how great his love for us was and is. If someone asked you to die tomorrow for people who were not being very nice to you, would you be ready to do this, or would you try and run away? This shows a bit how much he loves us.

Don't say you want to be confirmed by Mr. Head or prepared unless you really want to do so; it might well be better to leave it until you feel ready. But don't let that be a reason for being slack about thinking about God and your prayers; and to know him you must keep up your prayers; don't feel you have to say a lot; just read in a new translation a bit about Jesus and then think about it, and then remember those you love and people in trouble.

What did you get beaten for? Glad you didn't cry, but remember you are no longer a young bright boy who has shot up the school, but at the top and should be responsible now and not playing the fool.

14.7.67

Many, many happy returns: what an age: 12. How old and wise you are.

17.7.67

Thank you so much for your good letter. It is always a shock when someone pulls one up about one's life, but a very good thing if one takes the lesson and then changes and improves. Ma and I are very glad Mr. Barham did say that about Monopoly and we have both had the impression that you have been rather childish and irresponsible for your age a lot this term, not only in work but games and general fooling about; you just won't get the best out of life like that and you know this well enough and must not be led away by other weaker examples. It will be a pity if you are seventh in final order and a sure sign of a slack term - but if you pull yourself together and start out determined to make it up next year then it will be all right. I think it was very difficult to come back to a term after Eton exams and this has reacted badly on you and I notice that it is you and Haag, the other Eton boy, who seem to have been so childish. So learn the lesson and do better and forget about it.

But also don't just be a spectator in life; it doesn't matter if you can't do any of these competitions well; just try them and don't just watch, watch and muck about. We never do anything well without trying from scratch. Where is the cub who got his Leaping Wolf before most others? You didn't just say, 'I didn't enter for anything, as I can't do it'. You can if you try.

20.9.67

Thank you for such lovely holidays. I was proud of the way you have grown up so much in thoughtfulness, etc.

28.9.67

How good about the debate. Try and speak early before all the points are made.

FOR living in England:

(a) an uncertain climate that helps make people tough and resilient, instead of easy hot weather all the time.

(b) a good health service, so that no-one in need or want goes without medical care. We don't realise what this means till we go abroad and find out how much all this costs.

(c) in spite of all criticisms, a great Christian basis still in the general attitude of the people. André Maurois, the great French historian, said you could tell England was a Christian country still as you drove up from the coast seeing the milk bottles outside the doors in trust and honesty; in other countries they would be pinched.

(d) the good position women have, compared with, say, a Muslim country where they are still subservient to men.

(e) all the new ideas in the country and in the church at the moment; a new period of Reformation going on. An exciting time to be English, if a difficult one. New services, new cathedrals, Oxfam, Christian Aid - all helping others.

AGAINST:

(a) bad weather so much of the time; can't plan what you want to do ever. Too crowded, and a small overcrowded country is having to adjust itself to not being boss of an Empire, but just a small offshore part of Europe. 'England has lost an Empire and not discovered a new role for herself yet'; someone said that recently.

(b) The Welfare State, while good, makes people soft and too dependent on others and stops them working hard enough.

(c) England's great days are over and it is always better to live in a new developing country than a decadent one whose role is past.

There. I hope this gives you a few ideas; no time for more. I am off to Salisbury to take the Ordination Retreat till Sunday.

31.1.68
We worship God because we offer all our worth to him, because we try to love him. You try to do your best for Ma and me or anyone you love; in that sense we worship people - but God above all we offer our wor(th)ship to, and so want to say sorry for failure and to thank for his love.

22.2.68
I'm glad about Confirmation.

Try and think of God as a friend and find time to think about him by reading a little bit about him in the Bible every day. If you don't give time to a friend you slowly cease to be friends and then religion won't be real to you. So find a little time each day for your prayers. If you want to ask any questions about Confirmation or Holy Communion, don't hesitate, will you?

9.3.68. [Written from S. Luke's Hospital, London, where Freddy was having a hernia operation]
I am so very very sorry not to be at your Confirmation: to miss it is very sad, but I shall sit quietly at 3pm that Sunday, thinking of you and God as shown in Jesus, who is glad and happy to have you as a friend. Life is a very strange and mysterious thing; why are we here on this earth? Some poor, some unhappy through no fault of their own, some dying young like Mike, some like yourself who would never have been born if he hadn't died as it needed a lot of courage for Ma to have another baby after two difficult births. So you are specially precious. God can't be proved, but he also can't be disproved scientifically. Everywhere else in life we work by purpose: you are at school. Why? To learn - not just by chance. I'm in hospital. Why? Not by chance, but to have an op. So the most reasonable thing is to believe that there is an all-powerful purpose behind the world, who created it and controls it. This power all religions call God. Religion can be a frightening thing unless it is Christian and it is true that God really cares and loves each one of us so completely that he wants our *free* love in return, even being ready to be killed by us on the Cross. For we kill God in a way each time we do something horrid.

And the story of Jesus with Easter Day and the certainty that nothing you and I or anyone else can do defeats his love for us is the great 'good news' of the world. It is *never* easy to be a Christian; we'll always be a minority and it is specially difficult in England at the moment, which is in a bad mood. But elsewhere in the world, particularly in Africa and South America, Christianity is spreading fast. Holy Communion itself is quite simply in acting form taking the love of God given unto death by breaking the bread, right into ourselves by eating and drinking the simplest food and wine (it isn't caviare and champagne) - not by ourselves, but by sharing with others, and so becoming that love in the world. Don't worry if there are periods when it all seems dull and dead; God brings us through that.

14.3.68

I am getting better. I am so terribly sorry to miss Sunday: I hate it, but I shall sit quietly, munching a bit of bread and butter and sipping a cup of tea, which we have at 3, praying for everything that is good to be showered on you, and that no matter what may come in your life, you'll know that God is there as guide, master and friend. We are giving you a nice NEB, but I hope you still follow lessons in your Greek Testament.

No news really, except my love and longing for you to be all I know you could be and I'm sure will be; you've given us so much happiness already in your life.

10.5.68

Lovely; only a fortnight till we see you. Much too long. All well here. I had a nice time in Chester on the Church and State Commission. On Monday I was at the Leprosy Council and next week at Convocation. We saw 'Guess Who's Coming To Dinner?' today. It was very good indeed. We wept a lot and wished you'd been sobbing beside us.

7.6.68

How good to have got the scholarship: marvellous. Ma and I enjoyed hearing the clapping and cheering when you went to tea. We were *very* proud.

I am taking the Ordination Retreat in Bristol, staying at the Bishop's House. Ma is with the Pauls in Bristol. I had to pay 4/6d on your raincoat in stamps. Don't forget it again!

14.9.68. [Freddy's first letter to Stephen at Rugby]

We *hated* leaving you, but I hope all goes well. We *long* to hear about your form and your sets for science etc., about games and music, etc. - and who is nice and how the study goes, and biking to games. There will be so many new things to experience and learn about. I think of you such a lot and wonder how it all is. We are a quiet old pair here again now. Try and write a really newsy letter. Make the most of Rugby; ask about anything you don't understand or know, won't you?

16.9.68

Just got your letter. I know exactly how you feel; I did too. But come a fortnight and you'll know the details of each thing and it won't be new. It is a marvellous school but you will feel bewildered for a few weeks by it all. But learn early not to worry about the future too much; cope with each thing as it comes. We both flew at your letter. Ma burst into tears and said, 'Poor fellow; how very good it is for him, but I know how he's feeling; but he'll soon be all right.'

17.2.70

About the Resurrection: the empty tomb is quite good evidence; all the opponents of Jesus had to do was to produce the body of Jesus and there would have been no Christian religion; and we know they tried to do so. The tomb was well guarded and it is the last thing the disciples would have tried to do to steal the body as they thought everything had come to an end. So all the different bits of evidence make up such a strong case: the behaviour of the disciples who felt all had ended and that God had even deserted Jesus - for it was a disgrace for a Jew to be crucified, and the appearances and the change in James, Jesus' brother, a strong Jew, whom we know from the apocryphal gospels had an appearance. If you have not read it, you should read 'Who Moved The Stone?' by Frank Morison; it is told most excitingly by someone who did not want to believe but found the evidence made him.

7.3.70

We have got up later this morning as we were at the Mayoral Ball last night. Mother looked ravishingly beautiful as one would expect. When we got to the Ball we found we were to join the Mayor for supper, which was very nice of him. We met the MP, Ward, and his wife - very young, and he wears a frilly shirt. Also various other Mayors; the Mayor of Chippenham is a charming young married woman who chose as her Mayoress her young husband; he said he was the poor man's Prince Philip.

13.3.70

I could write a book on what is wrong with the Church. But the main thing to remember is that the Church is not the building but the folk who compose it. It is a very tough and yet a very radical organisation; nearly all the criticism of it comes from folk in it, who want it to be more lively, etc. It needs to be more flexible and able to go wherever it is needed more; it ought to be easier to get rid of buildings no longer needed when population has moved, etc. The Communion Service needs continually to be brought back again to the simple thing it is of eating and drinking simple food and thinking about what God is ready to do for us and has done. Human beings are always adding this and that to what they value and then a reformation sweeps things away, back to a more alive simplicity. You are going to see a great deal of change in the Church I think, in fact a new reformation, which won't be easy and won't mean large numbers - but the Church has always been at its most alive when it has been smaller. After all, Christ worked with twelve, and not with the five thousand.

23.6.70

Thank you so much for your letter and telling us about the dorm. Don't get too worried about sex; it is one of the most wonderful appetites that God has given us, which is a good and creative part of life. In fact it is the way human beings are made, and so quite rightly it is a thrilling, exciting and enjoyable thing in marriage, to be used and understood. It is one of the more powerful instincts and appetites, and so it is quite natural that all boys as they grow up find it exciting and are curious about it. It is reckoned that a great majority of men pass through a slight homosexual phase as they grow up, but most grow out of it as they approach manhood. Things you describe have always been prevalent in every public school or boarding school; they were in my prep school and very much so at Rugby in my time. So it is not a terrible thing to do now and then; it is better not, if possible, but some find that easier than others, in the same way as some find it easier than others not to eat too much or drink too much.

But like all appetites it can grow if not kept in control, and become demanding - and then it spoils a character, in the same way that someone who eats too much or drinks too much or smokes too much is not a well-balanced character; but sex is stronger than that, so is easier to get out of control and spoil things. Also in marriage it is the wonderful way two people show their love for each other and if it has been used often and frequently in a loose way, it spoils things later for real love. The problem is that physically a boy and girl are ready to make love by the time they are fifteen or so, but on all other sides of their nature they are not mature enough to marry till much later.

So this demands considerable control and discipline of themselves. So it is something worth keeping well under disciplined control, as far as possible - but don't get overwhelmed with guilt if now and then it is too difficult; it won't harm you in any way physically; in my day there were lurid stories about what would happen if anyone masturbated at all. Look on sex as one of the good, exciting appetites you have been given, to be kept under disciplined control as far as possible, till it can be given its proper scope in marriage - but a failure to do this now and then is not terrible and is very common.

I thought I would write before Saturday so you know how we felt about your letter. It is lovely you feel ready to tell us, and don't hesitate either to talk in the hols or write about it. We are not at all worried; it is one of the powerful instincts that grow inside us which we have to learn to control and then enjoy at the right time.

20.9.70

Don't be bored; it is the sign of a little mind and one who is not ready to get interested deeply in anything. It only needs taking up something fully to be really interested. Ancient History can be real fun if you lunge into it really hard; otherwise it can be a little dull - so go at it.

11.10.70

Try to like folk whom you instinctively find it difficult to like at the beginning. It is surprising what a real effort to see what are good points in someone can do; otherwise one goes through life at the mercy of one's instinctive reactions, which is a pity.

25.7.71

We don't of course know why we are here, except that we believe that a God of love naturally wants free human beings to love him and each other, and that is something infinitely worthwhile. But then comes the problem of suffering. I should read 'The Problem of Pain'; it is good. In so far as one can understand it, it is that God has given us freedom and however much someone argues that we are all determined either psychologically, socially or physically, in the end there is a basic element of self-will which determines our actions *forward* in terms of desires or goals to go for; and this makes for freedom. Well, you can't have freedom unless the natural world is ordered and obeys certain laws; I can only write to you if I am fairly sure of the law of gravity and that this typewriter will stay on the table and not fly to the ceiling. Yet this same law will mean that if I freely walk under a tottering chimney pot when there is a wind, it may fall on my head and damage me. People can freely live in a place which through certain laws of nature suddenly has an earthquake or erupts. This is part of the stern price of freedom - a hideous price for any religion that says that God has stayed out of it all and done nothing about it, but only all right for the Christian who believes that in Christ God has come into the world and shared all the pain and suffering and understands it all.

So glad you see the point of Rugby as a place to learn all you can about everything, to be prepared for work in the world for God and others. This all may not answer your questions; if so, ask next time.

I proposed the Mayor's health today at the Mayor's Lunch and they laughed in the right places.

17.9.71

It was so good to get your letter and know that now things were better; it is always very difficult after a happy summer holidays and they *were* fun; thank you for them. You give us both so much happiness.

I hope the work is fun and interesting. If you get the feeling that what you are studying is remote, let me put it this way: you don't want to work with figures or with things but with people, and so a really good course in classics and then philosophy is the very best for this as it demands a much better training of the mind than sociology or modern history; it is much easier just to waffle in them - and still some of the best thinkers have been the Greek and Latin philosophers. And what you are doing now is really the basis for a really good course at University; and even if you get accepted in Classics, you could, if you wanted, always change to another humanities course when there. This is quite all right.

I have been away at a television course at Bushey this week where we were in-terviewed on subjects without knowing what the questions would be. I do not think I did mine very well, but it was fun and there were nice folk there. I planned to come back on Wednesday morning, but woke up early at 5 and could not get to sleep, so got up and sped back through the empty roads to have to wake poor Mother up at 7.15 when she had read till after midnight, with me being away! I have been in Bristol and am now off to Swanwick, past Derby. I shall come by Rugby, but sadly no time to see you. So life is very full and I have not had time to do very much in the garden. Mother has not had time to practice on her moped; she did just what you did on that dodgem car and shot into the fence by the roses while the Dugdales were just the other side; luckily, no damage to fence or anyone.

3.12.71

Don't forget that it is *your main Christian job* this next year to equip yourself really well for the next stage at university, which I think you will love. There you will find the discussion and argument on all these things tremendous. It will be impor-tant you read a lot so that you are not floored and discouraged when you meet the best arguments there are against Christianity; they can be countered and defeat-ed, but need really thinking out.

31.5.72

A dinner party at X the other night; the hosts were pleasant but there were two rich widows who were intolerable, but they were rather sad really as they were fundamentally unhappy. I argued with much of what they said, which startled them at a dinner party. But it may make them think.

Next morning your good letter arrived; yes, one always has to face ridicule and fun about one's beliefs, but if you can keep normal, smiling and like the folk still, without becoming smug, all of which you do, then all is well at the end.

Last night Mother took us [Mina was home] to the bistro part of the Bell Inn at Ramsbury; a lovely evening and drive by side roads and a pleasant meal in a place that Mother pronounced had ATMOSPHERE; so that was all right.

13.10.72

I hope all goes well and that the new boy is not being too difficult; it is tiring and draining being responsible for folk who behave strangely; this is something that goes on through life. I hope you are not too depressed too often; one so often is depressed with oneself; then the great thought is that God never gets fed up with us and goes on hoping and loving and not demanding more than we can manage. I sympathise with you so much; my diaries of your age were full of gloom about myself.

23.5.73

I have been raking out all the old family crosses with any jewels in them to sell, in order that my bishop's ring should not cost too much; it will cost about £80, but with some exchanges I should get it down to about £30; better have a coffee morning for it???

We were at a party of a young couple on Saturday, terribly wealthy and masses of drink - the sort of party neither of us care for very much.

8.7.73

Remember that God always moves on ahead of us from time to time, and when he seems far away it is a sign for us to bestir ourselves in some way or another and get up out of that resting place and continue on our spiritual journey - and then somewhere out amid the rock and stones he will find us and take us on to the next; but so many people get stuck along the route.

11.8.73

I do feel for you leaving the school and saying goodbye, etc. These partings are always horrid and also, even at your age, the feeling that a chapter of life is closing irrevocably and moving on. The only thing then is to realise that death is the entry into something far more exciting and venturesome. All life is so much death and resurrection; each ending is a little death and then a new beginning starts.

28.8.73

I shall be most interested to hear more about your visit to the Pentecostal church. There is a great deal in some of what this stands for: a freedom and readiness to live by the Spirit - but so often, alas, the danger with some Pentecostalists is that they seem to think that the most important Christian thing is to speak in tongues and that you are not really converted if you do not. This is what one of St. Paul's letters to the Corinthians, 1 Corinthians 13, is all about - that love in its deepest form is far more important than any speaking in tongues. If one is given this gift from God then you accept it gratefully and the freedom it expresses, but it does no-one but oneself any good, and I would myself rather have gifts of patience, understanding, truth and courage than the gift of tongues - and I would always reckon as more deeply Christian someone who had these gifts rather than someone who kept telling us they spoke in tongues. I think we should all be freer and more open and sometimes in real worship this will lead to ecstasy and ecstatic utterance, but I myself would not go deliberately in search of it. I think there is a danger of seeking God for emotional kicks rather than solid service and love for him and our fellow men.

This is where I think 'Charisma' was wrong in seeking the gift as something special above all. As St. Paul says, love is far more important. And I look always as a guide to Jesus for what is the standard, and I don't see much sign of speaking with tongues in him. It belongs to the Old Testament more, and of course is there in the first great experience at Pentecost when it is genuine - but it is never deliberately sought by the apostles and St. Paul has to speak quite severely to the Corinthians about it.

Now we get ready for the very exciting autumn. It is quite humbling trying to think and pray about how one can best be of service as a Bishop, and guide and help and lead people to more knowledge of God.

4.11.73

Your letter means a great deal to me: I was most moved you wrote like that. It was a lovely day in every way. It will be a far more wonderful sphere of work. I'm sure, when I can shed the finance and building committees, there will be many more retreats and conferences, trying to help and inspire folk to see more and live more fully: all of which will need more time of quiet and prayer to prepare. It will have to be a life of quality rather than quantity.

Friday, a sermon to a full Cathedral in Bristol, Colston Girls, then a meeting with a possible vicar at Brinkworth and the Bankers' Dinner in the evening. Then yesterday an Alcoholics Conference all day; v. interesting. Today, 2 preachings and next week General Synod all week. Life is a bit too full to be right.

13.11.73

It is very seldom that any extreme convinced position has been really well thought out; truth is usually somewhere more in the middle, and yet one has to keep the fire and enthusiasm going as well. That is why I wasn't so violently pro-Charismatic as you, because I see its good points but also believe that the Holy Spirit is always at work and gives many other gifts as well. I think that feeling, joy and exuberance is something needed as a corrective at the moment - but then soon after someone will have to discover again the discipline, suffering and Man of Sorrows that Christ was and is; and in a way, thank heaven for this, as most of the world is in suffering and sad, so a Christ who understands that will appeal to more of the world than an affluent, indulgent West. Our own family is a good example of the fact that the best brains have tested Christianity and found it true through all the criticism - Uncle William and Grandfather Frederick beside the others. Even scientists and philosophers will agree that it is as true as any other theory of life - and then it is in living it out that you and I know that it is true. Old illustration: Mother is biologically 85% water, but I know her as the most wonderful wife, mother and person by living with her; but it can't be philosophically *proved*.

15.11.73

Thank you so much for your letter. I would be far more worried if you felt that you could take the whole of the Bible quite literally, because of course very few sane and balanced people do. It is a historical document just like any other and must be sifted and examined historically and critically like any other document. Jesus was an historical figure and it is just pure magic to believe that suddenly some simple apostles afterwards wrote down something that was totally inspired and accurate with no mistakes in it. Also it is quite clear that, to start with, things were passed on by word of mouth and then got written down much later on, and you have only to compare the three synoptic gospels, that is the first three, to realise how different some of their accounts are. I should get the warden [of Keble College, Oxford], Denis Nineham, to talk to you about this, as he takes a very highly critical view of the scriptures and yet he is a convinced Christian.

It is very clear, for instance, that the Nativity stories have not nearly as much value as the Passion and Crucifixion. I think it is true that if you use the Bible as a quarry for texts, then you can pick out whatever you want to believe. There are some parables showing that there will be a judgement for us, but there are also strands which show that God loves everyone and wants everyone to be saved. This is again a case of where one has to hold both points of view. I think it is important to hold on to the idea of Hell for oneself and believe that one's choices do have a real effect, and that God will let one go on one's own if one wants to - but also believe that his love will conquer in the end. So I hold a doctrine of Hell and final judgement for myself, but of conquering love for everyone else. The major thing to hold on to is that you know that you have a real mission and knowledge of Christ and his friendship, and that you will try in your own way to do what he calls you to do. There is absolutely no reason why you need to go along a set pattern of all these extra bits that these other people so facilely pick up. The Bible is certainly not infallible and I can't see any good argument as to why it should be thought to be so. I think you are quite right that the major thing is to accept Jesus and to believe in the Crucifixion and the Resurrection; this is the fundamental point. I hope you are going much more to SCM and also mixing with other Christians who question things, as it does seem that Keble is a hotbed of rather simple fundamentalism. This is certainly not typical of most Christians, so don't get battered into thinking it is. We read the Bible in order to get as far as we can a glimpse of this wonderful figure who strode the world and taught these simple, wonderful truths - but was clearly desperately misunderstood both during his lifetime and probably afterwards. Original sin is nothing especially to do with sex, but it is the sin of the origo of the species, and in that way is selfishness or the fact that each one of us is bound at start, with self-consciousness, to look out on the world from our own point of view. This will inevitably be biased and need to be changed with a death and resurrection experience.

1.11.74

Why not stop going to St. Ebbe's and St. Aldate's if the diet no longer satisfies? Try St. Mary's in the evenings - and SCM, where they question more and probe more?

I think one of Uncle William's books would interest you now, or John Baker's 'Foolishness of God': v.g. It will be in your library. I enclose his lecture at Lee Ab-bey, which you might enjoy. I think you need for your faith some leading up the paths of theology: the 'simple' Bible won't satisfy. Anyhow, it *isn't* simple; and Uncle W or Baker or Bishop Oliver would show you how the deepest questions can still be satisfied or led on by questing theology. And then I think you see a bit more point in philosophy: a good grounding in philosophy helps you to think bet-ter about God - and all intelligent Christians want to do that.

28.1.75
I do hope it's not all too depressing and that you don't feel now and then too lost as to what life is about. Take heart: all sensitive and alert Christians do. It is a very facile and narrow view that it is all so simple, sure and certain. St. Paul certainly wasn't so sure, dying daily and asking people to pray that he finally be not cast away. So don't pay too much heed to OICCU folk. The traditional Christian pat-tern is that it is a long slog of prayer, discipline, fasting (i.e. not much emotion about it), with small bouts of wonderful vision and certainty that make it all worthwhile.

9.10.75
Good of you to write as you did: yes, I was very frightened of you those 5 days. I felt all I did irritated or annoyed you.

I think I would advise dropping St. Aldate's for a time as I think that you have through them got the Christian faith all the wrong way round. It is primarily ei-ther the truth about the world or quite false. It is not 'demands' to be met or reject-ed. It is the belief that this life of Jesus is the truth about God (the power or being who creates and upholds the world); the incredible belief that this power loves each of us and so hopes, not demands, the best from each of us, by showing that love right to the Cross. So it is for any intelligent person an *enormously* difficult thing to swallow: so many questions to ask and answer: God? Who? Why? How? The life of Christ so outrageous in so many ways: the arrogant claims if not true, 'I am the Truth, the Way, the Life', etc. etc. Yet some of the ablest men, some of the most sensitive creatures, have found it true. So it is first finding out that God is Love, and not meaning this just as a trite phrase. Then, when one is loved, you *want* to be yourself and do all you can for others. Then Christian conduct is what you *want* to do, not a *demand*. 'Conduct tests prayer and gratitude'; prayer is not an aid to conduct. I have always felt what you had in the past was real but a bit shal-low and couldn't last. I'm really relieved it hasn't.

The Christian faith is a far bigger, more mysterious, uncertain venture than the slick thing some Evangelicals make it. Of course we are all to be ourselves: but when we are really loved, we do care, we do want to be courteous to others and even be tidy, as it's nicer for others. But remember prostitutes, being themselves, go into the Kingdom before the public school Pharisee. So don't go on being put off.

Uncle William's books would mean more to you now. Christianity is really to be really human; to be warm, open, genuine, not smug or living to an imposed standard. But also it's not really human to be dirty, untidy, swear and be rude; it's animal and selfish. I used to find Oxford a very difficult time because I found it such a fundamentally selfish time; I expected to plan my whole life as *I* wanted and couldn't see why I had to fit in with others in the vac. - being at home when my mother said I must, mowing the lawn, scrubbing the bath, polishing this and that - and so I went away when I could. So I can understand how difficult you must find it all.

15.10.75

Fascinated by your letter. No, I wouldn't think a sacrifice is something you don't want to do. In fact the best sacrifices are those you long and want to do: it is a making holy of an act out of love of God, usually by curbing the lower self and encouraging the better self to *want* it. We none of us freely do what we don't want to, but then it is a question of the will and desire: a love to want what is best for all.

26.10.75

I think it is only because it is the Evangelical point of view that you hear that you can't accept, 'No-one comes to the Father but by me'. But if the first half is true, 'I am the Way, the Truth, the Life', then the second must be. If Christ is the Word, the underlying Principle of Life, then anyone searching for Truth, Beauty, Goodness, is coming to God through Him. He is the light that lighteth *every* man, not just the man who has said, 'Jesus is Lord'. Any light to ideals anywhere is his. Socrates, Buddha, etc. all come to God through the true light. I believe Christ to be the highest personal expression of that light, so high as to be unique in quality. But the Bible and Hebrew thought is but one way to God and Greeks have added their ideas and interpretation to Christ; African and Chinese thinkers will add theirs. The trouble nowadays is so many Evangelicals *only* read theology and their bibles; in the past folk read Philosophy and History as well.

3.5.76

I am sure you are right that one needs patience both for oneself and others, and yet a striving as well; this is where the peace of God, the rope binding one to God, matters. I think you would find some form of disciplined religious life a help again, but it must be something you can find not too uncongenial. So, if you decide to start, don't set yourself too high a standard that then tails off. I am sure there will always be solid plodding on for much of the time; very few of us get the thrills and exaltation often.

What an interesting essay on Socrates being killed. An interesting change in

England is that when I was young we were proudly told our shores were always open and free for the oppressed from any dictatorship anywhere - and it was this marvellous mixture that made us such a fine strong breed of men. Now we have immigration quotas and are frightened of foreigners; historians will see it as a decline.

17.5.77
It is fun that you are starting to find philosophy fun. I wish this had fused with you earlier. I like your truth idea; at the Clergy School, Christopher Bryant plugged that Christ seldom told folk that they were sinful or guilty or good or bad - but stressed the plain folly or silliness of not following him: the man building on sand was just stupid and unrealistic. Christ did not say, 'I am Goodness', but 'the Way, the Truth, the Life': much more existential. As I understand you, you quite rightly reject the idea that only those statements are true that can be quantitatively verifiable. We none of us work on that basis; Mother is 85% water verifiably, but that is not the real truth about her, which is something poetic and unquantifiable.

?.10.83
Leaving here is going to be difficult, but beyond each dying is a resurrection with God there in it all; and life is really all a training of enjoying to the full and then releasing and letting go to be born again - until the final dying here for new birth.

5.8.90
Thank you so much for coming this weekend; it was lovely for all of us, but a bit dull for you. Mother suddenly in an angry mood this morning let out, 'Stephen feels the whole atmosphere in the cottage has changed.' I am so sorry as I thought we had some rather happy times all together. But, understandably, this has been and is a time of stress for us. The rushing in and out of hospital is a drama; and then my legs are another strain, especially with angina, meaning there could be a bad stoppage some time. On my side, even though I know in my head all the answers about God being in suffering and thousands being blind, I am finding coming to terms with incipient and steadily increasing blindness very frightening and frustrating; so that is why I am often rather difficult to live with. We each give a marvellous face to the outside world - 'so brave, such spirits, such cheerfulness', etc. etc. I fear it is only the family like you who see the other side. Mother keeps up with you and Mina, but naturally alone is often quite shattered.

Sorry for all this, but it's difficult to say, and we're so grateful for you coping with us so well.

7.3.91
I have had my eyes tested again at PMH. The young Dr. Low got me an appointment to see Mr. Ramsey, recommending that I be registered 'blind'. This would

mean quite a few perks, but still I find it quite a profound psychological shock to pass that landmark.

26.4.91

We went to another of the 'Thinking Lunches' in Swindon and heard an excellent Professor Norman Myers on 'The Environment and the Third World'. 13 million children die in the world a year, which could be prevented - the equivalent of a Jumbo Jet full of children crashing every 15 minutes. How the papers would react and people respond if they heard of various things governments could do, but won't because of expense, which, in Professor Myers' words, would be 'the equivalent of 2 days of the Gulf War'. For weeks our media has been all about the Kurds - and Africa is forgotten.

To another subject: Mother and I are thinking of giving our bodies when we die to anatomical research, instead of cremation. But we don't want to fix it without Mina's and your consent. Mina has said, 'Yes, if that's what you want', but I don't think thought through it. What happens is that the local undertaker takes the body away to his chapel and then the hospital takes it from there. They quietly cremate the remains when they've done with them. So there's no 'funeral' service with coffin and crematorium, etc., but a memorial thanksgiving service later. If the body being dissected seems macabre, it is no different to burning really and more useful. We did not want to spring it on you, so think about it and let us know. We have to put a note with our wills and let our GP know.

11.7.91

I am coming, I hope, to accept the blindness; much has to go, but there is still quite a full life to lead.

26.11.91

The 'soaps' keep lively. 'Brookside' has Barry confess to a priest that he was in part responsible for Sue and the baby's death. In 'Neighbours', Emma has had a motorbike accident and may lose a leg; also a young man's appeared claiming to be Jim's illegitimate son from when he was in Vietnam, and Todd and Carly have run away and not returned. So we keep lively.

23.2.92

'Coronation Street': Derek is still out of work.
'Brookside': The newcomers, wife a deputy head, are accused of fraud in the family business; really the brother's fault. Sinbad has found his mother, who still does not want to know him.
'Eastenders': 'Our Stella' has guessed about Mark's HIV.
'Neighbours': Todd has not come home yet. Jim now acknowledges his illegitimate son from the Vietnam war. Melanie failed to get off the ship when seeing

Paul and bride off on their honeymoon.

'Home and Away': Marilyn's aunt has left. Juliet's father has died and Nick has told her they are only 'friends'. Bobby's had to give back her foster-child.
So there you are!!

1.3.92

We saw a marvellous RSC production of Wilde's 'A Woman of No Importance'; such a good play with all the wit - and yet, tragic, serious bits in it. Mother says the scenery and dresses were magnificent.

20.5.93

We saw a good play at the Watermill, 'My Children, My Africa'. Most moving, about SA and apartheid. Mina was in tears at the end and Mother in floods. So, thoroughly enjoyable!! Then on the way to the car, Mother saw the girl who played the Afrikaner girl who was trying to understand it all, and so rushed across to tell her how marvellous it was - and more floods of tears. Quite different from a *ghastly* play we saw at Bath on Tuesday; no plot at all, just a drunk man, and everyone saying 'Fuck off', 'piss' and 'shit', at which the prim Bath audience tittered and sniggered. For the first time in our lives, we left in the interval.

15.10.93

Absolutely awful Tory conference: brutes; horrid. Women baying for blood over single parents, law and order. 6 new prisons to be built. We already put more folk in prison than any other EC country.

8.11.93

November 1st was a wonderful evening. Alan Woods had taken so much trouble; Barbara, his wife, wrote out the service very large and beautifully in her own hand: a peal of bells and the church beautifully decorated in colours I could see; marvellous eats, excellent sermon by Jeffrey Maples. John read the OT lesson; Mother read the NT lesson on what a bishop should be; she read brilliantly. 'A bishop not given to drink' - and looked at me; 'able to control his family' - and looked straight at Mina. As we processed out, Alan had suggested Joan come out and walk beside me, which was lovely. There were masses of cards and presents as well. The church was packed.

21.11.93

We had a night at Stratford; we saw 'Love's Labour Lost' on Wednesday night - very well done and very amusing - and next day, 'Rondo', on Elgar's life, brilliant and moving. Ma in floods of tears at the end, so a great success. A new Spoonerism in it which I'd not met before: 'The Sather, the Fun and the Golly Host'.

14.3.94

We had a *wonderful* service in Bristol Cathedral when 32 women were ordained priests. The Dean had kindly provided parking in the cloister garth; we arrived early and only a small space for Mother to back into. Myriads of reporters and photographers who, as soon as I appeared in purple cassock, kept snapping right and left - including Mother trying to park. She called out, 'Would one of you like to park this instead?' - but they clicked her all the more. I told them we'd been in Hong Kong, where the first woman was priested in the 40s. It was lovely meeting so many old friends who came up and told me who they were. There were no disturbances; the only group outside was the 'Catholic Women's League for Ordination', calling out, 'Please pray for us: that ours may come soon'. And one RC priest prayed in the service that his Church would soon follow.

23.9.94

This is my RNIB raised line paper to keep me straight, but I can't see it at all.

14.2.95

Mother will have told you about the Labour Party dinner, with Gordon Brown speaking quite well. The invitation read, 'Men: a suit; women: posh frock'.

1.3.95

We saw 'Goodbye Mr. Chips' at the Watermill; v.g. Had Mother in tears, so very good. We have seen 2 poor plays, one at Bath, one at Stratford. Saw them just because good people were in them. I've persuaded Mother we must concentrate on the play for choice, not the stars.

17.1.96

At a celebration luncheon yesterday, I had a friend of X opposite me, who, as Mother was cutting up chicken for me off a bone, said, 'I expect you really enjoy all this fuss over you'. So I was quite fierce and said, 'Please, never again make that sort of joke to people with disabilities. We hear it very often, and it's no help at all. When I hear people who are a bit deaf say, "I'm afraid I didn't hear", and then the reply comes, "You're lucky not to hear all the rubbish talked", I could brain them. So, please, *never ever* again.' After a silence she recovered well, apologised and talked well. But it may have taught a lesson.

25.1.96 [The last letter Freddy wrote to Stephen]

We had Chris and David to supper on Wednesday; pleasant. They have a deaf dog, which they have taught sign language!

Very much love. Father.

Index